# Adapting Minds

Evolutionary Psychology and the Persistent Quest for Human Nature

David J. Buller

D0068172

A Bradford Book
The MIT Press
Cambridge, Massachusetts
London, England

First MIT Press paperback edition, 2006
© 2005 Massachusetts Institute of Technology

MIT Press books may be purchased at special quantity discounts for business or sales
promotional use. For information, please e-mail special_sales@mitpress.mit.edu or
write to Special Sales Department, The MIT Press, 55 Hayward Street, Cambridge,
MA 02142.

This book was set in Stone sans and Stone serif by SNP Best-set Typesetter Ltd., Hong
Kong.
Printed and bound in the United States of America.

Library of Congress Cataloging-in-Publication Data
Buller, David J., 1959–
Adapting minds : evolutionary psychology and the persistent quest for human
nature / David J. Buller.
    p. cm.
"A Bradford book."
Includes bibliographical references (p. ) and index.
ISBN 978-0-262-02579-9 (hc. : alk. paper)— 978-0-262-52460-5 (pb. : alk. paper)
1. Evolutionary psychology. I. Title.

BF701.B85   2005
155.7–dc22

                                                                    2004057932

10 9 8 7 6 5

To Heide,
for giving me my life,
but mostly for giving me Dabi

# Contents

# Acknowledgments

The completion of this book came at the end of a long road that was frequently difficult to navigate, and along the way I received a lot of direction. I am deeply indebted to all who provided that direction, and to the extent that I am able in this forum I would like to repay those debts with some public displays of gratitude.

First, I have general intellectual debts that predate this book project but that significantly conditioned my approach to it. One of these is to Arthur Fine, my dissertation advisor of many years ago, well before I became interested in evolutionary biology and evolutionary psychology. Arthur taught me a great deal about the relation between science and philosophy, most of which didn't truly sink in until years after he ceased being my teacher and dissertation advisor. But his lessons are evident (at least to me) in all that follows. When working on my dissertation, I remember expressing concern to Arthur that I wasn't really doing *philosophy* in my dissertation. He responded with his usual warm-hearted laugh and the gentle comment, "Don't worry about that." Well, Arthur, as you'll see here, I've certainly stopped worrying about that! The other general intellectual debt is to David Hull, who succeeded in teaching me a lot about both biology and the nature of philosophy in the years since graduate school, despite what must have seemed my stubborn reluctance to learn. As with Arthur's lessons, many of David's often didn't take until well after the fact, much to his occasional frustration, I am sure. David also provided detailed and thoughtful comments on the whole manuscript for this book, and I am very grateful for his time and thoughtfulness in providing them.

Another general debt, of a very different sort, is to Philip Kitcher for his 1985 book *Vaulting Ambition: Sociobiology and the Quest for Human Nature*, which subjected the sociobiology of the day to scathing criticism. For, *in certain respects*, Kitcher's book was a conceptual model for mine—a fact to which this book's subtitle gives the nod. I say "in certain respects" for two reasons. First, Kitcher saw sociobiology as "rotten at every rung," finding nothing worth salvaging in the program of sociobiology, and was generally skeptical about applying evolutionary theory to human behavior. In contrast, I am unabashedly enthusiastic about efforts to apply evolutionary theory to human psychology. Indeed, in what follows I will often endorse one or another hypothesis about the evolution of some aspect of human psychology. For what I believe to be good reasons, my criticisms are aimed at a much smaller target than were Kitcher's. Second, since evolutionary psychology differs from sociobiology both theoretically and methodologically, Kitcher's critique of sociobiology doesn't apply to evolutionary psychology. Consequently, in what follows I don't pick up any of the threads of Kitcher's arguments—indeed, I don't discuss them at all. Despite parting ways with Kitcher, however, and despite not specifically discussing his contribution in what follows, I am indebted to *Vaulting Ambition* for the bedrock conception of this book.

I am also very grateful to several individuals and organizations whose support made this book possible. Perhaps the greatest of these debts is to Betty Stanton, the former editor of Bradford Books, for her enthusiasm for and faith in this project. Betty signed this book to MIT Press before a single word of it had been written, and that faith gave me a focus and direction that may have otherwise been lacking. Once the project was up and running, essential release time from teaching and other academic duties was provided by a grant from the National Science Foundation (Scholars Award number SES9985820), a sabbatical from Northern Illinois University, and a Summer Research and Artistry Grant from Northern Illinois University. Apart from these institutional forms of support, Dean Frederick Kitterle, of Northern Illinois University, found creative ways to support my work on this book on several occasions, and I am deeply indebted to him.

Several other individuals provided critical input to the writing of the book itself. Elliott Sober, Jonathan Kaplan, J. D. Trout, and Steve Downes read the entire manuscript and provided detailed, helpful, and challenging comments, which helped improve the finished product. Prior to reading the full manuscript, each of them also engaged in many educational e-mail exchanges and conversations with me as the ideas in this book were taking shape, and J.D. was almost always on call for a "reality check" when I was befuddled. I am also grateful to Valerie Hardcastle for her collaboration on chapter 4; I can't imagine a better collaborator. A number of other individuals also contributed very helpful discussions and e-mail exchanges. For these contributions I am grateful to Andre Ariew, Neil Blackstone, Harold Brown, Tessa Crume, Jeremy Freese, Peter Godfrey-

Smith, Todd Grantham, Kristen Hawkes, Wade Hazel, Joel Milner, Brad Sagarin, Terry Sullivan, Denis Walsh, David Sloan Wilson, and anonymous referees for the National Science Foundation. In addition, I am thankful to all the students in my seminars over the years, and to the students in Brad Sagarin's evolutionary psychology seminar, for providing feedback on the evolving ideas in this book. One former student, Wendy Parker, deserves special thanks for particularly incisive feedback in the formative stages of the project.

As you will see, in order to test some hypotheses in chapter 7, I had to conduct my own empirical study of patterns of child abuse in the United States. This wouldn't have been possible without the efforts of my collaborator in this endeavor, Elliott G. Smith, the Associate Director of the National Data Archive on Child Abuse and Neglect (NDACAN). Elliott was extremely generous and helpful, over several months, and I learned a great deal from working with him. On one level it was challenging and fun, but on another it was deeply depressing. I acquired a lot of respect for those who work full time, year after year, researching the horrible suffering that is inflicted upon children by those whom they love and depend on the most. This research is not easy to stomach, and those who subject themselves to it do so in an effort to improve our understanding of, and hopefully one day to mitigate, child abuse. They deserve our undying admiration.

My greatest debt is to my wife, Heide Fehrenbach, who provided me with loving support and encouragement throughout the long duration of this project, despite working at the same time on a book of her own. Heide also provided excellent editorial comments on parts of the manuscript. Finally, a list of my debts would not be complete without acknowledging our son, "Dabi," who brought some perspective to my life and taught me that writing a book is comparatively unimportant.

**Adapting Minds**

# Introduction

Several years ago, I spent a semester's leave in London, put up in a flat off Kensington Gardens on someone else's dime. During that semester, I was fortunate enough to spend my days reading evolutionary biology, pursuing applications of evolutionary theory to problems in contemporary philosophy of mind, and my nights in outstanding pubs or at home watching surprisingly superb British television. (It was always easier to find an interesting program on the four channels we received in our London flat than on one hundred American channels.)

One night at home, I happened into the end of an immediately gripping program on the BBC. In a scene I was convinced I would not have found on American television, a naked heterosexual couple was engaged in foreplay. Within moments, there was a jump cut to another scene, and I found myself taking a ride that Albert Einstein never imagined. In one of his famous thought experiments, you may recall, Einstein asked us to imagine how events would appear to an observer riding a beam of light. That's all very interesting, I suppose, but to someone with an abiding and not-strictly-professional interest in human sexuality, it simply doesn't compare to the ride I, as a suddenly devoted BBC viewer, was then taking. For a camera had been strapped to the male's erect penis, and I was riding the male's penis and viewing the copulatory act from within the female's surprisingly well lit vagina.

After a number of penile thrusts and vaginal contractions, the inevitable ejaculation came. Moments later, I (and no doubt countless other enraptured viewers in Britain) witnessed the female's cervix take several "dips" into the semen that had pooled at the back of her vagina. The narrator—whom I later discovered was Desmond Morris—explained that the cervix was "sucking" the semen up into the uterus in order to "increase the chances of fertilization."[1] We were then informed that a female can increase the chances of being fertilized by a particular partner by "varying the timing of her orgasms." If unfaithful, the narrator continued, a woman could "favor the sperm of a young healthy lover, while continuing to gain protection from a powerful older husband."

Even more remarkably, we were told that males had evolved a defense against this female strategy. In fact, the narrator confidently proclaimed, "new research has proved" that only a small percentage of the sperm in a male's ejaculate function to seek out and fertilize the egg. The remainder of a male's sperm are, instead, designed for "sperm wars" with the sperm that may have been deposited in his partner's womb by any ne'er-do-well with whom she may have recently dallied. Most of these warriors, the narrator said, are "killer sperm" that swim around looking for the sperm of other males, which they can detect with a chemical sensor. Indeed, this narration was accompanied by video of a sperm swimming from one sperm to another, stopping only at select sperm to impale them with the tip of its head, which bore an uncanny resemblance to the helmets worn by German officers in World War I. Then, in the narrative climax, we were told that "a man can unconsciously control the numbers of these killer sperm in his ejaculate, and that would depend on whether or not he believed he was the first or second male to mate with a particular woman." Apparently, Woody Allen's depiction of sperm (in *Everything You Always Wanted to Know About Sex but Were Afraid to Ask*), as rushing headlong and blindly toward the uterus in statistically vain hopes of smashing into the egg, couldn't have been more wrong. So much for the primary texts of my sex education.

Watching this remarkable footage, I recalled a vivid passage in Richard Dawkins's *The Selfish Gene* that describes us as "survival machines" for our genes, which "created us, body and mind; and their preservation is the ultimate rationale for our existence."[2] But this put a new spin on things. Sperm appeared so wily that they had hijacked an unconscious part of the male mind so that they could send an appropriately sized battalion to war. I then saw myself as a mere vehicle for transporting and delivering my sperm to its desired port. I had an epiphany that most of my behavior, and most of my unconscious mind that controls so much of my behavior, is merely in the service of my sperm and their puppet masters, my genes.

This was incredible stuff, and thanks to the BBC I had seen the evidence of "sperm wars" with my own eyes. Suddenly I felt that I had been wasting my time studying evolutionary biology in order to apply it to problems in "serious philosophy" (which virtually always means philosophy that only a few dozen other philosophers would bother to take seriously). For I had just witnessed direct and immediate applications of biology to human behavior, which promised to reveal many more truths about human psychology than abstruse philosophy of mind ever could. These applications of biology to human behavior promised to explain why we desire sex with some people but not others, why we marry the people we do, why we are sometimes unfaithful, why the number of sperm in a male's ejaculate varies with the amount of time his partner is out of sight, why we care so deeply for our children, why conflicts arise in all our intimate relationships, and why "men are from Mars and women are from Venus." And the best part was that many of the applications of biology to human behavior concerned human sexuality. At that moment, my research agenda was redefined. I immediately abandoned my suddenly boring research into whether evolutionary theory could explain the representational properties of mental states in order to explore instead what was becoming known as "evolutionary psychology."

Once I began to focus on evolutionary psychology, I seemed to encounter it everywhere I turned, especially in the popular media. During almost every wait in the supermarket checkout line, I would find reference to the evolutionary psychology of human mating on the covers of women's and men's magazines. On Sundays, I would often find articles in the *New York Times Magazine* or the *Chicago Tribune Magazine* about the evolutionary psychology of mating, parent-child relationships, or status seeking. And it seemed to be all over television, and not just on "high-brow" channels like PBS and the Discovery Channel. On a Saturday night, ABC aired an ABC News Special Report by John Stossel examining the evolutionary psychology of sex differences and their implications for early education. It appeared that evolutionary psychology was capturing the public consciousness and beginning to condition the human self-conception presented in popular culture.

Initially, I was completely captivated by evolutionary psychology, and I was certain that it was providing a deep and accurate understanding of human mentality and behavior. But after six months' research, it was unclear to me how everything that went by the name "evolutionary psychology" fit together, and I began having serious doubts about many of the confident claims made by evolutionary psychologists (such as Morris's claim that "research has *proved*" that the majority of sperm in an ejaculate function as sperm warriors). A year's research later, it was clear to me that there were distinctly different lines of research being conducted under the "evolutionary psychology" label, and I became convinced that the line of research that had garnered the most attention, both within academia and throughout the popular media, was wrong in almost every detail. This book emerged as my effort to sort the promising from the wrongheaded lines of research. Accordingly, I originally intended to write a book about the "strong" and the "weak" evolutionary psychology. As the project evolved, however, I found that there was too much to be said about the problems with the "weak" evolutionary psychology, and the project consequently became a critique of evolutionary psychology.

But at many junctures I felt that I didn't want to go public with a critique of evolutionary psychology. For, as my research progressed, I became disheartened over the scarcity of reasoned intellectual exchange regarding evolutionary psychology. I found that published criticisms of evolutionary psychology typically contained more vitriol than serious analysis of the reasoning and evidence behind the claims made by evolutionary psychologists, and I didn't particularly want to be associated with that. I found that critics of evolutionary psychology too often portrayed evolutionary psychologists as crude "biological determinists" who are so benighted as to have never heard of culture or as right-wing reactionaries seeking simple certainties in the face of the cultural and intellectual cataclysms of the late twentieth century. Accordingly, it was too easy to find critics attacking evolutionary psychology for its "directly political dimension" and its "culturally pernicious" political claims.[3] And, when evolutionary psychology wasn't being attacked on political grounds, it was easy to find critics dismissing evolutionary psychology for being built on a single "fatal flaw." For example, the late paleontologist Stephen Jay Gould disparaged evolutionary psychology as "pseudoscience" and "Darwinian fundamentalism."[4] Once evolutionary psychology was dismissed because of its "fatal flaw," there was no need to offer detailed critical examination of its specific claims. Thus, dismissing evolutionary psychology for its corrupt politics or for being based on "one big mistake" enabled critics to deflect attention from the *evidence* that evolutionary psychologists present and to avoid altogether any serious engagement with evolutionary psychology.

To a large extent, these critical tactics served to condition public perception of the issues at stake in the "debate" over evolutionary psychology, a fact that was driven home to me by a personal experience. Some time ago, I was contacted by a producer for a show on Chicago Public Radio, who wanted to vet me for appearance on a talk show with Steven Pinker, one of the foremost proponents of evolutionary psychology. The issue they wanted to explore on the show, I was told, was why people are so upset by evolutionary psychology. They wanted a discussion of whether undesirable ethical or political implications are intrinsic to evolutionary psychology or whether critics of evolutionary psychology merely read undesirable ethical or political implications into it. After some discussion, I explained that I had nothing to say about whether we should be upset by any possible ethical or political implications of evolutionary psychology, because I was interested in whether *there are good reasons to believe* the claims made by evolutionary psychologists. The producer granted that perhaps that was a legitimate interest, but reiterated that they were interested only in examining whether there are reasons to get worked up about the "political issues" at stake. To my ears, this implied that evolutionary psychology should be accepted or rejected on the basis of its purported ethical and political implications rather than on the basis of scientific standards of evidence. I believe, in contrast, that we should *first and foremost* give a fair and balanced hearing to the evidence that evolutionary psychologists present in support of their claims.

But I found no shortage of unfairness in evolutionary psychologists' responses to their critics, either. All too often I found evolutionary psychologists dismissing their critics as "antiscientific," "politically correct postmodernists," or closet creationists. Any skepticism about the claims of evolutionary psychology was typically portrayed as a product of dogmatic indoctrination in the social sciences, and of the attendant belief that all of human psychology is the product of "socialization," or else as evidence of a commitment to the "superstitious" belief that humans somehow managed to "transcend" the evolutionary process. Indeed, many critics have been dismissed as simply *not wanting to accept* the implications of the fact that humans evolved just like the beasts of the field. When critics questioned evolutionary psychologists' claim that stepparents abuse their children at far higher rates than genetic parents, for example, they were dismissed as suffering from "denial" because "there is something about the association between step-parenthood and child maltreatment that appears to be uniquely unpalatable."[5] (For the life of me, however, I haven't been able to understand why evolutionary psychologists think that people find more palatable the belief that genetic parents abuse their children to the same extent that stepparents do.) On a more personal level, resistance to evolutionary psychology was sometimes attributed to the purported fact that "it poses a serious threat to the status of those who have achieved success in their field using non-evolutionary approaches."[6] On an even more personal level, Gould was excoriated by virtually every evolutionary psychologist with access to a writing implement. For a time, it was very common to find evolutionary psychologists quoting a quip by the English evolutionary biologist John Maynard Smith in which Gould is described "as a man whose ideas are so confused as to be hardly worth bothering with."[7] Too much of the response to Gould then focused on his credentials as an evolutionary biologist instead of on the actual content of his arguments.

But the most insidious rhetoric employed by evolutionary psychologists in responding to their critics has involved the claim, often implied, that there are no *biological* grounds on which to criticize evolutionary psychology. Evolutionary psychologists have often defended some very specific hypothesis about human mentality or behavior by arguing that rejection of that hypothesis requires rejecting the very idea that human psychology has evolved along with everything else on the planet. If we are to accept that humans have evolved, the defense often goes, then we have to accept all of the "evolutionary" arguments offered by evolutionary psychologists and, consequently, all of the specific doctrines that derive from those arguments. As a result, very specific claims are presented as *entailed* by an evolutionary view of humanity. The view that males prefer nubile females and females prefer high-status males, for example, has been presented as "*the* evolutionary view" of human mating. Similarly, the view that there are evolved sex differences in the intensity of sexual jealousy has been called "*the* evolutionary theory of jealousy" by proponents and critics alike, as though taking an evolutionary view of jealousy *entails* the specific theory that there are evolved sex differences in sexual jealousy. Accordingly, the rhetoric sets up the following dichotomy: Either you accept biology, in which case you must accept the claims of evolutionary psychologists, or you don't. Critics have thus been portrayed as necessarily committed to scientifically empty theories from the social sciences, to some form of postmodernist relativism, or to creationism. No one who *truly* accepts evolution, the rhetoric goes, can seriously question any of the specific claims of evolutionary psychology.

I have found this lack of civilized, reasoned dialogue to be deeply lamentable. On the one side, evolutionary psychologists have not given their critics their due. In a (perhaps understandable) defensive posture toward their critics, they have too often simply circled the wagons and become entrenched in dogmatic views, rather than revising their views in light of genuine problems. This is not the path of scientific progress. As the philosopher of science Karl Popper put it, scientific progress consists of iterated rounds of "conjecture and refutation." To dogmatically reject all "refutations," by deflecting attention from the content of the criticism and toward the motives of the critic, is to hinder the growth of scientific knowledge. On the other side, critics have not given evolutionary psychology *its* due. Evolutionary psychology is a bold and innovative approach to understanding human psychology, and its ideas deserve to be taken just as seriously as any other scientific ideas. In this book, I intend to take them very seriously. Indeed, this book is an extended analysis of the *reasons* (the arguments and evidence) that evolutionary psychologists offer in support of their claims. Of course, I've already telegraphed that I think that much of evolutionary psychology is wrong, and I will argue throughout this book that it is often wrong on *evolutionary* grounds. But there is wrong, and then there is wrong. Some wrong ideas are unfruitfully wrong. The Church's insistence, during the trial of Galileo, that the earth is the stationary center of the universe was simply dead wrong, and it never led anyone toward a deeper and more accurate understanding of the heavens. Other wrong ideas, however, mark significant steps *forward* in our scientific understanding of the world. Copernicus's astronomy and Newton's mechanics were both wrong, but Copernicus and Newton supplied the shoulders on which Kepler and Einstein were able to stand. I believe that many of the ideas in evolutionary psychology, though wrong, will similarly lead us to a deeper understanding of human psychology once we come to terms with the precise ways in which those ideas are wrong. Failure to take evolutionary psychology seriously—failure to evaluate its claims on the basis of the evidence, rather than on the basis of its alleged political implications—constitutes, I believe, a failure to accept the shoulders on which tomorrow's scientists may stand.

Observing the vituperative exchanges between evolutionary psychologists and their critics did, however, impress on me the need for crystal clarity with respect to one special point. For I found that evolutionary psychologists and their critics often talked past one another because of a failure to be clear about how the term "evolutionary psychology" was being used. The typical pattern was this. A critic of evolutionary psychology would object to a claim made in the name of evolutionary psychology and conclude that "evolutionary psychology" was therefore mistaken. A respondent would then come along and argue that this criticism of "evolutionary psychology" was wholly unfounded because some different "evolutionary psychologist" wasn't committed to the criticized claim, so "evolutionary psychology" was untouched by the criticism. In these exchanges, the critic presented a narrow criticism as having broad applicability, but the respondent failed to address the criticism by retreating to a definition of "evolutionary psychology" that was broad enough to fall beyond its scope. What inevitably got lost in this rhetorical shuffle was whether the criticism was justified and whether a specific idea needed to be reevaluated. And the reason it got lost was that the parties to the "debate" failed to be clear about how they defined the term "evolutionary psychology." In order to forestall this kind of misunderstanding, and in order to be crystal clear about the target of my critique in this book, let's get clear about what evolutionary psychology is.

The term "evolutionary psychology" is sometimes used simply as a shorthand for "the evolutionary study of mind and behavior" or as a short-hand for theories "adopting an evolutionary perspective on human behavior and psychology."[8] When used in these ways, "evolutionary psychology" designates a *field of inquiry*, which is so broad as to cover work ranging from studies of foraging and birth spacing in traditional hunter-gatherer societies to studies of encephalization (the progressive increase in brain size relative to body size in the human lineage) and the evolution of altruism and language. If one examines all of the work that adopts "an evolutionary perspective on human behavior and psychology," one will find that it varies significantly in fundamental theoretical and methodological commitments. Indeed, such work is united only by a commitment to articulating questions about human behavior and mentality, and articulating hypothetical answers to those questions, with conceptual and theoretical tools drawn from evolutionary theory. This is why I say that all this work forms a *field of inquiry*. For fields of inquiry are defined not by specific sets of doctrines, but by sets of related questions. Fields of inquiry are defined not by specific answers to questions, but by the importance they place on particular kinds of question.

Many researchers in the field of evolutionary psychology often deliberately resist the "evolutionary psychology" label, however, preferring to classify their work as, for example, human ethology, human behavioral ecology, or evolutionary anthropology. The reason is that the term "evolutionary psychology" has increasingly come to be used to designate only work conducted within a specific set of theoretical and methodological commitments shared and articulated by a prominent and influential group of researchers, and many researchers outside this group often wish to distance themselves from it by rejecting the "evolutionary psychology" label. The most notable members of this influential group of researchers are the psychologists David Buss, Leda Cosmides, Martin Daly, Steven Pinker, and Margo Wilson, and the anthropologists Donald Symons and John Tooby. This group is united in the belief that adoption of an evolutionary perspective on human psychology immediately entails a number of very specific theoretical and methodological doctrines. These theoretical and methodological doctrines will be elaborated in detail in chapter 2, but a brief overview of them is useful here.

Since evolution by natural selection has created anatomical adaptations that are universal among humans, this group of researchers argues, it has undoubtedly created universal psychological adaptations as well. Our psychological adaptations are presumably rather complex traits, however, and the construction of complex adaptations typically requires hundreds of thousands of years of cumulative selection. Our ancestors spent the Pleistocene—the epoch spanning 1.8 million to 10,000 years ago—living in small hunter-gatherer groups, but only the past 10,000 years living as agriculturists and the past couple hundred years living in industrial societies. Consequently, these evolutionary psychologists argue, our psychological adaptations must have been designed during the Pleistocene to solve the adaptive problems faced by our hunter-gatherer ancestors. But the adaptive problems faced by our Pleistocene ancestors varied considerably. As a result, each adaptive problem would have selected for the evolution of its own specialized psychological adaptation. Thus, this group argues, the mind must consist of genetically specified "mental organs" or "modules," each of which is functionally specialized at solving a particular adaptive problem, just as the body consists of numerous organs that are each functionally specialized. Given the enormous number of adaptive problems our Pleistocene ancestors faced, these evolutionary psychologists argue, the human mind must consist of "hundreds or thousands" of such mental organs. And, since the human mind must be just as monomorphic as the human body, this group of evolutionary psychologists concludes that these mental organs must constitute a universal human nature.

The goal of evolutionary psychology, according to this group of researchers, is to discover the mental organs that constitute our universal human nature and to articulate how those mental organs function to solve evolutionary problems. However, because our mental organs evolved to solve the adaptive problems faced by our Pleistocene ancestors, and because the environments we now inhabit differ enormously from those inhabited by our Pleistocene ancestors, we can't discover the evolved design of the mind by studying human behavior and cognition in our modern environments. We must, instead, "reverse engineer" the evolved design of the mind by figuring out the adaptive problems our Pleistocene ancestors must have faced and then inferring the psychological adaptations that must have evolved to solve them.

This method has been applied to a number of areas of human behavior and cognition, and this group of evolutionary psychologists believes that it has already made significant discoveries about the evolved design of the mind. For example, David Buss has argued that, in our Pleistocene past, it would have been adaptively advantageous for males to prefer nubile females as mates and for females to prefer high-status males as mates. Buss, together with a large team of researchers, has conducted large-scale research that appears to support these hypotheses about mate preferences. Similarly, the husband-and-wife team of Martin Daly and Margo Wilson has argued that, in our Pleistocene past, it would have been adaptively advantageous for parents to selectively allocate their love and resources only to children they could be confident were their genetic offspring. And Daly and Wilson have gathered some provocative evidence of this "discriminative parental solicitude." Finally, the wife-and-husband team of Leda Cosmides and John Tooby has argued that, in our Pleistocene past, it would have been adaptively advantageous for people to be able to detect when someone was cheating them in a "social exchange." And they have made some interesting experimental discoveries, which they claim support the idea that we have a mental organ that is functionally dedicated to "cheater detection."

When the term "evolutionary psychology" is used to designate only work conducted under the auspices of the above theoretical and methodological doctrines, the term designates what the late historian and philosopher of science Thomas Kuhn called a *paradigm*. According to Kuhn, a paradigm emerges within a scientific field of inquiry when a significant and growing number of working scientists come to agreement about the fundamental doctrines that define their field. The paradigm is the cluster of fundamental doctrines on which scientists agree, and once a paradigm emerges within a field of inquiry it provides a large number of working scientists with a common research focus. For, having come to agreement about the fundamental doctrines that define their field, scientists can turn their attention away from debate about fundamentals and toward gathering detailed facts within the framework that the paradigm provides.

More specifically, according to Kuhn, a paradigm consists of the following aspects. First, a paradigm provides scientists with a shared *theoretical understanding* of the entities, mechanisms, and processes that make up the particular aspect of reality investigated by a field of inquiry. The above group of researchers, for example, shares a commitment to the theoretical claim that the human mind consists of numerous genetically specified mental organs that evolved to solve the adaptive problems of our Pleistocene ancestors and that these mental organs now constitute a universal human nature. Second, a paradigm provides scientists with a shared set of *methods* that are to be applied in the effort to arrive at further knowledge of the relevant aspect of reality. For example, this group of evolutionary psychologists is united in its conviction that we can discover the mental organs that constitute human nature only by reverse engineering the human mind from the vantage of our Pleistocene past, rather than from the vantage of human behavior in modern industrial environments. And, third, a paradigm involves one or more *exemplars*, which are specific examples of empirical research that the scientists working within the paradigm accept as significant achievements and as exemplary of how their science is to be done. For example, Buss's work on mate preferences, Daly and Wilson's work on "discriminative parental solicitude," and Cosmides and Tooby's work on "cheater detection" are accepted by this group of evolutionary psychologists as important discoveries that exemplify how evolutionary psychologists can acquire additional knowledge of the evolved design of the human mind.

When a paradigm becomes dominant within a field of inquiry, Kuhn claims, the paradigm virtually *defines* that field of inquiry, and scientists committed to the paradigm begin to write textbooks and establish research centers from which a new generation of scientists will be trained to view the field of inquiry from the perspective of the paradigm. In this respect, also, the work of this group of evolutionary psychologists possesses the hallmarks of a Kuhnian paradigm. The theoretical and methodological commitments of the group were forcefully articulated in an important 1992 manifesto, *The Adapted Mind*, which also reproduced the above-mentioned exemplars of empirical research conducted within the framework of its theoretical and methodological commitments. This manifesto was updated in David Buss's 1999 textbook, *Evolutionary Psychology: The New Science of the Mind*, which aims to be the source from which a growing number of future practitioners will be trained and to contribute "in some modest measure to the fulfillment of a scientific revolution that will provide the foundation for psychology in the new millennium."[9] To facilitate this revolution, centers at the University of California at Santa Barbara and the University of Texas at Austin have been established to train a new generation in this group's fundamental commitments, and fledgling programs have sprouted elsewhere.

This approach to evolutionary psychology has also benefited from having attracted a highly talented group of popular-science writers. The science writer and journalist Robert Wright introduced many of the ideas of this paradigm to a broad audience in his 1994 book *The Moral Animal: Evolutionary Psychology and Everyday Life*. This was followed by popular works by the most gifted and accessible writers among the paradigm's academic insiders. In his inimitable style, Steven Pinker articulated the theoretical underpinnings of the paradigm in two books written for a general audience, *How the Mind Works* and *The Blank Slate: The Modern Denial of Human Nature*. And presenting his own work on human mating, David Buss introduced the public to many of the details of the sexier aspects of the paradigm in his books *The Evolution of Desire: Strategies of Human Mating* and *The Dangerous Passion: Why Jealousy Is as Necessary as Love and Sex*. Indeed, because of the remarkable success of these popular works, if you've heard anything at all about evolutionary psychology, the chances are that what you've heard derives from the paradigm popularized by Pinker and Buss.

In fact, this group of researchers has been so effective in marketing its paradigm that it has become the single most dominant paradigm within the field of evolutionary psychology. As a result, when researchers in *the field* of evolutionary psychology deliberately call their work "human behavioral ecology," for example, they typically do so to distance themselves from *the paradigm* that has become known as "evolutionary psychology." So as to clearly distinguish the field of inquiry of evolutionary psychology from the evolutionary psychology paradigm associated with Buss and Pinker, throughout this book I will refer to the field of inquiry as "evolutionary psychology" (lower case) and the paradigm as "Evolutionary Psychology" (capitalized).

In light of this distinction, I can clarify that this book is a critique of Evolutionary Psychology. My target throughout this book is Evolutionary Psychology *the paradigm*, and my criticisms are neither intended nor assumed to apply to all the work conducted with the *field of inquiry* that is sometimes called "evolutionary psychology." In fact, I am unabashedly enthusiastic about evolutionary psychology as a field of inquiry, and in my arguments I will frequently draw on ideas from the field of evolutionary psychology in order to criticize aspects of the Evolutionary Psychology paradigm. To repeat, this book is a critique of Evolutionary Psychology—the paradigm associated with the work of Buss, Pinker, Cosmides and Tooby, and Daly and Wilson. This book is *not* a critique of the very idea that human psychology can be understood from an evolutionary perspective, the idea embodied in the field of inquiry known as "evolutionary psychology." So creationists will find no succor here.

Some of the arguments I present against Evolutionary Psychology, however, will apply beyond the Evolutionary Psychology paradigm. For some of the doctrines of Evolutionary Psychology are accepted by many researchers in the field of evolutionary psychology who otherwise dissent from the core commitments of the paradigm. For example, in chapter 5 I argue that there is no good evidence that women prefer high-status men as mates, which is an idea that is accepted by most evolutionary psychologists, not just by the adherents to the Evolutionary Psychology paradigm. But, insofar as my arguments apply more widely than Evolutionary Psychology, that application is strictly incidental to my purpose. At no point will I be concerned with detailing the precise contours of the scope of my arguments beyond the borders of Evolutionary Psychology. It will be a sufficiently taxing project just to clearly convey the many ways in which the Evolutionary Psychology paradigm is mistaken.

This project will begin, in chapter 1, Evolution, with an overview of evolutionary biology. Since Evolutionary Psychologists claim that their theories derive from the application of evolutionary theory to human psychology, it is essential to have a clear understanding of the basic principles of evolutionary biology before embarking on an analysis of the claims made by Evolutionary Psychologists. Chapter 2, Mind, will then provide a detailed introduction to the theoretical and methodological commitments of Evolutionary Psychology. In that chapter I will be concerned not with evaluating any of these theoretical or methodological commitments, but simply with presenting, in as persuasive a way as possible, the arguments underlying them.

These introductory chapters will be followed by two theoretical chapters. Chapter 3, Adaptation, will critique a number of claims that Evolutionary Psychologists make about the nature of psychological adaptations and the methods by which they must be discovered. In particular, I will argue that there is ongoing evolution in human psychological adaptations, so it is mistaken to believe that our minds are adapted to our Pleistocene past. Accordingly, I will reject Evolutionary Psychology's methodological doctrine that we must investigate the evolved design of the mind from the vantage of our evolutionary past. In chapter 3 I will also launch the first salvo against the idea that human psychological adaptations must constitute a universal human nature. I will demonstrate the problems with Evolutionary Psychology's arguments for a universal human nature and show that there is ample evidence of adaptive psychological variation in human populations. In chapter 4, Modularity, I will then present a case against Evolutionary Psychology's claim that the human mind consists of "hundreds or thousands" of genetically specified mental organs that are functionally specialized at solving specific adaptive problems. There are, in the adult mind, many neurological structures that are relatively specialized and that resemble mental organs. But these structures, I will argue, are not biological adaptations; they are flexible responses to the experiential conditions of an individual's life.

Chapters 3 and 4 will thus provide most of the meaning of the book's title, *Adapting Minds*, which is a riposte to the title of Evolutionary Psychology's manifesto, *The Adapted Mind*. For these chapters will argue that human populations are characterized by evolved psychological variation, *multiple minds*, rather than a single "mind" that is universal within human populations. And, rather than being *adapted* to our Pleistocene past, these chapters will argue that human minds are continually *adapting* in at least two senses. First, at the population level, human minds are continuously adapting to changing environments over evolutionary time; there continues to be evolution in human psychological characteristics. And, second, at the individual level, a human mind continually adapts to changing environments over the course of an individual's lifetime; it is not a static structure preprogrammed with the ways in which it will respond to different experiences it may encounter.

Some of the ideas I will criticize in these chapters have been criticized by others. The Norwegian Evolutionary Psychologist Leif Kennair has responded to these criticisms by claiming that they are rather empty. Kennair argues that Evolutionary Psychology should be evaluated on the basis of the empirical *results* it has produced, rather than criticized on purely abstract theoretical grounds. In particular, Kennair cites the three exemplars of Evolutionary Psychology discussed above: Cosmides and Tooby's work on "cheater detection," Buss's work on mate preferences, and Daly and Wilson's work on "discriminative parental solicitude." The theoretical principles of Evolutionary Psychology can't be wrong, despite appearances, Kennair argues, if they have led to such impressive results. Thus, he concludes, "I claim that these [exemplars] are what need to be addressed critically in any attempt at disqualifying Evolutionary Psychology."[10]

Throughout the central chapters of this book I will take up Kennair's challenge, providing detailed critiques of the exemplars he cites as well as some others. Cosmides and Tooby's work on "cheater detection" will be discussed in chapter 4. Chapter 5, Mating, will analyze the research that is believed to support the claims that males have an evolved mate preference for nubile females and that females have an evolved mate preference for high-status males. Chapter 6, Marriage, will then examine claims that Evolutionary Psychologists have made about human marriage and the psychological adaptations that have purportedly evolved with it. In particular, I will critically analyze the evidence for two purported psychological adaptations. First, I will discuss Evolutionary Psychologists' claim that females have a psychological adaptation for pursuing extramarital affairs in order to "favor the sperm of a young healthy lover, while continuing to gain protection from a powerful older husband" (as we saw Desmond Morris report in the opening paragraphs of this introduction). Second, I will evaluate Buss's claim that there are evolved sex differences in jealous reactions to infidelity. In chapter 7, Parenthood, I will then analyze the evidence offered in support of Daly and Wilson's theory of "discriminative parental solicitude." I will focus extensively on Daly and Wilson's claim that stepparents abuse their children at a higher rate than genetic parents, which purportedly supports their "evolutionary theory" that humans have psychological adaptations for discriminatively allocating parental care to children they can be confident are their genetic offspring. With respect to each exemplar discussed, I will argue that the evidence does not support the confidence that Evolutionary Psychologists have in them. The cumulative effect of these chapters will be to show not only that the theoretical and methodological doctrines of Evolutionary Psychology are problematic, but that Evolutionary Psychology has not, in fact, produced any solid empirical results.

In chapter 8, "Human Nature," I will then take a step back from the details of empirical research in order to engage some very broad theoretical ideas regarding the idea of human nature. I will argue not only that Evolutionary Psychology's theory of a universal human nature is mistaken, but that the very idea of human nature is incompatible with a genuinely evolutionary understanding of our species. If we are to have a successful evolutionary psychology, I will argue, we need to abandon altogether the quest for human nature.

These chapters will traverse some rugged theoretical and methodological terrain. But, although the ideas presented in the chapters to follow are intended to be challenging and provocative to researchers in the field of evolutionary psychology, my goal throughout is to present them in a way that is accessible to the same general audience that has been interested in the popular works written in support of Evolutionary Psychology. Indeed, the book is self-contained in the sense that every idea discussed in the book will be explained in the book. There are no prerequisites for understanding the arguments I will present. For I believe that it is important that everyone with an interest in evolutionary psychology be able to understand both sides to the story of Evolutionary Psychology. Evolutionary Psychologists have been very successful in conveying their ideas to a broader public, and I strive in this book to convey to the same broad public the other side of the story. Everyone should be able to understand the problems with Evolutionary Psychology and to understand why we must move beyond Evolutionary Psychology in order to one day achieve a better evolutionary psychology.

# 1 | Evolution

Evolutionary Psychologists claim that their account of human nature follows from applying the principles of evolutionary biology to the study of the human mind. Consequently, to truly understand Evolutionary Psychology, and to be in a position to critically evaluate it, it is essential to have a basic understanding of evolutionary theory. This chapter provides the necessary introduction to the fundamentals of evolutionary biology. For the initiate, this may be a slow go. But theoretical principles and concepts explained in this chapter will repeatedly turn up later in our examination of Evolutionary Psychology, so understanding them is a necessary first step toward understanding Evolutionary Psychology.

In developing their account of human nature, Evolutionary Psychologists build on (their interpretation of) the reigning orthodoxy in evolutionary biology. Aspects of this reigning orthodoxy are currently being challenged by a number of researchers in developmental biology. As a result, one could endorse one of these recent challenges and criticize Evolutionary Psychology for erecting itself on a mistaken biological foundation. Although some have taken this approach, I will not. For I think it is far too early to tell whether any of these challenges will fundamentally change the way we think about evolution. Instead, throughout this book I will take for granted the reigning orthodoxy in evolutionary biology, just as Evolutionary Psychologists do. Here, then, is a brief introduction to orthodox neo-Darwinian evolutionary biology.

## The Nature of Evolution

For Darwin, and for several generations of biologists after him, evolution was conceived of as *descent with modification*. Each component of this definition, *descent* and *modification*, requires some comment. Consider first descent.

According to this conception of evolution, evolution occurs only in *lineages*, which are populations of organisms that are related by descent. A population, in the biological sense, is a group of reproductively interacting organisms. As organisms in a population reproduce, they create a new generation, which itself reproductively interacts to spawn yet another generation of reproductively interacting organisms. This process creates a temporally extended sequence of populations, the later of which are descended from the earlier by reproduction, and such a temporal sequence of populations is a lineage. In a lineage, offspring tend to inherit their characteristics from their parents, so that offspring resemble their parents more than they resemble unrelated organisms in their lineage. "Descent," then, indicates a lineage of organisms that are characterized by hereditary similarity between parents and their offspring.

"Modification" refers to change across generations in the distribution of characteristics, or traits, in a lineage. A trait can be any one of an organism's observable properties, from an organ or bit of morphology to a form of behavior. As the organisms in a population reproduce to create a new generation, there may or may not be changes in the frequencies of traits from one generation to the next. If one generation of a human population is 65 percent brown-eyed, 25 percent green-eyed, and 10 percent blue-eyed, for example, and if the percentages of these eye colors are different in the next generation, then there has been "modification" of that lineage. Thus, for Darwin and several generations of biologists after him, evolution was change in the frequencies of hereditary characteristics across generations in a lineage. It is important to note that, according to this definition, evolution does not concern changes that individual organisms undergo during their lifetimes. Rather, evolution consists only in the changes *across generations* within a lineage in the frequencies of characteristics of organisms.

There were two important holes in this conception of evolution, which Darwin and his early successors did not adequately fill. First, descent with modification requires some mechanism of inheritance, which is causally responsible for the resemblance between parents and their offspring. But the process by which offspring inherit their characteristics from their parents was not successfully explained by Darwin or his early successors. Second, descent with modification clearly requires variation in populations, since the frequencies of hereditary characteristics cannot change from one generation to another unless those characteristics occur in more than one form. Further, the variation in a population occasionally includes evolutionary novelties, characteristics that didn't appear in a parent generation but that make their appearance in some members of the offspring generation, who can then transmit that characteristic to their progeny. The source of these evolutionary novelties was also not successfully explained by Darwin's theory.

As it turned out, the development of genetics in the twentieth century illuminated both of these issues. It was discovered, first of all, that offspring inherit their parents' characteristics because parents transmit their *genes* to their offspring in the process of reproduction, and genes causally influence the *phenotypes*—the anatomical structures, physiological states, or behavioral forms—that organisms exhibit. Thus, offspring resemble their parents because the genes that causally influenced parental phenotypes are directly transmitted to offspring, in whom those same genes causally influence the development of the same phenotypes. Genes were consequently recognized as playing a dual role in evolution: They are the units of heredity, which get directly transmitted from parents to offspring in reproduction, and they guide the development of organisms in ways that influence the phenotypes they possess. It was also discovered, however, that an organism's phenotype does not affect the genes it can transmit to its offspring. As a result, no modifications to an organism's phenotype during the course of its life affect the genes its offspring possess. So, genes were seen as the locus of two causal arrows, one running from the genes of an organism to its phenotypes and the other running from the genes of an organism to the genes of its offspring. But there is no causal arrow running from the phenotypes of an organism to the genes of its offspring. No matter how much body-building you do in your life, your babies won't be any stronger than they would be if you were a couch potato. Similarly, breaking your arm will not affect the bones of your offspring.

Developments in genetics also led to the discovery that, in the process of reproduction, genes sometimes *mutate* into new forms. Consequently, the evolutionarily novel phenotypes that occasionally appear in a lineage are the result of mutated genes, which produce novel phenotypes in the individuals with those genes. Once a mutated gene appears in a population, it can be transmitted to the offspring of organisms with that gene, and the novel phenotype it produces can be transmitted along with it.

Since genes are the key to both inheritance and the appearance of evolutionary novelties, they came to be seen as central to the process of descent with modification. Indeed, since phenotypes are produced by genes, and phenotypes have no effect on the genes available to be transmitted across generations, genes came to be seen as the very locus at which evolution occurs. The discoveries of modern genetics thus gave rise to a wholly new definition of evolution. According to this new definition, which is now standard within contemporary evolutionary biology, *evolution is change in gene or genotype frequencies (at a particular locus) across generations in a lineage*. Thus, by this genetic definition of evolution, transgenerational changes in the frequencies of phenotypes do not constitute evolution unless they reflect changes in gene or genotype frequencies.

There are a number of concepts in this last paragraph, however, that are so far undefined, and the modern definition of evolution will consequently make little sense to the initiate. In order to understand the modern genetic theory of evolution, it is necessary to take a brief excursion into elementary genetics. Since this book is about human psychology, I will focus on human genetics. But the initiate should be aware that there is far more in heaven and on (and under) earth—much of it incredibly bizarre—than can be captured by a brief introduction to human genetics. The initiate should also be aware that, while some of the following may not be especially titillating compared with the evolutionary psychology of human mating, for example, concepts to be introduced here will appear again later. (It should also be noted that the definition of "evolution" explained here is a definition of *microevolution*, evolutionary change *within* species. Macroevolution concerns the birth and extinction of species, and the mechanics of macroevolution are irrelevant to the topics discussed in this book.)

First, then, human bodies contain cells, the nuclei of which contain chromosomes, which are long strings of deoxyribonucleic acid, or DNA. DNA itself is a long string composed of the four nucleic acid bases adenine, guanine, cytosine, and thymine (known as A, G, C, and T, respectively). For heuristic purposes, a chromosome can be thought of as containing a sequence of slots, called *loci*, each of which is occupied by a *gene*, which is a short, replicable segment of DNA, or nucleic acid bases. The different forms of a gene that can occupy a locus are called *alleles*, which are alternative sequences of A, G, C, or T at a particular locus. Alleles can be thought of as "rivals" for occupying that locus.

The nuclei of the cells that make up a human body—the cells that form the liver, brain, skin, and so on—contain 23 pairs of chromosomes and are called *diploid* cells. In diploid cells, the pairs of chromosomes are aligned so that we can think of the opposing loci on paired chromosomes as a single (diploid) locus that is occupied by a pair of alleles, where the pair of alleles an organism has at a locus is called its *genotype*. If different genes occur at a locus in a population, then an organism can be either *homozygous* or *heterozygous* at that locus. For example, consider a simple case in which there are two different alleles, designated $A$ and $a$, that can occur at some locus in a population. Then a pair of these alleles can be a pair of identical alleles (the pair $AA$ or the pair $aa$) or a pair of different alleles (the pair $Aa$). If an organism has the same allele in each opposing slot, if it has the $AA$ or $aa$ genotype, it is a *homozygote*; and if it has different alleles in the opposing slots, if it has the $Aa$ genotype, it is a *heterozygote*.

In addition to diploid cells human bodies contain some *haploid* cells, the nuclei of which contain 23 single, unpaired chromosomes. These cells, called *gametes*, are formed by a process called *meiosis*. In meiosis a diploid cell first undergoes a process of DNA replication, which generates another copy of each chromosome contained in the nucleus. This is followed by two rounds of cell division, in which the chromosomes separate from one another and divide into four haploid cells. To make this less abstract, consider the process of meiosis with respect to a single locus containing the $Aa$ genotype. Meiosis is a process whereby that single diploid $Aa$ cell replicates and divides to produce two haploid cells containing $A$ and two haploid cells containing $a$. Consequently, the result of meiosis is that an organism's DNA gets split in half: Half of the genes in a diploid cell take up residence in one haploid cell and the other half take up residence in a different haploid cell. Thus, while all an organism's diploid cells are genetically identical (with the exception of cells in which there has been a mutation), its gametes are routinely genetically different from one another.

The gametes produced in meiosis are important in the process of reproduction, since they form the egg cells in females and the sperm cells in males. During fertilization an egg cell and sperm cell fuse to form a new diploid cell, called a *zygote*, from which a new organism develops. Reproduction is thus a process whereby each of two parents contributes a gamete, which contains half of the parent's genes, to the formation of a diploid cell that will develop into an organism of the next generation. Half of the genes in the diploid cells that form that newly developing organism's body will thus have come from its mother's egg (which contains half of the mother's genes) and the other half from its father's sperm (which contains half of the father's genes).

Now consider how zygote genotypes are determined. For simplicity, consider again a single locus at which the three genotypes $AA$, $aa$, and $Aa$ occur in a population. And suppose that mating in this population is *random*— that is, there is no overall statistical tendency for like genotypes to mate with one another. If two $AA$ organisms reproduce, each will contribute only $A$ gametes, which will fuse to form $AA$ zygotes; so all the offspring of two $AA$ organisms will also be $AA$. Similarly, all offspring of two $aa$ organisms will also be *aa*. If an *AA* organism reproduces with an *aa* organism, on the other hand, all their offspring will be heterozygotes with the *Aa* genotype.

Things are more complicated, however, when reproduction involves heterozygotes. Recall that half of an *Aa* organism's gametes will be *A* and the other half *a*. (There are exceptions to this, but they need not concern us here.) If an *Aa* organism reproduces with an *AA* organism, 50 percent of all possible zygotes created through their matings will be *AA* and the other 50 percent will be *Aa*. This is because the *AA* organism will contribute only *A* gametes to their union, which will fuse with the 50 percent *A* gametes contributed by the heterozygote to form the *AA* zygotes and with the other 50 percent *a* gametes from the heterozygote to form the *Aa* zygotes. Similarly, if a heterozygote reproduces with an *aa* organism, 50 percent of all possible zygotes created through their matings will be *Aa* and 50 percent will be *aa*. If two heterozygotes mate with one another, on the other hand, half the female's eggs will be *A* and half *a*, and half the male's sperm will be *A* and half *a*. Of the *A* eggs, half will thus be fertilized by *A* sperm and half by *a* sperm, so 25 percent of the fertilized eggs will be *AA* and 25 percent *Aa*. Similarly, of the *a* eggs, half will be fertilized by *A* sperm and half by *a* sperm, producing an additional 25 percent of the fertilized eggs that are *Aa* and 25 percent that are *aa*. In total, then, 25 percent of the zygotes will be *AA*, 50 percent will be *Aa*, and 25 percent will be *aa*.

I've spoken as though all an organism's gametes go to form zygotes. This, of course, is false; many parents have only one child, for example. If heterozygote parents have one child, it will be just one of the three possible genotypes. The way the above principles apply to such cases is in terms of probabilities. That is, there is a 25 percent chance that a child of two heterozygotes will be *AA*, a 50 percent chance that it will be a heterozygote like its parents, and a 25 percent chance that it will be *aa*. This use of probabilities assumes that the genotypes of zygotes in an indefinitely large population of heterozygotes would occur in the 25/50/25 percent frequencies mentioned above, even if many heterozygote pairs in that population produce only one child.

You will have noticed that, while matings between two *AA* organisms and between two *aa* organisms produce only *AA* and *aa* offspring respectively, matings between heterozygotes can produce both heterozygous and homozygous offspring. This has implications for the understanding of evolution as change in gene or genotype frequencies across generations. For suppose that there is a very small population of heterozygotes that reproduces in replacement numbers—that is, each couple produces only two offspring. Since we are supposing that each organism in this population has the *Aa* genotype, there are two alleles, *A* and *a*, that occur at the locus that interests us. Further, since every organism is *Aa*, half the alleles that occur at that locus are *A* and half are *a*; in other words, the frequency of *A* is 50 percent and the frequency of *a* is 50 percent. Now, although unlikely, it is possible for each couple to produce one *AA* and one *Aa* offspring. In that case, in the offspring generation the frequency of the *A* allele will increase to 75 percent (since three out of every four slots in the diploid locus are occupied by *A*) and the frequency of the *a* allele will decrease to 25 percent. Under the modern genetic definition of evolution, this constitutes significant evolution.

While this example of a change in gene frequencies also involves a change in genotype frequencies (since the population evolved from 100 percent *Aa* to 50 percent *AA* and 50 percent *Aa*), it is possible for there to be a change in genotype frequencies across generations without a corresponding change in gene frequencies. To see how, suppose there is a population consisting of just eight organisms—three *AA*, three *aa*, and two *Aa* organisms. The alleles *A* and *a* each occur with a frequency of 50 percent in this generation of the population. (There are six copies of *A* from the three *AA* organisms and two copies of *A* from the two *Aa* organisms; and there are six copies of *a* from the three *aa* organisms and two copies from the two *Aa* organisms. There are thus eight copies each of *A* and *a*, out of a total of sixteen alleles at the locus.) Now suppose that two *AA* organisms mate with each other as do two *aa* organisms, and one *Aa* organism mates with the remaining *AA* organism while the other *Aa* organism mates with the remaining *aa* organism. Suppose further that each of these pairs produces just two offspring, so the next generation of the population also contains just eight organisms. We know that the offspring from the homozygote matings will be homozygotes of the same genotype and that there is a 50 percent chance that the offspring from the heterozygote-homozygote matings will also be homozygotes. Suppose that in fact the heterozygote-homozygote pairs produce only homozygotes. Then the next generation of the population will consist of four *AA* organisms (two from the *AA-AA* mating and two from the *AA-Aa* mating) and four *aa* organisms (two from the *aa-aa* mating and two from the *Aa-aa* mating). Although the gene frequencies have not changed, both *A* and *a* remaining at 50 percent, the genotype frequencies have. For whereas 37.5 percent of the parental generation was *AA*, 37.5 percent *aa*, and 25 percent *Aa*, the offspring generation is 50 percent *AA* and 50 percent *aa*. Under the modern genetic definition of evolution, this also constitutes significant evolution.

The kinds of evolution we have just considered can also produce changes across generations in the frequencies of phenotypes in a population. The reason is that genes regulate the synthesis of proteins, the stuff of which our bodies are made, and differences between bodies or between parts of the same body are a product of differences in the proteins of which they are made. By regulating protein synthesis, genes consequently guide the development of organisms, and this influences the phenotypes that organisms possess. When a gene influences a particular phenotype in this way, biologists say it is a *gene for* that phenotype. Thus, a change in gene or genotype frequencies can produce a change in the frequencies of the phenotypes influenced by those genes or genotypes.

But why do I say that genes "influence" phenotypes, rather than saying that genes "determine" phenotypes? This is because, by themselves, genes don't determine anything. One can't simply put some carefully selected genes in a petri dish, for example, and grow a cute little button nose. For how a gene affects the phenotype of an organism depends on precisely when (or if) it is switched on and off in the process of development, and that in turn depends on the properties of the gene's environment. The environment of a gene includes not only the environment outside the organism (which affects the surface of the organism), but also the cells surrounding the one in which the gene resides (which can affect gene action, sometimes as a result of cascading effects from the environment outside the organism) and the other genes within the same cell (whose patterns of activity can affect when a gene is switched on or off). In short, the development of an organism is not simply a matter of gene action, but a matter of causal *interaction* between genes and their environment.

For this reason, there is no straightforward relationship of "determination" between genotypes and phenotypes. Indeed, given the interaction between genes and environment in development, even if two individuals possess the same genotype, they can differ in phenotype as a result of developing under different environmental conditions. For example, if we plant corn seeds of the same genotype in different soil conditions, and fertilize and water those plants differently, the resulting corn plants can differ significantly in phenotypes such as height of plant and sweetness of kernels. So the same genotype can produce a range of different phenotypes across a range of different developmental environments. Some genotypes tend to produce the same phenotype across a very wide range of different environments. But rarely is there a straightforward one-to-one relation between a genotype and a phenotype. Genotypes typically produce different phenotypes if developmental conditions are varied sufficiently.

But, if this is true, what sense does it make to speak of a "gene for" a particular phenotype? To say that a gene or genotype G is "for" a phenotype P means first of all that, other things being equal, an organism with G is more likely to have P than is any organism without G (that is, with a possible rival allele of G). The clause "other things being equal" is important here, since it includes the environments in which the organisms develop. The point is to compare organisms within developmentally similar environments to see whether having G makes a difference with respect to having P. For, if we compared organisms with G in one developmental environment to organisms without G in a different developmental environment, then any difference among them with respect to their having P could be due to the differences in their developmental environments. The clause "other things being equal" enables us to focus on how a change in having G produces a change in having P, rather than on how a change in the environment produces a change in having P. But this first condition is purely correlational, requiring that G be correlated with P in relevant environments in order to be "for" P. Consequently, this condition alone fails to distinguish the case in which G actually produces P from the case in which G produces some other phenotype that is correlated with P. Thus, to say that G is "for" P means, second, that G must play a causal role in the development of P (in those organisms with P). When these two conditions are met, it is perfectly sensible to speak of genes or genotypes as being "for" phenotypes.

The fact that phenotypes are produced by the interaction of genes and environment has a couple of implications with respect to understanding the connection between evolution at the genetic level and changes across generations in the phenotypes of organisms in a lineage. First, if a gene increases in frequency across generations, the phenotype that it is the gene for can increase in frequency only if the developmentally relevant aspects of the environment remain relatively constant. This is because there will only be a particular range of developmental environments in which that gene will produce the phenotype it is for. So, if the environment changes so as to fall outside the range in which that gene produces that phenotype, then any increase in the gene's frequency will not be accompanied by an increase in the frequency of the phenotype it is for. Thus, in order for patterns of phenotypic change across generations to parallel patterns of evolution at the genetic level, the developmentally relevant properties of the environment must remain relatively stable across those generations.

Second, because genotypes can produce different phenotypes in different developmental environments, it is possible for there to be phenotypic change across generations in the absence of genetic evolution. This can occur simply in virtue of changes in the environment in which genotypes develop. For example, even if we control the genes of corn plants from one generation to the next, so that there is no genetic change, it is still possible to produce taller corn plants in the later generation by altering how much the plants are fertilized and watered. Such transgenerational changes in the environment can produce what I will call *phenotypic evolution* in the absence of any underlying genetic evolution. Thus, phenotypic evolution—changes across generations in phenotype frequencies—can be strictly environmentally driven. This happened in many human populations during the twentieth century, when improved diets produced an increase in average height over the course of the century.

## The Causes of Evolution

So far we have been concerned with what evolution *is*. But what *causes* evolution? As mentioned earlier, evolution can occur only if there is *variation* in a population. For, if evolution is change in gene or genotype frequencies, there must be at least two genotypes occurring at a particular locus in a population, the frequencies of which then get altered across generations. So, if a population is composed of organisms that are genetically identical, the only way that evolution can occur is if a new genetic variant gets introduced into the population. With this in mind, the causes of evolution can be divided into two very broad types: One type of cause introduces new variants into a population and the other changes the frequencies of already existing variants. Consider these in turn.

There are two main processes that cause evolution by introducing new variants into a population, one of which is mutation. Recall that the first stage of meiosis involves the replication, or copying, of the genes on each chromosome in a diploid cell. In the process of gene replication, there are occasional copying errors, in which one of the nucleic acid bases in a sequence gets translated incorrectly—for example, an A in a sequence of bases gets copied as T. The result is a new gene—a new sequence of bases—that differs from the gene from which it was copied at that one position in the sequence of bases. A copying error of this kind is called a *mutation*. The mutation is then shuttled into one of an organism's gametes where it can be transmitted to one of its offspring, in whom the new mutant gene can then produce some novel phenotype.

The other process that causes evolution by introducing new variants into a population is *recombination*. To illustrate, consider a double heterozygote, an organism with the *Aa* genotype at one locus and the *Bb* genotype at another locus, where *A* and *B* occur on one chromosome while *a* and *b* occur on the other. In such a double heterozygote, meiosis without recombination produces two *AB* gametes and two *ab* gametes. (Recall that *A* and *B* are alleles at different loci on the *same* chromosome, as are *a* and *b*. So *AB* is not a genotype; it is a chromosome type.) Sometimes, however, after chromosome replication but before the first cell division, chromosomes align themselves and exchange genes in a process called *crossing over*. For example, an *AB* chromosome may align with an *ab* chromosome and exchange its *B* with its partner's *b*, thereby transforming the *AB* chromosome into an *Ab* chromosome and its partner into an *aB* chromosome. The second stage of meiosis will then produce four distinct gametes: *AB*, *Ab*, *aB*, and *ab*. In this process, genes get recombined, and new genetic variants get introduced, specifically the *Ab* and *aB* chromosomes.

Recombination has a significant effect in reproduction. For, in the absence of recombination, if two double heterozygotes—that is, two *AaBb* organisms—reproduce, their offspring have a 25 percent chance of being *AABB*, a 50 percent chance of being *AaBb*, and a 25 percent chance of being *aabb*. But, if recombination occurs during meiosis in one of these organisms, their offspring have instead a 12.5 percent chance of being *AABB*, a 25 percent chance of being *AaBb*, a 12.5 percent chance of being *aabb*, and an additional 12.5 percent chance each of being *AABb*, *AaBB*, *Aabb*, and *aaBb*. And, if recombination occurs during meiosis in both parents, there are further possibilities. Recombination can thus introduce into an offspring generation significant genetic variation that wasn't in the parent generation. The difference between this and mutation is that mutation introduces new variants by creating *new genes*, while recombination does so by creating *new combinations* of genes on a chromosome.

It is important to note that both mutation and recombination are *nondirected*, or *random*, processes. This means that the fact that a new variant might be beneficial to an organism does not increase the probability that it will be produced. Indeed, the overwhelming majority of mutations are either neutral or detrimental. Thus, the processes that generate new variation in a population operate independently of the processes that determine what is beneficial or detrimental to the organisms in that population. But, while new variants are random in origin, their frequency in a population once they have arisen may or may not be random, as we are about to see.

There are also two main processes that cause evolution by altering the frequencies of already existing variants in a population. One of these is *natural selection*, which is a process that occurs when three conditions obtain in a population. First, there must be preexisting *phenotypic variation* in the population. Second, the variant phenotypes must be *hereditary*—that is, there must be genes for each of the variant phenotypes, which parents transmit to their offspring. Third, these hereditary phenotypic differences must be responsible for *differences in fitness*.

This third condition requires some explaining. *Fitness*, as it is most commonly characterized, is a measure of an organism's ability to survive and reproduce. Thus, if one organism is fitter, or has greater fitness, than another, the former has a greater ability to survive and reproduce than the latter. This does not mean that the fitter organism actually will survive longer and reproduce more than the less fit organism. You may be better able than I to lift 300 pounds, but your greater ability may never have the chance to show itself in actual performance, since you may never have the opportunity to attempt to lift 300 pounds. Similarly, one organism may be better able than another to survive and reproduce even though it doesn't actually outlive and outreproduce the other. It may die from a freakish accident before puberty, for example. So fitness is not a measure of an organism's *actual* survival and reproduction, but a measure of its *ability* to survive and reproduce.

In addition, an organism's ability to survive and reproduce depends not simply on its physical characteristics, but on how well adapted those characteristics are to the environment the organism inhabits, which in turn depends on the precise nature of the environmental demands, or *selection pressures*, an organism faces. For heuristic purposes (and with serious qualifications to be discussed in chapter 3), we can think of these selection pressures as posing *adaptive problems*, which an organism must solve in order to survive and reproduce. Such problems would include finding food, avoiding predators, and attracting mates. An organism's phenotypes can then be thought of as providing potential "solutions" to these problems. Some organisms may thus be endowed with a phenotype (for example, greater running speed) that provides a better solution to an adaptive problem (escaping predators) than the phenotypes with which other (slower) organisms are endowed. To say that fitness is a measure of an organism's ability to survive and reproduce, then, is to say that fitness is a measure of how well an organism's characteristics solve the adaptive problems posed by its environment. Thus, an organism's fitness is always relative to its environment; its characteristics may make it better able to survive and reproduce in one environment than in another.

As many biologists have pointed out, however, conceiving of fitness as a measure of the ability to survive and reproduce in an environment is a little misleading. For survival, in itself, means nothing in evolutionary terms. Surely, if one fails to survive a childhood illness, one will not contribute to the gene pool of the next generation. But one's impact on future gene pools is no greater if one is a THINKER (half of a couple with Two Healthy Incomes, No Kids, and Early Retirement). What's important in evolution is whether one *reproduces*; survival matters only insofar as it enables reproduction. But the evolutionary significance of reproduction, in turn, lies in the fact that, in contributing offspring to the next generation, one is transmitting (half of) one's genes to that generation and thereby affecting the gene and genotype frequencies in that generation. Once we reconceive fitness as a measure of the ability to survive *to* reproduce, then, and recognize that reproduction is a matter of transmitting one's genes to the next generation, we can redefine "fitness" as a measure of an organism's *expected genetic contribution* to future generations. In this refined definition, the term "expected" reflects the degree to which an organism's characteristics enable it to reproduce: Its ability to reproduce is measured as the *probability* of its reproducing. And the term "genetic contribution" reflects how many copies of its genes an organism contributes to future generations via the number of its offspring. Thus, to say that the organisms in a population differ in fitness is to say that they differ in their expected genetic contributions to future generations (in the specific environment they inhabit). Given this definition, we can then define the fitness of a genotype or phenotype as the average fitness of all the organisms with that genotype or phenotype.

Returning now to the three conditions under which natural selection occurs, when (1) phenotypic variation is (2) hereditary and (3) responsible for fitness differences in a population, the phenotypic traits that enhance fitness in that population (that is, the phenotypic traits that make their possessors *fitter than* organisms possessing alternative traits) will increase in frequency across generations. This is because organisms with a fitness-enhancing trait will, *on average*, outreproduce the other organisms, thereby transmitting more of their genes to the next generation than those other organisms transmit. These genes, of course, will include the gene for the fitness-enhancing trait. And, as more copies of that gene get transmitted to the next generation, proportionately more of the population will develop the fitness-enhancing trait, and it will thereby increase in frequency in the population. This process is natural selection, and it changes the frequencies of genes in a population as a function of the phenotypic effects they produce, increasing in frequency those genes with fitness-enhancing phenotypic effects and decreasing in frequency those genes with fitness-reducing phenotypic effects. Of course, as it changes the frequencies of the genes with these phenotypic effects, it also changes the frequencies of the phenotypes they produce. When a phenotypic trait increases in frequency as a result of natural selection in this way, biologists say that there has been *selection for* that trait—that the trait has conferred a *selective advantage*, or *reproductive advantage*, on its bearers.

It is worth noting that some biologists apply the term *natural selection* only to selection for traits that affect survival, while applying the term *sexual selection* to selection for traits that affect the ability to attract and mate with members of the opposite sex. In other words, traits that are solutions to adaptive problems posed by members of the opposite sex evolve under sexual selection, whereas traits that are solutions to adaptive problems posed by the rest of the environment evolve under natural selection. Other biologists treat sexual selection as an aspect of natural selection. But distinguishing the two can be useful when analyzing some traits, since some traits are detrimental with respect to survival, yet enhance reproductive success by appealing to members of the opposite sex. The classic example is the peacock's tail, which is detrimental to survival (since it attracts predators and impairs the ability to escape), yet appeals to peahens and, hence, increases the mating ability of well-endowed peacocks. For the most part I will simply use the term *selection*, encompassing both natural and sexual selection. But, when necessary, I will refer specifically to natural or sexual selection.

Finally, the other process that can cause evolution by altering the frequencies of already existing variants in a population is *genetic drift*, which is due to two types of chance event: random survival and random sampling of gametes.

Random survival is due to random events—for example, floods, fires, or lightning strikes—that kill a much larger number of organisms with one allele than those with the rival allele. This would have the effect of making the latter allele more frequent in the next generation, since its bearers would have survived to reproduce at a higher rate than the bearers of the unlucky allele. This would constitute evolution, but it would be due to chance rather than to differences in fitness.

We have already touched on the random sampling of gametes. Recall that every organism produces many more gametes than will go to form zygotes. We can thus think of fertilization as a process that randomly "draws" one gamete from the total pool of gametes created by each parent organism. When a population contains *Aa* organisms, which produce gametes that are 50 percent *A* and 50 percent *a*, the random drawing of their gametes, *in each case*, has a 50 percent chance of yielding an *A* and a 50 percent chance of yielding an *a*. But there is a possibility that the total number of drawings of gametes from heterozygotes in a population will contain many more copies of one allele than of the other. This is analogous to flipping a coin a number of times. Each coin toss has a 50 percent chance of landing heads and a 50 percent chance of landing tails. Nonetheless, it is possible that a string of twelve coin flips will yield nine heads and three tails. When the random sampling of gametes draws a greater number of one allele than of its rival in this way, there is a change in allele frequencies across generations, but it is due strictly to a randomness built into the process of fertilization rather than to selection for one allele over the others.

Drift is a causal force in evolution in every generation, since random survival and random sampling of gametes occurs in every generation. But frequently the effects of drift are offset by selection. In order for drift to be the cause of a *long-term evolutionary trend*, the rival alleles at a locus must be *selectively neutral* (that is, no one of the alleles can confer a selective advantage on its bearers). When rival alleles are selectively neutral, the frequencies of those alleles can change greatly over many generations due strictly to genetic drift. Indeed, drift can drive an allele to fixation, or extinction, in a population just as surely as selection can, since the effects of drift can be compounded over many generations just like the effects of selection. But these effects of drift are greatest in small populations. This is because in larger populations the frequencies of alleles in the pool of actually sampled gametes more closely approximate the frequencies of those alleles in the total pool of gametes available to be sampled. This, again, is analogous to the coin-flipping case. A three-to-one ratio of heads to tails is more common in series of twelve coin tosses than in series of twelve thousand coin tosses. As the number of tosses in the series increases, there are more and more series in which the frequency of heads and tails closely approximates 50 percent. Similarly, drift is far more likely to have significant effects in small populations than in large ones, since the alleles in the actually sampled heterozygote gametes in large populations more closely approximate a 50/50 frequency. In large populations, therefore, selection tends to be the primary cause of long-term evolutionary trends.

## Adaptation

These are the nuts and bolts of evolution, but how do they fit together to build all the complex, functionally integrated organisms that we see in the world? For organisms are composed of numerous and diverse parts that are well adapted to one another and to particular features of the world, and that appear very intricately designed for their functionally specialized roles. Darwin called such functionally specialized parts of organisms "organs of extreme perfection and complication" and, in illustration, marveled at the human eye, "with all its inimitable contrivances for adjusting the focus to different distances, for admitting different amounts of light, and for the correction of spherical and chromatic aberration."[1] The eye, of course, is merely one of many examples of such "perfection and complication." The wings of birds are very well designed for flight, the echolocation (sonar) system of bats is very well designed for detecting flying insects at night, and the coloration of many species provides excellent camouflage from predators.

Such "organs of extreme perfection and complication" appear to be designed for a *purpose*. Echolocation, for example, appears to be designed precisely so that bats can detect the flying insects that make up their diet. And to say that a part is designed for a purpose is to say that an organism possesses it *because* that part solves a particular adaptive problem. So, bats appear to possess echolocation precisely because possessing echolocation enables them to eat. But, if all apparent design in nature is the product of evolution, rather than the product of creation by some intelligent being, how can there be such design-for-a-purpose in nature? How, in other words, can the processes discussed so far account for the apparent purposeful design of functionally specialized "organs of extreme perfection and complication"?

Whether it is a matter of building a trait that appears well designed for solving some adaptive problem or building an entire organism composed of numerous such traits that are all functionally integrated, the process is the same: iterated cycles of modifying a preexisting structure and retaining the modification. This process created all of the world's diverse organic forms out of simple replicating molecules. Of course it took a very long time. But this book is not about the origins of species. For our purposes, it is sufficient to understand how complex traits that solve adaptive problems are created by the causes of evolution just discussed—to understand how traits can develop *within* a species that make organisms well adapted to the specific demands of their environment. Consider first how such traits can evolve under selection, then consider whether they can evolve under drift.

Suppose there is a population of birds whose beaks vary slightly in size. The sole food supply for this population is seeds that are digestible only once they have been extracted from their hulls. To extract the seeds, the birds must use their beaks. Suppose that birds with the slightly broader beaks are the most efficient at hulling the seeds, hence get the most nutrition, and consequently enjoy a slight reproductive advantage over the other birds in the population. The gene for the broad beak will thus increase in frequency in the population, as will the broad beak itself.

But suppose also that the broader beak would be even more efficient at hulling seeds if it had slightly sharper edges. And suppose that there is a gene in the population that would produce sharper-edged beaks if it mutated. Of course, since mutation is random, the fact that sharper beaks would be beneficial doesn't increase the probability that the desirable mutation will occur. Also, since mutation is random, the mutation for sharper-edged beaks is just as likely to occur in a bird without the broad beak as it is to occur in a bird with the broad beak (in whom it would be most beneficial). But, as the gene for the broad beak becomes ever more frequent in the population, there is an increased probability that, if the mutation for sharper-edged beaks occurs, it will occur in conjunction with the gene for the broader beak, and thereby provide a beak that is even better designed for hulling seeds. This increased probability of a better beak is analogous to rolling dice. Suppose you need a three to turn up on a rolled die. If you roll just one die, there is a one-sixth probability of getting a three. And, if you roll twelve dice, each die has a one-sixth probability of turning up three. But your odds of getting a three are greatly improved if you can roll twelve dice rather than one die. Similarly, as the gene for a broad beak spreads in the population, there is an increased probability that a mutation for sharper edges might occur with it and, hence, further modify the beak in a way that makes it even better designed for hulling seeds. If the beak does get further modified in this way, the improved beak will become more frequent in the population over succeeding generations. And so on.

This process—a new mutation introduces a beneficial modification that is retained by selection—can be repeated many times over a very long period of time. After a very large number of generations, the population can come to be composed of a large number of birds with beaks that are extremely well designed for hulling seeds, beaks that have a shape that conforms to the demands of the seed hulls and are powered by muscles that exert efficient force in cracking those hulls. And that design will have been produced by a process of cumulative retention of slight design improvements introduced by random mutations. (Of course, there may have been many other mutations that impaired design; but they would have been selected against and driven to extinction.) In this way, the combination of mutation (which adds modifications to preexisting traits) and selection (which preserves the new modifications that are beneficial and subtracts those that are not) can build traits of great complexity, which make their bearers highly adapted to their environment and highly successful at solving adaptive problems related to survival and reproduction.

Note that what is essential to building complex traits is the process of cumulative retention of modifications that further elaborate the design of the trait. In principle, such cumulative retention of design elaborations could be accomplished by genetic drift. For drift can increase the frequency of a design-elaborating allele in a population and thereby increase the probability that another design-elaborating mutation could occur in conjunction with it. But, if this process is guided by drift alone, by definition each new modification must be *selectively neutral*. If a modification provides a reproductive advantage to its bearers, then by definition it is undergoing selection, not drift. In addition, if each new modification were affected by drift alone, it would be as likely to drift to extinction as to drift to near fixation. (Actually, since each new modification would be introduced by an initially rare allele, the initial rarity of the allele would make it more likely to drift to extinction than fixation.) Thus, it would be monstrously unlikely that drift alone would accumulate a *whole series* of modifications to build a trait as complex as the human eye, for example. When a modification provides a selective advantage, however, selection is a force that favors its persistence, and typically proliferation, in the population and actively works against the possibility of its extinction. Since selection preserves modifications to traits that are advantageous to their bearers, it increases the probability that organisms in a population will develop complex traits that serve a purpose.

This is the crux of the issue about whether drift can create traits that solve adaptive problems so effectively as to give the appearance of having been designed for the purpose of solving those problems. For recall that, insofar as a trait's *purpose* is to serve a particular function, it is present in organisms *because of* the beneficial function it serves. A trait that has evolved under drift, however, is present in the organisms in a population only because of chance, even if it is the result of cumulative modification. In fact, even if a trait that has evolved under drift provides some benefit to the organisms that currently possess it, they possess that trait only because the gene for it has randomly drifted to a high frequency in the population, not because of the benefit the trait provides. When a trait evolves under selection, in contrast, organisms possess that trait because it provided a benefit to their ancestors from whom they inherited the gene for that trait—specifically, the benefit because of which the trait was selected. The benefit the trait provides is thus the reason why the trait spreads or persists in the population; that benefit *is* the purpose of the trait, since the trait's providing that benefit is the reason organisms possess the trait (via inheritance from ancestors in whom the trait was selected for).

A trait that is present in a current population because it performed a function (solved an adaptive problem) that enhanced fitness in an ancestral population, and was thus preserved or proliferated under selection for it, is called an *adaptation*. In other words, an adaptation is a trait that has a history of having been preserved, and possibly modified, by selection for the beneficial role it plays in an organism. Thus, an adaptation is a trait that contributed to its own persistence or proliferation; for, by enhancing the fitness of its bearers, an adaptation contributed to the reproductive success of its bearers, which contributed to the transmission of the genes for that adaptation, which in turn contributed to the development of that trait in other organisms. Adaptations, in short, are self-perpetuating design features of organisms. Organisms have those traits *because* they were beneficial to their ancestors.

It is important not to confuse adaptation with adaptiveness. A trait is adaptive if it enhances fitness, but it is an adaptation if it is possessed by organisms in a current population because they inherited it from ancestors in whom that trait enhanced fitness. As the philosopher of biology Elliott Sober so nicely puts it: "To say that a trait is an adaptation is to make a claim about the cause of its presence; to say that it is adaptive is to comment on its consequences for survival and reproduction."[2]

This distinction is important to bear in mind because of the following two implications. First, just because a trait is adaptive doesn't mean that it is an adaptation. A trait could evolve in a population under drift, but then come to enhance the fitness of its bearers if the environment of the population changes so as to make the trait useful. In such a case, the trait would be adaptive, but since it did not evolve under selection it would not be an adaptation. For adaptation is a historical concept, applying only to traits with the right sort of evolutionary history. Second, a trait could be an adaptation yet fail to be adaptive. This, too, could result from a change in a population's environment. A trait could evolve under selection, and even go to fixation in a population, yet the environmental demands to which that trait was responsive could cease, thereby rendering the trait useless. In such a case, the adaptation would no longer be adaptive. For adaptiveness is an ahistorical concept, applying only to traits that currently enhance fitness. A trait is adaptive, then, if it has *current utility*; it is an adaptation if it had *past utility*, if it evolved and is present in a current population because it *was adaptive*.

The fact that organisms possess adaptations because of the benefits those traits provided to the organisms' ancestors means that questions about why an organism possesses a particular adaptation are always ambiguous, admitting of two very distinct types of answer. To illustrate, suppose we ask why black-headed gulls remove the eggshells from their nests after their fledglings have hatched. We could answer in terms of the functioning of the neurophysiological behavior-control mechanisms in the gull and how those mechanisms respond to stimuli in the gull's environment. This would answer in terms of the immediate causal antecedents, the *proximate causes*, of the eggshell-removal behavior. We could also trace these causes back a little further in time and answer in terms of the developmental processes by which a gull comes to have the mechanisms that control eggshell removal. While this would cite causes that are not the immediate antecedents of the phenomenon to be explained, it would nonetheless explain that phenomenon by citing causes within the lifetime of the individual gull whose eggshell-removal behavior we are explaining. In that sense, it would still be an explanation citing proximate causes.

In sharp contrast, however, we could explain the eggshell-removal behavior in terms of the history of selection that caused that behavior to become widespread in, and characteristic of, black-headed gulls. Such an explanation in terms of selection would cite the fitness-enhancing benefit provided by eggshell removal, because of which eggshell removal increased in frequency in ancestral gull populations. This explanation would consist in pointing out that eggshells are conspicuous and attract the attention of birds that prey on gull fledglings; thus, removing eggshells from the nest helps protect fledglings against predation. Consequently, gulls that removed eggshells from their nests made a greater genetic contribution to subsequent generations than gulls that didn't remove their eggshells; so eggshell removal evolved to (near) fixation in gull populations. This would be an explanation in terms of the *ultimate causes* of eggshell removal, what caused the evolution of eggshell removal in gull populations. Unlike the explanation in terms of proximate causes, the explanation in terms of ultimate causes explains a gull's eggshell-removal behavior in terms of causes that acted during the evolutionary history of the lineage leading up to that gull, not in terms of causes acting during that gull's lifetime.

It is important to note that proximate explanations (those citing proximate causes) and ultimate explanations (those citing ultimate causes) do not compete with one another. It's not the case that, if one explanation is right, the other must be wrong. Rather, they complement one another by providing different kinds of information about the same phenomenon. Indeed, one could see ultimate explanations as explaining why particular proximate causes are operative. For example, the ultimate explanation of eggshell removal explains why gulls have neurophysiological mechanisms that respond to particular stimuli in a way that results in eggshell removal. But that doesn't mean that the ultimate explanation can *replace* a proximate explanation. Knowing the ultimate causes of eggshell removal doesn't give us any information about how eggshell removal gets accomplished by any individual gull. Similarly, a proximate explanation doesn't exclude an ultimate explanation, since knowing how a particular neurophysiological mechanism causes eggshell removal doesn't inform us about the causes of the evolution of eggshell removal. Thus, every adaptation can be explained in terms of both proximate and ultimate causes, where the former cites the immediate antecedent "mechanistic" causes and the latter cites the evolutionary causes.

## Phenotypic Variation

Up to this point, I have spoken of selection as a process in which some trait consistently enhances the fitness of its bearers over a very large number of generations. When this occurs, in each new generation the fitness-enhancing trait will increase in frequency in the population. If this process continues for enough generations, the trait will eventually go to *fixation* (become possessed by every organism) in a population, thereby wiping out all rival traits. While selection does sometimes drive traits to fixation in this way, it doesn't always act to eliminate phenotypic variation and create a uniform population. Indeed, there are several reasons why selection doesn't always eliminate phenotypic variation.

First, mutation and recombination introduce new variation into a population in every generation. Thus, even if selection reduces variation in each generation, by increasing the frequency of the fittest variant, it may never completely eliminate variation, since new variation is continually introduced.

Second, some phenotypic variation is selectively neutral, in which case selection won't favor any of the variants over the others (or won't favor any of the variants that are within a certain range over the others in that range). For example, population members may vary in height or weight in ways that don't affect their fitness. In such a case, selection won't winnow this variation, since no one of the variants is fitter than any of the others.

(Of course, it could be the case that extreme heights or weights would be selected *against*, while all of the nonextreme variation in height and weight would be selectively neutral.)

Third, even if a genotype for a fitness-enhancing phenotype goes to fixation under selection, the fact that the same genotype can produce different phenotypes under different developmental conditions means that the phenotype it's for won't necessarily go to fixation also. For a genotype to be selected, it needn't always produce the fitness-enhancing phenotype. It is only necessary that the *average fitness* of all the phenotypes it produces (under all its developmental conditions) be higher than the average fitness of all the phenotypes produced by alternative genotypes (under all their developmental conditions). So, even a genotype that is increasing in frequency under selection can sometimes produce phenotypes that provide no selective advantage or are positively maladaptive. Indeed, even if that genotype goes to fixation, it might still, in certain developmental conditions, produce a phenotype other than the fitness-enhancing phenotype it was selected for producing. Thus, variation in developmental conditions can produce phenotypic variation even when a beneficial genotype has gone to fixation.

These are cases in which phenotypic variation persists in a population in spite of selection, as it were. More interesting, however, are the ways in which selection can actively maintain phenotypic variation in a population. There are several ways in which selection can maintain phenotypic variation, but only two of these will be relevant to later discussions. So here I'll confine my discussion to those two ways: frequency-dependent selection and adaptive plasticity.

Consider first *frequency-dependent selection*. To get a really good handle on frequency-dependent selection, it is best to take a brief excursion into cost-benefit analyses of fitness.

Fitness, recall, is a measure of the ability to survive and reproduce in a particular environment. Many activities in which organisms engage enhance or diminish that ability. For example, female black-tipped hangingflies mate with males who offer them edible insects. When the male presents the insect, the female feeds on it while copulation occurs. Consequently, a male hangingfly enhances his ability to reproduce by capturing an insect that will entice a female. Capturing an insect is thus a *fitness benefit* for male hangingflies. Conversely, if a female lays eggs to be fertilized by a male who turns out to be sterile, she diminishes her ability to reproduce as a function of the lost eggs. Losing the eggs is for her a *fitness cost*.

Fitness costs and benefits need not be so drastic or so obvious. Each meal that we eat contains nutrients that sustain us and thereby enhances our ability to survive and reproduce relative to the ability we would possess in the absence of receiving those nutrients. We can thus think of very simple acts such as eating an apple as having an associated, yet small, fitness benefit, measured in terms of the nutrients the apple provides and the role those nutrients play in facilitating survival and reproduction. Similarly, the very act of engaging in some activity has metabolic costs, diminishing the energy available for engaging in other activities. Three hours spent in fruitless foraging diminishes one's energy store for fruitful copulations. So every activity has an associated, though perhaps small, fitness cost, measured in terms of the depletion of energy available for other activities essential to survival and reproduction.

The fitness costs and benefits of some activities in which organisms engage are independent of the behavior of other members of the organism's population. The energy gained from eating a particular food item, for example, is independent of what other individuals in the population are eating or doing. For male dung flies, there is an optimal amount of time spent copulating, which maximizes the rate of egg fertilization per unit of copulation time, and for any given male this optimum is independent of how long other males spend copulating. And for many animals there is an optimal amount of time spent foraging for food, which maximizes the energy intake per unit of foraging time, and this optimum is independent of how long other population members spend foraging. An activity with fitness costs and benefits that are independent of how other population members behave has *frequency-independent fitness*, since its fitness is independent of the frequency of that activity in a population—independent, that is, of how many population members engage in that activity.

But the fitness costs and benefits of many activities in which humans and other animals engage are not independent of the behavior of other population members. For example, in some species males fight with one another for territory. If most males in such a species only engage in threatening displays and retreat when attacked, a tactic of extreme aggression might accrue high fitness benefits to any male adopting it. However, if most males are extremely aggressive in conflicts, then aggression could exact the fitness costs of injury or death. So the fitness costs and benefits of any particular form of behavior in a conflict depend on the tactics adopted by other males in the population. Similarly, when members of one sex compete to mate with members of the opposite sex, the best tactic to employ to attract members of the opposite sex can depend on what other members of your own sex are doing to attract mates. If all other members of your sex send roses, rather than competing to find the best roses, you may be better off sending orchids, which are easier to obtain since they aren't in demand. It may pay just to be different. In fact, in general, the fitness costs and benefits associated with any activity that involves competition with some other population members will be a function of how one's competitors behave. Such an activity has *frequency-dependent fitness*, since its fitness is dependent on the frequency of that activity in a population. Consequently, the fitness of an activity with frequency-dependent fitness changes as the frequency of that activity in a population changes.

When activities have frequency-dependent fitnesses, selection often maintains a particular proportion of alternative variants. To see how this can occur, consider a simple model known as the "Hawk-Dove game," which was first developed in a classic article by the evolutionary biologists John Maynard Smith and Geoffrey A. Parker. For purposes of illustrating the game, we'll represent fitness costs and benefits by whole numbers, or "fitness points," where benefits are represented by positive numbers and costs by negative numbers.

The Hawk-Dove game is a contest for a resource worth +40 points, and contestants can "play" either Hawk or Dove in competing for the resource. Hawks always attack and fight aggressively until they win or get seriously injured. Doves always exhibit a threatening display, but never attack, and retreat if attacked by their opponent. Since Hawks immediately attack and Doves retreat when attacked, Doves always immediately lose to Hawks. But we'll assume that Hawks have a 50 percent chance of defeating another Hawk and that Doves have a 50 percent chance of defeating another Dove. Finally, we'll assume that the cost of a serious injury is –60 points and that wasting time and energy in a very prolonged contest costs –10 points.

Given these assumptions, neither Hawk nor Dove can evolve to fixation and remain there. To see why, consider first a population of Doves. Since Doves never attack and only retreat when attacked, the absence of attack in every Dove-Dove contest results in a very prolonged contest of display, so each Dove accrues –10 points. The eventual winner, however, gets +40 points for acquiring the resource. Since each Dove has a 50 percent chance of winning, the average payoff for a Dove in a population of Doves is thus +10 (+40 times 50 percent, plus –10 for wasting time and energy). But suppose that a mutant Hawk arises in this population. This Hawk will win every contest, so it will enjoy an average payoff of +40 compared to the Dove average of +10. Consequently, Hawks will begin to increase in frequency in subsequent generations in the population. So Dove can never evolve to and remain at fixation.

But neither can Hawk. In a population of Hawks, nature is truly red in tooth and claw, for a pair of competing Hawks will attack one another aggressively, and the contest will end only when one of them is injured. The winner scores +40 points for acquiring the resource, but the loser accrues –60 points for injury. Since each Hawk has a 50 percent chance of winning (hence of losing) the contest, the average payoff for a Hawk in a population of Hawks is –10 fitness points (+40 times 50 percent, plus –60 times 50 percent). Now suppose a mutant Dove arises in this population. The Dove never wins, but it also never pays the cost of injury. So it averages 0 compared to the Hawks' –10. Consequently, Doves will begin to increase in frequency. So Hawk can't evolve to and remain at fixation either.

Interestingly, given the fitness costs and benefits assumed in this simple model, selection will favor an evolutionarily stable mix of 75 percent Hawks and 25 percent Doves, since Hawk and Dove have equal fitnesses when coexisting in this ratio. For, given this ratio of Doves to Hawks, 75 percent of one's contests are against Hawks and 25 percent are against Doves, so the average payoff to both Hawk and Dove is +2.5 fitness points. This proportion of Hawks to Doves is thus *evolutionarily stable* because any departure from it—caused by drift or mutation—will be corrected by selection, and the three-to-one ratio will be restored. This is because the fitnesses of both Hawk and Dove are dependent on the frequencies of those two phenotypes in the population. If the proportion of Hawks drops below 75 percent, then Hawks will enjoy proportionately more contests against Doves, so Hawks will have higher fitness than Doves; and, if the proportion of Hawks rises above 75 percent, then Hawks will have proportionately more potentially costly contests with one another, so Doves will have higher fitness than Hawks. Since selection will favor the phenotype with highest fitness, which phenotype selection favors thus depends on their frequencies in the population. This is *frequency-dependent selection*. And, in this example, frequency-dependent selection will maintain a three-to-one ratio of Hawks to Doves, because that is the ratio at which both Hawks and Doves enjoy equal fitness. (Of course, if we assumed different costs and benefits the stable ratio would be different.)

Note that the evolutionarily stable ratio results in no one's enjoying the greatest possible fitness. The average payoff to a Dove in a population of Doves is +10, but a population of Doves is not evolutionarily stable. Evolutionary stability, instead, turns out to be a three-to-one ratio of Hawks to Doves in which the average payoff is +2.5. It would clearly be best to be a Dove in a population of Doves, but the best in this case can't evolve, since it isn't evolutionarily stable.

I've illustrated how selection can maintain a balanced ratio of alternative types with reference to behavioral types. But frequency-dependent selection can maintain an evolutionarily stable ratio of alternative phenotypes of any kind. For example, variation in eye color, variation in size, variation in the age at first reproduction, variation in number of offspring produced, and the sex ratio in a population could all be maintained by frequency-dependent selection. It doesn't act only on behavior.

A consistent result of mathematical models of frequency-dependent selection is that balanced proportions of alternative phenotypes, rather than just single phenotypes, turn out to be evolutionarily stable. But such balanced proportions of phenotypes can be achieved in two very different ways. To see this, consider the balanced proportion of Hawks and Doves described above. What is essential to the evolutionarily stable three-to-one ratio of Hawks to Doves is having 75 percent of one's contests against Hawk and 25 percent against Dove. One way this can be achieved is in a *mixed population*—that is, a population in which 75 percent of individuals are dedicated Hawks and 25 percent are dedicated Doves. But it can also be achieved in a population of individuals who are identical in playing a *mixed strategy*—that is, a population of individuals who randomly play Hawk 75 percent of the time and Dove 25 percent of the time.

When a mixed population is evolutionarily stable it is called a *stable polymorphism*. In a stable polymorphism, there is a genotype for each alternative phenotype, and selection maintains a stable ratio of the alternative phenotypes by maintaining a stable ratio of the alternative genetic types in the population. Thus, a genetic polymorphism—a locus at which different genotypes occur—is essential to each stable polymorphism. When a population consists of individuals playing a mixed strategy, on the other hand, the individuals in the population are genetically *monomorphic*—they share the same genotype—for that strategy. This genotype produces some mechanism that is capable of randomly generating the alternative phenotypes, and selection just sets the frequencies at which the alternative phenotypic forms are randomly generated. In both stable polymorphisms and mixed strategies, however, the alternative phenotypes have equal fitness.

Mathematical models of frequency-dependent selection are typically neutral with respect to whether an evolutionarily stable ratio of alternative phenotypes is a polymorphism or a mixed strategy. But, in nature, mixed strategies are probably rarer than stable polymorphisms (although there are a couple of documented examples of mixed strategies, the most well known of which is the determination of the sex of offspring). The best evidence for this claim is the simple paucity of documented cases of mixed strategies compared to the number of documented cases of stable polymorphisms. This comparative paucity is evident in the numerous studies of alternative within-sex reproductive behaviors (that is, alternative behavioral tactics for attracting mates and securing copulations). Although there is intrasexual variation in reproductive behaviors in most major taxa, there is not a single documented case of a mixed reproductive strategy. In contrast, there are a number of documented cases of stable polymorphisms of alternative within-sex reproductive behaviors.

One particularly well documented case derives from the work of the biologist Stephen Shuster on *Paracerceis sculpta*, a marine isopod crustacean. Males of this species come in small, medium, and large, and these sizes perfectly correlate with distinct mating behaviors. Large males secure and "guard" harems of females in the recesses of sponges, acquiring their copulations with the females in the harem. Small males are unable to compete with large males for the acquisition of a harem, so they acquire copulations by "sneaking" past inattentive large males and thereby gaining access to the females in the harem. Medium males morphologically resemble females, so they "mimic" the female courtship display to a large male; thinking he is acquiring another female for his harem, the large male allows the medium male to enter the harem, where the medium male then copulates with some of the females inside. These three mating strategies have equal reproductive success, and the genes underlying them have been identified. So this is a clear case of a stable polymorphism. Similar polymorphisms have been found in the swordtail, *Xiphiphorus nigrensis*, the field cricket, *Gryllus integer*, a tree lizard, *Urosaurus ornatus*, and the ruff, *Philomachus pugnax*.

A second way in which selection can maintain phenotypic variation is through *adaptive plasticity* (sometimes called a *conditional strategy*). Adaptive plasticity is the capacity of a single genotype to produce more than one phenotype—more than one anatomical form, physiological state, or behavior—in response to environmental conditions. Like a mixed strategy, then, adaptive plasticity involves a single genotype that produces multiple phenotypes. But adaptive plasticity differs from a mixed strategy in two very important ways. First, the alternative phenotypes of a mixed strategy are produced *randomly*; they are not produced in response to environmental conditions. That is, in a mixed strategy a particular phenotype gets produced just because "its number has come up," not because that phenotype is especially suited to the particular environmental conditions in which the organism happens to find itself. In contrast, the alternative phenotypes produced by adaptive plasticity are generated nonrandomly, in response to the conditions that obtain in the organism's environment; the phenotypes are produced to match the environmental conditions. Second, the alternative phenotypes of a mixed strategy have equal fitness at their evolutionarily stable ratio. In contrast, the alternative phenotypes produced by adaptive plasticity need not have equal fitness; in fact, the alternative phenotypes can vary significantly in their fitnesses. It need only be the case that the fitness of each phenotype is greater, in the environment in which it occurs, than any of the alternative phenotypes would be in that same environment. This is compatible with one of the alternative phenotype's having lower fitness than the others; it just means that, *in those circumstances*, all the other phenotypes would have even lower fitness.

In biology, the concept of adaptive plasticity is applied to a very wide range of phenomena. But I will discuss just two distinct forms of adaptive plasticity, *developmental plasticity* and *phenotypic plasticity*. These two forms of adaptive plasticity don't exhaust the phenomena, but they are the forms that will be important in later discussions. Before elaborating this distinction, however, I should issue a caveat. I will not be using the terms *adaptive plasticity*, *developmental plasticity*, and *phenotypic plasticity* in a way that conforms with standard usage in biology. The reason is that there simply is no standard usage of these terms in biology. Indeed, discussions of plasticity in the biological literature are characterized by widespread terminological inconsistency. Some biologists use all three of the above terms interchangeably, while other biologists distinguish developmental plasticity from general phenotypic plasticity. In what follows, then, I will be defining these terms so as to serve my purposes. And, for my purposes, I will treat developmental plasticity and phenotypic plasticity as distinct forms of the more general phenomenon of adaptive plasticity.

To illustrate developmental plasticity, consider the caterpillars of the moth *Nemoria arizonaria*, the larvae of which develop in oak trees. Caterpillars hatched in spring feed on the staminate flowers of the oak and develop to strongly resemble those flowers. Caterpillars hatched in summer feed on the leaves of the oak and develop to strongly resemble twigs on the oak. A difference in diet, due to a difference in chemical composition of the flowers and the leaves, is responsible for the development of the very different "flower" and "twig" phenotypes. And each phenotype is adaptive in its circumstances, since each serves the function of camouflaging the caterpillars and thereby protecting them against predation. Overall, however, the "flower" phenotype has the highest fitness, so it is definitely better to be a "flower" than a "twig" in the spring. But, since developing the "flower" phenotype in the summer would be maladaptive (because it would be conspicuous to predators in an oak without staminate flowers), it is more beneficial to be a "twig" than a "flower" in the summer, even though being a "twig" is suboptimal overall. As Richard Dawkins colorfully puts it, "twigs" are simply "making the best of a bad job." Consequently, a single genotype has evolved in this species that is capable of producing both phenotypes, and it does so by selectively matching the phenotype to the environment in response to chemical cues in the caterpillars' diets during development.

Similarly, bryozoans, or "sea moss," are sometimes preyed upon by sea slugs. Sea slugs are detectable by a chemical cue that is present in the water around them. So, when bryozoans develop in the presence of this chemical cue, they grow spines that deter predation by sea slugs. In the absence of this chemical cue, they do not grow spines. However, since the growth of the spines is developmentally very costly (detracting from the allocation of resources to other aspects of bryozoan life history), nonspiny bryozoans have higher overall fitness. But, it would be clearly maladaptive not to grow spines in an environment populated by predatory sea slugs. Here again, a single genotype has evolved that is capable of producing two different phenotypes, each of which has higher fitness *in its circumstances* than the other, but one of which has the highest overall fitness. A similar developmental plasticity is present in aphids. If aphids develop in very crowded populations, which are likely to run out of food, they grow wings that enable migration. If they develop in uncrowded populations, they don't grow wings.

For developmental plasticity to evolve by selection, several conditions must be met. First, there must be variation in a population's environment. That is, there must be at least two different environmental conditions that affect fitness and that are consistently encountered across many generations of the population. Second, this environmental variation must be predictable. If a population's environment varied, but in unpredictable ways, no hereditary mechanism could evolve to "match" offspring phenotypes to their environmental conditions, because those conditions would likely not have been encountered by ancestral generations. Third, a mix of alternative phenotypes, each occurring in its own environmental conditions, has to have a higher average fitness than any single phenotype would have across the range of variable environmental conditions. If some particular phenotype had the highest fitness in each of the different environmental conditions, then that single phenotype would be selected. Finally, there must be "cues" in each of the different developmental conditions that are reliable predictors of the selection pressures to be encountered in the environment and to which some mechanism of adaptive plasticity can respond. If there were no waterborne chemical cue correlated with the presence of sea slugs, for example, bryozoans would not "know" when it is appropriate to grow spines and when not. The presence of sea slugs would then be unpredictable, and no developmental mechanism could evolve to *selectively* grow spines in response to the presence of sea slugs.

If all these conditions are satisfied, a genotype that is capable of producing alternative phenotypes that match alternative environmental conditions can be favored by selection over competing genotypes. In such a case, selection could drive that genotype to fixation. But, given the developmental plasticity of that genotype, selection for it would actually maintain variation at the phenotypic level as a function of the environmental variation encountered by a population. And the phenotypic variation maintained by selection in this way would be adaptive.

In cases of developmental plasticity, then, a genotype can produce two or more phenotypes, and the genotype is responsive to particular environmental cues during development in "deciding" which of those phenotypes to produce. In cases of *phenotypic plasticity*, in contrast, the genotype produces a phenotype that is capable of phenotypic change or reorganization in response to changing conditions in the organism's environment. An example of phenotypic plasticity in the Hawk-Dove game would be an organism that played Hawk against all smaller opponents, but played Dove against all opponents of equal or greater size. In such a case, the organism's behavioral phenotype would vary flexibly in response to fluctuating environmental demands.

A nontheoretical example of phenotypic plasticity is provided by the African cichlid fish, *Haplochromis burtoni*. There are two sexual phenotypes among *H. burtoni* males: territorial and nonterritorial. Territorial males are brightly colored, maintain and defend visually isolated territories, have mature testes, are reproductively active, and allocate all of their energy to defending their territories and reproducing. Nonterritorial males are cryptically colored, swim in schools with females, do not have mature testes, are not reproductively active, and allocate all of their energy to somatic growth. Territorial males accrue the direct fitness benefits of reproduction, which nonterritorial males do not accrue. However, because of their bright coloration, territorial males suffer far higher rates of predation than do nonterritorial males, so they also incur greater fitness costs than nonterritorial males. Conspicuous coloration is worth its high costs only if a male is actively reproducing.

The territories defended by territorial males typically lie within the recesses of vegetation or behind leaves. In a natural environment, such territories prove highly unstable. Leaves move, territories are exposed, and other areas become visually isolated, hence suitable candidates for defensible territory. When these changes occur, nonterritorial and displaced territorial males compete for new territories. If a nonterritorial male captures a territory, within days it becomes brightly colored and develops mature testes. If a displaced territorial male fails to secure a new territory, within days it loses its bright coloration, becoming cryptically colored, and its testes begin to atrophy. As a displaced territorial male makes the transition to nonterritorial male, it begins to once again allocate all of its energy to somatic growth in preparation for later competition for new territories. If their habitats fluctuate greatly, male *H. burtoni* can cycle several times in this way through the territorial and nonterritorial phenotypes.

In order for such phenotypic plasticity to evolve by selection, there must be variation in some aspect of a population's environment that is relevant to fitness, just as with the evolution of developmental plasticity. But, in order for phenotypic plasticity rather than developmental plasticity to evolve in response to environmental variation, the environmental variation must occur relatively rapidly and unpredictably. That is, a population must face several different environmental conditions within the course of a single generation, there must be no reliable pattern in the order in which those different environmental conditions are encountered, and each different environmental condition must be of uncertain duration. In short, there must be *fluctuation* in some aspect of a population's environment that is relevant to fitness. Finally, the ability to vary phenotype in response to these fluctuating conditions must have higher average fitness than any single phenotype would have across all of the conditions. If it weren't better to revert to the nonterritorial phenotype when not holding a territory, for example, *H. burtoni* males would be brightly colored with mature testes throughout adulthood.

The following illustration will help to make the distinction between developmental plasticity and phenotypic plasticity less abstract and more intuitive. The phenomena to which I am applying the label *developmental plasticity* tend to conform to the following model: Organisms can encounter one of two types of environment, either an environment characterized by round holes or one characterized by square holes. A genotype then evolves to build round pegs in the round-hole environment and square pegs in the square-hole environment. The phenomena to which I am applying the label *phenotypic plasticity*, however, tend to conform to the following, rather different model: Organisms encounter both round holes and square holes in their environment, in random order, and in sometimes rapid succession. A genotype then evolves to build Silly Putty, which can take the shape of a round peg or square peg as needed. In the case of developmental plasticity the genotype exhibits a flexible response to different environmental conditions, whereas in the case of phenotypic plasticity the phenotype itself exhibits the flexible ability to remake itself in response to fluctuating environmental demands. But both types of plasticity result in alternative phenotypes that are uniquely adapted to their circumstances.

In conclusion, then, selection can maintain phenotypic variation in a population by maintaining genetic variation in the population (a stable polymorphism) or by maintaining a genotype that adaptively produces alternative phenotypes (through a mixed strategy or adaptive plasticity). But, although I have explained each of them separately, you shouldn't infer that these different mechanisms of phenotypic variation are mutually exclusive. Indeed, it is possible to have a stable polymorphism of different mixed strategies, or a stable polymorphism of two "pure" phenotypes and one mixed strategy, or a stable polymorphism of two adaptively plastic genotypes, and so on. Life can be exceedingly complex. But we have seen enough of it to be able to move on.

Chapter 1 was an introduction to evolutionary biology. This chapter is an introduction to Evolutionary Psychology, explaining how Evolutionary Psychologists attempt to build a theory of the human mind on the foundation of evolutionary biology. Those familiar with Evolutionary Psychology primarily through its popularized theories of human mating and stepparental child abuse may find this chapter rather densely theoretical. Although the popularity of Evolutionary Psychology among those who don't specialize in studying human behavior and mentality is due to such captivating theories, to focus solely on them is truly to miss the forest for the trees. For the popularized theories of human mating, and so on, aren't a disjointed collection of random evolutionary speculations regarding aspects of everyday human life; they stem from, and are systematically united by, a common underlying theory about the evolution and nature of the human mind. Reading about this theory isn't anywhere near as titillating as reading about sexual attraction, promiscuity, infidelity, and sperm competition; however, anyone who wants to fully understand Evolutionary Psychology's claims about those phenomena needs to understand the underlying theory of the evolution and nature of the human mind.

This chapter will explain that theory, focusing solely on the fundamental theoretical tenets of the Evolutionary Psychology paradigm and leaving discussion of topical, explanatory applications of the paradigm (to human mating, for example) for later chapters. This chapter will also be purely expository, reserving critical discussion for later chapters. My goal in this chapter is to give a good sense of the theoretical foundation of Evolutionary Psychology before going on to critique it.

## The Evolution of Behavior

When a gene has a phenotypic effect that enhances the fitness of its bearers (that makes its bearers fitter than population members without the gene), it tends to increase in frequency in a population, and as a result so does its fitness-enhancing phenotypic effect. So, a gene that makes a gazelle a faster runner than others in its population, and hence better able to escape predators, will increase in frequency in a gazelle population and thereby increase the average running speed of the population. And a gene that makes its bearers immune to a common and deadly disease will similarly increase in frequency. In both cases, the gene codes for a protein that makes its bearers' bodies different from those without the gene. In the former case the effect is on musculature and in the latter on antibody production.

A gene can also increase in frequency by making its bearers more likely than nonbearers to perform some fitness-enhancing behavior. For example, females of many species choose a mate based on the quality of male courtship displays. If the courtship displays of males differ in quality and a genetic difference underlies the display difference, the gene for the superior display will increase in frequency. Of course, courtship behaviors are not the only behaviors that affect fitness. If parents differ in the quantity of care they give to their offspring, if the quantity of care affects the viability of offspring, and if a genetic difference underlies this difference in parental care, then the gene for higher quantity care will increase in frequency. So, as long as a gene makes some fitness-enhancing behavior more likely, that gene will increase in frequency in a population, and as a result the behavior may increase in frequency as well. For this reason, biologists frequently say that, from the standpoint of evolutionary biology, "behavioral traits are like any other class of characters."[1]

But treating behavioral traits as just like other traits obscures a fundamental difference between the way genes affect morphological traits like stronger muscles and the way they affect behavioral traits like courtship displays. For muscles are made of proteins, and genes affect the strength of muscles by coding for the proteins of which they are made. This is a stable and relatively long-lasting *condition* of an animal's body, which is not reactive to the rapidly changing conditions in an animal's environment. Behavior, on the other hand, isn't made of proteins; it is what an animal does in the world with its body. It consists in relatively fleeting *events* that are caused by an animal's brain in reaction to rapidly changing conditions (although in simple animals behavior is merely reflexive, caused by a rudimentary, brainless nervous system). Thus, while the strength of my arm muscles remains relatively constant month after month and doesn't change in reaction to the demands of the moment, the brain-controlled movements of my arms often last but a split second and change in reaction to relatively rapidly changing conditions.

The conditions that are relevant to how an animal's brain produces behavior are of two types. First, there are the current conditions of the animal's environment, which may change rapidly and about which its brain is constantly updating information. Second, there are the current conditions of the animal's own brain—in particular, its representations of desires, goals, or (in cognitively sophisticated animals) plans and its representations of what needs or remains to be done to achieve these ends. Information about what needs to be done to achieve ends is also subject to rapid change as an animal acts in, and thereby changes, its environment, and the brain also constantly updates this class of information. Behavior is thus an event, of relatively short duration, which is the output of an information-processing brain reacting to informational input about the current conditions in an animal's environment and brain.

Of course, precisely how an animal reacts to the information about these current conditions depends on the design of its brain. It depends, that is, on what kinds of goals and plans the animal's brain is designed to entertain and on how its brain is designed to process information about the environment and its own states (and, to some extent, on how the rest of its nervous system is designed to react to both afferent and efferent stimuli). In short, an animal's behavioral response to current conditions depends on the nature of the *cognitive and motivational mechanisms* in its brain—it depends, that is, on the nature of what Evolutionary Psychologists call the *proximate mechanisms* that regulate and control the animal's behavior. Differences between animals in the nature of their proximate behavior-control mechanisms account for many of the behavioral differences between them. If two animals are both hungry and are both receiving information from the environment that a rat is present, any behavioral difference between them (eating the rat versus running away in disgust) is due to functional differences in their proximate mechanisms.

This puts us in a position to see exactly how genes affect behavior. For an animal's brain is made up of numerous interconnected neurons, which signal one another through electrical impulses and the release of neurotransmitters. In addition, the release of hormones in the brain affects the activities of neurons. The neurons and the connections among them are made of proteins, and the neurotransmitters and hormones are made of amino acids (the building blocks of proteins). By coding for the amino acids and proteins of which these things are made, genes can affect the neuronal structure and functioning of the proximate mechanisms that make up the brain (by affecting the goals that the brain entertains or how the brain processes information relevant to achieving those goals). And this could make an animal with a particular gene more likely than one without it to produce a particular type of behavior.

It must not be forgotten, however, that behavior is reactive to current conditions, some of which are external conditions of the environment, and genes don't directly affect those external conditions. For example, Thomson's gazelles exhibit a behavior called *stotting*, which consists in repeatedly jumping a couple of feet off the ground in plain sight of a predator, a behavior apparently designed to communicate something like this to the predator: "I see you watching me and I'm prepared to run if you charge; but I have very strong leg muscles, as demonstrated by how high I'm jumping right now, so you would be ill advised to bother trying to catch me." A gazelle's genes don't affect whether there are predators in its current environment and, consequently, don't affect one of the conditions essential for stotting to be exhibited. But a gene can affect a gazelle's brain so that it is more likely to stott *when it sees a cheetah*. Thus, while genes cannot directly affect behavior, they *can* affect proximate mechanisms in such a way that certain behavioral responses become more likely under certain conditions.

Since there can be genes for behaviors in this (indirect) way, the full range of evolutionary causes discussed in the last chapter can produce behavioral evolution in a population. But a fitness-enhancing behavior may not actually increase in frequency in a population. This is because the external conditions to which the behavior is reactive may *decrease* in frequency, even if only temporarily. If this happens, behavior that provides a selective advantage one generation may actually be less frequent in the next generation. Suppose that there is selection for stotting in a gazelle population, which increases the frequency of the gene for stotting, but that the population of gazelle predators is suddenly wiped out by some natural disaster. Gazelles would then cease stotting, but only because the external conditions to which stotting is a response would be lacking, not because the population would no longer be composed of gazelles with a disposition to stott. Indeed, because of the selection for stotting, more gazelles would possess the proximate mechanism that underlies the disposition to stott, so more gazelles would possess the tendency to stott when they see a predator. They just wouldn't see predators.

So, when a behavior has evolved under selection, there is an important sense in which it is not the behavior itself that has been selected for, but rather the proximate (cognitive or motivational) mechanism underlying the tendency to exhibit that behavior. This is because only traits that are hereditary—traits that are passed directly from parents to offspring—can evolve under selection. And, as we see with the stotting example, stotting itself is not inherited; only the *tendency* to stott is inherited via transmission of the gene that affects the proximate mechanism that causes stotting. The stotting behavior itself is exhibited only when the inherited proximate mechanism receives information from the environment that stotting is appropriate. To see this even more clearly, suppose that, after a couple of generations of living free from predators, the gazelles encountered a new predator population in their environment. Gazelles would then begin stotting again. Although this behavior would be the result of inheritance, it would not be due to continuous transmission of stotting behavior; for there would have been continuous transmission only of the proximate mechanism that causes stotting. Thus, as the Evolutionary Psychologists Leda Cosmides and John Tooby say: "To speak of natural selection as selecting for 'behaviors' is a convenient shorthand, but it is misleading usage. . . . Natural selection cannot select for behavior per se; it can only select for mechanisms that produce behavior."[2]

This fact has implications for understanding the emergence of adaptation through behavioral evolution. An adaptation, recall, is a trait that is possessed by organisms in a current population because of selection for that trait in ancestral populations. Since adaptations are traits that were selected for, and since behavioral evolution involves selection for the proximate mechanisms that produce behavior (not selection for behavior itself), the adaptations that emerge in the process of behavioral evolution under selection are the mechanisms that produce fitness-enhancing behavior (not the fitness-enhancing behaviors themselves). To put it briefly, behavior evolves under selection because of adaptive evolution *in the brain's proximate mechanisms*.

## The Adapted Mind

But is there any reason for thinking that human behavior has evolved under selection? In other words, is there any reason for thinking that the human brain is an adaptation? Evolutionary Psychologists answer this question with a strong affirmative (although, as we will see later in this chapter, they claim that the brain is not a single adaptation, but a network of many specialized adaptations).

Their argument is simple and compelling. The human brain, which is capable of producing highly sophisticated and appropriate behavior in response to an indefinite variety of circumstances, is without doubt the most complex organ possessed by any species. For reasons we saw in chapter 1, the probability that something of this complexity would have evolved purely by random, undirected processes (such as genetic drift) is so infinitesimally small that such processes can be ruled out as an explanation of the complex design of the human brain. The human brain is undoubtedly the result of a long period of selection, in which a series of fitness-enhancing modifications to the brain's cognitive and motivational mechanisms were retained and accumulated. But selection retains modifications only when they provide new or better solutions to adaptive problems. Thus, the brain must have been designed by selection to produce behavioral solutions to the adaptive problems faced by human populations. "The evolutionary function of the human brain," as Cosmides and Tooby say, "is to process information in ways that lead to adaptive behavior."[3] In short, the brain is an adaptation for producing adaptive behavior. Understanding the evolutionary process that designed the brain should thus enable us to understand its functional, information-processing design, to understand what selection designed the brain *to do*. The real question, then, is *what kind of functional design* the brain has evolved under selection. Since Evolutionary Psychologists follow the overwhelming majority of cognitive scientists in identifying the mind with the functional, information-processing design of the brain, this question is tantamount to asking *what kind of mind* has evolved in the human lineage.

One possibility is that selection designed the brain to monitor the current environment and produce whatever behavior maximizes fitness. According to this view, as the psychologists John and Stamati Crook endorse it, "humans are endeavouring consciously or unconsciously to optimize their reproductive success."[4] This leads to the prediction that humans in current populations should be engaging in behavior that is designed to maximize reproductive success.

The Evolutionary Psychologists David Buss and Donald Symons argue that this prediction is everywhere disconfirmed, for contemporary human behavior too often fails to maximize fitness. For example, donating one's sperm or eggs to cryobanks is an obvious way to maximize reproductive success, but few people pursue this practice. Further, if humans had an evolved behavioral tendency to maximize reproductive success, the use of contraception wouldn't be as widespread as it is, and there wouldn't be so many people deliberately remaining childless. From the standpoint of reproductive success, contemporary human behavior is frequently *maladaptive*. So the human brain cannot be designed to maximize fitness in current environments.

This does not imply, however, that the human brain was not designed by selection. To draw that inference would be to presuppose that selection designs only fitness-maximizing mechanisms, and this, as Symons points out, is to commit the fallacy of conflating adaptiveness with adaptation. A trait is adaptive, recall, if it currently enhances fitness; it is an adaptation if current organisms possess it because it enhanced the fitness of their ancestors. Thus, the brain's being an adaptation is compatible with its not currently producing adaptive behavior.

But is this merely a semantic distinction, or can adaptations really fail to be adaptive? Moreover, how can the brain fail to produce adaptive behavior if, as Evolutionary Psychologists claim, it is an adaptation specifically *for* producing adaptive behavior?

To answer these questions, recall how adaptations are built by selection. First a mutation must occur that modifies some preexisting structure in a way that enhances fitness. Its bearers will then, on average, have greater reproductive success than other organisms in the population, and the beneficially modified structure will begin to increase in frequency. How long it takes this beneficial modification to spread from the initial mutant(s) to a very high frequency in the population will depend on how great a reproductive advantage the beneficial modification confers. If, for example, organisms with the beneficial modification produce approximately 5 percent more offspring on average than organisms without, according to standard calculations the mutant gene will spread to virtual fixation in a population in approximately one thousand generations. If the reproductive advantage is greater or less than 5 percent, the number of generations to near fixation will be respectively less or greater. Of course, the more frequent the beneficial trait becomes, the greater the probability that another mutation will occur in conjunction with it, modifying the trait and making it even more beneficial. If this happens, the improved trait will then increase in frequency.

For this sequence of events to occur, however, there must be constant selection for each new modification, which requires that the environment remain relatively constant, so that a fitness-enhancing modification continues to enhance fitness. But the environment to which a population adapts also undergoes change (although ocean-bottom environments have changed relatively little over evolutionary time). For example, the physical environment of terrestrial animals undergoes climatic changes, which sometimes devastate a population's food resources. More significant, however, are the changes in a population's biological environment, which consists of other species that are themselves undergoing evolution—in particular, parasite, predator, and prey species. For example, if a cheetah population increases its average running speed, the population of gazelles on which it preys faces a new adaptive problem (that of escaping faster cheetahs).

When the environment inhabited by a population changes, what was previously beneficial, and increasing in frequency under selection, may cease to be beneficial. When this happens, the population can adapt to the new environment, but how quickly it does so depends on the extent and nature of the variation in the population when the environment changes. If there is significant variation and one of the existing variants provides a reproductive advantage in the new environment, that variant will begin to spread in the population. If the existing variants in the population have equal fitness, on the other hand, so that no one variant provides a reproductive advantage over the others, then the population will only begin to adapt after a mutation occurs that enhances fitness in the new environment. Either way, it can take another several hundred to several thousand generations for the population to adapt to the new environment—depending on whether a new mutation is required, if so how long it takes before a *beneficial* mutation occurs, and how great a reproductive advantage is provided by the beneficial variant. During these generations, the population as a whole will exhibit a lack of fit between its adaptations (the traits that are present in the population because they *were* adaptive in ancestral populations) and its current environment. In short, during this time its adaptations will not be adaptive.

In the case of the brain, this lack of fit between adaptation and current environment has a particular character. For, if the brain is an adaptation, as Evolutionary Psychologists argue, then at some point in human evolutionary history there was selection for brain mechanisms that transformed information about environmental conditions into behavioral output that was adaptive to those environmental conditions. Of course, there was selection for these mechanisms because of how they responded *to the environment prevailing at the time they were selected*. If environmental conditions are now different, the informational inputs to the brain are different also; consequently, the brain may respond to this new information by producing behavior that is not adaptive to the new conditions.

There are at least two ways in which this failure of adaptiveness could occur. In the simple case, the brain could continue to produce the same old behavior under the new conditions, but that behavior may fail to have the beneficial consequences under the new conditions that it had under the old. On the other hand, the brain could produce some new behavior in response to the new informational inputs, but the new behavior could fail to be adaptive. This latter phenomenon is common to a wide range of mechanisms that are reactive to the conditions around them: They are designed to respond well to certain circumscribed conditions; but, when those conditions change, they respond in ways their designers did not expressly intend. For example, sophisticated computer programs, which are designed to perform a variety of complex tasks, are programmed to produce "adaptive" outputs (on the monitor or to a peripheral device) in response to certain key or key-combination inputs. But a novel key-combination input can cause the program to give some nonsensical or undesirable ("nonadaptive") output—a phenomenon that is all too familiar to Windows users. The program wasn't *designed* by the program-mers to give this output; but, given how the program was designed, this output is an incidental response to an unanticipated input. Similarly, a proximate mechanism that produced adaptive behavior under the condi-tions in which it was selected may fail to produce adaptive behavior when it no longer encounters the informational inputs it once responded to adaptively.

The assumption that humans have an evolved behavioral tendency to maximize reproductive success, Evolutionary Psychologists argue, conflates the claim that the human brain was designed by a history of selection (adaptation) with the claim that it functions to maximize reproductive success (adaptiveness). The fact that the brain was designed by selection entails only that it is designed to solve the adaptive problems posed by the environment in which there was selection for that brain design; it doesn't entail that the brain is designed to produce fitness-maximizing behavior in present environments. For human environments may have changed since there was selection for the brain's design, and much contemporary human behavior could thus be maladaptive because of a "time lag" between human brain design and the environment.

But is there any reason for thinking that the human mind is lagging behind modern environments in this way? Evolutionary Psychologists argue that the answer is yes, and largely because of environmental changes produced by human action. The invention of agriculture some 10,000 years (four hundred generations) ago; the industrialization of Western societies some 200 years (eight generations) ago; the attendant rise of the modern metropolis and megalopolis, which resulted in humans living in unprecedentedly large groups; the proliferation and increased availability during the last century of contraceptives hitherto unrivaled in effectiveness—all of these, Evolutionary Psychologists argue, have changed the selectively relevant environment for humans in profound and far-reaching ways. These are changes with which human genetic evolution, and consequently human psychological adaptation, could not possibly have kept pace; for, since those changes took place, they argue, there have been too few generations for significant genetic evolution to have occurred. For these reasons, among others to be discussed in the next section, Evolutionary Psychologists think it overwhelmingly likely that the human mental design built by selection will frequently fail to produce adaptive behavior in modern environments.

Evolutionary Psychologists conclude that an evolutionary approach to understanding the design of the human mind should not lead us to look for fitness-maximizing behavior but should lead us to investigate the adaptive *history* that shaped the mind. Thus, the central premise of Evolutionary Psychology is the idea that the brain's design was produced by a history of reproductive success, rather than the idea that the brain is designed to produce reproductive success. This prompts Evolutionary Psychologists to say that humans are not "fitness maximizers," but "adaptation executors," which means that human behavior is produced not by a brain that is attempting to maximize fitness, but by a brain functioning in ways that were selected for because of how they maximized fitness *in the past*. And, because our psychological adaptations may fail to produce adaptive behavior in modern human environments, Evolutionary Psychologists believe that "studies of the adaptiveness of human behavior are ineffective in illuminating human psychological adaptations."[5]

## The Environment of Evolutionary Adaptedness

Qua adaptation, the brain is designed to produce behavioral solutions to adaptive problems. The adaptive problems that the brain evolved to solve, however, are those of the *past* environments in which it evolved, not those of the current environments in which it now functions to produce behavior. According to Evolutionary Psychologists, then, in order to understand the design of the mind—that is, the functional design of the brain—it is necessary to get a fix on the *environment of evolutionary adaptedness*, the past environment to which the mind *is* adapted.

The environment of evolutionary adaptedness (or EEA), according to Evolutionary Psychologists, is not a specific place (for example, eastern Africa) or habitat (for example, savanna), although specific places and habitats may be incidentally part of the EEA. Rather, as Tooby and Cosmides put it, the EEA is a "composite of the adaptation-relevant properties of the ancestral environments encountered by members of ancestral populations."[6] In particular, it is a "composite of environmental properties of the most recent segment of a species' evolution that encompasses the period during which its modern collection of adaptations assumed their present form."[7] A species' EEA, then, is the set of environmental properties that prevailed during the period in which its adaptations ceased to be modified under selection and came to be maintained at or near fixation by selection. For this is the period in a species' evolution during which its adaptations enjoyed a good "fit" with its environment. The environmental properties prevailing during this period defined the adaptive problems faced by a species and thus defined the problems that its adaptations are designed to solve.

Evolutionary Psychologists contend that the human EEA consists in the set of environmental conditions encountered by early human populations during the Pleistocene, the epoch stretching from 1.8 million to 10,000 years ago. According to Evolutionary Psychologists, from the beginning of the Pleistocene epoch early human populations occupied the savannas of eastern Africa, living as hunter-gatherers in bands whose populations ranged from fifty to three hundred individuals. *Homo sapiens* evolved from one of these populations in a speciation event that occurred approximately 150,000 years ago. *Homo sapiens* continued to live a hunter-gatherer lifestyle in eastern Africa until some populations began to disperse into Europe, Asia, and Australia some 50,000 years ago. Thus, according to Evolutionary Psychologists, the human EEA is the set of environmental conditions encountered by Pleistocene hunter-gatherers, and the human mind is designed to solve the adaptive problems faced by these early human hunter-gatherers. Psychologically, Evolutionary Psychologists claim, we are walking fossils of our Pleistocene hunter-gatherer ancestors. Or, as Cosmides and Tooby so colorfully put it, "our modern skulls house a Stone Age mind."[8]

Aspects of this theory of human origins have recently been challenged. Some paleoanthropologists argue, for example, that the early human population from which *Homo sapiens* descended may have spent much of the early Pleistocene in heavily forested areas of Asia before migrating back to eastern Africa where *Homo sapiens* emerged. But none of the recent challenges to this standard view of human origins significantly affects the conclusions that Evolutionary Psychologists draw about the human EEA. For the Pleistocene conditions that constitute the human EEA are not just the physical conditions of the habitats of early human populations. While those conditions are certainly factors to which some human traits are adapted, the most significant conditions with respect to human psychological adaptation are the social conditions that typified Pleistocene hunter-gatherer populations, regardless of their physical habitats. For, although withstanding drastic climate change is necessary for survival, negotiating the social order of one's band, which may include individuals capable of extreme violence, is just as necessary for survival and must be dealt with on a daily basis. Moreover, in order to reproduce one must attract a member of the opposite sex, and this involves competition with members of one's own sex.

With respect to human psychology, then, the selectively relevant features of the human EEA are primarily those of Pleistocene hunter-gatherer *social life*. And Evolutionary Psychologists argue that there is a great deal about human social life that hasn't changed significantly since the Pleistocene. Just like our Pleistocene ancestors, for example, we modern humans must attract and retain mates, provide care for our children, understand the motives of those with whom we engage in social exchange, and navigate ever-present status hierarchies in ways that promote our own interests. Thus, although much human behavior is maladaptive because of a time lag between our Pleistocene minds and our modern environments, Evolutionary Psychologists claim that a great deal of our interpersonal behavior is reactive to social situations that would not be all that foreign to our Pleistocene ancestors.

To illustrate the claim that the mind is adapted to Pleistocene conditions, consider one of the favorite examples of Evolutionary Psychologists. In current human populations there is a widespread fear of snakes. This fear isn't well designed for contemporary human environments, since many of us who fear snakes spend our lives in environments where we are virtually never exposed to them. But the relatively snake-free environments of densely populated and industrialized urban and suburban areas are a very recent phenomenon on the time scale of human evolution. The vast majority of human evolution was spent in Pleistocene environments where there would have been frequent enough encounters with venomous snakes. A fear of snakes, which produces snake-avoidance behavior, *is* well designed for those environments. Further, if there is a genotype that produces a fear of snakes, and if that genotype was selected for during the

Pleistocene, it would still be present in contemporary human populations; for there have been too few generations since the Pleistocene for genetic evolution to have eradicated that genotype. Thus, the widespread human fear of snakes is a product of a mind that is adapted to the conditions of human evolution during the Pleistocene and that is lagging behind the rapid environmental changes that have occurred since then.

The Evolutionary Psychologist Steven Pinker argues that something similar is true of many human fears: "The other common fears are of heights, storms, large carnivores, darkness, blood, strangers, confinement, deep water, social scrutiny, and leaving home alone. The common thread is obvious. These are the situations that put our evolutionary ancestors in danger."[9] Strikingly absent from this catalog of human fears are the things humans *should* be afraid of in contemporary environments. The sight of a car or a gun, for example, should strike far more fear into the heart of a modern human than does the sight of a snake, for cars and guns kill far more people than do snake bites. In spite of this, humans tend to have a greater fear of snakes. From an evolutionary standpoint, argue Evolutionary Psychologists, this should be expected. For there have been too few generations since the invention of guns and cars for selection to proliferate any recently emerged genotype for a fear of guns or cars.

Evolutionary Psychologists do not simply marshal numerous examples of this sort in support of their claim that the human mind is adapted to Pleistocene environments. There are, rather, some general theoretical considerations that motivate their claim. The argument is as follows.

The human mind is undoubtedly a highly complex trait, one of what Cosmides, Tooby, and Barkow term "complex functionally integrated designs."[10] And the evolution of a complex functionally integrated design, like the human eye, is a very slow process of cumulative modification under selection, which requires vast stretches of evolutionary time. The 10,000 years since the end of the Pleistocene, they argue, "is only a small stretch in evolutionary terms, less than 1% of the two million years our ancestors spent as Pleistocene hunter-gatherers. For this reason, it is unlikely that new complex designs—ones requiring the coordinated assembly of many novel, functionally integrated features—could evolve in so few generations."[11] In other words, there have been only four hundred generations since the end of the Pleistocene, and that is too few, they argue, for genetic evolution significant enough to "assemble" complex psychological mechanisms that are adapted to modern environments. Thus, they conclude, our psychological adaptations must have evolved, instead, during the Pleistocene.

Further, if human adaptations could have been formed in the 10,000 years since the Pleistocene ended and agriculture was invented, contemporary agricultural populations would differ in their evolved adaptations from populations that have continued to live as hunter-gatherers in the post-Pleistocene period. But, Evolutionary Psychologists argue, the anthropological evidence shows that contemporary agricultural and hunter-gatherer populations do not differ in their evolved adaptations. Whatever complex functionally integrated designs humans possess, then, must be adapted to Pleistocene conditions, not to post-Pleistocene agricultural and industrial conditions.

But what, specifically, were some of the adaptive problems defined by Pleistocene conditions to which our ancestors evolved psychological adaptations? Tooby and Cosmides offer a long list of Pleistocene adaptive problems, from which I'll excerpt several of the most interesting. In order to survive and reproduce, Pleistocene humans needed to: "avoid incest, . . . identify plant foods, capture animals, acquire grammar, attend to alarm cries, detect when their children needed assistance, be motivated to make that assistance, . . . select mates of high reproductive value, induce potential mates to choose them, . . . interpret social situations correctly, help relatives, . . . inhibit one's mate from conceiving children by another, deter aggression, maintain friendships, . . . recognize emotions, [and] cooperate."[12]

According to Evolutionary Psychologists, early Pleistocene humans differed in the degree to which their behavior was successful in solving these problems. Those possessing proximate mechanisms that produced the most successful behavioral solutions to these and other adaptive problems enjoyed the greatest reproductive success during that period. Consequently, the proximate mechanisms responsible for their greater reproductive success increased in frequency throughout the Pleistocene epoch until they became fixed in early human populations. These proximate mechanisms have been inherited by modern humans, in whom they are not always still adaptive, and they are what make us walking psychological fossils of our Pleistocene hunter-gatherer ancestors.

We can now be more specific about why Evolutionary Psychologists believe that much contemporary human behavior is maladaptive. Human behavior in contemporary environments is caused by cognitive and motivational mechanisms that are designed to produce adaptive behavior in response to Pleistocene environmental conditions. When and where contemporary environments resemble Pleistocene environments, these proximate mechanisms will produce adaptive behavior. But, when and where contemporary environments differ from Pleistocene environments, the proximate mechanisms we've inherited from our Pleistocene ancestors will produce either Pleistocene-appropriate behavior (which will fail to be adaptive under contemporary conditions) or novel nonadaptive or maladaptive behavior (as per analogy with the computer program given a novel input to which it was not designed to respond).

To illustrate, consider some examples of maladaptiveness mentioned earlier. Why don't more people maximize their reproductive success by donating their sperm or eggs to cryobanks? Because these reproductive options weren't available in the Pleistocene, and we have minds designed to maximize reproductive success only under Pleistocene-like conditions. In the Pleistocene, reproductive success was achieved through the pursuit of copulation, not through the donation of gametes to cryobanks. Proximate behavior-control mechanisms in modern humans, which have been inherited from our Pleistocene ancestors, are thus directed at the pursuit of copulation; they are relatively insensitive to information about reproduction via donation to cryobanks. But why do so many people thwart their reproductive success by using contraceptives? Because contraceptives were unavailable in the Pleistocene, so proximate mechanisms directed solely at the pursuit of copulation were sufficient to achieve reproductive success. Now that contraceptives are so freely available, we contemporary humans are able to uncouple copulation from reproduction in ways that our Pleistocene ancestors were not. All the while, however, our proximate mechanisms enjoin pursuit of copulation just as they did in our ancestors.

## Modularity and the Adapted Mind

Evolutionary Psychologists claim that the human mind is an adaptation designed to process information in ways that will produce adaptive behavior under Pleistocene-like conditions. As mentioned earlier, however, Evolutionary Psychologists do not think that the mind is just a single monomorphic adaptation. Rather, they claim that it is a network of many psychological adaptations, each specialized at processing information in ways that solve a specific adaptive problem or set of closely related adaptive problems. As Pinker says, "the mind is organized into *modules* or mental organs, each with a specialized design that makes it an expert in one arena of interaction with the world. The modules' basic logic is specified by our genetic program. Their operation was shaped by natural selection to solve the problems of the hunting and gathering life led by our ancestors in most of our evolutionary history."[13] These modules, according to Evolutionary Psychologists, are our evolved proximate behavior-control mechanisms.

To get a handle on this modular view of the mind, it is most useful to begin by contrasting it with the view it is intended to supplant. During the first half of the twentieth century, it was widely accepted that the mind comes equipped with just a few general reasoning abilities, which are employed in learning everything we come to know about the world. These few abilities were considered to be *domain general*, in that they were assumed to be applicable to any problem domain that might be encountered—everything from the acquisition of language or mathematical skill to the ability to play chess or ride a bicycle. In this view, the mind doesn't bring any specific knowledge of a particular problem domain *to* the process of learning in that domain. Rather, all the information the mind possesses about a particular problem domain is extracted *from* the world by its few domain-general reasoning abilities.

This is the view that most (but not all) cognitive scientists—and Evolutionary Psychologists along with them—now reject in favor of a view of the mind as consisting of a number of psychological modules. Since different cognitive scientists attribute different sets of properties to modules, it is important to enumerate the properties of modules that are significant to Evolutionary Psychology.

First, according to Evolutionary Psychologists, the single most important property of a module is that it is *domain specific*—that is, it is specialized to deal only with a restricted problem domain. As such, its information-processing procedures are activated only by information about a particular aspect of the world, and they are unresponsive to information about other aspects of the world. This is much like how the eye is responsive only to light of specific wavelengths, and the ear is responsive only to acoustical disturbances of specific vibratory frequencies.

Second, a module develops in the absence of any explicit instruction in the problem domain with which it is specialized to deal. This is not to say that a module develops in the absence of *any* environmental stimulus, for some kind of triggering stimulus is typically required. But the environmental stimuli that trigger development of a module always contain less information than the fully developed module employs about its problem domain. The linguist Noam Chomsky argues that this is true of our knowledge of the rules of grammar. A child must be exposed to linguistic stimuli in order to acquire a language. But a child is exposed to only a relatively small, finite number of grammatical sentences and to virtually no explicit instruction in the rules of grammar. Yet by the age of five or six a child's knowledge of grammar, as exhibited in its speech, is highly complex and sophisticated.

This is because, third, a module comes equipped with certain "innate knowledge" about the problem domain with which it is specialized to deal and an "innate" set of procedures for applying that knowledge to solve problems in its special domain. That is, rather than needing to extract all its information about its problem domain through experience during the course of an individual's life, a module contains "unlearned" information and procedures about its problem domain, which it employs in its problem solving.

Fourth, modules are comparatively fast. That is, they solve problems in their special domains in far less time than general cognitive processes take to solve a problem for which there is no dedicated module. For example, whereas you may spend minutes to hours puzzling over how to reassemble your car's carburetor, you can understand a long and complex sentence as soon as it's uttered. If we were to develop computer programs to solve both problems, however, we would likely find that the processes involved in reassembling the carburetor are no more computationally complex than the processes involved in determining the syntactic structure of the long sentence. What makes the difference, according to most cognitive scientists, is that the human brain has psychological modules dedicated to speech perception, but none dedicated to automotive repair. So, while problems in automotive repair have to be figured out, problems in sentence processing are solved automatically.

What accounts for the problem-solving speed of modules is the fact that they are, to varying degrees, *informationally isolated* from psychological processes external to them. That is, a module doesn't have access to the full range of information available in an organism's brain, even when some of that information is relevant to solving problems in its specialized problem domain. In particular, it tends to have access only to the outputs of other modules and not to the information employed by other modules in generating their outputs. Instead, a module stores internally its own restricted body of information and tends to employ only that information in processing its inputs. As Tooby and Cosmides say: "In order to solve its characteristic domain of problems, a module is designed to interpret the world in its own pre-existing terms and framework, operating primarily or solely with its own specialized 'lexicon'—a set of procedures, formats, and representational primitives closely tailored to the demands of its targeted family of problem."[14] This informational "tunnel vision" allows modules to function faster than they would if they had to sort through the entire range of information available in the brain.

Informational isolation entails that much of what one learns can fail to affect the way that modules process information and go about solving problems. To borrow an example from the cognitive scientist Jerry Fodor, optical illusions persist even after you learn that they are merely illusions. You *know* that there is no puddle on the desert road ahead, yet you see one anyway; you *know* that the lines in the Müller-Lyer illusion are of equal length, but that doesn't prevent you from seeing them as having different lengths. This is because our vision modules are informationally isolated in the extreme. What we come to know about the world doesn't affect the way that our vision modules function in constructing representations of the spatial layout and orientations of objects in the world. Similarly, due to their informational isolation, evolved modules process information in ways that are unaffected by much of what we learn, even when some of what we learn is relevant to the adaptive problems those modules have evolved to solve.

Evolutionary Psychologists support this view of the mind with both general theoretical considerations and some empirical evidence. Let's begin by considering three theoretical arguments in support of this view.

First, as we have seen, the adaptive problems faced by our Pleistocene ancestors varied widely in character, ranging from identifying edible plant matter and avoiding deadly predators to selecting a reproductively valuable mate and cooperating with others in a status hierarchy. Symons argues that, given the diverse characters of these problems, what constitutes a successful solution to one problem is very different from what constitutes a solution to another. So no single general-purpose problem-solving strategy can successfully generate solutions to all of the problems in such a diverse array; instead, each problem requires its own domain-specific problem-solving strategy. Thus, our Pleistocene ancestors could not have evolved minds consisting of a single all-purpose problem-solving mechanism, but must have instead evolved distinct domain-specific mechanisms, each dedicated to solving a specific adaptive problem posed by the Pleistocene hunter-gatherer lifestyle. As Symons says: "It is no more probable that some sort of general-purpose brain/mind mechanism could solve all the behavioral problems an organism faces (find food, choose a mate, select a habitat, etc.) than it is that some sort of general-purpose organ could perform all physiological functions (pump blood, digest food, nourish an embryo, etc.)."[15]

Second, in order for a complex problem-solving adaptation to evolve and become prevalent in a population, Tooby and Cosmides argue, there must be "recurrent structure" both in the environment and in the organisms in the evolving population. That is, in order for selection to do its slow work of fashioning a "fit" between organismic properties and environmental properties over the course of many generations, there must be both a trans-generationally stable environmental structure (which is adapted to) and a hereditarily recurring organismic structure (which selection adapts to the environmental structure). But, while there is recurrent environmental structure associated with each adaptive problem taken individually, there is virtually no recurrent environmental structure in common between two very different adaptive problems (for example, choosing a mate and choosing a green leafy plant). So, if we lumped all adaptive problems together, we would find no recurrent environmental structure common to all of them. In the absence of common environmental structure, there is nothing to which selection can adapt an organismic structure. So a strictly domain-general mind could not have evolved, since there is no structure to a "general domain." As Symons pithily states the argument: "There is no such thing as a 'general problem solver' because there is no such thing as a general problem."[16] Thus, according to Evolutionary Psychologists, the very nature of adaptation requires mechanisms that specialize in solving particular adaptive problems, rather than a general-purpose problem-solving mechanism.

Third, all knowledge possessed by a strictly domain-general mind would have to be derived from experience. But information about which behaviors will effectively solve an adaptive problem cannot possibly be derived from experience. As Cosmides and Tooby say, "adaptive courses of action can be neither deduced nor learned by general criteria alone because they depend on statistical relationships between features of the environment, behavior, and fitness that emerge over many generations and are, therefore, often not observable during a single lifetime."[17] So selection has fashioned a mind consisting of numerous domain-specific mechanisms, since only these come preequipped with knowledge of which courses of action are adaptive in their proprietary problem domains.

In addition to these theoretical arguments, cognitive scientists have presented empirical evidence for the existence of a number of modules. In addition to modules for each of our five senses (which typically involve modules within modules, in the way that the "vision module" involves modules for analyzing color, depth, shape, movement, and so on), cognitive scientists have presented evidence of modules for face recognition, language, the motions of inanimate objects, the classification of plants and animals, and the interpretation and explanation of human behavior. The only real difference between Evolutionary Psychologists and the majority of cognitive scientists, in this respect, concerns the number and nature of postulated modules. For, in addition to those mentioned above, Evolutionary Psychologists postulate that there are "a face recognition module, a spatial relations module, a rigid object mechanics module, a tool-use module, a fear module, a social-exchange module, an emotion-perception module, a kin-oriented motivation module, an effort allocation and recalibration module, a child-care module, a social-inference module, a sexual-attraction module, a semantic-inference module, a friendship module, a grammar acquisition module, a communication-pragmatics module, a theory of mind module, and so on."[18] Indeed, given the extraordinarily large and diverse number of adaptive problems faced by our Pleistocene ancestors, Tooby and Cosmides speculate that "our cognitive architecture resembles a confederation of *hundreds or thousands* of functionally dedicated computers (often called modules)."[19]

But Evolutionary Psychologists do not claim that the mind consists *solely* of evolved modules. In fact, a wholly modular mental organization would be impossible. For, since modules are relatively informationally isolated from one another, in a wholly modular mind information from separate modules would never be collated into a single, coherent interpretation of all the task demands of one's current situation. For example, Cosmides conducted an interesting series of experiments that purportedly demonstrate the existence of a module for detecting cheaters in social exchanges (which will be discussed in detail in chapter 4). In these experiments, Cosmides presented subjects with a number of conditional statements, such as "If you are drinking beer, then you must be over twenty-one." Cosmides claims that such conditionals activate a cheater-detection module, which evaluates whether someone is in violation of the rules expressed in the conditionals. Without any domain-general processes, a subject in Cosmides' experiments would have some understanding of the verbal instructions from the experimenter and the written conditionals (understanding derived from processing in the language module), and the subject would perhaps have some understanding of whether a conditional rule was being violated (derived from processing in the hypothesized cheater-detection module). But, without any domain-general processes, the subject would be unable to integrate all of these tasks into an action sequence designed to comply with the experimenter's instructions. Consequently, there must be *some* domain-general processes that operate on the information delivered by the modules to form an understanding of one's (possibly unique) current situation and formulate plans for one's immediate and distant future.

Evolutionary Psychologists claim only that, for every adaptive problem consistently encountered by early human populations in the Pleistocene, selection has fashioned a module that is dedicated to processing information about that adaptive problem in ways that produce adaptive behavior in Pleistocene-like environments. Evolutionary Psychologists expect there to be "hundreds or thousands" of such modular mechanisms in the human mind; and, as Buss says, "the central task according to Evolutionary Psychologists is to discover, describe, and explain the nature of those mechanisms."[20]

This theoretical perspective entails a specific method for discovering the design of the mind. The method is *evolutionary functional analysis*, and it involves determining what the mind's design must be on the basis of an analysis of the problems it must have evolved to solve. For "a central premise of Evolutionary Psychology is that the main nonarbitrary way to identify, describe, and understand psychological mechanisms is to articulate their functions—the specific adaptive problems they were designed by selection to solve."[21] Indeed, according to Tooby and Cosmides, "one can easily use the definition of an adaptive problem to generate hypotheses about the design features of information-processing mechanisms."[22] Evolutionary functional analysis, then, is a method of inferring the proximate causes of behavior (the functioning of our proximate mechanisms) from premises about the ultimate causes of our behavior.

Evolutionary functional analysis proceeds as follows. It begins with speculation about the nature of the EEA in order to ascertain the specific adaptive problems Pleistocene humans faced. Once an adaptive problem is identified, a *task analysis* is performed to break down the adaptive problem into a number of subproblems whose solutions collectively constitute a solution to the adaptive problem. For example, early human males in the EEA faced the problem of intrasexual competition for reproductive access to females. Solving this problem required solving the subproblems of acquiring the resources required by potential female mates, successfully courting potential mates, and retaining mates, among other things. Once the task analysis is completed, the next step is to identify the forms of behavior that would have solved each of the subproblems under Pleistocene conditions. A module is then postulated, which is assumed to respond to environmental input about the subproblems by generating the behavioral solution(s) to them. The final step is to determine the information-processing procedures, or decision rules, by which the module generates its behavioral solutions.

The information-processing procedures employed by evolved modules are commonly called *Darwinian algorithms*. The concept of an algorithm comes from artificial intelligence research, where it denotes an information-processing procedure that takes a prespecified problem as input and produces a correct solution to the problem as output. Since Evolutionary Psychologists view evolved modules as solutions to adaptive problems, they claim that the input to an evolved module is a representation that "specifies to the organism the particular adaptive problem it is facing" and that the "output (a) regulates physiological activity, provides information to other psychological mechanisms, or produces manifest action and (b) solves a particular adaptive problem."[23] A Darwinian algorithm, then, is a set of decision rules that transforms a representation of an adaptive problem into a solution to that adaptive problem. So the goal of evolutionary functional analysis is to discover the Darwinian algorithms that are executed by evolved modules.

There are two criteria that a hypothesized Darwinian algorithm must satisfy. First, it must generate behavior that would have been adaptive in the EEA, since only such an algorithm could have evolved at all. Second, it must generate the full range of behavior that we actually observe humans to perform in modern environments, even when that behavior is maladaptive. For, of all the Darwinian algorithms that could have evolved, only one that generates current maladaptive behavior could be the one that did in fact evolve. Any hypothesized Darwinian algorithm that satisfies both of these criteria, according to Evolutionary Psychologists, is a highly plausible account of the functioning of an evolved psychological module.

**"Human Nature"**

Evolutionary Psychologists argue that Pleistocene humans possessing a module that effectively solved an adaptive problem would have enjoyed a reproductive advantage over population members not possessing the module. Further, they argue, since the Pleistocene was a vast stretch of evolutionary time, there was ample opportunity for selection to drive each beneficial module to fixation in early human populations. Consequently, the modules that evolved to solve Pleistocene adaptive problems now constitute "an array of psychological mechanisms that is universal among *Homo sapiens*."[24] Since this array of modules was fashioned during the

Pleistocene, it "reflects completed rather than ongoing selection,"[25] and it forms "a single, universal panhuman design, stemming from our long-enduring existence as hunter-gatherers."[26] These modules are thus "the psychological universals that constitute human nature."[27]

There are two apparent difficulties with this idea of a universal human nature. First, there is obvious and significant cultural diversity in the world, which would appear inconsistent with the claim that "human nature is everywhere the same."[28] Second, even within a single culture, there are obvious and significant individual differences, which also appear inconsistent with the existence of a universal human nature. But Evolutionary Psychologists explain away both of these apparent difficulties.

In the first place, Evolutionary Psychologists claim only that our psychological adaptations are species universals, not that all psychological characteristics are. Just as many selectively neutral morphological characteristics, such as hair color and amount of body hair, are free to vary among individuals without being affected by selection, so too are many selectively neutral psychological characteristics free to vary. Much of the psychological variation within and across human cultures may be selectively neutral. And such variation is not included in the scope of what Evolutionary Psychologists consider human nature, since human nature is constituted only by our psychological adaptations.

Second, Evolutionary Psychologists argue, cultural diversity has been greatly exaggerated. Indeed, they claim, many of the landmark studies in cultural anthropology that were responsible for the idea of radical cultural diversity have recently been shown to suffer from methodological defects. It was once widely accepted among cultural anthropologists that there are radical differences between cultures in such things as the classification of colors, concepts of time, the facial expressions of emotion, attitudes toward promiscuity, the incidence of rape, and jealousy over sexual infidelity. But such claims are no longer accepted as uncritically as they once were. Indeed, in some cases, reexamination of available evidence and collection of further evidence have shown significant cultural uniformity underlying the apparent cultural differences.

Finally, even where there is genuine cultural diversity, that diversity may simply mask an underlying psychological uniformity. For example, since different languages are spoken in different cultures, it may appear that language is determined wholly by the culture in which one is raised. But the work begun by Chomsky, and continued by Pinker, appears to show that a common set of structural rules, known as *universal grammar*, underlies every one of the world's languages. Further, many cognitive scientists argue that this universal grammar is encoded in language-acquisition modules in every human being who has learned or can learn a language, and that it explains how an individual is able to acquire the grammar of a specific language. Thus, as Tooby and Cosmides argue, although the specific language one learns is determined by the linguistic culture in which one is raised, that language is learned through the activation of language-acquisition modules that are common to inhabitants of all cultures. The surface cultural variability in spoken language is therefore a result of a common language-acquisition mechanism responding differentially to different linguistic inputs during the process of language learning. "So what at the behavioral level appears variable ('speaks English,' 'speaks Kikuyu'; or, even, 'speaks a language,' 'does not speak any language') fractionates into variable environmental inputs and a uniform underlying design, interacting to produce the observed patterns of manifest variation."[29]

The idea that variation can result from a common nature responding to different conditions provides Evolutionary Psychologists with a robust and general solution to the problem of reconciling individual differences with a universal human nature. The analogy is with a computer program. Since the output of a program is a product not only of the nature of the program but also of its input, the same program will produce different outputs in response to different inputs. Thus, even where there is actual cultural diversity, cultural differences in behavior and attitudes could be the product of common psychological adaptations responding differently to different cultural inputs. Even more generally, differences in behavior and attitudes between individuals in the same culture could be the product of common psychological adaptations responding differently to different developmental or current conditions.

Evolutionary Psychologists do not claim, then, that there are universal human behaviors or even universal human attitudes or preferences. Our putative universal human nature does not consist in our behaving the same or having the same likes and dislikes. We do, in fact, differ from one another behaviorally and attitudinally. Evolutionary Psychologists claim only that our psychological adaptations are universal. Consequently, they claim, behavioral and attitudinal differences among normal humans do not reflect differences in underlying psychological adaptations, but merely reflect differences in the inputs to common underlying adaptations. Thus, an Evolutionary Psychologist "observes variable manifest psychologies or behaviors between individuals and across cultures and views them as the product of a common, underlying evolved psychology, operating under different circumstances."[30]

Tooby and Cosmides offer two arguments to show that human psychological adaptations must be universal. One argument is what I will call "the argument from *Gray's Anatomy*." As Tooby and Cosmides put it, "the fact that any given page out of *Gray's Anatomy* describes in precise anatomical detail individual humans from around the world demonstrates the pronounced monomorphism present in complex human physiological adaptations. Although we cannot yet directly 'see' psychological adaptations (except as described neuroanatomically), no less could be true of them."[31] The point is simply that, since selection has designed our minds as well as our bodies, we should expect selection-designed psychological traits to be just as universal as selection-designed morphological traits.

This argument is largely a rhetorical appeal to common sense, but Tooby and Cosmides offer another, more theoretical argument, which I will call "the argument from sexual recombination." It first appeared in their 1990 article "On the Universality of Human Nature and the Uniqueness of the Individual: The Role of Genetics and Adaptation," and it has been repeated and refined in several of their subsequent publications. It has become accepted among Evolutionary Psychologists as definitive proof of a universal human nature, and it is repeated without modification by Buss, Pinker, and Symons. The argument is as follows.

Adaptations are complex traits, which possess parts that are functionally interconnected. (Think of how the cornea, pupil, lens, retina, and so on, of the eye must be functionally interconnected in order for the eye to perform its function of transmitting information about objects in the world to the brain.) Being so complex, such traits "require coordinated gene expression, involving hundreds or thousands of genes to regulate their development."[32] Since sexual reproduction is a process in which random halves of each parent's genes are "recombined" to form the genome of a zygote, if parents differed in any of their complex adaptations, the random sexual recombination of the genes for those adaptations would make it highly improbable that their offspring would receive all the genes necessary for developing any of the parental adaptations. In other words, given the randomness inherent in sexual reproduction (in particular, in crossing over and gamete sampling), "it is improbable that all of the genes necessary for a complex adaptation would be together in the same individual if the genes coding for the components of complex adaptations varied substantially between individuals."[33] As a result, if individuals differed in the genes underlying adaptations, no adaptation would be reliably reproduced across generations, and this in turn would mean that no adaptive trait would persist long enough to be modified by selection in the direction of greater functional effectiveness. "Therefore, in order for a complex adaptation to exist, all of the genes . . . required to construct it must be present in the genomes of all individuals of the species. Hence, all of a species' complex adaptations must be of essentially uniform design."[34] So "the psychic unity of humankind—that is, a universal and uniform human nature—is necessarily imposed to the extent and along those dimensions that our psychologies are collections of complex adaptations."[35]

Consequently, Evolutionary Psychologists do not believe that there are any stable polymorphisms of psychological phenotypes in human populations. Rather, they argue, "characteristics in which individuals differ because of genetic differences . . . are generally limited to quantitative variation in the components of complex, highly articulated, species-typical psychological mechanisms."[36] For example, while all humans possess the fear-of-snakes adaptation, genetic differences among individuals may correlate with differences in the threshold at which the fear response is activated. Analogously, Tooby and Cosmides argue, while all humans have stomachs, genetic differences among individuals may correlate with differences in stomach size. In general, then, most effects of genetic differences will be confined to quantitative variation within each qualitatively distinct universal adaptation. All other effects of genetic differences will have no impact on the form or functioning of our adaptations.

As mentioned, however, some individual differences are due to our common psychological adaptations responding differentially to varied inputs. According to Tooby and Cosmides, our universal psychological adaptations are designed in such a way that individual differences in "manifest psychologies or behaviors" can be produced by differences in either "situational assessments," "environmental cues," or "genetic switches." Individual differences due to differences in situational assessments are a function of different inputs to the same psychological mechanism, whereas individual differences due to differences in environmental cues or genetic switches are a function of different inputs to the same developmental program. Consider each in turn.

Two individuals may have the same psychological mechanism, yet that mechanism may cause them to exhibit different behaviors in response to differences in their current situations. For example, two individuals may both have an operative module for jealousy, as Evolutionary Psychologists postulate. But, if the mate of one individual shows signs of infidelity while the mate of the other does not, then that jealousy module will cause the former, though not the latter, individual to experience jealousy. Thus, although the two individuals share the same psychological mechanism, this difference in their affective responses is a function of differences in their respective situations. Tooby and Cosmides attribute such a behavioral difference to a difference in *situational assessment*.

Of course, the above example is extremely simple. Our psychological mechanisms are responsive to a broad array of information. In addition, our behavior is typically the result of complex interactions among several of our psychological mechanisms, and these complex interactions can compound the effects of situational differences. As a result, even very small differences in situational assessments can produce significant differences in manifest psychological and behavioral responses among individuals who possess the same array of psychological mechanisms. So, many individual differences could be a function of even small differences in situational assessments.

There are two important things to note about individual differences due to situational assessments. First, the mechanisms that perform situational assessments monitor changes in the *current* environment in real time. Consequently, individual differences that are due to differences in situational assessments change as the situations in which individuals find themselves change. Second, any differences that are due to differences in situational assessments *alone* would be eliminated by exposing the differing individuals to the same situation. That is, if two individuals possessed exactly the same array of operative psychological mechanisms, they would exhibit exactly the same behavior and attitudes if exposed to identical situations.

As a matter of empirical fact, of course, different individuals don't always respond to identical situations in the same way. That's because of differences in the developmental conditions of those individuals, which are a function of differences in either environmental cues or genetic switches.

Environmental cues can cause individual differences in two basic ways. First, in order for an adaptation to develop properly at all, it may be necessary for an individual to be exposed to an environmental cue that "triggers" the development of that adaptation. In such cases, there may be a "critical period" during development at which the environmental cue is necessary for that adaptation to emerge, and after which it is no longer possible to develop that adaptation. According to many psycholinguists, the development of our language module is dependent on exposure to linguistic input at a critical period of development. Given linguistic input from parents and others during early childhood, our language module develops normally. But, if a human child is not exposed to any linguistic input by early adolescence, that child will be unable to acquire any mastery of even rudimentary grammatical structures (although the child may be able to learn a number of words). Thus, environmental cues can be necessary for the development of a psychological adaptation. When they are, an individual not exposed to the proper cue during development can lack a psychological adaptation possessed by those exposed to that cue.

Second, different environmental cues at a particular point during development can shunt development down alternative paths, and this can result in individuals' differing with respect to the form of their developed psychological adaptations. For example, the anthropologists Patricia Draper and Henry Harpending found a strong correlation between a woman's mating strategy and the degree to which she experienced paternal investment during childhood. On average, women raised in a home without the presence of an investing father pursue an "opportunistic" reproductive strategy, which is characterized by early sexual activity, multiple partners, and early and frequent reproduction in the context of short-term relationships. In contrast, women raised in a home with an investing father pursue an "investing" reproductive strategy, characterized by later sexual maturation, fewer sexual partners, and a lower rate of reproduction that occurs within a long-term partnership.

This difference in reproductive tactics, according to Evolutionary Psychologists, is due to the same developmental program's encountering different environmental cues during development about the stability of mateships. In response to those different cues, the developmental program produces differently functioning psychological mechanisms. "The environmental input during development—presence versus absence of investing fathers and the reliability or unpredictability of resources—presumably provides information about the probability of securing a high-investing, committed mate and hence whether or not the pursuit of a series of short-term mates might be more advantageous."[37] "An absent father indicates a polygynous society, and activates a coordinated adaptive strategy of early sexuality, promiscuity, high fertility, and low levels of parental investment per child; a present father indicates a monogamous society, and activates an adaptive strategy of later and more selective sexuality, lower fertility, and high levels of parental investment per child."[38]

There are two important things to note about individual differences that are due to differences in environmental cues during development. First, the mechanisms that respond to such environmental cues do not monitor and respond to changes in the environment in real time. They are selectively responsive to particular environmental cues at particular stages of development, and they shunt an individual's development down one of a number of alternative developmental pathways. In other words, these are developmental mechanisms that are executing a conditional strategy, "locking in" to a particular developmental outcome on the basis of an environmental cue (much like how *N. arizonaria* caterpillars develop into "twigs" or "flowers" on the basis of a chemical difference in their diets during early development).

As a result, second, differences in environmental cues during development produce individuals who differ in the psychological mechanisms they possess or who differ in how their psychological mechanisms function. Someone who is not exposed to an environmental cue necessary for the development of a particular psychological adaptation simply lacks the psychological mechanism possessed by those exposed to that cue. Similarly, female children who have investing fathers develop a psychological mechanism that assesses prospective mates for investment, whereas female children who don't have investing fathers develop a psychological mechanism that seeks early and multiple matings. Thus, when different environmental cues shunt individuals down alternative developmental pathways, individuals can develop psychological mechanisms that *differ in their patterns of situational assessment*. When this occurs, individuals do not assess the same situations in the same way, and they do not necessarily behave the same when exposed to identical current environmental inputs.

This is important to bear in mind when thinking about Evolutionary Psychology's claim that there is a universal human nature. For that claim is ambiguous. On the one hand, when Evolutionary Psychologists speak of our "common, underlying evolved psychology," they typically mean the array of evolved *modules*, which obtain information from the environment, process it through evolved Darwinian algorithms, and then cause our behavior. This is the sense of "common, underlying evolved psychology" that is at work in Cosmides, Tooby, and Barkow's claim that "there is a universal human nature, but that this universality exists primarily at the level of *evolved psychological mechanisms*, not of expressed cultural behaviors."[39]

Because of differences in environmental cues during development, however, we have seen that our evolved modules are *not* universal. This is why, in one punctilious moment, Tooby and Cosmides explicitly say that "common, underlying evolved psychology" refers primarily to evolved *developmental programs* and not to the modules that are produced by those developmental programs. As Tooby and Cosmides put it, "when we use terms such as 'evolved design,' 'evolved architecture,' or even 'species-typical,' 'species-standard,' 'universal,' and 'panhuman,' we are not making claims about every human phenotype all or even some of the time; instead, we are referring to the existence of evolutionarily organized developmental adaptations, whether they are activated or latent."[40]

The Evolutionary Psychologist Charles Crawford draws a distinction that is helpful here. Crawford distinguishes what he calls "operational adaptations" from "innate adaptations." "The *operational adaptation* consists of the anatomical structures, physiological processes, and psychological processes that develop because of interactions with the environment and that actually do the work of helping the organism survive and reproduce."[41] An operational adaptation, then, is a *developmental outcome*—in particular, an outcome that enhanced ancestral fitness. Thus, our fully developed psychological modules are operational adaptations. In contrast, "the *innate adaptation* is the information encoded in the genes that mediates the development of the operational adaptation."[42] The "information" encoded by our innate adaptations constitutes a set of *developmental programs*, which "are designed to assemble (either conditionally or regardless of normal environmental variation) evolutionarily designed . . . mechanisms that are then present to be activated by appropriate cues."[43] Each such "developmental mechanism, by virtue of its physical design, embodies a specification for how each possible state of the developmental environment is to be [developmentally] responded to, if encountered."[44]

There may, then, be some developmental experiences that are necessary for an evolved module to develop (or to develop correctly). If so, an individual who fails to have those experiences will fail to (correctly) develop a module that is an operational adaptation in those of us in whom it does develop. Nonetheless, according to Tooby and Cosmides, this individual still shares with the rest of us an underlying innate adaptation, which encodes the instructions for developing the operational adaptation they lack. For this reason, Tooby and Cosmides say that our "universal human nature" should be thought of as the entire constellation of "the evolved developmental mechanisms and the psychological mechanisms they reliably construct."[45] Although we may differ with respect to our operational adaptations, we are all alike in the sense that we all share the same innate adaptations, the same set of developmental adaptations for developing a psychology.

Different environmental cues, however, are not the only factors that can shunt these universal developmental programs down different developmental pathways. According to Tooby and Cosmides, our common developmental programs can respond differently to different "genetic switches," and theoretically individuals can differ in the genetic switches they possess. A genetic switch initiates a cascade of developmental events by activating a particular genetic subsystem of our developmental program. Individuals who possess alternative alleles of some genetic switch, then, may develop very different phenotypes, and those alternative phenotypes may even be adaptive. But, Tooby and Cosmides argue, it is important to realize that a genetic switch "does not contain the information necessary for building the alternative designs; it acts only as a switch, in a binary fashion, activating one of two extensive functionally integrated genetic subsystems, both of which are simultaneously present in all humans."[46] Thus, like environmental cues, genetic switches merely act as inputs to our universal developmental program.

Tooby and Cosmides argue that genetic switches are very rare in nature, especially when it comes to the determination of alternative psychological phenotypes. For "a genetic switch determines an individual's future at conception, so that individual has one set of adaptations and not another regardless of how suited they might be to the local situation. A far more effective system, in general, is to determine what to be as a response to what environment one finds oneself in. . . . An individual can better tailor its morphology and behavior to its local environment by relying on environmental cues, or by assessing the relationship between itself and its environment."[47] If, for example, the alternative female reproductive strategies discussed above were determined by alternative alleles of a genetic switch, and those alternative alleles were present in all populations, then some females would nonadaptively seek high-investing, committed mates in a polygynous society, while others would nonadaptively pursue a strategy of noninvesting promiscuity in a monogamous society. By relying on an environmental cue instead, a female's reproductive strategy can be adaptively tailored to her environment. Consequently, Tooby and Cosmides argue, when alternative phenotypes are equally adaptive, selection will almost always favor mechanisms of situational assessment or mechanisms that rely on environmental cues over genetic switches for determining which phenotype to be.

Evolutionary Psychologists do, however, grant two major exceptions to the claim that human psychological adaptations exhibit a "species-typical design." First, they count male and female morphologies as alternative adaptive forms of our species, and sex determination is under the control of a genetic switch. For sex is determined by the presence or absence of a single gene, the *SRY* gene on the Y chromosome, which codes for a protein called "testis-determining factor." When this protein is produced, it triggers certain cells to release testosterone into the womb, and testosterone initiates the development of male reproductive organs. In the absence of a Y chromosome, hence the *SRY* gene, female reproductive organs develop. So sex is essentially determined by the presence or absence of a single gene. Further, Evolutionary Psychologists argue, the adaptive differences between males and females are not confined to morphology. Indeed, men and women must solve different sets of problems in order to successfully attract and retain mates and then reproduce (some of which will be discussed in later chapters). Throughout human evolutionary history, these differing problems created different selection pressures acting on the two sexes. As a result, men and women evolved distinct sets of psychological adaptations for solving the different reproductive problems they face. Thus, according to Evolutionary Psychologists, many aspects of human psychology are universal among normal human beings, but those aspects of human psychology that evolved to solve the problems of sexual reproduction exhibit sexual dimorphism.

Because these psychological differences are a function of biological differences in sex, which is under the control of a genetic switch, sex differences in psychological adaptations are also produced by different forms of that genetic switch, which activate different "genetic subsystems" that are present in both males and females of our species. Sex differences in psychological adaptations are thus actually "coded for" by these different "genetic subsystems," which have been modified by selection over evolutionary time to produce specialized female and male psychologies when activated by the appropriate form of the genetic switch.

This dimorphism in human sexual psychology is a function of different selection pressures on the two sexes. But the selection pressures on individuals within a sex also change across the course of the life cycle, and they have done so consistently throughout human evolutionary history. Adolescents face some adaptive problems not faced by children, middle-aged parents face some adaptive problems not faced by adolescents or elderly adults (for example, providing primary care for pubescent children), and elderly adults face some adaptive problems not faced by individuals in any other life stages (for example, assisting their children in providing care for their grandchildren). Consequently, the second major exception to a "species-typical design," Evolutionary Psychologists argue, is adaptive "coordinated design differences" at various stages of life.

These age-specific coordinated designs are the result of our innate adaptations' being timed to reliably construct throughout the life cycle those operational adaptations that are required for and appropriate to each stage in the life cycle. "Developmental processes continue to bring additional adaptations on line (as well as remove them) at least until adulthood. . . .

Thus, just as teeth and breasts are absent at birth and develop later in an individual's life history, perceptual organization, domain-specific reasoning mechanisms, the language acquisition device, motivational organization, and many other intricate psychological adaptations mature and are elaborated in age-specific fashions that are not simply the product of the accumulation of 'experience.' Consequently, psychological adaptations may be developmentally timed to appear, disappear, or change operation to mesh with the changing demands of different age-specific tasks."[48] While individuals of different ages may differ considerably in their "manifest psychologies or behaviors," such differences are due to the differential activation of common developmental programs as a function of different maturational cues. In this respect, such differences are very similar to individual differences that are due to differences in environmental cues during development.

All these adaptive differences among humans—different psychological phenotypes due to different environmental cues during development, different adaptive forms due to the genetic switch determining sex, and different morphological and psychological differences due to differences in stage of life cycle—are due merely to differences in input to a common developmental program, a common set of innate adaptations. For "the genetically universal may be developmentally expressed as different maturational designs in the infant, the child, the adolescent, and the adult; in females and males; or in individuals who encounter different circumstances."[49] If all of us shared the same form of the genetic switch determining sex, were the same age, and were exposed to the same environmental cues during development, our operational psychological adaptations would be identical. Thus, our "genetically universal" developmental program (innate adaptations) and the psychological modules it is designed to produce under normal conditions (operational adaptations) are what constitute our "universal human nature."

# 3 | Adaptation

As even a casual reading of the previous chapter makes clear, the concept of adaptation is central to Evolutionary Psychology. For Evolutionary Psychology's goal is to discover our psychological adaptations and explain how they function, and the paradigm holds that our network of psychological adaptations constitutes a "universal human nature" that is adapted to the lifestyle of Pleistocene hunter-gatherers. This focus on psychological adaptation to the Pleistocene EEA led the late paleontologist Stephen Jay Gould to criticize Evolutionary Psychology for being adaptationist and unscientific. Indeed, Gould claimed that adaptationism is "the fatal flaw of Evolutionary Psychology in its current form."[1]

Despite its influence in some circles, however, Gould's critique of Evolutionary Psychology is fallacious and misguided. In the next section, I will detail some of the problems with Gould's arguments in order to dispose of red herrings. As we carry the red herrings toward the garbage, though, we will be put on the scent of some legitimate problems with Evolutionary Psychology's claims about psychological adaptation, and they will be the focus for the remainder of the chapter.

## Adaptationism?

In their famous critique of adaptationism, Gould and his coauthor, the geneticist Richard Lewontin, characterize adaptationism as an attitude that "regards natural selection as so powerful and the constraints upon it so few that direct production of adaptation through its operation becomes the primary cause of nearly all organic form, function, and behaviour."[2] As a result, they say, adaptationists view virtually every trait of every organism as an adaptation, and they consequently see the principal function of evolutionary biology as providing ultimate explanations of traits. Gould claims that Evolutionary Psychology is adaptationist, since Evolutionary

Psychologists "confine evolutionary accounts to the workings of natural selection and consequent adaptation for personal reproductive success."[3]

Gould argues that this single-minded focus on psychological adaptation is deeply misguided, since it ignores the fact that many psychological traits may have evolved by means other than selection. Even psychological traits that enable us to solve many adaptive problems encountered in our daily lives may not be adaptations, Gould contends, since "some useful characters did not arise by selection for their current roles."[4] Many useful psychological traits are instead, he claims, *exaptations*.

The term "exaptation" was introduced by Gould and the biologist Elisabeth Vrba to designate traits that "evolved for other usages (or for no function at all), and [were] later 'coopted' for their current role."[5] As this definition entails, there are two kinds of exaptation. One kind is a *co-opted adaptation*, a trait that originated as an adaptation for one purpose, but then became used for some other adaptive purpose. In the evolution of birds, Gould argues, feathers originated as adaptations for thermoregulation. But, once feathers were in place they could be used for other purposes, one of which was flight. Thus, whereas feathers are an adaptation for thermoregulation, according to Gould, they are an exaptation (a co-opted adaptation) for flight.

The other kind of exaptation is what Gould and Lewontin call a "spandrel," a feature of an organism that originated by the "laws of growth" as a developmental by-product of an adaptation. Spandrels are features that originally had no adaptive purpose whatsoever, but that became co-opted for some adaptive function. For example, female spotted hyenas have unusually large clitorises, which look (to us, at least) very much like the penises of male spotted hyenas. Although the unusual size of the clitoris serves no apparent reproductive function, it plays a role in a meeting ceremony during which females spend ten to fifteen seconds licking one another's clitorises. The unusual size of the clitoris is not, according to Gould, an adaptation for this meeting ceremony. Instead, he claims, it is a by-product of high androgen levels in female spotted hyenas, which is apparently an adaptation for female behavioral dominance over males. So, while the large clitoris originated for no adaptive purpose whatsoever, it later became co-opted for the meeting ceremony.

Gould contends that "*most* of our mental properties and potentials may be spandrels," rather than adaptations.[6] As Gould says, "I will accept the most orthodox of Darwinian positions—that the human brain achieved its enlarged size and capacity by natural selection for some set of purposes in our ancestral state. *Large size is therefore an adaptation.* . . . Natural selection built the brain; yet, by virtue of structural complexities so engendered, the same brain can perform a plethora of tasks that may later become central to culture, but that are spandrels rather than targets of the original natural selection."[7] Thus, according to Gould, having a large brain is an adaptation, and virtually all other psychological features are by-products of a large brain.

To support his claim, Gould cites singing Wagner, reading, writing, consciousness of our own mortality, and the religious beliefs engendered by consciousness of mortality. It is absurd, Gould argues, to think that these were targets of selection, so they must instead be mere by-products of a large brain. Indeed, he claims, "for something so complex and replete with latent capacity as the human brain, spandrels must vastly outnumber original reasons, and exaptations of the brain must greatly exceed adaptations by orders of magnitude."[8] Therefore, Gould concludes, adaptationism is Evolutionary Psychology's "fatal flaw."

This salvo misses its target for a couple of reasons. First, the exaptations Gould cites—such as singing Wagner, consciousness of mortality, and religious belief—are beside the point. No Evolutionary Psychologist has claimed that consciousness of our own mortality and religious belief—not to mention singing Wagner—are adaptations. They agree that such things are spandrels. In addition, the exaptations Gould cites are all examples of specific behaviors, mental acts, beliefs, attitudes, and preferences. Such phenomena are the *outputs* of proximate mechanisms, generated in response to the inputs from experience. But Evolutionary Psychologists claim that our psychological adaptations are (some of) the *proximate mechanisms* that generate such outputs, not the outputs themselves. As Steven Pinker says, *"the major faculties of the mind* . . . show the handiwork of selection. That does not mean that every aspect of the mind is adaptive. From low-level features like the sluggishness and noisiness of neurons, to momentous activities like art, music, religion, and dreams, we should expect to find activities of the mind that are not adaptations in the biologists' sense."[9] Thus, whether psychological exaptations outnumber adaptations "by orders of magnitude" is irrelevant. In fact, if you count the outputs of our proximate mechanisms, Evolutionary Psychologists would quickly agree that psychological exaptations outnumber adaptations "by orders of magnitude." The question is whether our "major faculties of the mind" are adaptations, and Gould does not address this question.

Second, Gould argues that the fundamental psychological adaptation in humans is brain size and that our mental capacities are merely by-products of a large brain. But there was surely no adaptive advantage to largeness of brain per se. Rather, selection made the human brain large because of the specific cognitive capacities conferred by larger brains. As Pinker points out, the mere largeness of the human brain is purely detrimental. "If *anything* is a byproduct, it is the size of the human brain, which guzzles nutrients [18 percent of the body's energy intake, although it is only 2 percent of the body's weight], makes us vulnerable to blows and falls, compromises the biomechanical design of the woman's pelvis, and makes childbirth dangerous. Bigness of brain is surely a byproduct of selection for more complex (and hence hardware-demanding) computational abilities, ones that allowed our ancestors to deal with tools, the natural world, and one another."[10] Thus, Gould's claim about what *is* a psychological adaptation, which functions to separate adaptation from byproducts, gets things backwards.

This characterization may, however, be uncharitable to Gould. It is possible that what Gould means by "large brain" is "general-purpose intelligence." In that case, Gould's claim that most of our "mental properties and potentials" are spandrels would actually be a rejection of Evolutionary Psychology's modular view of the mind and an endorsement of the view that the mind's cognitive capacities are domain general. While this interpretation would charitably avoid attributing to Gould the absurd view that there was selection for big heads, it nonetheless fails to advance his case against Evolutionary Psychology, since Gould offers no reasons to doubt Evolutionary Psychology's modularity thesis or to accept domain generality. He simply doesn't address these issues. So, however one reads him, Gould fails to show that adaptationism is the "fatal flaw" of Evolutionary Psychology.

Of course, escaping Gould's charge of adaptationism unscathed is meaningless if Gould is correct in claiming that Evolutionary Psychology is unscientific. But what are Gould's grounds for that claim?

The claim is grounded in another aspect of Gould and Lewontin's classic critique of adaptationism. Gould and Lewontin argue that the assumption that a trait is an adaptation is often so powerful that it leads evolutionists to accept an ultimate explanation of a trait even in the absence of evidence for it. "Often, evolutionists use *consistency* with natural selection as the sole criterion [of hypothesis acceptance] and consider their work done when they concoct a plausible story" about how a trait may have evolved under selection.[11] But, "since the range of adaptive stories is as wide as our minds are fertile," Gould and Lewontin argue, it is always easy to concoct a story about how some trait was adaptive in the long-gone evolutionary past.[12] Given the ease with which such stories can be concocted, Gould pejoratively dubs them "just-so stories." What is needed, Gould argues, is not a

"just-so story," which explains how a trait *may* have evolved under selection, but some serious evidence of past selection to support the story.

Gould thinks that Evolutionary Psychology, however, has priced itself
out of the market for evidence to support its adaptive hypotheses. His argument is as follows. First, he rightly points out that Evolutionary Psychologists don't assume that "all prominent and universal behaviors must, *ipso
facto*, be adaptive to modern humans in boosting reproductive success."[13]
But, Gould claims, as a result "the task of evolutionary psychology then
turns into a speculative search for reasons why a behavior that may harm
us now must once have originated for adaptive purposes. . . . Much of evolutionary psychology therefore devolves into a search for the so-called EEA,
or 'environment of evolutionary adaptation,' that allegedly prevailed in
prehistoric times."[14] However, Gould argues, "claims about an EEA usually
cannot be tested in principle but only subjected to speculation."[15] For "how
can we possibly know in detail what small bands of hunter-gatherers did
in Africa two million years ago? These ancestors left some tools and bones,
and paleoanthropologists can make some ingenious inferences from such
evidence. But how can we possibly obtain the key information that would
be required to show the validity of adaptive tales about an EEA . . .?"[16] Since
we have no evidence of how selection acted on human populations in
the EEA, Gould concludes, "the chief strategy proposed by evolutionary
psychologists for identifying adaptation is untestable, and therefore
unscientific."[17]

Once again, however, Gould's salvo misses the mark. For Evolutionary
Psychology is unscientific only if it is untestable *in principle*, not simply if
it is untestable in practice. A theory or hypothesis is untestable in principle if there is no *possible* evidence that could count for or against it. To put
this another way, if a theory or hypothesis is compatible with *all possible*
evidence, then it is unscientific. For example, young-earth creationism,
which claims that the earth was created by God some six thousand years
ago, is unscientific because there is no possible evidence that can count
against it. If geologists find rock strata that appear to be billions of years
old, according to young-earth creationism that is simply because six thousand years ago God created the rock strata to appear to be billions of years
old. Any possible evidence that appears to count against the theory that
the earth was created six thousand years ago thus gets explained in such
a way as to be compatible with the theory. For that reason, young-earth
creationism is unscientific.

In contrast, a theory or hypothesis is untestable *in practice* if there is some
possible evidence that would count for or against it, and if all such

evidence is currently unavailable to us. But the mere fact that we are unable, in practice, to gather the evidence needed to test a theory or hypothesis does not mean that it is unscientific. Particle physics, for example, has a history of proposing hypotheses about Very Tiny Things. Often, at the time these hypotheses are proposed, we have no way to test them, since we lack the technology to gather the evidence needed to test them. But this does not make these claims "untestable, and therefore unscientific," for we typically know precisely what kinds of evidence *would* test the claims if only we could obtain it. In short, there *is* evidence against which the claims could be tested, so the claims *are* testable in principle; we just aren't able, in practice, to obtain that evidence. Indeed, in particle physics, knowing what evidence would be needed to test theories often guides the process of building ever more super particle accelerators and colliders, which then enable us to create the conditions necessary for testing hypotheses. When we build the new supercollider, a theory or hypothesis that was once untestable in practice becomes testable in practice; but all along it was testable in principle, hence scientific. A claim is truly unscientific only when there is in principle no evidence against which it can be tested.

Now, *in principle* we often know precisely what kinds of evidence would confirm or disconfirm Evolutionary Psychology's claims about the EEA. For example, Evolutionary Psychologists claim that, other things being equal, Pleistocene males who preferred mating with nubile females would have produced more offspring than Pleistocene males who preferred mating with prepubescent or postmenopausal females. As a result, they claim, human males would have evolved a preference for nubile females, and consequently this preference is an adaptation in contemporary human males.

This adaptive hypothesis has clear test implications regarding our EEA. If it is true, any observer stationed in our EEA should have observed males with a preference for nubile mates outreproducing males with a preference for prepubescent or postmenopausal mates (other things being equal). In principle we know exactly what kinds of evidence would confirm or disconfirm the adaptive hypothesis, so the hypothesis is testable in principle, contrary to Gould's claim. It's just that in practice we don't have access to the evidence needed to confirm or disconfirm the hypothesis, since we can't actually observe our Pleistocene ancestors. But, since such hypotheses are testable in principle, they aren't unscientific.

Of course, even though Evolutionary Psychology's adaptive hypotheses are testable in principle, Gould could still press the point that they are untestable in practice, that they make (explicit or implicit) claims about a period in human evolution for which we lack sufficient evidence for adaptive hypotheses. Thus, while perhaps not unscientific per se, Gould could still charge that Evolutionary Psychology "ranks as pure guesswork in the cocktail party mode."[18] For, again, Gould might say, "how can we possibly know in detail what small bands of hunter-gatherers did in Africa two million years ago?"[19]

But Gould's argument fails to substantiate even this weaker charge. For Evolutionary Psychologists answer Gould's question by claiming that there are three sources from which we can obtain information about the EEA: the design of our adaptations, studies of extant hunter-gatherer societies, and primate studies. So, showing that we can't possibly have any evidence for Evolutionary Psychology's adaptive hypotheses requires more than Gould's rhetorical question about how we can know what our ancestors did two million years ago; it requires examining the three sources of evidence that Evolutionary Psychologists claim can substantiate their adaptive hypotheses. Gould, however, fails to discuss these sources of evidence and their relevance to his argument.

Further, Gould writes as though a lack of evidence that a trait is an adaptation constitutes evidence that it is an exaptation. But this is simply false. In fact, Gould's "exaptive" hypotheses are no more testable than the adaptive hypotheses he deplores. This is because exaptations are either co-opted adaptations or spandrels, developmental by-products of adaptations. Thus, to have evidence that a trait is a co-opted adaptation, we need evidence that the trait was an adaptation for its original purpose *and* evidence that in our evolutionary past the trait was co-opted for another role. Similarly, if a trait is a spandrel, we need evidence of a developmental mechanism by which that trait develops as a by-product of another *and* evidence that the trait of which it is a developmental by-product is itself an adaptation. If all of Evolutionary Psychology's claims about adaptation in the human EEA are untestable for want of data, all claims about human psychological exaptation are similarly untestable, since all claims of exaptation rest on claims of adaptation *and* require additional, different evidence of co-optation or developmental by-production. So, if Evolutionary Psychology is simply a bunch of "just-so stories," Gould's claims about psychological exaptations are simply "just-ain't-so stories." Conversely, however, if there can be evidence for Gould's claims about exaptations, there can also be evidence for claims about psychological adaptations.

Second, and most important, Gould completely mistakes the logic of adaptive reasoning in Evolutionary Psychology. The reason stems from the fact that Gould wants to transpose his earlier critique of adaptationism in evolutionary biology to a critique of Evolutionary Psychology. The pattern of adaptive reasoning denounced in that earlier critique moves from an already identified morphological or behavioral trait to speculation about the history of selection that designed the trait. This pattern of reasoning begins with the observation of a purported adaptation and then attempts to reconstruct its evolutionary history. That Gould believes this form of adaptive reasoning prevails in Evolutionary Psychology is evident in his assumption that Evolutionary Psychologists are in the business of providing adaptive explanations of "prominent and universal behaviors." However, Evolutionary Psychology is not in the business of providing adaptive explanations of behavior at all. Instead, it is interested in the adaptive evolution of the proximate mechanisms that control behavior.

This makes a tremendous difference to the role of adaptive reasoning in Evolutionary Psychology. The reason is quite simply that we cannot observe our psychological capacities or mechanisms, and cognitive science has yet to discover them. So, adaptive reasoning in Evolutionary Psychology doesn't begin with the observation of a purported adaptation and then attempt to reconstruct its evolutionary history, for the simple reason that we don't know what the proximate mechanisms are that are candidate psychological adaptations. Indeed, what makes Evolutionary Psychology so initially captivating is its promise to *discover* our psychological adaptations and reveal the structure of the mind.

Adaptive reasoning in Evolutionary Psychology must be understood in this context of attempted discovery. For the psychological adaptations postulated by Evolutionary Psychologists are *inferred from* adaptive hypotheses about human evolution in the EEA, not identified prior to and independently of speculation about their adaptive evolution in the EEA. The typical pattern of adaptive reasoning in Evolutionary Psychology is that found in evolutionary functional analysis, the method for discovering our psychological adaptations. That pattern is as follows: If early humans faced such-and-such an adaptive problem in the EEA, then our species should have evolved this or that proximate behavior-control mechanism to solve that adaptive problem; so, if modern humans possess such a proximate mechanism, it is an adaptation. Evolutionary Psychologists then conduct standard sorts of psychological experiment in an attempt to determine whether people possess the inferred proximate mechanism.

This typical pattern of adaptive reasoning in Evolutionary Psychology is clearly exemplified in the following passage from David Buss. Noting that human females are not fertile at all stages in life, Buss argues that early human males would have faced the adaptive problem of choosing a fertile mate. "Under these conditions, males who happened to mate with females of ages falling outside the reproductive years would become no one's ancestors. Males who happened to mate with females of peak fertility, in contrast, would enjoy relatively high reproductive success. Over thousands of generations, this selection pressure would, unless constrained, fashion a psychological mechanism that inclined males to mate with females of high fertility over those of low fertility."[20] Buss then conducted a large-scale, cross-cultural survey of male mate preferences in order to determine whether males possess the predicted psychological mechanism.

Given that the pattern of adaptive reasoning in Evolutionary Psychology is precisely the reverse of what Gould criticizes, Evolutionary Psychologists have a ready defense of the scientific character of their enterprise. For Evolutionary Psychologists use adaptive reasoning to *predict* the presence of previously undiscovered psychological mechanisms in the human mind; this is the whole point of evolutionary functional analysis. Evidence that humans possess the predicted psychological mechanisms is therefore evidence for the adaptive hypotheses that entail the predictions. This is a standard mode of scientific reasoning. A hypothesis is formulated and a prediction is derived from it; if the hypothesis correctly predicts the existence of a previously undiscovered phenomenon, then the hypothesis is considered confirmed. In other words, the discovery of a previously undiscovered and unexpected phenomenon confers some degree of probable truth on the hypothesis that predicted it. Consequently, Evolutionary Psychologists could argue, discovering that humans have a psychological mechanism that is predicted by some adaptive hypothesis about human evolution in the EEA is evidence for that adaptive hypothesis. Since Gould mistakes the logic of adaptive reasoning in Evolutionary Psychology, he misses the fact that adaptive hypotheses can be supported by the confirmed predictions they make about human psychological mechanisms.

While this does mean that Gould's arguments fail to show that there is anything wrong with adaptive reasoning in Evolutionary Psychology, it doesn't mean that all is well with Evolutionary Psychology. Indeed, adaptive reasoning in evolutionary functional analysis involves three steps, and Evolutionary Psychology can face problems at each of these three steps. The first step involves the identification of the adaptive problems our ancestors faced. The second step involves inferring the psychological mechanisms that must have evolved to solve those adaptive problems. Since the psychological mechanisms that are predicted in the second step are not observable, the third step involves conducting experiments to determine whether humans possess the predicted psychological mechanisms.

In the next section, I will argue that there are serious obstacles to successful completion of the first two steps. But I will argue throughout later chapters that most of Evolutionary Psychology's problems lie in the third step, in the process of confirming the existence of predicted psychological mechanisms. Typically, Evolutionary Psychology's problems do not concern a lack of evidence that such-and-such a psychological mechanism is an adaptation, but rather a lack of evidence that humans in fact possess that psychological mechanism. Of course, to show this requires examining specific Evolutionary Psychological hypotheses and the evidence that has been offered in support of them. Those hypotheses must be examined on a case-by-case basis in order to determine whether the evidence is there. Gould would like to find a single "fatal flaw" of Evolutionary Psychology and expose it with a quick and simple argument. But there is no such single "fatal flaw" of Evolutionary Psychology, so it can't be dealt such a quick and easy death blow. Its devils lie in its details, and Gould doesn't address any of those details.

## Adaptation Hunting

Evolutionary Psychology claims that it's well on the way to discovering the psychological adaptations that form the human mind and that the job will soon be completed. As Tooby and Cosmides so boldly say, "just as one can now flip open *Gray's Anatomy* to any page and find an intricately detailed depiction of some part of our evolved species-typical morphology, we anticipate that in 50 or 100 years one will be able to pick up an equivalent reference work for psychology and find in it detailed information-processing descriptions of the multitude of evolved species-typical adaptations of the human mind."[21]

This confidence is based on faith in the method of evolutionary functional analysis, which is a kind of *reverse engineering*. Forward engineering is a process of designing a mechanism that will be capable of performing some desired task. Reverse engineering is a process of figuring out the design of a mechanism on the basis of an analysis of the tasks it performs. Evolutionary functional analysis is a form of reverse engineering in that it attempts to reconstruct the mind's design from an analysis of the problems the mind must have evolved to solve.

However, because our psychological mechanisms were designed to solve the adaptive problems faced by our Pleistocene ancestors, according to Evolutionary Psychologists, and because the environments we now inhabit often differ considerably from those inhabited by our Pleistocene ancestors, our psychological adaptations often fail to function as designed. As a result, Evolutionary Psychologists argue, our psychological adaptations consistently produce maladaptive thought, emotion, and behavior in our modern environments. So we can't reverse engineer the evolved design of the mind by studying contemporary human behavior and cognition, by studying the tasks that the mind performs in our modern environments. Instead, Evolutionary Psychologists claim, we must reverse engineer the mind from the vantage of our evolutionary past. Thus, evolutionary functional analysis begins with a specification of an adaptive problem that prevailed in our EEA and proceeds to the description of a domain-specific psychological mechanism that specializes in solving it. It is a method of inferring the existence of a psychological adaptation from a claim about a history of selection pressures.

Evolutionary Psychologists are confident that evolutionary functional analysis can lead to the discovery of unknown psychological adaptations, because, as Tooby and Cosmides say, a "selection pressure defines an information-processing problem that organisms will be selected to evolve mechanisms to solve. . . . Using this description of an adaptive problem as a starting point, one can immediately begin to define the cognitive subtasks that would have to be addressed."[22] "Because an adaptive problem and its cognitive solution—a mechanism—need to *fit together like a lock and a key*, understanding adaptive problems tells one a great deal about the associated cognitive mechanisms. Natural selection shapes domain-specific mechanisms so that their structure meshes with the evolutionarily stable features of their particular problem-domains."[23] Because of this alleged tight correspondence between adaptive problems and their psychological solutions, "evolutionary functional analysis guides the researcher step by step from a definition of an adaptive problem to the discovery and mapping of the mechanisms that solve it."[24]

I will argue that there are intractable obstacles to discovering our psychological adaptations via evolutionary functional analysis. For the method requires that we identify the adaptive problems faced by our ancestors and that we then infer the design of the psychological mechanisms that evolved to solve them. I will argue, first, that we can't specify the adaptive problems faced by our ancestors precisely enough to know what kinds of psychological mechanism would have had to evolve to solve them. I will argue, second, that no reliable chain of inference leads from ancestral adaptive problems to our psychological adaptations anyway.

With respect to the first problem, we simply don't know what adaptive problems our ancestors faced in our EEA. We don't even know the number of species in the genus *Homo*, which species were our direct ancestors, or in general how *Homo* species were related to one another, let alone details about the lifestyles led by those species. This was one of Gould's complaints against Evolutionary Psychology. But Gould oversimplified by ignoring the fact that Evolutionary Psychologists propose three sources of evidence from which we can obtain information about the adaptive problems faced by our ancestors. So how, according to Evolutionary Psychologists, can we obtain information about the adaptive problems faced by our Pleistocene ancestors?

One source of evidence is the design of adaptations. As the evolutionary biologist Randy Thornhill puts it: "The functional design of an adaptation is the record of the salient, long-term environmental problem involved in the creation of the functional design. Thus, we can actually scientifically go back in time and discover the creative selection pressures that were effective in human evolutionary history."[25] Following Thornhill's lead, David Buss argues that, although "we lack a videotape of the selective pressures" that affected human psychology, nonetheless "some selection pressures can be inferred from the . . . analysis of the current design of our mechanisms."[26]

The problem with this suggestion is that we are supposed to *discover* the "current design of our mechanisms" via evolutionary functional analysis, which is supposed to begin with a specification of the adaptive problems that have shaped human psychology. This suggestion instead requires antecedent knowledge of our adaptations, which is used as a source of information about the adaptive problems that have shaped them. But, while the mind may not be a wholly black box any longer, it still remains a dark shade of charcoal heather. So this suggestion is a nonstarter if, as in fact is the case, we haven't independently identified the psychological characteristics that are candidate adaptations.

A second potential source of evidence about the adaptive problems faced by our hunter-gatherer ancestors is the lifestyles of extant hunter-gatherer populations. Evolutionary psychologists argue that hunter-gatherer populations that have been unaffected by agriculturalization and industrialization live much as Pleistocene hunter-gatherers did. In effect, they argue, there has been a continuity of lifestyle from our ancestral hunter-gatherer populations to extant hunter-gatherer populations. Consequently, they conclude, the adaptive problems faced by extant hunter-gatherers should be the same as those faced by our Pleistocene ancestors.

There are, however, two problems with this proposal. First, it is naive to think that the social lives of extant hunter-gatherer populations have not changed significantly in the last 10,000 years. As the anthropologist Robert Kelly argues, "long before anthropologists arrived on the scene, hunter-gatherers had already been contacted, given diseases, shot at, traded with, employed and exploited by colonial powers, agriculturalists, and/or pastoralists. The result has been dramatic alterations in hunter-gatherers' livelihoods. . . . There can be little doubt that all ethnographically known hunter-gatherers are tied into the world economic system in one way or another; in some cases they have been so connected for hundreds of years. They are in no way evolutionary relics."[27]

Second, as the anthropologist Laura Betzig points out, there is considerable variation in the lifestyles of extant hunter-gatherer populations. Among these populations, the average daily caloric intake from foods gathered by women ranges from 2 percent to 67 percent, average paternal care ranges from ten minutes a day to 88 percent of the day, and mating systems vary. This variation is not restricted to differences between sub-Saharan hunter-gatherers and, for example, South American hunter-gatherers. There is considerable such variation among African hunter-gatherers in and around the region Evolutionary Psychologists believe was inhabited by our ancestors. Which of these populations should we take as our model of our Pleistocene ancestors? It makes a difference. If we choose a monogamous population, we will get a different picture of the adaptive problems that shaped human sexual psychology than if we choose a polygynous population. Similarly, a population that gets most of its calories from foods provided by women will give us a different picture of adaptive problems than a population that gets most of its calories from foods provided by men. Since it isn't at all clear which extant hunter-gatherer population we should take as our model, we can't reliably reconstruct the adaptive problems faced by our Pleistocene ancestors through a study of extant hunter-gatherers.

The third source of potential evidence about the adaptive problems faced by our Pleistocene ancestors is comparative analysis, the study of species related to ours. Evolutionary psychologists claim that we may come to understand the adaptive problems faced by Pleistocene humans by studying the adaptive problems faced by related nonhuman primates, since they share with us a common ancestor.

But there are problems with this suggestion too. First, the most recent ancestor common to us and our closest relative, the chimpanzee, lived 5 to 7 million years ago, a good 3 to 5 million years before the Pleistocene.

The ways in which our lineage diverged from that of our chimpanzee relatives before the Pleistocene, not to mention during the Pleistocene itself, are profound. By the time early humans emerged in the Pleistocene, the adaptive problems driving their evolution should have differed profoundly from the adaptive problems facing nonhuman Pleistocene primates. And, since nonhuman primates have been evolving since the Pleistocene as well, the adaptive problems faced by contemporary nonhuman primates should differ even more from the adaptive problems faced by early humans. As a result, even our closest relative's lifestyle holds few clues to the lifestyle of our Pleistocene ancestors.

Second, nonhuman primate species differ considerably with respect to foraging, parental care, and mating system. So we face the problem of which nonhuman primate to take as our model of Pleistocene humans. The lifestyle of our closest relatives won't necessarily provide the best clues to the adaptive problems that drove human psychological evolution. Studies of 178 mammal and 151 bird species have shown that closely related species are more similar with respect to morphological and life-history traits than are distantly related species, but that degree of relatedness isn't correlated with similarity in behavioral traits.[28] Rather, similarity of ecological conditions is a more important determinant of similarity of behavioral traits than is degree of relatedness.

Since human psychology would have evolved in response to selection's acting on behavior, the ecological conditions of our ancestors would have been a primary determinant of the evolution of human psychological traits. Consequently, rather than simply studying our closest primate relatives, we need to study the primate species whose ecological conditions most closely resemble those of our Pleistocene ancestors, for that species will provide the best guide to the adaptive problems faced by our ancestors. But, without knowledge of the ecological conditions of our Pleistocene ancestors, which is what we're trying to obtain, we can't determine which nonhuman primates live in ecological conditions similar to those of Pleistocene humans. Thus, the study of nonhuman primates is unlikely to shed light on the adaptive problems that helped shape human psychology.

These are all serious obstacles to the specification of adaptive problems that constitutes the first step of evolutionary functional analysis. Any specification of those problems will indeed rank as pure guesswork on the part of Evolutionary Psychologists, much in the way that Gould complains.

Of course, Evolutionary Psychologists will find this argument unduly skeptical, much as Pinker finds Gould's argument unduly skeptical. As Pinker says, "what makes Gould so certain that our ancestors' environment lacked written language—the basis for his argument that reading is a span-drel? Obviously it is the archeological record, which shows that writing is a recent invention. . . . It is precisely such evidence that leads Evolution-ary Psychologists to infer that the ancestral environment lacked agricul-ture, contraception, high-tech medicine, mass media, mass-produced goods, money, police, armies, communities of strangers, and other modern features—absences with profound implications for the minds that evolved in such an environment."[29]

But a list of things we know *did not* affect human psychological evolu-tion is a far cry from a positive account of the adaptive problems that *did* shape human psychology. Of course, Evolutionary Psychologists will still insist that they can say with some certainty what some of those adaptive problems were, since many of them seem to follow immediately from reflection on the demands of survival and reproduction. This is how Tooby and Cosmides arrived at their laundry list of Pleistocene adaptive problems discussed in chapter 2. As Tooby and Cosmides would argue, we can be quite confident that Pleistocene humans would have had to "select mates of high reproductive value" and to "induce potential mates to choose them," for example.

But here we encounter a problem concerning the "grain" at which these adaptive problems are described. It is true that we can always be certain that just about all sexually reproducing species face the adaptive problems of selecting mates of high reproductive value and inducing potential mates to become actual mates. These descriptions of adaptive problems are so coarse-grained, however, as to be wholly uninformative about the selec-tion pressures that act on a species. Consider, for example, what one need do to attract a mate. Male bowerbirds must build ornately decorated bowers, male hangingflies must offer captured prey as a nuptial gift, and male sedge warblers must sing a wider repertoire of songs than other males. The adaptive problem of attracting a mate thus takes very different forms depending on the species. For male bowerbirds, the adaptive problem that is describable at a very coarse grain as "attracting a mate" is, at a finer grain of description, the problem of building an ornately decorated bower. The finer-grained description is the one that captures the adaptive problem *for bowerbirds*. So, the problem is that, while it's true that we can be confident that Pleistocene humans needed to attract mates, that coarse-grained description doesn't inform us of the specific form of adaptive problem that helped shape human sexual psychology.

There is another way to think about this difficulty. Recall from chapter 2 that evolutionary functional analysis begins with a specification of an adaptive problem and then proceeds to a *task analysis* of that problem. The task analysis involves breaking down the adaptive problem into a number of subproblems, the solutions to which collectively constitute a solution to the adaptive problem. One purportedly solves the adaptive problem by solving the subproblems that constitute it, and psychological adaptations purportedly evolved to solve these subproblems. Seen in this light, simply knowing that Pleistocene humans needed to attract mates doesn't inform us of the subproblems that constituted that adaptive problem *for Pleistocene humans*. And it is those more specific subproblems that adaptations would have evolved to solve. In order to get the more fine-grained and informative description of the subproblems, however, we would need to have more detailed knowledge of the lifestyles of our ancestors. And that's knowledge we simply don't have.

There is even reason to think that we couldn't *possibly* have any knowledge of the finer-grained adaptive problems faced by our Pleistocene ancestors without knowing something about their psychology. The reason is that the finer-grained adaptive subproblems faced by a species are not independent of the morphology and psychology of that species. Indeed, the morphology and psychology of a species determine which aspects of the environment are adaptively relevant to the species. As the biologist Richard Lewontin says: "The bark of trees is part of the environment of a woodpecker, but the stones lying at the base of the tree, even though physically present, are not. On the other hand, thrushes that break snail shells include the stones, but exclude the tree from their environment. If breaking snail shells is a 'problem' to which the use of a stone anvil is a thrush's 'solution,' it is because thrushes have evolved into snail-eating birds, whereas woodpeckers have not. The breaking of snails is a problem created by the thrushes, not a transcendental problem that existed before the evolution of the *Turdidae*."[30] Which features of the environment pose adaptive problems for a species, in other words, depends on the "equipment" of the species, since that equipment will antecedently be attuned to certain features of the environment but not to others. And features of the environment to which a species' equipment is not attuned will generally be irrelevant to that species' subsequent evolution by natural or sexual selection.

This means that, without knowledge of the morphology and psychology of a species, we can never specify the adaptive problems confronting it with anything but the most coarse-grained descriptions, and these will not inform us of the specific selection pressures acting on it. So, in order to identify the selection pressures that helped shape human psychology, we would need to know something about ancestral human psychology. For our ancestors' motivational states and cognitive processes would have been selectively responsive to certain features of the physical and social environments, and only those features would have affected subsequent adaptive evolution of early human psychology. At this point we again collide with our ignorance of our early ancestors. And, given that psychologies don't fossilize, this ignorance is likely intractable.

So far I have argued that, without antecedent knowledge of our psychological adaptations, we're unlikely to ever be in a position to have the evidence required to make the identification of ancestral human adaptive problems anything more than pure guesswork. This is a problem for Evolutionary Psychology, which proposes to infer the nature of our psychological adaptations from the adaptive problems that shaped them. But my argument so far has merely suggested epistemic obstacles to evolutionary functional analysis, limitations of our knowledge that prevent us from identifying ancestral adaptive problems. There are, however, more principled reasons for being deeply skeptical of evolutionary functional analysis as a method of discovering our psychological adaptations—reasons for being skeptical *even if* all the epistemic obstacles I've mentioned could be overcome. For evolutionary functional analysis presupposes that there were relatively stable adaptive problems during human evolution to which selection very slowly tailored psychological solutions. The stability of these problems is supposedly reflected in the design of our psychological adaptations, and consequently we are supposed to be able to get a handle on the design of those adaptations by identifying the stable problems for which they were designed. But there are reasons for thinking that there were no stable adaptive problems driving the majority of human psychological evolution.

The most widely accepted account of the evolution of human intelligence, which is also accepted by Evolutionary Psychologists, is the social intelligence hypothesis (also known as the Machiavellian intelligence hypothesis). According to this hypothesis, most of human psychological evolution was driven by the human social environment, not by the physical environment. For the compelling problems whose solutions required true intelligence were those involved in social life: competing with members of the same sex for mates, competing with others for resources, recognizing and responding appropriately to deception and hostility, protecting and feeding offspring, and so on. In other words, the majority of adaptive problems that drove human psychological evolution were posed by other humans, who were themselves responding adaptively to the demands of human social life. The problems involved in competing for a mate were posed by the preferences of the opposite sex and by the behavior of competitors of one's own sex. The problems involved in dealing with hostilities were posed by the wants, temperaments, and behavioral tendencies of other humans. In short, the need to better one another in social competition wielded the crop that drove the evolution of our intelligence. Put crudely, the primary driving force of human psychological evolution was *human psychology*.

As the philosophers of biology Kim Sterelny and Paul Griffiths point out, this state of affairs set up an "arms race" in human psychological evolution. In an evolutionary arms race, there is progressive modification not only in the solutions to adaptive problems, but in the adaptive problems themselves. "Improving" solutions are continually matched by ever more "difficult" problems, with evolution in either precipitating the evolution of the other. Many arms races are between predators and prey. As predators evolve to get better at catching their prey, this creates a selection pressure on the prey to become better at escaping the predator, which then creates a selection pressure on the predator to catch the more adept prey, and so on. As cheetahs become faster runners, gazelles are selected to become faster runners; but their running faster selects for faster cheetahs, which then selects for even faster gazelles, and so on. Arms races are common in predator-prey and host-parasite interactions, but they can also take place within a species or within a sex whenever conspecifics compete for the same resources.

This latter kind of evolutionary arms race would have characterized all of human psychological evolution that was responsive to the human social environment. For any evolution in human psychology would have changed the psychological composition of the population as a whole, which would have then created a new adaptive problem for human psychology to adapt to. But this means that, as human psychology evolved, the adaptive problems driving human psychological evolution would have evolved in lockstep, so that there would have been no stable adaptive problems driving human psychological evolution. As Sterelny and Griffiths put it, "when evolution is driven by features of the social structure of the evolving species, evolution transforms the environment of the evolving organism. The evolution of language, of tool use, and of indirect reciprocity are not solutions to preexisting problems posed to the organism. There are no stable problems in these domains to which natural selection can grind out a solution. The 'adaptive problem' is always being transformed in an arms race. As we evolve to detect cheaters, these honesty-mimics evolve better and better imitations of a trustworthy and honest face."[31]

Note that the force of this argument is somewhat sensitive to the grain at which adaptive problems are described. It may be true, for example, that the adaptive problem of attracting a mate has remained stable throughout human evolutionary history. But, as I argued earlier, this very coarse-grained description of the adaptive problem doesn't inform us of *what one must do* to attract a mate. A finer-grained description of the adaptive problem would specify the precise form the task takes. The adaptive problems that would have exhibited instability in an evolutionary arms race are those specified by such finer-grained descriptions. In other words, while the coarse-grained adaptive problem of attracting a mate may have remained stable, the finer-grained subproblems involved in the attracting would have undergone change. Thus, the adaptive subproblems that shaped human psychology would have been very fluid throughout human evolution.

But evolutionary arms races are not the only phenomenon that produces fluidity of adaptive problems. Organisms often actively construct their niches. When they do, they modify the selection pressures that drive their evolution. And the more actively they construct their niches, the more fluid are the selection pressures. An obvious example of niche construction is dam-building by beavers. But niche construction can take much simpler forms. Digging a burrow to escape the unusual cold of a severe winter is an act of constructing a new niche in which the selection pressures differ from those outside the burrow.

Humans have been supreme niche constructors. The development of agriculture, for example, greatly altered human niches. An acre of farmed land was able to feed many more mouths than an acre of wild land from which foods were gathered. As a result, population densities increased in agricultural areas and birthrates among agriculturists increased as well. At the same time, however, the transition to a diet composed primarily of starchy foods brought widespread malnutrition, and the higher population densities allowed diseases such as cholera to spread quickly to large numbers of people. The development of industry brought about similar changes in human niches, and developments in medicine have continually altered the toll of disease on survival and, as a consequence, opportunities to reproduce. On the psychological side, techniques of teaching, whether skill or information based, have altered the cognitive niche in which humans develop, and the recent development of information technologies is radically altering the cognitive niche to which future generations will have to adapt. These are some spectacular ways in which humans have modified their niches, but there are a multitude of less spectacular ways that we have done so, ranging from methods of food preparation and preservation (think of pasteurization, for example) to methods of shelter construction, from methods of contraception to systems of organized education. And we really don't know precisely how niche construction among our prehistoric ancestors may have continuously altered the adaptive problems they faced and helped shape and reshape the direction of human psychological evolution.

The evolutionary biologists Kevin Laland, John Odling-Smee, and Marcus Feldman offer the following simple nonpsychological example of how easily, and inadvertently, human niche construction can change selection pressures. A West African population "increased the frequency of a gene for sickle-cell anemia in their own population as a result of the indirect effects of yam cultivation. . . . [They] traditionally cut clearings in the rainforest, creating more standing water and increasing the breeding grounds for malaria-carrying mosquitoes. This, in turn, intensifies selection for the sickle-cell allele, because of the protection offered by this allele against malaria in the heterozygotic condition."[32] There can be little doubt that similarly subtle niche construction would have affected the direction of human psychological evolution.

Further, as populations of our direct ancestors diverged around 50,000 years ago (or earlier, depending on whose account you believe) and began to occupy different parts of the globe, the different habitats they encountered would have prompted different behavioral responses, at least some of which would have involved niche construction. Because niche construction would have taken different forms in the different habitats occupied by these early human populations, the adaptive problems faced by different populations would have diverged, and the problems would have been very fluid in each different habitat. And diversity in the ways early human populations formed environmental niches would have compounded the instability of the adaptive problems our ancestors faced.

Because of evolutionary arms races and niche construction, it is doubtful that there were many stable adaptive problems to which humans evolved psychological solutions. But, if there weren't stable adaptive problems driving human psychological evolution, there are no stable adaptive problems whose identification will give us a handle on the nature of our psychological adaptations. Once again, the necessary first step in evolutionary functional analysis—the identification of adaptive problems to which we evolved psychological solutions—appears unachievable.

So far I have argued that there are severe problems with the idea that we can identify the adaptive problems to which selection slowly tailored human psychological adaptations. Now I want to shift gears. Suppose, for the sake of argument, that we could overcome all the difficulties I have discussed so far. Suppose that we could compile an exhaustive list of all the psychologically relevant adaptive problems faced by our ancestors *throughout* human evolutionary history. What would that list enable us to infer about the nature of human psychological adaptations? Not much, I will now argue.

First, not every adaptive problem is solved by a population. It's true that some adaptive problems have a do-or-die character, such that failing to solve them results in failure to survive or reproduce. But not every adaptive problem absolutely *must* be solved. Steven Pinker has argued eloquently that language is an adaptation, and I have no doubt that he is right. That means that language solved certain adaptive problems for the early human population in which it evolved. But the ancestors of that population didn't go extinct because they lacked language, despite the fact that language would have provided them with all the adaptive advantages it provided their descendants. So the adaptive problems that language solved didn't *force* the evolution of a solution to them. Selection pressures, or adaptive problems, can only "pressure" a population to evolve when a variant emerges that is responsive to that pressure, and often a population can survive and reproduce without variation that is differentially responsive to some selection pressure. Thus, even if we could identify all the adaptive problems facing ancestral human populations, we still couldn't be assured that our ancestors evolved solutions to those problems.

This is important to bear in mind, because adaptive reasoning in Evolutionary Psychology typically proceeds only on the basis of hypotheticals, claims about what *would have* provided an adaptive advantage among our Pleistocene ancestors. But the fact that some trait would have provided an adaptive advantage is no guarantee that it has in fact evolved. Humans see very poorly in the dark, for example, even though it is easy to imagine adaptive advantages of night vision during the Pleistocene.

Second, even if our ancestors did evolve a solution to some adaptive problem facing them, that solution may not have a form that is easily inferable from the task demands of the adaptive problem. Evolutionary functional analysis presupposes that the properties of adaptive problems and the properties of their solutions "fit together like a lock and a key, [so that] understanding adaptive problems tells one a great deal about the associated [modules]."[33]

But selection never designs solutions to adaptive problems from scratch. Adaptations all emerge through modifications to preexisting structures.

The form of a solution to an adaptive problem, then, will always depend heavily on the form of the preexisting structure that got modified. Because selection does not design organisms with structures that *anticipate* specific future needs, the form of each preexisting structure will not have been designed specifically for the task for which it subsequently got recruited. Thus, given that selection always builds on what is already present, which is not designed to anticipate its future use, evolved solutions will have a much looser "fit" with their adaptive problems than keys have with the locks they open. Indeed, if survival and reproductive success are represented by entry to the house and adaptive problems by the lock on the door, then evolved solutions tend not to resemble keys that were cut to fit the lock, but to resemble drills that bore through the lock, saws that cut a hole in the door, or hammers that break the side window. Each of these solutions effectively gains entry to the house, but none of their forms can be predicted by examining the properties of the lock on the door.

Since selection builds solutions to adaptive problems by retaining modifications to preexisting structures, the form of a solution—an adaptation—will always be a function of the possible ways in which the preexisting structure could be modified. Consequently, we can never infer the structure of an evolved solution to an adaptive problem from the nature of the problem itself. We also need to know something about the preexisting structure that was recruited and modified to solve the problem. But, as argued previously, we simply don't know what kinds of preexisting psychological characteristics our ancestors possessed. In the absence of knowledge of ancestral human psychology, we will be misled about the form of our psychological adaptations if we attempt to infer them strictly from a description of the adaptive problems they purportedly evolved to solve. Thus, even if we could identify the adaptive problems that drove human psychological evolution, it is implausible to suppose that doing so would enable us to formulate reliable hypotheses about our psychological adaptations, as Evolutionary Psychologists claim. As a method for discovering our psychological adaptations, evolutionary functional analysis *is* pure guesswork.

Of course, as I have mentioned, if that guesswork correctly predicts the existence of a previously undiscovered psychological mechanism, then we have reason to believe the guess may be right. So, although these arguments offer reasons for skepticism regarding the discovery of our psychological adaptations via evolutionary functional analysis, we really need to examine the empirical evidence for the existence of specific predicted mechanisms to see whether evolutionary functional analysis can bear fruit.

If it's true, however, that the real proof of evolutionary functional analysis is in the pudding of empirical evidence for the psychological mechanisms it predicts, then why did I just argue extensively that evolutionary functional analysis is an unreliable method for the discovery of our psychological adaptations? Why not just turn directly to an examination of the empirical evidence of specific predicted psychological mechanisms and leave it at that?

The reason has to do with the grounds on which we are justified in accepting claims about new discoveries in science. Here is one typical pattern of justification for a claim that a new phenomenon has been discovered. We begin with some theoretical principles that we have independent reasons for accepting. We discover that these principles, perhaps together with some independent empirical data, entail the existence of a previously undiscovered phenomenon. We then reason that, if that phenomenon indeed exists, we should obtain certain results if we perform a particular kind of experiment. We then conduct the experiment to see if we obtain those results. If we do obtain those results, then we can be confident that we have discovered a new phenomenon.

Consider how this pattern would be ideally exemplified by evolutionary functional analysis. We begin with some general theoretical principles regarding the evolutionary process together with some claims about the selection pressures operative during human evolutionary history, which we should have independent reasons for accepting. We deduce from these the hypothesis that one or both of the sexes should have evolved a particular psychological mechanism. We then reason that, if people possess that psychological mechanism, we should obtain certain results if we subject people to a particular battery of tests or surveys. If we do obtain those results, we can be confident that people possess the relevant psychological mechanism—that is, we conclude that our hypothesis has been confirmed.

But what if we don't obtain the right experimental results or the results aren't entirely clear? A popular image of science is that a theory makes a prediction, the scientists check to see whether the prediction is accurate, and they jettison the theory if it's not. But this popular image is wrong. Science does not actually work that way, and it would not be a rational enterprise if it did. When theoretical principles are independently justified and have withstood the test of time, we're often more justified in doubting the empirical data that contradict them or their entailments than in doubting the theoretical principles themselves. When your experiments in high-school chemistry class failed to produce results that exactly matched those predicted by the textbook, you didn't reject the relevant aspects of chemical theory, but concluded that you had not done the experiment correctly at every stage. And, if your results came out *in the ballpark* of the predicted values, you considered the experiment a success and took it as further confirmation of the theoretical principles in the textbook.

Unfortunately, empirical data in science rarely speak loudly and unequivocally for or against a hypothesis. This is especially true of empirical data, like those in Evolutionary Psychology, that are gathered by forced-choice questionnaires, or other social psychological instruments, and then analyzed using statistical procedures. Data are often messy as a result of "noise" in the experimental procedure, factors that interfere with obtaining clean and unequivocal results that clearly confirm or disconfirm a hypothesis. Consequently, it often requires some work in order to know what the data are saying about a hypothesis.

Given the frequent messiness of data, how confident can we be in hypotheses that we derive from independent theoretical principles and assumptions? That depends on how confident we can be in either the theoretical principles that entailed the hypothesis or the empirical evidence gathered to test it. If we can be very confident in the theoretical principles from which we derive a hypothesis, then we can be confident in that hypothesis even if our empirical evidence for it isn't very good. In this case, as with high-school chemistry experiments, we can attribute a failure of exact match between predicted and obtained results to experimental "noise," and we can accept results that are merely in the ballpark as fair confirmation of our hypothesis. On the other hand, if we can't be confident in the theoretical principles from which we derive a hypothesis, then our degree of confidence in the hypothesis is going to derive almost entirely from the strength of the empirical evidence. In this case, to be confident in our hypothesis the empirical evidence does need to say very clearly that the hypothesis is accurate.

The moral of this digression is that confidence in a hypothesis can derive from two sources—the theoretical principles that entail the hypothesis and the empirical evidence gathered to directly test it. In the ideal case, we can be confident in both the theoretical principles (when they have a lot of independent evidence in their favor) and the empirical evidence, for then we can be maximally confident that our hypothesis is accurate. But we can nonetheless enjoy a lower degree of confidence in our hypothesis if we can be confident of either the theoretical principles that entail it or the empirical evidence for it, even though the other is somewhat dubious.

Thus, the point of my argument that evolutionary functional analysis is pure guesswork is to show that we should have very little or no confidence in the theoretical claims about human evolution from which Evolutionary Psychologists derive their hypotheses about the psychological mechanisms we possess (for example, that males have a psychological mechanism for detecting and preferring nubile females as mates). If we are to be at all confident in these hypotheses, the confidence must derive *entirely* from the empirical evidence that allegedly confirms them. If the empirical evidence is weak, we should be skeptical of the hypotheses, since they aren't derived from a body of sound and independently confirmed theoretical principles. In the case of Evolutionary Psychology's claims about what psychological adaptations humans have evolved, the empirical evidence for the existence of those adaptations is *everything*. Without it, there is no sound theory for the hypotheses about psychological adaptations to fall back on. In later chapters, I will examine the empirical evidence for each of Evolutionary Psychology's most prominent claims about the psychological adaptations we possess.

### "Our Modern Skulls House a Stone-Age Mind"

As we have seen, one thing, though not the only thing, that gets evolutionary functional analysis into trouble is its attempt to reverse engineer the mind from the vantage of our prehistoric past. For it attempts to reverse engineer the mind by starting from the adaptive problems faced by our Pleistocene ancestors, and there are severe obstacles to identifying those adaptive problems. But why do Evolutionary Psychologists think that we need to begin the process of reverse engineering the mind from our insufficiently knowable Pleistocene past? The reason is that Evolutionary Psychologists believe that our psychological adaptations were designed during the Pleistocene to solve the problems of hunter-gatherer life and that there has been no significant psychological evolution since the Pleistocene. Consequently, Evolutionary Psychologists believe that the evolved structure of the mind "reflects completed rather than ongoing selection."[34] The psychologist Henry Plotkin calls this "the thesis of ancient provenance," since it claims that our minds were fixed by "ancient" selection processes. In this section, I will argue that the thesis of ancient provenance is unjustified.

Recall, from chapter 2, why Evolutionary Psychologists think that our psychological adaptations are adapted to Pleistocene, rather than modern, environments. The sole reason is a general theoretical argument about how long it takes for complex adaptations to evolve. The 10,000 years since the end of the Pleistocene, they argue, "is only a small stretch in evolutionary terms, less than 1% of the two million years our ancestors spent as Pleistocene hunter-gatherers. For this reason, it is unlikely that new complex designs—ones requiring the coordinated assembly of many novel, functionally integrated features—could evolve in so few generations."[35] The four hundred generations since the end of the Pleistocene are too few for genetic evolution significant enough to "assemble" complex psychological modules that are adapted to modern environments. Thus, our psychological adaptations must have evolved, instead, *during* the Pleistocene and hence must be adapted to the Pleistocene conditions under which they evolved.

There are, however, several problems with this argument. First, the issue is not whether "*new* complex designs" that require the "coordinated assembly" of many features could have evolved in the 10,000 years since the Pleistocene. Without doubt, selection could not build a human mind from scratch in a mere four hundred generations. But, from the fact that a "new complex design" could not have evolved since the Pleistocene, it doesn't follow that the psychological adaptations of contemporary humans are identical to those of our Pleistocene ancestors. For the issue is whether *old* complex designs, which evolved during the Pleistocene, could have been *modified* by selection in the last 10,000 years. Since the argument doesn't address this possibility, it fails to show that our psychological adaptations must have *remained* adapted to Pleistocene conditions.

Second, as the evolutionary biologist David Sloan Wilson points out, "it makes no sense to express evolutionary time as a proportion of the species history (e.g., 1%). If the environment of a species changes, the evolutionary response will depend on the heritability of traits [roughly, the proportion of variation in traits that is due to genetic variation], the intensity of selection, and the number of generations that selection acts. The number of generations that the species existed in the old environment is irrelevant, except insofar as it affects the heritability of traits."[36] In other words, it doesn't matter whether a lineage spends only 1 percent of its evolutionary history in a new environment, what matters is what kinds of change occur during that 1 percent of its evolutionary history. Thus, Wilson concludes, "rather than marvelling at the antiquity of our species, we should be asking what kinds of evolutionary change can be expected in 10, 100, or 1000 generations."

Finally, the thesis of ancient provenance does indeed underestimate the kinds of evolutionary change that may have occurred since the end of the

Pleistocene. In considering what kinds of evolutionary change may have occurred in the last 10,000 years, we need to distinguish two different questions. First, we need to ask whether the environments inhabited by human populations have changed significantly since the Pleistocene. This question is important because, if the environment inhabited by a population remains unchanged, selection will favor the status quo in the population. On the other hand, if the environment changes, and with it the adaptive problems faced by the population, selection will pressure the population to adapt to the changing environment. Second, if the environment has changed, we need to ask whether there has been sufficient time for human populations to respond to the change. For, even if the environment has changed, it may be the case that the change has been too recent and too rapid to be tracked by an evolutionary response in human populations.

So, have the environments inhabited by human populations changed enough since the Pleistocene to have created a selection pressure for change in some features of human psychology? The answer to this question is undoubtedly yes. Such changes can be seen most clearly by considering those human populations that became agriculturalized and industrialized, for the agricultural and industrial revolutions changed environments in radical ways, as we saw in the last section. Evolutionary Psychologists argue that, despite these changes, humans have still needed to live in groups and that the adaptive problems posed by human *social life* have remained largely unchanged from Pleistocene hunter-gatherer populations. But this is false. The agricultural and industrial revolutions precipitated fundamental changes in the group sizes and social structures of human populations, which in turn altered the selection pressures on a variety of interpersonal behaviors.

For example, Evolutionary Psychologists argue that women have an evolved preference for mates who can provide the resources essential to child rearing, such as food and shelter. If they are right, this preference, over our evolutionary history, would have sexually selected for males with the ability to provide those resources. Let's assume, just for the sake of present argument, that Pleistocene women had this preference and that modern women do too, so that men since the Pleistocene have had to solve the adaptive problem of providing food and shelter. As we saw earlier, even if this coarse-grained adaptive problem has remained constant for men since the Pleistocene, it doesn't follow that the *subtasks* involved in solving that adaptive problem have likewise remained constant. If the subtasks have changed, then any Darwinian algorithms that effectively solved the subtasks before the changes will not necessarily be effective after the change. So, if the subtasks involved in acquiring food, for example, have changed, there has been selection pressure for evolution in the Darwinian algorithms involved in acquiring food.

To see how such subtasks have changed, consider that in a hunter-gatherer population a man must find and kill an animal in order to acquire food for a (potential) mate and offspring. But what a man must do to acquire food in an agricultural population differs considerably. And what a man must do to acquire food within a barter system, or as a wage laborer in a capitalist system, differs even more. Wage-Laborer Man needs to obtain a job (often in a large population characterized by intense competition for jobs), perform the tasks required of that job, manage his wages, locate a purveyor of food, and negotiate the rules required to obtain the food from the purveyor (then navigate the traffic back home to the wife and kids). So, even if Hunter Man and Wage-Laborer Man faced the same coarse-grained adaptive problem of acquiring food for a mate and offspring, the subtasks required of each to solve this problem differ significantly. So any Darwinian algorithm executed by Hunter Man would not be effective in acquiring food in the world of Wage-Laborer Man. Consequently, changes in human social structures would have created intense selection pressure favoring changes in any psychological mechanisms that Pleistocene males may have evolved to solve the adaptive problem posed by female preference.

This is just one example, among many possible, of how changes in human social structures since the Pleistocene would have changed the selection pressures on psychological mechanisms—even if we assume that the very coarse-grained adaptive problems faced by humans have not changed. Such changes in social structures are forms of niche construction, and they rapidly change the adaptive problems a population faces. As these changes in social structures occurred, however, humans would have needed to compete with one another within these changing environments for the resources essential to survival and reproduction, including members of the opposite sex. These forms of intraspecific and intrasexual competition within rapidly changing environments would have in turn spawned evolutionary arms races with respect to psychological solutions to the problems faced. Thus, it is safe to conclude that radically changed environments since the Pleistocene have created strong selection pressures favoring psychological evolution.

But has there been sufficient time since the Pleistocene for an evolutionary response to these environmental changes? Let's be clear about the question, since Evolutionary Psychologists typically are not. The question is *not* whether there has been enough time since the Pleistocene for human populations to evolve minds that are adapted to twenty-first-century environments. The question, instead, is whether there has been sufficient time for *modification* to whatever psychological adaptations Pleistocene humans possessed.

Consider first that there are clear cases of post-Pleistocene adaptive evolution in physiological and morphological traits. Laland, Odling-Smee, and Feldman point out that "the persistent domestication of cattle, and the associated dairying activities, did alter the selective environments of some human populations for sufficient generations to select for genes that today confer greater adult lactose tolerance."[37] Indeed, they argue, niche construction typically accelerates the pace of evolution as successive generations continually modify the sources of selection acting on themselves and subsequent generations. There is little doubt that human niche construction has been radical in this regard. And there is no reason to think that such evolution must have been confined to physiological and morphological traits. In fact, the fundamental assumption of Evolutionary Psychology is that selection has shaped both mind and body. So, any evidence of post-Pleistocene evolution in physiological and morphological traits should create a presumption that there has been evolution in psychological traits as well.

Moreover, the idea that human psychological adaptations cannot have evolved since the end of the Pleistocene depends on a false assumption about the rate at which natural selection can alter traits in a population. Recent work by the biologist David Reznick and his colleagues has shown that evolution by natural selection can occur very rapidly. Reznick and his colleagues split populations of guppies living in high-predation environments, leaving a part of each population in its high-predation environment and moving the other part to a low-predation environment. They found that life-history traits of the transplanted guppies evolved significantly within a mere eighteen generations. The descendants of the transplanted guppies matured to a larger size and achieved reproductive viability at a later age than the nontransplanted guppies. More significantly, they produced fewer litters, with fewer and larger offspring in each litter, and they allocated less of their total resources to reproduction during their early reproductive lives. And Reznick and his colleagues were able to identify both the genetic basis of this change and the mechanism by which selection drove it (namely, differential mortality by predation). If this much evolution can occur in eighteen generations, the nearly four hundred human generations since the end of the Pleistocene has certainly been sufficient time for selection-driven evolution in human psychological traits.

Thus, it is overwhelmingly likely that there has been some adaptive psychological evolution since the end of the Pleistocene, which has rendered contemporary humans psychologically different from their Pleistocene ancestors. There is no reason to think that contemporary humans are, like Fred and Wilma Flintstone, just Pleistocene hunter-gatherers struggling to survive and reproduce in evolutionarily novel suburban habitats. If we are to reverse engineer the adaptive structure of the human mind, then, it would be a mistake (not to mention impossible) to attempt to begin with the adaptive problems of our Pleistocene ancestors. The best place to begin reverse engineering the evolved structure of the mind is from the vantage of the decisions that affect survival and reproduction made by real people here and now. As we will see in chapter 4, however, if we do so, the psychological adaptations we are likely to find will not take the form that Evolutionary Psychologists expect.

## Psychological Differences and Our "Common Nature"

So far we have followed a trail of issues that arose out of problems with Gould's critique of Evolutionary Psychology. Now I want to consider one other issue before leaving the discussion of Evolutionary Psychology's focus on psychological adaptations and its theoretical treatment of them. For perhaps the strongest claim that Evolutionary Psychologists make about human psychological adaptations is that they are, of necessity, universal in the species. As Tooby and Cosmides say, "the psychic unity of humankind—that is, a universal and uniform human nature—is *necessarily* imposed to the extent and along those dimensions that our psychologies are collections of complex adaptations."[38] This is allegedly demonstrated by the argument from sexual recombination discussed in chapter 2, which purports to show that the genes underlying complex adaptations must be universal in our species and, hence, that the adaptations they underlie must be universal as well. If the argument is correct, genetic differences among humans never produce differences in psychological adaptations—that is, there are no stable psychological polymorphisms in human populations.

There is, nonetheless, obvious variation in psychological phenotypes in human populations, and a significant portion of that variation shows signs of being adaptive. For example, the "opportunistic" and "investing" female reproductive strategies discussed in chapter 2 appear to coexist stably in human populations, and the evolutionary psychologists Steven Gangestad and Jeffry Simpson argue convincingly that they are the product of frequency-dependent selection. In addition, introverts and extroverts appear to have long coexisted in human populations, and David Sloan Wilson argues that they embody alternative strategies for extracting fitness benefits from different kinds of situation. An extrovert "who thrives on risk may be the one to seize the moment but may also be unable to function effectively in highly structured situations that offer opportunities without risk," whereas an introvert can reap the benefits of structured low-risk opportunities while avoiding high-risk situations.[39] Further, individual differences in degree of "Machiavellianism," the tendency to manipulate and exploit others for personal gain, have long coexisted in human populations. Wilson also argues that the coexistence of "high-Machs" and "low-Machs" shows classic signs of frequency-dependent selection for alternative strategies in social interactions. Finally, Gangestad and Simpson also argue that individual differences in the ability to control facial expressions of emotion are a product of genetic differences, and that the alternative genotypes are probably a stable polymorphism resulting from frequency-dependent selection for strategies of deception and honesty in social interactions.

These examples no doubt merely scratch the surface of adaptive variation in human psychological phenotypes. However, if adaptive variation is not due to genetic differences, as the argument from sexual recombination claims, then all adaptive psychological variation is the product of adaptive plasticity (where a common genetic makeup produces multiple adaptive phenotypes in response to different developmental or current circumstances). This leads Evolutionary Psychologists to claim that all adaptive variation in behavioral and psychological phenotypes is "the product of a common, underlying evolved psychology, operating under different circumstances."[40]

There are two sides to the viewpoint I've just sketched. One side concerns the source of adaptive individual differences in psychological traits. According to this side, genetic differences are not the source of adaptive individual differences. Rather, all adaptive psychological variation arises from adaptive plasticity. The flip side is a particular account of the "common nature" that underlies our individual differences. According to this side, the "common nature" that is invariant across all manifest psychological variation is a "universal evolved psychology," which produces differences "between individuals when different environmental inputs are operated on by the same procedures to produce different manifest outputs."[41]

I will argue that there are problems with both sides of this viewpoint. In particular, I will argue that there likely are some stable psychological polymorphisms in human populations and that there simply is no "universal psychology" underlying manifest individual differences. To root out these problems, we must begin by reexamining the argument from sexual recombination, which supports the idea that human psychological adaptations are universal in the species.

The argument from sexual recombination, recall, is as follows. "Complex adaptations are intricate machines . . . that require coordinated gene expression, involving hundreds or thousands of genes to regulate their development."[42] Since sexual reproduction is a process in which random halves of each parent's genes are "recombined" to form the genome of a zygote, if parents differed in any of their complex adaptations, randomly recombining the genes for those adaptations would make it highly improbable that offspring would receive all the genes necessary to build any of the adaptations. Consequently, if individuals differed in their complex adaptations, no adaptation could be reliably reproduced across generations. "Therefore, in order for a complex adaptation to exist, all of the genes . . . required to construct it must be present in the genomes of all individuals of the species. Hence, all of a species' complex adaptations must be of essentially uniform design."[43] It follows that no adaptive psychological differences result from genetic polymorphisms maintained by selection, since such polymorphisms would constitute alternative adaptations. And this entails that all adaptive differences result from adaptive plasticity.

But the argument is fallacious. The random genetic reshuffling inherent in sexual reproduction, on which the argument relies, is not unique to humans. It characterizes reproduction in every sexually reproducing species. Thus, as David Sloan Wilson points out, if the argument "were correct, then complex genetic polymorphisms would be absent from all sexually reproducing species."[44] However, stable polymorphisms have been documented in a number of species, some of which were mentioned in chapter 1. Since the argument would preclude such polymorphisms, it is clearly mistaken.

Wilson doesn't go further and pinpoint the fallacy in the argument, but it's not hard to spot. The argument mistakenly assumes that, since adaptations require hundreds or thousands of genes for their development, if two individuals had different adaptations, they would also have to differ with respect to hundreds or thousands of genes, which, the argument purports to show, could not possibly be transmitted collectively intact to offspring. But the genetics of sex determination in humans shows the problem with this assumption. The reproductive organs of each sex clearly constitute a complex suite of functionally coordinated adaptations: in males, the testicles, vas deferens, seminal vesicles, prostate, penis, and so on; in females, the ovaries, fallopian tubes, uterus, vagina, and so on. Yet the difference between these coordinated suites of adaptations is the result of a single-gene difference, the *SRY* gene on the Y chromosome. Males and females don't have to differ in hundreds or thousands of genes to differ profoundly in their reproductive anatomy.

Of course, male reproductive anatomy is not built by the *SRY* gene alone. Both male and female reproductive organs do, indeed, require the coordinated interaction of hundreds or thousands of genes in order to develop, and the *SRY* gene produces male reproductive anatomy only in interaction with hundreds or thousands of genes that males and females share. But, against the genetic background shared by males and females, a single genetic switch initiates a cascade of developmental events that results in a coordinated suite of male reproductive adaptations, which differs profoundly from the coordinated suite of female reproductive adaptations.

If such differences in whole suites of adaptations can result from a single genetic switch, then many less profound differences in adaptations could result from alternative forms of a genetic switch. In such cases, alternative genotypes at a single locus would causally interact with other, shared genes to shunt development down alternative pathways leading to different adaptive phenotypes. Since the argument from sexual recombination fails to show that there cannot be stable polymorphisms produced by alternative forms of a genetic switch, the argument fails to show that adaptations must be species universals. Consequently, the argument fails to show that no psychological variation in human populations results from genetic variation maintained by selection. In fact, single-locus polymorphisms could underlie a significant amount of adaptive psychological variation in human populations.

Tooby and Cosmides actually acknowledge that the differences in adaptations between males and females result from a single genetic switch, and they grant that single-gene adaptive differences are an exception to the argument from sexual recombination. But they misinterpret the way that single-gene differences can function. As Tooby and Cosmides say: "An adaptation wholly coded for by a single gene can survive this filter [of sexual recombination] without any problem. . . . As a result, arguments that genetic differences are adaptations depend on the proposed adaptation being coded for on a single gene (or at most a few genes). . . . Complex adaptations resting on genetic diversity cannot survive the destructive filter of recombination, and so cannot be a significant factor explaining human genetic diversity."[45]

As the example of sex determination shows, however, differences in adaptations don't have to be "*wholly* coded for" on a single gene; they can be complex adaptations that require a multitude of genes for their development. Differences in adaptations require only different forms of a single genetic switch interacting with shared genes, and such a genetic switch *can* "survive the destructive filter of recombination."

Tooby and Cosmides hope to forestall this line of argument, however, on the grounds that genetic switches are very rare in nature. They argue that selection consistently favors adaptive plasticity over polymorphic genetic switches as a method of producing adaptive differences. As they say, "a genetic switch determines an individual's future at conception, so that individual has one set of adaptations and not another regardless of how suited they might be to the local situation. A far more effective system, in general, is to determine what to be as a response to what environment one finds oneself in."[46]

But this argument, as well, is problematic. First, there simply is no such law of nature to the effect that adaptive plasticity is consistently favored by selection over polymorphic genetic switches. Although sex in mammals is determined by a genetic switch, in many reptiles it is determined by the incubation temperature of eggs. And many fishes "choose" their sex in response to observed conditions of the social environment, such as the sex ratio in the population (changing to the rarer sex in order to maximize the number of available mates) or their relative size (since, in some species, the average reproductive output for large males is greater than that for large females). So it is biologically possible to determine what sex to be in response to one's "local situation." Yet sex in mammals is determined by a genetic switch. So selection doesn't consistently favor adaptive plasticity over genetic switches.

No doubt the evolution of a genetic system of sex determination in mammals had much to do with other demands of the development and life history of early mammals. Within the overall context of early mammalian development—which included the need for coordinated developmental timing of numerous physiological systems—genetic sex determination was probably the "most effective" system. So which system of sex determination was most effective had a lot to do with the role of sex determination within the development and life history of early mammals. In general, then, whether a genetic switch or adaptive plasticity is the more effective system for determining alternative phenotypes depends on which phenotypes we're talking about, the role they play in the life history of the organism, and the role their development plays in the overall development of the organism. Whether adaptive plasticity or a genetic switch is more effective can't be determined for all phenotypes *in general* by a simple a priori argument.

Considerations of development and life history show that the effectiveness of adaptive plasticity or a genetic switch in producing particular alternative phenotypes is relative to a number of other factors "internal" to the organism. Sometimes adaptive plasticity is more effective, and can be favored by selection, and at other times a genetic switch is more effective. But which system is more effective is also relative to factors "external" to the organism. Tooby and Cosmides' argument presupposes that a polymorphic genetic switch will always be less adaptive to the "local situation" than a mechanism of adaptive plasticity that relies on cues from the environment. But this ignores the question of precisely which aspects of the "local situation" are being *adapted to*.

Some "local situations" can favor a genetic switch. For example, when the fitness of a phenotype depends on its frequency in a population, then the environment to which that phenotype is adapted is one containing an evolutionarily stable ratio of alternative phenotypes. Recall the Hawk-Dove game. If the evolutionarily stable ratio is 75 percent Hawks and 25 percent Doves, then Dove and Hawk are each well adapted to an environment containing 75 percent Hawks and 25 percent Doves. In such circumstances, a genetic polymorphism maintained by frequency-dependent selection is just as effective as a system of adaptive plasticity for maintaining an evolutionarily stable ratio of alternative phenotypes. There would be no improving on a genetic polymorphism by "deciding" which phenotype to possess based on information gathered from the environment, since those "decisions" would still have to result in the same stable ratio that is produced by the genetic polymorphism. So adaptive plasticity will entail no greater benefit in such cases.

In addition, a system for "choosing" the phenotype based on conditions of the environment requires some method of ascertaining the condition of the environment. This is particularly apparent in cases like sex "choice" in fishes. If sex is "chosen" based on the sex ratio in the local population, there must be some mechanism that monitors the local sex ratio and then causally generates the sexual phenotype. Such mechanisms must themselves develop in the organism, and their development draws from the total resources available to a developing organism. The operation of such mechanisms must also be maintained in the organism, and this will exact metabolic costs. (Think again of how the human brain utilizes 18 percent of the body's energy intake, while constituting only 2 percent of its weight.) Thus, systems of adaptive plasticity will often exact costs not exacted by genetic switches, while proving no more effective than genetic switches at maintaining evolutionarily stable ratios of alternative phenotypes. So, in certain simple cases of frequency-dependent fitness, genetic switches will be more effective from a cost-benefit standpoint than systems of adaptive plasticity.

On the other hand, there are some circumstances to which systems of adaptive plasticity are better adapted than genetic switches. In particular, when the environment is rapidly changing and unpredictable, the flexibility provided by *phenotypic plasticity* will clearly be a greater asset to an organism than a genetic switch. That is, if the environmental features being adapted to are highly variable from one generation to another, so that the phenotype determined by a particular form of a genetic switch would be effective at some times but not others, then phenotypic plasticity, which can produce phenotypes that are adaptive in each of the variant environments, will clearly be more effective than a genetic switch.

Earlier in this chapter I argued that our ancestors no doubt evolved in environments that were rapidly changing in many ways, so that many adaptive problems faced by our ancestors would not have been stable throughout human evolutionary history. This, I argued, provides reason to doubt that we can ascertain the adaptive problems faced by our ancestors and then simply infer the psychological adaptations that must have evolved to solve them. But one shouldn't overgeneralize from these considerations and conclude that, since our ancestors evolved in rapidly changing environments, phenotypic plasticity must have consistently been favored throughout human evolution over genetic switches. For, again, it all depends on which features of the environment are being adapted to. Both genetic switches and systems of phenotypic plasticity could have evolved in humans, and they could have coevolved by interacting in interesting ways.

For example, consider again the coexistence of "high-Machs" and "low-Machs." Suppose, as Wilson argues, that the coexistence of high-Machs and low-Machs is maintained by frequency-dependent selection for alternative strategies in social interactions. Suppose also that these two personality types result from alternative forms of a single genetic switch (which can pass through the "destructive filter of recombination"). Under these conditions, the coexistence of high-Machs and low-Machs is a stable polymorphism. Suppose further that the current stable ratio of high-Machs to low-Machs has been stable for, say, the last 100,000 years. Nonetheless, throughout that period, high-Machs could have been constantly upgrading their techniques of manipulation and exploitation. This would have created selection pressure on low-Machs for upgraded techniques of detecting and avoiding manipulation and exploitation, which would have in turn created selection pressure on high-Machs to further upgrade their techniques. That is, there could have been an evolutionary arms race between high-Machs and low-Machs with respect to techniques of manipulation and exploitation and the detection and avoidance of those. This arms race could have selected for phenotypic plasticity in the mechanisms that solve the problems of how to exploit or avoid being exploited by others. Thus, while the alternative personality types could be the product of a stable genetic polymorphism, the cognitive mechanisms that solve the problems those personality types pose for one another could be the product of phenotypic plasticity. This kind of interaction between alternative phenotypes controlled by genetic switches (for example, personality types) and those controlled by phenotypic plasticity (for example, cognitive techniques of problem solving) could be widespread in human psychology.

Thus, again, whether a genetic switch or adaptive plasticity underlies a particular dimension of adaptive variation depends heavily on the specifics of the case. The relative effectiveness of either system will vary from case to case. Contrary to Tooby and Cosmides' argument, then, there simply is no general rule to the effect that adaptive plasticity will be consistently favored over genetic switches. So there are no sound reasons for thinking that polymorphic genetic switches are not responsible for some of the adaptive psychological variation that is observed in human populations. Given this fact, the argument from sexual recombination simply fails to show that adaptations *must* be species universals. Whether there are polymorphic psychological adaptations in human populations can be decided only by empirical research into each adaptive dimension of human psychology.

Tooby and Cosmides make an additional claim that is worth examining here. They grant that genetic differences may affect psychological adaptations, but they maintain that genetic differences do not actually produce different adaptations. Rather, they claim, genetic differences produce only "quantitative variation in the components of complex, highly articulated, species-typical psychological mechanisms," in the way that genetic variation may produce quantitative differences in the size of the stomach from one person to another, but not a qualitative difference between having and not having a stomach.[47]

To illustrate this principle, Tooby and Cosmides ask us to suppose that all humans have a complex psychological mechanism that regulates aggression, but that genetic differences among individuals correlate with variation in the threshold at which the mechanism is activated, so that some people have a "shorter fuse" than others. In this case, Tooby and Cosmides argue, the adaptation is the universal aggression-regulating mechanism, and "the *variations* in the exact level at which the threshold of activation is set are probably not adaptations. . . . Those features of the system that can be described in terms of uniform design are likely to be adaptations, whereas the heritable variations in the system are not."[48]

This assumes that selection acts on *qualitative* features of organisms to create qualitative uniformity in adaptations, while quantitative properties of those qualitative adaptations are free to vary because they are selectively neutral. But the distinction between qualitative traits and their quantitative properties doesn't mark a divide between (possible) adaptations and nonadaptations, for selection can act on and maintain quantitative differences in traits within populations. Indeed, although the two sexes in dimorphic species now appear qualitatively distinct, they are the result of very ancient selection on gamete size, which favored each of the extreme gamete sizes over intermediate-sized gametes. Very small gametes were favored for their mobility, while very large gametes were favored for their ability to store nutrients. Selection on gamete size thus forced a division in the quantitative continuum of gamete sizes, creating and maintaining a system in which only very small and very large gametes are present. As a result, males (with their reproductive anatomy specialized for delivering a payload of small, mobile gametes) and females (with their reproductive anatomy specialized for storing and nurturing the large, nutrient-rich gametes) got built up around that division in gamete size. Thus, variation in the quantitative properties (such as size) of a shared qualitative feature (such as gametes) can be grist for selection's mill, and when it is quantitative differences can become differences in adaptations.

Of course, sexual dimorphism is an extreme example of how selection can create alternative adaptations from quantitative variation in a shared qualitative feature. But, if alternative gamete sizes can be alternative adaptations, different "fuse lengths" in a shared aggression-regulating mechanism and differences in degree of Machiavellianism can be alternative adaptations as well.

I am not, however, arguing that either of these quantitative differences *are* alternative adaptations. These are issues to be decided by future empirical research. My point is that, even if genetic variation produces only differences in the quantitative properties of a shared feature, it doesn't follow that those quantitative differences are not alternative adaptations. Whether variation of any kind—quantitative or qualitative—represents alternative adaptations can be determined only by empirical investigation into the specifics of the case. The argument from sexual recombination inappropriately attempts to substitute armchair reasoning for the necessary empirical research.

Of course, the fact that an argument is fallacious means only that its conclusion doesn't follow from its premises; it doesn't mean that its conclusion is false. But it is, indeed, highly improbable that there are *no* psychological polymorphisms in human populations. By the best estimates, humans are genetically polymorphic at 20 to 25 percent of all loci. That's a significant amount of genetic variation, and it would be truly remarkable if none of that variation underlies adaptive psychological variation, since comparable degrees of genetic variation underlie adaptive variation in other species. So the odds are very good that there are *some* polymorphic psychological adaptations in human populations. It just remains for empirical research to discover what they are.

So far I've focused on Evolutionary Psychology's claim regarding the source of adaptive psychological differences—that all adaptive differences arise from adaptive plasticity rather than from genetic differences. I've argued that Evolutionary Psychology's claim that human psychological adaptations are universal in the species is unjustified. Indeed, I've argued, given the degree of genetic polymorphism in human populations, it is quite likely that there are some polymorphic psychological adaptations in human populations, which future empirical research will discover. Now I want to focus on the flip side of the claim regarding the source of adaptive individual differences. The flip side is a particular account of what humans have in common beneath their differences, an account of what is invariant across the full range of adaptive psychological variation. For, as Tooby and Cosmides say, an Evolutionary Psychologist "observes variable manifest psychologies or behaviors between individuals and across cultures and views them as the product of a common, underlying evolved psychology, operating under different circumstances."[49] But what is this "common, underlying evolved psychology"?

The first thing to note is that it's not a *psychology* at all. This follows relatively straightforwardly from facts that Evolutionary Psychologists accept. To see why, suppose that one psychological adaptation is a mechanism dedicated to detecting cheaters in social exchanges, as Evolutionary Psychologists claim. First, the cheater-detection mechanism, like all psychological adaptations, will develop only in individuals exposed to the right developmental environments—in particular, those developmental environments encountered by most humans throughout the period in which the cheater-detection mechanism evolved. Individuals exposed to developmentally impoverished environments, which lack the environmental cues or metabolic resources necessary for the proper development of the mechanism, will not develop the cheater-detection mechanism. Second, not all individuals are in fact exposed to the right developmental environments; some individuals develop in impoverished environments. Consequently, some individuals' psychologies include a cheater-detection mechanism, whereas other individuals' psychologies don't. Since this will be the case for every psychological adaptation, there simply is no psychology common to all humans.

This argument relies on differences in developmental environment that result in some individuals' lacking an adaptation that other individuals possess. But psychological differences can also be produced by differences in environmental cues, which shunt psychological development down alternative pathways, and by genetic switches, which produce differences in psychological adaptations. Since psychological characteristics are phenotypic, individuals who have different psychological phenotypes, for any of these reasons, ipso facto have different psychologies. Consequently, individual differences that are due to different environmental cues during development or to different forms of a genetic switch are *psychological differences*, which are irreducible to some underlying psychological commonality. So there simply is no universal human *mind*.

To a certain extent this is acknowledged by Evolutionary Psychologists. The acknowledgment is implicit in Charles Crawford's distinction between innate and operational adaptations. Operational adaptations, according to Crawford, are "the anatomical structures, physiological processes, and psychological processes that develop because of interactions with the environment and that actually do the work of helping the organism survive and reproduce."[50] Since differences in developmental environment can produce differences in operational adaptations, Crawford claims that what we really share are innate adaptations, where an "*innate adaptation* is the information encoded in the genes that mediates the development of the operational adaptation."[51]

The acknowledgment that there is no universal human psychology is pretty much explicit in Tooby and Cosmides' statement that, "when we use terms such as 'evolved design,' 'evolved architecture,' or even 'species-typical,' 'species-standard,' 'universal,' and 'panhuman,' we are not making claims about every human phenotype all or even some of the time; instead, we are referring to the existence of evolutionarily organized *developmental adaptations*."[52] These developmental adaptations, which Tooby and Cosmides also call "developmental programs," "are designed to assemble (either conditionally or regardless of normal environmental variation) evolutionarily designed . . . mechanisms that are then present to be activated by appropriate cues."[53] The assembled mechanisms are our psychological characteristics.

Consequently, despite Evolutionary Psychology's bold advertisements promising the discovery of an "array of psychological mechanisms that is universal among *Homo sapiens*," there simply is no universal array of *psychological* mechanisms.[54] The fine print in the advertisements reveals that Evolutionary Psychology really claims that what we have in common beneath all our individual differences is a set of "developmental programs," which produce our psychological mechanisms. Each developmental program, according to Tooby and Cosmides, "embodies a specification for how each possible state of the developmental environment is to be responded to, if encountered."[55] In other words, each developmental program is a set of conditional rules to the effect, "If encountering developmental environment A, produce phenotype X; if encountering developmental environment B, produce phenotype Y; and so on." It is this "specification" of how to respond to each developmental environment that accounts for the adaptive plasticity of psychological development, for the rules that constitute the developmental programs specify adaptive phenotypes across a range of different environments. And the set of all these developmental programs for constructing psychological mechanisms work together as one big developmental program for the construction of the human mind.

The "common nature" that Evolutionary Psychology is truly promising to discover, then, is the developmental program that produces the full range of psychological types observable in human populations. That is, our "universal human nature" does not actually consist in universal cognitive processes, or Darwinian algorithms, that cause behavior (since there are no such universal cognitive processes), but in allegedly universal *developmental rules* for building a human mind.

But there are also problems with this account of our "common nature" as a developmental program for building the human mind. I will focus on just two of these problems. First, Evolutionary Psychologists render the idea of a universal developmental program for the human mind plausible only by treating genetic switches as *external* to the putative universal developmental program. In particular, genetic switches are treated as a form of "minimal genetic *input*" to the program, rather than as parts of the developmental program.[56] This simply *defines* "universal developmental program" in terms of whatever genes humans share, and thus, by definitional fiat, relegates nonshared genes to mere "inputs" to the shared program. This line of reasoning, however, is problematic. For, to the extent that alternative forms of genetic switches produce alternative psychological adaptations, the "gene complexes" that produce the resulting adaptations include the genetic switches. The genetic switches are part of the "programs" from which the alternative psychological adaptations develop. Consequently, individuals with different forms of a genetic switch simply have different developmental programs for building their minds. If, as I have argued is likely, there are some differences in genetic switches that affect human psychological adaptations, then there simply is no universal developmental program for the human mind.

Second, there is a problem with the very idea of a developmental program, as that is conceived by Evolutionary Psychologists. Tooby and Cosmides characterize the developmental program as a set of conditional rules specifying "how each possible state of the developmental environment is to be responded to, if encountered."[57] But development is not the execution of a set of conditional rules stored in a developmental program.

To see why, suppose that development *is* the execution of a set of conditional rules stored in our developmental program. If this is true, then the information contained in those rules is itself something that had to evolve, presumably through a gradual elaboration of the rules. The developmental program couldn't have contained information that *anticipated* evolutionarily novel environments and specified how to develop in response to them. Rather, as our species evolved and encountered new environments, those individuals who developed adaptively in response to the new environments left more offspring, and as a result the developmental rule by which they developed became a part of the species' developmental program. In other words, the rule for how to develop adaptively in a particular environment became part of the species' developmental program only after the species had evolved through that environment. Thus, the "developmental program" can only contain information about how to develop in an environment the species has already encountered in its evolutionary history.

But surely there have been some radical changes in developmental environments at particular points throughout the evolutionary history of our species. That is, there must have been at least some occasions on which a population encountered an evolutionarily novel developmental environment. Since humans did not go extinct, some individuals must have developed adaptively in that evolutionarily novel environment. Further, it is implausible to suppose that, on such occasions, only a random mutant or two survived the radical environmental change. Instead, most individuals were able to develop in the novel environment. But that means that most individuals were able to develop adaptive phenotypes in an environment for which their developmental programs could not possibly have contained a rule specifying an adaptive response, since developmental programs cannot contain rules for evolutionarily novel environments.

If the foregoing is correct, then there have been some occasions in our evolutionary history on which individuals have developed adaptive phenotypes *without the need for a rule* specifying "how each possible state of the developmental environment is to be responded to, if encountered."[58] But, if adaptive phenotypes can develop in some environments without the need for a rule, they can develop in all environments without the need for a rule. This means that the notion of a set of rules embodied in a developmental program guiding development is idle; it plays no genuine role in explaining how development occurs. When we develop differently, it is not because something that is *the same* in us simply responds differently in a programmed way to differences outside us.

Not only is the notion of a "program" guiding development idle in explaining how development occurs, the goal of discovering such a program has been altogether abandoned by researchers in genetics. The geneticist Sydney Brenner has spent decades studying the genetics and development of a simple nematode, *Caenorhabditis elegans*, which has only 959 cells in its body. Given the simplicity of this organism and the regular way in which it develops, Brenner believed it to be an ideal research subject and expected that study of its development would quickly reveal the "program" guiding it. Even though Brenner and his team discovered the complete developmental history of every cell in the nematode's body, and every connection in its nervous system, nowhere did they discover an orderly pattern of developmental events that gave the appearance of unfolding in accordance with "programmed" rules. After decades spent in search of the "developmental program" of *C. elegans*, Brenner finally concluded that there simply is no such thing and "that there is hardly a shorter way of giving a rule for what goes on [in its development] than just describing what there is."[59] Development happens, but it doesn't happen because it's guided by a set of rules stored in a "developmental program."

Thus, our "universal human nature" can't be "an array of psychological mechanisms that is universal among *Homo sapiens*," since differences in developmental environments and genetic switches produce widespread psychological differences among humans. It also can't be a universal "developmental program," consisting of a set of rules specifying how to build a human mind in each possible developmental environment, for there simply is no such universal developmental program. In certain cases, our psychological differences may be due to differences in our developmental environments. In those cases, our differences may appropriately be described as the result of a common *genotype's* responding adaptively to different developmental circumstances. Such differences are produced by an encounter between a common genetic makeup and different environmental inputs. But what is true in these particular cases cannot be generalized to account for all psychological differences. We have our differences, you and I, and many of those differences are adaptive psychological differences, which cannot be reduced to some characteristic that we share.

# 4 | Modularity

## (with Valerie Gray Hardcastle)

Evolutionary Psychologists claim that human psychological adaptations take the form of modules, special-purpose "minicomputers," each of which is dedicated to solving problems related to a particular aspect of survival or reproduction in the human environment of evolutionary adaptedness (EEA). Summarizing this view, Steven Pinker says, "the mind is organized into modules or mental organs, each with a specialized design that makes it an expert in one arena of interaction with the world. The modules' basic logic is specified by our genetic program. Their operation was shaped by natural selection to solve the problems of the hunting and gathering life led by our ancestors in most of our evolutionary history."[1] Given that Evolutionary Psychologists claim that there are "hundreds or thousands" of modules comprising the human mind, this view of the mind has been called the "massive modularity thesis."

This chapter will critically examine this view, beginning with a review of the massive modularity thesis and an argument that it is inconsistent with what we know about the brain. Contrary to Evolutionary Psychology's claims, the brain actually is a kind of general-purpose problem solver. This will prompt a reexamination of the arguments and evidence that Evolutionary Psychologists have offered in support of the massive modularity thesis. The arguments and empirical evidence appear compelling at first glance, but closer scrutiny reveals that they do not support Evolutionary Psychologists' claims about the modularity of the mind. The chapter will conclude with a discussion of what it means for the brain to be a "general-purpose" problem solver.

## Evolutionary Psychology, Meet Developmental Neurobiology

For the reasons discussed in chapter 2, Evolutionary Psychologists reject the idea of a general-purpose mind that employs just a few basic domain-independent cognitive procedures in acquiring all its knowledge of the world. Evolutionary Psychologists argue, instead, that "our cognitive architecture resembles a confederation of *hundreds or thousands* of functionally dedicated computers (often called modules)."[2] In this view, the human brain is "composed of a large collection of circuits, with different circuits specialized for solving different problems. One can think of each specialized circuit as a minicomputer that is dedicated to solving one problem."[3] "Over evolutionary time, the brain's circuits were cumulatively added because they reasoned or processed information in a way that enhanced the adaptive regulation of behavior."[4] Each of these circuits is a module.

Modules, you'll recall from chapter 2, are characterized by the following properties. First, they are domain specific, functionally dedicated to solving a restricted range of very closely related adaptive problems. They are like highly trained specialists who are incapable of performing effectively outside of their areas of specialization. Second, they develop in the absence of explicit instruction in the problem domains in which they specialize. This is because, third, modules "embody 'innate knowledge' about the problem-relevant parts of the world."[5] That is, they are "equipped with 'crib sheets': They come to a problem already knowing a lot about it."[6] Fourth, a module is, to some degree, informationally isolated from cognitive processing occurring in other parts of the mind, "operating primarily or solely with its own specialized 'lexicon'—a set of procedures, formats, and representational primitives closely tailored to the demands of its targeted family of problems."[7] In other words, modules tend not to access information employed by other modules or in nonmodular cognitive processing. Finally, informational isolation enables modules to be comparatively fast at solving problems in their special domains. For, rather than having to "figure out" how to solve a problem, which is typically a process of determining which of the many things one knows will help to solve a problem, modules solve problems in their special domains automatically by following their "crib sheets" and ignoring all other information.

Given these properties, modules strongly resemble what were traditionally called *instincts*. "In fact," Cosmides and Tooby say, "one can think of these special-purpose computational systems as *reasoning instincts* and *learning instincts*. These systems make certain kinds of inferences just as easy, effortless, and natural to humans as spinning a web to a spider."[8] In this view, human intelligence is due not to a few powerful general-purpose problem-solving abilities, but to an extraordinarily large number of such reasoning instincts. As Tooby and Cosmides say, "what is special about the human mind is not that it gave up 'instinct' in order to become flexible, but that it proliferated 'instincts'—that is, content-specific problem-solving specializations."[9]

It is important to consider precisely how, according to this picture, these instincts-as-modules "proliferated" in the human mind. First, according to Evolutionary Psychologists, each module (or "brain circuit") was "added" to the mind at some point in human evolutionary history and then subsequently "shaped" by selection to be highly effective at solving adaptive problems in its proprietary domain. This "shaping" consisted in selection's retaining successive modifications to the existing design of the module, each of which made the module more effective in solving its adaptive problems. Second, since Evolutionary Psychologists claim that each module was shaped by selection pressures specific to the adaptive-problem domain in which it specializes, each module must have evolved independently of every other. This does not mean that no two modules evolved during the same period of human evolution, but only that separate modules evolved in response to independent selective forces and were functionally modifiable independently of other modules.

These two claims entail that each module evolved as a result of numerous mutations over human evolutionary history, each of which added or modified a specialized "brain circuit," and all of which were preserved by selection as the gene complex that regulates the development of the module. In short, each module must be the developmental product of its own gene complex, which, as Pinker puts it, is that part of the "genetic program" that "specifies" the "basic design" of that "mental organ."[10]

This is not to say that each module's gene complex has developmental effects on that module alone; genes often have multiple developmental effects. But, if modules were added and modified by selection independently of one another, it is highly unlikely that any single mutation would have added more than one module to the brain or that any single mutation would have produced a beneficial modification to more than one module. Think of this in terms of Evolutionary Psychologists' favored comparison of modules to bodily organs: It is highly unlikely that any single mutation would "add" both a kidney and a liver to human anatomy or enhance the functional effectiveness of both the stomach and the heart. Thus, if the picture proposed by Evolutionary Psychologists is accurate, as modules proliferated in the human brain and became shaped by selection, the number of genes for features of the human brain would have had to increase proportionately. More and more of the human genome would have had to become involved in building the growing number of modules in the human brain.

Now, it is true that the adult human brain contains numerous (relatively) special-purpose brain circuits, which possess some properties that are similar to those Evolutionary Psychologists ascribe to modules. But Evolutionary Psychology's account of these special-purpose brain circuits, and of how and why adult brains come to possess them, does not square with our knowledge of the brain. To see why, begin by considering some facts about human brain development.

Estimates of the number of genes in human DNA currently range between 30,000 and 90,000 genes, and many geneticists believe that a figure near 70,000 is the safest bet. It is also estimated that perhaps 50 percent of these genes are involved in building the brain. Yet fully 4 percent of the genes involved in brain development are concerned with building the sensory cells inside the nose. We can assume that roughly as many are concerned with building sensory cells in our ears and on our tongues, but that many more are involved in building the cells in our far more complex eyes and all the sensory cells in our skin. As systems, however, our sensory receptors are surely less complex than the brain systems devoted to higher cognitive functions. For our sensory receptors just reformat and transfer information from the world into the brain, whereas the brain systems devoted to higher cognitive functions process that information in ways designed to make adaptive decisions. Yet despite the fact that our brain systems outnumber our sensory receptors and are undoubtedly more complex, there appears to be disproportionately greater "genetic specification" of our sensory receptors. Our genes seem to worry more about making sure our sensory receptors are constructed properly than about building more central brain structures. Indeed, given the complexity of the brain, it appears that its higher cognitive structures are vastly *underspecified* genetically compared to its more peripheral sensory structures.

Moreover, as the neuroscientist Terrence Deacon argues, if our brains consisted of numerous modules, each of which was "specified" by a gene complex, we would expect some positive correlation between brain complexity and the number of genes in a genome. Yet when we look at the cross-species data we find no such correlation. We find, instead, that genome size is fairly constant across a very wide spectrum of brain complexity. In fact, despite our vastly more complex brains, the house mouse has roughly 80,000 genes, at least as many as humans, though perhaps even more than we humans. Of course, there may be a lot of nonfunctional DNA in mice. And given the discussion in chapter 3 of how single-gene differences can produce significant differences in adaptations, it is possible for significant phenotypic differences to be produced by relatively small genetic differences. But these are merely reasons for thinking that we shouldn't expect to find a *perfect* cross-species correlation between genome size and brain complexity. The remarkable thing is that there is *no correlation whatsoever*. Species with very complex brains simply don't have more "genetic information" available for building those brains than do species with relatively simple brains.

But, if the complex structure of the human brain isn't "genetically specified," how does it develop? If each special-purpose brain circuit in an adult brain isn't constructed in accordance with a "genetic program" that "specifies its design," how do such complex and functionally effective circuits develop?

From the time the human brain begins to develop in utero, at about twenty-five days after conception, it increases by a remarkable 250,000 cells per minute, and this rate of cell production continues until birth. The production of these cells takes place in two different "zones," the ventricular and the subventricular. The cells that make up the evolutionarily oldest parts of the brain are produced in the ventricular zone. These are the cells that make up the midbrain and the limbic system, which are regions of the brain controlling motor coordination, sexual response, and emotion (such as the fear response). In contrast, the cells produced in the subventricular zone make up the evolutionarily most recent addition to the brain, the neocortex, which carries out the "higher" cognitive functions.

These two cell-production zones also have different modes of operation. As the ventricular zone produces cells, newly formed cells simply push older cells outward from the zone of production. So cell production in the ventricular zone builds brain structures by adding cells to already existing layers of cells, in much the way that other parts or organs of the body are formed. All the building of these structures is done by cells working at very close quarters, and it appears to be under rather rigid genetic control. While this is the method for building the evolutionarily older parts of the brain, the development of the evolutionarily more recent cortex is a very different matter. Since Evolutionary Psychologists claim that their postulated modules are complex information-processing mechanisms, which execute sophisticated "Darwinian algorithms" in solving adaptive problems, these modules would most likely be found in the cortex. So cortical development will be the principal focus in what follows, although there will be a brief discussion later of subcortical structures.

Unlike the cells produced in the ventricular zone, the cells produced in the subventricular zone, which make up the cortex, must actively "migrate" to their final destinations in the brain, wending their way through a thicket of other cells. Once they reach their final destinations, they grow branching axons that form connections with other cells. Much of this development is also undoubtedly under rather rigid genetic control, since it is uniform across individuals who develop in very different environments. But this is true only of the development of the major structures of the brain and their primary subdivisions; it is not generally true of the development of the more fine-grained brain structures that perform specialized cognitive functions. Indeed, whereas the major cortical structures and their primary subdivisions are in place at birth or shortly thereafter, the functionally specialized circuits that characterize an adult brain are not. But the transition from infant to adult brain is not a matter of *adding* fine-grained specialized circuits to the developing brain in the way that adaptations such as teeth and breasts are added to the developing organism in time to meet new age-specific adaptive demands. In fact, since the adult brain contains fewer cells and connections than the infant brain, the transition is actually a matter of *subtracting* connections and cells. And the primary mechanism of subtraction is cell competition and cell death.

For a simple illustration of this mechanism, consider the development of motor neurons, which transmit information from the central nervous system to muscle fibers. In an adult, each motor neuron is connected to at least one, though usually more than one, muscle fiber, yet each muscle fiber is innervated by only one motor neuron. But this one-many connection pattern is not present in the developing embryo. Instead, many motor neurons are connected to many muscle fibers in a vast proliferation of connections that is not present in the adult. Over the course of development, the ends of most of the motor neurons retract until only one neuron controls each muscle fiber. The best explanation to date of the mechanism for this sort of neuronal pruning is that motor neurons *compete* with each other for sole activation rights of muscle fibers. The neuron with the strongest activation wins, and the cells that lose the competition lose their connections to other cells and eventually die.

This process of pruning the overabundance of connections and cells forms the brain circuits that carry out our specialized cognitive functions. Central to this process is cell competition and death, in which the cells with the strongest patterns of innervation retain their connections and the other cells die. And two types of innervation are relevant in the competition for cellular survival: spontaneous neural firings internal to the brain itself and the brain activity produced by sensory inputs. Indeed, without both sorts of activity, functional brain circuits simply do not develop. If we chemically block spontaneous firing of the cells that protrude from the retina, the structures that relay information to the visual cortex do not develop in a way that enables normal vision. Similarly, if you keep one eye closed as your visual system is developing, so that your brain receives little input from one retina, you will end up functionally blind in that eye. As a result, even though the cells projecting from the retina produce normal outputs after you reopen the eye, the areas in the cortex to which they feed will no longer respond appropriately to visual inputs. Other brain regions are similarly dependent on environmental stimuli. If infants are deprived of auditory inputs, they are subsequently unable to process speech or understand language without special intervention (teaching them a signed language, for example, or artificially stimulating their central auditory cortex).

Thus, the precise patterns of environmental stimuli to which the developing cortex is exposed play an essential role in shaping the brain circuits, and the functional properties of those circuits, that are connected most directly to our sensory receptors. But, as we have seen, patterns of activity internal to the brain are essential in shaping the circuits and functional properties of less peripheral cortical mechanisms. Indeed, the shaping of the less peripheral circuits in the cortex is almost entirely dependent on innervation from other brain cells, rather than from sensory receptors. The structures in which those other cells reside will have themselves been shaped either by patterns of innervation from other brain cells or by patterns of innervation from sensory receptors. And so on. Eventually, however, we get to structures that were shaped primarily by sensory innervations. Since patterns of innervation from sensory receptors are propagated inward in this way, even circuits that are shaped primarily by patterns of innervation from other brain cells are ultimately, though indirectly, shaped by the patterns of environmental stimuli encountered during development. In short, environmental inputs to the brain shape the more fine-grained cortical structures by determining the outcome of cell competition.

The cognitive scientist Jeffrey Elman and his colleagues draw a distinction between *additive* and *subtractive* events that is very helpful in thinking about the process of brain development. Additive events are the formation of neurons, their migrations to their final locations in the brain, and their axonal branching to establish connections with other neurons. Subtractive events are axonal retraction (whereby neurons lose their connections to other neurons) and cell death. Cortical development consists of additive events, which *overproduce* neurons and connections, followed by subtractive events, which *selectively eliminate* neurons and connections. Additive events provide a large mass of clay, which subtractive events sculpt into functional form.

This process of "proliferate-and-prune" can produce relatively stable brain circuits that specialize primarily in particular information-processing tasks. In other words, the process of proliferate-and-prune can produce brain circuits that closely resemble Evolutionary Psychology's postulated modules. Some of these circuits even function to solve adaptive problems, and they *can* even be produced with some regularity across populations and down lineages, even more closely resembling Evolutionary Psychology's postulated adaptive-problem-solving modules. However, the degree to which different brains develop similar cortical circuitry is due more to their encountering similar environmental inputs during development than to a "genetic program" that "specifies" recurrent developmental outcomes. Thus, although an adult human brain can be characterized by "modular" information-processing structures, these are *environmentally shaped*, not "genetically specified," outcomes of development. For it is primarily environmental inputs to the brain that determine the subtractive events that shape its cognitive-processing structures.

Of course, Evolutionary Psychologists don't deny that environmental inputs are essential to the development of modules. Indeed, they frequently repeat the truism that all traits, including modules, are a product of causal interaction between genes and environment. However, Evolutionary Psychologists consign environmental inputs to one of two roles in the development of modules. They treat them either as "triggers" that activate the development of a module in accordance with a "developmental program" that is coded in the genes, or as "cues" that determine which of a limited number of information-processing "settings" a module will have (in the way that the presence or absence of an investing father allegedly cues a female's mate-choice module to pursue an "investing" or "opportunistic" reproductive strategy). The picture is that genes encode the information for constructing a module, but that they await a "trigger" or "cue" from the environment telling them to begin constructing the module or which of a limited number of "settings" to apply in constructing it.

This is a picture in which modules are *added* to the brain by elaborately timed developmental programs that are triggered or cued by inputs from the environment. As Tooby and Cosmides say, "just as teeth and breasts are absent at birth and develop later in an individual's life history, perceptual organization, domain-specific reasoning mechanisms, the language acquisition device, motivational organization, and many other intricate psychological adaptations mature and are elaborated in age-specific fashions that are not simply the product of the accumulation of 'experience.' Consequently, psychological adaptations may be *developmentally timed to appear*, disappear, or change operation to mesh with the changing demands of different age-specific tasks, such as parenting, emotional decoding of the mother's voice, language acquisition, . . . and so on."[11]

But environmental inputs do not "trigger" the *addition* or "appearance" of various information-processing structures or "cue" the development of their properties. Instead, during cortical development we find a diffuse proliferation of neural connections, which later brain activity, guided by interaction with the environment, sculpts into its "final" form. Brain functions in infants are widely distributed across a variety of cortical areas, and as children mature some of these same functions become localized to particular structures. In this process, neurons compete with one another for the sort of information-processing structure they are going to be, and *brain activity*, guided by environmental inputs, determines which neurons win this competition, hence which processing roles they end up playing. The processing roles of neurons are not laid down in advance by a "developmental program" encoded in our genes.

Genes do, of course, play an essential role in this process. Gene expression—the switching on and off of genes and the protein synthesis effected by this process—is absolutely central to the *additive* processes in brain development (the formation of neurons, the growth of their axonal branches, and the formation of connections among neurons). But additive processes merely provide the raw material that subtractive processes sculpt into form, and the subtractive processes are guided by brain activity, which is ultimately guided by environmental inputs. Genes do determine the physical properties of cells, which in turn determine the conditions under which cells will die (how cells will react to various physical stimuli or their absence). But gene expression does not guide the sculpting process that selects which cells will die and which will live to fire another day. So our genetic endowment does not explain the "final" form that our cortical structures take. Insofar as we have modularized cortical structures, they are not "specified" by our genes.

The Nobel Prize–winning neurobiologist Gerald Edelman points out that the process of proliferate-and-prune is structurally similar to the process of evolution by natural selection. Natural selection involves a process that overproduces variation (which is provided by mutation and recombination) followed by a process that retains those variants that are doing the best job. Through repeated cycles of variation overproduction followed by selective retention of the fittest variants, natural selection builds anatomical structures that perform highly specialized functions. Similarly, Edelman points out, cortical development involves a process that overproduces neurons and connections followed by a process that retains those neurons and connections that are most responsive to the environmental inputs to which the developing organism is exposed (although, unlike natural selection, it does not involve the reproduction of successful structures). And, as with natural selection, the conjunction of these processes can build brain structures that perform highly specialized functions. In another parallel with natural selection, these structures emerge without the need of intelligent design or information (as in the form of a "genetic program") that guides the process toward its outcome. As Terrence Deacon pithily puts it, "evolution builds brains using evolution itself as a design tool."[12] In other words, evolution has not designed a brain that consists of numerous prefabricated adaptations, but has designed a brain that is capable of *adapting* to its local environment.

This is no mere analogy between evolution by natural selection and cortical development via proliferate-and-prune. There is, indeed, a deep structural relation between the two processes, and that relation illuminates why it is that our genetic endowment doesn't explain the forms of our developed cortical circuits. Think about how we explain the complex structure of the human eye. The additive processes of mutation and recombination by themselves simply cannot explain how that structure evolved, since those processes generated all kinds of variation that didn't end up getting incorporated in the structure of the eye. Of course, those processes did generate all of the elements that *did* end up getting incorporated in the structure of the eye, but only the subtractive process of selection (which retained only the most adaptive of the variants generated by mutation and recombination) explains the precise structure of the eye. And that explanation ultimately refers to the environmental demands that were effectively met by just a small fraction of the overproduced variation.

Similarly, the genetically guided additive processes in cortical development don't explain the forms of the brain circuits that emerge from development, since those additive processes overproduce the materials for those circuits. In fact, the result of this overproduction simply doesn't have much specific form at all. Only the subtractive processes explain the precise forms of our cortical circuits, and those processes are driven by the environmental inputs encountered during development. In both cases, it is not the source that overproduces the raw materials that explains the final form, but the particular environmental demands that prune those materials that explain it. In short, it is simply *not* the case that "our mental organs owe their basic design to our genetic program," which evolved during the evolutionary history of the species.[13] They owe their basic design to environment-guided brain activity, which occurs during the lifetime of the individual organism.

This developmental flexibility of the cortex is known as *neural plasticity*. Although the concept of neural plasticity is related to the concept of adaptive plasticity discussed in chapter 1, in that both denote forms of flexibility, the two concepts have different meanings, and it is worth being clear about this difference. Adaptive plasticity, recall, is the ability of a single genotype to produce more than one adaptive phenotype, producing the phenotype that is the fittest in its environment. This is a sort of flexibility of the genotype. The concept of neural plasticity, in contrast, refers to the ability of brain regions to perform different functions, so that a given brain region has the capacity take on the function of any other region. This kind of flexibility entails not only the possibility of multiple developmental outcomes, which are contingent on the environment, but also the possibility of change or reorganization of structure in response to changes in the environment. In other words, the concept of neural plasticity refers not to a genotype's ability to produce different adaptive phenotypes, but to *the brain's* ability to remake itself in response to changing environmental demands. This makes neural plasticity an instance of *phenotypic plasticity*. The concept of phenotypic plasticity, in contrast with the concept of developmental plasticity, refers to cases in which a genotype builds a mechanism or process that is capable of producing phenotypic change or reorganization in response to changing conditions in the organism's environment. Thus, although the concept of neural plasticity differs in meaning from the concept of adaptive plasticity in general, and from the concept of phenotypic plasticity in particular, neural plasticity is actually a form of phenotypic plasticity.

In fact, neural plasticity isn't confined to what we mark off as the process of development from infancy to adulthood. Our brains are changing all the time, quite rapidly and profoundly. We now know that the number of neurons in several areas of the cortex increases throughout life, continually providing neurons and connections to be further pruned by exposure to environmental demands. In addition, not only do our brains continue to grow (at least in some places), but they continually reorganize themselves in response to environmental demands. If a finger is lost, the cortical region that used to respond to its input will decrease in size and the neighboring regions will expand until nothing is left of the functional brain area at all. The converse is true as well. If a digit is overstimulated for a while, its corresponding area in the cortex increases in size. These changes occur outside of any "critical period" of development and can occur within a matter of days or even hours. Indeed, it appears that our brains change enough over our lifetimes that, by the time we are old, we use regions in our brains that are different from the ones we used as young adults to accomplish the same tasks.

How can our brains maintain a plasticity that allows for changes of function within hours? The evidence now indicates that regions once thought to be dedicated to a single information-processing task actually receive inputs from more than one source. When the median nerve of the hand is severed in adult owl or squirrel monkeys, areas of the cortex that normally respond to medial nerve stimulation begin almost immediately to respond to inputs from other nerves in the hand. Currently, the best explanation of the rapidity of this response is that silencing the inputs to the medial nerve "unmasks" secondary inputs from other nerves. Other animal studies, human behavioral studies of phantom-limb patients, and functional magnetic resonance imaging (fMRI) studies of the human cortex all indicate that brain mechanisms process overlapping inputs. In each case, areas of the cortex allegedly dedicated to processing one sort of information are revealed to process very different sorts of information as well.

Perhaps the most striking research that supports this blurring of information-processing streams concerns how our brains compensate for vestibular disturbances. If we remove the semicircular canals in our ears (which help us maintain balance), so that our vestibular system no longer receives any orientation information, we recover our sense of balance very quickly, much faster than we could form new neural connections. Single-cell recordings show that vestibular processing is not rerouted elsewhere in the brain; the same neurons in the brain stem that respond to normal vestibular inputs are also used in recovery. Obviously, they must be getting orientation information from somewhere other than the missing semicircular canals. Some other sensory system must already be feeding into the vestibular system. One hypothesis is that brains use a form of sensory substitution to compensate for such information loss. In this case, the brain would use internally generated signals from the visual system to compensate for the loss of inputs from the semicircular canals. It would substitute computations from a visual pursuit system (involved in tracking objects as they move across the visual field), which probably reconstructs information about head movement, for inputs from the semicircular canals. Perhaps as animals try to orient toward targets, error signals from the retina help the vestibular system compute head location. Ongoing work is exploring this possibility.

Research in neural plasticity also dovetails with recent data that highlight *cross-modal* connections—that is, connections between different sensory modalities, such as sight and smell. For example, if you touch someone's body on the same side and at the same time as you present them with a visual stimulus, activation in the visual cortex is significantly greater than when the visual stimulus is presented alone. Imaging studies of this phenomenon indicate that the somatosensory cortex (which processes information about touch, pressure, and joint position) projects back to the visual cortex, telling the visual cortex about tactile stimuli received. The extent of cross-modal communication among our alleged sensory "modules" is still a matter of investigation, though we do know that auditory and visual areas of the cortex exchange a lot of information regarding speech perception.

So what do all these facts tell us about Evolutionary Psychology's massive modularity thesis? First, if information processing about different sensory domains overlaps in our various brain circuits, and if even "modality-specific" processing receives inputs from other sensory modalities, there is little sense in which even our most basic cognitive processes are informationally isolated in the way that the massive modularity thesis implies. And, if this is true of our most basic cognitive processes, which function primarily to convey information about the ambient environment, it is undoubtedly true in spades for the "higher" cognitive processes involved in adaptive-problem solving of the sort that interests Evolutionary Psychologists. The degree of informational overlap in our brains shows that brain circuits are not "domain specific," but that they are domain *dominant*. One sort of processing in a brain circuit may be more prominent than others, but other processing is still occurring. Our brain circuits are not so specialized that they deal only with restricted domains. Instead, they deal *mostly* with particular domains, and they do so only contingently; the dedication of a brain circuit to a particular task is subject to change as the inputs to that circuit change.

Second, even if our species was faced with recurrent adaptive problems throughout a significant portion of its evolutionary history, distinct "genetically specified" brain circuits were not required to solve those problems. Our brains hit on a different, domain-general solution: a plasticity that allows particular environmental demands to participate heavily in tailoring the cortical circuits that process information about those demands. Our ancestors may have encountered diverse adaptive problems, but we didn't evolve a separate, genetically specified brain circuit for each adaptive-problem domain encountered in our evolutionary history. We evolved a plastic system capable of forming specialized brain circuits in response to the demands of its local environment.

Such a general solution, by the way, is not unique to the brain. The immune system constantly faces threat from a structurally diverse array of pathogens. Like Evolutionary Psychologists, we could reason that the immune system must have evolved separate, genetically specified "immuno-modules," each of which is specialized to solve the adaptive problem posed by a particular pathogen. But the immune system has, in fact, hit upon a general solution to the multitude of specific problems posed by pathogens. Through a single, elegant process, B cells assemble antibodies in response to each invading pathogen, and these are built "from scratch." In fact, B cells don't even have genes for each antibody. Rather, they possess mere gene fragments from which they assemble, on the spot, the genes necessary for building antibodies. So there is no sense in which each antibody is genetically specified. If we were to look at the antibody population in any given adult human, however, we would find a dazzling variety of antibodies, each specialized at attacking a specific pathogen. But this "structure" within the antibody population of a mature adult has been shaped by interaction between the antibody-assembly process and the pathogenic environment to which the individual has been exposed. The "structure" of the antibody population, in short, is a product not of genetic specification, but of interaction between the immune system and the environment.

The fact that our functionally specialized cortical circuits are plastic and environmentally shaped, rather than "genetically specified," means that they simply are not biological adaptations, just as specific antibodies are not biological adaptations. To see why, let's quickly review some of the basics of evolutionary biology. By definition, adaptations are traits that have a history of preservation and modification by selection. And selection occurs only when there is phenotypic variation that is responsible for fitness differences and that is *hereditary*. The requirement that the phenotypic variation be hereditary means that the phenotypic differences that are responsible for fitness differences must be due to genetic differences. Thus, if a trait is an adaptation, we know three things about it. First, at some point in the evolutionary history of the lineage with that trait, there was variation with respect to possession of the trait; some individuals had it and some didn't. Second, the individuals with the trait, because of having that trait, had higher fitness, on average, than those without it. And, third, the difference between having and not having the trait was due (at least in part) to a *genetic difference* between individuals with and without the trait. This is why evolutionary biologists say that "adaptive evolution is caused by natural selection acting on genetic variation."[14] Thus, adaptations are traits that are present in current individuals because of an evolutionary history in which selection acted on genetic differences between individuals, preserving the genes for those traits and weeding out the genes for alternative traits.

Consequently, differences between individuals that are due to environmental differences are not grist for selection's mill and, hence, do not form the basis of biological adaptation. Indeed, (micro)evolution, you'll recall, just *is* change in gene or genotype frequencies across generations in a population. So transgenerational phenotypic changes that are due to environmental changes—such as the increase in average height in the developed world during the twentieth century, which was due to improved nutrition—are not even biological evolution, let alone adaptive evolution. Only phenotypic changes across generations that are driven by underlying genetic changes are adaptive evolution.

But why does this matter? It matters because, for the reasons discussed, our functionally specialized cortical circuits are the product of a plastic system's response to its local environment. In other words, differences between individuals with respect to their functionally specialized cortical circuits are due to environmental differences between them, not to genetic differences (with the exception of mutations that disrupt development so severely that "normal" cortical plasticity is lost). And, as it is for us in this respect, so it was for our ancestors. Consequently, such functionally specialized brain circuits cannot have formed the basis of adaptive evolution. They are not present in current individuals because of an evolutionary history in which selection acted on genetic differences between individuals with certain functionally specialized brain circuits and those without. They are present in individuals because of a plastic brain's response to its local environment. In short, even though an adult human brain has many functionally specialized cortical circuits, which resemble in certain respects what Evolutionary Psychologists call modules, those circuits are not adaptations, and they do not owe their basic design to our "genetic program." To put this the other way around, whatever our psychological adaptations are, they are not modules.

However, the brain's plasticity—the process by which it forms functionally specialized circuits in response to environmental demands—*is* an adaptation. Similarly, the immune system's antibody-assembly process is an adaptation. Both of these systems are present in current humans because of past selection for their abilities to produce adaptive responses to the demands of the local environment. And both systems were undoubtedly shaped by selection to be ever more exquisitely responsive to those demands. But here is the critical point: In both cases, we need to distinguish the process from its products. The processes (antibody assembly and brain plasticity) are biological adaptations, but their products (antibodies and functionally specialized brain circuits) are not. The products of these processes are, instead, simply the adaptive responses of adaptations to the local environment. Thus, rather than slowly adapting specialized structures in the brain to environmental demands over the course of evolutionary time, selection has designed a brain whose adaptation is its ability to adapt to local environmental demands throughout the lifetime of an individual, and sometimes within a period of days, by forming specialized structures to deal with those demands.

This is actually analogous to Evolutionary Psychologists' own argument regarding behavior. As we saw in chapter 2, Evolutionary Psychologists argue that, since behavior is the contingent response of brain mechanisms to their current environments, behaviors themselves are not adaptations. Rather, they argue, the adaptations are the mechanisms that produce behavior conditional on the current environment. Further, they claim, those behavior-control mechanisms have been shaped by selection for their ability to respond flexibly to changes in the environment. So, behaviors themselves are not adaptations, but are the products of behavior-control mechanisms, which are flexible adaptations. The argument here is similar. Since cortical mechanisms are contingent responses of cortical plasticity to its local environment, cortical mechanisms themselves are not adaptations; the plasticity that produces them in response to rapidly changing environmental demands is the adaptation.

But it is possible that this is true primarily of the cortex, which performs virtually all of our "higher" cognitive functions. For, as noted earlier, the process by which cortical neurons are generated and put in place differs from that by which the neurons that make up the evolutionarily older parts of the brain are generated and put in place. Indeed, it appears that development of the brain regions that control sexual and emotional responses is primarily under the control of additive events, unlike cortical development in which subtractive events play such a large role. If this turns out to be correct, then certain sexual and emotional responses may indeed be adaptations themselves, rather than the products of a plastic system's response to its local environment. That is, certain sexual and emotional responses may be more like the liver or the kidneys than like antibodies, the result of selection's having acted on genetic differences between individuals, preserving the genes for those sexual and emotional responses while discarding the genes for their alternatives. Consequently, Evolutionary Psychologists may be right about some of our more basic emotional adaptations, but nonetheless wrong in its claims that we possess a lot of *cognitive* adaptations devoted to very specific forms of problem solving.

So cortical plasticity is no doubt not our only psychological adaptation. Some of our affective responses, subserved by circuits in the midbrain and limbic system, may be adaptations as well. At the same time, it may be that the emotional adaptations we find in the limbic system are not the sort of precisely honed psychological adaptations that interest Evolutionary Psychologists. Our limbic system produces fear in response to dangerous phenomena in the environment, such as coiled snakes. The limbic system alone, however, is not very sophisticated in the way it produces these fear responses, since it reacts to all coiled shapes (hoses, ropes, a circular pile of brush) with the same fear response. Only when the limbic system is conjoined with our higher cortical structures do we get more specific responses, such as "Danger! Rattlesnake!" But such specific message contents derive largely from the functioning of the cortex. The fear response itself derives from the limbic system, which is simply too crude to do anything more than react in a rough-and-ready fashion.

There are additional things that we should count among our psychological adaptations, since brain function is not determined solely by the brain's neural circuitry, by how the brain is "wired." Neurotransmitters and hormones also affect how the brain's circuits function and thus contribute to the regulation and control of behavior. We know that the brain regions regulating sexual desire and response are affected by levels of the sex hormones in the brain and that these levels sometimes vary cyclically. For example, although human females are sexually receptive throughout their menstrual cycles, there is a marked increase in sexual fantasy and female-initiated sexual activity around ovulation, and this increase is produced by peaking levels of estrogen around ovulation. This is undoubtedly an adaptation, selected for its effects on sexual behavior. Consequently, neurotransmitters and hormones, or specific levels of these, also number among our psychological adaptations (although specific patterns of their timed release could be adaptations as well).

So we do possess psychological adaptations in addition to brain plasticity. But the question so far has been what accounts for the functionally specialized brain circuits that subserve our higher cognitive functions—the circuits that process information in complex ways and make decisions about action and action plans. And the answer has been that they are not "innate" modular adaptations, as Evolutionary Psychologists claim, but the products of the brain's plastic response to its environment. What form is taken by those additional psychological adaptations is a question to be addressed in the next section.

## The Arguments for Modularity Reconsidered

Chapter 2 reviewed several arguments Evolutionary Psychologists have given for the massive modularity thesis. These arguments seemed compelling at the time, and they directly contradict the arguments of the previous section. It may appear that we have arrived at a tie: There are good arguments both for and against the massive modularity thesis, with no independent considerations enabling a choice between the two sides. If it appears this way to you, it is because you are presupposing that Evolutionary Psychology's arguments for massive modularity are sound. They are not. Let's reexamine each of the arguments for massive modularity, and we'll see where they go wrong.

One argument for massive modularity is as follows. The adaptive problems faced by our ancestors were very diverse in character, ranging from identifying edible plant matter and avoiding deadly predators to selecting a reproductively valuable mate and cooperating with others in a status hierarchy. Given the diversity of these problems, what constitutes a successful solution to one problem is very different from what constitutes a solution to another. No single general-purpose problem-solving mechanism could successfully solve each of the problems in such a diverse array; instead, each problem requires its own domain-specific problem-solving mechanism. As Donald Symons says: "It is no more probable that some sort of general-purpose brain/mind mechanism could solve all the behavioral problems an organism faces (find food, choose a mate, select a habitat, etc.) than it is that some sort of general-purpose organ could perform all physiological functions (pump blood, digest food, nourish an embryo, etc.)."[15] Thus, "there must be as many domain-specific cognitive mechanisms as there are domains in which the definitions of successful behavioral outcomes are incommensurate."[16]

The crucial step in this argument is clearly the claim that no general-purpose problem-solving mechanism could solve a diverse array of problems. But what does this mean and why should we believe it? Cosmides and Tooby answer these questions in a couple of passages. Here's one: "A woman who used the same taste preference mechanisms in choosing a mate that she used to choose nutritious foods would choose a very strange mate indeed."[17] Here's the other: "Suppose our hypothetical domain-general learning mechanism guiding an ancestral hunter-gatherer somehow inferred that sexual intercourse is a necessary condition for producing offspring. Should the individual, then, have sex at every opportunity? In fact, such a design would rapidly be selected out. There are large fitness costs associated with incest, to pick only a single kind of sexual error."[18] We are presumably left to imagine this individual attempting sex with the nearest object when confronting any adaptive problem.

In both of these passages Cosmides and Tooby are arguing against the effectiveness of a general-purpose, or domain-general, problem solver, but in neither passage do they describe a problem-solving strategy that is truly domain general. Rather, they gesture toward a domain-specific strategy that is *overgeneralized* (a woman who applies criteria for selecting fruit to the problem of selecting a mate; an individual who tries to use sex to solve every problem). But Cosmides and Tooby give us no reason to think— indeed, there *is* no reason to think—that a domain-general problem solver would simply apply a solution that works in one problem domain to every other domain it encounters.

Part of the problem here is that Evolutionary Psychologists never provide a clear and detailed account of how the domain-general mechanisms they are rejecting might work. The most that Tooby and Cosmides say is that the alternative to a mind that is massively modular is a mind that consists "of a few, general-purpose mechanisms, like operant conditioning, social learning, and trial-and-error induction."[19] Such a mind possesses only a few domain-general mechanisms, which operate in every problem domain in an effort to generate solutions in those domains.

But consider the domain-general "mechanism" of social learning, which involves observation of models (such as parents or teachers) followed by imitation of the observed behavior of those models. Suppose a female employs social learning in figuring out how to select nutritious peaches: She observes her parents selecting plump and juicy peaches, and she does the same. If she now switches problem domains to the selection of a mate, the mechanism of social learning would clearly not guide her to search for a plump and juicy mate. Rather, it would guide her to observe and imitate the mate-selection behavior of female role models, and this would lead to the acquisition of mate-selection criteria that are specific to the problem domain of selecting a mate. So domain-general social learning wouldn't result in the overgeneralization of an acquired domain-specific solution, it would result in the acquisition of (imitated) solutions specific to each problem domain in which it operated. In short, the domain-general mechanism would generate domain-specific solutions.

The point here is not to defend social-learning accounts of behavior, for they undoubtedly have very restricted application. The point is, rather, that Cosmides and Tooby fail to show that domain-general mechanisms can't generate domain-specific solutions because their arguments rely on a misrepresentation of how a domain-general problem solver would function in different problem domains. Consequently, the crucial step in the argument for massive modularity is unsupported, so we're given no reason to believe that the mind can't be a general-purpose problem solver.

This shows that Cosmides and Tooby's arguments fail even given their own sketchy characterizations of "domain-general mechanisms." But we needn't accept their characterizations. The previous section described a mechanism of neural plasticity, which allows the environment a crucial role in forming brain circuits that specialize (though not exclusively) in solving problems in particular domains. This mechanism is domain general, or "domain neutral," in that it is not specialized to respond to the demands of any specific problem domain in particular. Its function, rather, is to form brain circuits that solve the problems posed by specific domains. Thus, neural plasticity is a domain-general mechanism that produces more highly specialized mechanisms, which in turn solve the problems specific to the domains that have been involved in shaping them.

In light of this, it's worth reconsidering Symons's claim that no "general-purpose brain/mind mechanism could solve all the behavioral problems an organism faces." Think again about the immune system. It's true that each pathogen requires a separate and specialized mechanism to deal with it. These specialized mechanisms are the antibodies. Antibodies, however, are created by an assembly mechanism that is *not* specialized to deal with any particular pathogen, but that is "pathogen general." In one sense, then, the problem posed by a pathogen is solved by a "domain-specific" mechanism, the antibody. However, since the antibody is produced by a pathogen-general mechanism, there is another sense in which the problem is solved by a "domain-general" mechanism.

Similarly, the problems that require behavioral solutions may require specialized mechanisms to produce those behavioral solutions. These specialized mechanisms are domain-dominant brain circuits. They are formed, however, by a mechanism of neural plasticity that is *not* specialized to deal with any particular behavioral problems. Neural plasticity, which forms functionally specialized circuits in response to demands of the local environment, is a *domain-general* mechanism with respect to behavioral response. So, even if we accept the argument that specific problems require specialized problem solvers, it simply doesn't follow that those specialized problem solvers must be adaptations, rather than mechanisms that are manufactured as needed by a plastic system in response to environmental demands.

Consider now a second argument for massive modularity. In order for an adaptation to evolve and become prevalent in a population, Tooby and Cosmides argue, there must be "recurrent structure" in both the environment and the organisms in the evolving population. That is, there must be both a transgenerationally stable environmental structure (which is adapted to) and a hereditarily recurring organismic structure (which selection adapts to the environmental structure). But, although there is recurrent environmental structure associated with each adaptive problem taken individually, there is virtually no recurrent environmental structure in common between two very different adaptive problems (for example, choosing a mate and choosing a fruit) and absolutely no recurrent environmental structure common to all of them. So a strictly domain-general mind could not have evolved, since there is no recurrent structure to the "general domain" to which it would have to be adapted. As Symons says, "there is no such thing as a 'general problem solver' because there is no such thing as a general problem."[20]

This argument presupposes that there were stable adaptive problems, which drove human psychological evolution, and that the mind evolved adaptations to each of them. As argued in chapter 3, however, there probably weren't many stable adaptive problems driving human psychological evolution, since most of the features of the environment that called for behavioral responses were changing rapidly during human evolution. And, when the environment changes rapidly, there is selection for phenotypic plasticity, rather than for transgenerationally stable organismic structures that can be shaped to recurrent environmental demands.

The argument also presupposes that a general-purpose mechanism could evolve only by becoming adapted to a "general problem" or "general domain" (which, the argument purports to show, is an absurd notion). But, when mechanisms of phenotypic plasticity evolve, it is not because they are adapted to some "general" feature of the environment, but because they are capable of producing *a variety of specific responses* to the environment, each of which is appropriate to the environment in which it appears. Mechanisms of phenotypic plasticity are thus appropriately describable as "general purpose" or "domain general," in that they are not committed to producing any given specific response prior to interaction with the environment. But they always do produce domain-specific solutions to the problems they encounter in their local environments. So, the fact that there is no "recurrent structure" to a "general domain" doesn't entail that a "general-purpose brain/mind mechanism" could not have evolved.

The other argument for massive modularity sketched in chapter 2 is this. All knowledge possessed by a strictly domain-general mind would have to be derived from experience, for domain-general mechanisms "are limited to knowing what can be validly derived by general processes from perceptual information."[21] But knowledge of which behaviors will effectively solve an adaptive problem cannot possibly be derived from experience. As Cosmides and Tooby argue: "Because the promotion of fitness means differential representation of genes in subsequent generations, the time at which the consequences of an action can be assessed is remote from the time at which the action must be taken. Adaptive courses of action can be neither deduced nor learned by general criteria alone because they depend on statistical relationships between features of the environment, behavior, and fitness that emerge over many generations and are, therefore, often not observable during a single lifetime."[22] Modules, however, come equipped with knowledge of which courses of action are adaptive in their proprietary problem domains, since this knowledge has been built into them by selection. Thus, a general-purpose mind could not have evolved; only a massively modular mind, with a module specialized at solving each adaptive problem, could have evolved.

This argument commits a single, simple mistake. As the cognitive scientist Jerry Fodor and the philosopher Richard Samuels independently point out, the most this argument shows is that the human mind must come equipped with some *innate knowledge*; it doesn't show that that knowledge must be contained in "hundreds or thousands" of innate modules. Evolutionary Psychologists claim that modules are "genetically specified," domain specific, informationally isolated, equipped with innate knowledge, equipped with domain-specific rules of reasoning, and relatively fast. But these properties are independent of one another; it is possible for a mechanism to possess one of the properties without possessing the others. Consequently, an argument that shows that the mind must possess innate knowledge of which behaviors are adaptive in particular circumstances (since it wouldn't be able to glean this knowledge from experience) doesn't entail that the mind must consist of "hundreds or thousands" of distinct domain-specific *mechanisms*. For a general-purpose mind could possess innate knowledge. In short, the very first premise of the argument—that all knowledge possessed by a strictly domain-general mind would have to be derived from experience—is false, so the argument fails to support massive modularity.

The crucial point here is the distinction between information and the mechanisms in the mind that process that information. The mind could come equipped with innate knowledge about particular adaptive problems—for example, that snakes are dangerous or that you should sacrifice your own resources to benefit others only in proportion to the degree to which others are related to you. Fodor and Samuels think that Evolutionary Psychology's argument establishes this much. But Evolutionary Psychologists also claim that the mind possesses a specialized mechanism, or "minicomputer," for each adaptively important body of domain-specific information. Each of these mechanisms, they claim, specializes in processing a particular body of domain-specific information, and it processes that information with a domain-specific body of rules, which applies only to that information. These are the claims that Fodor and Samuels contend don't follow from the argument. For the mind could consist primarily of a single general-purpose mechanism (supplemented by modules for sensory inputs), which employs rules of reasoning that apply to information independently of the problem domain that the information is about. Paradigms of such domain-independent rules of information processing are the rules of deductive logic and the probabilistic rules of hypothesis testing. Thus, according to Fodor and Samuels, the picture that emerges from the argument is one of a mind that is equipped with some innate *domain-specific information* that is processed by a *domain-general mechanism* employing *domain-general rules*, which are also used in acquiring additional information about the world.

While Fodor and Samuels are right about the fallacy in the argument, they're too quick to accept that the argument actually demonstrates the necessity of innate knowledge. All the argument really shows is that a strictly domain-general mechanism, which employs only domain-general learning rules, must be given a head start on learning in certain adaptively crucial domains. Without any head starts, domain-general learning would face the insoluble problem of learning which of the world's features are worth learning about before they set about learning about them. For there are an overwhelmingly vast number of things in the world that a general-purpose mechanism could learn about. On entering the world, should it pay more attention to the walls of the nursery or to mother's face? Should it spend hours watching for and documenting subtle changes on the backs of its hands or should it focus on the noises coming from mother's mouth? Since there are far too many features of the world that could be foci of domain-general learning, a wholly unconstrained general-purpose learning mechanism would be overwhelmed by useless data unless it had some built-in "data filters." Thus, if a general-purpose mechanism as plastic as the brain is to develop the right problem-solving specializations, there must be some constraints on its possible courses of development. In short, its development must be "channeled" in the right directions.

Innate knowledge of adaptively important features of the world is certainly one way to ensure that a general-purpose mechanism comes to know the right stuff, since it's "preequipped" with the knowledge it will need. But innate knowledge is not the only way to ensure coming to know the right stuff. *Initial biases* in the mechanism, which channel attention to particular environmental inputs more than others, can be all that is required to get it learning about the right stuff. These initial biases can be far short of actual knowledge about a problem domain. They can be mere predispositions to apply domain-general learning to certain special classes of environmental inputs.

To illustrate the role of initial biases in learning, consider the phenomenon of face recognition. In an adult human, a significant portion of the brain is involved in processing information about human faces, and the ability to accurately distinguish our conspecifics from one another and detect subtle facial cues of emotional state has undoubted adaptive value. (Think of the problems you'd have if you couldn't distinguish people who have previously helped you from those who have hurt you, or if you couldn't tell whether someone was angry or happy with you.) Because of this, some cognitive scientists, including Evolutionary Psychologists, have proposed that there is a genetically specified module for face recognition, which embodies a lot of innate knowledge about human faces.

But Jeffrey Elman and his colleagues propose an alternative, according to which face recognition becomes gradually and progressively "modularized." This process, however, has a head start in development. An experiment with human newborns has shown that they preferentially attend to stimuli consisting of three high-contrast blobs in the triangular configuration of two eyes and a mouth. Interestingly, newborns don't prefer actual faces over pictures of three high-contrast blobs until a little later in development, and even at six months infants show no discrimination of human faces from monkey faces. Only later still do infants begin to pay attention to and discriminate among movements internal to the face. Thus, infants appear to gradually learn about human faces, but learning is aided by an initial bias to attend to stimuli consisting of three triangulated high-contrast blobs. As a result, face-recognition abilities become gradually more domain specific: Beginning with attention to the domain of three high-contrast blobs, they become progressively more specific until they specialize in the domain of human faces.

The mechanism that accomplishes this trick appears to be distributed across two face-recognition devices, one subcortical and the other cortical. The subcortical device is up and running at birth, and it is tuned to selectively respond to three high-contrast blobs. Its outputs feed into and help "train up" the highly plastic cortical device, which learns to discriminate among faces and facial expressions and to discriminate between faces and other stimuli that appear in the form of three high-contrast blobs. The cortical device does most of the real work of face recognition, yet it gets a head start in learning to recognize faces by the initial bias in its inputs from the subcortical system, and because of its plasticity its functioning is heavily dependent on the nature of the outputs from the subcortical system. Ranchers use the cortical device to distinguish among the cows in their herds, and dog breeders use this area to discern different dogs. But most of us use this area just to recognize human faces, and as a result most cows' faces look alike to us. Thus, our face-recognition capacity can be fine-tuned in many different ways, depending on the particular inputs to which we are primarily exposed. And, if we are totally deprived of exposure to stimuli consisting of three high-contrast blobs during development, the highly plastic cortical device that is used for face recognition in most people will be taken over and used for other task demands.

In the case of face recognition, the initial bias is built into a "hardwired" subcortical device, which feeds into the cortical device that learns to recognize faces. But, according to the best model we have now, initial biases could also be realized in the cortex in the initial connection strengths among neurons. Stronger initial connections would enjoy an advantage in cell competition, since they would require less activation to consolidate their connections than would weaker initial connections. This would make certain circuits easier to stabilize than others. These biases would make the cortex predisposed to develop circuits that specialize in bias-directed inputs more quickly and easily than circuits that specialize in other classes of input. But, if the environment offers little in the way of bias-directed inputs, the cortex's general plasticity will soon overcome the initial biases, and circuits will develop that are specialized in dealing with whatever environmental inputs are most salient. While this allows for relatively quick "modularization" into circuits built around initial biases, unlike a massively modular brain it accomplishes the trick with very minimal initial structure built into the brain. For, rather than needing to build in a complex specialized circuit for a particular task, or a developmental mechanism to "add" that circuit at a particular point in development, it merely needs to build in a bias to preferentially attend to a restricted class of inputs.

The initial biases built into the brain, of course, may themselves have been shaped by selection (indeed, they could even be the product of frequency-dependent selection). So our psychological adaptations would consist not only in brain plasticity, neurotransmitters, hormones, and some affective responses, but in the brain's specific initial biases as well. It is worth noting, however, that the biases needn't be as domain specific as Evolutionary Psychology's modules, so they needn't be as precisely attuned to adaptive-problem domains as Evolutionary Psychologists believe modules to be. For, again, face recognition can be accomplished by starting with learning about three high-contrast blobs. This can solve the adaptive problem of needing a mechanism that recognizes *faces*, but the initial bias pertains to a far wider domain than that of human faces; in fact, the initial bias isn't even about faces per se. Thus, while initial biases number among our psychological adaptations, they cannot be easily inferred from the highly specialized cognitive abilities exhibited by adult humans. All that initial biases need do is start the functioning of a general-purpose mechanism down a path that will lead, in standard developmental environments, to a brain circuit that specializes in an adaptive-problem domain.

These points are important enough to belabor a little, so consider them from another angle. Many cognitive scientists have claimed that there is a strong similarity between learning and the growth of scientific knowledge. Like the growth of scientific knowledge, learning appears to be a process in which hypotheses about a particular domain of phenomena are tested against evidence derived from experience and rejected or revised when that evidence conflicts with them. And, in both cases, the goal is to arrive at hypotheses about the world that enable us to accurately anticipate the course of experience (to make accurate predictions).

In an argument that long predated Evolutionary Psychology's argument for innateness, the philosopher of science Karl Popper argued that *some kind* of hypotheses always had to precede the gathering of data in science, since data gathering that is not guided by hypotheses would be overwhelmed by the literal infinity of "facts" that could be recorded. Imagine recording everything that you can observe right now. As you become more absorbed in this exercise, you'll quickly realize that there is an infinity of minutiae that you could record. Without some way of filtering this infinity of minutiae, you would never know which of all the many observations you could record will be *relevant* to predicting events in the immediate future. Only antecedent hypotheses about which features of the world are relevant to predicting future events can provide the basis for meaningful data gathering. So, Popper concluded, in science hypotheses must always come before the evidence; speculation, or "conjecture," must always precede observation. Further, he argued, this must also be true of how the mind learns about the world; there must always be some innate hypotheses about the world guiding our experiential accumulation of the data against which those hypotheses are tested.

This sounds like Evolutionary Psychology's argument, but there are a couple of very important differences. First, the logic of hypothesis testing and evidence evaluation doesn't differ depending on whether we're studying quarks, planets, or neurons. Indeed, the method of hypothesis testing in science is the very paradigm of a domain-general method, and anyone who thinks that domain-general problem-solving methods are too weak to generate richly structured knowledge simply hasn't been paying attention to the history of science over the past few centuries. Of course, as Popper argued, in order for a domain-general scientific method of hypothesis testing to effectively arrive at knowledge of the world, it has to be guided by hypotheses that are prior to the gathering of evidence, not derived from the evidence. So science can work effectively only when its domain-general method of hypothesis testing is combined with prior hypotheses about various aspects of the world. This is analogous to the sort of mind that Fodor and Samuels imagine we have: a domain-general problem solver equipped with some innate domain-specific knowledge.

But, second, nothing in Popper's argument requires that the hypotheses with which we begin be *right*, or even close, in order to facilitate acquiring knowledge of the world. We now know that the atomic weight of an oxygen atom is 15.9994 atomic mass units, but oxygen, as a "substance," wasn't discovered until the late eighteenth century, and the discovery that "substances" are composed of atoms wasn't made until much later. In fact, oxygen wasn't even a *concept* to early eighteenth-century chemists; many of the chemical reactions we attribute to the properties of oxygen were explained by them by appeal to "phlogiston," which we now know doesn't exist. Nonetheless, there is a continuous chain of iterated cycles of what Popper called "conjectures and refutations" connecting our current scientific knowledge with the false starts of Enlightenment scientists. In order to arrive at our current scientific knowledge, it wasn't necessary that early scientists possessed exactly the right hypotheses. In fact, they had radically mistaken hypotheses, many of which weren't even about the "domains" of phenomena that scientists now study, but were about "domains" of nonexistent phenomena. But, even by beginning with those radically mistaken hypotheses, domain-general scientific methods were able to produce all of our richly detailed scientific knowledge of the world.

Similarly, in order for a domain-general mechanism to arrive at richly detailed knowledge of a particular problem domain, it isn't necessary that it begin with full-blown innate knowledge of that domain. It is often sufficient that it begin merely with the right minimal initial bias, which will initiate a sequence of "conjectures and refutations" culminating in the knowledge that it is adaptively important to have. In this light, we can think of face recognition as beginning in the newborn with the hypothesis "Triangulated high-contrast blobs are very important" and culminating in richly detailed knowledge of human faces. The initial "hypothesis" doesn't even need to be *about faces* or even very detailed. It just needs to be an effective starting point for domain-general knowledge acquisition. Thus, initial biases can be exceptionally minimal nudges in the right direction, which needn't even be about the things of which adults have knowledge.

There is another consideration underlying Evolutionary Psychology's massive modularity thesis, which is closely related to the third argument for massive modularity just considered. That argument, recall, claimed that domain-general learning mechanisms can't learn how to behave adaptively, since information about whether a behavior is adaptive isn't available during an individual's lifetime. This doesn't purport to show that domain-general mechanisms couldn't learn what they need to *even if* they had access to information about the future reproductive consequences of behavioral choices. The argument alleges only that the necessary information is there but out of reach, not that domain-general mechanisms are not powerful enough to learn what they need to learn from the information.

But Evolutionary Psychologists do believe that, even if the necessary information were available to a domain-general learning mechanism, it would be *unable to learn* from that information how to solve the problems that humans are in fact capable of solving. As Tooby and Cosmides say, "a psychological architecture that consisted of nothing but equipotential, general-purpose, content-independent, or content-free mechanisms could not successfully perform the tasks the human mind is known to perform or solve the adaptive problems humans evolved to solve."[23]

In this passage, once again, Tooby and Cosmides conflate a few distinct properties. As we have seen, a general-purpose mechanism need not necessarily be "content free" or "content independent." A general-purpose mechanism can have initial biases that are "content dependent," *about* particular things in the environment that are important targets of learning, and these can facilitate the acquisition of adaptively crucial information. Even granting this, however, Tooby and Cosmides would remain unconvinced that learning is driven by domain-general rules. For the real worry underlying their claim is that a domain-general learning mechanism would be unable to acquire certain crucial *domain-specific rules*.

Everyone agrees that human problem solving routinely employs rules that are domain specific. Figuring out the best move in chess involves rules that are specific to chess; not only must one have learned the rules of chess, but one must have rules for reasoning about which moves are most effective in which circumstances, and these rules will apply only in chess games. Similarly, figuring out the best strategic maneuver at a critical point in a baseball game involves use of rules that are highly baseball specific in their content, and figuring out how to solve an equation in algebra involves use of rules of inference that are specific to algebra. Thus, learning isn't simply a process of acquiring information about the world; it is also a process of acquiring many domain-specific rules, which are used in solving problems in their proprietary domains. And the conviction of Evolutionary Psychologists is that a mind equipped with only domain-general learning rules would be unable to acquire the repertoire of domain-specific rules that characterizes adult human problem-solving abilities. So, they believe, the human mind can't consist solely of domain-general mechanisms, but must contain some domain-specific mechanisms that are preequipped with rules of reasoning specific to their proprietary domains.

Obviously, however, humans do acquire chess-specific and baseball-specific rules of problem solving. Since no one would argue that humans possess innate rules that are specific to these domains, they must be acquired through some domain-general mechanism. So what is the source of Evolutionary Psychologists' conviction that a domain-general learning mechanism couldn't learn to perform the problem-solving tasks that humans routinely perform? The conviction is based on a widely accepted view concerning language acquisition and an assumption that what is true of language acquisition is true of the acquisition of most complex human competences. So consider language acquisition.

Adult speakers of a language are capable of understanding and generating a potentially infinite number of grammatical sentences. According to the received view in psycholinguistics, this capacity can be explained only by supposing that adult speakers know the grammatical rules that generate all of the infinitely many grammatical sentences of their languages. The problem of explaining language acquisition, then, is the problem of explaining how individuals acquire knowledge of the grammatical rules of their languages.

Now, suppose that individuals are equipped only with domain-general learning rules. We can then suppose that learning involves formulating hypotheses about the grammatical rules of one's language and testing those hypotheses against the linguistic data encountered in one's experience (the sentences uttered by others, corrections of one's own uttered sentences, and any explicit instruction in the rules of grammar). And suppose further that hypothesis formation and testing employs only domain-general rules of reasoning—for example, those of probability theory and deductive logic. Could an individual equipped only with such domain-general learning rules acquire knowledge of the grammatical rules of their language?

According to the received view, the answer is no, for the following reasons. During the course of linguistic development, children are exposed primarily to speech containing incomplete and ungrammatical sentences and to comparatively few utterances that are grammatically correct. In addition, they are exposed to virtually no "positive evidence" of grammatical rules (being told what the rules are) and to very little "negative evidence" of the rules (being told that their utterances are grammatically incorrect and having them corrected). In short, during the course of linguistic development, the average language learner is exposed to precious little evidence about the grammatical rules of their language. If language acquisition involved the employment of domain-general rules in forming and testing hypotheses about grammatical rules, hypotheses would have to be tested against this very small body of evidence regarding grammatical rules. Since the evidence is always necessarily sparse compared to the number of grammatical sentences in a language, however, it would always be compatible with several competing hypotheses about the rules of grammar. As a result, a language learner guided solely by domain-general learning rules would be unable to learn which among several competing hypotheses about the rules of grammar is the correct hypothesis. Yet native language speakers *do* arrive at knowledge of the grammatical rules of their languages, so they can't be acquiring this knowledge through domain-general learning rules. Consequently, language acquisition must have a head start in the form of *domain-specific learning rules*, which are designed specifically to facilitate acquisition of the grammatical rules of one's native language. And these domain-specific learning rules are assumed to be a Universal Grammar, which is innately encoded in a small network of modules known as the *language acquisition device*.

According to the received view in psycholinguistics, then, language is simply *unlearnable* by domain-general rules, because the experiential data from which those rules would learn underdetermine the end state of learning (knowledge of grammar). Tooby and Cosmides believe that what is true of language acquisition in this respect is true of most of the complex problem-solving competences that humans possess, including competences to solve adaptive problems. Most of the complex tasks that people can perform, they contend, are simply unlearnable by domain-general rules from the available experiential data.

But there are three problems with this conviction. First, even if the received view of language acquisition is correct (and it's not without its detractors), language learning could be the exception, rather than just an instance of the rule. Indeed, Fodor, who wrote the seminal work on modularity, argues that we have modules only for our five senses and for language. So, even if there is a module—or, more accurately, a small network of interconnected modules—for language, the massive modularity thesis doesn't follow. For the received view of language acquisition is the result of extensive empirical investigation and formal modeling of language learning. Similar conclusions can't be drawn about other areas of learning without similar extensive research, and Evolutionary Psychologists have yet to do that research for each of the domains for which it claims we must have evolved modules. Thus, while we may well have an innate language-acquisition module, it simply doesn't follow that we must also have modules for mate choice, parenting, aggressive threat, cooperation, or food selection.

Second, language involves a very complex system of rules. If it is unlearnable by domain-general learning rules, this is because of its great complexity. The things for which Evolutionary Psychologists claim that we have modules typically don't exhibit anything remotely like the complexity of language. For example, Evolutionary Psychologists claim that human males have an evolved mate-preference module that leads them to find reproductive-aged females maximally attractive. The module allegedly responds to cues of youth, since youth is correlated with reproductive capability. But being sexually attracted to cues of youth isn't a complex capacity to acquire; and, given the wealth of data about sexual relations available in a maturing male's environment, it's rather implausible that a domain-general learning mechanism couldn't acquire from that data a sexual attraction to young females. Chess is far more complex than sexual attraction to young women, yet we learn chess without the benefit of an innate chess module. Since the majority of the adaptive "tasks" that Evolutionary Psychologists claim we perform are similarly much less complex than speaking a language, it is a mistake to assume that what is true of language acquisition must be true of learning in each of these other domains as well.

Third, even if learning in certain nonlinguistic domains requires a head start in the form of domain-specific learning rules, given the lack of complexity in these domains, the necessary domain-specific learning rules could take the form of minimal initial biases. The initial bias described in greatest detail earlier was a bias to attend to certain stimuli, but initial biases could also take the form of dispositions that physically embody a domain-specific rule. Thermostats, for example, are physically constituted in such a way that, when set at seventy degrees, they behave in accordance with the rule, "Turn the furnace on when the temperature falls below seventy degrees, and turn it off when the temperature rises above seventy degrees." Thus, while it remains to be demonstrated that learning in any area other than language requires a head start in the form of innate domain-specific learning rules, if such head starts are required, they could be provided by initial biases.

So far we've been examining Evolutionary Psychology's arguments for massive modularity, and we've found that none of them demonstrates that the brain is massively modular in the way Evolutionary Psychology claims. But there is also a good theoretical reason to think that the brain *could not possibly* be massively modular in the way Evolutionary Psychologists claim. Indeed, there is reason to think that most of the modules postulated by Evolutionary Psychologists couldn't function without the assistance of a domain-general mechanism.

To see why, consider Evolutionary Psychology's claim, to be examined in detail in chapter 5, that women have an evolved mate-choice module that implements rules "designed to detect and prefer high-status men."[24] According to Evolutionary Psychologists, modules are activated by the environmental cues that are specific to the domains in which they specialize. So a woman's mate-preference module is activated when exposed to high-status men, and it functions to produce attraction to those men. But status is not directly observable in the way that baldness is; it has to be inferred from other properties that are observable. Thus, in order to produce attraction to high-status males, the female mate-preference module must be activated by *signs* that are positively correlated with high status. That is, its *input* must be a sign of high status in males.

Signs of status, however, vary considerably across cultures. What is accorded high status in one culture may be denigrated in another. As Robert Wright, Evolutionary Psychology's most effective popularizer, vividly puts it: "The range of things that can bring status in different cultures and subcultures is astonishing. Making beads, making music, delivering sermons, delivering babies, inventing drugs, inventing tales, collecting coins, collecting scalps. . . . [T]he Zuni [Native Americans of New Mexico] confer status on those who don't seek status too fiercely, and deny status to those who do. . . . In a monastery, serenity and asceticism can be sources of status. In *some strata* of Victorian England, a nearly ludicrous amount of gentility and humility could help earn status."[25] In spite of this, Symons says: "The particular correlates or indexes of male status do, of course, vary; what is invariant is the psychological adaptation that specifies the rule 'prefer signs of high status.'"[26]

Since signs of high status can be so varied, however, information from any number of domains could be relevant to determining which among all the many observable properties are the signs of high status in one's local environment. If delivering sermons or delivering babies could be signs of high status, then information from "the religion domain" (to determine who's the best preacher) or "the obstetric domain" (to determine who's the best obstetrician) would be relevant to detecting high-status males. But, since the mate-preference module employs only narrow domain-specific rules that are specialized to process information about signs of high status, it will be unable to wander across an unprincipled variety of domains with those rules in order to figure out which are the local signs of high status. For, in order to function, it must be *given* a sign of high status. Thus, some domain-general mechanism must be involved in ascertaining the local signs of high status. But, if a domain-general mechanism has to mediate between environmental inputs and the inputs to modules, and if it can effectively perform the tasks necessary in this capacity, it's very unclear why we would need highly specialized modules to do the easy jobs after a domain-general mechanism has done the hard jobs. A domain-general mechanism that can effectively mediate between the environment and modules should also be able to perform as well as modules on the specialized tasks that Evolutionary Psychologists attribute to them.

Fodor calls this the *input problem*. The input problem arises when the properties to which a module is allegedly responsive aren't things that can be directly detected by the senses but must be *inferred* from things that can be detected by the senses—properties such as *having high status* and *being a social exchange*. For, as Fodor puts it, there is no "Lurking Benevolence" that paints high-status males or social exchanges readily perceptible, proprietary colors. And most of the modules postulated by Evolutionary Psychologists deal with properties that can't be detected by the senses, but must be inferred. Since such properties must be inferred, and since information from any number of domains could be relevant in inferring them, they can't simply be *detected* by modules. So domain-specific mechanisms cannot perform their putative functions without the prior assistance of a more powerful domain-general mechanism feeding them their inputs. But the necessity of this more powerful domain-general mechanism undermines claims that domain-specific mechanisms are necessary for performing the tasks attributed to them.

## The Empirical Evidence for Modularity Reconsidered

The last section examined strictly theoretical arguments for and against massive modularity, finding none that supports it and one that poses serious problems for it. But these are just arguments. Nothing convinces quite like good empirical evidence; the proof is in the experiments. And Evolutionary Psychologists believe that there is strong empirical evidence for some of the modules they postulate. For example, Evolutionary Psychologists believe that there is currently very strong empirical evidence for the existence of language modules. As argued earlier, however, language is atypically complex, and acquiring it may require a language acquisition device. Since nothing would follow from this about the *massive* modularity of the mind, we need to examine the empirical evidence for other modules.

Apart from language modules, Evolutionary Psychologists widely tout two other postulated modules as having very strong empirical evidence in their favor. One is Cosmides' "cheater-detection module," which was discussed briefly in chapter 2, and the other is the so-called "theory-of-mind module." Let's examine each of these, beginning with the cheater-detection module.

As we saw in chapter 1, many activities in which organisms engage have associated fitness costs and benefits. Foraging for food expends energy, which exacts a fitness cost from the forager, but finding food provides the forager with a fitness benefit. From a cost-benefit standpoint, then, we should expect organisms to forage for food in ways that minimize fitness costs and maximize fitness benefits. Indeed, in general, we should expect organisms to act in ways that maximize the fitness returns on their acts. We should not expect organisms to perform costly acts that will not lead to any possible fitness benefit. Yet in many species, including ours, organisms appear to perform such acts on a routine basis. In particular, organisms can often be found performing altruistic acts. In a biological context, an *altruistic act* is an act that exacts a fitness cost from the actor while providing a fitness benefit to another individual who is unrelated to the actor. In our species, the glorious examples of altruistic acts are those whereby one individual risks death in order to save the life of another, unrelated individual. But there are numerous more mundane examples of altruistic acts, such as one individual's providing food for another. Since there should be selection against costly acts that provide no fitness benefit to the actor, from an evolutionary standpoint it is puzzling how altruism could evolve.

In a classic paper published in 1971, the evolutionary anthropologist Robert Trivers argued that altruism can evolve if it is *reciprocal*. That is, individuals in a population can evolve a propensity to perform altruistic acts if there is a strong likelihood that the recipients of altruistic acts will reciprocate by performing altruistic acts that benefit those who have benefited them. The fitness costs incurred by an individual who performs an altruistic act are thus recovered when the recipient of that individual's altruism responds in kind. But, Trivers argued, reciprocal altruism can evolve only if there are many opportunities for altruistic exchanges within the same small group of individuals. For, if individuals encountered one another only once, an individual who performed an altruistic act would incur the fitness costs of that act without any possibility of receiving the fitness benefits of a reciprocated act of altruism. In that case, there would be selection against any propensity to perform altruistic acts. If individuals encounter one another repeatedly in the same relatively small group, however, there will be many opportunities for individuals to repay acts of kindness. In that case, the likelihood of reciprocity is increased, and the likelihood of altruism is increased along with it.

But, of course, it is not sufficient simply that individuals encounter one another frequently within the same relatively small population. At the end of the day, altruism must pay. That is, in order for A to perform an altruistic act that benefits B, A must accrue a fitness benefit that outweighs the cost incurred by acting to benefit B. And, in order for altruism to pay in this way, the following conditions must be met. First, A must perform an act that benefits B at some cost to A. Second, B must reciprocate by performing some act that benefits *A* at some cost to *B*. Third, the fitness benefit to *A* of *B's* act must be greater than the fitness cost to *A* of *A's* act. Fourth, the fitness benefit to *B* of *A's* act must be greater than the fitness cost to *B* of *B's* act. When these four conditions are met, *A* and *B* both come out ahead by performing acts that benefit one another, and selection then favors their propensities to perform altruistic acts. Any interactions that have the above cost-benefit structure are an instance of what Trivers calls *reciprocal altruism* and what Cosmides calls a *social exchange.*

Once individuals evolve propensities to perform altruistic acts, however, selection can favor what Trivers calls "cheating," the failure or refusal to reciprocate an altruistic act. As Cosmides puts it, a *cheater* is thus someone who *accepts the benefit* of another's altruistic act *without paying the cost* of reciprocation. In a population of altruists, a mutant cheater would enjoy the highest fitness, since the cheater would accrue the benefits of the altruistic acts of others without ever paying the costs of reciprocation. So cheaters would begin to increase in frequency in such a population. As cheaters increased in frequency, however, the number of individuals performing altruistic acts would decrease until there were no more altruistic acts from which cheaters, or anyone else, could benefit. Thus, reciprocal altruism appears to be evolutionarily unstable. "Given this unstable character of the system, where a degree of cheating is adaptive," Trivers argues, "natural selection will rapidly favor a complex psychological system in each individual regulating both his own altruistic and cheating tendencies and his responses to these tendencies in others. As selection favors subtler forms of cheating, it will favor more acute abilities to detect cheating."[27]

In keeping with Evolutionary Psychology's claim that distinct adaptive problems select for distinct solutions, Cosmides argues that these selection pressures would have selected for a module dedicated to detecting cheaters in social exchanges. This module, she argues, should be designed to detect and process information about social exchanges using its own proprietary body of principles of reasoning that apply specifically to social exchanges. These principles of reasoning would include "algorithms that produce and operate on cost-benefit representations of exchange interactions" and "inferential procedures that make one very good at detecting cheating."[28] The latter inferential procedures would be designed to detect when someone has failed "to pay a cost to which one has obligated oneself by accepting a benefit, and without which the other person would not have agreed to provide the benefit."[29] The module that implements the inferential procedures to look for those who have accepted a benefit without paying a cost in a social exchange is what Cosmides calls the "cheater-detection module."

Cosmides and others have gathered some interesting empirical evidence to support the hypothesis that humans possess a cheater-detection module. This evidence derives entirely from experiments in which subjects perform what is known as the *Wason selection task*, so named after the psychologist Peter Wason, who devised the task. In a Wason selection task, subjects are given a so-called *conditional rule* (a rule of the form *if P, then Q*) together with four two-sided cards that contain information on one side about whether the antecedent condition of the rule (*P*) holds and on the other side about whether the consequent condition (*Q*) holds. Subjects are allowed to see only one side of the cards, and they are instructed to turn over those cards necessary in order to determine whether the conditional rule is true. For example, in one of the original Wason selection tasks, subjects were given four cards, the visible sides of which displayed *E, K, 4,* and *7.* Subjects were told that each card had a letter on one side and a number on the other, and they were instructed to turn over only those cards necessary in order to determine whether the following "conditional rule" is true: "If a card has a vowel on one side, then it has an even number on the other." Thus, the *E* and *K* cards display information about whether the antecedent (the "if" clause) of the conditional rule is true, and the *4* and *7* cards display information about whether the consequent (the "then" clause) of the conditional is true.

Drawing on elementary propositional logic, Wason reasoned that a conditional rule of the form *if P, then Q* is false only when its antecedent, *P*, is true and its consequent, *Q*, is false; in other words, *if P, then Q* is false only if *P* and *not-Q* are both true. So the "logically correct" response to the above task is to turn over the *E* card (since an odd number on the other side would prove the rule false) and the *7* card (since a vowel on the other side would prove the rule false). Since only a vowel together with an odd number would falsify the conditional rule, subjects should not turn over the *K* card or the *4* card. To put this more abstractly, the logically correct response to a Wason selection task is to turn over the *P* card (the card that makes the antecedent of the conditional rule true) and the *not-Q* card (the card that makes the consequent of the conditional rule false) in order to see whether either of those cards conjoins *P* with *not-Q*.

Cosmides and others have conducted numerous experiments with the Wason selection task, and there are three principal findings that appear to support the hypothesis that humans have a cheater-detection module. One of these findings, which is rather robust, is that the frequency with which subjects give the logically correct response to the Wason selection task appears to vary as a function of what the conditional rules are about. For example, in response to the Wason selection task described above, typically only 10 percent of subjects choose the *E* and *7* cards. Most subjects choose the *E* card alone or the *E* and *4* cards, despite the fact that no matter what is on the other side of the *4* card it cannot falsify the conditional rule "If a card has a vowel on one side, then it has an even number on the other." In contrast, most subjects choose the logically correct cards when presented with the "drinking-age problem," for which subjects are instructed to imagine being a "bouncer" in a bar, whose job is to identify and eject violators of the conditional rule "If a person is drinking beer, then they must be at least twenty-one years old." Subjects are then given the following four cards, which contain partial information about four customers: *drinking beer, drinking Coke, twenty-five years old,* and *sixteen years old.* Typically, 75 percent of subjects choose the *drinking beer* and *sixteen years old* cards, the cards that represent the *P* and *not-Q* conditions.

Many psychologists, Evolutionary Psychologists among them, conclude that these results indicate a "content effect" in the Wason selection task. For it appears that the conditional rules in both problems have the same *logical form* and that they differ only in their *content*, in what the rules are *about*. The fact that the drinking-age problem elicits a high rate of logically correct responses, while the letter-number problem elicits a very low rate of logically correct responses, appears to indicate that the content of the problems accounts for the difference in performance. There must be something about the drinking-age problem that facilitates subjects' reasoning in a way that the letter-number problem does not.

Cosmides and Tooby argue that the "content effect" is due to the fact that the drinking-age problem exemplifies a *social-contract rule*, whereas the letter-number problem does not. Cosmides and Tooby define a *social contract* as "a situation in which an individual is obligated to satisfy a requirement of some kind, usually at some cost to him- or herself, in order to be entitled to receive a benefit from another individual (or group). The requirement is imposed because its satisfaction creates a situation that benefits the party that imposed it. Thus, a well-formed social contract expresses an intercontingent situation of mutual benefit: To receive a benefit, an individual (or group) is required to provide a benefit. Usually (but not always) one incurs a cost by satisfying the requirement."[30] In the drinking-age problem, Cosmides and Tooby argue, drinking beer represents a "benefit" that is supposed to be available only to those who have satisfied the "requirement" of being over twenty-one years old. That requirement, in turn, is imposed by the social group because it benefits by restricting the drinking of alcohol to mature adults. Checking to see whether individuals who are drinking beer are at least twenty-one, Cosmides and Tooby claim, is consequently a matter of checking to see whether those who have accepted a benefit have satisfied the requirement that the social group has imposed as a precondition for receipt of that benefit. Since those who accept a benefit without paying the cost or satisfying the requirement that is a precondition for receiving that benefit are in violation of a social contract, this is actually a matter of checking for cheaters. Thus, Cosmides and Tooby conclude, subjects perform better on the drinking-age problem than on the letter-number problem because the former activates the cheater-detection module, which evolved in order to detect cheaters in social exchanges, whereas there is no module specialized to deal with problems such as the latter.

Of course, the letter-number problem is rather abstract and not the sort of problem one encounters in daily life, while the drinking-age problem is familiar to virtually all subjects, especially the college students who serve as subjects in these psychological experiments. It's possible that cognitive faculties deal more effectively with familiar than unfamiliar problems. So, perhaps subjects perform better on the drinking-age problem than on the letter-number problem simply because the former is more familiar than the latter.

To rule out this possibility, Cosmides conducted a couple of experiments with unfamiliar social-contract rules and unfamiliar non-social-contract conditionals. She reasoned that, if subjects perform better on the drinking-age problem simply because it is familiar, performance with unfamiliar conditional rules should be as low as performance on the number-letter problem. On the other hand, Cosmides argued, if humans possess a cheater-detection module, it should be activated even by unfamiliar social-contract rules, in which case performance on unfamiliar social-contract problems should be as high as on the drinking-age problem. Thus, if subjects routinely perform better on unfamiliar social-contract problems than on unfamiliar non-social-contract problems, it is evidence of a cheater-detection module, and the familiarity of the problem must not be affecting performance.

In one of these experiments, Cosmides asked subjects to imagine being members of a Polynesian island culture with strict sexual mores that prohibit sex between unmarried people. In order to readily distinguish married from unmarried men, all men in this culture get facial tattoos upon getting married. The island has a native plant called "cassava root," which is a very powerful aphrodisiac that makes the men who eat it irresistible to women. Given the prohibition on sex between unmarried people, the island's elders have thus enacted the following rule: "If a man eats cassava root, then he must have a tattoo on his face." Of course, because cassava root is such a powerful aphrodisiac, many bachelors in this culture "are tempted to cheat on this law whenever the elders are not looking."[31] Cosmides then presented subjects with four cards that read *eats cassava root, eats molo nuts, tattoo,* and *no tattoo.* Subjects were instructed that these cards described four men and that they were to turn over the necessary cards in order to determine whether any of these four men were in violation of the rule.

Cosmides paired this unfamiliar social-contract problem with the following unfamiliar non-social-contract problem. Subjects were asked to imagine being anthropologists studying an African hunter-gatherer band whose members like to eat duiker meat, the meat of a small antelope, and who like to use ostrich eggshells, which are very light, as canteens to carry water. Subjects were asked to imagine overhearing the natives frequently say, "If you eat duiker meat, then you have found an ostrich eggshell." The natives' rationale for this saying is that duikers frequently feed on ostrich eggs, so duikers and ostrich eggshells are typically found in close proximity. Cosmides then presented subjects with four cards that provided information about four locations with caches of eggs. One side of the cards described the type of eggshell found at that location, and the other side described mammal tracks found at that location. The cards read, *duiker, weasel, ostrich eggshell,* and *quail eggshell.* Subjects were instructed to turn over the necessary cards in order to determine whether the natives' conditional saying is true.

Cosmides found that 75 percent of subjects turned over the logically correct P and *not-Q* cards (*eats cassava root* and *no tattoo*) in response to the unfamiliar social-contract problem, but that only 21 percent of subjects turned over the logically correct cards (*duiker* and *quail eggshell*) in response to the unfamiliar non-social-contract problem. In a second, similar experiment, Cosmides obtained similar results, finding that 71 percent of subjects selected the logically correct P and *not-Q* cards in response to the unfamiliar social-contract problem, while only 25 percent of subjects selected the logically correct cards in response to the unfamiliar non-social-contract problem. Thus, she concluded, the "content effect" is robust; subjects reason more effectively about social-contract rules, even when they are unfamiliar, than about logically identical non-social-contract rules. In short, social-contract rules "facilitate" performance on the Wason selection task.

But why is this finding significant? Cosmides argues that, if the human mind does not consist of numerous domain-specific psychological mechanisms, then it must apply the same set of logical principles to solve all reasoning problems, regardless of what those problems happen to be about. In that case, she claims, the mind would apply precisely the same logical principles to all problems that have the same logical structure. In particular, if subjects solved Wason selection tasks by applying logical principles, they would apply the same logical principles to all logically identical tasks, in which case subjects should perform with the same degree of proficiency on all problems that are logically identical. The fact that subjects don't perform with the same degree of proficiency on all logically identical problems, Cosmides argues, indicates that they are not simply applying logical principles in solving those problems, which in turn entails that the human mind does not employ a single set of logical principles to solve all reasoning problems. In contrast, Cosmides argues, if humans have an evolved cheater-detection module, any context that presents a social contract should activate that module to look for cheaters, but contexts that do not present social contracts should not activate the module. Thus, Cosmides concludes, the robust social-contract "content effect" in performance on Wason selection tasks is evidence of a cheater-detection module.

The second finding that supports the cheater-detection hypothesis is that subjects appear to systematically select logically incorrect cards in selection tasks when those cards represent cheating, taking a benefit without paying a cost. This result was obtained in "switched-conditional" experiments conducted by Cosmides and "perspective-switching" experiments conducted by the evolutionary psychologists Gerd Gigerenzer and Klaus Hug.

In one of Cosmides' "switched-conditional" experiments, subjects were given precisely the same background information and instructions that they were given in the experiment described above. The only difference was that the conditionals that subjects were asked to evaluate were switched around. Thus, in the "switched" cassava-root problem, subjects were asked to select those cards necessary to discover any violations of the rule "If a man has a tattoo on his face, then he eats cassava root." And, in the "switched" duiker-meat problem, subjects were asked to select those cards necessary to determine whether "If you have found an ostrich eggshell, then you eat duiker meat" is true.

Cosmides argued that the logically correct responses to these problems are to select the $P$ and *not-Q* cards. But, she claimed, if the "switched" social-contract conditional activates a cheater-detection module, it should cause subjects to select the *not-P* and Q cards (*no tattoo* and *eats cassava root*), since those cards represent cheating, accepting a benefit without meeting the appropriate requirement. In this case, unlike the "unswitched" problem, the "logically correct" solution differs from the detection of a cheater. Thus, if subjects choose the *not-P* and Q cards, Cosmides argued, it can't be due to facilitated effectiveness in applying logical rules, but must be due to the fact that subjects are sensitive to the conditions that represent cheating, regardless of the logical form of the conditional in which those conditions appear. But, if this is true, Cosmides argued, we should also expect subjects *not* to choose the *not-P* and Q cards in the "switched" non-social-contract problem, because those cards are neither logically correct nor representative of cheating.

Interestingly, the results conformed to Cosmides' predictions. Sixty-seven percent of subjects chose the "logically incorrect" *not-P* and Q cards in response to the "switched" social-contract problem, whereas only 4 percent chose the *not-P* and Q cards in response to the "switched" non-social-contract problem. In a second "switched-conditional" experiment, she obtained similar results, finding that 75 percent of subjects selected the *not-P* and Q cards in response to the "switched" social-contract problem, whereas no subjects selected the *not-P* and Q cards in response to the "switched" non-social-contract problem.

Gigerenzer and Hug obtained results that seem to lend further support to Cosmides' argument. Gigerenzer and Hug reasoned that, if we possess a cheater-detection module, it should be activated by situations that present the possibility of *being cheated*, but not by situations that present the possibility of cheating others. For it is the possibility of being cheated in a social contract that presents an individual with potential fitness costs. Many social contracts, however, involve a *bilateral cheating option*. That is, in many social contracts each party to the contract has the option of cheating the other. In such cases, what counts as being cheated depends on the *perspective* that a party to the social contract occupies. Given this fact, Gigerenzer and Hug argued, if we possess a cheater-detection module, it should be sensitive to *perspective switching* on social-contract rules. That is, if we possess a cheater-detection module, the cards a subject selects in a Wason selection task involving a social-contract rule with a bilateral cheating option should be a function of which perspective on the social-contract rule (which role in the social contract) the subject occupies.

To test this hypothesis, Gigerenzer and Hug presented subjects with the following "day off" rule: "If an employee works on the weekend, then that person gets a day off during the week." This rule was presented with two different background stories, one that cued the subject into the perspective of the employee, and one that cued the subject into the perspective of the employer. "The employee version stated that working on the weekend is a benefit for the employer, because the firm can make use of its machines and be more flexible. Working on the weekend, on the other hand, is a cost for the employee. The context story was about an employee who had never worked on the weekend before, but who is considering working on Saturdays from time to time, since having a day off during the week is a benefit that outweighs the costs of working on Saturday. There are rumours that the rule has been violated before. The subjects' task was to check information about four colleagues to see whether the rule has been violated before."[32] In the employer version, subjects were given the same rationale, but were cued into the perspective of the employer by being told to check whether any of four employees had violated the rule before. The four cards giving information about the four employees in both tasks displayed *worked on the weekend, did not work on the weekend, did get a day off*, and *did not get a day off.*

Gigerenzer and Hug argued that the application of domain-general logical principles should lead to selecting the *P* and *not-Q* cards (*worked on the weekend* and *did not get a day off*) regardless of a subject's perspective on the conditional rule. On the other hand, a cheater-detection module should lead subjects to select whichever pair of cards represents being cheated from the perspective they occupy. Thus, subjects cued into the perspective of the employee should select the *P* and *not-Q* cards (*worked on the weekend* and *did not get a day off*), since they represent the conditions under which an employee was cheated by the employer. In contrast, subjects cued into the perspective of the employer should select the *not-P* and *Q* cards (*did not work on the weekend* and *did get a day off*), since they represent the conditions under which the employer was cheated by an employee. And, indeed, Gigerenzer and Hug found that 75 percent of the subjects cued into the perspective of the employee chose the *P* and *not-Q* cards and that 61 percent of the subjects cued into the perspective of the employer chose the *not-P* and *Q* cards. Gigerenzer and Hug conclude that these results clearly provide evidence of a cheater-detection mechanism.

The third finding that is taken as evidence of a cheater-detection module was obtained in an experiment conducted by the Evolutionary Psychologist Lawrence Fiddick along with Cosmides and Tooby. In this experiment, subjects were all presented with the following scenario: "You are a South American farmer. At the end of the harvest you find you have more potatoes than you need so you pack up some of them and travel to the neighboring village. When you get to the village four different people approach you, and though you don't speak the same dialect, you recognize that each of them is telling you. . . ."[33] At this point, half the subjects were presented with the following "conditional version" of the problem: "If you give me some potatoes, then I will give you some corn." The other half of the subjects were presented with the following "want version" of the problem: "'I want some potatoes.' You, in turn, know a little bit of their dialect, and tell them 'I want some corn.'" Then all subjects were given the same four cards, each providing information about one of the four people, and were instructed to turn over only those cards necessary in order to determine whether any of the four people had cheated "you." The four cards read *you gave this person potatoes, you gave this person nothing, this person gave you corn*, and *this person gave you nothing*.

Fiddick, Cosmides, and Tooby argued that, if subjects apply domain-general logical principles in solving these problems, there should be a significant difference in the frequency with which subjects choose the *P* and *not-Q* cards in the two versions of the problem. Of course, in the "conditional version," subjects should select the *P* and *not-Q* cards (*you gave this person potatoes* and *this person gave you nothing*), since they represent the logically correct solution to the problem. But, they argued, since there is no logical connective connecting the statements "I want some potatoes" and "I want some corn" in the "want version" of the problem, there is nothing in the "want version" to which logical principles can apply. As a result, card selection in the "want version" should be random. Indeed, since there are sixteen possible ways of selecting cards in response to the problem, the selection of both *you gave this person potatoes* and *this person gave you nothing* shouldn't be any more likely than any of the other fifteen possible responses. Thus, they concluded, if subjects apply domain-general logical principles in the selection task, vastly more subjects should choose the *P* and *not-Q* cards (*you gave this person potatoes* and *this person gave you nothing*) in the "conditional version" than in the "want version."

Interestingly, Fiddick, Cosmides, and Tooby found that 67 percent of subjects chose the *P* and *not-Q* cards in response to the "conditional version" of the problem and that 50 percent chose the same cards in response to the "want version" of the problem. Although this can't be accounted for by the hypothesis that people employ domain-general logical principles in reasoning about social contracts, they claimed, these results are precisely what we should expect if humans have an evolved cheater-detection module. For a cheater-detection module would represent both scenarios as social exchanges, and consequently in both scenarios it would represent *you gave this person potatoes* and *this person gave you nothing* as a situation in which "you" are being cheated. Thus, they concluded, the fact that the *P* and *not-Q* response rate is nearly as high in the "want version" of the selection task as in the "conditional version" of the task is strong evidence of the existence of a cheater-detection module.

To summarize the discussion so far, there are three principal findings, each deriving from experiments with the Wason selection task, that are taken to provide evidence of a cheater-detection module. First, there appears to be a robust "content effect." Subjects appear to reason more effectively about social contracts than about non-social-contract facts. Second, the fact that subjects choose the "logically incorrect" cards in response to "switched" conditionals and "switched perspectives" on conditionals appears to indicate that subjects ignore the logical properties of the conditionals they're evaluating and focus exclusively on whether someone is receiving a benefit without paying the corresponding cost. Third, the fact that subjects choose the same cards in response to a "want version" of a social-contract problem (which contains no logical connectives) as they choose in response to a "conditional version" of the same problem appears to show that subjects do not respond to the logical features of the problem, but merely focus on whether someone has taken a benefit from them without paying to them the cost for receipt of that benefit.

I will now argue that each of these findings has been vastly *overinterpreted* and that none provides convincing evidence of a cheater-detection module. Before I turn to a detailed examination of these experimental results, however, a broader issue concerning the relation between the experimental findings and the theoretical derivation of the cheater-detection hypothesis requires comment.

Cosmides derives the hypothesis of a cheater-detection module from Trivers's argument that reciprocal altruism is evolutionarily unstable unless parties to reciprocal exchanges of benefits have the ability to detect when someone is taking a benefit from them without providing them a benefit in turn. Reciprocal altruism concerns what Cosmides calls *social exchanges*, which occur when two individuals perform acts that *benefit one another at a cost to each*. Social exchanges are thus relations between two individuals, and cheating in a social exchange involves benefiting from an act performed by another individual without performing an act that benefits that individual. Virtually all of the experimental results that purportedly provide evidence of a cheater-detection module, however, derive from selection tasks involving what Cosmides and Tooby call *social contracts*, which is a much broader class of phenomena than the class of social exchanges. For a social contract, as Cosmides and Tooby define it, is "a situation in which an individual is obligated to satisfy a requirement of some kind, usually at some cost to him- or herself, in order to be entitled to receive a benefit from another individual (*or group*)."[34] Social contracts thus include situations in which an individual must *satisfy a requirement* in order to *receive a benefit from society*. Indeed, this is the kind of situation embodied in the drinking-age problem and the cassava-root problem. In the drinking-age problem, individuals must satisfy the requirement of being at least twenty-one years of age before society bestows the benefit of being able to drink beer, while in the cassava-root problem males must be married (as signified by a facial tattoo) before society bestows the benefit of being able to eat cassava root. Social contracts are thus relations between individuals and society, in which society makes the satisfaction of a particular requirement a precondition for the receipt of a certain benefit. Cheating on a social contract thus involves taking a benefit from society without satisfying the requirement that is a precondition for receipt of that benefit.

There is, therefore, a disconnect between the *theoretical support* for the cheater-detection module and the *experimental results* that purportedly provide evidence of its existence. The theory behind the cheater-detection module should lead us to expect a mechanism that is specialized in detecting cheaters *in the domain of social exchanges*. But the experimental results that purportedly support the existence of a cheater-detection module involve detecting cheaters *in the domain of social contracts*. This poses the following dilemma for Evolutionary Psychology's claim that there is strong empirical evidence of an evolved cheater-detection module. On the one hand, even if the experimental results provide evidence of a module for detecting cheaters in social contracts, there is no theoretical support for predicting that humans have an evolved module that specializes in social contracts. The reason is that, although we have a well-developed theoretical understanding of how social exchanges evolved, we have no comparable theoretical understanding of how social contracts evolved (and Evolutionary Psychologists offer no theory about the evolution of social contracts). We consequently have no well-developed theoretical basis for any hypotheses regarding the psychological mechanisms, if any, that have evolved to deal with social contracts. On the other hand, even if we have good theoretical reasons to expect that humans have an evolved psychological ability to detect cheaters in social exchanges, the experimental results obtained to date provide no evidence of a mechanism that is specific to the domain of social exchanges. The reason is that all the evidence pertains to social contracts, and the domain of social contracts is far broader than the domain of social exchanges. So there is no evidence to date of the appropriate level of domain specificity of psychological functioning. In sum, theory and evidence regarding the cheater-detection module fail to match up appropriately.

This is a "big-picture problem" with Evolutionary Psychology's claim to have demonstrated the existence of a cheater-detection module, but there are devils in the details as well. None of the three experimental findings demonstrates the operation of a cheater-detection module. Indeed, all of the findings are compatible with the operation of a mind that applies the same set of logical principles to solve problems across a multitude of problem domains. To see why, let's examine each of the experimental findings that purportedly provide evidence of a cheater-detection module.

The first of those findings is the alleged "content effect" in performance on Wason selection tasks. I will argue that there is no genuine "content effect," but that differential performance on selection tasks is due to a difference in the *logical properties* of the tasks. Subjects apply different logical principles in different types of task, and it is the facility with which they apply these principles that accounts for the difference in performance. Thus, the results are fully compatible with the operation of a mind that applies the same set of logical principles to solve reasoning problems. Consequently, the results don't demonstrate that there is a psychological mechanism that is dedicated to reasoning about social contracts.

The idea that there is a "content effect" in performance on Wason selection tasks presupposes that so-called social-contract conditional rules and non-social-contract conditionals have the same logical form and differ only in their content. This presupposition is occasionally made explicit. For example, Fiddick, Cosmides, and Tooby say that the conditionals in Wason selection tasks always possess the same "logical structure" into which different kinds of "contents" can be substituted.[35] Indeed, they go so far as to say that identical "discourse structures"—different natural-language sentences with the same surface grammar—all possess the same "logical form."[36] Under this presupposition, the sentence "If a card has a vowel on one side, then it has an even number on the other" has the same logical properties as the sentence "If you are under the age of twenty-one, then you must not drink alcohol." Given the presupposition that these sentences have the same logical form, any difference in the way that subjects respond to them gets interpreted as due to a difference in what the sentences are about.

But this presupposition is false. Not all conditionals are alike. Indeed, it is a commonplace among most philosophers of logic that there are several different kinds of conditional. Two of these are important for present purposes, *indicative conditionals* and *deontic conditionals*. Indicative conditionals are formed by making the truth of one fact-stating sentence, $Q$, conditional upon the truth of another fact-stating sentence, $P$. The indicative conditional *if P, then Q* then makes a conditional assertion, another statement that purports to be true. In short, indicative conditionals are used to make *assertions of fact*. The conditional sentence "If a card has a vowel on one side, then it has an even number on the other" is an example of an indicative conditional. In contrast, deontic conditionals are used to *impose obligations*. Rather than making the truth of one statement conditional upon the truth of another, they make an obligation conditional upon the truth of a fact-stating sentence. The conditional sentence "If you are under the age of twenty-one, then you must not drink alcohol" is an example of a deontic conditional. In the Wason selection tasks we've discussed, all of the conditionals that elicited a low frequency of $P$ and *not*-$Q$ selections are indicative conditionals, whereas the conditionals that elicited a high frequency of $P$ and *not*-$Q$ selections are deontic. Indeed, all of the so-called social-contract rules are deontic conditionals, although the class of deontic conditionals is broader than the class of so-called social-contract rules that are used in Evolutionary Psychologists' experiments.

Indicative conditionals and deontic conditionals actually have different logical properties, and the difference in their logical properties affects the logic of the Wason selection tasks in which the two types of conditional are embedded. This can be seen by comparing the problems in Cosmides' first experiment. In the duiker-meat problem, subjects are asked *to evaluate the truth* of the conditional "If you eat duiker meat, then you have found an ostrich eggshell." The so-called *not*-$Q$ card reads *quail eggshell*, which is elliptical for "you have found a quail eggshell," which (in the context of the background story) entails "it is not the case that you have found an ostrich eggshell." Thus, the "quail eggshell" card is elliptical for the *negation* of the consequent of the conditional whose truth the subjects are to evaluate. In contrast, in the cassava-root problem, subjects are asked *to determine whether any men are violating the rule* "If a man eats cassava root, then he must have a tattoo on his face." The so-called *not*-$Q$ card in this problem reads *no tattoo*. This card, however, does not represent the negation of the consequent clause of the conditional rule. There are two ways in which a negation can be inserted into the consequent clause of the rule. We can either negate it by saying, "it is not the case that he must have a tattoo on his face," which removes the obligation to have a facial tattoo, or we can insert a negation by saying, "he must not have a tattoo on his face," which imposes an obligation to *not have* a facial tattoo. The *no tattoo* card, however, corresponds to neither of these. Rather, the *no tattoo* card is simply elliptical for "this man has no facial tattoo." Consequently, the *logic* of the cassava-root problem, which contains a deontic conditional, differs from the *logic* of the duiker-meat problem, which contains an indicative conditional.

Other commentators have made roughly the same point in a different way. For example, the evolutionary anthropologists Dan Sperber, Francesco Cara, and Vittorio Girotto point out that, in the indicative-conditional versions of the Wason selection task, "subjects are asked to reason *about* the rule," to determine whether it is true, whereas "in true deontic versions they are asked to reason *from* a rule given as axiomatic," to determine whether someone is in conformance with the rule.[37] What Sperber, Cara, and Girotto fail to drive home, however, is that the reason that the logic of the tasks differ in this way is that the conditionals embedded in the tasks differ in their logical properties.

But, if deontic conditionals have a different logical form than indicative conditionals, what is it? For it certainly looks like the logical form of "If you are under the age of twenty-one, then you must not drink alcohol" is *if P, then Q*. Fodor has an interesting suggestion, which I believe is correct. Fodor argues that, in an important sense, deontic conditionals aren't true conditionals at all. Rather, Fodor argues, deontic conditionals categorically impose obligations (in their Q parts), while also indicating on whom the obligations fall (in their P parts). For example, on Fodor's analysis, the above conditional actually has the form "Thou shalt not drink alcohol, and this prohibition falls on those under the age of twenty-one." An equivalent way of viewing this is to see the *P* part of deontic conditionals as negatively indicating a class of individuals who are *exempted* from the obligation imposed in the Q part. In this equivalent formulation, the above deontic conditional actually asserts "Thou shalt not drink alcohol—unless you happen to be at least twenty-one." On Fodor's analysis, then, all deontic conditionals have the logical form of Old Testament commandments. For, in the Old Testament, God's commandment "Thou shalt not kill" actually had the form "Thou shalt not kill—unless, of course, I command you to make a sacrifice of your son or to smite all the inhabitants of Jericho."

But how does this different logic account for the fact that subjects perform better on deontic versions of the selection task than on indicative versions? The reason, Fodor argues, is that, since deontic conditionals actually require Q (under the condition that P), attention is immediately drawn to the *not-Q* case. For example, in the drinking-age problem, the deontic conditional actually prohibits drinking alcohol (under the condition that individuals are under twenty-one), so subjects immediately begin looking for those who are drinking alcohol, since they violate the prohibition. Subjects then examine the violators in order to determine whether they are among those on whom the prohibition against drinking alcohol actually falls. Thus, the increase in the frequency with which so-called *not-Q* cards are selected in the deontic versions of Wason selection tasks is due to the fact that the *not-Q* cards represent direct violations of the obligations that are categorically imposed by the deontic rules.

In an effort to refute Fodor, the psychologist Philip Beaman conducted Wason selection tasks in which subjects were presented with "social-contract rules" formulated in the usual way and also reworded in accordance with Fodor's analysis. If Fodor's analysis is right, Beaman argued, making the logical form of the deontic conditionals even more perspicuous in accordance with Fodor's analysis should facilitate performance on "social-contract" selection tasks even more. Rather than refuting Fodor's analysis, however, Beaman found that rewording deontic conditionals in accordance with Fodor's analysis did, indeed, facilitate performance. Whereas approximately 67 percent of subjects selected the P and *not-Q* cards in response to the usually formulated "social-contract rule," a full 90 percent of subjects selected those cards in response to the Fodorized rule. This indicates that Fodor's analysis has tapped the logic that subjects are responding to in "social-contract" versions of the Wason selection task and that, when that logic is made fully explicit, they perform even better.

Thus, the results from the Wason selection tasks don't demonstrate a "content effect" according to which subjects are able to reason more effectively about social contracts than about non-social-contract facts. Rather, the results demonstrate a *logic effect*, according to which subjects grasp the different logical properties of indicative and deontic conditionals, and then select the so-called *not-Q* cards with greater frequency in response to the latter because the appropriateness of that response is made more perspicuous by the *logical form* of deontic conditionals.

But doesn't Evolutionary Psychology still win, even if there isn't a cheater-detection module per se? For doesn't the greater facility with deontic reasoning at least show that there is a domain-specific mechanism devoted to deontic reasoning, rather than a domain-general mind that applies the same set of logical principles in solving a variety of problems? In short, no. Conjunctions, statements of the form *P and Q*, have a different logical form than indicative conditionals, and subjects might reason more effectively about conjunctions than indicative conditionals. But it wouldn't follow that there is a mechanism that is specific to the domain of conjunctions. Standard propositional logic consists of a single set of principles for reasoning about both conjunctions and (material) conditionals, and some principles in that set apply to conjunctions while others apply to conditionals. For example, the inference rule *simplification* allows inferring Q from the conjunction *P and Q*, and the inference rule *modus ponens* allows inferring Q from P together with the conditional *if P, then Q*. Simplification applies only to conjunctions and modus ponens applies only to conditionals. Indeed, one could say that simplification is a domain-specific inference rule (applying only to conjunctions) and that modus ponens is a domain-specific inference rule (applying only to conditionals). Despite that, both rules are elements of the *same set* of inference rules that apply to *all truth-functional inferences*. And, if people apply logical principles in making truth-functional inferences, their mental logics undoubtedly are similar in consisting of a single set of inference rules, some of which apply to sentences of one logical type and others of which apply to sentences of another logical type, but the whole set of which applies to *all* truth-functional inferences. There needn't be a special domain-specific mechanism to apply the appropriate inference rules to each type of statement with its own logical form.

Cosmides could respond to the above argument by objecting that the principles of propositional logic draw no distinction between indicative conditionals and deontic conditionals (for example, that modus ponens applies to both) and that, consequently, difference in performance on selection tasks involving the two types of conditional must be due to a "content effect." But this objection would simply betray an ignorance of logic. Although standard propositional logic involves but a single type of conditional, standard propositional logic is only one of many logical systems, and it is the weakest of all. For standard propositional logic also can't represent the difference between "All rectangles are not squares" and "Not all rectangles are squares." But first-order predicate logic can. And as logical systems become more powerful and more complex (including modal and deontic logics), they become capable of representing differences between logically distinct types of conditional. If people solve reasoning problems by applying a single set of logical principles, their mental logics are undoubtedly far more complex than standard propositional logic. Indeed, mental logic would assuredly be equipped with the means of representing all logical types of conditional and with principles for reasoning about all those logically distinct conditionals. Thus, we may be equipped with a single set of logical principles for reasoning about problems such as those embodied in Wason selection tasks. Some of these logical principles would apply to deontic conditionals, and others would apply to indicative conditionals. The fact that we might reason more effectively about deontic conditionals in certain highly regimented task situations doesn't show that we must have a separate psychological mechanism dedicated to those reasoning tasks.

Some commentators on Evolutionary Psychology have claimed that all that Evolutionary Psychologists mean by speaking of distinct psychological "mechanisms" for distinct problem domains is that, in solving problems in certain types of problem domain, the mind applies principles that are specific to the problem domain in question. But this takes the *mechanism* out of talk of psychological mechanisms and reduces domain specificity to a property of *reasoning principles*, rather than a structural property of the mind. In addition, it makes talk of domain specificity trivially true, for all principles of reasoning are domain specific in this sense. Modus ponens is specific to the domain of conditionals, and simplification is specific to the domain of conjunctions. For that matter, statements about cows are specific to the domain of cows. It is *trivially true* of all statements and principles that they are specific to the domain that they are about, because it is in the nature of symbolism in general that it *represents* what it is about to the exclusion of everything else. In this sense, *of course* applying modus ponens to reasoning about conditionals is domain-specific reasoning. But nothing follows from this trivial fact about the structure of the mind. And Evolutionary Psychologists claim that their empirical findings reveal to us something about the evolved *structure* of the mind, not just something trivially true about the nature of all symbolic representation.

But there is an additional reason why there is no genuine "content effect" in Wason selection tasks. I've discussed only indicative and deontic conditionals, but most philosophers of logic believe that there are other types of conditional, such as counterfactuals (subjunctives) and causal conditionals, each with its own unique logical properties. For example, some conditionals are logically entailed by the negations of their antecedents, whereas others are not. Similarly, the negations of some conditionals logically entail their antecedents, whereas the negations of other conditionals (counterfactuals) do not logically entail their antecedents. In short, different types of conditional play different types of role in logical inference. Given the fact that there are several different types of conditional, the act of comprehension of a conditional sentence of a natural language requires the evaluation of semantic and contextual information in order to determine the logical type of the conditional sentence. In other words, in comprehending a natural-language conditional, language-comprehension mechanisms take the natural-language conditional sentence as input and produce a representation of the logical form of that sentence as output. The representation of the logical form of the sentence then features in mental operations regarding that sentence (drawing inferences, solving problems, and so on). If semantic and contextual information is insufficient to determine a unique representation of the logical form of the conditional sentence, then logical reasoning about that natural-language conditional is hampered.

All of the indicative conditionals in the experiments we've discussed (including those in Cosmides' unfamiliar non-social-contract problems) embody *arbitrary* relations between the antecedent condition and the consequent condition. In the letter-number problem, for example, there is an arbitrarily stipulated connection between vowels and even numbers. In Cosmides' duiker-meat problem, there is an arbitrarily stipulated connection between eating duiker meat and having found an ostrich eggshell. One important feature of *real-life* conditionals is that they do not embody arbitrary relations between their antecedent and consequent conditions. When we say, "If she missed the flight, then she won't be here for dinner," there is a natural connection, which we all comprehend, between the antecedent condition and the consequent condition. When we say, "If you're late for work one more time, then you'll be fired," there is a conventional connection between being late for work and being fired. Indeed, in *real life* we always trade in conditionals in which there is some kind of natural or conventional connection between the antecedent and consequent conditions. The indicative conditionals in the Wason selection tasks we've discussed, however, don't conform to this real-life model for natural-language conditional sentences.

Given this fact, one distinct possibility is that few subjects choose the "logically correct" *P* and *not-Q* cards in response to Wason selection tasks with indicative conditionals because these conditionals embody an arbitrary connection between antecedent and consequent conditions, and the background stories in which the conditionals are embedded provide insufficient contextual information to make the connection appear sensible. In other words, the semantic and contextual information on which subjects normally rely in order to represent the unique logical type of a natural-language conditional sentence is lacking in Wason selection tasks involving arbitrary indicative conditionals. Because that information is lacking, subjects don't know which logical type the conditional sentence is an instance of, and they are consequently unable to perform appropriate logical tasks with respect to the conditional. In short, the reason subjects perform poorly in Wason selection tasks involving arbitrary indicative conditionals is that most subjects don't fully comprehend the conditionals in those tasks. If this is the case, the low frequency with which the $P$ and $not$-$Q$ cards are chosen together is not really due to a difference in the facility with which subjects apply deontic logical principles and indicative logical principles, but is due to the fact that most subjects don't recognize the arbitrary conditionals as ones to which the logical principles governing indicative conditionals apply, whereas they do recognize the "social-contract rules" as conditionals to which deontic logical principles apply.

Under this hypothesis, the conditional in the letter-number problem is actually a *degraded cognitive stimulus*. A degraded stimulus is a stimulus that falls under a concept possessed by a subject, but appears to the subject in a "degraded" form, a form in which some of its paradigmatic features are missing. For example, an array of dots configured to form the letter $H$, but hidden inside a busy picture, is a degraded stimulus. An interesting fact of cognitive psychology is that subjects are often able to correctly identify stimuli even when they are severely degraded. But often subjects can't identify degraded stimuli, for it's like trying to identify the person walking toward you in the fog. Indicative conditionals that embody arbitrary connections between antecedent and consequent conditions, and that are presented within very sketchy and artificial background stories, do not appear with a sufficient number of the informational properties on which subjects normally rely in representing the logical type of a conditional utterance. Such conditionals are thus *cognitively degraded*, in that they don't possess sufficient properties to facilitate the cognitive processing that results in accurate representation of logical form. And that's why few subjects choose the $P$ and $not$-$Q$ cards in tasks involving those conditionals. In contrast, the deontic selection tasks are comparatively clear. They are all clearly cases in which an obligation is imposed, and the conditionals are comparatively clear in how they are imposing those obligations. Thus, for the reasons

Fodor suggests, subjects are able to accurately focus in on the *P* and *not-Q* cards in those tasks.

If this hypothesis is correct, then if subjects were presented with more natural indicative conditionals, embedded within background stories that made very perspicuous the connection between antecedent and consequent conditions, they would select the *P* and *not-Q* cards with as high a frequency as they're selected in deontic selection tasks. Interestingly, Sperber, Cara, and Girotto have conducted some experiments that confirm this prediction.

Sperber, Cara, and Girotto conducted three experiments in which some subjects were presented with the standard Wason selection tasks involving conditionals with arbitrary connections between antecedent and consequent conditions, and other subjects were presented with more natural indicative conditionals. The more natural conditionals were presented in what they called "relevance conditions," background stories that served to make perspicuous the logic of the conditionals being presented. In each of the experiments, the "relevance conditions" conformed to the following pattern. In the background story, either a character in the scenario or the experimenter asserted that there are cases of *P and not-Q*. Another character in the scenario then denied this assertion by claiming, *"If P, then Q."* Subjects were then asked to turn over the necessary cards in order to evaluate the truth of *if P, then Q*. The interesting feature of all of the "relevance conditions" is that they present *if P, then Q* as being the *contradictory* of *P and not-Q*. This serves to make it very clear that the logic of the conditional is that of an indicative, which is falsified by conjunctions of *P* with *not-Q*.

In their first experiment in this vein, they presented some subjects with the standard letter-number problem, which represented the "nonrelevance condition." The other subjects were presented a problem in a "relevance condition." This problem involved a scenario in which a religious leader is suspected of trying to create an elite group of virgin mothers. The religious leader dismisses the suspicion by asserting, "If a woman has a child, she has had sex." Subjects were then given four cards that read *children: yes, children: no, sex: yes,* and *sex: no.* They were instructed that these cards described four women in the religious group and that they were to determine whether the religious leader's claim is true. In this particular experiment, Sperber, Cara, and Girotto found that 78 percent of subjects chose the *P* and *not-Q* cards (*children: yes* and *sex: no*), which is as high as the frequency normally obtained in deontic selection tasks. In contrast, only 26 percent of subjects chose the *P* and *not-Q* cards in the "nonrelevance" letter-number problem. In the two other, similar experiments, they obtained similar results. In the "relevance conditions," 65 percent of subjects chose the P and *not-Q* cards in the first of these experiments and 70 percent chose them in the second. In contrast, in the "nonrelevance conditions," only 16 percent of subjects chose the P and *not-Q* cards in the first experiment and only 25 percent chose them in the second.

There are a few interesting features of these experiments. First, the conditional "If a woman has a child, she has had sex" expresses a natural connection between the antecedent and consequent conditions, which contrasts with the arbitrary connection in the letter-number problem. This in itself should facilitate comprehension of the former compared to the latter. The "relevance-condition" conditionals in the other two experiments were similarly natural in comparison with the "non-relevance-condition" conditionals. Second, the "relevance condition" stories rubbed subjects' noses in the logical properties of the conditionals whose truth they were asked to evaluate, since they clearly presented *if P, then Q* as the contradictory of *P and not-Q*. Thus, when background information made the logical properties of the indicatives clear, subjects reasoned as effectively about them as about deontic conditionals. Third, rather than pairing an arbitrary indicative conditional with a deontic conditional, as did Evolutionary Psychologists' experiments, each experiment paired an arbitrary indicative conditional with a natural indicative conditional. The difference in results thus demonstrates that performance with indicatives can be as high as performance with deontic conditionals, provided that the indicatives are natural. Since performance with indicatives was as high as performance with deontic conditionals, the results also demonstrate that the so-called "content effect" obtained in Evolutionary Psychologists' selection tasks is an artifact of pairing deontic conditionals with arbitrary indicative conditionals. If deontic conditionals were paired with natural indicatives, the difference in performance on the two types of task would disappear.

Thus, the performance differentials found in Wason selection tasks do not represent a "content effect," for at least two reasons. First, the selection tasks that elicit high performance involve deontic conditionals, whereas the selection tasks that elicit low performance involve indicatives. Evolutionary Psychologists argue that, if subjects solve selection tasks by applying a single set of logical principles, they would have to apply *the same logical principles* to both types of problem; and, since performance on different problems differs, subjects must not be solving the problems by applying logical principles. But the fact that deontic and indicative conditionals differ in their logical form means that subjects would apply different logical principles in solving problems involving the different types of conditional, just as subjects would apply different logical principles in solving problems involving conjunctions than in problems involving conditionals. So, differential performance on different types of selection task simply doesn't entail that subjects are not solving those tasks by applying logical principles; it just means that they are applying different logical principles in different types of task. Second, the fact that a logic effect was obtained in early experiments was largely an artifact of pairing *arbitrary* indicative conditionals with deontic conditionals. When subjects are given selection tasks with natural, rather than artificial, indicatives, they are just as effective in applying logical principles to solve those selection tasks as when they are presented with deontic conditionals. Thus, since there is no genuine content effect, the "content effect" doesn't provide evidence of a domain-specific mechanism dedicated to reasoning about cheating in social exchanges and social contracts. Indeed, the experimental results are fully compatible with the operation of a domain-general mind that applies a single set of logical principles to solve problems.

The second finding that purportedly provides evidence of a cheater-detection mechanism is that subjects will select the "logically incorrect" cards in social-contract selection tasks when those cards clearly represent cheating. Since the "logically incorrect" solutions correspond to the detection of cheating, Evolutionary Psychologists argue, subjects must simply be looking for cheating in social-contract situations, rather than applying logical principles to solve the problems. This conclusion, however, rests on the assumption that a small change in the wording of the selection tasks changes subjects' representations of the logical properties of the tasks. In Cosmides' "switched-conditional" experiments, the background stories and the instructions were unchanged. The only difference was that Cosmides changed the order of the antecedent and consequent conditions in the conditional—for example, asking subjects to determine whether any of four men violated the rule "If a man has a tattoo on his face, then he eats cassava root." Cosmides argued that "switching" the conditional changes the "logically correct" solution to the problem, so that in the "switched" problem the *P* and *not-Q* cards (which were the *not-P* and *Q* cards in the "unswitched" problem) are "logically correct."

But simply "switching" the conditional is insufficient to change how subjects *represent* the *logic* of the problem. As I mentioned above, comprehension of conditionals (and other statements, for that matter) involves taking a natural-language sentence as input and producing a mental representation of the logical form of the sentence as output. It is the mental representation of logical form that subsequently plays a role in any inferences a subject draws regarding the statement made by the natural-language sentence. Thus, what determines subjects' inferential processes in selection tasks are the *mental representations* of the logical forms of the conditionals provided by experimenters, not the written forms of those conditionals. Cosmides assumes that "switching" the natural-language conditional will change the logic to which subjects respond in solving the selection tasks. But there are problems with this assumption.

First, note that the "switched" conditional isn't truly a simple switching around of the antecedent and consequent conditions. The conditional from the "unswitched" cassava-root problem is "If a man eats cassava root, then he must have a tattoo on his face." Cosmides' "switched" conditional is "If a man has a tattoo on his face, then he eats cassava root." The "switched" conditional no longer expresses an obligation, and in particular it no longer attaches an obligation to having a facial tattoo. This is because a true "switching" of the conditional would be nonsense. As even Cosmides admits, "a switched version of the cassava root rule would read 'If a man *must* have a tattoo on his face, then he eats cassava root', however, the modal 'must' was left out of the 'If' clause in the switched version because it violates standard English usage."[38] But the obligating "must" is also not attached to eating cassava root in the "switched" version. So, subjects were presented with a background story that clearly obligates eaters of cassava root to having facial tattoos, but were then asked to evaluate compliance to a conditional rule that didn't make sense in the context of that story.

Under such circumstances, the natural thing for subjects to do is to process the conditional *together with the background information* in a way that produces a representation of the logical form of the conditional that makes sense given the background information. Indeed, this is what we all do, every day, when we interpret the utterances of others. Consequently, in the "switched" cassava root problem, since subjects are given a background story that makes having a facial tattoo obligatory for those eating cassava root, they "normalize" the "switched" conditional to one that expresses that obligation—namely, the "unswitched" conditional of the original cassava root problem. Given that subjects represent the *logic* of both the "switched" and "unswitched" conditionals the same way, the "logically correct" solution to both problems is to select the "eats cassava root" and "no tattoo" cards. Thus, subjects aren't actually selecting the "logically incorrect" cards in the "switched" version; they are selecting the "logically correct" cards relative to their representation of the (deontic) logical form of the conditional. Consequently, the results of Cosmides' "switched-conditional" experiments don't show that subjects ignore logic in favor of a focus on cheating. Subjects are simply applying logic in a way that makes sense in the context of the problem.

But isn't this a bit of a stretch by way of explaining away results that clearly seem to favor Cosmides' hypothesis? Hardly. What is actually a stretch is the presupposition that underlies Evolutionary Psychologists' interpretation of these experimental results. That presupposition is that, when subjects interpret the logical form of a given rule, "the rule must be assigned a logical form in accordance with the discourse structure and the rules of logic alone."[39] In other words, the presupposition maintains that representations of the logical form of utterances is a simple matter of directly mapping the surface grammar ("discourse structure") of an utterance onto a logical form. But this presupposition is falsified numerous times a day by each of us in interpreting the utterances of others. For example, your house burns down and a friend says to you, "All is not lost; you still have your family." According to the surface grammar of the utterance "all is not lost," the logical form is "for every $x$, $x$ is not lost." This entails that your house was not lost. But not a single one among us interprets the utterance as entailing that. Not a single one among us would berate the friend for stupidly implying that our house hadn't just been lost in a fire. Rather, we process the utterance as having the logical form "it is not the case that, for every $x$, $x$ is lost," which is logically equivalent to "for some $x$, $x$ is not lost." In other words, and more colloquially, we all *always* interpret "all is not lost" as meaning "not all is lost." The logical form that we interpret the utterance as having is not at all the form that its surface grammar indicates it has.

And this isn't an isolated example. My lovely and charming wife, who hails from New Jersey, has a quirky way of expressing that the floor is dirty. She says, "There is all dirt on the floor." Being the logic teacher in the family, I'm always quick to point out that that's false, since there is still some dirt outside. "There may be *some* dirt *all over* the floor," I say, "but there is definitely *not* all dirt on the floor." Of course, neither I nor anyone else really represents the *logic* of my wife's utterance as "*all* dirt is on the floor." The utterance is "normalized" to a logical representation that makes sense in the context and that is the same one that my wife attaches to the utterance. And we do this with one another's utterances all day, every day. It's just part of verbal comprehension. Thus, it is simply *not* the case that subjects map the surface grammar of natural-language statements directly to logical forms. Rather, subjects *interpret* natural-language statements as having logical forms that make sense in the contexts in which those statements are made. And often that process of interpretation involves assigning the statement a logical form that does not accord with the surface structure of the natural-language statement. Indeed, this is precisely how logicians apply logic to natural languages and how they teach their students to apply logic to natural languages. As a result, simply "switching" a conditional or making minor changes to the wording of selection tasks is insufficient to change the way that subjects represent the logical forms of the conditionals in those tasks.

In fact, the results that Cosmides obtained in the "switched" selection tasks support the hypothesis that subjects "normalize" the switched conditionals and select cards appropriate to the normalized conditionals. In the "unswitched" cassava-root problem, 75 percent of subjects selected the *eats cassava root* and *no tattoo* cards, which were the logically correct cards in that problem. In the "switched" version of the problem, however, only 67 percent of subjects selected those cards. If subjects were ignoring the logic of the conditionals, and focusing only on whether a man accepted a benefit without meeting a requirement, what accounts for the drop in performance? If subjects don't really care about logic in these problems, and are simply looking to select the *eats cassava root* and *no tattoo* cards, then why didn't the full 75 percent of subjects choose those cards in the "switched" version of the problem? Cosmides offers no answer to this question. But I think that the answer is obvious. The answer is that subjects are focusing on logic, but that the logical form of the "switched" conditional doesn't correspond to its surface grammar, so it's harder to interpret. While 67 percent of subjects "normalize" the "switched" conditional, and then select the cards that are logically correct relative to the normalized conditional, some subjects are simply stymied by the task of evaluating compliance with a conditional rule that doesn't really make sense in the context of the problem. Thus, even though subjects are responding to the same mental representation of logical form in both the "switched" and "unswitched" versions of the problem, there is a decline in performance on the "switched" version of the problem because that logical form is harder to represent in the context of the problem.

A similar phenomenon accounts for the results obtained by Gigerenzer and Hug. Rather than "switching" the conditional to which subjects were instructed to determine compliance, Gigerenzer and Hug made minor modifications to the instructions in order to "switch" the perspective from which subjects were asked to evaluate the same conditional. In the "employee version" of the problem, subjects were asked to imagine being an employee who wants to know whether the employer has violated the rule "If an employee works on the weekend, then that person gets a day off during the week." In the "employer version," subjects were asked to imagine being the employer who wants to know whether any employees have violated the identically worded rule. But instructing subjects that they are to adopt the perspective of an employer looking for cheating employees will affect more than simply the "perspective" that subjects adopt on the conditional rule. Indeed, it should induce subjects to assign the conditional a logical form that makes sense of the task they are given. For "employees," that form will correspond to the surface grammar of the conditional given. But, for "employers," the given conditional imposes no obligation on employees, *if that conditional is simply taken literally.* "Employers," however, are instructed to find cases of cheating *by employees.* If they are to execute that task meaningfully, they need to find cases in which employees have violated a deontic conditional that actually imposes an obligation *on employees.* Working with the wording in the problem, the only deontic conditional that would actually impose a sensible obligation on employees is "If an employee gets a day off during the week, then that employee must work on the weekend," which would be the "normalized" form of the conditional given (relative to the perspective of an employer). Relative to the normalized conditional, then, the logically correct response from an "employer" is to select the *did not work on the weekend* and *did get a day off* cards, which is what 61 percent of the "employers" did.

So "employers" aren't actually violating the logic of the conditional by simply looking for whatever represents being cheated from their perspective; they are reasoning logically about the only sensible representation of the logical form of the conditional in the context of the task they're assigned. And, again, evidence of this is the fact that "employees" perform better on the task than "employers." For, if subjects simply look for an instance of being cheated in a social contract, what accounts for the fact that 75 percent of "employees" identify the cards that represent their being cheated by the employer, whereas only 61 percent of "employers" identify the cards that represent their being cheated by employees? If subjects ignore the logic of the problem, and look only for cases in which someone has accepted a benefit without paying a cost, "employers" should perform as well as "employees" in the task. On the other hand, if subjects apply logical principles to solve the problems, then the version of the problem that doesn't *literally* make sense should elicit a lower performance from subjects, because they have to first assign the conditional rule a logical form that makes sense given the task demands. Thus, a significant number of "employers" simply get stymied by a nonsensical task, although 61 percent of them "normalize" the conditional to a deontic conditional that makes sense given their task and choose the logically correct cards relative to that normalized conditional.

In sum, the results from Cosmides' "switched-conditional" experiments and Gigerenzer and Hug's "switched-perspective" experiments simply do not show that subjects are looking for cheaters rather than applying logical principles in solving the selection tasks in those experiments. Cosmides' interpretation of the results rests on the mistaken supposition that, if subjects apply logical principles, they do so *without interpreting* the linguistic input in the problems. But verbal comprehension tasks routinely involve interpreting statements as having logical forms that differ from the forms of their surface grammar, particularly when such interpretation is necessary to make sense of a statement or a task. Cosmides' "switched-conditional" problems and Gigerenzer and Hug's "switched-perspective" problems are precisely instances of tasks that don't make logical sense. In order to make sense of the problems, subjects interpret the conditionals as having logical forms that differ from their surface grammar, and then they select the logically correct cards relative to their mental representations of logical form. Thus, the findings fail to demonstrate that subjects do not apply logical principles in solving selection tasks involving social contracts.

The third finding that purportedly provides evidence of a cheater-detection module is Fiddick, Cosmides, and Tooby's finding that subjects select cards that represent cheating even in a version of the problem in which no conditional rule is provided, but in which two individuals merely state their wants. Fiddick, Cosmides, and Tooby argue that, if subjects solved the problem by applying logical principles, they would be unable to solve this "want version" of the problem, because it contains no logical connectives to which logical principles can apply. But, again, this argument wrongly presupposes that, if subjects are not *given* statements whose surface grammar contains apparent logical form, they will not *interpret* the statements as having a logical form. Again, for the purposes of drawing logical inferences in Wason selection tasks, however, it's not the surface grammar of the conditionals (or want statements) that matters, but the subject's *mental representation of the logical form* of the conditionals (or want statements). And, in the "want version" of the selection task that Fiddick, Cosmides, and Tooby conducted, there is a clear, albeit implicit, logical form, and that logical form is the same as the logical form of the conditional in the "conditional version" of the task with which it was paired.

In the "conditional version," recall, subjects were given the conditional "If you give me some potatoes, then I will give you some corn," and they were then instructed to turn over the necessary cards to determine whether "you" have been cheated. In the "want version," *the instructions are identical*, but subjects were to imagine hearing another person say, "I want some potatoes," and replying, "I want some corn." In the "conditional version," 67 percent of subjects selected the *you gave this person potatoes* and *this person gave you nothing* cards, while 50 percent of subjects selected those cards in the "want version." Of course, against the background of being instructed to determine whether "you" *have been cheated*, subjects will naturally represent the "want version" of the problem as embodying a deontic logic. In particular, subjects will represent the want statements as establishing an agreement that "If you give me some potatoes, then I will give you some corn," which imposes an obligation on "me." They will probably also represent those statements as establishing an agreement that "If I give you some corn, then you will give me some potatoes," which imposes an obligation on "you." But the instructions are clear that subjects are to determine whether "you" have been cheated, so it is the former deontic conditional that will be operative in their thinking about the problem, since that is the only sensible representation of the situation in accordance with which it is possible that "I" can cheat "you" by not giving "you" corn when "you" give "me" potatoes. Again, Fiddick, Cosmides, and Tooby mistakenly assume that, if subjects apply logical principles to selection tasks, they apply those principles to the surface grammar of the English, rather than to the mental representations of the logical form of the English that are the output of verbal comprehension.

And, again, if subjects are sensitive only to accepting benefits without paying costs, and not to the logical properties of the selection tasks they're presented, it's unclear why the 67 percent response rate in the "conditional version" of the problem should drop to 50 percent in the "want version." In both versions, the acceptance of the benefit without paying the cost is the same. What is *not* the same in the two versions is the explicitness of the *logic* of the problem. In the "conditional version," the logic of the problem is explicit in the surface grammar of the conditional. But in the "want version," the logic of the problem is only implicit, and subjects must perform complex cognitive processing in order to comprehend the logic of the situation. Given this fact, if subjects apply logical principles to solve the problem, it is to be expected that subjects will perform better when the logic of the problem is explicit than when it is merely implicit. For, in the latter case, the cognitive processing required to comprehend the logic of the problem introduces an additional level of processing into which error can creep. Thus, whereas Cosmides' theory offers no principled explanation of why performance would differ in the two versions of the problem, this differential performance is a principled consequence of the hypothesis that subjects apply logical principles to mental representations of logical form in order to solve the problems. Consequently, the results from the "want version" of the social-exchange selection task fail to demonstrate the operation of a cheater-detection module.

Thus, none of the principal findings that Evolutionary Psychologists tout as strong evidence of a cheater-detection module in fact demonstrate the existence of such a module. Indeed, all of the findings are compatible with the hypothesis that the human mind solves problems by applying a single, domain-general *set* of logical principles, the elements of which are selectively applied to the problems to which they are logically appropriate. In sum, if we are looking for empirical evidence of massive modularity, it's not to be found in the research on the cheater-detection module.

Let's turn our attention, then, to the so-called "theory-of-mind module" and the experimental results that have been cited as evidence of its existence.

We routinely explain one another's behavior by citing beliefs and desires. We say, for example, that Sue opened the refrigerator because she wanted orange juice and believed that some was in the refrigerator. By the age of three or four, the vast majority of children have mastered such explanations, though before this age they appear to lack certain concepts that are essential to the explanations. Our everyday explanations of behavior are sufficiently patterned that many cognitive scientists believe that a "theory of mind" or "folk psychology" underlies their use. Some of these cognitive scientists, Evolutionary Psychologists included, go further and postulate that we have a module that specializes in interpreting and explaining behavior. According to this hypothesis, all of our belief-desire explanations of one another's behavior are generated by a theory-of-mind module, whose sole function is to make sense of the behavior of fellow human beings.

Of course, the mere fact that we offer such explanations is, in itself, insufficient evidence that the explanations are generated by a module. But, if they are generated by a theory-of-mind module, there should be another way to gather evidence for its existence. An essential characteristic of

modules is that they function independently of one another. Consequently, if a module is impaired or malfunctioning, highly specific forms
of cognitive or behavioral deficit should result. These deficits should be
confined to the domain of the module and should not affect cognitive or
behavioral performance in other domains. For example, if we have syntax
modules, people with impaired syntax modules should exhibit syntax-
specific deficits; they should be unable to construct or understand
syntactically complex utterances, although they should still be able to
understand the semantic content of words or short phrases (the things that
can be stored in and recalled from non-language-specific memory). In contrast, the reasoning goes, if our mind is general purpose, cognitive and
behavioral deficits shouldn't exhibit such domain specificity; cognitive
impairments should produce deficits that cross a wide variety of problem-
solving domains.

Following this reasoning, the Evolutionary Psychologist Simon Baron-
Cohen has argued that autism is evidence of a theory-of-mind module.
This claim is based on a number of experiments involving the "false-belief
test." The idea behind the experiments is that the concept of belief is
central to our everyday explanations of behavior, but that a grasp of the
concept of belief requires understanding that beliefs can be false. When
someone's beliefs are at odds with reality, what matters with respect to
explaining their behavior is what they believe about the world, not the
way the world really is. Anyone who doesn't grasp this fact simply doesn't
understand the concept of belief and consequently will be unable to make
sense of the behavior of others. So false-belief tests are designed to detect
whether a subject grasps the distinction between reality and someone's
(possibly false) beliefs about reality.

In a typical false-belief test, a subject watches two individuals, *A* and *B*,
in a room. *A* places an object inside a covered box, then *B* leaves the room.
While *B* is gone, *A* removes the object from the covered box and places it
inside a covered can. *B* then returns to the room, and the subject is asked
where *B* will look for the object. "Normal" three-year-old children answer
that *B* will look in the can, thereby demonstrating that they haven't
grasped the concept of belief, since they don't understand that one can be
in a position to have only partial or mistaken information about the world.
By the age of four, however, "normal" children answer that *B* will look in
the box, thereby demonstrating a full grasp of the concept of belief.

A battery of false-belief tests conducted with "normal" children, autistic
children, and children with Down syndrome turned up some interesting
evidence. Although autistic children often performed as well as other

children when solving problems about inanimate objects, even preteen children with autism failed the false-belief test that most four-year-olds passed. In contrast, children with Down syndrome passed the false-belief test, even when their overall "mental age" (as measured by comparing their task performance with that of "normal" children of a specified age group) was much lower than their chronological age. Thus, autistic children appear to have a cognitive deficit that is specific to understanding the mental states of others. In short, they appear to view other humans as objects, rather than as subjects. If there is a theory-of-mind module, then its malfunctioning should lead to precisely such deficits, and this is why Baron-Cohen argues that autism is evidence for a theory-of-mind module.

There are, however, two problems with Baron-Cohen's argument. First, the well-known inability of autistic children to interact effectively with others is by no means limited to an inability to understand the mental states of others. Autistic children have flattened and inappropriate affect, and they eschew contact with others to the point of not even liking to be touched. They have a hard time looking directly at objects in their environment, they are extremely stressed by environmental change or complexity, they prefer quiet and calm over activity, they seek routine and predictability, and they are easily irritated. So the difficulties that autistic children have with coping are not even restricted to animate objects, let alone other beings whose behavior is caused by mental states.

Rather than being simply an inability to understand the minds of others, autism appears instead to prevent individuals from being able to damp down the total array of irrelevant inputs to the brain. All of us are constantly bombarded with stimuli from our environment, most of which our brains either ignore and leave unprocessed or actively suppress. Autistics don't seem to be able to do either of these things, which is why they seek simple and predictable environments. This also explains why autistics engage in so much repetitive behavior, such as hand flapping, rocking, and spinning disks; for repetitive behavior is an external way of damping down environmental stimuli.

Thus, while autism does involve an inability to pass false-belief tests, it encompasses a wide-ranging array of cognitive and affective deficits relevant to understanding others. The strongest confirmation of the theory-of-mind module hypothesis would come from a deficit that disrupted theory of mind but left all other abilities intact. Autism, however, is by no means such a deficit. Indeed, if a theory of mind were acquired from some more general learning abilities, rather than being embedded in a module, it would not be surprising that autistic children fail to acquire a theory of mind given their avoidance of interaction with other people and their inability to attend to complex and changing environmental stimuli. For acquiring a theory of mind would surely require a great deal of extended interaction with others, since learning mechanisms would require a lot of data about the behavior of others and how others explain their behavior, and this could only be acquired through extended interaction. But that interaction in turn would require an attention to environmental complexity that autistic children can't give.

The philosopher Philip Gerrans points out that autistic children are not alone in this respect. "Deaf children of hearing parents as well as congenitally blind children suffer autistic-like deficits in social, communicative, and imaginative abilities, as well as selective incapacity to pass reasoning tasks with a mentalistic component."[40] Indeed, the psychologists Candida Peterson and Michael Siegal report that deaf children of hearing parents perform comparably to autistic children on the false-belief test. The reason, Peterson and Siegal found, is that hearing parents do not attempt to communicate with their deaf children about abstractions such as mental states. Virtually all communication between hearing parents and deaf children, instead, concerns objects that can be easily pointed to in the visual environment. In other words, deaf children of hearing parents, like autistic children, do not have ready access to information about the mental states of others, which is a prerequisite for the kinds of learning necessary to acquire a theory of mind. Consequently, it's really not clear what we can infer about the theory-of-mind module hypothesis from the fact that autistic children can't pass false-belief tests.

Second, Baron-Cohen's tests of the theory-of-mind module hypothesis take the false-belief test as a criterion for possessing a theory of mind. But, as the cognitive scientists Paul Bloom and Tim German argue, it's not at all clear that the false-belief test in fact tests specifically for the possession of a theory of mind. On the one hand, they argue, the ability to pass the false-belief test requires more than just a theory of mind; and, on the other hand, possessing a theory of mind involves more than the ability to pass the false-belief test.

Consider first why passing the false-belief test involves more than a theory of mind. As noted earlier, three-year-olds typically fail the false-belief test, while four-year-olds typically pass. The same is true, however, of the "false-photograph" test. In the false-photograph test, children are taught how to use a Polaroid camera. They are then instructed to take a picture of a scene in which a stuffed cat is sitting on a chair next to a bed. After the picture is taken, and the snapshot is removed from the camera, the cat is moved to the bed. The child is then asked two questions: "Where was the cat when you took the photograph?" and "In the photograph, where is the cat?" Three-year-olds typically answer that, in the photograph, the cat is on the bed, despite saying that the cat was on the chair when the photograph was taken, while four-year-olds typically answer both questions correctly.

Passing the false-photograph test clearly doesn't involve reasoning with a theory of mind, yet children typically either fail both it and the false-belief test or pass both. If three-year-olds passed the false-photograph test but failed the false-belief test, then their failure on the false-belief test could reasonably be attributed to their not having developed a theory of mind. Conversely, if four-year-olds passed the false-belief test but failed the false-photograph test, then their success with the false-belief test could reasonably be attributed to their having developed a theory of mind but not more general principles of sophisticated reasoning. Since children pass or fail both tests at the same stages of development, however, it appears that success in both tests is the result of having acquired sophisticated principles of counterfactual reasoning that apply to more than just beliefs.

Indeed, one of the first things that a child beginning to understand mental states would learn is that beliefs are a way of tracking the way the world is. Consequently, one of the first useful heuristics a child would acquire is that people's beliefs tend to be true. That is, a child will typically reason that Daddy says that he thinks there's milk in the refrigerator because there is milk in the refrigerator. Only subsequently, and as a result of ample experience, will a child learn that people's beliefs can deviate, sometimes wildly, from the way the world is. But this step involves more than simply reasoning about beliefs. It involves reasoning about two states of affairs—one's beliefs, and the aspects of the world those beliefs are about—*and* sophisticated counterfactual reasoning about what *would* happen *if* the world changed. These principles of counterfactual reasoning go beyond mere reasoning about beliefs, and they appear to be operative in the false-photograph test in addition to the false-belief test.

Interestingly, older autistic children typically pass the false-photograph test, while still failing the false-belief test. This has been taken, by Baron-Cohen and others, as evidence that autistic children specifically lack a theory of mind—that they are like "normal" three-year-olds with respect to reasoning about human behavior, but are like "normal" peers in their abilities to reason about inanimate objects. But this isn't necessarily evidence that autistic children have an impaired theory-of-mind *module*. Perhaps those autistic children who are able to pass the false-photograph test have acquired some principles of counterfactual reasoning, which accounts for their success in this task. Nonetheless, given their impoverished interactions with others and their inability to attend to the behavior of others, it is possible that they simply lack sufficient data about other people to effectively apply those principles of counterfactual reasoning to human behavior. Knowing certain principles is one thing, and knowing how to apply them in particular cases is another. Perhaps autistic children simply haven't learned how to apply counterfactual principles in all of the same ways as "normal" four-year-olds have.

Consider now why possessing a theory of mind involves more than the ability to pass the false-belief test. Bloom and German argue that children even younger than two begin showing signs of understanding other minds. They can initiate and understand pretend play, they can imitate the *intended* actions of others (even when those actions aren't completed), and they can attribute goals to others. By the time children are three, they deftly manipulate the actions of others (especially their parents), and they deftly engage in extended pretense. All of these require some understanding of the minds of others, despite the inability to pass the false-belief test. In addition, in all of these respects, "normal" three-year-olds differ considerably from autistic children. When the false-belief test is used as a test of whether children possess a theory of mind, however, "normal" three-year-olds and autistic children get grouped together as simply individuals who lack a theory of mind. And this merely shows why the false-belief test can't be taken as a criterion for whether an individual possesses a theory of mind.

Thus, there simply isn't strong empirical evidence for the hypothesis that we possess a theory-of-mind module. The experiments that have been taken as confirmation of that hypothesis have relied on the false-belief test, but performance on the false-belief test is not a good indicator of possession of a theory of mind, let alone a theory-of-mind *module*. Further, autism isn't an example of the sort of highly specific deficit that would provide evidence of a theory-of-mind module. If we're looking for a good example of an empirically demonstrated module, which can be held up as a model of how the rest of the mind must be organized, the alleged theory-of-mind module isn't it.

## On Domain-General Mechanisms

This has been a wide-ranging chapter, so it might pay to take stock of where we've arrived. We've seen that none of the arguments for the massive modularity thesis succeeds in showing that the mind is massively modular. All of those arguments are designed to show that domain-general learning mechanisms are incapable of learning some things that humans routinely learn and that consequently the human mind must be composed of numerous "genetically specified" domain-specific mechanisms (or modules). But, as we saw, the first two of those arguments simply fail to show that domain-general learning is incapable of acquiring domain-specific competences. The last two arguments, though, did show that domain-general learning rules are too weak to learn some of the things that humans learn, but they entail only that domain-general learning must be accompanied by initial learning biases.

We've also seen that, although a process of "modularization" does occur during brain development, the resulting "modules" are not genetically specified, but rather are shaped by a plastic brain's interaction with its local environment via the process of proliferate-and-prune. Consequently, the "modules" that emerge from brain development, like the antibodies that are present in the immune system, are not biological adaptations, although they do possess properties similar to those that Evolutionary Psychologists ascribe to modules. The brain's plasticity itself, however, is a biological adaptation, as are some of the initial biases in brain development, certain (levels of) hormones and neurotransmitters involved in regulating behavior, and no doubt some of our sexual and emotional responses (which are subserved by subcortical circuits). Finally, we saw that cortical plasticity is *domain general* in the sense that it is capable of producing brain circuits that are specialized for a wide range of task domains, while not itself being specialized for any of those task domains. This is analogous to the immune system's being "pathogen general" in the sense that it is not specialized for combating any particular pathogen, although it is capable of producing antibodies that do combat specific pathogens.

This account may appear to be a return to the old-fashioned view of the mind as "general purpose," and the tidal wave of opinion in cognitive science for the past few decades holds this view to be immensely implausible. Part of the reason this view has been rejected is that "general purpose" has typically been equated with behaviorism's operant conditioning or eighteenth-century empiricism's association of ideas, and these have clearly been shown to be implausible as general models of how the mind works. But the domain-general, or general-purpose, conception of cortical plasticity explained here is in fact not a return to the old-fashioned "general-purpose mind," although it may be hard to tell. The reason it may be hard to tell is that Evolutionary Psychologists conflate two different conceptions of what it means for the mind or brain to be "domain general."

The conflation of these different conceptions is evident in Evolutionary Psychologists' typical characterizations of the old-fashioned view that they reject. For example, Tooby and Cosmides describe the domain-general conception of the mind as maintaining that "any evolved component, *processing, or mechanism* must be equipotential, content-free, content-independent, general-purpose, domain-general, and so on."[41] But "processing" and "mechanisms" are two different things. "Processing" concerns information and the rules for reasoning with information. "Mechanisms," on the other hand, are physical systems that function in lawlike ways; they *can* be systems that *perform* information processing, but they need not be. If you look again at the arguments for massive modularity considered earlier, you'll find a constant slippage in the arguments: They move from arguing that domain-general cognitive *rules* ("processing") are incapable of learning what humans learn to a conclusion that domain-general *mechanisms* can't acquire human competences. As noted earlier, some of the arguments, which claim that at least some human competences can't be acquired through learning using solely domain-general rules, are correct. But it simply doesn't follow that the human brain can't be a domain-general *mechanism*. For a domain-general mechanism can function in ways that don't involve applying domain-general learning rules.

Indeed, the system of plasticity by which the cortex organizes and structures itself is precisely a domain-general mechanism that doesn't operate by applying domain-general learning rules. The mechanism of proliferate-and-prune forms brain circuits that perform specialized functions and that solve problems in particular task domains (such as face recognition and the explanation of behavior). But it isn't a process that forms those specialized circuits through learning by applying domain-general rules, such as "Observe and imitate the behavior of role models." Rather, our functionally specialized cortical circuits emerge automatically from the process of proliferate-and-prune, without the need for any guidance by "learning rules."

This may sound deeply mysterious, since it doesn't conform to the orthodox belief, deeply ingrained in the psychological tradition of the last several centuries, that we acquire our specialized competences through *learning* (through either acquiring information or acquiring rules for reasoning with information). To demystify this idea somewhat, reflect again on the structural similarity between the process of proliferate-and-prune and the process of natural selection.

In the process of natural selection, mutation and recombination generate variation, which is then winnowed by environmental demands. This
process is very wasteful in the sense that an overabundance of variation is
generated—that is, more variants are generated than will successfully meet
the environmental demands. But the overabundance hedges against environmental uncertainty, since the more distinct variants there are in a population, the more distinct environments the population can evolve into.
Since the process of variation production followed by selective winnowing
repeats every generation, natural selection has the opportunity to sample
a vast supply of variation over the course of evolutionary time, retaining
the fittest variants of each generation to build on in subsequent generations. The result is a long series of successive minor modifications to
preexisting structures, which produces very complex traits that perform
highly specialized functions. Livers, hearts, and kidneys are created by this
process as the anatomy of a species adapts to the demands of the species'
environment. But these specialized organs are not generated within the
body via the body's applying some sort of "general-purpose" rules for learning how to grow organs. They emerge automatically from cycles of variation overproduction followed by selective winnowing.

Similarly, our specialized brain circuits emerge automatically from the
process of proliferate-and-prune, and they do so in the absence of any
"general-purpose" rules for learning how to produce them. Additive
processes in cortical development create an overabundance of neurons and
connections, which is then pruned by the subtractive processes of cell
competition and cell death. Just as the anatomy of a species adapts to its
environment through the process of natural selection (by forming and
modifying specialized bodily organs), so the brain *adapts* to its environment through the process of proliferate-and-prune (by forming functionally specialized brain circuits). These circuits are formed not by applying
antecedently possessed, domain-general learning rules to the data encountered in experience, but by a process that allows environmental demands
to tailor circuits that specialize in dealing with them. The process by which
the brain adapts is structurally very similar, then, to the process by which
a species' anatomy adapts. It just takes place during the lifetime of an individual, rather than over the course of a species' evolutionary history. But
it is no more mysterious than the process of natural selection itself. Indeed,
just as selection can build complex adaptive structures without needing
to be guided by a divine intelligence, neural plasticity can build complex
adaptive cognitive structures without needing to be guided by "genetic
specification."

None of this is to say that the human brain doesn't learn. It surely does. It is merely to say that the traditional concept of learning doesn't adequately capture the process by which the brain forms the specialized circuits that perform cognitive functions. It is also not to say that the brain's circuits don't process information. They surely do. Some of them process information using domain-specific rules, and some process information using domain-general rules. It is merely to say that we don't come by our specialized competences *solely* through a process of applying rules to information in order to generate and acquire more rules and information. Essential to the process of acquiring specialized competences is the process of forming the brain circuits that subserve those competences, and essential to that process in turn is the process of proliferate-and-prune by which the brain *adapts* to its local environment. This process gives rise to domain-dominant information-processing circuits in the brain, which in turn give us the highly specialized cognitive structures that are similar to Evolutionary Psychology's modules.

At this point Evolutionary Psychologists may be tempted to respond that brain plasticity isn't actually inconsistent with the massive modularity thesis. What matters, they could argue, is not *how* the brain succeeds in developing and organizing itself into functionally specialized brain circuits, but only *that it succeeds* in doing so, even if the method it employs to do so is proliferate-and-prune. As long as functionally specialized mechanisms, which function to solve adaptive problems, *somehow* emerge during the course of development, and somehow have regularly emerged throughout human evolutionary history, these mechanisms can still be adaptations, having been tailored by natural selection to solve their respective problems. For, as Tooby and Cosmides argue, "it is primarily the information-processing structure of the human psychological architecture that has been functionally organized by natural selection, and the neurophysiology has been organized insofar as it physically realized this cognitive organization."[42] Thus, Evolutionary Psychologists might conclude, details about brain plasticity don't refute the massive modularity thesis, since that thesis concerns the *information-processing structure* of the mind; and as long as the right information-processing structure emerges, the physical process by which it emerges is irrelevant.

But there are two problems with this line of argument. First, as explained in detail earlier in this chapter, characteristics that emerge from the interaction between a plastic system and its environment—such as antibodies or functionally specialized brain circuits—are not biological adaptations. So the details about brain plasticity do undercut Evolutionary Psychology's claim that our functionally specialized brain circuits are adaptations. Those circuits simply don't have the right kind of causal history to count as biological adaptations. They weren't shaped by selection over our species' evolutionary history; they are shaped by the local environment during the course of an individual's lifetime.

Second, the response presupposes that selection can build adaptations at an abstractly functional level, without bothering with the details about how to build the physical structures that implement the functions. But, as explained earlier, adaptations are traits that have been preserved and modified by selection. Selection, however, acts only on *genetic* differences between individuals. Thus, an adaptation is a trait that has been shaped by selection through a process in which selection retained the genes that beneficially modified the trait and discarded genes that detrimentally modified it.

Genes, however, affect only the protein structures in an organism's body. They can affect the functions that are performed by some body part only by affecting the physical structure of the part that performs the function. To build an organism that digests, genes must build a physical structure that performs the function of digestion; they can't build digestion in some ethereal, abstract functional space in the organism. Thus, the genes that were preserved by selection because of their effects on human psychology had their effects only by altering the neurophysiology of the brain in such a way that it performed beneficial psychological functions. Genes simply can't affect information processing without affecting the neurophysiology of the brain. Consequently, selection shaped human psychology only by altering the neurophysiology of the brain over evolutionary time. In contrast to Tooby and Cosmides' claim, it is the neurophysiology of the brain that has been organized by selection, and it has been organized in the way it has because of the functional benefits of that neurophysiology.

Thus, rather than being an irrelevant detail along the way to the development of functionally specialized brain circuits, cortical plasticity has been a primary focus of selection's creative energy throughout human psychological evolution. Consequently, it is a mistake to assume that the *products* of brain development—the functionally specialized brain circuits that emerge during the course of brain development—are cognitive adaptations. Our primary *cognitive* adaptation is, instead, the *process* that continually generates and modifies these specialized brain circuits. However "modularized" a human brain becomes in the course of development, it simply doesn't contain "hundreds or thousands" of modules that are biological adaptations.

# 5 | Mating

So far we have explored a number of rather abstractly theoretical issues regarding the evolution and structure of the mind and haven't paid much attention to the *contents* of the mind, the specific ways that people think and feel. But what makes Evolutionary Psychology so fascinating is how it applies its abstract theoretical principles to generate specific hypotheses about human psychology. For it holds the promise of revealing the nature of, and evolutionary reasons for, the psychology underlying our intimate relationships with others—why we desire sex with some people but not others, why we marry or cohabitate with the people we do, why we are sometimes unfaithful, why infidelities elicit jealousy, and why we care so deeply for our children. Unlike the more abstractly theoretical issues we have so far considered, these claims concern issues that occupy the overwhelming majority of our daily lives.

This is the first of three chapters that will examine Evolutionary Psychology's specific hypotheses, and the evidence offered in their support, regarding the psychology of mate choice, infidelity, jealousy, and parental care. This chapter will focus on the psychology of mate choice.

Evolutionary Psychology has offered a number of interesting hypotheses regarding sex differences in the psychology of human mating. But this chapter will focus exclusively on two core hypotheses that have become shibboleths of Evolutionary Psychology. Men, Evolutionary Psychologists claim, have an evolved preference for mating with young women, and women have an evolved preference for mating with high-status men. These preferences are supposedly implemented in evolved modules that are also designed to detect signs of youth and status, respectively.

Evolutionary Psychologists claim to have gathered overwhelming empirical evidence that confirms both of these hypotheses, and this chapter will examine that evidence. Since chapter 4 argued that we don't have evolved modules for all the functions Evolutionary Psychologists claim, I will not be concerned here with evaluating any evidence for modularity. My focus, instead, will be on the preferences themselves—on whether men have evolved to detect and prefer young women and whether women have evolved to detect and prefer high-status men—regardless of the kind of mechanism that implements them. The question is: How good is the evidence for Evolutionary Psychology's core hypotheses about male and female mate preferences? But before examining the evidence let's briefly examine the theoretical foundation of the hypotheses.

### "The Evolution of Desire"

As we saw in chapter 1, life (in the biological, not existential, sense of the term) is all about reproductive success—how many copies of one's genes one contributes to future generations via the bodies of one's offspring. We also saw in chapter 1 that many activities have fitness costs and benefits, which respectively diminish and enhance fitness. Producing offspring, the very sine qua non of fitness, is no exception. Indeed, producing offspring is a costly endeavor.

First of all, barring very recently invented reproductive technologies (which are too new to have affected evolved motives and preferences), in sexually reproducing species such as ours, you've got to have sex with a member of the opposite sex in order to produce offspring. But, unfortunately, members of the opposite sex don't have sex with you just because you want them to. They've got to be enticed into it, one way or another, and the cost of enticement can range from the metabolic costs of producing a come-hither wink to the costs of building a bower or obtaining and presenting gifts over an extended period. Once a partner has been enticed, the sex act costs the energy involved in doing it (plus the contents of an ejaculate if you're male). Then, if sex results in conception and you're a female, you've just begun to pay. If you're a human female, you pay the costs of a nine-month gestation, which exacts an enormous physiological toll on your body. And, throughout most of our evolutionary history, ancestral women paid the additional metabolic costs involved in breast-feeding for several years.

So here is one of Nature's great inequities. If you're a woman, the absolute minimum cost for producing a single offspring is quite high. Not only do you pay the costs of gestation and lactation, but you also pay the cost of forgoing any other possible reproductive opportunities with males other than the father of your offspring—possibly *better* males than the father of your offspring—during the period of pregnancy and lactation. If you're a man, on the other hand, the absolute minimum cost for producing a single offspring is the energy expended in copulation and the contents of a single ejaculate (an inexpensive 300 million sperm and three milliliters of semen). After a fruitful copulation, a man can get up and pursue reproductive opportunities with other women, whereas a woman is committed to the costly act of childbearing. This is a radical asymmetry in the minimum costs the sexes must pay in order to produce a single offspring.

Although the costs are real, it's not like flushing money down the toilet, since you do get an offspring out of the deal. So these expenditures are really an investment—what is called *parental investment*. Parental investment is standardly defined as any characteristics or behaviors of a parent that enhance the ability of an offspring to survive and reproduce at a cost to the parent's fitness, including diminishment in the parent's future abilities to mate or care for other offspring. Thus, one way of describing the above asymmetry between the sexes is that the *minimum obligatory parental investment* for women is vastly higher than that for men.

Evolutionary Psychologists derive their hypotheses about evolved mate preferences from this fact about minimum obligatory parental investment, and the derivation begins in the work of the evolutionary anthropologist Robert Trivers. In a classic article, Trivers argued that, when there is a sex asymmetry in parental investment, selection will tend to make the higher-investing sex choosier in the mating market, because that sex stands to lose more by making a poor choice of mate. This greater choosiness on the part of the higher-investing sex will force members of the other sex to compete among one another to be chosen. As a result, the higher-investing sex will appear more cautious in the mating market, while the lower-investing sex will appear more eager and more intensely competitive in its attempts to attract mates. For example, if males invest nothing beyond the act of copulation and an ejaculate, leaving females to cover all costs of parental care, females will be very selective in choosing a mate. Under these circumstances, males are little more than sperm transport, so a male's quality is solely a function of the genes he can provide. Females will then hold out for males who show signs of having "good genes"—signs such as good health and bodily symmetry (a purported sign of developmental stability). And males will compete among themselves to be chosen by females, attempting to present the best advertisements of "good genes."

Trivers's theory is supported by observations of the mating habits of many species. Some of the strongest support for the theory comes from species in which males provide greater parental investment than females, since males in those species tend to be more selective in choosing mates and females are more competitive. But Trivers's theory also predicts that, if the parental investment in both sexes is relatively high, both sexes will be highly selective in choosing mates, holding out for mates who demonstrate the ability to provide a fairly high level of parental investment.

Humans are among a small minority of species in which both sexes invest heavily in offspring. Of course, as we've seen, the physiological investment by females vastly exceeds that by males. But, as we saw in chapter 1, merely bringing offspring into the world is no guarantee of genetic immortality. In some species, offspring are born sufficiently developed that they can survive on their own almost immediately. But human offspring are heavily dependent on parental care for many years after birth. Indeed, in the early years they are entirely incapable of caring for themselves, requiring very intensive parental care. Since reproductive success requires that offspring themselves survive to reproduce, human offspring need to be nurtured at least until they're able to survive on their own.

And this, according to Evolutionary Psychology, is where male parental investment comes in. During our evolutionary history, Evolutionary Psychologists argue, a female who had to spend all her days tending to a suckling infant would not have been able to adequately provide for herself and her infant. So it was necessary for males to provide their mates and offspring with food, shelter, and protection. Further, the demands of survival among our ancestors required learning the skills involved in foraging for food and making shelter, and the demands of reproduction required learning the skills involved in negotiating one's social group. So males could also enhance the survivability and subsequent reproductive success of their offspring by playing a role in teaching them such skills. On average, then, the rate of survival and subsequent reproductive success of offspring of ancestral "single mothers" would have been lower than that of offspring who enjoyed both maternal care and a high level of male parental care. Thus, Evolutionary Psychologists argue, the extraordinarily heavy dependence of human offspring on parental care created strong selection pressure for a fairly high level of male parental investment. (There are reasons, which I will discuss in chapter 6, for believing that this is not why male parental investment evolved.)

Despite the relatively high level of male parental investment in our species, however, the postnatal parental investment provided by females still exceeds that provided by males in every culture. This is what we should expect, Evolutionary Psychologists argue, given another sex asymmetry in our species. With internal fertilization, a female can always be 100 percent certain that the offspring she births are hers. But no male can be 100 percent certain that the offspring birthed by his mate are his. For we are a species in which internal fertilization is coupled with concealed ovulation. This contrasts with other primates, such as chimpanzees. When a chimpanzee female is ovulating, her genitals swell and become red, a clear sign to chimpanzee males that it is time to take action. If a chimpanzee male wants to sire an offspring, he merely needs to ensure that he sexually monopolizes a female during her fertile period. Ancestral human males, in contrast, had no idea when females were ovulating, so they could never be sure whether they were inseminating a fertile female or not. So, in order to sire an offspring, they had to copulate with ancestral females round-the-month. But a lot can happen in a month. The demands of survival would have required frequent periods during which mates were out of one another's sight foraging, for example. A female who had been out of sight for a mere twenty minutes could have been carrying internally the inseminate of another male. Even if her mate copulated with her immediately upon their reunion, there was never any sure way to know exactly what was going on in there. As a result, any issue from her womb was of uncertain provenance from a male's perspective. This is known as the problem of *paternity uncertainty*.

Given the possibility that a male's putative offspring are not truly his own, there is always the chance that the male is investing in another male's offspring, thus squandering resources that could be better spent in a competition to fertilize other females. A female, in contrast, never faces the potential problem of squandering her parental investment on offspring she mistakenly believes to be hers. Thus, Evolutionary Psychologists argue, since human male parental investment can be misspent in a way that human female parental investment cannot, selection should have designed males to deliver a lower level of parental investment than females as a hedge against the possibility of misspending it. In fact, Evolutionary Psychologists further predict, the degree of male parental investment should be a function of the degree to which a male feels confident in his paternity of offspring.

Nonetheless, because human males provided a fairly high level of parental investment throughout our evolutionary history, they, like human females, have evolved to be very selective in choosing a female with whom they will jointly invest in offspring. However, because the two sexes provided different forms of parental investment throughout human evolutionary history, Evolutionary Psychologists argue, each sex has evolved to prefer as mates those members of the opposite sex who show signs of being able to provide the forms of parental investment in which that sex specialized in human evolutionary history.

As the Evolutionary Psychologists Douglas Kenrick and Richard Keefe put it: "Males invest relatively more indirect resources (food, money, protection, and security), and females invest relatively more direct physiological resources (contributing their own bodily nutrients to the fetus and nursing the child). For this reason, females who are choosing mates are assumed to pay particular attention to a male's ability to provide indirect resources, and males are assumed to pay special attention to signs of a female's apparent health and reproductive potential."[1] Thus, females should have evolved to prefer males who can provide indirect resources, whereas males should have evolved to prefer females of peak reproductive potential.

But this poses a "detection problem" for both sexes: How can each sex detect the members of the opposite sex who possess the preferred qualities? A male's ability to provide indirect resources cannot be directly detected in the way the length of his nose can. Similarly, as David Buss says: "The number of children a woman is likely to bear in her lifetime is not stamped on her forehead. It is not imbued in her social reputation. Even women themselves lack direct knowledge of their reproductive value."[2] Therefore, Evolutionary Psychologists argue, women should have evolved to be attracted to *detectable qualities* of men that are *correlated with* the ability to provide indirect resources, and men should have evolved to be attracted to detectable qualities of women that are correlated with peak reproductive potential.

Women, according to Evolutionary Psychologists, solved their detection problem by evolving a preference for high-status males. For, as the Evolutionary Psychologist Bruce Ellis says: "In general, the higher a male is in status (i.e., the higher the level of esteem and influence accorded to him by others), the greater his ability to control resources across many situations. . . . Since control of positional resources is both a sign and a reward of status, natural selection could be expected to have favored evaluative mechanisms in women designed to detect and prefer high-status men."[3] Hence Evolutionary Psychology's core hypothesis about female mate preferences.

Men, on the other hand, needed to solve the problem of detecting peak reproductive potential. Reproductive potential involves two things. On the one hand, it involves *fertility*, which is a measure of the likelihood of being able to conceive and carry a pregnancy to term, and a human female's fertility typically peaks in her mid-twenties. On the other hand, reproductive potential involves *reproductive value*, which is a measure of the remaining number of offspring that a female can produce. The younger a fertile woman is the greater is her reproductive potential, since the greater is the number of years she has remaining in which to produce offspring. So women with the highest fertility don't have the greatest reproductive value and vice versa. But women in their very early twenties are near the peaks of both fertility and reproductive value, so they have the highest overall reproductive potential—that is, the greatest ability to immediately provide the physiological resources necessary for bearing many offspring.

Of course, as Buss notes, "even age must be inferred, as it cannot be assessed directly."[4] To further complicate matters, this preference for women of peak reproductive potential evolved well before calendars and even before counting, so it wasn't possible to simply ask about a woman's age during the evolution of these preferences. Males, Buss argues, also had to evolve a solution to the detection problem for age. Thus, "according to evolutionary psychologists, the evolutionary model predicts that what men desire is not youth per se, but rather features of women that are associated with reproductive value or fertility."[5] These features are "full lips [since lips thin with advancing age], clear skin, smooth skin, clear eyes, lustrous hair, good muscle tone and body fat distribution."[6]

The qualities of full lips, good muscle tone, and so on, are perhaps self-explanatory. But body fat distribution requires some comment. Before puberty, Evolutionary Psychologists argue, boys and girls are shaped much alike, with a waist-to-hip ratio of roughly 0.90 (which means that the girth of the waist is 90 percent of that of the hips). At puberty, however, the release of estrogen in females causes fat to be deposited on the hips and upper thighs. As a result, females' hips become even wider after puberty, with the waist-to-hip ratio decreasing to around 0.70. Pregnancy, however, often leaves a lasting deposit of fat on the waist, increasing the waist-to-hip ratio. Further, as women approach middle age and undergo menopause, more body fat gets deposited in the waist, thereby further increasing the waist-to-hip ratio. Thus, according to Evolutionary Psychologists, a waist-to-hip ratio of around 0.70 indicates a fertile female who has yet to bear a child; and, throughout much of human evolutionary history a fertile, yet childless, female would have been very close to her peak reproductive potential. So, Evolutionary Psychologists conclude, males have evolved a preference for females with waist-to-hip ratios around 0.70.

We see, then, how Evolutionary Psychologists arrive at the hypotheses that women have an evolved preference for high-status men and that men have an evolved preference for young women (that is, women with physical features that are correlated with peak reproductive potential). These hypotheses are derived from general theoretical considerations regarding the nature of parental investment in our species.

It is worth noting, however, that these preferences are for the qualities of *long-term mates*. According to Evolutionary Psychologists, when people are in the market for short-term mates (one-night stands, for example), their preferences shift. Men still like fertile women as short-term mates, Evolutionary Psychologists claim, but men's standards for short-term mating typically drop so low that they're willing to copulate with pretty much anything that is self-moving (since, after all, sperm is cheap). Women, on the other hand, are less interested in status and more interested in intelligence and good looks when seeking a short-term mate. In what follows, I will not examine these claims about short-term mate preferences, but will focus exclusively on the two core hypotheses regarding long-term mate preferences.

Each of the hypotheses about long-term mate preferences is separable into two independent claims. One is a claim about *what* people prefer, and the other is a claim about *why* they prefer it. Each hypothesis, that is, contains a claim that a particular universal preference has evolved in each sex and a claim that that universal preference evolved because of selection for it in our evolutionary past (that it is an adaptation). These claims are typically not separated, because empirical studies in Evolutionary Psychology are presumed to test both claims simultaneously.

To illustrate, consider the male preference for youth. As Buss says, "because male reproductive success in humans depends heavily on mating with reproductively capable females, selection over thousands of generations should favor those males who prefer to mate with reproductively capable females."[7] Here a hypothesis about *what* males prefer (reproductive capability) is derived from a hypothesis about how selection has acted during human evolutionary history, which would explain *why* males have that preference (it is an adaptation). If we get confirmation of the derived (preference) hypothesis, it seems to be simultaneous confirmation of the hypothesis (about past selection) from which it was derived. So, if the evidence shows that males indeed prefer youth, that appears to confirm the hypothesis that the preference is an adaptation.

Universality enters the picture because, for the reasons discussed in chapters 2 and 3, Evolutionary Psychologists believe that adaptations are, of necessity, species universals. This is why, in attempting to confirm hypotheses about evolved mate preferences, Buss conducted a massive cross-cultural study (to be discussed below) to determine whether the predicted preferences are indeed universal. According to Buss, the evidence shows that "men universally prefer younger women as wives" and that "women worldwide desire financial resources in a marriage partner."[8] Thus, Evolutionary Psychologists believe that the evidence shows that male preference for young females and female preference for high-status males are adaptations.

I've belabored the distinction between a hypothesis about *what* people prefer and a hypothesis about *why* people have those preferences because it helps clarify two different ways in which Evolutionary Psychology's hypotheses about mate preferences can be questioned. On the one hand, one could ask: How good is the evidence that male preference for youth and female preference for high status are adaptations? That is, how good is the evidence for Evolutionary Psychology's claims about *why* people have these preferences? A number of critics of Evolutionary Psychology have asked this question and answered it in the negative, arguing that Evolutionary Psychology falls far short of providing convincing evidence that these preferences are adaptations. Indeed, this is the line of argument that Gould consistently urges against Evolutionary Psychology. According to this line of argument, selection isn't the only explanation for the existence of these preferences, so merely finding the preferences doesn't confirm that they are adaptations, since it doesn't rule out nonadaptationist explanations of the preferences.

But this line of argument presupposes that Evolutionary Psychologists have provided convincing evidence that males indeed prefer youth and that females indeed prefer high status. So, on the other hand, one could ask: How good is the evidence that males prefer females of peak reproductive potential and females prefer high-status males? That is, how good is the evidence about *what* people prefer in mates? I believe that this question has not received the attention it deserves, and it will be the focus of the sections to follow. I will argue that there is no convincing evidence for either hypothesized universal mate preference.

Before turning to these arguments, however, a comment is in order on the notion of universality. We have already discussed some of the complexities of this notion in Evolutionary Psychology, and we have seen that when Evolutionary Psychologists use the term "universal" they are implicitly referring to a developmental program shared by all "normal" human beings, not to manifest or observable preferences, beliefs, attitudes, or behaviors. So, if push came to shove, Evolutionary Psychologists would admit that their claims regarding mate preferences do not mean that each and every human male prefers young women and that each and every female prefers high-status men. It is always possible that certain individuals have unusual developmental experiences and end up not possessing the predicted preferences. But, if there is a truly universal developmental program that has been designed by selection to reliably produce a preference for young females in men and a preference for high-status males in women, that developmental program should produce those preferences across a very wide range of conditions. Thus, Evolutionary Psychologists would maintain, to say that those preferences are "universal" means that they are observable *in all cultures, all historical periods, all economic or political systems, all social classes, all religious groups, all "races" or ethnicities, and all relevant ages of the life cycle.* It is this more restricted sense of "universal" that is operative when Buss claims that female preference for high-status, resource-holding mates is universal. As Buss says, "women across all continents, all political systems (including socialism and communism), all racial groups, all religious groups, and all systems of mating (from intense polygyny to presumptive monogamy) place more value than men on good financial prospects."[9]

I will argue that, even in this more restricted sense of "universal," the data on human mate preferences fail to provide convincing support for claims of a universal male preference for youth and a universal female preference for high status. Indeed, I will argue, the mate preferences in which Evolutionary Psychologists are interested tend to vary with age and social class, among other things. If this is right, then something is wrong with the hypotheses about human evolution from which Evolutionary Psychology derives its claims about mate preferences. Let's turn now to the evidence for Evolutionary Psychology's core mate-preference hypotheses, focusing on the studies that are standardly cited in support of those hypotheses.

## Men Seeking Women

In collaboration with a bevy of social psychologists from around the world, David Buss gathered survey data about mate preferences from 4,601 men and 5,446 women (a total of 10,047 subjects), who comprised thirty-seven survey samples from thirty-three countries located on six continents and five islands. The sheer scale of this study is remarkable, and the study has become an exemplar of empirical research in Evolutionary Psychology.

Among other things, Buss's survey asked subjects to give the age at which they'd prefer to marry, and he found that, on average, males preferred to marry at 27.49 years of age. He also asked subjects to give the preferred age of their mates relative to their own ages. So males were asked to state how much younger or older than themselves their ideal mate would be. He found that in every one of the thirty-seven samples males indicated a preference for younger mates, with average preferences ranging from 0.38 to 7.38 years younger. Pooling all the samples, Buss found that, on average, males preferred a mate who was 2.66 years younger. "By subtracting the mean age difference preferred between males and their mates (2.66 years) from the age at which males prefer to marry (27.49 years), it can be inferred that males in these samples prefer to marry females who are approximately 24.83 years old. This age preference is closer to peak female fertility than to peak reproductive value."[10]

Without splitting hairs about peak fertility versus peak reproductive value (or peak reproductive potential, which incorporates both), an average preferred age of 24.83 years is clearly near the height of female reproductive potential. Given the large cross-cultural scale of Buss's study, this appears to show that male preference for females with high reproductive potential is universal. And this, in turn, appears to confirm the hypothesis that selection has designed male mate preferences to be highly sensitive to female reproductive potential.

As Buss recognizes, however, males may indicate preferences on a survey questionnaire that don't accord with the actual decisions they make in choosing a mate. In addition, offspring are produced not by preferences for mates with certain qualities, but by actual matings. Consequently, selection cannot have acted on male preferences unless males throughout human evolutionary history actually mated in accordance with their preferences. In particular, a preference for fertile young women could not increase in frequency in a population unless there was a strong correlation between that preference and actually mating with fertile young women. Thus, there can't have been past selection for a male *preference* for young women unless males with that preference actually produced more offspring, by actually mating with fertile young women, than did males with alternative preferences.

To confirm that the preferences for young women that males reported on his questionnaire are (and presumably were in our evolutionary history) reflected in actual mating behavior, Buss compared the age-preference data with the actual ages at marriage of men and women in thirty of his thirty-seven samples. He found that the average age at marriage was 28.2 years for males and 25.3 years for females, only slightly higher than males' preferred ages of 27.49 years and 24.83 years respectively.

Of course, it takes two to mate. So, while males may prefer mates who are 24.83 years old, females have their own preferences, and females expressed a preference to marry at 25.4 years to a man of 28.8 years. Thus, the discrepancy between males' preferred ages of self and spouse at marriage and the actual ages at marriage appears to be a product of compromise with female preference. Indeed, Evolutionary Psychologists argue, we should expect all actual mating decisions and behaviors to differ from the preferences of both sexes, since the preferences of the sexes will typically differ; and, when preferences of the mating parties differ, actual mating decisions and behaviors will reflect a compromise between the preferences. Despite the expected compromise, however, the actual average age of women at marriage is very close to the male preference, so male preferences for young women do indeed appear to be reflected in actual mating behavior. Therefore, Buss concludes, the preference data together with the marriage data provide strong "support for the evolution-based hypothesis that males both prefer *and* choose females displaying cues to high reproductive capacity."[11]

But Buss's analyzed data do not clearly confirm this hypothesis. Buss's analysis of his preference data consists in subtracting the average preferred age difference between male respondents and their female mates (2.66 years) from the average age at which his male respondents said they preferred to marry (27.49 years). Since the average age of his male respondents was 23.49 years, this shows only that *young* men *say* that they prefer to marry relatively *younger* women and to do so at a fairly young age. As Buss recognizes, what males *say* they want in a mate stands in need of a validity check, which his analysis of his marriage data purportedly provides. But Buss's analysis of his marriage data consists only of comparing the *average age* of males at marriage (28.2 years) with the *average age* of females at marriage (25.3 years). While this does show that on average males marry fairly young women, it also shows that on average the males marrying them are themselves young—only 2.9 years older than their brides.

If males both prefer and choose young women as mates, however, this preference should be present across the male life cycle. Older males should exhibit a preference for young women just as young males do. Since Buss's analysis employs only the averages from his samples, it doesn't show that older males prefer and choose young women as mates. The mate preferences of older males disappear into the averages, and the averages present a profile of the mate preferences of relatively young males. But, to confirm that males have an evolved preference for young women, it is not enough to show that *young men* prefer young women.

The reason is that there is a large body of sociological evidence that shows the most robust mate-choice phenomenon to be what social scientists call *homogamy*. Homogamy is the tendency for people to mate with those similar in race or ethnic background, age, socioeconomic status, educational background, and religious orientation. Homogamy is a form of what biologists call *assortative mating*, which is preferential mating with other organisms with like phenotype(s). In the case of homogamy, mating is assortative with respect to social characteristics rather than morphological or behavioral phenotypes. And a very recent large-scale study of mating in the United States, conducted by the sociologist Edward Laumann and his colleagues, found that similarity in age is even more important in mate choice than similarity in religious orientation.

But why should age similarity be important in mating? The Evolutionary Psychologists Douglas Kenrick and Richard Keefe argue that there may have been selection for assortative mating by age in our evolutionary past. "Extended interactions over long periods between mates would have been easier if the partners had similar expectations, values, activity levels, and habits. A preference for similarity in age, all else being equal, would have made the long-term cooperation of mates more feasible and thus adaptive. . . . Thus, humans may have evolved with a preference for similar mates, including similarly aged mates, because of the advantage to parenting effort this would have contributed."[12] This simple hypothesis of age homogamy—that human mating is assortative by age—appears sufficient to explain Buss's finding that young men prefer young women.

Of course, assortative mating by age doesn't explain why Buss found a consistent *age difference* in both his preference data and his marriage data. If people merely seek similarly aged mates, in a very large sample such as Buss's we should expect the average male preference to be for similarly aged mates (rather than for mates 2.66 years younger) and the average age difference between spouses at marriage to be close to zero (rather than 2.9 years). Why do males consistently prefer and mate with younger women, while women prefer and mate with older men? According to Buss, this age difference reflects the fact that men seek young women as mates, because of their reproductive capacity, and women seek older men as mates, because older men tend to have greater resources than younger men. Thus, the consistent age difference between mates appears to tell in favor of the hypothesis that males have an evolved preference for young women and against the hypothesis of age homogamy.

But, if Buss is right, why should the average age difference be as small as it is? Why shouldn't twenty-eight-year-old males on average prefer twenty-year-old females, who have greater reproductive potential than twenty-five-year-old females? Similarly, why shouldn't twenty-two-year-old females prefer thirty-five-year-old males, since they tend to have greater resources than twenty-five-year-old males (whom they actually prefer), yet still have a fairly long life ahead of them in which to provide resources for a female and her offspring? Age similarity does seem to be a factor in mate choice. Perhaps some variation on the hypothesis of age homogamy would account for the age difference that Buss found, while providing a better explanation of Buss's data than the hypothesis that males simply have an evolved preference for young women.

Consider the following variation on the hypothesis of age homogamy. Let's begin by supposing that selection favored assortative mating by *similar* age for the reasons that Kenrick and Keefe suggest (although, in chapter 6, I will present reasons for thinking that this preference was driven by sexual selection rather than natural selection). We need now to explain why, within this general constraint of age similarity, there should be a consistent age difference of just a few years between mates. The zoologist Janet Leonard suggests that this relatively small average age difference between mates is due partly to the fact that human males achieve reproductive maturity later than females. In fact, males lag behind females in reaching puberty and full adult growth by two years, on average. In addition, she argues, because competition among males for mates is slightly greater than competition among females, males require more time than females after reaching physiological maturity to hone their competitive skills and become successful at acquiring mates. This would further increase the age difference between mates. So, if humans paired up strictly as a function of similar age (for the reasons Kenrick and Keefe suggest), but offset similarity in age by sex differences in the achievement of reproductive maturity (for the reasons Leonard suggests), males would be a few years older, on average, than the females with whom they pair. And this corresponds closely with the average age difference Buss found in his marriage data.

This age difference could be the result of evolution's having equipped males with a simple preference for females who are a little younger and females with a simple preference for males who are a little older. These preferences could have been adaptive in our evolutionary past by helping to ensure matings between individuals of comparable reproductive maturity at the point in life at which reproduction typically began, which in turn helped ensure extended cooperation in providing parental care.

Let's call this alternative hypothesis the *hypothesis of adjusted age homogamy*. Like Buss's hypothesis, this hypothesis makes a prediction about mate preferences and provides an evolutionary explanation of those preferences. The hypothesis of adjusted age homogamy predicts that males and females both prefer similarly aged mates, but that the preferred ages are adjusted for sex differences in age at reproductive maturation. This entails that males prefer females who are a few years younger than themselves and that females prefer males who are a few years older. This hypothesis thus explains why Buss found that males prefer and mate with females who are a few years younger. More interestingly, however, it also explains why age similarity—albeit adjusted age similarity—would be such a robust effect in human mating.

We have, then, two hypotheses to consider. One is Evolutionary Psychology's hypothesis that males have an evolved preference for young women because young women have the greatest reproductive potential. The other is the hypothesis of adjusted age homogamy, according to which males have an evolved preference for females who are, on average, a few years younger than themselves. These hypotheses make competing predictions regarding the preferences of forty- or fifty-year-old males. Evolutionary Psychology's hypothesis predicts that males of all ages should prefer—and, when possible, mate with—women in their early twenties. The hypothesis of adjusted age homogamy, on the other hand, predicts that forty-year-old males should prefer women in their late thirties, while fifty-year-old males should prefer women in their late forties. Both hypotheses, however, predict that males in their late twenties should prefer mates in their early midtwenties. Buss's finding that marriages occur between twenty-eight-year-old males and twenty-five-year-old females, on average, and that this accords closely with the stated preferences of young males, is actually compatible with both hypotheses. Thus, Buss's findings don't actually confirm Evolutionary Psychology's hypothesis, since they don't rule out the competing hypothesis of adjusted age homogamy.

But Kenrick and Keefe conducted a study that does appear to show that males do, indeed, have a preference for young women, not simply for slightly younger women. Rather than averaging the ages at marriage of all the subjects in their samples, Kenrick and Keefe examined the average age differences between spouses at marriage for separate age groups—for individuals who married in their teens, twenties, thirties, forties, fifties, and sixties.

Kenrick and Keefe expected that age similarity would be a large factor in mate choice, for the reasons already discussed, but expected that males would also prefer females of peak reproductive potential. Consequently, they hypothesized that males weigh both age similarity and reproductive potential in mate choice, with the result that actual choices of mate strike a balance between the two potentially competing considerations.

This has some interesting implications. For a male in his twenties, like Buss's average respondent, similarly aged females are also those near their peak reproductive potential, so males in their twenties should prefer females in their early twenties. But, as males age, similarly aged females are increasingly further from their peak reproductive potential, so older males must trade off the increasingly competing considerations of age similarity and reproductive potential. Thus, Kenrick and Keefe predicted, "whereas aging males should prefer progressively older women (because of similarity), they should also prefer women progressively younger than themselves (to maximize reproductive opportunities)."[13] That is, as males get older, the average age difference at marriage between self and spouse should gradually increase. While the age difference at marriage should be relatively small for males in their twenties, it should be fairly large for older males, who must choose females no older than their forties in order to have mates with some remaining, albeit small, reproductive potential.

Kenrick and Keefe examined all the marriages that took place in Seattle in January 1986 and a sample of those in Phoenix in January and May 1986. To ensure that their results would not simply be an artifact of 1980s America, they also examined a sample of one hundred marriages in Phoenix in 1923. And to further ensure that these combined results would not simply be an artifact of American culture, they examined all marriages on the Philippine island of Poro between 1913 and 1939.

Kenrick and Keefe found the same pattern in all their samples. The 1986 samples were virtually identical. In these samples, on average, males who married in their twenties married females a year or so younger; males in their thirties married females a few years younger; males in their forties married females about six years younger; males in their fifties married females about nine years younger; and males in their sixties married females about ten years younger. The sample of Phoenix marriages in 1923 showed the same pattern for males in their twenties and thirties, but there were even greater age differences between older males and their spouses. In 1923 Phoenix, males in their forties married females about thirteen years younger, and the age difference between spouses increased a year for each decade of male age after that. Finally, in Poro, on average, males in their twenties married females three years younger; males in their thirties married females about nine years younger; males in their forties married females about twelve years younger; males in their fifties married females fifteen years younger; and males in their sixties married females a full twenty years younger.

Although these data appear to provide straightforward confirmation of Kenrick and Keefe's hypothesis that males weigh both age similarity and reproductive potential in selecting a mate, thus striking a balance between the two considerations, things are not quite that simple. First, as the psychologist Kim Wallen points out, the principal period of fecundity for women is between the ages of twenty and forty, and the average age of menopause is fifty. But the data show older males, on average, marrying women who are past the period of principal fecundity and much older males marrying women who are in their postreproductive years or very nearly so. If reproductive potential is a significant factor in male mate choice at all, regardless of the male's age we should not find males marrying women who are at or very near the end of their reproductive careers.

Of course, males aren't the only ones doing the choosing. It may be that males in their late fifties and older are unable, for the most part, to attract and marry women with significant remaining reproductive potential. So the fact that older males marry women with little or no reproductive potential could simply be a result of compromise in the mating market. Perhaps older men would rather marry significantly younger women, but they can't, so they settle for women who are postmenopausal or very nearly so.

But Kenrick and Keefe also gathered data from personal ads, in which advertisers indicated a preferred age or age range for their respondents, and the pattern of average preferred age differences from the ads closely matched the pattern of average age differences in the marriage data. As the age of male advertisers increased, the average age difference between them and their desired respondents also increased. However, although men in their fifties and sixties did express a preference for much younger women, *on average*, the ages they preferred still fell near the end of or beyond female reproductive potential. So, on average, older males not only marry women who are postreproductive or nearly so, but *seek them* as well.

This is not what we should expect given Kenrick and Keefe's hypothesis. Even if males choose mates by weighing both age similarity and reproductive potential, when a potential mate has little or no reproductive potential, age similarity should count for little or nothing in mate choice. For, by Kenrick and Keefe's account, age similarity factors into male mate choice only because it facilitates extended cooperation in providing parental care. But, if a postreproductive mate is chosen, there will be no

offspring for whom to provide parental care. So a preference for age similarity can facilitate parental cooperation only if it plays second fiddle to
the preference for reproductive potential. However, Kenrick and Keefe's
marriage data and preference data appear to show that a preference for age
similarity among older males virtually trumps any preference for reproductive potential.

A second problem is that the samples of marriages of males in their fifties
and sixties consist almost entirely of males who are remarrying, as Kenrick
and Keefe acknowledge. Evolutionary Psychologists argue that it is enlight-
ening to examine the choices that males of those age groups make when
they are seeking new mates. But their mating decisions present only a
partial picture of the mating decisions of males in those age groups.

Consider the fact that the National Marriage Project of 2000 found that
40 to 50 percent of all marriages end in divorce. Suppose we adopt the
extreme estimate that 50 percent of marriages end in divorce. Some of
these divorces are attributable to serial marriers (or serial divorcers, depending on whether you're a romantic or not), for whom two out of three, three
out of four, or even seven out of eight marriages end in divorce. So, even
if as many as 50 percent of all marriages end in divorce, it is not the case
that 50 percent of all those who marry end up getting divorced. *At least*
50 percent of all men who marry do *not* get divorced, hence never remarry,
so about half of all men in their fifties and sixties have decided to remain
married. Since this half will have married much earlier in life, by Kenrick
and Keefe's own data, their wives will be relatively close to their own ages.
The divorce data, and independent data about the frequency of infidelity,
however, shows that married people frequently have the option of taking
up with a new mate. So, these males are making genuine *choices* to remain
married, since they always have the option of divorcing and looking for a
new mate. Remaining married is actually a continual *choice of one's spouse*
over others. Thus, half the older male population is choosing to remain in
mateships with women who are no longer capable of bearing children. A
hypothesis about male mate preferences can't be tested exclusively on the
males who choose to remarry after fifty. The choices of males who remain
in mateships with no reproductive potential have to be considered as well.

Third, Kenrick and Keefe's analysis of the data suffers from a problem
that plagues Buss's analysis as well. They base their analysis entirely on the
*averages* in their samples and ignore the variation. But, as Kenrick and Keefe
admit: "Individual subjects showed wide variation in their preferences,
however, and in their choice of marriage partners. There were older men
who sought, and others who married, women their own age."[14]

Kenrick and Keefe don't report the variation in their data, but the evolutionary psychologist Karl Grammer reconstructed the variation from their personal-ad data. Grammer found the variation to be much higher than one would expect if males prefer mates with high reproductive potential. Consider a couple of examples. Among 53-year-old males, preferences for mate age ranged from 35 to 57, and among 56-year-old males they ranged from 46 to 52. The marriage data undoubtedly exhibit similar ranges, although they aren't reported by Kenrick and Keefe. This means, however, that a significant number of males in their fifties and sixties *both prefer and choose* postreproductive women as mates. And this doesn't conform to Kenrick and Keefe's predictions.

Apart from these specific problems with Kenrick and Keefe's hypothesis, there is a general reason why it's problematic to test hypotheses about mate preferences against sample averages alone, as both Buss and Kenrick and Keefe do. As we saw in chapter 1, variation is not only the fuel on which selection burns, but is itself often produced and maintained by selection. As a consequence, patterns of variation can be highly significant, because they can indicate that different, possibly frequency-dependent, strategies are being pursued. To put this another way, Evolutionary Psychologists assume that each hypothesis about past selection entails a prediction about a single adaptation that evolved in response to it. As a result, Evolutionary Psychologists tend to focus only on the sample average to see whether it conforms to the phenotypic value they derive from their hypothesis about past selection. But hypotheses about past selection can entail the coexistence of multiple adaptive phenotypes in a population. In such cases, phenotypic values in a population may be bimodally (or trimodally) distributed. Such distributions, however, are concealed when only sample averages are calculated. So, rather than collapsing variation inside sample averages, we should always ask whether there is a potential explanation of the variation itself.

There is not sufficient data at this point to strongly confirm any hypotheses about the precise nature and source of variation in male preferences regarding age differences between themselves and their mates. But there is sufficient data to suggest a possibility. Let's review a few of the relevant facts.

First, even if we focus only on the *average* age differences between males and their mates, we find that older males, on average, both prefer and mate with females who are very near or at the end of their reproductive careers. So, if males are weighing both age similarity and reproductive potential in choosing their mates, they are placing too great a weight on age similarity *if* they are still looking to reproduce. Second, when we consider the variation in the data, rather than just the averages, we find that many older males both prefer and choose postmenopausal females as mates. Third, the older males in Kenrick and Keefe's preference data and marriage data are either on the market for mates or remarrying, respectively. This group fails to represent that larger portion of older males who have chosen to remain in mateships with postreproductive females.

When these facts are considered together, they seem to call into question Evolutionary Psychology's standard depiction of the mating life of the human male. Evolutionary Psychologists typically focus only on the fact that a female's reproductive career is limited by menopause while a male can, theoretically, produce offspring well into old age. This focus portrays males throughout the life cycle as virile and sexually heroic.

Although it is, indeed, *possible* for most males to sire offspring even into old age, the fact is that precious few males do sire offspring in old age, even in hunter-gatherer populations. A fertility study of the !Kung of the Kalahari Desert showed that male fertility peaks at thirty, declines slightly to the age of forty, then declines rapidly. Although 25 percent of all individuals born survive to age sixty, fifty-year-old males have only about a 3 percent chance of siring an offspring, and by age fifty-five male fertility drops to zero. In addition, a British fertility study of 8,515 couples found that males over thirty-five were half as likely as males under twenty-five to impregnate their partners within twelve months, even after the study controlled for their partners' age and health. Moreover, male sex drive peaks in the twenties, then declines continually throughout the rest of life. Accompanying this decline in sex drive is a reduction in the size of the testes, a reduction in the volume and force of ejaculation, and a significant reduction in the number of motile sperm in an ejaculate. The above facts hardly paint a picture of a well-oiled sex machine designed to impregnate females even on a deathbed. There is a very real degradation in male sexual function beginning in middle age and continuing throughout the latter part of the life cycle. Might this change be accompanied by a shift in male reproductive effort?

*Reproductive effort* refers to the allocation of physiological resources among the component demands of survival and reproduction. It is expended throughout the life cycle and includes factors such as growth. For our purposes, we can consider just the strategic allocation of resources between *mating effort* and *parenting effort*. Mating effort, of course, is effort expended to mate. An organism that mates indiscriminately and invests nothing in the spawn of its matings allocates all of its reproductive effort to mating effort. In contrast, an organism that mates only until offspring are produced, then forgoes any further mating in order to invest itself fully in caring for its offspring, allocates part of its reproductive effort to mating effort and the majority to parenting effort.

Parenting effort, recall, is essential to reproductive success. For, if one's children fail to reproduce, one has hit a genetic dead end just as surely as if one failed to have children. Reproductive success requires providing care and resources for one's children in an effort to ensure that they in turn reproduce. But it's just as important that one's grandchildren and great-grandchildren reproduce as well, for precisely the same reasons. So, wherever selection favors parental investment, it should also, and for the same reasons, favor *some* investment in one's remoter descendants in an effort to help ensure their survival and reproduction. Of course, life is limited, and in humans the opportunity to invest in descendants is typically limited to grandchildren. Since the lifespan is long enough to overlap with the lives of one's grandchildren, however, there is an opportunity to allocate some reproductive effort to *grandparenting effort*—to caring or providing resources for, or aiding one's children in caring or providing resources for, one's grandchildren.

The anthropologist Kristen Hawkes and her colleagues have found that, through caring and providing resources for their daughters and their daughters' children, grandmothers can promote their reproductive success more than if they were to have more offspring themselves. By providing care and resources to her daughter and her daughter's children, a grandmother enables her daughter to resume childbearing more quickly than she would if she had to care for herself and her children on her own. And the number of additional children this enables the daughter to produce exceeds the number of children the grandmother would be able to produce and successfully care for were she to continue having offspring of her own. In other words, *even if* postmenopausal women could still have children, they would nonetheless increase their expected genetic contribution to future generations more through grandparenting effort than through continued mating effort.

No one has studied grandfathering to a fraction of the extent that Hawkes and her colleagues have studied grandmothering. But the psychologists Harald Euler and Barbara Weitzel did a study of grandparental investment in Germany. Euler and Weitzel asked adult subjects to indicate on a seven-point scale, ranging from 1 (not at all) to 7 (very much), how much each of their grandparents had provided care for them up to the age of seven years. Euler and Weitzel were primarily interested in whether paternity uncertainty affected the degree of grandparental investment. They reasoned that the father's parents should invest less than the mother's parents because of the possibility of mistaken paternity. They also reasoned that grandfathers should invest less than grandmothers because of their own possibly mistaken paternity of their putative children. As a consequence, they claimed, paternal grandfathers should invest the least of all due to the possibility of two counts of mistaken paternity. Euler and Weitzel did find that maternal grandmothers invested more than maternal grandfathers, that paternal grandmothers invested more than paternal grandfathers, and that the maternal grandfather invested more than the paternal grandmother. These patterns seem to support their hypothesis that paternity uncertainty affects grandparental investment.

What is most interesting for our purposes, however, is their finding that grandfathers were rated as significantly investing in their grandchildren. The average rating of investment by maternal grandmothers was 5.09, whereas the average rating of investment by maternal grandfathers was 4.51. Similarly, the average rating of investment by paternal grandmothers was 4.20, whereas the average rating of investment by paternal grandfathers was 3.80. Clearly, grandmothers were more investing than grandfathers. However, the difference between grandmothers' averages and grandfathers' averages is not very large. And this is not simply an artifact of grandfathers' being pressed into service by nagging grandmothers, for the average investment rating of widowed grandfathers was still fairly high. Widowed maternal grandfathers got an average rating of 4.17, and widowed paternal grandfathers got an average rating of 3.89. Thus, although grandmothers are clearly more investing than grandfathers, there is still evidence of significant grandparenting effort on the part of older males, especially on the part of fathers of daughters with children.

This at least raises the possibility that, like grandmothers, though to a lesser extent, grandfathers can enhance their reproductive success through grandparenting effort. This could be the case if the rate of return on grandparenting effort exceeded the rate of return on continued mating effort. This seems possible given the decline in sexual function in older males and the fact that most older males are simply not as attractive as younger men to young women (so they cannot compete as successfully for matings with young fertile women). So, for most older males, continued mating effort would likely not pay. Further, since the rate of return on joint grandparenting effort would be greater than that on single grandparenting effort, it might pay older males to remain in mateships with their postmenopausal spouses and continue joint investment in their children and grand-children.

If all of this is correct, then we should see shifts in the distribution of reproductive effort across the male lifespan. Upon reaching reproductive maturity and intrasexual competitive success, a male's reproductive effort should, of course, be wholly directed to mating effort. Upon the birth of a child, some reproductive effort previously directed to mating should be redistributed to parenting effort, and each new child should effect further such redistributions. With advancing age, the diminishing returns on mating effort should effect a further redistribution of reproductive effort from mating to parenting. And the birth of grandchildren should further diminish the effort devoted to mating in favor of increased parenting and grandparenting effort.

These shifts in the distribution of reproductive effort would entail shifts in the importance attached to a mate's age. At the peak of mating effort, a male should place greatest weight on the reproductive potential of a mate. Since this will occur fairly early in a male's reproductive career, we should find males in their twenties exhibiting a preference for similarly aged, though slightly younger, mates. As mating effort diminishes with advancing age, however, we should find males' placing less emphasis on youth and a greater emphasis on qualities that facilitate joint parenting and grandparenting effort. Since age similarity may facilitate such joint efforts, we should expect males to begin exhibiting a preference for ever older females. The overall effect, then, would be one in which young men exhibit a preference for slightly younger, fertile females, mating with such females, then sticking with them *out of preference* in order to jointly invest in children and grandchildren.

I am not suggesting, however, that this strategy is universal. Kenrick and Keefe's data clearly demonstrate that some males continue to allocate most of their reproductive effort to mating effort, even as they age. And a male dedicated to mating effort should pursue females with reproductive potential. But, for the reasons discussed, such males represent only a fraction of their sex. The majority of males either remain in mateships or, when they reach their fifties and sixties, prefer and choose postreproductive females as mates. It is possible that these males are pursuing an investing "grand-father strategy," while the older males who prefer and choose much younger women as mates are pursuing a strategy dominated by mating effort. The former would conform to the predictions of the hypothesis of adjusted age homogamy, while the latter would conform to the predictions of Evolutionary Psychology's hypothesis that males have an evolved preference for young women.

One question this account might raise is why the older males who remarry would still choose older females, since they are clearly no longer in jointly investing mateships with the grandmothers of their grandchildren (if they have any). There are a couple of possibilities. First, they may still be investing in their grandchildren, and to expend mating effort with a new female could detract from that grandparenting effort in a way that may not have a clear reproductive advantage. (In this connection, it would be interesting if a disproportionate number of males who remarry to older women have daughters with children, since they appear to invest more heavily in their grandchildren than do males with sons with children.) Second, the different male strategies could be a function of different personality types. In that case, males who are of the "mating effort" personality type will consistently get divorced more often and attempt to remarry fertile young women, whereas males who are of the "investing grandfather" personality type will remarry slightly younger women on average.

Of course, as I say, there is insufficient evidence at this point to confirm any of these speculations. What is clear, however, is that the data don't fit Evolutionary Psychology's simple hypothesis that males prefer and choose females of high reproductive potential. In fact, when variation in the data is taken into consideration, along with the reproductive choices of all those males who remain in mateships even when their mates can no longer bear offspring, a hypothesis that there are different male reproductive strategies at work in the populations studied fits the overall data much better. In particular, the data are compatible with the hypothesis that some males pursue a strategy of trading mating effort for parenting and grandparenting effort as they age (and hence don't continue to pursue young women), whereas other males pursue a strategy of trading parenting and grandparenting effort for mating effort (and continue to pursue young women even as they age). Though much more evidence needs to be gathered, once it is in, male reproductive strategies will no doubt appear far more complex than Evolutionary Psychology makes out. It is doubtful that the desire for fertile young women is as ineluctable a part of male psychology from puberty to death as Evolutionary Psychologists claim.

The hypothesis that many males will shift reproductive effort from mating to parenting and grandparenting as they age, placing less importance on youth in a mate as they age, can also explain other results that Evolutionary Psychologists claim support their hypothesis. Kenrick and

Keefe and their colleagues conducted a study to test whether males actually prefer females who are near peak reproductive potential or whether they simply prefer slightly younger females. They argued that the preferences of adolescent males provide a crucial test of these alternative hypotheses. For, if adolescent males prefer *older* females, they claimed, the preference for females of peak reproductive potential must be deeply ingrained in male sexual psychology.

Kenrick and Keefe and their colleagues interviewed 103 males between the ages of twelve and eighteen, asking them to "think of the most attractive person you could possibly imagine" going on a date with and to indicate how much older or younger than the respondent that person is.[15] They also asked their male subjects to indicate the minimum and maximum acceptable ages of a potential date, again in terms of a difference from the respondent's age. They found that males from twelve to sixteen indicated that females who were 3 to 4 years older were most attractive, and that seventeen-year-old males indicated that females 6 years older were most attractive. They also found that, averaged across ages, these young males were willing to date females who were between 1.57 years younger and 6.0 years older than themselves.

Both results seem to indicate an adolescent male preference for somewhat older females, especially females near peak reproductive potential. "The most interesting feature of these data," the authors say, "is that adolescent males expressed an interest in females substantially older than themselves, despite the fact that older females' age preferences showed no evidence of a reciprocal interest in younger males."[16] Thus, since these preferences couldn't possibly be experientially induced by reciprocal female interest, they concluded that the results had to indicate an evolved preference for peak reproductive potential.

But, according to the hypothesis of shifting reproductive effort, these results are instead a by-product of the fact that adolescent males, who have yet to reproduce, represent pure, unadulterated mating effort. And, when reproductive effort is devoted exclusively to mating, we can expect males to prefer fertile females. Thus, rather than indicating that male preference is focused laser-like on the female years of peak reproductive potential, these results only reinforce that, when preferences are a function of mating effort alone, males will prefer fertile young females.

Further, these results are not as surprising as Kenrick and Keefe and their colleagues make out. They claim that their results show the robustness of male preference for fertile young females because adolescent males cannot possibly have been encouraged in these preferences by having experienced reciprocal interest from females in their early twenties. But, given the conditions of the interview, there is nothing at all surprising about the fact that the adolescent males responded as they did. For the interviewers primed the subjects with the following instructions: "I'd like you to think for a second about what type of person you would find attractive. Imagine you were going to go on a date with someone. *Assume that the person would be interested in you. . . .*"[17] Here the interviewers are explicitly instructing the respondents to imagine a situation *of reciprocal interest*, not the real world in which older females aren't interested in adolescent males. If the adolescent subjects hadn't been explicitly instructed to assume reciprocal interest on the part of *any female they could imagine*, their responses may have been different. Indeed, if they were responding on the basis of their real-world preferences, they may have indicated a preference for females closer to their own ages.

One other study deserves comment before we turn our attention to female mate preferences. In *The Evolution of Human Sexuality*, Donald Symons argues that the preferences of homosexuals provide an "acid test" for evolutionary hypotheses about mate preferences. For, according to Symons, the two sexes bring very different sets of desires to the act of mating, and these differences in desire engender conflict. As a result, heterosexual mating, Symons argues, always involves both parties' compromising their true desires in order to form a less-than-perfect union. But homosexuals need never compromise, since both parties bring the same sets of desires to homosexual unions. Thus, Symons claims, the preferences of homosexual men and women should reveal the pure, uncompromised evolved desires of each sex.

Playing off this idea, the anthropologist William Jankowiak and his colleagues had both heterosexual and homosexual men and women rank photographs of members of their desired sex on the criterion of physical attractiveness. They found that both heterosexual and homosexual men consistently ranked the photographs of younger individuals as most attractive, while both heterosexual and homosexual women placed no emphasis on youth in their attractiveness rankings. Consequently, in *The Evolution of Desire*, Buss takes the fact that homosexual men placed such a clear emphasis on youth in their attractiveness rankings as clear evidence of an evolved male preference for youth in a mate.

But it's not at all clear what to make of this result. For recall that Buss says, "according to evolutionary psychologists, the evolutionary model predicts that what men desire is not youth per se, but rather *features of women that are associated with reproductive value or fertility*."[18] One of the features allegedly associated with reproductive value, recall, is a waist-to-hip ratio of roughly 0.70. Needless to say, young males typically don't have waist-to-hip ratios of 0.70, and the males featured in gay men's magazines embody very masculine, muscular physiques, not pseudo-feminine physiques. Since male preference for youth in mates is supposed to be subserved by a module designed to detect signs of youth in women, that module would have evolved to detect things like a 0.70 waist-to-hip ratio and then to signal the desirability of the creature with that feature. Thus, the detection equipment that allegedly evolved to aid males in detecting young women can't possibly be at work in gay male judgments of the attractiveness of young males. So gay male attractiveness judgments can hardly be evidence of an evolved preference for features associated with fertility in women.

On the other hand, it may not be the case that men have an evolved preference for a 0.70 waist-to-hip ratio. The idea that they do comes from studies by the psychologist Devendra Singh. Singh showed his subjects line drawings of females with four waist-to-hip ratios in each of three weight categories. He found that Caucasian male college students, older Caucasian males, Indonesian male students at the University of Texas, and African-American male college students all found females with a 0.70 waist-to-hip ratio to be the most attractive. Evolutionary Psychologists quickly inferred that the preference is universal, since the samples were ethnically mixed and there appears to be an adaptive rationale for the preference (that a 0.70 waist-to-hip ratio is correlated with peak reproductive potential).

But these results have come under scrutiny, and it is anything but clear that there is a universal preference for a 0.70 waist-to-hip ratio (and the youth putatively associated with it). Though tapping different ethnicities, all of Singh's subjects were living in the United States. Even though some were Indonesian, they were a self-selected group who chose to attend college in the United States, possibly indicating an antecedent psychological affinity for American culture. To attempt to control for the effects of American culture on the responses, the biologist Douglas Yu and the anthropologist Glenn Shepard presented Singh's line drawings to males in an isolated indigenous population in southeast Peru. Males in this population consistently rated the "overweight" female with a 0.90 waist-to-hip ratio as most attractive. In fact, the females with a 0.70 waist-to-hip ratio were described as having "had diarrhea a few days ago" or having "had fever, lost weight, especially in the waist." Similarly, in a study of the Hadza, a hunter-gatherer population in Tanzania, the anthropologists Frank Marlowe and Adam Wetsman found that male Hadza exhibited a preference for "overweight" females with a high waist-to-hip ratio. Interestingly, both of these counterexamples come from hunter-gatherer populations, which Evolutionary Psychologists believe provide good models of the ancestral human populations in which our mate preferences evolved.

Further, the psychologists Louis Tassinary and Kristi Hansen argue that Singh's line drawings confound waist-to-hip ratio with mere waist size relative to overall body size. Tassinary and Hansen constructed a new, more numerous set of line drawings designed to separate the factors of weight, hip size, and waist size (whereas Singh's drawings had separated only weight and waist-to-hip ratio). Presenting their line drawings to a sample of American undergraduate males, they found that overall weight and hip size relative to overall body size were more significant factors in attractiveness judgments than waist-to-hip ratio. In short, by varying the line drawings presented to subjects, Tassinary and Hansen were unable to replicate Singh's results.

So it's anything but clear that males are most attracted to females with a 0.70 waist-to-hip ratio, which is supposedly correlated with peak reproductive potential. This doesn't mean, however, that the gay male attractiveness judgments can be unproblematically reintroduced as evidence of an evolved male preference for youth. For reasons to be discussed in chapter 6, it is very unclear how homosexual preferences fit into Evolutionary Psychology's scheme of evolved psychological sex differences. For these reasons, gay male attractiveness judgments don't conclusively demonstrate anything about heterosexual male mate preferences.

### Women Seeking Men

"Choosing a mate is a complex task," David Buss says, "and so we do not expect to find simple answers to what women want. Perhaps no other topic has received as much research attention in evolutionary psychology, however, and so we have some reasonably firm answers to this long-standing question."[19] Indeed, female mate preferences have been the focus of roughly twice as many studies in Evolutionary Psychology as male mate preferences. But, despite the efforts on this front, Evolutionary Psychology's answer to the question of what women want is not exactly firm.

As we have seen, Evolutionary Psychologists claim that women have an evolved preference for high-status men because, "in general, the higher a male is in status . . . the greater his ability to control resources across many situations" and to invest those resources in his mate and their offspring.[20]

This presupposes that, throughout our evolutionary history as hunter-gatherers, males have been the primary providers of food and other resources to their mates and their offspring and that, as a consequence, females evolved to prefer the males who excelled in this role.

As I pointed out in chapter 3, however, there is significant variation among hunter-gatherer populations with respect to male contributions to the diets of their young. In some hunter-gatherer populations female foraging provides a full 67 percent of the total daily caloric intake. And Kristen Hawkes found that a Hadza woman and her children receive more food from her mother than from her mate. As I argued, it's not clear which of the various hunter-gatherer populations we are to take as representative of our Pleistocene ancestors, or even whether Pleistocene hunter-gatherers led a uniform lifestyle.

This fact poses a problem for the claim that females have evolved a universal preference for males who show signs of being able providers. For, if ancestral hunter-gatherer populations were just as variable as contemporary hunter-gatherer populations with respect to the degree of male provisioning, then a preference for high-status males may have evolved in populations with high male provisioning, but not in populations where males provided relatively little in the way of essential resources. Given our lack of knowledge of our ancestors' lifestyles, as detailed in chapter 3, we simply don't know whether selection would have favored and made universal a female preference for high-status, resource-holding males.

In keeping with this skepticism, a number of researchers—for example, Linnda Caporael, Alice Eagly, and Sarah Blaffer Hrdy—have challenged Evolutionary Psychology's account of female mate preferences. They argue that female preference for high-status males results from current economic inequality, not past selection. In this view, a preference for males with resources is a rational response to a social situation in which males control economic resources, since in such circumstances a female can gain access to economic resources only through her choice of mate.

Evolutionary Psychologists have dubbed this view the "structural (or economic) powerlessness hypothesis." They argue that this hypothesis entails the prediction that women in high-paying professions should place less emphasis on status in mate choice than unemployed women or women in low-paying jobs. Evolutionary Psychologists claim to have shown this prediction to be false. Thus, they claim, the evidence favors the evolutionary hypothesis over the structural powerlessness hypothesis.

What's at stake here is whether female preference for high-status males is an adaptation. Evolutionary Psychologists claim it is, and the structural powerlessness hypothesis claims it isn't. As I mentioned earlier, this debate is not my central concern. For, despite their disagreement with Evolutionary Psychology, advocates of the structural powerlessness hypothesis still accept that there is a robust female preference for high-status males. But, in what follows, I will argue that there is no good evidence of such a robust preference among women.

Before examining that evidence, it is worth asking what *status* is. Status "refers to an individual's relative position in a social group; it is a measure of where one stands among one's peers and competitors."[21] This definition is very abstract, and its abstractness poses two problems. First, women would have had to evolve a mechanism to detect status. Second, Evolutionary Psychologists have to construct experimental instruments that can detect whether women prefer high-status men; so they need measures of male status that can be incorporated into their questionnaires and experiments and used to elicit a female preference for high-status men.

Evolutionary Psychologists have analyzed the concept of status into two more readily measurable characteristics, and it is typically assumed that these are the concrete indicators of status on which women rely in assessing males. The first concrete indicator of status is *dominance*, which is "a measure of one individual's ability to prevail over another in competitive encounters," since "the higher a male is in dominance . . . , the greater his access to a variety of fitness-enhancing resources."[22] The second concrete indicator is *socioeconomic status* (SES), which includes earning power and occupational prestige. Thus, when Evolutionary Psychologists test to see whether women prefer high-status males, they construct experimental instruments designed to determine whether women prefer dominant or high-SES males. So let's look at the studies. The first we'll examine employs the criterion of dominance, while the others employ the criterion of high SES.

The Evolutionary Psychologists Edward Sadalla, Douglas Kenrick, and Beth Vershure presented 86 female undergraduates with descriptions of dominant and nondominant males. The dominant male was described as follows:

John is 5'10" tall, 165 lbs. He has been playing tennis for one year and is currently enrolled in an intermediate tennis class. Despite his limited amount of training he is a very coordinated tennis player, who has won 60% of his matches. His serve is very strong and his returns are extremely powerful. In addition to his physical abilities, he has the mental qualities that lead to success in tennis. He is extremely competitive, refusing to yield against opponents who have been playing much longer. All of his movements tend to communicate dominance and authority. He tends to psychologically dominate his opponents, forcing them off their games and into mental mistakes.[23]

The nondominant male was described as follows:

John is 5'10" tall, 165 lbs. He has been playing tennis for one year and is currently enrolled in an intermediate tennis class. Despite his limited amount of training he is a very coordinated tennis player, who has won 60% of his matches. His serve and his returns are consistent and well placed. Although he plays well, he prefers to play for fun rather than to win. He is not particularly competitive and tends to yield to opponents who have been playing tennis much longer. He is easily thrown off his game by opponents who play with great authority. Strong opponents are able to psychologically dominate him, sometimes forcing him off his game. He enjoys the game of tennis but avoids highly competitive situations.[24]

Sadalla, Kenrick, and Vershure then asked their female subjects to rate the sexual attractiveness and dating desirability of both males. Subjects used a seven-point scale with 7 being highest. On the dimension of sexual attractiveness, John the Dominant received an average rating of 5.37, while John the Nondominant received an average rating of 4.05. On the dimension of dating desirability, John the Dominant received an average rating of 4.56, while John the Nondominant received an average rating of 3.49. Sadalla, Kenrick, and Vershure concluded that females are most sexually attracted to dominant males and find them most desirable as mates.

You'll note, however, that the experiment fails to include a male who is described as neither dominant nor nondominant. One description depicts John as *dominating* the other males with whom he competes, while the other depicts him as *easily dominated by* his competitors. But there is no description of a male who neither easily dominates nor is easily dominated by others. So the psychologists Jerry Burger and Mica Cosby decided to run the experiment again and include the "missing control condition."

Burger and Cosby had 118 female undergraduates read the same two descriptions that Sadalla, Kenrick, and Vershure used, but they added the following "control" description, which says nothing about whether John is dominant or nondominant:

John is 5'10" tall, 165 lbs. He has been playing tennis for one year and is currently enrolled in an intermediate tennis class. Despite his limited amount of training he is a very coordinated tennis player, who has won 60% of his matches.

Burger and Cosby then had their subjects rate the sexual attractiveness and dating desirability of all three males. Subjects used a seven-point scale, but this time 1, rather than 7, was highest (so, in this study, lower scores are better).

Like the previous study, Burger and Cosby found that, on the dimension of sexual attractiveness, John the Dominant received an average rating of 3.63, although John the Nondominant received an average rating of 4.11. Also like the previous study, they found that, on the dimension of dating desirability, John the Dominant received an average rating of 3.72, while John the Nondominant received an average rating of 3.97. However, John the Control, who was described as neither dominant nor nondominant, received an average rating of 3.19 on the dimension of sexual attractiveness and 3.11 on the dimension of dating desirability. Not only are these scores higher than John the Dominant's scores, but they are significantly higher. These results indicate that, although women may prefer dominant males to males who are easily dominated, they may prefer males who are neither to both of the others.

The concept of dominance, however, may carry negative connotations, which may have influenced how female subjects responded to the descriptions they were given. Given only the descriptions provided, female subjects may have (unconsciously) inferred that John the Dominant's dominance and competitiveness would be directed at his mate as well. And this may have made John the Dominant appear less desirable than a male who is not depicted as so aggressively dominant, especially when that male is also not depicted as a pushover. It may be that females actually do desire mates who are toward the top of the male status hierarchy, but that they just respond negatively to the connotations of the concept of dominance employed in these experiments. So let's look at the battery of studies that have used the other concrete indicator of high status, high SES.

The most fun studies purporting to demonstrate that females prefer high-SES males were conducted by the anthropologist John Marshall Townsend and the psychologist Gary Levy. The procedures and results of these studies were almost identical, so I will focus primarily on one of them, since it is representative of the others and discussion of it applies equally to the others.

In Townsend and Levy's study, 112 white female undergraduates from Syracuse University were shown photographs of two male models, who were selected for this purpose because an independent group had rated one as very handsome and the other as very homely. In the photographs, each male model was dressed in each of three different "costumes." One was the uniform of a Burger King employee, intended to depict low SES. Another was a plain off-white shirt, to depict medium SES. And the third was "a white dress shirt with a designer paisley tie, a navy blazer thrown over the left shoulder, and a Rolex wristwatch showing on the left wrist," to depict high SES.[25]

The female subjects were asked to indicate their degree of willingness to enter six types of relationship, ranging from very casual to very serious, with "someone like" the models. The six types of relationship were described as "coffee and conversation," "date," "sex only," "serious involvement, marriage potential," "sexual and serious, marriage potential," and "marriage." Subjects were instructed to indicate their degree of willingness on the following five-point scale: (1) very willing, (2) willing, (3) undecided, (4) unwilling, and (5) very unwilling.

To simplify discussion, I'll focus on three representative relationship types: "date," "serious involvement, marriage potential," and "marriage." The average ratings from the female subjects for these three relationship types are presented in table 5.1.

Townsend and Levy found two aspects of the results in table 5.1 to be significant. First, at each level of involvement (from date to marriage), each model got better ratings in the high-SES costume than in the other costumes. The sole exception was that the handsome model was a slightly more desirable date in the medium-SES costume than in the high-SES costume. As the level of involvement became more serious, however, even

**Table 5.1**
Average Female Willingness to Enter a Relationship as a Function of Male "Costume"

*Handsome model*

| Level of involvement | Costume | | |
|---|---|---|---|
| | High SES | Medium SES | Low SES |
| Date | 2.16 | 1.94 | 2.82 |
| Serious involvement | 2.58 | 2.74 | 3.87 |
| Marriage | 2.53 | 2.77 | 3.84 |

*Homely model*

| Level of involvement | Costume | | |
|---|---|---|---|
| | High SES | Medium SES | Low SES |
| Date | 2.57 | 4.00 | 3.69 |
| Serious involvement | 3.20 | 4.35 | 4.13 |
| Marriage | 3.17 | 4.38 | 4.18 |

the handsome model scored better in the high-SES costume than in either of the other costumes. Second, high status appears to compensate for homeliness, since the high-SES costume raised the homely model's acceptability at every level of involvement over that of the handsome model in the low-SES costume. Townsend and Levy conclude that females prefer high-status mates. And the Evolutionary Psychologist Bruce Ellis interprets the experiment as showing that "status and economic achievement are highly relevant barometers of male attractiveness, more so than physical attributes."[26]

But, if we look at the data in a different way, we see a different barometer. For, at every level of involvement and at every status level, the handsome male is preferred over the homely male. In fact, the handsome male in the medium-SES costume scored better than the homely male in the high-SES costume, despite the fact that the latter can presumably provide more resources than the former. So the results could equally well be interpreted as showing that physical attributes are "highly relevant barometers of male attractiveness," more so than male status.

In addition, although Townsend and Levy claim that status compensates for homeliness, since the homely model in the high-SES costume scored higher than the handsome model in the low-SES costume, the homely model scored 3.20 and 3.17 for serious involvement and marriage respectively. Both of these scores lie between "undecided" and "unwilling" in the scale used to indicate degree of willingness to enter a relationship with someone like the model. So high SES doesn't appear to make females *willing* to enter a serious relationship with someone they find homely. (Also, the homely model inexplicably scored better in the low-SES costume than in the medium-SES costume, despite the fact that medium-SES males can provide resources that low-SES males can't. There is no doubt some fashion advice lurking here about who should wear plain off-white shirts.)

While Evolutionary Psychologists typically deemphasize the role of male physical attractiveness in female mate preferences, both of these objections could easily be accommodated simply by claiming that women weigh both physical attractiveness and status in choosing a mate. The data, it could be claimed, demonstrate that both have significant effects on female mate preferences. Thus, the data don't have to be a perfect fit to the prediction that females prefer high-status males, they only need to show that status plays a role in female mate preferences. And the data do seem to demonstrate this.

But there is a problem with the data nonetheless, which is due to the fact that Townsend and Levy's subjects were all university students. As we have seen, homogamy is the most robust mating phenomenon, and status homogamy is second only to race homogamy in the strength of its effect on mate choice. There are two possible explanations for this. First, it may be that everyone competes for high-status mates, but only high-status individuals succeed in attracting high-status mates. This effect could trickle down to other status levels, with the result that everyone ends up with a mate of comparable status. Second, it may be that people actually prefer mates of comparable status, and status homogamy results from this preference. The sociological evidence actually favors the second explanation. People mate with those of comparable status primarily out of preference, rather than settling for a mate of comparable status because of an inability to get a mate of higher status.

But why would anyone prefer to mate with a fellow medium-status individual, say, rather than a high-status individual? The reason could well be the one that Kenrick and Keefe give for why age similarity is important in mate choice. Recall that Kenrick and Keefe argued that *all forms* of similarity between mates may facilitate long-term parental cooperation, since homogamously mated individuals have "similar expectations, values, activity levels, and habits."[27] Consequently, they suggested, selection may have favored homogamous mating—a "birds of a feather mate together" principle—among our ancestors. If this is right, then we should expect people to prefer mates of comparable status in addition to mates of similar age. As a consequence, assortative mating by status would be fairly robust, which in fact it is.

Studies of status homogamy have considered four different dimensions of status: education level, cultural status of occupation, income level, and social-class origins. Of these, educational homogamy is the most robust. Overwhelmingly, people select mates who have achieved (or will achieve) a comparable level of education. Indeed, one of the boundaries that is very rarely crossed in mating relationships is the boundary between those who have some college education (like Townsend and Levy's female subjects) and those who have only a high-school education (presumably like Townsend and Levy's Burger King employee). Consequently, the fact that Townsend and Levy's subjects preferred medium- to high-SES males over low-SES males could simply be an artifact of assortative mating by status. The results could simply be due to the fact that the female subjects perceived the low-SES model as uneducated and tended to consider only males of probable comparable education level as prospective mates.

This explains why the models would score so low in the low-SES costumes, but why would they score higher in the high-SES costumes than in the medium-SES costumes? Is this also the effect of status homogamy, or does it reveal a genuine preference for high-SES males?

To know for sure, we would need status information about Townsend and Levy's female subjects, and Townsend and Levy don't report having gathered such information. But recall that status involves social-class origins and cultural status of occupation in addition to level of education. The relevant information about respondent status would thus include information about social-class origins. Respondents with higher class origins should be expected to favor the high-SES models. Relevant information would also include not simply education level achieved at the time of response (which was sufficient to already place a social barrier between the respondents and the low-SES models), but also *anticipated* achieved level of education. Similarly, it would include anticipated occupation. Status homogamy should lead us to expect that all of these factors would influence female preference. And, if more of Townsend and Levy's female respondents were themselves high SES than medium SES, and if all respondents gave the highest score to the models from their own SES, then the average ratings of the high-SES models would be higher than the medium-SES models, even if all medium-SES respondents rated the medium-SES models highest.

There is reason to think that Townsend and Levy's sample *was* composed predominantly of high-SES females (or at least females who were toward the upper end of the SES continuum). For all the female subjects were white female undergraduates at one of the nation's most expensive private universities, and at least half of them belonged to sororities (half were interviewed in sororities). So it is highly probable that females with upper-middle-class origins were overrepresented in the sample. Further, there should be a correlation between these class origins and higher levels of anticipated educational achievement and anticipated occupational status. And females who are high-SES along these dimensions would prefer the high-SES models on the basis of status homogamy alone. Since the sample was no doubt composed predominantly of high-SES females, then, it should be expected that the average ratings of the high-SES models would exceed those of the medium-SES models.

Interestingly, Townsend repeated this experiment with 82 female law students, this time supplementing the pictures with descriptions. The model in the Burger King uniform was described as training to be a waiter who would earn a starting salary of $15,000 a year, the model in the off-white shirt as training to be a teacher who would earn $22,000 a year, and the model in the Rolex as training to be a doctor who would earn $80,000 a year. Guess what. The female law students preferred the doctor. But this doesn't necessarily indicate a preference for high SES per se. For this preference is precisely what we should expect if female law students were choosing mates of comparable education level, comparable cultural status of occupation, and comparable projected income level.

Further, the female law students rated the high-SES models higher than the college students had. This is also precisely what we should expect from assortative mating by status, since the law students form a more homogeneously high-status sample than the undergraduates. Because the undergraduate sample was less status homogeneous, containing a higher ratio of medium-SES respondents, they gave a lower average score to the high-SES model. In short, the Townsend and Levy data fit the preference ratings that would result from status homogamy alone.

Thus, given the composition of the subject groups in these experiments, none of the experiments can distinguish whether female respondents were indicating a genuine preference for a mate with high SES or whether their ratings were a product of simple assortative mating by status. Given the independently documented robustness of status homogamy, we already know that, if you ask medium- and high-SES females what they want in a mate, they will show a preference bias against low-SES males. In order to distinguish a genuine preference for high status from assortative mating by status, we would need data on the preferences of low-SES females. We would also need a subgroup analysis by status of female preferences; that is, we would need to see female preference orderings broken down by SES of female respondent. Evolutionary Psychologists have provided no such data, but it would be needed to substantiate their claim that females desire high-SES males. For without this data, there is no evidence that medium-SES females don't prefer the medium-SES model over the ostentatious high-SES model, or that low-SES females don't find the handsome model in the Burger King uniform most desirable of all. Only if low-SES females systematically indicate a preference for high-status males can we infer a real preference for high status. However, the independent evidence of status homogamy suggests that the latter preference pattern would not be found.

Of course, it is entirely possible that women actually have an evolved preference for high-status men, but that the experiments conducted by Evolutionary Psychologists have simply failed to reveal that fact because their results are confounded by status homogamy. This could be the case, for example, if dominance and high SES, as those are articulated in the experimental instruments used by Evolutionary Psychologists, are poor measures of the kind of status that women have evolved to prefer. After all, this preference is supposed to have evolved long before people had education levels and incomes or had careers as doctors and lawyers. And the ability to easily dominate opponents in tennis matches, which weren't played in the Pleistocene, may not set off alarms in women's evolved status-detection modules. So maybe Evolutionary Psychologists have simply used experimental procedures that are incapable of detecting female preference for high-status mates, though it is there waiting to be detected.

Although this is a possibility, I doubt it's true. As Evolutionary Psychologists standardly define the concept, status "refers to an individual's *relative position in a social group;* it is a measure of where one stands among one's peers and competitors."[28] If selecting a high-status mate had, and continues to have, significant fitness consequences for women, as Evolutionary Psychologists claim, we should expect women to have evolved techniques of detecting *social relations* among males. They should have evolved to be sensitive to the structural features of male interactions, detecting how males form a hierarchy in their interactions with one another, regardless of which particular intrinsic male qualities are correlated with high or low status. And, if women have evolved to be sensitive in this way to where a male stands in relation to other males, and to prefer those who are in the upper strata of male hierarchies, the kinds of experiment we've discussed should detect that preference. So, the fact that the results of these experiments are confounded by status homogamy probably isn't due to the experiments' making use of cues that didn't indicate status in the Pleistocene.

At this point Evolutionary Psychologists could respond that assortative mating by status cannot explain the sex differences they consistently find. For studies of mate preferences consistently find that women place a greater emphasis on a potential mate's status than do men. If female preferences for high status are simply a by-product of the fact that the female experimental subjects are relatively high status themselves and are merely indicating a preference for males of comparable status, then we should expect male experimental subjects (who tend to be from the same social classes as female subjects) to place a comparable emphasis on a potential mate's status. For, if people prefer mates of similar status, that should be evident not only in female preferences, but in male preferences as well. But study after study finds that a potential mate's status doesn't matter to men in the way that it matters to women.

The studies showing a sex difference with respect to preferences for high-status mates have focused on the income dimension of status, finding that women care more about a potential mate's earning capacity than men do. One such study was conducted by Douglas Kenrick in collaboration with the psychologists Edward Sadalla, Gary Groth, and Melanie Trost. Kenrick and his collaborators provided 64 female and 29 male undergraduates with a list of characteristics and asked them how they would weigh those characteristics in choosing a partner for a date, for steady exclusive dating, and for marriage. "Participants were asked to give the minimum and maximum percentiles of each characteristic that they would find acceptable in a partner at each level of involvement. Several examples were given to clarify any questions about the percentile concept, e.g., 'A person at the 50th percentile would be above 50% of other people on [the characteristic] kind and understanding, and below 49% of the people on this dimension.' "[29]

The primary evidence supporting the claim that females desire high-status mates came from responses regarding *minimum acceptable earning capacity*. With respect to this characteristic, average responses for each sex were as presented in table 5.2, and these results do appear to show that male earning capacity plays a strong role in female mate choice. Indeed, in accordance with Evolutionary Psychologists' expectations, as the level of involvement becomes more serious, and consequently a male's ability to provide resources becomes increasingly important, females appear to place increasing weight on earning capacity. And this result appears to confirm that women prefer high-SES males.

Again, however, the female subjects were all American undergraduates, hence, on average, of medium SES or higher. (Education level alone would make them of medium SES, but some may be higher because of higher social-class origins, anticipated high-status occupations, or anticipated high income levels after college.) Thus, again, it is not clear whether the results actually demonstrate a preference for high status per se, or whether they merely reflect status homogamy. For, again, if the subjects are predominantly from the upper half of the socioeconomic continuum, and if

**Table 5.2**
Average Minimum Acceptable Earning Capacity of a Potential Partner

| Level of involvement | Earning capacity (expressed as percentile) | |
| --- | --- | --- |
| | Female respondents | Male respondents |
| Date | 44.58 | 23.79 |
| Steady dating | 61.08 | 36.86 |
| Marriage | 67.17 | 42.21 |

they express preferences for same-status males, their average preference rating will fall in the upper half of the socioeconomic continuum.

But what about the sex difference in the results? Males clearly placed much less emphasis than females on earning capacity, although males did, like females, place greater emphasis on earning capacity as the level of involvement increased. If the results are a product of assortative mating by status, we should expect males to express the same preferences as females: Medium- to high-SES males should indicate a preference for females whose earning capacities fall in the medium- to high-SES range. But, in fact, the average minimum acceptable earning percentiles preferred by males run a full 20 to 25 percentile points lower than female averages. Doesn't this show that the results are not an artifact of status homogamy and that females have a genuine preference for high status per se in a mate?

In short, no. Recall that status has four dimensions: education level, cultural prestige of occupation, social-class origins, and income level. In American society (from which the subjects in this experiment were drawn), earning capacity is a cue to, or a predictor of, other dimensions of a male's status in a way that it is not for a female. In American society, women hold only about one-quarter of the jobs in professions paying over $40,000 a year. And, in professions and trades where women hold a larger fraction of the jobs, women earn only about three-quarters as much as men performing the same job. Given this significant economic inequality between the sexes, a medium-SES male seeking a medium-SES female can expect his prospective mate to earn significantly less than he does, even if they are perfectly matched on other dimensions of status. Consequently, even if upper-SES subjects chose mates by employing the criterion of similar status alone, females should specify significantly higher minimum acceptable earning percentiles for prospective mates than males, since income is a better predictor of other dimensions of male status than it is of other dimensions of female status.

If people select mates of comparable status because people of comparable status have "similar expectations, values, activity levels, and habits," and these similarities facilitate parental cooperation (as per Kenrick and Keefe's argument), surely education level, occupation, and social-class origins are better indicators of one's values and so on than income level alone. Social-class origins and the education level one achieves play a role in shaping personality, expectations, and values, and chosen occupation is a reflection of one's values and expectations in life. One's income, in itself, is much less a reflection of one's values and character than the other dimensions of status. So, education level, occupation, and social-class origins should be more important factors in mate choice than income level. And the sociological evidence of status homogamy does show these factors to have a stronger effect on mate choice than income level. Since economic inequality between the sexes makes income level a better predictor among males than females of these other dimensions of status, if subjects are asked specifically to rate the importance of income level in mate choice, we should expect females to accord it greater weight than males. Thus, under conditions of economic inequality between the sexes, a sex difference in the importance attached to a potential mate's earning capacity is fully consistent with simple assortative mating by status.

In addition, if you reread the instructions given to participants in Kenrick's study, which I quoted above, you'll see that subjects were instructed to provide percentile rankings for each characteristic *relative to the whole population* ("50th percentile would be above 50% of other people"), not just relative to the sex of a potential mate. So males indicated a preference to marry a woman whose income is in the 42nd percentile of all Americans, not just in the 42nd percentile of American women. Similarly, females indicated a preference to marry a man whose income is in the 67th percentile of all Americans, which includes the lower-earning female half of the population. Thus, if the earning-capacity percentile rankings were adjusted to accommodate the economic inequality between the sexes, the sex difference in the rankings would virtually disappear.

My argument sounds suspiciously like the structural powerlessness hypothesis, but it's not exactly the same. According to the structural powerlessness hypothesis, women desire high-SES mates because, under conditions of economic inequality between the sexes, the only way a woman can gain access to economic resources is through her mate. The suggestion I'm making is that, in the results obtained by Kenrick and his collaborators (and in similar studies), women only *appear* to desire high-SES mates because only upper-SES women have been asked about their preferences, and the economic inequality between the sexes results in a sex difference in the percentiles assigned to the characteristic *minimum acceptable earning capacity*. The structural powerlessness hypothesis takes the reality of a female preference for high earning capacity for granted, and I'm suggesting that females merely appear to prefer high earning capacity, but that the data don't provide good evidence that they in fact do. Nonetheless, my suggestion is similar enough to the structural powerlessness hypothesis to warrant examining the evidence that Evolutionary Psychologists present against the latter.

Evolutionary Psychologists contend that the structural powerlessness hypothesis entails that female preference for high earning capacity should vary with a female's own economic power, so that women with a high earning capacity should place less emphasis on earning capacity in choosing a mate than do women with a low earning capacity. Evolutionary Psychologists claim that two studies have shown this to be false. First, from his large survey, Buss had data on personal income and class background for 100 of the female respondents from his United States sample. Among this group, he found that "women who make *more* money tend to value monetary and professional status of mates *more* than those who make less money."[30] Second, the Evolutionary Psychologists Michael Wiederman and Elizabeth Allgeier asked 637 female undergraduates and 167 women in two Ohio communities to rate the importance of several characteristics in the selection of a husband, one of which was *good financial prospect*. They also asked them to indicate the annual income they expected to earn in the following year or in the years immediately after finishing college. They found that "the more personal income the women in the sample expected to earn, the more likely they were to value good financial prospects in a mate."[31] Evolutionary Psychologists claim that both results directly contradict the prediction entailed by the structural powerlessness hypothesis and support their evolutionary hypothesis.

But there are a few problems with this claim. First, it's not clear that the structural powerlessness hypothesis in fact entails the prediction tested. The structural powerlessness hypothesis claims only that females will prefer high-income mates under conditions of economic inequality, in which women gain access to economic resources primarily through their mates. One way that a preference for high-income mates could become prevalent among women under such conditions is through "socialization" during formative childhood and teen years. Women could be encouraged by their family members, friends, or other advisors to select high-SES mates (doctors, lawyers, or the like). There is no reason why a preference formed through twenty or so years of such socialization should disappear simply because a woman finds herself earning a good salary. So, the structural powerlessness hypothesis doesn't actually entail that high-paid women will not share a preference for high-SES mates with other women.

Second, it's not at all clear how the data support Evolutionary Psychology's hypothesis. If women have an evolved preference for high-status males, which translates into a preference for high-income males in contemporary societies, they should prefer as high an income as they can get in a mate, regardless of their own income. Evolutionary Psychology's hypothesis doesn't entail that medium-SES women should have lower standards for income in a potential mate than high-SES women.

However, third, if women prefer males in their own socioeconomic group, then medium-SES women will, on average, exhibit a preference for medium-SES males, which will appear as a preference for a moderate ability to provide resources. High-SES women, on the other hand, will exhibit a preference for high-SES men, which will make them appear to desire an even greater ability to provide resources than is desired by medium-SES women. Such preference patterns are precisely those that assortative mating by status should lead us to expect. So, again, the data are unable to demonstrate a female preference for high status per se rather than simple assortative mating by status.

Of course, all the studies so far considered have involved only American female subjects. So perhaps the results of these studies are confounded by status homogamy simply because the studies made use of unrepresentative samples. If so, a much larger, cross-cultural study should be able to provide results that are not confounded by status homogamy.

This larger study would obviously be Buss's cross-cultural study, in which he had his male and female respondents rate the importance of eighteen characteristics in choosing a mate. Respondents used a four-point scale, ranging from 0 (irrelevant or unimportant) to 3 (indispensable). In thirty-six of Buss's thirty-seven samples, females valued the characteristic *good financial prospect* significantly more than did males. In the remaining sample (Spain), females valued it more than males, but the difference was not significant. In the entire study, the average female rating of *good financial prospect* was 1.76 and the average male rating was 1.51. This appears to show that female preference for high-SES mates is not an artifact of unrepresentative American samples, but is in fact a robust universal preference.

Despite the size of Buss's sample, however, and despite the number of cultures sampled, the sample is still not representative in the way that would be needed to distinguish a preference for high SES per se from simple assortative mating by status. As Buss himself admits: "The samples obtained cannot be viewed as representative of the populations in each country. In general, rural, less-educated, and lower levels of socioeconomic status are underrepresented."[32] But these underrepresented groups are precisely those who might, on average, place much less emphasis on earning capacity because of status homogamy. In fact, the preference ratings of these groups could significantly lower the average rating of *good financial prospect* and thereby remove the appearance of a female preference for high-SES mates. For, as we have seen, in samples that are skewed toward the upper half of the socioeconomic continuum, assortative mating by status biases preference ratings in favor of males in the upper half, and against males in the lower half, of the socioeconomic continuum.

Further, the psychologists Alice Eagly and Wendy Wood reanalyzed Buss's data and compared it with transnational data on economic inequality between the sexes gathered by the United Nations. They found that the sex difference in ratings of *good financial prospect* by Buss's subjects was greater in societies with greater economic inequality between the sexes. Where there was less economic inequality between the sexes, the sex difference in ratings of *good financial prospect* was smaller.

If, as I have argued, income is a better predictor of other dimensions of status among males than among females under conditions of economic inequality between the sexes, this is precisely the result we should expect. For, under conditions of strict economic equality between the sexes, income will be as good a predictor of other dimensions of status for one sex as for the other, and the sex difference in emphasis on earning power will disappear. The fact that Eagly and Wood found a correlation between degree of economic inequality across societies and the strength of the sex difference in emphasis on *good financial prospect* is thus fully consistent with assortative mating by status. Therefore, since low-SES groups are strongly underrepresented in Buss's study, and since the sex difference in emphasis placed on *good financial prospect* diminishes as economic inequality between the sexes diminishes, even Buss's study fails to demonstrate a female preference for high-SES mates per se.

So far we have considered studies that ask females to indicate the qualities they prefer in a mate, and I have argued that none of these studies demonstrates a preference for high-status males, since all their results are confounded by assortative mating by status. There is, however, another way in which evidence of female preference for high-status mates can be gathered. Rather than asking females what their preferences are, we could ask males how they are doing in their mating efforts. If we find that high-status males enjoy greater mating success than lower-status males it would presumably be evidence of a female preference for high-status males.

This approach was taken in a study by the anthropologist Daniel Pérusse. Pérusse had students at two major French-speaking universities in the Montreal area distribute questionnaires to their native French-speaking friends and relatives, thereby apparently avoiding the problem that plagues samples of college and university students. Respondents were asked to report education level achieved, occupation, and income, which were used as the measures of status. They were also asked to report the number of coital partners during the previous twelve months and the number of coital acts per partner. The information about coital partners and coital acts per partner was used to construct a measure of mating success, which Pérusse called *number of potential conceptions (NPC)*. Mating success was thus represented by the formula

$$NPC = [1 - (1 - p^{P_1})] + [1 - (1 - p^{P_2})] + \ldots + [1 - (1 - p^{P_n})]$$

where $P_i$ is the number of coital acts with the $i$th partner, and $p$ is an estimated probability of conception per coital act, which for a variety of reasons Pérusse set at 0.03.

Pérusse found a very weak correlation between status and mating success (that is, the higher a male's status, the higher his NPC) in the whole sample and no correlation whatsoever between status and mating success for men over forty. The latter was a particularly surprising result, since men older than forty have typically achieved higher occupational and income levels than younger men have; so, if higher-status males enjoy higher mating success, men over forty should show a strong correlation between status and mating success. Given that the correlation between status and mating success for the entire sample was lower than Pérusse expected, he surmised that the over-forty group was responsible for weakening the correlation in the entire sample. Pérusse also speculated that the lack of correlation between status and mating success in the over-forty group was due to the fact that the majority of men over forty were married, hence presumably monogamous, thereby lowering their overall mating success regardless of status.

To test these speculations, Pérusse divided the over-forty sample into married and unmarried groups. Since there were too few unmarried males over forty on which to base a comparison of the two groups (there were 8), Pérusse expanded the two groups to include all married and unmarried respondents between the ages of thirty and forty-nine. Pérusse then compared the correlation between status and mating success for the unmarried males in this age group with the correlation for married males. He found a strong correlation between status and mating success for unmarried males and no correlation for married males.

This seemed to confirm his suspicion that the lack of correlation between status and mating success among married males was due to their presumed monogamy. Married males, Pérusse suggested, "may not be in a position to translate socioeconomic advantages into mating success as freely as uninvolved men would."[33] Thus, he argued, the hypothesis that high-status males have greater mating success—and, by inference, that they are preferred by females—should be tested only against the group of males that is *able* to translate high status into mating success. Since there was a strong correlation between status and mating success among the unmarried males between thirty and forty-nine, Pérusse concluded that high-status males have the greatest mating success. And Evolutionary Psychologists have often cited Pérusse's study as strong confirmation that females prefer high-status males.

There are, however, a number of problems with Pérusse's conclusions. First, his measure of mating success (the formula defining NPC) is flawed. By Pérusse's measure, a male who has evenly spaced one-night stands with ten women over the course of a month has a 30 percent chance of conception. By contrast, a male who has sex with a single mate on the same schedule over the course of a month has only a 26 percent chance of conception. Given that sperm can survive in the womb for five days, a male who inseminates his mate every three days is guaranteed to have sperm present in her womb during the entire fertile phase of her cycle. In contrast, the odds of inseminating a woman during her fertile phase through a one-night stand are far lower. As a result, a male who inseminates his mate every three days should have a higher probability of conception than a male who copulates only once with a number of women and who has a low probability of insemination during the fertile phase with each. Indeed, if this weren't the case, monogamy would never have evolved in the human lineage, since it would never have paid males to stick with a single mate (a point that I will elaborate further in chapter 6). Thus, Pérusse's measure of mating success is inappropriately designed to assign a higher degree of mating success to unmarried males with multiple partners than to (presumably monogamous) married males. Consequently, Pérusse didn't have good grounds for excluding the married males from the sample against which his hypothesis was tested. Of course, when they are included, the correlation between status and mating success is very weak.

Second, Pérusse's argument that married men are less able than unmarried men to translate status into mating success rings hollow. As already noted, the divorce rate is very high, a fact that can't possibly be lost on unmarried women. If high-status males are truly so attractive to women, we should expect some women to pursue even married high-status men in the hope of luring them away from their mates and into a new mateship. If high-status men are pursued in this way, we should also expect many of them to use the promise of leaving their wives as a means of enticing their pursuers into extramarital affairs. Since there is no shortage of extramarital affairs in this world, if there is a correlation between status and mating success, we should thus expect married high-status males to engage in extramarital affairs more frequently than lower-status males and thus to still report greater mating success than their lower-status counterparts. But Pérusse's data show no evidence of this.

Interestingly, in this connection, the psychologist Steven Gangestad and the biologist Randy Thornhill did a study of the frequency of extrapair copulation. Gangestad and Thornhill had the men and women involved in 203 heterosexual relationships complete a questionnaire asking them, among other things, to report how many extrapair sex partners they had had (that is, how many sex partners they had had outside a primary relationship during that relationship) and how many people had chosen them as extrapair sex partners (that is, how many sex partners they had had who were seriously involved in other relationships at the time). Gangestad and Thornhill found no correlation whatsoever between the number of extrapair partners or the number of times chosen as an extrapair partner and male SES or expected income (typical measures of status). If women truly prefer high-status men, however, high-status men should have a greater frequency of extrapair copulations.

Third, and most important, the sample of unmarried males between thirty and forty-nine in which Pérusse found a strong correlation between status and mating success consisted of only 18 males. This is far too small a sample on which to base any meaningful subgroup analysis, such as comparing the mating success of males of differing statuses, for the analysis is then based on just a few males from each status level. Thus, no meaningful conclusions can be drawn from Pérusse's data.

Another study sometimes cited by Evolutionary Psychologists as indirect evidence of a female preference for high-status mates was conducted by the sociologist Glen Elder. Published in 1969, Elder's study was based on an "exchange theory" of human mating, according to which women offer what males desire in exchange for the male characteristics they desire. Elder took for granted that males desire youth and attractiveness in a mate and that females desire high status in a mate, so he expected to find very attractive women mated to higher-status men. Among 76 married women he studied, he found a correlation between female attractiveness and husband's status. Indeed, he concluded that very attractive lower-class women were often able to use their attractiveness to "marry up" and secure a high-status husband.

Commenting on this study, Buss says: "High-status men, such as the aging rock stars Rod Stewart and Mick Jagger and the movie stars Warren

Beatty and Jack Nicholson, frequently select women two or three decades younger. . . . Men who are high in occupational status are able to marry women who are considerably more physically attractive than are men who are low in occupational status."[34] Presumably, the attractive young women are in very high demand, so the greater ability of high-status men to marry them attests to the fact that women desire them more. Indeed, women with the attractiveness that men desire appear to use it to bag the high-status husbands that every woman wants.

There is, however, a problem with this argument. For Elder's study obtained attractiveness ratings for the female subjects, but not for their husbands. Indeed, the only measure of the husbands' desirability that Elder used was status level. This raises the possibility that Elder's findings were confounded by male physical attractiveness. To test this idea, the sociologists Gillian Stevens, Dawn Owens, and Eric Schaefer analyzed the wedding announcements of 129 couples that appeared in the major daily newspaper of a small city. Each wedding announcement contained information about the education levels and occupations of the bride and groom, plus a wedding photograph. The images of bride and groom in these photographs were separated, so that spouses didn't appear together, and a mixed-sex panel rated each bride and each groom for physical attractiveness. Since all couples were dressed in formal wedding attire in the photographs, differences in attractiveness judgments weren't affected by differences in the everyday attire of the brides and grooms. So there were no "Burger King uniform" effects in the attractiveness judgments.

Stevens and her colleagues found a strong correlation between the attractiveness ratings of spouses. Very attractive females married very attractive males, average-looking females married average-looking males, and unattractive females married unattractive males. Indeed, there was a much stronger correlation between the attractiveness of spouses than between female attractiveness and male social status. They concluded that "physical attractiveness plays a large and an approximately equal role in marriage choices for men and for women."[35] In short, mating is strongly assortative by degree of attractiveness.

Further, a number of independent sociological studies have demonstrated a strong positive correlation between attractiveness and both income level and occupational achievement.[36] Highly attractive people have better jobs and make more money, on average, than do average-looking people, who in turn have better jobs and make more money than people who are judged to be homely. Perhaps contrary to what you'd expect, this effect is even stronger among men than among women. Thus,

Elder's finding that higher-status men tended to be married to more attractive women may simply be a by-product of a correlation between high status and high attractiveness among men. Attractive women marry attractive men, who incidentally tend to be more successful than less attractive men. Thus, Elder's study doesn't actually provide the support that Buss claims it does for the idea that women prefer high-status men.

Finally, there is significant evidence from a much larger sample that directly contradicts Evolutionary Psychologists' claim that high-status males enjoy greater mating success (as a result of female preference for high-status males). The sexologists Martin Weinberg and Colin Williams analyzed the data collected by Alfred Kinsey from 5,460 white males in the United States between 1938 and 1963, which remain the most comprehensive data ever collected on sexual behavior. Analyzing sexual behavior by social class of male respondents in the Kinsey data, Weinberg and Williams found a *negative correlation* between social status and mating success (that is, the higher one's social status, the lower one's mating success). They found that low-SES males had coitus at a significantly younger age than high-SES males and that they had more coital partners than high-SES males. The averages, broken down by three social classes, are presented in table 5.3. Weinberg and Williams subsequently conducted a study, in 1969–1970, of 284 white males, that replicated these findings.

Although neither the Kinsey sample nor Weinberg and Williams's sample is truly representative of the general population, they are certainly closer to being representative than the extremely small sample in which Pérusse found a correlation between status and mating success. And these larger, more representative samples present a picture of the relation between male status and mating success that is directly at odds with Evolutionary Psychology's claim that females preferentially mate with high-status males. Indeed, this evidence seems to indicate that sexual activity is greater among low-status males than among high-status males. *Somebody* must like low-status males.

**Table 5.3**
Mating Success of Males by Class

|  | Social class | | |
|---|---|---|---|
|  | Low SES | Medium SES | High SES |
| Age at first coitus | 17.3 | 17.8 | 20.5 |
| Number of partners | 18.9 | 10.5 | 9.6 |

Now, if the evidence for the claim that females prefer high-status males is as weak as I've made out, why is the claim so widely accepted? I think the reason is that we are captivated by a particular picture of the relation between sex and status among our primate relatives, and this picture affects our perception of human mating. It is widely accepted that among non-human primates high-status males have greater mating success than males lower in the status hierarchy. This belief is due partly to the popularity of the engaging work of the primatologist Frans de Waal, who has been one of the main purveyors of this idea. Once we're convinced of the strength of the correlation between status and mating success among our primate relatives, the standards of evidence that are required to convince us of a correlation in humans get lowered considerably. As de Waal says: "In monkeys and apes there is a clear link between power and sex. High-ranking males enjoy sexual privileges, and are more attractive to the opposite sex. We need only look at recent events in the White House (and at a television spectacular like 'Who Wants to Marry a Multimillionaire?') to see how much the link exists in us too."[37]

But there are two problems with this viewpoint. First, to determine whether there is a correlation between male status and mating success in humans, we need do much more than simply look at the Lewinsky scandal and a single sensationalistic television show on the Fox network. We need the same amount and quality of evidence concerning humans that has been gathered about nonhuman primates before we can conclude that we humans are like our primate relatives in this respect. Of course, Evolutionary Psychologists have presented much more than just two items of anecdotal data. But, as I've argued, their evidence fails to demonstrate that females prefer high-status males. It appears more convincing than it is because a conviction about a link between status and sex in primates leads us to think that it *must* also be true that human females prefer high-status mates.

Second, the primate literature is far from definitive in showing a correlation between status and mating success among nonhuman primates. The sociologist Lee Ellis did a literature survey of all studies published on the correlation between status and sex among nonhuman primates. The studies reviewed employed two primary measures of mating success: number of copulations and number of copulations with a female in estrus. Ellis found that two-thirds of all published studies reported a positive correlation between status and one of these measures of mating success, while one-quarter reported no correlation, and the remainder reported a negative correlation. Although more studies report a positive correlation than either no correlation or a negative correlation, there are still more studies that found no positive correlation than would be expected if there were such a strong link between status and mating success among nonhuman primates.

Moreover, there are reasons to think that the studies reporting a positive correlation indicate little about female preference. First, a number of studies that reported a positive correlation were based on observations of captive groups containing only two to four males. This represents a significant restriction on female choice, which would not be faced in the wild. Consequently, the fact that females copulated more with the higher-ranking of two or three males doesn't necessarily indicate that they would prefer those males if given the wider choice they would normally enjoy in noncaptive settings. (Recall how John the Control scored higher than John the Dominant once women were given the option of choosing him.)

Second, one study of macaques found that females in estrus spent more time in close proximity to lower-ranking males than to higher-ranking males, despite the fact that higher-ranking males had higher copulation rates with females in estrus. One could argue that females might prefer the lower-ranking males "as friends," but prefer to mate with the higher-ranking males when it counts. But there is another possibility. Often, among primates, higher-ranking males secure copulations with females by physically driving away lower-ranking males and physically coercing the female. As the biologist Pascal Gagneux and his colleagues say, in such situations, "the degree to which females are able to choose their mates is unclear as the physically stronger males can force them to copulate and even coerce them to enter into a consortship."[38] So the mating success of high-status males in such cases is more a reflection of their ability to control sexual access to females in estrus than it is a reflection of female preference for them. Thus, many of the studies that show a positive correlation between status and mating success indicate nothing about a female preference for high-status males.

An analogous argument can be made regarding studies of status and reproductive success among humans, some of which have found that high-status human males enjoy greater reproductive success than lower-status males. For example, in a well-documented study, the anthropologist William Irons found that, among the Turkmen of Persia, males in the wealthier half of the population left 75 percent more offspring than males in the poorer half of the population. Buss cites several studies like this as indicating that "high status in men leads directly to increased sexual access to a larger number of women," and he implies that this is due to the greater desirability of high-status men.[39]

But, among the Turkmen, women were *sold* by their families into marriage. The reason that higher-status males enjoyed greater reproductive success among the Turkmen is that they were able to buy wives earlier and more often than lower-status males. Other studies that clearly demonstrate a reproductive advantage for high-status males are also studies of societies or circumstances in which males "traded" in women. This isn't evidence that high-status males enjoy greater reproductive success because women find them more desirable. Indeed, it isn't evidence of female preference *at all*, just as the fact that many harem-holding despots produced remarkable numbers of offspring is no evidence of their desirability to women. It is only evidence that when men have power they will use it to promote their reproductive success, among other things (and that women, under such circumstances, will prefer entering a harem to suffering the dire consequences of refusal).

Thus, although we have long been held captive by a picture in which high-status primate males are the preferred mates of primate females, there are reasons for thinking that the picture has been largely an illusion. If we let go of that picture, we will also let go of the reflexive expectation that the link between male high status and female preference exists in us, too. And, if we let go of that reflexive expectation, we will not be so easily convinced by impoverished evidence that human females prefer high-status males. We will then be able to look at the evidence with eyes unclouded by an antecedent conviction regarding what we'll find. When we do, as I have argued, we will see that there is no convincing evidence of a robust female preference for high-status males. Just as male mate preferences will turn out to be more complex than Evolutionary Psychologists have claimed, female mate preferences will no doubt turn out to be more strongly tied to physical attributes of males (physical attractiveness, bodily symmetry, or chemical signaling of histocompatibility) than Evolutionary Psychologists have claimed. Indeed, evidence of this association is already beginning to accumulate.

## Concluding Skeptical Remarks

I have argued that there isn't good evidence for Evolutionary Psychology's two core claims regarding human mate preferences. Although my arguments have pointed out a number of specific problems with those claims, there is a single general reason for skepticism regarding Evolutionary Psychology's core hypotheses about mate choice. The reason is a general argument that selection probably did not act on ancestral human populations in the way that Evolutionary Psychologists have claimed.

To see why, begin with Evolutionary Psychology's concept of *mate value*, which is a measure of "one's overall desirability to members of the opposite sex."[40] An individual's mate value, or overall desirability to the opposite sex, is a function of how much that individual can contribute to the reproductive success of members of the opposite sex. For, since it takes two to make an offspring, and since one's own reproductive success depends on the ability of one's offspring to survive and reproduce, one's own reproductive success is affected by the fitness of one's chosen mate. To get a handle on the concept of mate value, you can think in terms of the crass one-to-ten rating system you were introduced to in high school. Since mate value is a measure of desirability to the opposite sex, a female's mate value is a function of male mate preferences, while a male's mate value is a function of female mate preferences. Since males desire women of peak reproductive potential, according to Evolutionary Psychologists, young women with an hourglass figure, full lips, clear skin, clear eyes, and lustrous hair are "tens" (like Bo Derek in the movie *10*). And, since women desire high-status men, wealthy, powerful men like Donald Trump are tens. As a consequence, working-class males tend to be fours, fives, or sixes, just as women of average attractiveness, or women approaching middle age, with "good personalities," tend to be fours, fives or sixes.

Evolutionary Psychologists look on human mating and see a world in which everyone has an evolved desire to mate with a ten. Since competition for tens is so stiff, however, and since other tens also want to mate with tens, for the most part only other tens get to mate with tens. So wealthy, powerful men mate with beautiful young women; Hollywood producers mate with young starlets. This leaves everyone else competing to mate with the next best thing, the nines. Of course, competition is also stiff for the nines, and since other nines want to mate with nines (because they can't mate with tens), for the most part only other nines get to mate with nines. And so on. As a result, people tend to mate with others of comparable mate value, and working-class males end up marrying average-looking women.

According to Evolutionary Psychologists, although this is the way that mateships play out, it isn't actually necessary that each of us be kicked down the scale of mate value by rejections until we reach our level and find a mate. Experience in the mating market as teenagers and young adults quickly gives us a sense of our own mate value, and we then tend to pursue those with comparable mate value, having learned that pursuing those of higher mate value is futile. In short, you come to realize that you're a six, and you confine your mating efforts to other sixes, occasionally taking a stab at a seven in the hope that you'll bag a mate with slightly higher mate value and thereby enhance your reproductive prospects, however slightly.

In this vision of human mating, tens are the target of evolved human desires, but actual matings involve *compromising* one's desires in the light of realistic assessments of what one is likely to get on the mating market. But here's the catch. As even Evolutionary Psychologists admit, a pair of well-matched fives or sixes (an average-looking woman with a working-class husband) can have just as many offspring as a pair of nines or tens (a supermodel with a rock-star husband). This can happen in different ways. They could, of course, have just as many children. But they could also have fewer children who nonetheless provide them with the same number of grandchildren as are enjoyed by the pair of nines or tens. Similarly, they could have fewer children and grandchildren, but nonetheless have just as many great-grandchildren.

This entails that a six can have just as much reproductive success by "compromising" and mating with another six as by mating with a ten. One doesn't necessarily compromise one's reproductive success by "compromising" one's desires for a mate of maximal mate value. There is nothing about modern environments, however, that should make this fact an evolutionary novelty, an unprecedented quirk of our modern age. Our ancestors who were sixes should have had available the option of "compromising" their desires for tens and mating with fellow sixes, yet nonetheless producing just as many offspring as they could have produced by mating with nines or tens. But, if this is the case, there could not have been strong selection for a *desire* for tens in the first place. For selection could not have distinguished between sixes who desired—*whether requited or not*—to mate with tens and sixes who simply desired and mated with other sixes. In other words, desires for members of the opposite sex over a range of "mate values" would have had equal fitness. Thus, selection would not have favored and driven to fixation a desire for mates of the highest "mate value."

Of course, there is undoubtedly a limit to how far down the scale of putative mate value one can trade before encountering a precipitous decline in reproductive success. It may be that males at the very bottom of the status hierarchy, who can provide absolutely *nothing* in the way of resources, would significantly impair the reproductive success of any females who chose them as mates. The Evolutionary Psychologist Bruce Ellis suggests this when he cites George Orwell's depiction of the lives of homeless males in *Down and Out in Paris and London*. "These men lived a near sexless existence, not by choice, but by virtue of their social position: They were at the very bottom of society and had almost nothing to offer females."[41] (Of course, diminished opportunities for personal grooming may have played some role in their unattractiveness to women, irrespective of status issues.) Similarly, women of nonreproductive ages would no doubt severely impair the reproductive success of any males who consistently chose them, and only them, as mates.

If those who have "almost nothing to offer" members of the opposite sex would significantly impair the reproductive success of those choosing them as mates, we can expect that selection would have designed human mate preferences to discriminate strongly against them. But this process could result in a far less finely graded preference scheme than the one envisioned by Evolutionary Psychologists, for it could primarily divide the opposite sex into those who have something to offer reproductively and those who have almost nothing to offer. The "have-nothings" would not be desired as mates, while the "have-somethings" would be; but *evolved* preferences would not carefully rank the have-somethings in order of their putative potential contributions to one's reproductive success. The reason, as I have argued above, is that matings between different pairs of have-somethings can achieve equal reproductive success, even if those different pairs have different ranks in Evolutionary Psychology's scale of mate value.

Within limits, this is true even with respect to female reproductive potential. Suppose that one could produce five children by marrying a woman in her early twenties, but only two children by marrying a woman in her midthirties. That sounds like a large reproductive differential, but what matters most, of course, is what happens in subsequent generations. If the parents of the two children invest heavily in them and in their offspring, but the parents of the five children don't, the two children could produce just as many, if not more, great-grandchildren as the five children. In short, there are lots of ways to achieve reproductive success.

Evolutionary Psychologists make it sound as though there aren't, since they argue somewhat intuitively that selection would consistently favor those who produce more children by younger women over those who produce fewer by older women. But the crucial fact to bear in mind is that selection will act this way *only if* these propensities to mate with younger or older women are *inherited*—only if sons exhibit the same mating patterns as their fathers. If sons of men who mated with older women themselves mate with younger women, and sons of men who mated with younger women themselves mate with older women, then selection will not drive any particular preference to fixation. Since equal reproductive success can be achieved by matings with women in a range of ages in each generation, as I have argued, selection will not have severely constrained the available choices in each generation. Each generation will have enjoyed a range of flexibility in choosing mates, with equal reproductive success within that range.

Thus, since it should have been possible throughout human evolutionary history to achieve as much reproductive success by mating with a six (a medium-status male or a slightly older, less than stunningly beautiful woman), say, as with a ten, selection will not have designed human mate preferences to be targeted quite so laser-like on the so-called tens. However, we can expect selection to have designed mate preferences that discriminate against those at the bottom of Evolutionary Psychology's scale of mate value.

Of course, this argument is highly sensitive to which characteristics one takes as defining mate value. The argument only works for cases in which one can "trade down" the scale of putative mate value without thereby negatively affecting one's reproductive prospects. There are certainly some characteristics of members of the opposite sex that one cannot trade down very far while still achieving similar reproductive success. If mate value were defined by pathogen resistance, for example, with higher mate value reflecting a greater ability to fight off pathogens, we would certainly find those who mated with sixes leaving fewer offspring than those who mated with nines or tens.

The real question, then, is whether male status and female youth are characteristics that females and males respectively can "trade down" while still achieving comparable reproductive success. My skeptical argument presupposes that, within limits, they are. Evolutionary Psychology's view of human mate preferences presupposes, in contrast, that male status and female youth are characteristics that couldn't have been traded down by our ancestors without a corresponding decline in reproductive success.

Part of the reason to be skeptical of Evolutionary Psychology's view of human mate preferences is that Evolutionary Psychologists have no evidence for this presupposition. In fact, Evolutionary Psychologists have priced themselves out of the market for the evidence they'd need. Typically, the way to test the idea would be to gather evidence about the reproductive success over several generations of males of different status and females of different ages (in all the permutations of their intermating). But, as we saw in chapter 2, Evolutionary Psychologists contend that studies of reproductive success can shed no light on human psychological adaptations, since in modern environments human psychological adaptations can lead to maladaptive behavior. But, for reasons discussed in chapter 3, we also can't have any evidence regarding differential reproduction among our ancestors in the EEA. The most that Evolutionary Psychologists have by way of evidence is their *hypothetical* claims about reproductive success in the EEA—for example, that males who preferred females of peak reproductive potential *would have* outreproduced males who preferred other females. Such hypothetical claims, however, are not evidence. Without evidence that males who mated with young women and females who mated with high-status men produced the most offspring, skepticism is the most reasonable attitude to take toward the claims that males prefer young women and females prefer high-status men as mates.

# 6 | Marriage

Leaving behind the issue of which characteristics people seek in their long-term mates, let's focus now on what long-term mate preferences are *for*. According to Evolutionary Psychology, the function of long-term mate preferences is to select a partner for marriage. Of course, this concept of marriage doesn't involve white flowing dresses, tuxedoes, Wagner's "Wedding March," churches, or the county clerk's office. Even in societies with codified laws, there are legally recognized marriages between people who have never taken vows before a judge or minister. In the United States, these are known as common-law marriages, which are recognized in several states and which, once recognized, must also be recognized as legal marriages by all other states under the full faith and credit clause of the Constitution. Further, in most cultures without systems of codified laws, long-term mateships are ritually sanctioned by the community. If we are not to have too provincial a conception of marriage, these mateships should also count as marriages. But, given the diversity of cultural and legal practices in which long-term mateships are embedded, what makes them all *marriages*?

## What Is Marriage?

Anthropologists have often debated how to define "marriage" so as to capture what all long-term mateships have in common beneath the diverse array of cultural and legal practices built around them. Proposed definitions have focused on cohabitation, the ritual solemnization of a relationship before a community, the nature of the rights possessed by children born of the union, obligations to provide domestic services, rights of mutual sexual access, the social regulation of sexual access to women, and male trafficking in women, among other things.

Unfortunately for the anthropologists proposing the definitions, there has always seemed to be a culture whose long-term mateships didn't fit the proposed definition. This has led some anthropologists to abandon altogether the attempt to define the concept of marriage and others to adopt the idea that it is a family-resemblance concept. According to this latter idea, there is no feature or set of features that all and only marriages have in common. Rather, the relationships in various cultures that anthropologists usefully call marriages merely resemble one another in varying respects—much as two members of the same family can have the same nose but very different eyes, each having eyes that resemble third and fourth family members respectively (who, in turn, may share the same mouth, but have very different eyes and ears).

While there continues to be disagreement among some anthropologists about how or whether to define "marriage," there is consensus among Evolutionary Psychologists that, in its essence, "marriage represents an implicit reproductive contract."[1] The Evolutionary Psychologists Margo Wilson and Martin Daly elaborate this consensus viewpoint as follows: "Marriage is a cross-culturally ubiquitous feature of human societies, notwithstanding variations in social and cultural details of the marital relationship. What this means is that men and women everywhere enter into *individualized reproductive alliances*."[2] These alliances, Daly and Wilson argue, are characterized by the following features: "There is some degree of mutual obligation between wife and husband. There is a right of sexual access (often but not invariably exclusive). There is an expectation that the relationship will persist through pregnancy, lactation, and child rearing. And there is some sort of legitimization of the status of the couple's children."[3] Further, they say, these characteristics serve to distinguish human marriages from the sexual alliances typical among mammals: "The enduring aspect of marriage and its attendant implication of biparental obligations contrast with the usual mammalian state of affairs. Admittedly, marriages fail, but, unlike most mammalian sexual alliances, they are nowhere entered into with the expectation or intent of dissolution when conception or some other reproductive landmark has been attained. Notwithstanding its variable aspects, then, marriage is everywhere intelligible as a socially recognized alliance between a woman and a man, instituted and acknowledged as a vehicle for producing and rearing children."[4]

This conception of marriage has some interesting empirical evidence in its favor. First, in some societies—in the Andaman Islands, in rural Japan, and among the Tiv of eastern Nigeria, for example—a mateship isn't considered a marriage by the community, or entered as a marriage in village records, until it produces a child. Second, in a study of data collected by the United Nations on hundreds of millions of people from 45 societies between 1950 and 1989, the anthropologist Helen Fisher found that childless couples were half again as likely to divorce as couples with a single child, twice as likely to divorce as couples with two children, and four times as likely to divorce as couples with three or more children. Similarly, in a study of 160 societies from around the globe, the anthropologist Laura Betzig found infertility to be the second leading cause of divorce. Clearly, failure to reproduce increases the odds of marital dissolution, which should be expected if marriage is an implicit contract to reproduce. Third, Betzig also found the leading cause of marital dissolution worldwide to be infidelity. If marriage is an implicit reproductive contract, this should be no surprise, since infidelity creates the possibility of both reproduction outside of the union and abandonment; hence, infidelity breaches the "biparental obligations" and "expectation of persistence" that Wilson and Daly see as partly constituting the marital contract.

Defining marriage as an implicit reproductive contract may nonetheless strike you as unduly "reductionist," defining what seems essentially a cultural phenomenon in biological terms ("*reproductive* contract" or "*reproductive* alliance"). Discounting for the moment those cultures in which mateships aren't considered official marriages until the birth of a child, you may wonder what Evolutionary Psychology says about the many couples who become legally or ritually married, but who remain deliberately and steadfastly childless throughout life. If marriage is an implicit reproductive contract, are the unions of nonreproducing couples not marriages, by Evolutionary Psychology's definition, despite their legal or ritual status? Or what about couples who legally or ritually enter their unions without any intention of having children, but later decide to have children? By Evolutionary Psychology's definition, are their unions not actually marriages until the decision to reproduce, despite having been legally or ritually recognized as marriages? On the flip side, you might wonder, what about people who reproduce through brief sexual relationships, which neither party ever intended to be long lasting, let alone reproductive? Does the fact of reproduction make such individuals married?

Consider the latter worry first. According to the "implicit reproductive contract" conception of marriage, the mere fact of reproduction indeed does not constitute a marriage between the reproducing pair, even if reproduction is a consciously intended consequence of the relationship. To be a marriage, a union must be a reproductive *alliance*, not merely a reproductive *dalliance*. And to be an alliance, the parties must share something that parties to dalliances artfully avoid: commitment. It's commitment that involves what Wilson and Daly call "mutual obligation"—obligations of continuance, sexual fidelity, and joint investment in offspring—and that leads to the social recognition of the pair as "a couple." And a relationship characterized by commitment constitutes a *reproductive* alliance because reproduction is the *purpose* of a committed mateship.

This, however, seems to bring us back to the first worry. What about those who are committed to one another, being even legally or ritually married, but who deliberately and concertedly avoid reproducing? In what possible sense is reproduction the *purpose* of their mateship? That is, in what possible sense can two people who have explicitly agreed *not* to have children actually have an implicit contract *to have* children? And, if reproduction isn't the purpose of their long-term mateship, don't such culturally married couples fail to fit Evolutionary Psychology's "reductionist" definition of marriage? And doesn't the existence of such mateships show that it is wrong to conceive of marriage as an implicit reproductive contract?

The answer is no, because reproduction is the purpose of marriage in the functional, not the psychological, sense of the term *purpose*. That is, the claim is not that, consciously or unconsciously, people have the goal of reproduction in mind when they marry. In a great many cases people clearly do have that goal in mind, but whether they do is inessential to whether reproduction is the purpose of marriage. For to say that reproduction is the purpose of marriage is to say that, regardless of one's intentions or desires upon marrying, reproduction is the evolutionary *function* of marriage. And, as discussed in chapter 1, this means that marriage evolved because it enhanced the reproductive success of those who married. Thus, the claim that reproduction is the purpose of marriage doesn't imply that all married *individuals* have the *psychological purpose* of reproducing, that all codified marriage laws make explicit mention of reproduction, or that the social customs that solemnize marriages mandate reproduction. Rather, it implies only that socially recognized sexual and biparental alliances became a cultural universal because they promoted reproductive success.

But how did marriage enhance the reproductive success of those who married? That is, why did mateships characterized by rights of mutual sexual access, biparental obligations, and expectation of long-term persistence evolve in the human lineage? Why, in short, did marriage evolve? To a limited extent, we touched on this issue in the discussion of mate preferences in chapter 5, but it's time to take a closer look at it.

The traditional view of the evolution of marriage takes as its point of departure the fact that human offspring are extraordinarily dependent on parental care for many years. For several years, children are utterly unable to survive without intensive parental provisioning and care. Even after the period of most intensive parental care, children need to learn the complex skills involved in foraging for food and negotiating the social group in order to successfully care for themselves and compete to attract and retain mates. Our large brains presumably evolved in order to acquire and process all the information required for these material and social skills, and during the long developmental period stretching from the toddler years to puberty children need to have their brains filled with instruction in these essential skills. For this reason, according to the traditional view, children who received biparental care during our evolutionary history had a higher rate of survival and subsequent reproductive success, on average, than children who received only maternal care. And, since one's own fitness depends on the ability of one's offspring to survive and reproduce, anything that enhances the fitness of one's offspring thereby enhances one's own fitness. As a result, "pair bonds" evolved as the mechanism by which humans provided long-term biparental care.

There is a subtle aspect of this traditional view that will provide the point of comparison with other theories of the evolution of marriage, but in order to see it clearly we have to approach the problem from another angle. Recall the vast sex asymmetry in minimum obligatory parental investment discussed in chapter 5, and consider the role this asymmetry would have played in the evolution of marriage. Way back when, before marriage evolved, a male's minimum obligatory parental investment was the act of copulation resulting in conception, after which the male could abandon the female and refuse further investment in the offspring. In contrast, conception obliged a woman to pay the cost of a nine-month pregnancy. Once a woman gave birth, of course, she had the option of terminating her investment by abandoning the infant. But, in a population of noninvesting males, this would have consistently resulted in the infant's death. Once an infant was on the scene, then, a female faced a choice between abandonment, which entailed no fitness benefit, or continued investment, which would yield a fitness benefit. Given the lengthy dependency of human offspring, however, continued investment would have obligated women to costly monoparental care for many years. Nonetheless, selection would have favored mothers who sometimes chose continued investment over those who consistently chose abandonment. Thus, human females have always been stuck with long-term parental care in a way that human males haven't. Indeed, in general, in species with internal fertilization the sex that carries prenatal offspring internally (almost always the female) invests far more in offspring than the sex that simply deposits the "fertilizer." In many such species, females provide *all* the parental care and males simply go about copulating. But humans are not such a species, and the puzzle is why.

To solve this puzzle, we need to understand why the sexes would have struck what many throughout history have considered a Faustian bargain. We need to understand the fitness payoffs to each sex for "agreeing" to the marital contract. For women, the payoff for "agreeing" to marriage seems clear. By "agreeing" to enter marriage, women got help caring for their offspring, rather than being stuck with long-term monoparental care, which made their offspring better off, which enhanced their own fitness. (Biparental care also appears to have decreased the interval between births, thereby enabling women to increase their total number of offspring.) But why did *males* choose to enter contracts to provide long-term parental care? Why didn't males simply stick with the minimum obligatory parental investment of copulation and devote all their time to trying to impregnate as many women as possible? The payoff to males is less clear than that to females, and so many have taken the real puzzle to be, What was the fitness payoff to males for marrying?

When the problem is seen in this way, the traditional view about the evolution of marriage can be seen as claiming that the fitness payoff to males was really the same as that to females. Males evolved to marry because the offspring of those males who provided parental care had greater survivability and subsequent reproductive success, on average, than the offspring of males who didn't provide parental care. In short, males enhanced their own fitness by providing parental care, since their parental care enhanced the fitness of their offspring.

Evolutionary Psychologists accept this traditional view about the fitness payoffs to the sexes for marriage, but they think the evolution of marriage was rather more complicated than the traditional view makes out. As we saw in chapter 1, an organism's activities have associated fitness costs, which include the costs of forgoing the fitness benefits of alternative activities. Parental care is no exception. In fact, parental care is a very costly endeavor, involving the expenditure of the energy required to obtain food and provide protection, among other things. Further, parental care takes time away from the pursuit of matings. The time and energy spent helping one child along could instead be spent making another. A male, then, pays significant fitness costs by providing parental care. If that care is provided to the offspring of another male, then the care-giving male pays the costs of providing care without receiving any of its fitness benefits, since those benefits go to the male whose offspring receive the care. So, Evolutionary Psychologists argue, a male can enhance his fitness by providing parental care *only if* the children he's caring for are in fact his own. Thus, in order for males to accrue fitness benefits from providing care for their offspring, they first needed to *solve the problem of paternity uncertainty*, to maximize the likelihood that the offspring for whom they provided care were in fact their own.

According to Evolutionary Psychologists, males "agreed" to marriage because it helped as much as possible to solve the problem of paternity uncertainty. Through marriage, with its mutual sexual obligations, males achieved round-the-month sexual access to a female, and by the implicit marital contract this sexual access was typically exclusive. To put it in more sinister terms, marriage allowed ancestral males to *monopolize* the reproductive careers of their wives. They would have been content, perhaps, to simply attempt to monopolize females during their fertile periods each month, as chimpanzees attempt to do, but concealed ovulation denied them that possibility. So they had to establish a long-term monopoly over their mates' sexuality, and marriage provided that long-term monopoly. By entering marriages—that is, by forming implicit contracts with females for sexual access and exclusivity—ancestral males were able to reduce their paternity uncertainty and thereby reap the fitness benefits of sowing parental care among only their own offspring.

Thus, whereas the traditional view sees ancestral males as having "agreed" to marriage simply in order to accrue the fitness benefits of biparental care of their offspring, Evolutionary Psychology sees ancestral males as having "agreed" to marriage only on the condition that the investment of parental care that they cast upon children would return *unto them* rather than benefiting some other male. On both accounts, the fitness benefit to males is the same at the end of the day, but according to Evolutionary Psychology the bargain struck between the sexes was more complicated than the traditional view acknowledges.

The anthropologist Kristen Hawkes and her colleagues Alan Rogers and Eric Charnov argue, however, that both accounts are mistaken about the fitness payoff to males of paternal care. Hawkes and her colleagues constructed a number of game-theoretic models in which males have to "decide" how much of their reproductive effort to allocate to parental care of their offspring and how much to allocate to effort to secure as many matings as possible with as many women as possible. In all of the models, males evolve to allocate very little effort to parental care and to allocate the vast majority of their effort to mating, because the potential fitness payoff of parental care is never high enough to offset the potentially very high fitness payoff of increased mating opportunities. Even in those models in which the payoff of paternal care is very large, the evolved allocation to paternal care remains small, because the potential payoff for promiscuous mating is always larger.

The most interesting finding by Hawkes and her colleagues is that, even in a model of a pair-bonded population in which males are assured of paternity, and hence assured that their paternal care isn't misspent, males still allocate very little effort to parental care and the vast majority of their effort to promiscuous mating. To see why this would be so, suppose that a pair-bonded population in which males are assured of paternity was invaded by a mutant "Cad" male who eschewed all parental care and devoted all of his time to widely playing the field of already-mated females. This male would pay the absolute minimum for every offspring he produced, since those offspring would be cared for by the males he cuckolded, while the average payoff of parental care to other males in the population would decrease, since some of them would now be providing parental care to the Cad's offspring rather than their own. So, the overall fitness payoff to the mutant Cad would be greater than the average fitness payoff of the pair-bonded "Dads." As a result, Cads would increase in the population. In order to protect their investments, this would force Dads to allocate much of their time to "guarding" their mates against the charms of the Cads, thus reducing their allocation to parental care. This, however, would reduce the overall biparental care received by offspring in the population, which would in turn reduce the fitness payoff that Dads had been enjoying for being dads, causing Dads to lose further ground against the Cads. In order to keep up, Dads would have to begin allocating some of their effort to pursuing promiscuous matings, which would further reduce their allocation to parental care. Thus, Hawkes and her colleagues found, even in a population in which males are assured of paternity, the evolutionarily stable state is for males to allocate very little reproductive effort to parental care. Consequently, they argue, the benefit that accrues to a male's offspring because of paternal care, hence the fitness benefit that accrues to the male for providing that care, is insufficient to account for the observed level of parental care that human males provide. To put it crudely, during our evolutionary history males didn't "agree" to marriage because of the fitness benefits they accrued from caring for their offspring.

If Hawkes and her colleagues are right, however, what accounts for the evolution of marriage? For, in order for marriage to evolve, both sexes had to have "agreed" to the long-term biparental obligations that characterize marriage. If Hawkes and her colleagues are right, it's puzzling why males would have ever "agreed" to the institution of marriage. But the psychologists Barbara Smuts and David Gubernick have a solution to this puzzle. According to Smuts and Gubernick, long-term male parental care evolved because of *sexual selection* by females for males who provided child care. As in the traditional view, females stood to benefit by choosing care-giving males because of the enhanced survivability and subsequent reproductive success of their offspring. So it paid females to select for care-giving males. But why did males go along with this deal and become care-giving? Because females rewarded care-giving males with ongoing mating opportunities, *hence ongoing opportunities for paternity of offspring.* Thus, males evolved to provide long-term parental care not because of the direct fitness benefits that accrued to their offspring because of that care, but because of the increased opportunities for paternity that they earned from the mothers of the offspring to whom they provided care. In short, according to Smuts and Gubernick, long-term male parental care actually evolved as a form of mating effort, not as a pure form of parenting effort. Accordingly, Smuts and Gubernick call this hypothesis regarding the evolution of marriage the *mating effort hypothesis.*

Smuts and Gubernick's mating effort hypothesis doesn't deny that males accrue fitness benefits from providing parental care to their own offspring. In fact, if a female accrues fitness benefits from the biparental care her offspring receive, then the father of those offspring thereby accrues the same fitness benefits. Smuts and Gubernick merely argue, like Hawkes and her colleagues, that those benefits are insufficient to explain why males would have ever "agreed" to the institution of marriage. The deal-making benefit for males, they claim, was the increase in paternity opportunities provided by the mothers of the children for whom they provided care. Of course, once a female preferentially mates with a male who cares for her offspring, that increases that male's odds of paternity of her next offspring, which increases the odds that his continued parental care will eventually be directed to his own offspring. So, even if a male begins the process by caring for another male's offspring, he can eventually reap the fitness benefits of caring for his own offspring. But, Smuts and Gubernick argue, this fitness benefit was actually a *by-product* of the evolution of male parental care, not the ultimate cause of it.

This presents a slightly different picture of the evolution of marriage than the other views considered. In the traditional view, marriage evolved because both sexes stood to reap precisely the same benefit of biparental care of offspring, so the sexes "agreed" to enter implicit contracts to have offspring and provide them with that care. In Evolutionary Psychology's view, both sexes stood to gain from biparental care, but males "agreed" to provide it *only* on condition that they could be assured of the paternity of the children for whom they provided care. In other words, according to Evolutionary Psychology, marriage evolved as an exchange of parental care (provided by males) for paternity certainty (provided by females). According to the mating effort hypothesis, in contrast, marriage evolved as an exchange of parental care (provided by males) for paternity opportunities (provided by females).

There is significant evidence that favors the mating effort hypothesis over Evolutionary Psychology's hypothesis about the evolution of marriage. First, there is the theoretical finding by Hawkes and her colleagues that the fitness benefit of biparental care, even when conjoined with paternity certainty, is insufficient to account for the observed level of paternal care in humans. This tells against Evolutionary Psychology's hypothesis, but is compatible with the mating effort hypothesis, since according to the latter males are actually securing additional paternity opportunities by providing parental care. Second, there is a large body of empirical evidence that shows there to be no correlation between paternity certainty and male care in primates. Although gibbons are monogamous, and gibbon males enjoy a very high level of paternity certainty, male care is wholly absent in eight of nine gibbon species. In addition, many primate species are characterized by groups in which a single male defends and mates with a number of females. In such species, paternity certainty is very high, yet with one exception, the mountain gorilla, all such species are characterized by an absence of male care. In contrast, there is a high level of male care in many species in which many males live with many females, each of whom typically mates with several of the males in the group during estrus, thereby ensuring that no male enjoys a very high level of paternity certainty with respect to the young for whom he provides paternal care. If male parental care evolved in humans *only on condition* of female assurance of paternity, because of the severe fitness costs of providing paternal care to another male's offspring, then paternity certainty should also be a necessary condition for paternal care in other primate species, since males of those species should also suffer the costs of providing care for another male's offspring. But the correlation simply isn't there. Moreover, in several of the species mentioned, a positive correlation *has* been found between a male's mating with a female and his providing care for her offspring, regardless of whether the male was their father. Consequently, the mating effort hypothesis provides a more plausible account of the evolution of marriage than does Evolutionary Psychology's paternity certainty hypothesis.

Since Smuts and Gubernick claim that ancestral women selected for men who provided child care, however, the mating effort hypothesis may appear to support Evolutionary Psychology's claim that women have an evolved preference for males who control, and are hence able to provide, a lot of resources (that is, "dominant" or "high-status" males). But Smuts and Gubernick's hypothesis concerns actual hands-on care—feeding, carrying, holding, grooming, and protecting. Their idea is that females preferred males who actually spent a lot of time caring for children, not that females preferred males who spent a lot of time away from the nest fighting for control of "resources" that could be triumphantly brought back home to the wife and kids at the end of the day. In contemporary terms, this is not like preferring an ambitious man who will spend long days at work in order to earn a high income, but like preferring a man who will change diapers, give baths, and take the children to the playground. So their hypothesis about the evolution of marriage differs significantly from Evolutionary Psychology's claims about the evolution of mate preferences.

The respect in which the mating effort hypothesis does not differ from Evolutionary Psychology is in its fundamental conception of marriage as an implicit reproductive contract. Indeed, according to the mating effort hypothesis, marriage is an implicit contract whereby paternal care is exchanged for paternity opportunities. The difference between the mating effort hypothesis and Evolutionary Psychology's hypothesis regarding the evolution of marriage won't be significant, however, until we discuss jealousy in the final section of this chapter. So, for the remainder of this section, I would like to return to the fundamental conception of marriage as an implicit reproductive contract, which Evolutionary Psychology shares with the mating effort hypothesis.

As mentioned earlier, saying that marriage evolved as an exchange of paternal care for paternity certainty or paternity opportunities does *not* mean that ancestral members of either sex were consciously or unconsciously motivated by a desire to exchange paternal care for paternity certainty or paternity opportunities. It does *not* mean that males in any way calculated odds of receiving increased paternity certainty or paternity

opportunities by providing parental care or that females in any way calculated the odds of receiving continued paternal care by providing males
with ongoing paternity opportunities. Hypotheses about the evolution of
marriage are *not* hypotheses about the *motives* that caused ancestral
humans to enter and remain in marriages. They are hypotheses about the
*beneficial effects* of marriage because of which the sexes evolved to enter
marriages. But, of course, long-term mateships characterized by "biparental
obligations" and "expectations of persistence" couldn't have evolved in
the human lineage unless each of the sexes had *some* actual motives that
inclined them toward entering and remaining in such mateships. In other
words, marriage couldn't have evolved unless each of the sexes had desires
and emotions that made them *want* to get married and remain married;
marriage couldn't have evolved unless it actually satisfied certain *felt needs*
for each of the sexes. So, if marriage is an adaptation, we can expect that
some of our desires and emotions became or remained a part of our psyches
because they were the motivational impetus that promoted marriage
among our ancestors.

Since Evolutionary Psychology is concerned with the evolved nature of
the mind, its real interest is in the evolved emotions and desires that underlie human marriage. As Donald Symons says, Evolutionary Psychology's
focus is the question, "What species-typical mental mechanisms underpin
marriage and divorce?"[5] Gesturing toward a partial answer, Symons continues: "In various times and places, the following seem to have been
common motives for getting or staying married: recognition in the community; material well-being; status, or power; children; companionship, or
friendship; 'attachment'; the state of being in love, or romantic love; sexual
desire, or *eros*; love, or *agape*."[6] But the cluster of psychological states that
serves to keep us in marriages probably also includes our desires for and
expectations of our mates' fidelity and continued affection, as well as
actual *felt obligations* to provide fidelity and continued affection to our
mates in return.

When thinking pretheoretically about the nature of marriage, we tend
to focus on the mutual satisfaction of the above-mentioned cluster of
desires and emotions, the commitment engendered by these desires and
emotions, or the social customs that acknowledge and formalize this commitment. And this, I think is one reason why the *implicit reproductive contract* conception of marriage might appear unduly reductionist. But the
desires and emotions that draw us into and cause us to remain in marriages are the *proximate causes* of human marriages. Focusing on them tells
us why particular individuals are motivated to marry, but it doesn't tell us

why humans have motives to marry in the first place. While Evolutionary Psychology acknowledges the role of these proximate causes in human marriage, its conception of the nature of marriage seeks the *ultimate cause* of human marriage. And, insofar as we have motives that impel us to commit to marriages, Evolutionary Psychology seeks the ultimate causes of those motives as well. If the traditional view of the evolution of marriage is right, the ultimate cause of marital motives in both sexes is increased survivability and subsequent reproductive success of offspring. If Evolutionary Psychology is right, these were operative ultimate causes, but paternity certainty was also among the ultimate causes of marital motives in men. If the mating effort hypothesis is right, survivability and subsequent reproductive success of offspring is the ultimate cause of marital motives in women, but the ultimate cause of marital motives in men is increased paternity opportunities. The hypotheses about the evolution of marriage that we have just considered suggest the ultimate causes of why people have the desires and emotions that proximately cause them to become and remain married even when they don't want children. But none of the hypotheses implies that any of these desires or emotions are themselves *directed at* increased survivability of offspring or increased mating opportunities.

To make this point very clear, suppose we just had a single, simple *desire to marry*, to form a long-term, committed, sexual relationship with someone for whom we feel deep affection and friendship and who reciprocates those feelings. Suppose also that this simple desire evolved because those with the desire tended to act on it and thereby enjoyed greater reproductive success, on average, than those without the desire. In that case, the desire to marry has the *function* or *purpose* of reproduction. This does not mean, however, that we possess that desire as a means to achieving the desired end of reproduction (in the way that I often desire to go to the supermarket because it is a means to obtaining the desired end of having ice cream). It also doesn't mean that our desire to marry is merely the conscious manifestation of an unconscious desire to reproduce (in the way that Freud thought that a girl's desire to play boys' baseball, for example, is perhaps merely the conscious manifestation of the unconscious desire to have a penis). Indeed, it doesn't necessarily mean that we desire to reproduce *at all*. Rather, the desire to marry is nothing more than the desire to marry. Reproduction is the purpose of the desire to marry only in the functional sense, according to which that desire enhanced the reproductive success of our ancestors. Reproduction is then the *ultimate cause* of the desire to marry, but this doesn't mean that the desire to reproduce is among any of the *proximate psychological causes* of marriage, working alongside or behind the desire to marry (although it certainly is in many cases).

Although you may now be convinced that the *implicit reproductive contract* conception of marriage is not unduly reductionist, you may be starting to suspect that Evolutionary Psychology's conception of marriage is actually narrower than it seemed at first glance. For Evolutionary Psychology presupposes that *individuals have motives that cause them to desire and choose a marriage partner* and that these motives evolved because marriage enhanced the reproductive success of our ancestors. This, you might think, is rather provincial, since in many, if not most, societies throughout recorded human history marriages were arranged by parents, or other close relatives, rather than chosen by the principals to the marriage. This appears to mean that, during our evolutionary history, the opportunities for individuals to choose their own mates were few and far between. Consequently, you may argue, the opportunities for personal choice in mate selection have been too infrequent for selection to have favored individual psychological motives with a specifically marital function. Evolutionary Psychology's conception of the evolution of marital motives appears to be based on historically recent and geographically Western notions of romantic love between individuals, you may conclude, rather than on the historical facts about how marriages have actually occurred in human societies.

But this argument is misguided. First, even though many societies in recorded history have or had systems of arranged marriages, recorded history is but a drop in the bucket of human evolutionary history, and the phenomenon of marriage (or pair bonds) undoubtedly predates recorded history. We don't have any good evidence that human groups in prerecorded history had systems of arranged marriages like those documented by societies in recorded history. It is true that a number of hunter-gatherer populations have systems of arranged marriages, but in chapter 3 I gave several reasons for caution about inferring how our ancestors lived based on observations of how *some* extant hunter-gatherer populations live.

Second, and more important, the fact that social custom within a society dictates that marriages are to be arranged by the families of the individuals to be wed does *not* mean that the motives of the principals play no role in the process. Social custom dictates that Michael Jordan's agent arrange the details of his playing contract and all of his endorsement contracts, but it would be a mistake to infer that Michael Jordan himself is a mere pawn in the hands of his agent. Ultimately, Michael Jordan makes the decisions. Similarly, even where marriages are arranged by parents, it is typically done at the behest of one of the principals (as among the Kgatla of South Africa) or it is the culmination of a successful "blind date" arranged by the parents. As Helen Fisher says: "in the vast majority of cultures, the views of both the boy and girl are sought *before* wedding plans proceed. Modern Egyptians provide a good example. Parents of potential spouses design a meeting between the youths; *if the two like each other*, parents begin to plan the marriage."[7]

There are, nonetheless, some societies in which parents or other relatives arrange marriages without consulting the principals about their desires. But these arranged marriages are actually the exceptions that prove the rule that individuals have their own very strong, and arguably evolved, desires regarding whom they marry. The most poignant example of this is the practice of *sim-pua* marriage in Taiwan, in which a family gives a young daughter, typically under the age of three, to the family of a young boy to whom she will later be married. The two are then raised by the boy's family until they are old enough to form a conjugal union, at which point the boy's father announces one night over dinner that the two are henceforth husband and wife. The anthropologist Arthur Wolf found that, upon hearing this declaration, many of these young men and women simply refuse to go through with the planned marriage and run away. When they do proceed with the marriage plans, Wolf found that the large majority of these couples never consummate their marriages, that *sim-pua* marriages are characterized by far more extramarital affairs than other marriages in the culture, that they produce far fewer children, that children who are born in such marriages are nearly always known by the community to have been fathered by a man other than the husband, and that they have a far higher divorce rate than other marriages in the culture. And failure is not specific to this extreme type of arranged marriage. As Fisher points out, where arranged marriages "can be dissolved, as in New Guinea, on atolls in the Pacific, in much of Africa and Amazonia, people regularly divorce and remarry mates they choose themselves."[8] While certain cultural representations of romantic love may be specifically Western and recent, the reality is that people everywhere are strongly motivated by their own sense of whom they want as a mate, and these desires are not easily manipulated by those who would arrange their marriages for them. This is why, in the vast majority of societies practicing arranged marriage, the principals are actively involved in the process of determining whom they are to marry.

Now, one could continue to play the game of arguing that Evolutionary Psychology's conception of marriage and its hypotheses about the motives that underpin marriage are culturally or historically provincial. But I will not play that game in what follows. I think that the *implicit reproductive contract* definition of marriage is at least as good as any that has ever been offered, and it has implications that have led Evolutionary Psychologists down some interesting paths of inquiry. So in this chapter I want to explore two implications of this conception of marriage, each of which concerns the *contractual* nature of marriage. For, as a contract, marriage should share some general features of contracts.

One very general feature of contracts is the agreement between two parties to provide one another with certain "services." Indeed, this is the very essence of contracts. People enter contracts precisely because, by their calculations, receiving the benefit of the "services" provided by the other party outweighs the cost of providing that other party with the "services" they desire. Of course, Evolutionary Psychology doesn't suppose that people enter marriage contracts because they have calculated the fitness benefits they will receive from doing so. Rather, people enter marriage contracts because they believe that getting married will satisfy certain of their desires and emotional needs. Those desires and needs aren't concerned with the calculation of fitness benefits, but they have evolved because they prompted our ancestors to enter marriages, and our ancestors thereby received fitness benefits from acting on those desires and emotions. Figuratively speaking, *selection* calculated the fitness benefits of the motives among ancestral populations and then selected those motives that consistently had the highest average fitness benefits. Those motives now cause us to enter marriages, to our average benefit, without *our* needing to calculate, or even be aware of, fitness benefits.

One way to examine the contractual nature of marriage, then, would be to examine in detail the emotions and desires that cause humans to marry, such as those mentioned by Symons. These are surely some of the more exalted aspects of the human psyche, and it would no doubt be edifying to plumb their depths, as many poets have. But I will focus, instead, on the "negative" side of the contractual nature of marriage. For, on the negative side are two very general features of real-world contracts. First, wherever there is a contract, there is always the possibility that one of the parties will breach the contract if they perceive that it is in their best interest to do so. Second, because of this possibility, wherever there is a contract, there is some method of detecting and punishing violations of the contract. If marriage is an implicit reproductive contract, then in the case of marriage we should expect to find both calculated breaches of the contract and methods of detecting potential breaches. Let me explain.

Consider first contractual breaches. Typically, when a contract is breached, it is because the reneging party has determined that there is some benefit to be gained from violating the contract. Sometimes the benefit is so great that the reneging party is willing to pay the cost of openly dissolving the contract. For example, sometimes a sports team will fire a coach in midcontract, buying him or her out of the remainder of the contract, in order to hire another coach. In such cases, management has calculated that the benefits of having the new coach will outweigh the costs of buying the old coach out of the contract. At other times, however, the benefit of reneging on a contract merely outweighs the *weighted cost* of dissolving the contract—that is, the cost of dissolving the contract weighted by the probability that the breach will be detected and, hence, that the contract will actually be dissolved by the violated party. In these cases, the reneging party has no desire to dissolve the contract. Indeed, the reneging party desires to continue receiving all the benefits of the services provided by the other party, but merely seeks to gain some additional benefit that would accrue to a hopefully undetected contractual violation. For example, suppose a remodeling contractor will be paid $7,000 for the labor and materials for a job, but only if the job is performed using the materials specified in a written estimate. The contractor might realize that $500 could be shaved from the up-front costs by using materials inferior to those specified in the estimate and that there is only a 5 percent chance of getting caught using the inferior materials. In this case, the contractor's weighted cost of violating the contract is $350 (a 5 percent chance of losing $7,000), which is outweighed by the $500 to be gained by breaching the contract.

If marriage is an evolved implicit reproductive contract, we should find marital analogues of these situations. But, since evolutionary costs and benefits are calculated in the currency of fitness, violations of the marital contract should occur under circumstances where the fitness benefits of the violation outweigh the fitness costs. And indeed, Evolutionary Psychologists argue, we don't have to look far to find such violations. Often an individual will dissolve a marriage in order to marry someone else. Typically when this happens, according to David Buss, one of two things is going on. First, the couple may have drifted apart and stopped having sex, in which case leaving the marriage for another, more passionate marriage is a matter of leaving a marriage that has no reproductive potential for one that does, a clear fitness benefit. Second, one spouse may be dissolving the marriage in order to "marry up," to marry someone with higher perceived "mate value" than the abandoned partner, in which case the new partner represents enhanced fitness benefits for the spouse who is dissolving the marriage. Further, Buss argues, infidelity is sometimes a means of shopping for a new mate of higher "mate value" before actually paying the cost of divorcing one's partner. In such cases, infidelity is actually part of a long-term mating strategy, since it is a means of seeking a "new and improved" long-term mate while continuing to accrue benefits from the current long-term mateship. Whatever the details of the case, however, dissolving a marriage in order to remarry is an analogue of breaching a contract when the benefit to be gained from openly dissolving the contract outweighs the cost of losing the services provided by the "jilted" party.

But infidelity isn't always a long-term mating strategy, a means of shopping for a new long-term mate. Many unfaithful spouses desire to preserve their marriages, but also to surreptitiously pursue extramarital sex, or what Evolutionary Psychologists artfully call *extrapair copulations*. For often a married couple may have children to care for, or have excellent reproductive prospects together, so that the fitness benefits of the marriage are high for both parties and a divorce would be costly for both. Nonetheless, there may be certain circumstances under which an undetected short-term infidelity would have potential fitness payoffs for a married individual. In such cases, infidelity is a short-term mating strategy pursued in conjunction with the long-term strategy of remaining married. Thus, according to Evolutionary Psychologists, when *short-term infidelity* occurs it is an attempt to reap the fitness benefits of both extrapair copulations and a stable marriage. But, if short-term infidelity is analogous to a contractual breach, we should find that it is typically committed when the benefits of an extrapair copulation outweigh the cost of marital dissolution weighted by the probability of detection (and the consequent dissolution of the marriage at the hands of the cheated-on spouse). And this, Evolutionary Psychologists claim, is what we do in fact typically find. So short-term infidelity is the marital analogue to the second type of contractual breach.

As I pointed out earlier, however, if marriage is an implicit reproductive contract, we should find not only breaches of the contract in order to accrue fitness gains, but also some method of detecting when breaches occur or are likely to occur. Since infidelity is one of the most common ways in which an implicit reproductive contract is breached, we should find that people are relatively adept at detecting it. As Buss says: "It's unlikely that love, with the tremendous psychological investment it entails, could have evolved without a defense that shielded it from the constant threat from rivals and the possibility of betrayal from a partner."[9] The defense that evolution has equipped us with, according to Evolutionary Psychologists, is the emotion of *jealousy*. Jealousy, they claim, is an *emotional alarm* that is designed to go off whenever we detect signs of a partner's potential infidelity and to mobilize us to avoid or minimize our losses. As Buss says: "Sexual jealousy consists of emotions that are evoked by a perceived threat to a sexual relationship. The perception of a threat leads to actions designed to reduce or eliminate that threat. These can range from vigilance, which functions to monitor the mate for signs of extra-pair involvement, to violence, which inflicts a heavy cost on the mate or rival for signs of defection or poaching."[10]

Thus, there do appear to be marital analogues to the negative general facts about contractual violations and methods for detecting them. In the remainder of this chapter I will discuss some of what Evolutionary Psychologists have had to say about these phenomena. In the next section, I will examine some of Evolutionary Psychology's claims about the psychology of short-term infidelity and the circumstances under which it occurs. Then, in the following section, I will examine some of Evolutionary Psychology's claims about the psychology of jealousy.

**Keeping Myself Only unto You**

According to Evolutionary Psychologists, when marital infidelity is pursued as a short-term mating strategy, rather than as a long-term-mate replacement strategy, it is because the unfaithful partner's marriage provides fitness benefits that would be very costly to lose. So, short-term infidelity should occur when the potential fitness benefit of infidelity is greater than its fitness cost, where the cost of infidelity is the cost of losing the marriage weighted by the chances that the marriage will end as a result of the infidelity.

However, according to Evolutionary Psychologists, the fitness costs and benefits of short-term infidelity are different for the two sexes, even if the fitness cost of losing a marriage is constant (which, of course, it isn't, although that is a complication that needn't concern us here). Part of this sex difference in the cost-benefit structure of short-term infidelity derives from the sex difference in minimum obligatory parental investment, since this produces a sex difference in *maximum potential lifetime reproductive output*. For, during a pregnancy that provides both a man and a woman with an offspring, the woman is unable to bear any more offspring, while the man can produce a theoretically large number of additional offspring simply by copulating with other, unimpregnated women. Thus, a woman's maximum potential lifetime reproductive output is limited by the number of pregnancies she can carry to term during her reproductive years, whereas a man's maximum reproductive output is limited only by the number of women he can impregnate. A woman, then, can achieve her maximum reproductive output with a single mate, whereas a man can achieve his theoretical maximum only with multiple mates.

This means, argue Evolutionary Psychologists, that even a man in a sexually active marriage with a fertile mate can always increase his number of offspring by having extrapair copulations—indeed, at the theoretical limit, he can increase his number of offspring by one for every extrapair copulation with a new partner. "A married man with two children," as Buss says, "could increase his reproductive success by a full 50 percent by one short-term copulation that resulted in conception and birth."[11] Thus, Evolutionary Psychologists argue, we can expect that men have an evolved psychological mechanism that inclines them to pursue short-term infidelity whenever the potential costs of the infidelity are low. In short, men have an evolved tendency to cheat with as many women as possible as often as they think they can get away with it.

Of course, this only tells us what everyone already thinks that they know about men. Conventional wisdom has long held that men, married or not, will pursue sex with virtually any willing woman. As Mark Twain remarked, in a wry commentary on the seventh commandment, "by temperament, which is the *real* law of God, many men are goats and can't help committing adultery when they get a chance; whereas there are numbers of men who, by temperament, can keep their purity and let an opportunity go by if the woman lacks in attractiveness."[12] This witticism was subsequently matched by the following ditty, variously attributed to William James and to Dorothy Parker:

Hogamous, higamous,
Men are polygamous.
Higamous, hogamous,
Women monogamous.

And several scientific studies have seemed to many to demonstrate that folk wit and wisdom are right about men. In Alfred Kinsey's famous studies, 50 percent of married men, as opposed to only 26 percent of married women, reported having engaged in extramarital sex. Subsequent studies appeared to confirm men's greater promiscuity, although these studies came up with rather different numbers. In an extensive survey by the sociologist Edward Laumann and his colleagues, 24.5 percent of married men, but only 15 percent of married women, admitted to extramarital affairs.

And, in an analysis of data compiled by the General Social Survey of 1994, the psychologist Michael Wiederman found that 23 percent of married men, but only 12 percent of married women, admitted to having at least once had extramarital sex. While Kinsey's numbers are roughly double those of the later studies, in all studies nearly twice as many men as women admit to marital infidelity.

So it's by no means new, hence not particularly interesting, to claim that males have a propensity toward infidelity. Of course, Evolutionary Psychology does provide an evolutionary *explanation*, rather than simply a restatement, of what everyone already believes about men. But, while significant, explaining what we already know or think that we know is less impressive than predicting unexpected results that are subsequently confirmed. Truly impressive scientific victories are achieved by telling us something new and surprising that subsequently gets backed up by data. What Evolutionary Psychology has had to tell us about male short-term infidelity is neither new nor surprising. On the other hand, Evolutionary Psychologists have made some new and surprising claims about female short-term infidelity, and they have presented some very interesting evidence for their claims. If the evidence truly supports their claims, they can boast a significant theoretical victory. Unfortunately, I think that their claims go far beyond the evidence. So, in what follows, I will focus on Evolutionary Psychology's claims about female short-term infidelity and the evidence cited in their favor.

To approach these claims, let's rethink the survey data that show men to be twice as likely as women to engage in extramarital sex. Figures such as these have often been taken to confirm the folk wisdom that men are more promiscuous than women. But, as the entomologist Robert Smith points out, "males could not have been selected for promiscuity if historically females had always denied them opportunity for expression of the trait."[13] So, if men have evolved to pursue short-term matings, women throughout our evolutionary history must have engaged in short-term mating as well. And, as Helen Fisher argues, "since the vast majority of adults in almost all of the world's societies are married, logic upholds the proposition that when a married man is sneaking into the bushes in Amazonia, behind a rock in the Australian outback, or into a hut in Africa or Asia, he is most likely copulating with a married woman."[14] The same is presumably true not only of populations in which most extramarital sex occurs on beds, but of ancestral populations as well.

If Fisher is right, though, what accounts for the gender gap in the reported incidence of extramarital involvements? One thing to note in thinking about this question is that this gender gap parallels a gender gap in the reported number of lifetime sexual partners. A consistent result of sex surveys is that males report an average of two to four times as many lifetime (opposite-sex) sex partners as women. The problem with these results is that every new (opposite-sex) sex partner for a man is a new sex partner for a woman. So, the *average* number of lifetime (opposite-sex) sex partners has to be the same for both sexes. There have been a variety of explanations of this gender gap in survey data, but the consensus among sex researchers is that the gender gap is due to a combination of male over-reporting and female underreporting of number of lifetime sex partners (although there is disagreement about the mechanism that gives rise to male overreporting and female underreporting). So, it is possible that male overreporting and female underreporting similarly account for the gender gap in the reported incidence of extramarital involvements.

One possible problem with this explanation, however, is that males may actually underreport extramarital affairs despite overreporting lifetime number of sex partners. Kinsey and his colleagues found that male subjects were very reluctant to answer questions about extramarital sex: "There is probably nothing in the histories of older married males who belong to better educational and social levels that has more often been responsible for their refusal to contribute to the present research. Many of the persons who have contributed only after some months or years of refusal to do so, prove to have nothing in their histories that would explain their original hesitancy except their extra-marital intercourse. Even those who have contributed more readily have probably covered up on this more often than on any other single item."[15] So the incidence of extramarital affairs among men is probably at least as high as that reported in surveys. Whether that real incidence is as high as that reported by Kinsey or only about half that, as reported in later studies, or whether the incidence varies with era or culture, is something we will probably never know with any degree of certainty.

Thus, if the large majority of the women with whom males have extramarital affairs are themselves married (as Fisher argues), and if the gender gap in the reported incidence of extramarital involvements is not due to male overreporting (as Kinsey's work implies), then the bulk of the gender gap has to be due to underreporting of extramarital liaisons on the part of women. The actual incidence of extramarital involvements among women is no doubt significantly higher than is revealed by self-reports in survey data. Indeed, the actual incidence of extramarital affairs among women is surely well more than half the incidence of extramarital affairs among men.

Further evidence of female short-term infidelity, which is frequently cited by Evolutionary Psychologists, is the apparent incidence of "nonpaternity" or "paternal discrepancy." Paternal discrepancy occurs when a woman's husband, and the putative father of her children, is not in fact the biological father of one or more of her offspring. Data on the incidence of paternal discrepancy have typically been obtained as a by-product of studies of the inheritance patterns of various diseases. Researchers type the blood of family members for one purpose, for example, but then discover that one or more of the children in the family have a blood type that is incompatible with having been fathered by their mother's husband (their familial father). Such studies have revealed incidences of paternal discrepancy varying between 1.4 and 30 percent (meaning, for example, that 30 percent of children studied were not the biological offspring of their familial fathers). The spermatologists Robin Baker and Mark Bellis found the median incidence of paternal discrepancy across all studies to be 9 percent. Since most of these studies relied on blood typing, rather than DNA fingerprinting, however, they were unable to control for a potentially significant number of "false positives" (that is, mistaken assignments of paternity to the familial father, as in cases in which the familial father and biological father had the same blood type). Thus, the overall incidence of paternal discrepancy is surely higher than 9 percent, although standard genetics textbooks cite a conservative estimate of 10 percent. But, since the data are a by-product of other investigations, they haven't been collected with the rigor expected of scientific studies; so there are serious questions about the reliability of the data. Nonetheless, there is a substantial degree of paternal discrepancy, and it demonstrates a significant level of female infidelity. After all, it typically takes quite a lot of sex to make a baby, so nonpaternity rates as high as 10 percent imply infidelity rates *far* higher.

So, one of the interesting things that Evolutionary Psychologists have had to tell us is that female infidelity is probably much more common than either the conventional wisdom or the standard sex surveys have long led us to believe. But this merely begs a puzzling question, which we have already touched on in passing: What possible fitness benefit could women accrue from short-term infidelity? After all, as we saw when reasoning through the sex difference in maximum potential lifetime reproductive output, it appears that a woman can achieve her maximum reproductive output with a single mate. It appears that there could be no possible benefit to acquiring additional mates once a woman is already in a long-term mateship. As Buss says, an ancestral woman "could have had sex with hundreds of partners in the course of a single year and still have produced only a single child. Unless a woman's regular partner proved to be infertile, additional sex partners did not translate into additional children."[16] Given this apparent fact, how could selection ever have favored the female pursuit of short-term infidelity?

One possibility is that the assumption that females can't increase their total number of offspring by adding extramarital partners is mistaken. It is possible, for example, that females can increase their odds of getting pregnant during a menstrual cycle by having multiple mates. Conception is a very tricky business in even the best of circumstances. A fertile female's ovum can fail to be fertilized even when she has frequent unprotected sex with a fertile male throughout her menstrual cycle; and, if her egg does get fertilized, it can often fail to implant properly in the uterus. It is possible that having two or more partners with different genetic profiles during a cycle would increase the odds of successful conception. If so, that would get a female pregnant sooner, which in turn would allow her to shorten the times between pregnancies and thereby increase her total number of pregnancies. In fact, studies of a number of animal species have found that "multiple mating" does increase the odds of a successful pregnancy. A study of Gunnison's prairie dogs, for example, found that females who mated with three or more males while in estrus had a pregnancy rate of 100 percent, whereas females who mated with one or two males had a pregnancy rate of only 92 percent. Of course, humans aren't prairie dogs; we don't even have a similar reproductive physiology or mating system. And no studies have been done of humans to see whether females can increase their odds of pregnancy through multiple mating. So, while it's an interesting possibility that females could increase their number of children by taking extramarital partners, there is currently no evidence that they can do so.

Another possibility is that, while females can't increase the quantity of their offspring through extramarital affairs, they can increase the *quality* of their offspring. This is the possibility that has been central to Evolutionary Psychology's understanding of female short-term infidelity. David Buss has most fully articulated Evolutionary Psychology's theory about the role that offspring quality plays in female short-term infidelity, so I will focus on his account. Here is how the story goes.

The quality of offspring is a function of their fitness, and offspring fitness is largely determined by parental fitness. For parents have genes that influence their ability to survive and reproduce, and parents pass their genes on to their offspring, in whom those genes influence the ability of offspring to survive and reproduce. Individuals with higher-than-average fitness have "good genes," and by inheriting those "good genes" their offspring inherit their higher-than-average fitness. So, if a woman has a child from an extramarital affair with a male who has "better genes" (higher fitness) than her husband, that child will have higher fitness than a child she would have had by her husband. As Buss says: "Women can acquire better genes from higher value extrapair matings than from their regular mates. Good genes may bring better resistance to disease, increasing the health and hence survival of their children."[17] Good genes may also make a woman's children more attractive to the opposite sex and, hence, increase her number of grandchildren. Thus, a woman can potentially increase the fitness (quality) of her offspring through a short-term infidelity with a male who has "better genes" than her husband.

But, if women can increase their offspring's prospects, hence their own fitness, by mating with males with good genes, wouldn't they simply choose those males as their husbands, rather than simply as extrapair partners? The answer is yes—all other things being equal. Of course, all other things are virtually never equal. A woman also wants a husband who is going to invest in her offspring, whether through providing direct parental care (as Smuts and Gubernick claim) or through providing her with a high level of resources (as Evolutionary Psychologists claim). Ideally, women want husbands who have good genes *and* who contribute a high level of parental investment. But those males will be in very high demand, so they will be able to be highly selective and take as wives only women with very high mate value. Thus, a woman of middling mate value, according to Buss, will only be able to marry a man of middling mate value—for example, a man who is a good father, providing a lot of parental care, but who has only so-so genes. So most women aren't able to marry the men with the really good genes.

This leaves the average married woman in the position of having access to high-quality males only through short-term matings. Of course, high-quality males can increase their number of offspring by providing short-term matings to the average married woman. In fact, given that the minimum obligatory parental investment for males is so low, even a high-quality male who is married may be predisposed to readily oblige a married woman seeking *discreet* extramarital sex, since the potential payoff for the male dwarfs the costs. And, even though the offspring that a high-quality male can sire through such extramarital affairs won't have the quality of those he sires with his equally high-quality wife, they are still extra offspring. So, not only is there a potential fitness benefit to female short-term infidelity (an increase in offspring quality), but women should have sexual access to the high-quality males who can provide this benefit.

But securing good genes for her child is only part of the way in which a married woman can benefit from an extramarital affair. For, as a married woman, she also has a long-term mate who will invest in her offspring. So, as long as she can keep her extramarital affair concealed, a woman who has an extramarital affair with a male with good genes gets the fitness benefits of both worlds: She obtains superior genes for a child who can then be reared on the secured paternal investment provided by her cuckolded long-term mate with inferior genes. Thus, Buss says: "Some women pursue a 'mixed' mating strategy—ensuring devotion and investment from one man while acquiring good genes from another."[18]

Of course, this "mixed" mating strategy was available to ancestral women as well. Presumably some ancestral women pursued this strategy while others didn't. And, since ancestral women who had a propensity to pursue short-term infidelities with males with good genes would have produced higher-quality offspring, on average, than ancestral women who lacked that propensity and remained faithful to their long-term mates, over the course of human evolution selection "forged a female psychology of infidelity."[19] That is, not only did selection design the female mind to pursue the attraction and retention of a long-term mate, but selection designed the female mind to pursue extrapair sex under specific conditions—in particular, when paternal investment has already been secured from a long-term mate, when the extrapair sex is likely to go undetected, and when the extrapair partner has better genes than the long-term mate. The mind of the married woman, then, is designed to ascertain when these conditions are satisfied and to feel sexual desire for an available high-quality male. As Buss says: "Women's sexual psychology, *including their desire to stray*, exists today solely because that's what benefited ancestral women."[20] In other words, the female propensity toward short-term infidelity is an *adaptation*.

Buss claims that several lines of evidence converge to support the claim that female short-term infidelity is an adaptation. First, there is the previously mentioned fact that, by standard estimates, the rate of paternity discrepancy in humans is at least 10 percent. So a significant portion of children born within marriages are sired by women's extrapair partners. Of course, if female short-term infidelity is an adaptation for producing higher-quality offspring, it is not enough that contemporary women engage in significant extrapair coupling; adaptation requires that ancestral women pursued extrapair copulations as well. And there is indirect evidence that they did. Comparative studies of several nonhuman primate species have shown a correlation between male testes size in a species and the degree to which females of that species pursue multiple matings. In species in which females have multiple mates, inevitably the sperm of one or more males will be simultaneously present in a female's reproductive tract. In that event, the paternity advantage (other things being equal) will go to the male who inseminated the female with the most sperm. This will typically be the male with the largest testes, since the larger a male's testes, the more sperm his ejaculates contain. Thus, multiple mating by females in a species creates selection pressure for males of that species to evolve larger testes. As a result, for example, chimpanzee males have very large testes relative to their body size, since female chimpanzees typically mate with several males while they are in estrus. Though the average testes size (relative to overall body size) of human males is much lower than that of chimpanzee males, it is nonetheless higher than that of males in species in which females do not have multiple mates. And this is typically taken as evidence that ancestral human females did pursue multiple matings, though to a far lesser extent than their chimpanzee cousins. So, it does appear that female short-term infidelity occurred throughout human evolutionary history.

But why should we believe that women's extrapair mates typically have (or had) "better genes" than their long-term mates? To support the claim that women harvest "good genes" through their extrapair matings, Buss appeals to the results of a number of experiments conducted by the psychologist Steven Gangestad and the biologist Randy Thornhill. Gangestad and Thornhill argue that good genes are correlated with a high degree of bilateral symmetry. An individual with perfect bilateral symmetry is one in whom each side of the body is the perfect mirror image of the other. Of course, no such individual exists. We are all at least a little asymmetrical, with slightly crooked smiles, feet of slightly different lengths, or noses that curve a little to one side. Often these asymmetries are barely perceptible. You've no doubt seen facial photographs that have been doctored for perfect symmetry. A face that is not obviously asymmetrical suddenly becomes so when a photograph of it is presented alongside a picture in which a photograph of one half of the face has been joined with its mirror image to create a perfectly symmetrical face. Often the chimeric face created by joining the left half with its mirror image looks like a totally different person than the chimeric face created by joining the right half with its mirror image. Since the two sides of our bodies are not controlled by different genes, but develop from the same sets of genes, asymmetries are thought by some biologists to be the result of "developmental perturbations," which can be caused by a deleterious mutation or by exposure to pathogens or toxins during development. Symmetry, Gangestad and Thornhill argue, is thus a sign of *developmental stability*, a sign of a genetic constitution that is able to resist the deleterious effects of pathogens, toxins, and minor mutations. In short, a high degree of bodily symmetry is a sign of good genes.

If this is so, and if women choose men with good genes as extrapair partners, then we should expect women to show a decided preference for symmetrical men. And, indeed, in an experiment involving 203 heterosexual couples who had been in a relationship for at least a month, Gangestad and Thornhill claim to have found precisely that. Gangestad and Thornhill measured the widths of the left and right side of each participant's feet, ankles, hands, wrists, elbows, and ears, and they also measured left and right ear lengths. They then constructed a composite index of total asymmetry based on the differences between the left and right measurements for each trait. Photographs were then taken of each participant, and these photographs were rated for attractiveness on a scale of 1 to 10 by an independent panel. Finally the subjects completed a questionnaire, which asked, among other things, whether they had ever had extrapair sex partners (that is, whether they had ever had sex with someone other than their partner during their relationship with that partner) and whether they had ever been an extrapair sex partner (that is, whether they had ever had sex with someone else who was involved in a relationship at the time). When subjects answered in the affirmative, they were asked to list the number of extrapair partners or the number of people for whom they had been an extrapair partner. Gangestad and Thornhill found that, on average, the more symmetrical a male, the higher his attractiveness rating by female panelists. More interestingly, they found that highly symmetrical men, on average, reported having been chosen as an extrapair partner more often than less symmetrical men. The latter result, in particular, appears to show that, when women take extrapair partners, they prefer an extrapair partner with good genes.

But this finding supports the claim that female short-term infidelity is an adaptation for improving offspring quality only if women can potentially become pregnant by their extrapair partners. If women have extrapair sex, but do so only during infertile phases of their menstrual cycles, for example, then no amount of extrapair sex with symmetrical men is going to improve the quality of their offspring. In another experiment, however, Thornhill and Gangestad found that female preference for symmetrical men is actually stronger during ovulation than during the infertile phase of the menstrual cycle.

In this experiment, Thornhill and Gangestad made use of the fact, which has been known for some time, that both sexes respond to subliminal scents (or *pheromones*) emitted by members of the opposite sex. Thornhill and Gangestad issued their male participants T-shirts that had been washed in unscented laundry detergent. Male participants were instructed to refrain from using scented soaps or colognes for a two-day period, during which they were also to refrain from eating spicy foods, drinking alcohol, smoking, and having sex. They were required to wash their bedsheets in unscented laundry detergent at the beginning of the two-day period and to sleep in the T-shirt each of the two nights of the experimental period. Each male subject then returned his T-shirt in a sealed plastic bag, to be sniffed by the female participants (who were not taking hormone-based contraceptives that prevented natural ovulation). Females smelled all T-shirts in a random order both during ovulation and during the infertile phase of their menstrual cycles, and they rated each T-shirt on a scale of 1 to 10 for "pleasantness" and "sexiness" of smell. Thornhill and Gangestad found that scents of the T-shirts of highly symmetrical men were rated highest—but only by women who were ovulating. During the infertile phases of their menstrual cycles, women did not prefer the scent of symmetrical males' T-shirts over that of relatively asymmetrical males' T-shirts.

Thus, it appears that women do prefer males with good genes, but only during that phase of their menstrual cycles when they stand to benefit from sex with males with good genes. This, of course, seems to make sense from an evolutionary cost-benefit standpoint. For women can reap the benefits of extrapair sex with men with good genes only when they are fertile, but they can pay the costs of extrapair sex (loss of the cuckolded long-term mate) at any time throughout their menstrual cycles. So, Gangestad and Thornhill say, "selection may have shaped female interest in men who possess indicator traits of good genes such that it *changes* across the cycle: increases when women are fertile . . . and decreases when not."[21] Putting it more bluntly, Buss says: "Women detect the scent of symmetry, prefer that scent when ovulating, and choose more symmetrical men as affair partners."[22]

Another source of evidence that Buss cites to support the claim that female short-term infidelity is designed to tip the odds of paternity in favor of the extrapair partner derives from the work of the spermatologists Robin Baker and Mark Bellis. In a nationwide survey of 3,679 British women who were not taking hormone-based contraceptives, Baker and Bellis asked women to report whether they were having extrapair copulations, to provide information about the frequency and timing of their in-pair and extrapair copulations, and to provide details about their last copulation. The women who reported extrapair involvements also reported that approximately 60 percent of their copulations during the fertile phase of their menstrual cycles took place with their extrapair partners, whereas about 60 percent of their copulations during the *infertile* phase of their cycles took place with their *in-pair* partners. So, when women have affairs, their sexual activity with their affair partners is higher during the fertile phase of their menstrual cycles than during the infertile phase, and more of their sexual activity during the fertile phase occurs with their affair partners than with their long-term mates. Further, of the women who reported extrapair involvements, those whose last copulation was with their extrapair partner reported a higher incidence of "copulatory orgasms" than did those whose last copulation was with their in-pair partner (where Baker and Bellis define a female "copulatory orgasm" as one that occurs between one minute before and forty-five minutes after male ejaculation). This is significant, according to Baker and Bellis, because a copulatory orgasm increases sperm retention, since the contractions of orgasm cause the cervix to dip down into the pool of semen ejaculated at the back of the vagina and "suck" sperm up into the uterus where they have greater access to the oviducts. Thus, Buss concludes: "Women have more 'high sperm retention' orgasms with their affair partner than with their regular partner. . . . Furthermore, women seem to time their orgasms with their affair partners to coincide more closely with when they ovulate."[23]

Finally, in a study done with their colleague Randall Comer, Thornhill and Gangestad performed their standard measurements of seven bilateral traits (to compile an index of overall degree of asymmetry) on 86 heterosexual couples and had each member of each couple complete a questionnaire about the female's orgasms. They found a moderate correlation between the male and female reports of female orgasms, except in a handful of cases in which the women reported that they always faked orgasm and the men took them to be the real thing. Combining the male and female reports for the correlated cases, and using only the female reports for the other cases, they constructed an orgasm profile for the female of each couple. And they found that women whose partners had a high degree of bodily symmetry had more copulatory orgasms than women whose partners had a lower degree of bodily symmetry. Further, they found that this wasn't because women whose partners were symmetrical had more orgasms overall, since the symmetry of a woman's partner didn't correlate with the total number of orgasms she experienced (including those from oral sex or manual manipulation). It was simply that women whose partners were highly symmetrical experienced more copulatory orgasms, more of the allegedly "high-sperm-retention" orgasms, than other women.

This is a lot of merely circumstantial evidence, but it is *a lot* of merely circumstantial evidence, and Buss thinks that the combined evidence provides rather definitive support for the following picture. Women have a long-term mating psychology, which leads them to seek a long-term mate who will provide parental investment (which, according to Buss, is desired in the form of a high level of resources). But, once they have secured a long-term investing mate, women become motivated by "an evolved EPC [extrapair-copulation] psychology that is distinct from their long-term mating psychology."[24] This evolved extrapair-copulation psychology consists in "a psychological mechanism in women specifically designed to promote short-term mating."[25] So, if a woman's husband is a little weak in the genes, and if an opportunity for a discreet short-term infidelity with a male with good genes (a symmetrical male who smells sexy) presents itself, this psychological mechanism will cause strong sexual desire for that male and the woman will likely act on the desire. If an affair is begun with a male with good genes, this evolved mechanism will cause intensified desire for the extrapair partner during the fertile phase of the menstrual cycle, since the extrapair partner will then be especially sexy smelling, and this will lead the unfaithful woman to pursue more copulations with her extrapair partner than with her husband while she is fertile. Since the evolved mechanism will have caused her to choose a symmetrical male as an extrapair partner, she will also experience more copulatory orgasms with her affair partner than with her husband; and, since the majority of these copulatory orgasms with the affair partner will occur while she is fertile, she will be more likely to become pregnant by her extrapair partner than by her husband. If she does become pregnant by her extrapair partner, she will have a child with better genes than those her husband could have provided, and she will be able to raise that child on the already secured resources provided by her cuckolded husband. This, in turn, will enhance her reproductive success. And, as it is for modern women, so it was for ancestral women. Thus, the desire for and pursuit of short-term infidelity with males with good genes is a human female psychological adaptation.

Now, I think that the claim that women have a psychological adaptation for short-term infidelity goes well beyond the evidence. In fact, I will argue that the pattern of female short-term infidelity described above is best explained as a *by-product* of how *other* psychological and physiologi-cal adaptations operate under particular circumstances, rather than as a direct result of an adaptation specifically *for* short-term infidelity. Thus, I will *not* be arguing that Evolutionary Psychology is wrong to give a bio-logical explanation of female short-term infidelity, but that it is wrong to give an adaptationist explanation of it. The disagreement concerns the *kind of biological explanation* that should be given of female short-term infidelity, and I will argue that a *by-product explanation* provides the simplest account of all the data.

The case for Evolutionary Psychology's adaptationist explanation looks pretty convincing, however. Indeed, we have just examined a complex web of evidence with female adaptation for short-term infidelity at its center. In order to substantiate an alternative explanation, this web of evidence will have to be disentangled and rewoven around a new explanatory center. In the process, a lot of the strands of evidence that appear to support Evolutionary Psychology's explanation of female short-term infi-delity will have to be explained or explained away. And there will be a lot of explaining to do. In particular, the following questions will have to be answered. Why do women cheat at all if it's not because they are follow-ing an evolved script for increasing offspring quality? Why does sexual activity with extrapair partners increase during the fertile phase of the menstrual cycle? Why do women appear to choose symmetrical men as affair partners if their choice of affair partners isn't an adaptation for increasing offspring quality? And why do women experience more copu-latory orgasms with symmetrical men? Let's begin with the question of why women cheat at all.

The psychologists Shirley Glass and Thomas Wright found a robust sex difference in motives for extramarital involvements. In their surveys, of the men and women who reported having had extramarital sex, well over half of the men also reported having very happy marriages, whereas the vast majority of the women reported being dissatisfied with their mar-riages. For men infidelity was linked primarily to a desire for sexual variety and adventure, whereas for women it was linked primarily to marital dis-satisfaction. But, Glass and Wright wondered, what *kind* of marital dissat-isfaction was involved in female infidelity?

To answer this question, Glass and Wright asked their subjects not only about extramarital sexual involvements but also about extramarital emo-tional involvements, in which an emotionally intimate, yet nonsexual, relationship develops with someone other than one's spouse. They also dis-tinguished sexual dissatisfaction in the marital relationship from emotional dissatisfaction, and they asked those of their subjects who cited extramarital involvements to indicate which form of marital dissatisfaction they felt led to the extramarital involvement. Glass and Wright found a strong correlation between the type of marital dissatisfaction experienced by women and the type of extramarital relationship they became involved in. Women who developed extramarital emotional involvements reported emotional dissatisfaction in their marriages. But women who were emotionally dissatisfied in their marriages were not significantly more likely to develop extramarital sexual involvements than were women who reported being happy in their marriages. Similarly, women who reported extramarital sexual involvements reported sexual dissatisfaction in their marriages. And women who were sexually dissatisfied in their marriages were far more likely to develop extramarital sexual involvements than women who reported happy marriages. Thus, Glass and Wright found, it is not simply marital dissatisfaction that prompts the vast majority of women's extramarital sexual affairs, but specifically *sexual dissatisfaction* in marriage.

Glass and Wright's findings replicate the findings of a number of previous studies. In a 1938 study of 1,250 California couples, the psychologist Lewis Terman found that 27.2 percent of women who rated their marriages as unhappy reported that they "sometimes" or "very frequently" desired extramarital sex, whereas only 5.2 percent of the women who rated their marriages as happy reported similar levels of desire for extramarital sex. Further, he found that 19.4 percent of women who "never" or "sometimes" experienced orgasm with their husbands reported that they "sometimes" or "very frequently" desired extramarital sex, while only 7.8 percent of women who "usually" or "always" experienced orgasm with their husbands reported the same level of desire for extramarital sex. In a 1956 survey of 6,251 English women, the sociologist Eustace Chesser found that 25 percent of women who "always or frequently" had orgasm during sex with their husbands "occasionally" desired extramarital sex, and only 3 percent of them "frequently" desired extramarital sex. In contrast, of women who "rarely or never" had orgasm with their husbands, 38 percent reported "occasionally" desiring extramarital sex, and 10 percent reported "frequently" desiring it. In a 1974 study of 2,372 married American women, the sociologists Robert Bell and Dorthyann Peltz found that, of women who reported having had extramarital intercourse, 48 percent said that sex with their husbands was "poor" or "very poor," whereas 18 percent said that sex with their husbands was "very good." Further, they found that, of women who reported having had extramarital sex, 40 percent reported "never" having orgasm during sex with their husbands, while 24 percent reported having orgasm with their husbands "at least sometimes" (which, of course, is a widely inclusive category). Finally, in a 1975 survey of more than 100,000 female readers of *Redbook* magazine, the psychologists Carol Tavris and Susan Sadd found that only 22 percent of women who rated sex with their husbands as "very good" reported having had extramarital sex, but that 48 percent of women who rated their marital sex as "poor or very poor" reported having had an extramarital affair. While each of these samples is limited in one way or another, the findings are remarkably consistent: Sexually dissatisfied married women are far more likely than sexually satisfied married women to both desire and have extramarital sex.

Two studies by Buss and his colleague Heidi Greiling corroborate all of these findings. In one study, 101 women were given a list of forty-seven different life circumstances and were asked to rate how likely it would be that they would develop an extrapair sexual involvement in each of those circumstances. The results showed that the leading factor that would motivate female extrapair sexual involvements was retaliatory. Women said that discovering a partner's infidelity would make it somewhat likely that they would have extrapair sex themselves. But, in very close second and third places were motivations related to sexual dissatisfaction. Women rated "current partner is unwilling to engage in sexual relations" and "sexual relations with current partner have been unsatisfying for a long time" almost as high as discovery of a partner's infidelity. In the other study, Greiling and Buss asked 90 women to imagine a woman who was in a committed long-term relationship but who chose to have a short-term sexual relationship with another man. The participants were then given a list of twenty-eight possible benefits that the woman might derive from her short-term infidelity. The top-rated benefit, which was rated significantly higher than the second-rated benefit, was "likelihood of receiving sexual gratification." Given that sexual dissatisfaction in the current relationship ranked second and third among the leading motivations for extrapair sexual involvement in the previous study, it is reasonable to assume that the participants in the second study imagined the hypothetical unfaithful woman to be motivated by sexual dissatisfaction. If so, the results of the second study indicate that women perceive that a woman who is sexually dissatisfied in her marriage is likely to be able to find sexual gratification in an extramarital sexual involvement and that sexual gratification is a worthwhile benefit of an extramarital sexual involvement.

Thus, there is exceptionally strong evidence that, for women, sexual dissatisfaction in marriage is a leading factor in the occurrence of short-term extramarital sexual involvements. Of course, this in itself isn't incompatible with Evolutionary Psychology's adaptationist explanation of female infidelity. For Evolutionary Psychology's explanation isn't formulated in motivational terms. That is, Evolutionary Psychology isn't claiming that the *desire* for higher-quality offspring is what *motivates* women to pursue short-term infidelities with symmetrical males. The claim is that, *whatever the motives that drive women to short-term infidelities*, those motives evolved to work the way that they do because ancestral women with those motives benefited by having higher-quality offspring. In short, the studies cited above merely inform us of the *proximate cause* of female short-term infidelity, whereas Evolutionary Psychology's adaptationist explanation of female short-term infidelity informs us of the *ultimate cause*. So the two aren't incompatible.

Nonetheless, if the motives underlying female short-term infidelity evolved because they promoted an average increase in offspring quality, we should expect to find the *mere opportunity* for a short-term infidelity with a symmetrical male to be the leading factor in female short-term infidelities. That is, if offspring quality is why female short-term infidelity evolved, both sexually satisfied and sexually unsatisfied married women should pursue extrapair copulations with symmetrical males to an equal extent when given the opportunity. There should be no reason why sexually dissatisfied married women should pursue extrapair copulations to a greater extent than their sexually satisfied counterparts. Of course, one possibility is that the sexually satisfied women are already married to symmetrical men, and that's why they're sexually satisfied, whereas the sexually unsatisfied women are married to relatively asymmetrical men, so they need to seek their sexual satisfaction in extrapair copulations with symmetrical men. But there's simply no evidence that the partners of symmetrical men are more sexually satisfied than the partners of less symmetrical men. In their study of female orgasm, even Thornhill, Gangestad, and Comer found that the partners of highly symmetrical men were *not* more orgasmic, or more sexually satisfied, overall than the partners of less symmetrical men. So, while the motive of sexual dissatisfaction isn't exactly incompatible with Evolutionary Psychology's adaptationist account, it doesn't fit well with it.

It's reasonable to ask, then, whether female short-term infidelity, prompted by sexual dissatisfaction in marriage, might result from something other than the workings of a psychological mechanism specifically *for* short-term infidelity with symmetrical males. In looking for an alternative underlying cause of female short-term infidelity prompted by sexual dissatisfaction, we should postulate as little as possible in order to explain the phenomenon and then add to or modify that minimal explanation as necessary in order to account for other related phenomena. And we needn't look far to find an alternative explanation. The link between sex and reproductive success is too strong to require much comment. It's not implausible to suppose that ancestral individuals who desired a regular and fulfilling sex life, and who acted so as to ensure the satisfaction of that desire, produced more offspring, on average, than individuals who either lacked a desire for a regular and fulfilling sex life or failed to act so as to satisfy their desire for a regular and fulfilling sex life. This is just to say what many have taken to be obvious—that what I will call the "sex drive," for lack of a better term, is an adaptation. And, given the sex drive, if one finds oneself in a marriage in which one's "current partner is unwilling to engage in sexual relations" or in which "sexual relations with current partner have been unsatisfying for a long time," it is very likely that one will seek sexual satisfaction with extrapair partners. Thus, since women who cheat tend to be sexually dissatisfied in their marriages, their extra-marital sexual involvements can be seen, most simply, as the causal product of the sex drive—an adaptation to pursue sexual satisfaction—rather than as the product of a psychological mechanism specifically for short-term infidelity.

Of course, as I said, this account is just the bare minimum necessary to explain why women have extramarital sex at all, given that those who do are likely to report sexual dissatisfaction in marriage. It certainly doesn't explain the full panoply of phenomena that Evolutionary Psychology's adaptationist explanation explains. In particular, while it may explain why women take extramarital sex partners, it doesn't explain why their sexual activity with their extrapair partners increases during the fertile phase of their menstrual cycles. Here again, however, the behavior can be explained as the product of a more general adaptation, rather than as the product of an adaptation specifically *for* increasing the odds of bearing the child of a symmetrical extrapair partner.

For decades reproductive biologists stressed the fact that, unlike the females of other species, the human female is sexually "receptive" through-out the menstrual cycle, rather than just during the fertile phase of the cycle. This has always been one of the peculiarities of human sexuality that any evolutionary account of human sexual behavior had to explain, since it departs from the mammalian norm. But to ask why women are sexually "receptive" throughout their menstrual cycles is to conceive of women as *receptacles* in the sex act, rather than as sexual *agents*. Only relatively recently did a group of researchers turn from asking about when women are "receptive" to sex to asking questions about variations throughout the menstrual cycle in *female desire* for sex, *female fantasy* about sex, *female masturbation*, and *female initiation* of sex. This shifted away from a focus on sexual acts involving females, which could often be initiated by a male partner at a time when the female is not particularly interested, to a focus on female-determined sexual *activity*. And this shift in focus engendered some very interesting research, which consistently found a peak in the levels of female desire for sex, fantasy about sex, masturbation, and initiation of sex during the fertile phase of the menstrual cycle.[26] The rise in female-initiated sexual activity during the fertile phase is probably an adaptation, since it is too well designed for reproduction to be an accident or by-product of something else. So, the increase in sexual activity with extra-pair partners during the fertile phase of the menstrual cycle is really just a by-product of a generalized increase in female-initiated sexual activity during that period.

Evolutionary Psychologists are aware of this research, and they grant the reality of an increase in female sexual desire and female-initiated sex during the fertile phase of the menstrual cycle. They even grant that this is an adaptation, but they argue that it can't explain the facts about female short-term infidelity. For Baker and Bellis didn't find an increase in overall level of sexual activity during the fertile phase or an increase in sexual activity with in-pair partners. They found a more targeted increase in sexual activity. It was only sexual activity with extrapair partners that increased during the fertile phase. "Hence," Gangestad argues, "it appears that women's heightened sexual desire midcycle is not an increase in sexual desire in general. Rather, the data suggest that it motivates sexual behavior toward specific kinds of partners, in particular (pending further research) those who may have promised genetic benefits ancestrally."[27] So, if the by-product explanation is correct, why is there a *selective* increase in sexual activity with extrapair partners during the fertile phase?

The reason for this is relatively mundane. First, as we've seen, the vast majority of women who have extramarital sexual affairs are sexually dissatisfied in their marriages. Second, if a sexually dissatisfied married woman is seeking sexual gratification through an extrapair involvement, she will be unlikely to repeat extrapair sexual encounters with men who fail to provide her with the desired sexual gratification. As we've seen, there are potential costs to short-term infidelity, and if the desired benefit of sexual gratification isn't to be had with a particular male, a woman is not going to continue a sexual involvement with that male. So, any male who is a *regular* extrapair partner of a married woman is very likely a man with whom sex is gratifying in a way it's not with her husband. Therefore, when a woman experiences an increased desire for sex during the fertile phase of her cycle, she is far more likely to arrange to have sex with her extra-pair partner, with whom the sex is gratifying, than to have sex with her husband, with whom it's not. That is why there is an increase in sexual activity with extrapair partners during the fertile phase of women's men-strual cycles.

Still, Evolutionary Psychologists (or their sympathizers) will argue, that can't be the whole story. For none of this explains why women tend to choose *symmetrical men* as their extrapair partners. Evolutionary Psychol-ogy's adaptationist hypothesis explains this part of the overall picture as well, whereas the by-product explanation doesn't account for this fact. So, why *do* women tend to choose symmetrical men as affair partners if it's not because they are following an evolved script for enhancing offspring quality through short-term infidelity?

First, it's not clear that women *are* consistently choosing symmetrical men as affair partners. Although Gangestad and Thornhill did find a sta-tistically significant correlation between male symmetry and the number of women for whom a male has been an extrapair partner, this is the result of only one study with a relatively small sample. Their results haven't been replicated with larger samples or in a variety of different cultures. Second, the correlation that Gangestad and Thornhill found was actually relatively weak. A weak correlation between male symmetry and extrapair success could be found even if a significant number of relatively asymmetrical men had a high level of extrapair success and a significant number of highly symmetrical men had no extrapair success. Thus, the jury is still out about whether women really do choose symmetrical men as affair partners to a significantly greater degree than they choose less symmetrical men.

But, although it can't be considered "scientific fact" that women choose symmetrical men as affair partners, the evidence is intriguing. Further, cor-relations between high symmetry and high fitness and between high sym-metry and mating success have been fairly well documented in a number of other species. So I'm willing to grant for the sake of argument that (at least many) women do have an evolved preference for symmetrical men. This doesn't entail, however, that the preference for symmetry is specifi-cally part of an evolved mechanism for short-term infidelity.

To see why, recall that Buss claims that women seek symmetrical men as affair partners because, due to the "logic of the mating market," most women are unable to land a husband who is both symmetrical and invest-ing. This entails that symmetry is one of the things that women seek in a *long-term mate* because of the "good genes" signaled by symmetry. So, the fact that women have affairs with symmetrical men doesn't support Buss's claim that their choice of symmetrical men is produced by "an evolved EPC [extrapair copulation] psychology that is *distinct from* their long-term mating psychology."[28] For suppose, to simplify, that women seek long-term mates who have only two qualities—symmetry and a propensity for high parental investment. When a woman seeks a partner for a short-term infidelity, the same preference structure can be operative in her choice of partner, but parental investment becomes irrelevant. (This would not be the case if the infidelity is actually part of a long-term-mate replacement strategy, but we are considering only female short-term infidelity at the moment.) When parental investment drops out of the equation, the pref-erence for symmetry is the only preference left. Thus, even if women have an evolved preference for symmetrical men, this preference can be part of a *single set of mate preferences*, which is operative in choosing both long-term and short-term mates. Symmetry becomes more significant in con-texts of short-term infidelity only because women don't need to strike the best trade-off among their preferences in the way they need to when select-ing a long-term mate.

In sum, then, here is the by-product explanation of the discovered behavioral pattern of female short-term infidelity. Suppose, as the evidence seems to indicate, that the minds of many women contain the following three adaptations, among others: the "sex drive" (the desire for a regular and fulfilling sex life, together with the patterns of planning and acting so as to ensure the satisfaction of that desire), a peak in sexual desire during the fertile phase of the menstrual cycle (with its attendant increase in female-initiated sexual activity), and a preference for symmetrical males (which may be just one of several mate preferences). These three adapta-tions can causally interact in the following way. When a woman is sexu-ally dissatisfied in her marriage, there is increased probability that she will begin an extramarital sexual involvement if a desirable opportunity for such an affair presents itself. This is due to the standard operating proce-dures of the "sex drive." Since the potential costs of infidelity are high, however, she will be selective in choosing an extrapair partner. In select-ing an extrapair partner, the same preferences that were operative in choos-ing a long-term mate will also be operative, but some of them (for example, a propensity for parental care) will be irrelevant to the specifically sexual role for which the extrapair partner is being selected. As irrelevant preferences drop out of the selection process, the preference for symmetry will come to loom large in the selection of an extrapair partner. As a result, if a woman begins an extramarital affair, there is increased probability that she will select a high-symmetry male as her extrapair partner. But this is due to the standard operating procedures of her unitary set of mate preferences, rather than to a set of preferences specifically tailored to short-term infidelities. Then, once a woman begins an extramarital affair, her peaking desire for sex during the fertile phase of her menstrual cycle will cause an increase in the number of sexual encounters that she initiates. Since, by this hypothesis, she began the affair because sex with her husband is less gratifying than sex with her affair partner, the sexual encounters that she initiates will be directed almost exclusively toward her affair partner. As a result, the copulations with her highly symmetrical affair partner will tend to be concentrated during the fertile phase of her menstrual cycle. But this will be due to the standard operating procedures of her fertile-phase peak in sexual desire. Thus, the three adaptations can conspire, under circumstances of sexual dissatisfaction in marriage, to produce a pattern of behavior that appears to be the direct result of an adaptation specifically for short-term infidelity.

Two of the adaptations postulated in this alternative scenario (the fertile-phase peak in sexual desire and the preference for symmetrical men) are explicitly accepted by Evolutionary Psychologists, and the third (the sex drive) is a commonplace and nowhere explicitly rejected by Evolutionary Psychologists. And the data can be explained by appeal to these three adaptations without the need for Evolutionary Psychology's postulation of an adaptation specifically for female short-term infidelity. In short, the by-product explanation is simpler, since it postulates fewer adaptations overall, and it accounts for the same facts; therefore it is to be preferred to Evolutionary Psychology's explanation on grounds of parsimony.

The by-product explanation does, however, appear to leave a thread loose. For one strand of the web of evidence woven around Evolutionary Psychology's adaptationist hypothesis is Thornhill and Gangestad's results that appear to show that women have more "high-sperm-retention" copulatory orgasms with highly symmetrical men than with less symmetrical men. Those results seemed to lend further credence to the idea that women are designed to reap genetic benefits for their offspring through the pursuit of extrapair copulations. If extrapair copulations with highly symmetrical men are simply the by-product of interacting adaptations, rather than the result of an adaptation specifically for extracting good genes, what accounts for the higher incidence of copulatory orgasms with highly symmetrical men?

The by-product explanation does, in fact, leave this thread loose, but it's not at all clear that it's a thread that needs to be woven into any adequate explanation of female short-term infidelity. For there are good reasons for skepticism regarding the claims made for the role of female orgasm in Evolutionary Psychology's account of female short-term infidelity.

First, although Baker and Bellis claimed to find that female copulatory orgasms resulted in higher sperm retention relative to copulation without female orgasm, all of their evidence indicated that this allegedly higher level of sperm retention did *not* in fact increase the probability of conception. So, even if women have more copulatory orgasms with highly symmetrical men, there is no evidence whatsoever that that translates into higher levels of paternity for highly symmetrical men. In order to preserve the claim that female copulatory orgasm is facilitating paternity by symmetrical males, Thornhill and Gangestad are forced to argue that female copulatory orgasm merely functions to draw more of the extrapair partner's sperm into the uterus than the in-pair partner's sperm. Thus, while not directly increasing the odds of conception, female copulatory orgasm is supposed to give the extrapair partner more "lottery tickets," in effect, than are given to the in-pair partner. She thereby increases the odds that, *if* she becomes pregnant, he will be the father. But, if sucking up sperm into the uterus through copulatory orgasm doesn't increase the odds of conception over not sucking up sperm into the uterus, it's hard to see how sucking up the extrapair partner's sperm, while not sucking up the in-pair partner's sperm, is supposed to increase the odds that any resulting pregnancy will be due to the extrapair partner's sperm. In addition, if the extrapair partner does enjoy an advantage in the competition to impregnate a woman having an extramarital affair, this is no doubt due to the fact that she has more sex with him during her fertile phase than she does with her husband, as Baker and Bellis's data show. Thus, there's no evidence that a female's copulatory orgasms play any role in determining the paternity of her offspring.

Second, there are problems in the way that "copulatory orgasm" is defined in the study by Thornhill and Gangestad. Baker and Bellis claimed to find that *any female orgasm* that occurred between one minute before and forty-five minutes after ejaculation into the vagina sucked sperm up into the uterus and thereby resulted in higher sperm retention. Following this finding, Thornhill and Gangestad asked their subjects to report the incidence of any female orgasms that occurred in one of three time segments *during copulation*: before the male's ejaculation, at the same time as ejaculation, and within forty-five minutes after ejaculation. Thornhill and Gangestad then considered only the simultaneous and postejaculation orgasms to be high-sperm-retention "copulatory orgasms." And, as noted, they claimed to find that their female subjects reported having more of these orgasms with highly symmetrical men than with less symmetrical men.

But the biologist Nicholas Pound and the Evolutionary Psychologist Martin Daly point out that there are two significant problems in this procedure. First, the study only compared the orgasm profiles of women whose partners were highly symmetrical with those of women whose partners were less symmetrical. It didn't compare a woman's orgasm profile with a highly symmetrical partner with *that same woman's* orgasm profile with a less symmetrical partner. So, their study failed to show that individual women varied their number of copulatory orgasms in accordance with the degree of symmetry of their sex partner; and that is what would need to be shown to support Evolutionary Psychology's adaptationist explanation of female short-term infidelity. Second, by asking only about postejaculation orgasms that occurred *during copulation*, Thornhill and Gangestad ignored a potentially significant number of high-sperm-retention orgasms. For, if any orgasm within forty-five minutes after ejaculation is a high-sperm-retention orgasm, as Baker and Bellis claim, women could have had many high-sperm-retention orgasms that were not "copulatory orgasms" as Thornhill and Gangestad defined them. Even women with extremely asymmetrical partners could have had manually or orally induced orgasms within forty-five minutes after ejaculation, and these would have been high-sperm-retention orgasms as well. So, Thornhill and Gangestad in fact failed to show that the partners of highly symmetrical men had more high-sperm-retention orgasms, as opposed to more high-sperm-retention orgasms *during copulation*, than the partners of less symmetrical men.

There is, then, no good evidence of a connection between male symmetry and female high-sperm-retention orgasm, and there is no good evidence of a connection between so-called high-sperm-retention orgasms and conception. Thus, no account of female short-term infidelity has to explain why women have more copulatory orgasms with highly symmetrical men than with less symmetrical men. The by-product explanation accounts for all the evidence that truly need be accounted for. And by postulating a female adaptation specifically for short-term infidelity, Evolutionary Psychology goes well beyond the available evidence.

## The Green-Eyed Monster

Regardless of whether individuals have psychological adaptations specifically *for* strategic fitness-enhancing acts of infidelity, there has certainly been no shortage of infidelity throughout human evolutionary history. And each act of infidelity breaches the implicit reproductive contract between mates by introducing the possibility that the unfaithful partner will be undertaking a reproductive venture with an interloper. A woman whose husband is unfaithful faces the possibility that her husband will sire another woman's child and potentially direct some of his parental care and resources to that child rather than to hers. Since her own fitness is tied to the reproductive success of her children, and since their survivability and subsequent reproductive success depends at least partly on the quantity and quality of parental care they receive, a decrease in her husband's investment in her children exacts a fitness cost from her. A man whose wife is unfaithful faces the possibility that his wife will bring another man's child into the family. If she does, some of her parental care will be directed to that child, rather than to his children, and some of his parental care and resources will be spent on another man's child. Thus, his children by his wife will receive a smaller portion of his wife's parental care, which reduces his fitness, and he pays the fitness costs of providing parental care to that child without seeing any returns in the currency of his genes.

Further, even when infidelities are undertaken with the simple goal of supplemental sexual satisfaction, they can unexpectedly evolve into something more. Sporting sex can transform into consuming love, which can spell the doom of a marriage. So, each act of infidelity also raises the specter of abandonment. Recall from chapter 5 that reproductive effort is divided between mating effort and parenting effort. If you're a married woman sharing the burdens of parental care, you allocate less of your reproductive effort to parenting than you would if you were a single parent, which allows you to allocate more of your reproductive effort to further mating. If your spouse abandons you, and you're left caring for the children, all of the assistance you're receiving in your current parenting effort vanishes along with all of your plans for future mating projects. If you're a married man sharing the burdens of parental care, and your spouse abandons you and your children, you face the same problems. If your spouse takes the children, then they receive less care than they would if you stayed together, and your future mating projects are scuttled until you can find another mate. Thus, regardless of your sex, if your spouse abandons you, your reproductive effort is negatively impacted to a very high degree on both the parenting and mating fronts.

Infidelity, then, has the potential to be highly detrimental to the reproductive effort, hence fitness, of a cheated-on spouse. Selection appears to have designed us with emotional and physiological alarms to warn us of some threats to our survival. Pain is a physiological alarm that warns of potential bodily damage and motivates withdrawal from the painful stimulus. Arguably pain evolved precisely because the warning it sends, and the withdrawal it motivates, helped our very remote, nonhuman ancestors avoid prolonged exposure to very harmful or potentially fatal situations. Similarly, fear appears to have evolved as an emotional alarm that warns us of the presence of potentially harmful situations and motivates withdrawal from them. The fear that we experience at the sight of things like snakes and tigers, and the careful avoidance maneuvers that fear motivates, may have saved many an ancestor from death or serious injury. Of course, survival matters only insofar as it enables reproduction. So, if pain and fear are alarms that evolved to promote our survival by warning us of threats to our survival, we should also have evolved emotional alarms that advance our reproductive interests by warning of threats to our reproductive efforts, which are after all the sine qua non of evolution. In particular, because the infidelity of one's spouse poses a potentially severe threat to one's reproductive efforts, hence fitness, we should have evolved an emotional alarm that warns of potential or actual infidelities and motivates action designed to minimize the threat to our reproductive efforts. Jealousy, Evolutionary Psychologists argue, is that emotional alarm.

In one of the earliest formulations of Evolutionary Psychology's theory of jealousy, Daly, Wilson, and Weghorst defined jealousy as follows: "jealousy may best be defined as a *state* that is aroused by a perceived threat to a valued relationship or position and motivates behavior aimed at countering the threat. Jealousy is 'sexual' if the valued relationship is sexual."[29] The perceived threats to a sexual relationship range from flirting with, spending a lot of time with, and kissing another person (which are cues to a developing romantic or sexual interest in someone else) to having sex with and falling in love with another person.

In a study of 105 subjects, David Buss found that jealousy made people more likely to engage in a variety of behaviors ranging from vigilance to violence. Jealousy makes people more likely to be hypervigilant of their mates' activities (checking on their mates' whereabouts), to monopolize their mates' time (accompanying them everywhere), to manipulate their mates' emotions (threatening suicide if abandoned), to derogate the rivals for their mates' affections (criticizing the rivals' appearance or intelligence), to enhance one's own personal appearance, to threaten or become violent toward the rivals, to increase the frequency of public displays of possession (holding hands with or putting an arm around their mates), to shower their mates with affection or gifts (saying "I love you" more frequently), to turn up the sexual heat in the relationship (initiating sex more frequently and making love more passionately), and to threaten or enact violence toward their mates. Most of these actions are designed to counter perceived threats to a sexual relationship by minimizing a mate's opportunities for infidelity, diminishing a mate's interest in the rival, or reinvigorating a mate's interest in oneself. Further, Buss found that each sex rated most of these tactics, when employed by the opposite sex, to be at least moderately effective in preventing a mate from straying.

Jealousy, then, appears to be triggered by perceived threats to a relationship, and it appears to motivate a number of actions that are effective in retaining a mate who may be straying or contemplating straying. Since jealousy is so closely tied to, and effective in promoting, our reproductive interests in these ways, Evolutionary Psychologists argue that jealousy shows significant signs of being an emotional adaptation designed to detect and thwart threats to our reproductive interests.

Evolutionary Psychologists further argue that, since men and women faced different threats to reproductive interests throughout human evolutionary history, the sexes have evolved distinct jealousy mechanisms. As Buss and his colleagues say: "The evolutionary hypothesis about sex differences in jealousy is domain-specific—it proposes that *the psychological mechanisms of each sex will contain dedicated design features, each corresponding to the specific sex-linked adaptive problems that have recurred over thousands of generations of human evolutionary history.* From an evolutionary perspective, the odds that the sexes will be psychologically identical in domains where they have recurrently confronted different adaptive problems over the long expanse of human evolutionary history are essentially zero."[30]

In particular, the psychological mechanisms of the sexes will differ with respect to "design features" that are dedicated to looking out for and responding to different kinds of cue about when reproductive interests are in jeopardy. As Buss says: "From an ancestral man's perspective, the single most damaging form of infidelity his partner could commit, in the currency of reproduction, would have been a sexual infidelity. A woman's sexual infidelity jeopardizes a man's confidence that he is the genetic father of her children. A cuckolded man risks investing years, or even decades, in another man's children."[31] As a consequence, Buss argues, male jealousy evolved "to focus on cues to sexual infidelity because a long-term partner's sexual infidelity jeopardizes his certainty in paternity."[32] In contrast, Buss says: "Our ancestral mothers confronted a different problem, the loss of a partner's commitment to a rival woman and her children. Because emotional involvement is the most reliable signal of this disastrous loss, women key in on cues to a partner's feelings for other women."[33] Thus, Buss concludes: "An evolutionary analysis leads to the prediction that although both sexes will experience jealousy, they will differ in the weight they give to the cues that trigger jealousy. Men are predicted to give more weight to cues to *sexual* infidelity, whereas women are predicted to give more weight to cues to a long-term diversion of investment, such as *emotional* involvement with another person."[34]

It's important to be clear about what this theory is *not* saying. When Evolutionary Psychologists say that males focus on cues of sexual infidelity *because* a female's sexual infidelity jeopardizes a male's paternity certainty, this does *not* mean that, when a male experiences jealousy, he either consciously or unconsciously processes information about the likelihood that he will have to invest in another male's offspring. In other words, it does *not* mean that calculations about the probability of misspent parental care are necessarily among the proximate causes of a male's jealousy. Rather, it means that the adaptive problem of paternity certainty is the *ultimate cause* of the proximate mechanism underlying male jealousy. Thus, the theory entails only that males experience jealousy under the circumstances they do because the experience of jealousy under those circumstances motivated ancestral males to perform actions that were moderately successful on average in preventing their mates from pursuing sexual infidelities, and that this had the *beneficial consequence* of ensuring that *they* fathered their mates' children, which in turn had the *beneficial consequence* that they reaped the fitness benefits of parental investment in their own offspring. Nonetheless, Evolutionary Psychologists argue, if the ultimate cause of male jealousy is paternity certainty, then males should have evolved a *proximate mechanism* that causes feelings of jealousy in response to events that are correlated with a decreased probability of paternity. Similarly, when women experience jealousy, they aren't necessarily thinking, either consciously or unconsciously, "Oh, no, I may lose his parental care of and resource investment in my children." But, Evolutionary Psychologists reason, if the ultimate cause of female jealousy is the need to secure and retain male parental investment, then females should have evolved a proximate mechanism that causes feelings of jealousy in response to events that are correlated with an increased probability of losing that investment.

It's also important to bear in mind that, although jealousy evolved within the context of relationships characterized by an implicit reproductive contract, this does *not* mean that the emotion can be experienced only within formalized marriages. As we saw when discussing the evolution of marriage, marriage evolved in humans along with emotions and desires that motivated humans to form pair bonds characterized by an implicit reproductive contract. These emotions and desires didn't necessarily have the explicit objective of forming reproductive unions. They merely had to bond a man and a woman together and motivate them to invest in their joint offspring. Jealousy evolved as an emotional alarm that goes off when there is a perceived violation of the desires, expectations, and emotions that hold people together in long-term sexual relationships. Consequently, people needn't be in a fully formalized marriage in order to experience jealousy. Rather, according to Evolutionary Psychology, whenever two people have a relationship cemented by the emotions and desires that coevolved with marriage, they can experience jealousy. Even if a couple have only been dating a few months, and even if neither wants to have children, their involvement with one another is still a product of the emotions and desires that promoted marriage among our ancestors; as such, even though the stakes in their relationship are not the same as the stakes in a marriage, they will experience jealousy under much the same circumstances as would a formally married couple.

Evolutionary Psychologists have cited three kinds of evidence in support of their claim that the sexes have evolved "design differences" in the psychological mechanisms of jealousy. First, a variety of questionnaire studies have shown that significantly more men than women report that the thought of a partner's sexual infidelity is more distressing than the thought of a partner's extrapair emotional involvement. Second, a physiological study found that male subjects showed a greater physiological response to imagining a partner's having sex with another man than to imagining a partner's falling in love with another man, whereas female subjects showed the opposite pattern of physiological response to the imagined scenarios. Third, there are similarities across cultures in laws concerning adultery. Female sexual infidelity is always legal grounds for divorce, whereas male sexual infidelity is only sometimes legal grounds for divorce. Further, many societies that punish murder exempt from punishment cuckolded males who murder their wives or their wives' lovers upon finding them in flagrante delicto. These legal "double standards," Evolutionary Psychologists argue, attest to the universal understanding that a female's sexual infidelity is harmful to her mate's reproductive interests in a way that a male's sexual infidelity is not harmful to his mate's reproductive interests. And that universal understanding, they conclude, indicates that our "folk psychology"—our everyday means of understanding the behavior of our fellow humans—implicitly acknowledges a sex difference in the causes of jealous distress.

All of these sex differences are taken as providing very strong confirmation of Evolutionary Psychology's theory of jealousy. Summarizing this evidence, Buss says that "men's jealousy appears to be more sensitive to cues of sexual infidelity and women's jealousy more sensitive to cues to emotional infidelity—results that were found across both psychological and physiological methods, as well as across cultures."[35] Since this evidence derives from several societies from around the world, and since the results are so consistent across those societies, Buss concludes that these "sexual differences in the causes of jealousy appear to characterize the entire human species."[36] And this, Buss believes, is evidence that there are sex-differentiated "design features" in the psychological adaptations of jealousy in humans. In fact, Evolutionary Psychologists frequently cite this theory of sex differences in the psychology of jealousy as one of their most solid results.

In my opinion, viewing jealousy as an emotional adaptation is one of the more interesting and significant contributions Evolutionary Psychology has made to our understanding of the human psyche. Those of us old enough to remember the late 1960s and early 1970s recall an era in which not only psychologists, but popular culture, viewed jealousy as an expression of pathological insecurity and possessiveness that no fully self-actualized individual would experience. If you really love someone, the litany went, you won't try to "possess" them, but will allow them the freedom to achieve self-actualization, no matter how many sex partners they require in their quest for personal enlightenment. Although Paul Mazursky subjected this attitude, and the culture of "free love" that accompanied it, to withering satire in his 1969 film *Bob & Carol & Ted & Alice*, such beliefs tenaciously remained in the popular imagination long after. In researching this book, I was bemusedly surprised to find that articles are still being published in academic journals examining the relationship between jealousy and degree of "self-actualization." To place jealousy under the lens of evolutionary analysis, and to ask whether it may be an evolved emotional alarm, rather than a pathological expression of "possessiveness," is a significant contribution and one that I believe is on the right track.

Unfortunately, I think that Evolutionary Psychology's contribution pretty much ends there. There are problems with its "evolutionary analysis" of jealousy and with its claim that there are sex differences *in the "design features"* of the psychological mechanisms of jealousy. Let's begin examining these problems by considering Evolutionary Psychology's "evolutionary analysis" of jealousy.

Evolutionary Psychology's theory of jealousy, with its hypothesis of evolved sex differences in the triggers of jealousy, is frequently called *"the evolutionary theory of jealousy."* In one sense, this is right: It is the only evolutionary hypothesis regarding jealousy that has been articulated and tested in the literature. In another sense, however, it is deeply misleading: There are other genuinely evolutionary theories that one could hold about jealousy, none of which has even been considered by Evolutionary Psychologists, let alone tested. For example, Kristen Hawkes has suggested to me that the ultimate cause of male sexual jealousy may be mere paternity competition, rather than paternity uncertainty. This suggestion doesn't deny an evolved sex difference in the triggers of jealousy, but it offers a different evolutionary analysis of that difference, a different account of what drove the evolution of the sex difference. Let's explore this alternative for a moment.

According to Evolutionary Psychology, marriage is an implicit reproductive contract according to which parental care (given by the male) is exchanged for assurance of paternity (given by the female). The assurance of paternity is crucial, according to Evolutionary Psychology, since that is what ensures a male that his parental care won't be misspent on the offspring of another male. Jealousy, then, has evolved as an emotional alarm that signals that one's mate is, or could be contemplating, violating the implicit reproductive contract. Since a female violates the contract by nullifying the assurance that her mate will have paternity of her offspring, Evolutionary Psychology predicts that the proximate mechanism underlying male jealousy will monitor contexts in which parental care is at issue for signs of potential sexual infidelity, since sexual infidelity entails the potential for misspent parental care. In contrast, since a male violates the implicit reproductive contract by withdrawing his parental care, female jealousy is supposed to function to detect the potential for withdrawal of parental care, which is supposedly signaled by the development of other emotional involvements.

As we saw in our discussion of marriage, however, there are both theoretical and empirical reasons for believing that the mating effort hypothesis—according to which marriage evolved as a contractual exchange of parental care (given by the male) for paternity opportunities (given by the female)—provides a better explanation of the evolution of marriage than the one provided by Evolutionary Psychology's theory. According to the mating effort hypothesis, males evolved to provide parental care because they got increased paternity opportunities in return, and assurance of paternity wasn't a precondition for the evolution of male parental care. If we assume that male mating psychology evolved within the context of this type of marital contract, rather than within the context of a contractual exchange of parental care for assurance of paternity, we won't be led to expect male sexual jealousy to be focused on contexts in which parental care and resources could potentially be invested in the offspring of other males. Rather, if marriage evolved as postulated in the mating effort hypothesis, male jealousy should have evolved to be triggered by cues that signal the potential loss of paternity opportunities, rather than by cues that signal the potential loss of parental resources to unrelated offspring. Thus, whereas Evolutionary Psychology sees the evolved function of male jealousy to be protection against misspending parental care, the mating effort hypothesis leads us to see the evolved function of male jealousy to be protection against losing paternity opportunities to another male. In short, from the perspective of the mating effort hypothesis, male jealousy evolved to promote *paternity competition* rather than to promote paternity certainty.

Although the *paternity competition theory* differs from Evolutionary Psychology's paternity certainty theory in its account of how jealousy evolved, both predict that male sexual jealousy will be triggered by cues to a partner's potential sexual involvement with another male (and, hence, that male jealousy differs in this way from female jealousy). For, under the paternity competition theory, female sexual infidelity entails serious fitness costs for a male who is expecting exclusive paternity opportunities. If a man's mate becomes pregnant by another male, the cuckolded male is unable to father a child by his mate for at least the nine months of his mate's pregnancy, although he may lose paternity opportunities for up to two years between his mate's pregnancy and lactation (with its attendant suppression of ovulation). This effectively costs a male one offspring by his mate. In addition, since reproductive effort has to be allocated between parental effort and mating effort, if a man's mate bears another man's child, that child will increase the amount of reproductive effort his mate must allocate to parental effort, correspondingly decreasing the amount she allocates to mating effort and further negatively impacting his own mating effort. Like Evolutionary Psychology, then, the paternity competition theory sees female infidelity as exacting serious fitness costs from cuckolded males. But the two theories calculate those costs differently.

Whereas Evolutionary Psychology calculates the costs in terms of lost resources (misspent on another male's child), the paternity competition theory calculates the costs primarily in terms of lost offspring. Both theories, however, predict male jealousy in response to cues of a partner's potential sexual involvement with another male.

As a result, it may appear that the paternity competition theory is empirically indistinguishable from Evolutionary Psychology's theory of jealousy, that no evidence could favor one theory over the other. But the two theories do entail some different predictions. According to Evolutionary Psychology, male sexual jealousy evolved to protect against the possibility of investing in another male's offspring, so Evolutionary Psychology's theory predicts that male sexual jealousy should be triggered in contexts in which the investment of parental care is at stake. In contrast, according to the paternity competition theory, male sexual jealousy evolved to protect against losing paternity opportunities, so the paternity competition theory predicts that male sexual jealousy should be triggered in any context in which desired or expected paternity opportunities get awarded to another male, *even if* there is no possibility of investing parental care or resources in another male's offspring. Thus, the paternity competition theory predicts that male sexual jealousy should be triggered in a broader range of circumstances than Evolutionary Psychology's theory predicts—in particular, in contexts in which paternity opportunities are at stake, but parental care is not. And there are three contexts, in particular, in which the occurrence of male jealousy would tell in favor of the paternity competition theory and against Evolutionary Psychology's theory.

First, in his own research, Buss discovered that male "sexual jealousy can be triggered even before a full-blown relationship has formed."[37] Buss cites a case of a male subject who developed a desire for a sexual relationship with a neighbor, though the two hadn't yet so much as kissed. The subject reported extreme jealousy when the neighbor began having sex with his roommate. This is a context in which there is no possibility of investment in another male's offspring. Rather, male jealousy is triggered because a woman is denying a male the desired sexual relationship and developing it with someone else instead. If the proximate mechanism of jealousy is designed to protect against the possibility of misspent parental care, it shouldn't be triggered in such circumstances. In contrast, if jealousy evolved to promote paternity competition, then jealousy is to be expected under such circumstances.

Second, consider an affair between a man and a married woman. The woman's sexual involvement with her husband poses no threat to the extrapair male's parental investment, since he is neither investing parental care nor pledging to invest parental care in the woman's offspring. In fact, if he impregnates the woman, his genes get a free ride on the parental care of his lover's cuckolded husband. So, if the proximate mechanism of jealousy evolved to protect against misspent parental care, it should not be triggered in such contexts. Indeed, not only should a male involved with a married woman not experience jealousy over her sexual relationship with her husband, but he should favor her continued sexual involvement with her husband, since that may trick the husband into believing that he is the father of any offspring born of his wife. In contrast, if the paternity competition theory is correct, we should expect a male involved with a married woman to experience jealousy when contemplating her sexual involvement with her husband.

Third, suppose a couple splits up and the woman begins a new sexual relationship with another man. Under such circumstances, the jilted male is no longer in a position of having to provide parental care to any offspring that woman bears. So, since parental investment isn't at stake, Evolutionary Psychology's theory of jealousy should not lead us to expect males to experience jealousy in such circumstances. In contrast, since the woman's new sexual relationship marks the diversion of paternity opportunities from the jilted male to the new male, the paternity competition theory should lead us to expect the jilted male to experience jealousy.

All of the data to test these competing predictions would be easily obtainable through the testing methods favored by Evolutionary Psychologists. Having lived among humans for quite some time now, having been around the block more times than I care to recount, and having experienced many of the human emotions firsthand, I confidently predict that the results would show that males often experience sexual jealousy in all of the above circumstances, even though there is no possibility of misspent parental care in such circumstances. If this prediction were borne out, it would favor the paternity competition theory over Evolutionary Psychology's theory.

Even if empirical results confirmed this prediction, however, there are two mutually incompatible ways in which Evolutionary Psychologists could explain away the results and thereby attempt to save their theory from disconfirmation. First, they could argue that the emotion elicited in the three contexts mentioned is not jealousy, but envy. For jealousy and envy are commonly distinguished from one another as follows. Jealousy is the emotional distress you feel in response to someone's threatening to take away something that you have and value, whereas envy is the emotional distress you feel in response to someone's having something that you want. Applying this distinction to sexual relationships, Buss says: "A man might experience envy of another man who has a beautiful wife. The envy is directed at the man who possesses what he wants, but lacks. The husband, however, may be jealous of his beautiful wife if he suspects that she is developing an interest in another man. Envy implies covetousness, malice, and ill-will directed at someone who has what you lack; jealousy, in contrast, implies the fear of losing to a rival a valuable partner that you already have."[38] Thus, Evolutionary Psychologists could argue, since the three scenarios mentioned above are all cases in which a male feels emotional distress regarding an implicit reproductive contract he desires, rather than one he already has, that male is, properly speaking, experiencing envy rather than jealousy.

But this argument is problematic for a couple of reasons. On the one hand, it is inconsistent with Buss's own claim, regarding the first scenario described above, that male sexual jealousy can be triggered even before a sexual or romantic relationship has developed. On the other hand, Evolutionary Psychologists define jealousy as *the state* that is caused by a perceived threat to a valued relationship and that causes actions designed to minimize that threat. Male sexual jealousy, then, is the state that is caused by cues that a female (with whom the male has a valued relationship) is developing or has developed a sexual interest in another male and that causes actions designed to protect the male's investment in that valued relationship (actions such as derogating the rival, lavishing gifts on the female, advertising or enhancing the male's own desirability, or manipulating the female's emotions). Whatever emotional state has these typical causes and effects is, by Evolutionary Psychology's own definition, jealousy. And, in the three scenarios mentioned, male emotional distress is caused by cues that a desired female is having a sexual relationship with another male, and the emotional distress in such cases would undoubtedly cause the male to exhibit the behaviors typical of jealousy. So the emotional state is jealousy, not envy, since it fits the causal profile that defines jealousy.

The idea that males in the three scenarios described are experiencing envy, rather than jealousy, is made intuitively plausible by the fact that these are cases in which the male is not actually in, but merely desires, a committed mateship with the female whose behavior is triggering the jealousy. While this distinction may be salient to a third party, it is a distinction that is unlikely to make an *emotional difference* to a male. For, if a male has invested reproductive effort in the pursuit of a particular female, that is a "valued relationship" from the perspective of that male, and anything that stands in the way of a mateship with that female is a threat to that valued relationship. What makes it a "valued relationship" for the male, in other words, is not whether the female has invested reproductive effort in the male, but simply whether the male perceives an investment of his reproductive effort in the female. (If you doubt this, think about the psychological profiles of stalkers and their "relationships" with their victims.) Thus, if you covet your neighbor's ox, you're envious. Similarly, if you covet your neighbor's beautiful wife in a general way, wishing that you too had a beautiful wife, you're envious. But, if you covet *your neighbor's wife*, if you're emotionally invested in having a sexual relationship *with her*, and if you're emotionally distressed by thoughts of her sexual relationship with her husband (or your other neighbors), then you're jealous, plain and simple.

The second way in which Evolutionary Psychologists could attempt to dismiss the predicted results is by arguing that, because of the severe threat to fitness that misspent parental investment presents for males, male sexual jealousy is on a hair trigger that can easily be tripped even under circumstances in which parental investment isn't at stake. This, indeed, is what Buss claims about the case study I cited in the first of the above scenarios. While this argument can be made, it constitutes an ad hoc adjustment to Evolutionary Psychology's theory in order to get it to fit data that it doesn't directly predict. The paternity competition theory, however, predicts in a principled way the occurrence of male sexual jealousy even under circumstances in which parental investment isn't at stake. Evolutionary Psychology's theory can be modified to provide an uncomfortable fit with the predicted data, but the paternity competition theory provides a perfectly tailored fit with that data. Consequently, if the evidence came in as predicted, the paternity competition theory would provide a more parsimonious explanation of it. There is, then, a viable *evolutionary* alternative to Evolutionary Psychology's theory of jealousy.

Like Evolutionary Psychology, however, the paternity competition theory assumes that there is an evolved psychological sex difference. Both theories claim that the male mind has evolved to place greater weight on cues to extrapair sexual involvements, whereas the female mind has evolved to place greater weight on cues to extrapair emotional involvements. Both theories, in short, claim that the minds of men and women *work differently*. An evolutionary account of jealousy, though, needn't require that the minds of men and women actually work differently in these ways. Indeed, there can be a genuinely evolutionary theory of jealousy according to which there is *no* sex difference in the "design features" of the male and female minds. I will first attempt to motivate this alternative theoretically, and then I'll attempt to motivate it empirically through a reexamination of the available evidence.

To begin, let's perform a little thought experiment. Suppose there is a population consisting of two types of people, type *A* people and type *B* people, each of which make up half the population. The individuals in this population engage in a series of one-on-one interactions in which favors are supposed to be traded in a way that benefits each party to the inter-action to a very small degree. Whenever *A*s interact with *B*s, however, each attempts to cheat the other, which escalates into a violent confrontation in which both sustain some injury. When *A*s interact with other *A*s and *B*s with other *B*s, though, everything goes swimmingly and favors are exchanged to the mutual, though small, benefit of each. Suppose further that the cost that each type incurs when interacting with the other type is far greater than the benefit that each type accrues from interacting with its own type. Under such circumstances, *A*s should clearly attempt to avoid interactions with *B*s and confine their interactions to other *A*s, and vice versa, so that they can reap the benefits of interactions with their own kind without paying the costs of interacting with the other kind. That is, it would clearly be beneficial for *A*s to evolve a mechanism for discriminat-ing *A*s from *B*s and a preference for interacting exclusively with *A*s, and vice versa. To put it simply, it would be beneficial for *A*s to evolve the policy "don't trust *B*s" and for *B*s to evolve the policy "don't trust *A*s." Will *A*s and *B*s evolve these policies? It all depends. There are a couple of situa-tions in which they wouldn't.

First, suppose that *A*s and *B*s have no way of telling one another apart until an interaction has already begun, at which point the cost for that interaction is ineluctable. Under such circumstances, a "don't trust *A*s" or "don't trust *B*s" policy will be ineffective, since no one can figure out which individuals should be trusted and which not. If, as we have supposed, the cost of interacting with the other type is greater than the benefit of inter-acting with one's own type, and there is a 50 percent chance that each interaction will be with the other type rather than one's own type, over the long run these interactions will prove costly to everyone. Even though everyone will benefit from the interactions with their own type, everyone will suffer even more from the interactions with the other type, and on the whole the costs will outweigh the benefits. Under such circumstances, it will actually be better for both *A*s and *B*s to evolve a "trust no one" policy, since that will lead everyone to avoid the costs involved in the totality of interactions. The payoff to As of the "trust no one" policy will consist in avoiding the costs of interactions with Bs, and the payoff to Bs will consist in avoiding the costs of interactions with As. In short, the same "trust no one" policy will have *different functions* for As and Bs. (If you're tempted to think that the policy has the same function for each—namely, that of avoiding being injured—just vary the thought experiment, to suit your imagination, so that the *kind of cost* that As impose on Bs is different from the kind of cost that Bs impose on As in their interactions, although the costs are equal. Then the "trust no one" policy functions in As to avoid one kind of cost, while it functions in Bs to avoid a different kind of cost.)

Second, suppose that As and Bs do have some way of telling one another apart prior to engaging in interactions. If As and Bs develop a way to distinguish one another, then they can selectively interact only with their own kind, thereby accruing the benefits of interacting with their own kind while avoiding the costs of interacting with the other kind. To do so, however, each has to develop some kind of *detection mechanism*, which functions to distinguish As from Bs. Adding this detection mechanism to their anatomy or psychology will, however, entail some form of developmental costs. Now here's the rub. If the benefits from interacting with one's own kind are sufficiently small, they won't cover the costs of developing the detection mechanism required to distinguish the individuals from whom one will benefit from the rest. In such an event, it will be cheaper overall for the individual not to develop a detection mechanism and to simply stick with a "trust no one" policy. For As, this policy is not as precise in its effects as a "don't trust Bs" policy would be, since it forecloses on the benefits of interactions with other As. But the added precision that a "don't trust Bs" policy would bring doesn't cover the costs of implementing that policy. Sometimes it doesn't pay to be too specific and precise.

Now let's apply this point to the evolution of jealousy. Let's suppose that infidelity imposes different kinds of cost on the two sexes. If a man's wife contemplates straying, he risks losing paternity opportunities or risks investing in another male's offspring. If a woman's husband contemplates straying, she risks losing the parental care and resources he does or could provide for her children. But, although the costs of infidelity are different for the two sexes, it doesn't necessarily follow that the two sexes must have evolved mechanisms *with different "design features"* that specialize in tracking only events that are correlated with the costs specific to one's sex. It's possible that both sexes possess the same mechanism, which operates at a slightly more general level than any possible mechanisms concerned only with sex-specific costs. In particular, suppose that both sexes have the same jealousy mechanism, which monitors the environment for, and is then triggered by, any event that poses a threat to *any relationship in which one has invested one's reproductive effort* (so that this would include the three contexts mentioned in the discussion of the paternity competition hypothesis). If this were the case, this single mechanism would nonetheless have somewhat different functions in the two sexes, since it would serve to protect each sex against the particular kind of cost that sex suffers from infidelity or abandonment. In males, it would function to protect against losing paternity opportunities or resources, whereas in females it would function to protect against losing a male's parental care and resources. And, like the "trust no one" policy, this single mechanism would be simpler to evolve in the human lineage than two sex-differentiated mechanisms, since it wouldn't require separate developmental mechanisms in the two sexes that have been perfected by selection over evolutionary time to perform highly sex-specific functions.

Let me put all this another way. The fact that there is a sex difference in the potential costs of infidelity doesn't entail that selection must have created a corresponding sex difference in the "design features" of the mind. The fact that men and women might stand to lose different things from a partner's infidelity or abandonment doesn't entail that selection must have designed the minds of the two sexes to *work differently*, to function in ways that are highly focused only on what each sex has to lose. Rather, selection could have designed the jealous mind to function exactly the same in both men and women: to become jealous in response to any event, such as a sexual infidelity, that provokes anxiety that one might lose a (potential) partner to another. Evolutionary Psychologists believe that each sex has its own sex-specific module for jealousy, which contains a lot of innate information about sex-specific threats to reproductive interests and domain-specific procedures for operating with that information. I'm suggesting, in contrast, a very minimal conception of the jealousy mechanism that selection has designed, according to which there is no "built-in" information about sex-specific threats to reproductive interests, but instead only a more general responsiveness to situations and events that pose a threat to a relationship in which one has invested one's reproductive effort. This doesn't mean, however, that this minimal jealousy mechanism can't generate some sex differences in the way that people respond to particular circumstances. It only means that those sex-differentiated responses aren't built in to the way that the minds of the two sexes work.

This proposal, of course, is highly theoretical and abstract at this point. We've already seen evidence that seems to favor Evolutionary Psychology's theory that there are evolved sex differences in the psychological mechanisms of jealousy, and it's not at all clear how this alternative suggestion is supposed to explain, or explain away, those differences. That will become clearer, however, as we take a closer look at the evidence that Evolutionary Psychologists have accumulated in support of their theory. So we turn now to a closer examination of that evidence.

Let's begin by examining the questionnaire data that Evolutionary Psychologists have gathered. In one question that appeared in the questionnaires, subjects were presented with the following "dilemma":

Please think of a serious committed romantic relationship that you have had in the past, that you currently have, or that you would like to have. Imagine that you discover that the person with whom you've been seriously involved became interested in someone else. What would distress or upset you more (*please circle only one*):

(A) Imagining your partner forming a deep emotional attachment to that person.
(B) Imagining your partner enjoying passionate sexual intercourse with that other person.[39]

This dilemma was originally administered by Buss and his colleagues in a 1992 study, but it has subsequently been used by a number of other researchers in a number of studies in a total of seven societies. That subsequent literature has taken to calling (A) an *emotional infidelity* and (B) a *sexual infidelity*. I will follow this convention for ease of discussion. The results of these studies are presented in table 6.1, where the numbers are the percentages of respondents who chose (B), the sexual infidelity.[40]

As part of their 1992 study, Buss and his colleagues also gave subjects the same scenario as above, but replaced the "dilemma" in the first question with the following "dilemma":

**Table 6.1**
Infidelity Dilemma 1: Percentage of Respondents Choosing Sexual Infidelity as More Upsetting by Survey Sample

| | Survey sample | | | | | |
|---|---|---|---|---|---|---|
| | USA | USA | USA | USA | USA | USA |
| Male | 60 | 53 | 61 | 55 | 76 | 73 |
| Female | 17 | 23 | 18 | 32 | 32 | 4 |

| | China | Netherlands | Germany | Korea | Japan |
|---|---|---|---|---|---|
| Male | 21 | 51 | 28 | 59 | 38 |
| Female | 5 | 31 | 16 | 18 | 13 |

(A) Imagining your partner trying different sexual positions with that other person.

(B) Imagining your partner falling in love with that other person.[41]

This question, in which the order of the sexual infidelity and emotional infidelity was switched from the original dilemma, was then used by a number of other researchers in several subsequent studies in a total of five societies. The results of the second set of studies are presented in table 6.2, where the numbers are the percentages of respondents who chose (A), the sexual infidelity.[42]

Notice that there is a significant sex difference in the results of these studies. In no study did more women than men report sexual infidelity to be more upsetting than emotional infidelity. Indeed, averaged across the results of all studies, in response to both dilemmas many more men than women reported sexual infidelity to be more upsetting than emotional infidelity—51 percent of the men versus 22 percent of the women in response to the first dilemma (table 6.1), and 38 percent of the men versus 13 percent of the women in response to the second dilemma (table 6.2). It is this sex difference that Evolutionary Psychologists have emphasized in their description of the results and that they have cited as providing strong support for Evolutionary Psychology's theory of jealousy.

But the simple existence of a sex difference is insufficient to support Evolutionary Psychology's theory. For the existence of a sex difference is actually an *indirect consequence* of Evolutionary Psychology's theory, being entailed by Evolutionary Psychology's primary claims regarding the adaptive problems that jealousy evolved to solve for each of the sexes. According to Evolutionary Psychology, the adaptive problem that male jealousy evolved to solve was that of protecting against misspent parental invest-

**Table 6.2**

Infidelity Dilemma 2: Percentage of Respondents Choosing Sexual Infidelity as More Upsetting by Survey Sample

|  | Survey sample | | | |
| --- | --- | --- | --- | --- |
|  | USA | USA | USA | USA |
| Male | 44 | 44 | 47 | 43 |
| Female | 12 | 12 | 12 | 11 |
|  | Netherlands | Germany | Korea | Japan |
| Male | 23 | 30 | 53 | 32 |
| Female | 12 | 8 | 22 | 15 |

ment. Since sexual infidelity undermines confidence in paternity whereas emotional infidelity does not, Evolutionary Psychologists claim that males focus on cues to sexual infidelity. Similarly, according to Evolutionary Psychology, the adaptive problem that female jealousy evolved to solve was that of ensuring that a mate's parental care and resources would not be diverted to another woman. Since a male's sexual infidelity may mean nothing whereas his emotional infidelity might lead to his leaving, Evolutionary Psychologists claim that females place greater weight on cues to emotional infidelity. That there should be a sex difference is actually a *by-product* of these primary entailments of the theory regarding the adaptive problems that jealousy evolved to solve. To confirm the theory, then, it is insufficient that there be a sex difference. To confirm the theory, it is necessary to show that males care more about sexual infidelity *than they do about emotional infidelity*, not simply that they care more about sexual infidelity *than females do*. For, if males actually care more about *emotional* infidelity than they do about *sexual* infidelity, despite caring more about sexual infidelity than females do, there is no clear confirmation of the hypothesis that male jealousy evolved to solve the problem of paternity uncertainty, since that problem is supposed to be generated *only* by a female partner's potential *sexual* infidelity.

When the data are viewed in this light, it's far from clear that they provide support for Evolutionary Psychology's theory. First, the average of responses to the first dilemma (table 6.1) shows only 51 percent of males reporting that they would be more upset by sexual infidelity than by emotional infidelity, which is the slimmest possible majority. Males, in fact, are pretty much evenly divided over whether sexual or emotional infidelity would be more upsetting. Further, the average of responses to the second dilemma (table 6.2) shows only 38 percent of males reporting that they would be more upset by sexual infidelity than by emotional infidelity. So a majority of more than 60 percent of males reported emotional infidelity to be more upsetting, in the second dilemma, than sexual infidelity. These results are hardly a ringing confirmation of the hypothesis that males have an evolved jealousy mechanism whose "design features" specialize in detecting and responding to cues to sexual infidelity.

Second, there is significant cultural variation in the results. While the percentages of males reporting sexual infidelity to be more upsetting than emotional infidelity in response to the first dilemma (table 6.1) are as high as 76 percent in a U.S. sample and 59 percent in the Korean sample, they are as low as 21 percent in the Chinese sample and 28 percent in the German sample. Similarly, although the percentages of males selecting sexual infidelity in response to the second dilemma (table 6.2) are as high as 47 percent in a U.S. sample and 53 percent in the Korean sample, they are as low as 23 percent in the Dutch sample and 30 percent in the German sample. These results hardly support Buss's claim that "men's jealousy appears to be more sensitive to cues of sexual infidelity" and that this is true "across cultures."[43] And, again, even though more men than women reported sexual infidelity to be more upsetting than emotional infidelity for both dilemmas and in all samples, this sex difference *in itself* does not support Evolutionary Psychology's claim that males have evolved to be especially sensitive to cues of sexual infidelity. The sex difference certainly does require explanation. But the fact that male responses do not consistently indicate the focused concern with sexual infidelity that Evolutionary Psychology predicts raises serious doubt about whether Evolutionary Psychology's explanation of the sex differences is correct.

So the very data that Evolutionary Psychologists cite as confirmation of their theory do not, in fact, provide clear support for it. But there are other data that provide further difficulties for Evolutionary Psychology. Buss's questionnaire dilemmas were administered to homosexual men and women in several studies, and the results from homosexual men are particularly puzzling from the perspective of Evolutionary Psychology's theory. The psychologists Virgil Sheets and Marlow Wolfe found that only 24 percent of homosexual men chose sexual infidelity as more upsetting than emotional infidelity in the first dilemma (choosing between a partner's forming an emotional attachment versus having passionate sex) and only 5 percent chose sexual infidelity as more upsetting in the second dilemma (choosing between a partner's falling in love with someone else versus trying different sexual positions). The psychologist Christine Harris administered only the second dilemma to a sample of homosexual men, of whom only 13 percent chose sexual infidelity as more upsetting than emotional infidelity. Finally, the psychologist Michael Bailey and his colleagues administered Buss's two dilemmas to both homosexual and heterosexual men and women and found that homosexual men were even less likely than heterosexual women to report sexual infidelity to be more upsetting than emotional infidelity. In sum, all of these studies found homosexual men to be far less likely than heterosexual men to find sexual infidelity more upsetting than emotional infidelity. Indeed, homosexual men rather overwhelmingly report emotional infidelity to be more upsetting than sexual infidelity.

This fact is difficult to reconcile with Evolutionary Psychology's claim that there are sex differences in the evolved "design features" of the psychological mechanisms of jealousy. For, at first glance, it seems that Evolutionary Psychology's theory entails that homosexual males, *being males*, possess the same jealousy mechanism as heterosexual males and that, consequently, sexual infidelity should be the primary trigger of jealousy in both homosexual and heterosexual males. Indeed, this is the view that Donald Symons defended in *The Evolution of Human Sexuality*. According to Symons: "There is no reason to suppose that homosexuals differ systematically from heterosexuals in any way other than sexual object choice."[44] Symons further argued that relationships between homosexual men are highly unstable precisely because male jealousy is triggered by sexual infidelity and homosexual men tend to be highly promiscuous. At the time that Symons made these arguments, the above data regarding homosexual male jealousy had not been gathered. In light of that data, however, his view is untenable.

But there are a couple of ways in which Evolutionary Psychologists could attempt to reconcile their theory of sex differences in the "design features" of jealousy with the data from homosexual males. On the one hand, Evolutionary Psychologists could argue that, contrary to Symons, a difference in sexual orientation is actually accompanied by a wholesale difference in all aspects of sexual psychology. According to this argument, whatever process determines one's sexual orientation during development may also determine the "gender" of one's sexual psychology, so that the modules underlying one's sexual psychology develop with the settings typical of the sex that shares one's sexual orientation. According to this argument, in effect, homosexuals are "cross-gendered" psychologically. If this were true, the sexual psychology of homosexual men would be similar to that of heterosexual women, and the sexual psychology of homosexual women would be similar to that of heterosexual men. Consequently, we would expect homosexual men to respond more like heterosexual women than like heterosexual men to jealousy-triggering situations—which, according to the available questionnaire data, they apparently do.

There is, however, a significant body of evidence to show that homosexuals are not simply "cross-gendered" individuals. In the vast majority of respects and on average, homosexual men are more like heterosexual men than like heterosexual women, and homosexual women are more like heterosexual women than they are like heterosexual men. More to the present point, if the "cross-gendered" theory of homosexuality were true, the responses of homosexual women to Buss's dilemmas should be very similar to those of heterosexual men. But all three studies cited above found no significant difference between the responses of homosexual and heterosexual women to Buss's dilemmas. Like heterosexual women, only a relatively small minority of homosexual women reported finding sexual infidelity more upsetting than emotional infidelity. Thus, the "cross-gendered" hypothesis of homosexual sexual psychology fails; so it doesn't provide a plausible way of reconciling Evolutionary Psychology's theory of evolved sex differences in jealousy with the data regarding homosexual male jealousy.

There is, however, another possible explanation of why homosexual males differ from heterosexual males with respect to jealousy triggers. It's possible that homosexual males do, in fact, possess the same jealousy mechanism as heterosexual males, but that the psychological mechanism is more sensitive to contextual information about whether a sexual infidelity actually threatens paternity. Evolutionary Psychology portrays the male jealousy mechanism as being rather blindly responsive to any sexual infidelities, since in the environment of evolutionary adaptedness sexual infidelities would have compromised certainty of paternity. But suppose that the mechanism calculates whether a sexual infidelity jeopardizes paternity before triggering a jealous reaction to sexual infidelity. Further suppose that, when the mechanism doesn't detect cues of jeopardized paternity, it reacts primarily to cues of emotional infidelity, since emotional infidelity signals potential abandonment. If homosexual and heterosexual males shared such a mechanism, males in heterosexual relationships would become jealous over a partner's sexual infidelity, since it would compromise paternity certainty, whereas males in homosexual relationships would not become jealous over a partner's sexual infidelity, since paternity, hence investment of parental care and resources, isn't at stake. Homosexual males, then, would focus primarily on cues to emotional infidelity. If the male jealousy mechanism functioned in this way, the data regarding homosexual male jealousy could be reconciled with Evolutionary Psychology's theory of evolved sex differences in jealousy.

The problem with this proposal is that it could also account for the difference between heterosexual men and women. For, if the above proposal is right, homosexual and heterosexual men possess the same psychological adaptation for jealousy, which simply reacts differently to the different circumstances faced by homosexual and heterosexual men. In particular, since the sexual infidelities of the partners of heterosexual males jeopardize paternity, whereas the sexual infidelities of the partners of homosexual males do not, sexual infidelity triggers the jealousy mechanism in heterosexual males but not in homosexual males. But if that is so, then the difference between heterosexual men and women could also be due to a difference in circumstances, rather than a difference in psychological adaptations. For suppose that men and women share the same jealousy mechanism and that it functions as described above. Then, since a male's sexual infidelity doesn't threaten his female mate's parental investment, her jealousy will be triggered primarily by emotional infidelity rather than sexual infidelity. Thus, if the difference between homosexual and heterosexual males is explained away as due to a difference in circumstances with respect to potential paternity, rather than to a difference in the underlying psychological mechanism, then the difference between heterosexual men and women can likewise be attributed to the same psychological mechanism's functioning differently under the different circumstances faced by heterosexual men and women. So, the proposal that homosexual and heterosexual males share the same context-sensitive jealousy mechanism doesn't provide a plausible way of reconciling the data from homosexual males with Evolutionary Psychology's theory of evolved *sex differences in the "design features"* of jealousy.

There are, then, three sources of difficulty for Evolutionary Psychology's theory of sex differences in the "design features" of jealousy. First, if male jealousy is so focused on sexual infidelity, we should not find merely the slimmest possible majority reporting sexual infidelity to be more upsetting in response to Buss's first dilemma, and we should not find a minority reporting sexual infidelity to be more upsetting in response to Buss's second dilemma. Second, there is wide variation across cultures in the percentages of males who choose sexual infidelity as more upsetting in response to both dilemmas, and in some cultures the percentages of males choosing sexual infidelity as more upsetting constitute a fairly small minority. Third, the available data concerning homosexual male jealousy are not what we should expect given an evolved sex difference in the "design features" of jealousy, and there is no plausible way of reconciling those data with the hypothesis of an evolved sex-linked psychological difference. There is, of course, a clear sex difference in the responses to Buss's questionnaire dilemmas. But, given these three problems with Evolutionary Psychology's theory, perhaps there is some better explanation of the sex difference.

One interesting alternative explanation of the sex difference is the so-called *double-shot hypothesis*. The double-shot hypothesis has been defended by the psychologists David DeSteno and Peter Salovey, who gave the hypothesis its name, and by the psychologists Christine Harris and Nicholas Christenfeld. According to the double-shot hypothesis, men and women are equally distressed by both emotional and sexual infidelity, but they differ in their beliefs about how closely the two forms of infidelity are linked in the minds and behavior of members of the opposite sex. Men, according to this hypothesis, believe that women are unlikely to have sex without being in love, but that they can be in love without having sex. Consequently, when a man suspects his partner of a sexual involvement with another man, he infers that she must be in love with him as well. In contrast, if he suspects his partner of an emotional involvement with another man, he doesn't necessarily infer a sexual involvement as well. For a man, then, a partner's sexual infidelity represents a "double shot" of infidelity, since the sexual infidelity is believed to be accompanied by an emotional infidelity, whereas her emotional infidelity does not represent a "double shot" of infidelity. Similarly, according to this hypothesis, women believe that men can easily have sex without being in love, but that they can't be in love without wanting sex. Consequently, when a woman suspects her partner of an emotional involvement with another woman, she infers that a sexual involvement with that other woman is likely or forthcoming as well. In contrast, if she suspects her partner of a sexual involvement with another woman, she won't automatically infer that he must also be in love with that woman. For a woman, then, a partner's emotional, but not his sexual, infidelity represents a "double shot" of infidelity. Thus, when faced with one of Buss's forced-choice questionnaire dilemmas, males choose sexual infidelity as more distressing because a female's sexual infidelity is more likely than her emotional infidelity to signal a "double shot" of infidelity, whereas females choose emotional infidelity as more distressing because a male's emotional infidelity is more likely than his sexual infidelity to signal a "double shot" of infidelity.

Of course, if the double-shot hypothesis is correct, we should find evidence that men and women differ in their beliefs about the connection between sex and love in the minds and behavior of members of the opposite sex. So DeSteno and Salovey and Harris and Christenfeld conducted a series of studies designed to determine whether the sexes' beliefs do differ in the predicted ways. The studies differed slightly in their details, but they all involved presenting subjects with two types of question. In one type, subjects were asked to suppose that their mates, or other members of the opposite sex, had become sexually involved with someone else. They were then asked to indicate (on a nine-point or five-point scale) how likely they thought it was that their mates, or those other members of the opposite sex, had become emotionally involved with that other person as well. In the other type of question, they were asked to imagine an emotional involvement and then asked how likely it was that that involvement would be accompanied by a sexual involvement. All studies found that men believe that, for women, sex implicates love more than love implicates sex and that women believe that, for men, love implicates sex more than sex implicates love. Indeed, the most dramatic finding was that women believe that it is not particularly likely that a man's having sex with a woman implies any kind of emotional involvement with her. Since such beliefs can be easily acquired through learning, and since they can explain the sex difference in responses to Buss's questionnaire dilemmas, the defenders of the double-shot hypothesis argue that the questionnaire results don't provide strong support for Evolutionary Psychology's claim that there is an evolved domain-specific mechanism for jealousy, let alone that there are evolved sex differences in the "design features" of jealousy.

Although the double-shot hypothesis does adequately explain the results from Buss's two questionnaire dilemmas, Buss and his colleagues have criticized it on several grounds. First, Buss and his colleagues administered another battery of questionnaires designed to provide a crucial test of Evolutionary Psychology's theory versus the double-shot hypothesis. The new questionnaires involved three new "dilemmas," all of which described contexts about which Evolutionary Psychology's theory and the double-shot hypothesis entail different predictions. Two of the new dilemmas were designed to separate the two forms of infidelity, so that subjects could not construe either form of infidelity as indicating the probable presence of the other form (so that neither form ever indicated a "double shot"). In these dilemmas, in effect, subjects were forced to choose which "single shot" of infidelity they found most distressing. The other new dilemma was designed to guarantee subjects that both forms of infidelity *had* occurred, but forced them to choose which form was most upsetting. With respect to all of these new dilemmas, Buss and his colleagues argued, Evolutionary Psychology predicts that subjects will exhibit the same old sex difference, whereas if the double-shot hypothesis is right the sex difference should disappear.

One of the new dilemmas was as follows:

Imagine that you discover that the person with whom you've been seriously involved became interested in someone else. What would upset or distress you more (please circle only one):

(A) Imagining your partner forming a deep emotional (*but not sexual*) relationship with that person.

(B) Imagining your partner enjoying a sexual (*but not emotional*) relationship with that person.[45]

Buss and his colleagues administered this dilemma to two groups of American subjects, while the psychologists Michael Wiederman and Erica Kendall administered a virtually identically worded dilemma to a group of Swedish subjects. The results of these studies are presented in table 6.3, where the numbers indicate the percentages of respondents who chose (B), the emotionless sexual infidelity.[46]

A second new dilemma replaced (A) and (B) above with the following:

(A) Imagining your partner having sexual intercourse with that person, but you are certain that they will *not* form a deep emotional attachment.
(B) Imagining your partner forming a deep emotional attachment to that person, but you are certain that they will *not* have sexual intercourse.[47]

Buss and his colleagues administered this dilemma to groups of American, Korean, and Japanese subjects, and the results are presented in table 6.4, where the numbers indicate the percentages of respondents who chose (A), the sexual infidelity.[48]

Finally, the dilemma that was designed to guarantee subjects of a double shot of infidelity, but to force them to choose which "shot" hurt the most, was as follows:

Imagine that your partner *both* formed an emotional attachment to another person *and* had sexual intercourse with that other person. *Which aspect* of your partner's involvement would upset you more?

(A) the sexual intercourse with that other person.
(B) the emotional attachment to that other person.[49]

Buss and his colleagues also administered this dilemma to groups of American, Korean, and Japanese subjects, and the results are presented in table 6.5, where the numbers are the percentages of respondents who chose (A), the sexual involvement.[50]

**Table 6.3**
Infidelity Dilemma 3: Percentage of Respondents Choosing Emotionless Sexual Infidelity as More Upsetting by Survey Sample

|  | Survey sample | | |
| --- | --- | --- | --- |
|  | USA | USA | Sweden |
| Male | 43 | 45 | 62 |
| Female | 18 | 19 | 37 |

**Table 6.4**

Infidelity Dilemma 4: Percentage of Respondents Choosing Emotionless Sexual Infidelity as More Upsetting by Survey Sample

| | Survey sample | | |
|---|---|---|---|
| | USA | Korea | Japan |
| Male | 65 | 54 | 75 |
| Female | 31 | 30 | 75 |

**Table 6.5**

Infidelity Dilemma 5: Percentage of Respondents Choosing the Sexual Aspect of Infidelity as More Upsetting by Survey Sample

| | Survey sample | | |
|---|---|---|---|
| | USA | Korea | Japan |
| Male | 61 | 47 | 33 |
| Female | 13 | 27 | 21 |

With the exception of the Japanese response to the second of these new dilemmas (table 6.4), there is a significant sex difference in subjects' responses, with more males than females reporting the sexual aspects to be more upsetting than the emotional aspects, as predicted by Evolutionary Psychology. However, the fact that a majority of American men reported a partner's "deep emotional (*but not sexual*) relationship" to be more upsetting than a "sexual (*but not emotional*) relationship" (table 6.3) is certainly contrary to Evolutionary Psychology's general predictions about the nature of male jealousy. Nonetheless, the fact that there is a consistent sex difference in these results does appear to falsify the double-shot hypothesis, since that hypothesis seems inconsistent with a sex difference in responses when only a "single shot" of infidelity is guaranteed.

Buss and his colleagues also raise a couple of theoretical objections to the double-shot hypothesis. First, they argue, the double-shot hypothesis relies heavily on the fact that the sexes differ in their beliefs about the connection between sex and love in the minds and behavior of the opposite sex, but it offers no explanation of this sex difference. In contrast, they argue, Evolutionary Psychology can explain the sex difference in beliefs. In particular, women believe that men frequently have sex without an emotional involvement, whereas men believe that women typically don't have sex without an emotional involvement, because *in fact* the sexes pursue different sexual strategies. This difference in sexual strategies is due to the sex difference in minimum obligatory parental investment noted in chapter 5. Since males need only invest in the act of copulation in order to potentially gain an additional offspring, males have little to lose by having "casual sex." As a result, males have evolved to pursue sex even in the absence of an emotional involvement. A single act of casual sex, in contrast, can leave a woman with a child to rear without the assistance and parental care of a mate. As a result, women have evolved to be more wary than men about embarking on sexual adventures in the absence of an emotional commitment from a male, a strategy that helps ensure a woman that any pregnancy will occur within the context of a long-term, investing relationship. Consequently, due to a sex difference in the cost-benefit structure of casual sex, men are much more likely than women to have sex in the absence of an emotional involvement. And, Buss and his colleagues argue, the sex difference in beliefs about the sexual strategies of the opposite sex merely reflects the evolutionary reality of a sex difference in sexual strategies. Since Evolutionary Psychology can explain why the sexes' beliefs differ, whereas the double-shot hypothesis can't, Evolutionary Psychology has an additional advantage over the double-shot hypothesis.

Second, Buss and his colleagues argue, the double-shot hypothesis fallaciously infers that, "if the sex difference is due to differing beliefs about conditional probabilities [concerning the likelihood that a member of the opposite sex is in love if they are having sex with someone] rather than to evolved psychological sex differences, then the sex difference is due to socialization or other socially derived inferences rather than to evolution."[51] In other words, just because the sexes differ in their beliefs about the connection between sex and love in the opposite sex, it doesn't follow that those beliefs are arrived at through learning or "socialization." Rather, they contend, those beliefs may, instead, be an innate part of our evolved psychological equipment for navigating the stormy seas of sexual relationships.

I think that the first of these criticisms is largely correct. The sex difference in beliefs about the sexual strategies pursued by the opposite sex may, indeed, be an accurate reflection of psychological and behavioral differences between the sexes, and those differences may be a by-product of the sex difference in minimum obligatory parental investment. But I think that the second criticism is a red herring. While it is, indeed, fallacious to *infer* that beliefs *must* have their origin in learning, the real issue is whether there is any reason to suppose that the particular beliefs in question are likely to be an innate part of our psychological equipment. And there is, in fact, no reason to suppose that they are. Indeed, since the beliefs in question are relevant only to an individual's decisions about sexual relationships, and since most humans don't embark upon sexual relationships until their midteens or later, individuals have ample opportunity to acquire the relevant beliefs through learning before those beliefs are implicated in life decisions. Human social life is brimming with information about romantic and sexual relationships, and adolescents are eager observers of those aspects of human social life, so it is hardly necessary to have such simple beliefs built in to the innate structure of our minds. This is an instance of what the cognitive scientist Andy Clark calls "the 007 principle." As Clark says: "In general, evolved creatures will neither store nor process information in costly ways when they can use the structure of the environment and their operations upon it [instead]. . . . That is, know only as much as you need to know to get the job done."[52] Since the information about sex differences in sexual strategies is easily extractable from the environment, by Clark's 007 principle we are unlikely to have evolved to store that information innately. Indeed, since the benefit of having those beliefs is easily obtainable through learning, it isn't necessary to pay the developmental costs of building them in to the innate structure of our psychological equipment.

There is, however, an additional problem with the double-shot hypothesis that Buss and his colleagues don't mention. According to the double-shot hypothesis, each sex picks as more distressing the form of infidelity that is most likely to signal a "double shot" of infidelity. So, according to the hypothesis, men are more upset by sexual infidelity because they actually take sexual infidelity to indicate that their partners have *also* been emotionally unfaithful. But the double-shot hypothesis doesn't explain why a double shot of infidelity should be of greater concern than the particular "single shot" of infidelity that is actually chosen as the more distressing of the two. In other words, the double-shot hypothesis doesn't explain why men, for example, should actually be focused on whether their partners have been *both* emotionally and sexually unfaithful rather than just on whether their partners have been sexually unfaithful. Perhaps it's supposed to be obvious that being cheated on both emotionally and sexually is worse than just being cheated on sexually. But I don't see that this is obvious, in much the way that I don't see that it is obviously worse to die from two gunshot wounds than to die from one gunshot wound alone.

Harris makes a passing comment that could be construed as an explanation of why a double shot of infidelity is supposed to be a more focal
concern than a single shot. Harris says: "the same basic process is involved
in jealousy that arises not just in sexual relationships but in other interpersonal relationships as well. Jealousy may motivate people to keep what
they perceive as rightfully theirs."[53] On this account, a double shot of infidelity is worse than a single shot because twice as much of what one perceives as rightfully one's own is being stolen by someone else. But this
depends on viewing sexual relationships as just one more kind of interpersonal relationship, and it seems clear that they are not. Some of our
evolved desires and motives are obviously specific to sexual relationships.
We are not driven to enter and remain in sexual relationships and long-
term mateships solely by the motivational mechanisms that cause us to
form friendships and acquaintanceships. Since some of our desires and
motives function specifically to cause us to enter sexual relationships, it is
implausible that none of our emotions function specifically to protect us
once we are in sexual relationships. When sexual relationships are seen as
unique, and mates are not viewed as just another kind of "property" that
can be stolen by someone else, it is less than obvious why a double shot
of infidelity, *in itself*, should be worse than a single shot.

There is a more plausible alternative to the double-shot hypothesis,
which nonetheless explains how the sex difference in beliefs about opposite-sex sexual strategies affects responses to Buss's jealousy dilemmas. To
approach this other hypothesis, consider some of what Symons had to say
about female jealousy in *The Evolution of Human Sexuality*: "A husband's
dalliance may have no effect whatsoever on his wife's reproductive success
or it may presage a liaison that will entail a reduction in the husband's
investment in his wife and her children; furthermore, today's paramour
may be tomorrow's co-wife. . . . I suggest that selection has favored the
female capacity to learn to distinguish (not necessarily cognitively) threatening from nonthreatening adultery, and to experience jealousy in proportion to the perceived threat."[54] Symons is suggesting that the female
mind actually tracks events that signal the likely end of a male's investment. In effect, the female mind is looking out for events that portend *the
potential termination* of the implicit reproductive contract. Since men often
engage in sexual relations with women with whom they have no emotional involvement, and since women know this, women are often able to
discount a casual sexual infidelity as *not* signaling the likely termination
of the relationship. A male's emotional infidelity, on the other hand,
signals a likely interest in a long-term relationship with another woman,

and so emotional infidelity is more likely than sexual infidelity to portend the likely termination of the relationship. If this is right, we should expect women to be more upset by emotional infidelity than sexual infidelity, which is precisely what women respondents to Buss's dilemmas consistently report.

Compare this elaboration of Symons's suggestion with the double-shot hypothesis. According to the double-shot hypothesis, women report emotional infidelity to be more upsetting than sexual infidelity because emotional infidelity is more likely than sexual infidelity to signal a double shot of infidelity. According to the above elaboration of Symons's suggestion, women report emotional infidelity to be more upsetting than sexual infidelity because emotional infidelity is more likely than sexual infidelity *to pose a threat to the relationship*. Symons suggests that women have evolved to determine which infidelities pose a realistic threat to the relationship, and which do not, and to experience jealous upset to a degree that is proportional to the likelihood that the infidelity will lead to the termination of the relationship. Women's belief that men often have no emotional involvement with their casual sex partners figures in their determination of which infidelities threaten a relationship, and it leads women to perceive emotional infidelities as more threatening to a relationship, on average, than sexual infidelities.

But what if men, too, have an evolved "capacity to learn to distinguish threatening from nonthreatening" infidelities, just as Symons suggests women have? How would this capacity function in men? On the one hand, men would perceive emotional infidelities to be every bit as threatening to a relationship as women perceive them to be, and for many of the same reasons. If your wife falls in love with another man, that clearly places the future of your relationship in doubt, and that in turn places your future reproductive prospects in doubt (at the very least for the entire period of time it takes to woo and win a new long-term mate). On the other hand, however, men would *also* find sexual infidelities to be threatening to a relationship, and there are at least three reasons why men would find sexual infidelities more threatening to a relationship than women find them to be.

First, as already noted, although men know that women often have casual sex, so that men can sometimes discount sexual infidelities in the way that women can, men do believe that women are not as likely as men to have sex with someone with whom they have no emotional involvement. Men will consequently take a female's sexual infidelity to be more likely than their own to indicate an emotional involvement as well. As a result, sexual infidelities will be more distressing to men than to women. This greater distress will *not* be due to the fact that a sexual infidelity signals a double shot of infidelity, as the double-shot hypothesis claims, but will be due to the fact that a combined sexual and emotional extrapair involvement signals a very serious *threat to the relationship*. That is, sexual infidelities can be distressing to men because a female's sexual infidelity signals a likely emotional infidelity as well, and a combined sexual and emotional infidelity signals a very serious threat to the relationship—a greater threat, in fact, than the possibility of an extrapair emotional involvement alone. Thus, men will find sexual infidelities more distressing than women do, because a female's sexual infidelity signals a potential threat to a relationship (via the likely combination with an emotional involvement) that is greater than the potential threat signaled by a male's sexual infidelity.

Second, even if a female's sexual infidelity is not likely to be accompanied by an extrapair emotional involvement, a female's sexual infidelity still probably signals a greater threat to a relationship than does a male's sexual infidelity. As noted earlier, sexual dissatisfaction in marriage is a primary force driving women to pursue extramarital sexual involvements. Indeed, the studies that have shown this have also shown there to be a significant sex difference in this regard. Men who stray typically report a mere desire for sexual variety as the motivating factor, whereas women who stray typically report dissatisfaction in their marriages as the motivating factor. A woman's sexual infidelity, then, is a cue to sexual dissatisfaction in the relationship, and people who are dissatisfied in their relationships are more likely to terminate those relationships than people who are satisfied, especially if they find new partners who provide them with the needed sexual satisfaction. Thus, even in the absence of an accompanying emotional involvement, a woman's sexual infidelity signals a threat to a relationship by signaling dissatisfaction in the relationship.

Third, Buss argues that one of the functions of female infidelity is "trading up" in the mating market. That is, sometimes women pursue affairs as part of a long-term mating strategy of searching for a "new and improved" mate from the secure vantage point of already having a mate. It's unclear how much female infidelity can be attributed to the "trading up" strategy, but if Buss is right that a significant portion of female infidelity does, in fact, represent a shopping spree for a new mate, then a woman's sexual infidelity can also signal a threat to a relationship by signaling the possibility that she is shopping for a new mate.

Thus, if men also have an evolved "capacity to learn to distinguish threatening from nonthreatening" infidelities, we should expect men to find emotional infidelities just as threatening to a relationship as women find them. In addition, we should expect men to find sexual infidelities threatening to a relationship, for the three reasons just mentioned. Indeed, if the foregoing is correct, we should expect men to be more distressed than women are by sexual infidelity, but *not* necessarily to be more distressed by sexual infidelity than by emotional infidelity, since both forms of female infidelity threaten a relationship. In fact, in light of the foregoing, we might expect men to be more distressed by emotional infidelities than by sexual infidelities, since emotional infidelities are *direct signals* of relationship jeopardy, whereas sexual infidelities are *indirect signals* of relationship jeopardy. That is, if a deep extrapair emotional involvement signals a threat to a relationship at all, it does so by directly signaling the possibility that one's partner has fallen in love with another, which poses a serious threat to a relationship. If an extrapair sexual involvement signals a threat to a relationship at all, however, it does so by virtue of signaling either an extrapair emotional involvement, sexual dissatisfaction in the relationship, or a strategy of "trading up." It is these latter three conditions that pose a threat to a relationship, so a sexual infidelity signals a threat to a relationship only *indirectly* by signaling one or more of these potential threats to a relationship.

On the basis of these considerations, consider what I will call the *relationship jeopardy hypothesis*, according to which both sexes *have the same evolved capacity* to learn to distinguish threatening from nonthreatening extrapair involvements and to experience jealous upset to a degree that is proportional to the perceived threat to a relationship in which one has invested one's reproductive effort (including the three contexts mentioned in our discussion of the paternity competition hypothesis). This same capacity leads the sexes to view infidelities differently, however, because the sexes acquire different beliefs about opposite-sex sexual strategies: Women acquire the belief that men often have loveless sex, so women learn that they can often "discount" a male's sexual infidelity, while men acquire beliefs that a woman's sexual infidelity can signal an accompanying emotional involvement, sexual dissatisfaction in the relationship, or a strategy of "trading up." When these sex-differentiated beliefs are processed by the capacity to distinguish threatening from nonthreatening infidelities, and when individuals are given Buss-style forced-choice dilemmas, individuals of each sex report as more distressing the single form of infidelity that they believe to be the most likely signal *that their relationship is in jeopardy*. Thus, according to the relationship jeopardy hypothesis, women will tend to find emotional infidelity more distressing than sexual infidelity, because it is more likely to signal that a relationship is in jeopardy. Men, on the other hand, will find both forms of infidelity distressing, since both are reliable signals that a relationship is in jeopardy, although they will find sexual infidelity more distressing than women find it.

The relationship jeopardy hypothesis, then, strikes a middle ground between the double-shot hypothesis and Evolutionary Psychology's theory. According to the double-shot hypothesis, there is no evolved psychological mechanism specific to jealousy in sexual relationships. Rather, jealousy in sexual relationships is part of more general perceptions of threats to interpersonal relationships of all kinds, and sex differences in jealousy are due simply to differences in acquired beliefs. In contrast, the relationship jeopardy hypothesis does take there to be an evolved emotional alarm specific to threats to relationships in which one has invested one's reproductive effort. But, like the double-shot hypothesis, the relationship jeopardy hypothesis claims that sex differences in jealousy are due to differences in what the sexes learn about one another, even though much of what they learn is an accurate reflection of evolved sex differences in sexual strategies. In this sense, the relationship jeopardy hypothesis doesn't go as far as Evolutionary Psychology, which views sex differences in jealousy to be a manifestation of sex differences in the "design features" of the minds of the two sexes. In short, according to the relationship jeopardy hypothesis, jealousy is not a by-product of some more domain-general mechanisms (as per the double-shot hypothesis), but is specific to the domain of relationships in which reproductive effort is invested; at the same time, the mechanisms of jealousy are not so domain-specific as to be focused in each sex only on threats to that sex's reproductive interests (as per Evolutionary Psychology's theory).

With the relationship jeopardy hypothesis in hand, let's look again at some of the data already considered. The relationship jeopardy hypothesis predicts that men will find sexual infidelity more distressing than women, and that is in fact what is found in the responses to the first two of Buss's dilemmas (tables 6.1 and 6.2). The relationship jeopardy hypothesis, however, does *not* entail that men will find sexual infidelity more distressing than emotional infidelity. In fact, since sexual infidelity is an indirect signal of relationship jeopardy, while emotional infidelity is a direct signal of relationship jeopardy, the hypothesis actually leads us to expect that men may place a slightly greater weight on emotional rather than sexual infidelity. In contrast, Evolutionary Psychology's theory of jealousy, as we saw, entails that men should place greater weight on sexual infidelity than on emotional infidelity (not simply greater weight on sexual infidelity *than women* place on sexual infidelity).

When the results in table 6.1 are considered again, they provide greater support for the relationship jeopardy hypothesis than for Evolutionary Psychology's theory. Averaged over all studies using that first dilemma, 51 percent of men chose sexual infidelity as more distressing. As noted earlier, this is not strong confirmation of Evolutionary Psychology's theory, but if the relationship jeopardy hypothesis is correct we should find men to be divided with respect to whether emotional infidelity is more distressing than sexual infidelity. More telling are the results in table 6.2, in which only 38 percent of men chose sexual infidelity as more distressing than emotional infidelity. These results don't confirm Evolutionary Psychology's theory, but they fit the relationship jeopardy hypothesis, because according to that hypothesis emotional infidelity is a direct signal of relationship jeopardy whereas sexual infidelity is an indirect signal, and we should expect more men to choose the direct signal as more distressing than the indirect signal. Even so, since subjects were instructed to "think of a serious committed romantic relationship that you have had in the past, that you currently have, or that you would like to have," the form of infidelity any particular male selected as more distressing undoubtedly depended on his beliefs about the particular relationship he was thinking about when answering the question (that is, whether his partner's sexual or emotional infidelity would signal a greater likelihood of relationship jeopardy in that particular relationship).

Even more telling than these numbers, however, is an examination of exactly what subjects were choosing between in the first two dilemmas. In the first dilemma (table 6.1), the choice is between "imagining your partner forming a deep emotional attachment" to another person and "imagining your partner enjoying passionate sexual intercourse with that other person." There is little ambiguity in the phrase "passionate sexual intercourse," but there is plenty in the phrase "deep emotional attachment." It's difficult to construe "*passionate* sexual intercourse" as indicating anything other than passion. But a "deep emotional attachment" can be construed as indicating romantic love or just a platonic opposite-sex friendship, which is known to happen in nature. Given the ambiguity, many male subjects might discount the emotional attachment as non-threatening, since it could simply be a close friendship between two individuals who are not sexually attracted to one another. But, since sexual infidelity is a more reliable indicator of love in women than in men, and since the dilemma asks subjects to imagine a sexual infidelity that is *pas-*

*sionate*, many male subjects could find it harder to discount the threat of a passionate sexual involvement. Given the descriptions of the two options, then, and given the supposition that subjects are reacting to cues of relationship jeopardy, it's easy to see how male subjects could be pretty much evenly divided in their interpretations of which of the two options is a more reliable indicator of relationship jeopardy.

Things become even clearer when we examine the second dilemma (table 6.2), in which subjects are asked to choose between "imagining your partner trying different sexual positions" with another person and "imagining your partner falling in love with that other person." "Falling in love" is not ambiguous in the way that "deep emotional attachment" is. As a result, if subjects are reacting to cues of relationship jeopardy, we should expect that they should find "falling in love" more threatening to a relationship than a "deep emotional attachment." And, in fact, averaged over all trials with the second dilemma, the percentage of males reporting "falling in love" to be more distressing than "different sexual positions" is 62 percent, an increase of 13 percent over the number of male subjects choosing the emotional infidelity as more distressing in response to the first dilemma. Interestingly, the percentage of female subjects choosing the emotional infidelity in the second dilemma also increases by 9 percent over the number choosing emotional infidelity in the first dilemma, which confirms that the language "falling in love" doesn't lend itself to being discounted as nonthreatening in the way that "deep emotional attachment" does. But, in that case, why isn't the percentage of male respondents who choose "falling in love" even higher than it is? Why isn't it as high as the percentage of female respondents choosing it? Because males believe that a female's sexual infidelity is still a strong signal of relationship jeopardy. But, since "falling in love" is a stronger signal of relationship jeopardy, we find more males reporting it to be more distressing than the sexual infidelity.

There is a similar effect in the responses to the third and fourth dilemmas reported above. In the third dilemma, subjects are asked to choose between "a deep emotional (*but not sexual*) relationship" and "a sexual (*but not emotional*) relationship." And in the fourth dilemma, subjects are asked to imagine their partners forming relationships and then to choose between "sexual intercourse . . . , but you are *certain* that *they will not form a deep emotional attachment*" and "a deep emotional attachment . . . , but you are *certain* that *they will not have* sexual intercourse." In the third dilemma, then, the choice is between emotional or sexual relationships that are *currently* not characterized by an additional sexual or emotional involvement respectively. But, in that choice, there is no guarantee that the relationships so described will not become combined emotional and sexual involvements. In the fourth dilemma, subjects are assured with "certainty" that the sexual and emotional relationships they are choosing between "will not" become combined emotional and sexual involvements. In other words, the emotional involvement described in the fourth dilemma is more easily interpretable as just a platonic friendship than is the emotional involvement described in the fourth dilemma. As a result, we should expect subjects to more readily discount the threat posed by the emotional relationship described in the fourth dilemma than that posed by the emotional relationship described in the third dilemma. And, in fact, averaged over all trials, 50 percent of male subjects and 77 percent of female subjects found the emotional infidelity more threatening in the third dilemma (table 6.3), while only 33 percent of male subjects and 55 percent of female subjects found the emotional infidelity more threatening in the fourth dilemma (table 6.4). As the threat posed by the emotional relationship becomes more easily discounted, however, the threat posed by the sexual relationship looms larger, so the number of subjects choosing sexual infidelity increases. And this is precisely what we should expect if subjects are in fact responding to cues of relationship jeopardy.

Some of Sheets and Wolfe's results provide further evidence for the relationship jeopardy hypothesis. Recall that Sheets and Wolfe administered Buss's first two dilemmas to groups of both homosexual and heterosexual men and women. In addition, however, they asked subjects to report a variety of beliefs about relationships and infidelity. Among other things, they asked all subjects whether they believed that sexual infidelity indicated emotional infidelity (as per the double-shot hypothesis), whether they believed that sexual infidelity indicated that the unfaithful partner would probably abandon them, whether they believed sexual fidelity to be of great importance in a relationship, and whether they were certain of their partner's sexual fidelity. Sheets and Wolfe then looked for correlations between degree of distress over a potential sexual infidelity and the beliefs that subjects had about their relationships. Across all four groups, the only significant correlation that emerged was a correlation between degree of distress over sexual infidelity and the belief that sexual infidelity indicated likely abandonment. In other words, all subjects—whether men or women, homosexual or heterosexual—were far more likely to be distressed by an imagined sexual infidelity if they believed that sexual infidelity portends the end of a relationship. If, in fact, jealousy is a reaction to cues to the possible termination of a relationship, as posited by the relationship jeopardy hypothesis, we should expect individuals to find sexual infidelity distressing to a degree proportional to their belief that it is a signal of potential abandonment.

Further, Sheets and Wolfe found that, of all four groups, heterosexual males were by far the most likely to believe that a sexual infidelity is a likely precursor to abandonment. Women, both homosexual and heterosexual, were far more likely than heterosexual men to "discount" a sexual infidelity as nonthreatening to a relationship, and homosexual men were even more likely than women to discount a sexual infidelity as nonthreatening. These results, I believe, help answer two of the principal questions that have run throughout this section. First, why are heterosexual men more likely than women to find sexual infidelity distressing? Because both men and women react with jealous distress to signals that a relationship is being threatened by an interloper, and men are far more likely than women to believe that a sexual infidelity with an interloper is a signal that the relationship is in jeopardy (for one or more of the three reasons discussed earlier). Second, why don't homosexual men exhibit the same degree of jealousy over sexual infidelity as heterosexual men? Because homosexual men are far less likely to believe that a sexual infidelity signals potential abandonment. Thus, the difference between heterosexual men and women, and the difference between heterosexual and homosexual men, isn't due to a difference in the "design features" of their psychological mechanisms, it is due to a difference in the beliefs processed by a single psychological mechanism that they share—in particular, a difference in beliefs about what poses a threat to a relationship.

The relationship jeopardy hypothesis makes a further prediction that is borne out by the available evidence. If there are cultural differences in the degree to which sexual infidelity is correlated with desertion by the unfaithful partner, then the members of a culture in which there is a weaker correlation between sexual infidelity and desertion should be less bothered by sexual infidelity than the members of a culture in which the correlation is stronger. In their 1996 study of jealousy in the United States, Germany, and the Netherlands, Buss and his colleagues noted that the German and Dutch "cultures have more relaxed attitudes about sexuality, including extramarital sex, than does the American culture" and that in the Netherlands "a majority feels extramarital sexual relationships are acceptable under certain circumstances."[55] Given this cultural difference, German and Dutch males should be less likely than American males to assume that a female partner's sexual infidelity portends desertion, and consequently they should be less distressed by sexual infidelity than

American males. And, in fact, averaged across all studies in the United States, 61 percent of American males reported sexual infidelity to be more distressing than emotional infidelity in response to the first dilemma (table 6.1), and 44 percent reported sexual infidelity to be more distressing in response to the second dilemma (table 6.2). In contrast, when German and Dutch responses are averaged, only 40 percent of German and Dutch males chose sexual infidelity in the first dilemma (table 6.1), and only 26 percent chose sexual infidelity in the second dilemma (table 6.2).

So far, however, in comparing the relationship jeopardy hypothesis with Evolutionary Psychology's theory of jealousy I've focused primarily on the heterosexual and homosexual responses to Buss's questionnaire dilemmas. We've seen that the relationship jeopardy hypothesis accounts for all the data that Evolutionary Psychology accounts for and for some of the data that Evolutionary Psychology can't account for (such as the jealousy data from homosexual males). But Evolutionary Psychologists have cited more evidence than this in support of their theory, and if the relationship jeopardy hypothesis is to be a contender it must explain or explain away this other evidence as well. So let's turn our attention now to some of the other evidence that Evolutionary Psychologists have cited in support of their theory.

Recall that Evolutionary Psychologists also appeal to findings regarding a sex difference in physiological arousal in response to imagining sexual and emotional infidelities. These results were obtained in a 1992 study in which Buss and his colleagues hooked up subjects to several gadgets and asked them to "imagine you find out that your partner is having sexual intercourse" with another person and to "imagine that your partner is falling in love and forming an emotional attachment to that person." Buss and his colleagues measured subjects' physiological responses to these imagined scenarios and found that male subjects showed a greater physiological response to the sexual imagery than to the emotional imagery, whereas females showed a greater physiological response to the emotional imagery than to the sexual imagery. This sex difference has been taken to indicate that males are cued in to sexual infidelity, whereas females are cued in to emotional infidelity.

Buss and his colleagues concluded their report with a few cautions that the study was "limited in ways that call for additional research." In particular, they said: "future studies could test the alternative hypotheses that the current findings reflect (a) domain-specific psychological adaptations to cuckoldry versus potential investment loss or (b) a more domain-general mechanism such that any thoughts of sex are more interesting, arousing, and perhaps disturbing to men whereas any thoughts of love are more interesting, arousing, and perhaps disturbing to women, and hence that such responses are not specific to jealousy or infidelity."[56] Despite recognizing the need for this "additional research" before a victory could be declared for Evolutionary Psychology's theory, in the decade since this caution was issued Evolutionary Psychologists have yet to conduct any studies designed to rule out the more domain-general hypothesis. This lack of evidence, however, has not prevented Evolutionary Psychologists from declaring victory for their theory that the sexes have distinct domain-specific psychological mechanisms adapted to sex-differentiated problems.

Christine Harris has done the called-for follow-up study, however, and her results tell against Evolutionary Psychology's theory. Harris instructed one group of male subjects to imagine the same scenarios that Buss and his colleagues used, and she instructed a second group of male subjects to "imagine that you and your partner are having sexual intercourse" and to "imagine that you and your partner are falling in love and forming an emotional attachment to one another."[57] For the group that was asked to imagine the infidelity scenarios, Harris's results replicated those of Buss and his colleagues. She found that males had a significantly greater physiological response to imagined sexual infidelities than to imagined emotional infidelities. But Harris also found that the males in the group that was asked to imagine sex with their partners and falling in love with their partners also exhibited a significantly greater physiological response to imagining sex than to imagining falling in love. Indeed, Harris found that there was no significant difference between the one group's physiological arousal in response to imagined infidelity and the other group's physiological arousal in response to imagined sexual intercourse.

Harris's results indicate that the results obtained by Buss and his colleagues are unquestionably confounded by the fact that males become more physiologically aroused by imagining events with sexual content, *in general*, than by imagining events with emotional content. This is in line with some findings by the Evolutionary Psychologists Bruce Ellis and Donald Symons regarding sex differences in sexual fantasy. Ellis and Symons found that men are more likely than women to have sexual fantasies and to have them more frequently. More interestingly, they found that women's sexual fantasies tend not to be so overtly sexual. When fantasizing about a sexual encounter, women tend to focus on details about the context of and emotions involved in the encounter. The fantasies of men, on the other hand, tend to focus on body parts and their interactions, while ignoring any emotional context of the fantasized encounter.

This sex difference in sexual fantasy, Ellis and Symons argue, accounts for sex differences in the consumption of sexual and romantic literature and imagery. Males are the principal consumers of hard-core pornographic videos and magazines that feature body parts in varying degrees of magnification, whereas women are the principal consumers of romance novels and films that provide rich descriptions of the emotional context of sexual encounters. Given this sex difference in the nature and content of sexual and romantic fantasies, it is not surprising that males react far more strongly to sexual imagery than to emotional imagery. Sexual imagery comes easily to most males in a way that emotional imagery does not. Similarly, emotional imagery comes easily to most females in a way that explicitly sexual imagery does not. So, males show greater physiological reactivity to imagined sexual infidelity than to imagined emotional infidelity not because of differences in the implications of the form of infidelity per se, but because sexual imagery is more vivid for males than emotional imagery.

With this in mind, now, reconsider the fifth dilemma. Recall that Buss and his colleagues posed a dilemma that guaranteed subjects that a double shot of infidelity had occurred and asked them which aspect of it they found most distressing. The results (table 6.5) show the usual sex difference, with males reporting the sexual infidelity to be more distressing than the emotional infidelity. But this is a "dilemma" in which there is really no dilemma. Subjects are presented with a situation in which their partner is in love and having a sexual relationship with someone else, which guarantees the maximum likelihood of abandonment. So, by the relationship jeopardy hypothesis, neither aspect of the infidelity should register as more distressing than the other in such a situation, since the principal object of concern, abandonment, is already signaled with the highest degree of likelihood by the description of the situation. But, in that case, why should there be a sex difference in the responses? Because, when subjects are asked which aspect of the *imagined* extrapair involvement is most distressing, they choose the aspect that presents itself with greatest vividness to their imaginations. As a result, males tend to choose the sexual aspect, since that is more vivid in male imagination than the emotional aspect, and females tend to choose the emotional aspect, since that is more vivid in female imagination than the sexual aspect. So, this particular result is likely due to the sex difference in sexual versus emotional imagination. Each sex is simply responding most strongly to the aspect to which they are best attuned. In short, the results from the fifth dilemma are also confounded by the fact that males are more responsive to sexual than emotional imagery in general and that females are more responsive to emotional than sexual imagery in general.

Indeed, it is quite likely that all of the questionnaire results are confounded to some degree by the fact that, for males, the act of imagining an event with sexual content elicits greater physiological arousal than the act of imagining an event with emotional content, and vice versa for females. For, even if males are more strongly inclined to find their partners' emotional involvements with other men to be more threatening to their relationships, and hence more jealousy inducing, than sexual-but-not-emotional involvements, the fact that subjects are asked to *imagine* their partners' forming both sexual and emotional involvements may bias the results. Even if all subjects have a jealousy mechanism that monitors signals of possible desertion by their partners, and even if males take emotional involvements to be stronger signals of possible desertion than sexual involvements, the experimental design used in the studies by Buss and his colleagues may not be eliciting unadulterated *jealousy* responses from male subjects. In fact, when Buss and his colleagues issued their caution regarding their results, they did not confine the scope of the caution to their physiological study. They claimed that all of their results, questionnaire results included, could be called into question by the discovery that "any thoughts of sex are more interesting, arousing, and perhaps disturbing to men whereas any thoughts of love are more interesting, arousing, and perhaps disturbing to women." Thus, the sex difference in imagination and reactivity to scenarios with sexual and emotional content could affect all the questionnaire results.

While it is perhaps impossible to determine the extent to which the questionnaire results are affected by the sex difference in imagination, and thereby determine the extent to which the results reflect solely on the jealousy reactions of subjects, it is doubtful that the apparent sex difference in the results would disappear if the sex difference in imagination could be controlled for. There are good reasons for thinking that a female's sexual infidelity signals a greater threat to her relationship than a male's sexual infidelity does to his. And, if both sexes have an evolved "capacity to learn to distinguish threatening from nonthreatening" infidelities, as per the relationship jeopardy hypothesis, we should expect male jealousy to be triggered by sexual infidelities to a greater extent than female jealousy. But, none of the evidence so far considered has shown this difference to be due to a sex difference in the "design features" of the psychological mechanisms of jealousy, rather than to a difference in the acquired (though perhaps accurate) beliefs about the sexual strategies of the opposite sex.

This brings us, then, to the final form of evidence that Evolutionary Psychologists have cited in support of their theory of jealousy, the evidence concerning cross-cultural similarities in laws concerning adultery. Daly and Wilson found that "cross-cultural and historical reviews of adultery law reveal a remarkable consistency of concept: sexual intercourse between a married woman and a man other than her husband is an offence."[58] In fact, in every one of the societies they reviewed, which were globally representative, they found a wife's adultery to be sufficient grounds for her husband to be granted a divorce. In contrast, in only a few of the societies reviewed was a husband's adultery considered either an offense or sufficient grounds for his wife to be granted a divorce. Further, they found, in a vast majority of societies, a wife's adultery is considered so severe an offense against her husband that the law accords her husband diminished culpability for any violent acts, including murder, that he commits upon finding his wife in flagrante delicto with a lover. As Wilson and Daly remark: "Throughout the English-speaking world, the common law recognizes three kinds of acts as sufficiently provoking to reduce murder to manslaughter, and they constitute a virtually exhaustive list of *fundamental threats to fitness:* assaults upon oneself, assaults upon close relatives, and *sexual contact with one's wife*. Several American states had statutes or rulings that made killing upon the discovery of wifely adultery no crime at all; although these were finally abolished in the 1970s, jury acquittals and discretionary refusals to prosecute persist."[59] Commenting on these findings, Buss says: "Lawmakers and everyday jurors apparently believe that stumbling upon carnal evidence of adultery is a provocation so severe that many 'rational' *men* would resort to extreme violence."[60] And this is because lawmakers and everyday jurors implicitly recognize that "a sexual infidelity may have inflicted such a severe cost on a man in the currency of paternity uncertainty and the associated misdirection of his investments, that killing the woman may have been a viable means of stanching the costs."[61]

What Evolutionary Psychologists find interesting about all these laws is the fact that they are so one-sided. Laws consistently grant men divorces from their wives for wifely sexual infidelity, but rarely do they grant women divorces from sexually unfaithful husbands on the ground of sexual infidelity alone. Laws consistently accord diminished culpability to men who murder the wives they have found in flagrante delicto with a lover, but they do not extend the same treatment to women who catch their husbands with a lover. This "double standard," Evolutionary Psychologists argue, is due to an implicit and universal recognition of a difference in the costs to men and women whose spouses are sexually unfaith-ful. While a wife's sexual infidelity imposes the "severe costs" of "pater-nity uncertainty and misdirection of investments" upon her husband, a husband's sexual infidelity *in itself* imposes no fitness costs on his wife, since he has an endlessly renewable sperm supply with which to provide his wife with offspring, and his sexual infidelity needn't necessarily dimin-ish his investment in his and his wife's joint offspring. This is why Wilson and Daly's "virtually exhaustive list of fundamental threats to fitness"—a list of fundamental threats to fitness *tout court*, notice, not a list of funda-mental threats to *male* fitness—includes female sexual infidelity but not male sexual infidelity. Thus, Evolutionary Psychologists argue, the cross-cultural legal double standard exists simply because laws are made by people who recognize that, as a result of a sex difference in the fitness costs of spousal sexual infidelity, a spouse's sexual infidelity inflicts greater psy-chological pain on men than on women. The fact that our universal "folk psychology"—our everyday understanding of the minds and behavior of others—recognizes that a spouse's sexual infidelity causes men greater psy-chological pain than women is evidence of an evolved sex difference in the emotional weight that male and female minds place on a partner's sexual infidelity.

There is, of course, a different explanation of the double standards concerning adultery in laws the world over. Throughout recorded history the world over, men have made the laws, and they have made them to promote their own interests, not women's interests. Thus, rather than reflecting a universal recognition that female sexual infidelity is more costly and distressing to men than male sexual infidelity is to women, laws merely reflect the self-serving interests of those who've made them. If women had made the laws, laws would either contain none of the double standards concerning adultery or they would contain a double standard that served women's interests.

It may seem that there is no way to test this explanation against Evolu-tionary Psychology's explanation of the cross-cultural similarities in adultery laws, but there is. The psychologists Luci Paul, Mark Foss, and MaryAnn Baenninger have conducted precisely such a test. Paul and her colleagues argue that, if legal double standards merely reflect a universal recognition that there is a sex difference in the pain caused by sexual infi-delity, due to a sex difference in the fitness costs of being cheated on, men and women should endorse the same double standards. That is, not only should men find female sexual infidelity to be a greater offense than male sexual infidelity, but women should concur that their infidelity imposes greater pain or costs on their partners than their partners' sexual infidelity imposes on them. In other words, if the double standards merely reflect a *real* sex difference in psychological pain or fitness costs, then both men and women should find male anger in response to female sexual infidelity to be more justified than female anger in response to male sexual infidelity.

Paul and her colleagues tested this prediction among 92 female and 80 male subjects. To both male and female subjects, Paul and her colleagues posed the following questions: "How angry should a guy be at a girlfriend who has cheated on him?" and "How angry should a girl be at a boyfriend who has cheated on her?" Subjects were asked to indicate an appropriate degree of anger on a seven-point scale, in which 1 was labeled "not at all," 4 was labeled "somewhat," and 7 was labeled "very." Female subjects indicated that women *should be* angrier at a cheating boyfriend (an average anger rating of 6.8) than men should be at a cheating girlfriend (an average of 6.5). And male subjects indicated that men *should be* angrier at a cheating girlfriend (an average of 6.6) than women should be at a cheating boyfriend (an average of 6.4). Thus, rather than both sexes' endorsing a double standard that reflects the alleged sex difference in degree of distress in response to being cheated on, both sexes endorsed *self-serving* double standards.

These results indicate that, if laws the world over had been made by women, the double standards they embody would be reversed. This means, however, that the existence of cross-cultural double standards in laws regarding adultery can't be taken as evidence of a universal understanding that males suffer greater costs than females as a consequence of a partner's sexual infidelity, and thereby as evidence of a sex difference in the "design features" of the psychological mechanisms underlying jealousy. The cross-cultural double standards are evidence of nothing more than the fact that men the world over have made self-serving laws and that men throughout history have had the power to impose those laws on women.

To conclude, then, we have seen that cross-cultural legal double standards provide no evidence for Evolutionary Psychology's claim that there are evolved sex differences in the "design features" of the psychological mechanisms underlying jealousy in humans. In addition, we have seen that the physiological evidence for a sex difference in the "design features" of jealousy is confounded by the fact that males exhibit greater physiological arousal in response to imagining *any* event with sexual content than to imagining any event with emotional content and females exhibit greater arousal when imagining events with emotional content than events with sexual content. As a result, the physiological study by Buss and his colleagues tapped more general features of the minds of its subjects, rather than features specific to those subjects' jealousy.

Further, we have seen that the vast array of questionnaire data actually poses some problems for Evolutionary Psychology's theory of sex-linked differences in the "design features" of jealousy mechanisms. Evolutionary Psychology's theory is unable to account for why males, on balance, place a greater emphasis on emotional infidelity than on sexual infidelity, why there are such widely ranging cultural differences in the degree to which males emphasize sexual infidelity, and why there is such a striking difference between homosexual and heterosexual males in this regard. Finally, we have seen that there is a genuinely evolutionary alternative to Evolutionary Psychology's theory of jealousy—the relationship jeopardy hypothesis—that accounts for all of the data that Evolutionary Psychology is unable to account for in addition to accounting for all of the data that appear to support Evolutionary Psychology's theory. Thus, jealousy may well be a human psychological adaptation, but there is simply no good evidence that men and women possess distinct psychological mechanisms that have been tailored by selection to perform different functions.

"First comes love, then comes marriage, then comes baby in the baby carriage." So the old ditty goes. Following its logic, chapters 5 and 6 dealt with love and marriage respectively, so naturally this chapter deals with the baby in the baby carriage. In chapter 5 we examined Evolutionary Psychology's claim that humans possess evolved preferences for long-term mates with high "mate value." In chapter 6 we considered Evolutionary Psychology's claim that these mate preferences exist for the purpose of selecting a partner for marriage. Marriage, Evolutionary Psychologists argue, is an implicit reproductive contract, which evolved along with a host of psychological adaptations specific to it: needs and desires that impel us to enter and remain in long-term unions, strategic desires for extrapair copulations, and emotional alarms that serve to detect signs of possible infidelity and to motivate actions designed to protect one's investment in one's mate. If we have psychological adaptations for love and marriage, which exist for the sake of reproduction, selection must also have designed psychological adaptations for caring for the baby in the baby carriage. And Evolutionary Psychologists claim that we do, indeed, have an evolved psychology of parental care. The most important and influential work on the evolutionary psychology of parental care has been done by the Evolutionary Psychologists Martin Daly and Margo Wilson, and that work will be the focus of this chapter.

## Discriminative Parental Solicitude

As we have seen from earlier discussions, reproductive success isn't simply about producing children. Your children have to give you grandchildren—and so on—in order for your reproductive ventures to be truly successful in the evolutionary long run. Human children, however, require many years of intensive parental care before they can be turned loose in the arena of reproductive competition. As a result, once you produce a child, it is essential to your reproductive success that your child receive a substantial amount of parental care. Your overall reproductive effort, however, is a finite resource. Parenthood consequently forces you to make a decision about the allocation of your reproductive effort. How much mating effort should you redirect to parental care? If you end up with more than one child, you face an additional decision about how much parenting effort to allocate to each of your children. Should you provide equal care to each child? Should you provide one child with more care than the other(s)? Should you withhold care from "the runt of the litter"?

In earlier chapters we have had repeated encounters with Evolutionary Psychology's general theory of how selection has equipped us to "make decisions" about matters that are essential to our reproductive success. The general theory is that some of our emotions and desires—some of our *motivational systems*—are behavior-control mechanisms designed to cause us to act in ways that promote our reproductive interests (at least in conditions that resemble the environment of evolutionary adaptedness, or EEA). Accordingly, "decisions" about whom to mate with get "made" by evolved mate preferences, which manifest themselves as felt attraction to some individuals but not others. "Decisions" about whether one's mate is being unfaithful, or is flirting with the possibility of doing so, get "made" as a function of whether and to what degree one experiences jealousy, which is an evolved emotional alarm that is sensitive to cues of potential infidelities. Similarly, Evolutionary Psychologists argue, "decisions" about how to invest parental care get "made" by evolved motivational systems that cause us to provide parental care in ways that tend, on average, to enhance our expected genetic contribution to future generations.

The principal "decision" facing all parents, which they typically "make" without even thinking about it, is whether to care at all for a newborn child. Providing the parental care required to get a child to the point where it can fend for itself is one of the costliest endeavors in a person's life. Yet typical parents unhesitatingly and happily expend the time and resources necessary to ensure the well-being and success of their children, frequently putting their children's needs above their own. We make sacrifices for our children that we wouldn't dream of making for others, and we find it *rewarding* to do so. The reason for all this self-sacrificing behavior, as most parents know, is the intense emotion of parental love. As Daly and Wilson put it: "Child-specific parental love is the emotional mechanism that permits people to tolerate—even to rejoice in—those long years of expensive, unreciprocated parental investment."[1] Parental love is the motivational mechanism that causes us to "decide" to allocate a substantial portion of our overall reproductive effort to the care of our children. Parental love is the psychological trick that selection has used to ensure that we provide the expensive care that is in our long-term reproductive interests.

Despite often being self-sacrificial, however, parental love and care is rarely unconditional. Many parents feel no strong bond with their children, many parents neglect and abuse their children, and many parents withdraw their love and care entirely when their children do things they find unforgivable. If parental love motivates the care that is in a parent's reproductive interests, failing to love and care for one's children appears tantamount to shooting oneself in the genes. But Daly and Wilson argue that more careful attention to the calculus of parental investment can reveal coldly rational, fitness-enhancing "decisions" beneath many seemingly self-defeating failures of parental love.

As we saw in chapter 1, every activity, including parental care, has associated fitness costs and benefits. Providing parental care to a child enhances that child's ability to survive and reproduce, and this in turn enhances the parent's expected genetic contribution to future generations. But there are fitness costs involved in providing parental care. There are both direct costs, which range from the metabolic costs of providing care to the expenditure of resources, and indirect costs, which stem from the fact that caring for a child reduces the reproductive effort available for further mating or for caring for other children. This is why *parental investment* is defined as any behaviors of a parent that enhance the ability of an offspring to survive and reproduce *at a cost to the parent's fitness*, where the costs to the parent's fitness include diminishment in the parent's future abilities to mate or to care for other offspring.

Daly and Wilson argue that selection should have designed parental psychology to motivate parental care in ways that tend, on average, to maximize the ratio of fitness benefits to fitness costs of providing care. That is, evolved parental psychology should be characterized by what Daly and Wilson call *discriminative parental solicitude*—motivational mechanisms that cause parents to be discriminating with respect to how and to whom they provide parental care or solicitude. As Daly and Wilson argue, "we may expect parental motivational systems to contain processes and structures that function as if mediated by a unitary parameter of offspring-specific parental love or solicitude, which is influenced by a variety of parental, offspring, and situational cues of fitness value (i.e., of the offspring-specific expected contribution to parental fitness), and which influences in its turn a variety of parental activities."[2] To put it less technically, the degree to which a parent is motivated to care for a child should be influenced by the likelihood that caring for that child will be a good fitness investment in the long run.

This leads Daly and Wilson to the following general prediction regarding parental love: "A's love of B will tend to be a positive function of B's expected contribution to A's fitness."[3] The greater a child's expected contribution to a parent's fitness, the more the parent will love that child. But how is a child's "expected contribution" to a parent's fitness to be measured? Daly and Wilson offer the following formula: "An offspring's expected contribution to parental fitness is the product of its reproductive value and its relatedness (r) to the putative parent."[4] Thus, Daly and Wilson's general prediction about parental love amounts to the following, which I will call their General Formula: *The strength of A's love of B will tend to be proportional to the product of B's reproductive value and B's relatedness to A.* To fully understand the General Formula, it is necessary to explain the concepts of *reproductive value* and *relatedness* (r). In addition, the role of relatedness in the General Formula derives from the concept of *inclusive fitness*, which also requires explanation. We thus embark on a bit of a digression.

An individual's reproductive value is the expected number of remaining offspring that individual can produce. Average reproductive value in humans increases steadily until pubescence, at which time it peaks; average reproductive value then decreases gradually between pubescence and the late twenties, at which time it declines more precipitously until the mid-fifties. Part of this pattern is obvious. The average reproductive value of a fifty-year-old is drastically lower than that of a twenty-five-year-old, for example, because twenty-five-year-olds, on average, can produce far more offspring over the remainder of their lives than can fifty-year-olds. The average increase in reproductive value from infancy to pubescence, however, may be less obvious, since infants appear to have far more of their reproductive lives ahead of them than do pubescent teens. But infants are not fertile until they become pubescent teens themselves. So, although infants have more remaining years in their lives than pubescent teens, they don't actually have more remaining *fertile years* in their lives. Many infants, moreover, do not survive to pubescence. The class of infants, then, includes not only those who survive to reproductive viability, but those who die in infancy as well, whereas the class of pubescent teens includes only those who have survived to reproductive viability. Consequently, the average reproductive value of infants is lower than that of pubescent teens. For similar reasons, average reproductive value increases each year between infancy and pubescence. Thus, Daly and Wilson predict that parental love will vary partly as a function of a child's reproductive value, because a child's reproductive value is, roughly, a measure of how many copies of parental genes the child is likely to transmit to the next generation in the form of grandchildren.

The other concept that appears in Daly and Wilson's General Formula is $r$, which is known as the *coefficient of relatedness*. To get a handle on this concept, begin by recalling from chapter 1 that we each develop from a zygote, in which half the alleles are *copies* (via meiosis) of our mother's alleles and half are copies of our father's alleles. To say that a particular allele is a copy of another allele, recall, is not simply to say that the two alleles consist of the same DNA sequence. It is to say, rather, that the former allele, the copy, possesses the same DNA sequence as the latter because it *descended* from the latter via genetic replication. Now, two offspring of the same parent may each possess copies of one of that parent's alleles, in which case those two copies have descended, via genetic replication, from the same allele. Of course, alleles can be related by descent in this way via several rounds of replication. For example, a grandchild may possess an allele that is a copy of a copy of a grandparental allele, and first cousins may possess alleles that are copies of copies of the same grandparental allele. When one allele has descended from another by a chain of copying processes or two alleles have descended via copying processes from the same (other) allele, biologists say that those alleles are *identical by descent*. For ease of expression in what follows, I will use the term *copy* more loosely and refer to alleles that are identical by descent simply as *copies* of the same allele. In light of this, the coefficient of relatedness, $r$, is the probability that any allele selected at random in one person is a copy of (identical by descent with) an allele at the same locus in another person. It is, roughly, a measure of how closely related two individuals are genetically.

Let's see how this works. An allele at a particular locus in a woman is present in half of her gametes, as we saw in chapter 1. Since that woman's offspring are made from her gametes (together with those of her mate), for any particular maternal allele there is thus a probability of 0.5 (a 50 percent chance) that a copy of that allele is present in any one of her offspring. Similarly, for any paternal allele there is a probability of 0.5 that a copy of that allele is present at the same locus in any one of that man's offspring. Conversely, for any (nonmutated) allele in an offspring, there is a probability of 0.5 that a copy of that allele is present in its mother and a probability of 0.5 that a copy of it is present in its father. Consequently, the relatedness ($r$) between human parents and their offspring is 0.5.

For full siblings, also, relatedness is 0.5. The sibling relationship is a little more complicated than that of parent to offspring, so we'll have to go back to some basics to see why this is the case. Suppose that the maternal genotype at a particular locus is $A_1A_2$ and that the paternal genotype is $A_3A_4$. (In this example, the numerical subscripts simply indicate distinct allele tokens on different chromosomes; they don't necessarily indicate alleles with different DNA sequences. So, $A_1A_2$ could be a homozygous genotype.) There will then be four possible offspring genotypes at that locus: $A_1A_3$, $A_1A_4$, $A_2A_3$, and $A_2A_4$. Suppose that one offspring has $A_1A_3$. Let's select one of the alleles from this individual at random—$A_1$, say. Now, what is the probability that a full sibling of this individual also has a copy of $A_1$? Since the sibling will have one of the above four genotypes, two of which contain $A_1$, the probability that the sibling also has $A_1$ is 0.5. Similar reasoning would reveal that it doesn't matter which of the four genotypes we assume to be possessed by the target offspring or which allele we select from the assumed genotype in order to determine the probability that a sibling has a copy of that allele. Thus, relatedness between full siblings is 0.5.

I won't go through the reasoning involved in calculating relatedness for each of the other types of familial relationship. But it is worth pointing out the values of $r$ for some other human familial relationships. For half siblings, who share only one parent, relatedness is 0.25. The relatedness between grandparents and their grandchildren is also 0.25, as is the relatedness between aunts or uncles and their nieces or nephews. The relatedness between first cousins and between great-grandparents and their great-grandchildren is 0.125. And the relatedness between second cousins and between great-great-grandparents and their great-great-grandchildren is 0.0625. Finally, relatedness between two individuals whose most recent common ancestor was many generations ago is effectively zero.

The late English biologist William D. Hamilton showed that the coefficient of relatedness has significant and interesting implications with respect to how selection operates. As we saw in chapter 1, selection is a process whereby fitness-enhancing genes increase in frequency, and to say that a gene increases in frequency is just to say that it increases the number of its copies relative to the number of copies of alternative alleles. We also saw that genes can increase in frequency by affecting their bearers' phenotypes in ways that enhance the ability to reproduce. But Hamilton showed that this is not the only way that genes can affect their bearers so as to increase their own frequency. For suppose that I have the allele $A$. If I reproduce, there is a 50 percent chance that my child has a copy of $A$. But, if my parents reproduce and give me a sibling, there is also a 50 percent chance that my sibling has a copy of $A$. So, although $A$ could increase its number of copies by enhancing my reproductive ability, it could also increase its number of copies by influencing me to act in ways that increase the chances that my parents will give me a sibling. From the "perspective" of $A$, it doesn't really matter whether I or my parents reproduce.

Indeed, in general, from the "perspective" of $A$, it doesn't matter whether it is I who reproduce or any other individual with a copy of $A$. This brings us back to the coefficient of relatedness, which gives the probability that another individual has copies of my genes. As we have seen, the other individuals who are likely to have copies of my genes are my kin—my parents, my siblings, my children, my nieces and nephews, my grandchildren, my cousins, and so on. Thus, if $A$ influences me to aid the reproductive efforts of my kin, it can be just as successful in increasing its number of copies as it would be if it influenced my own reproduction. This led Hamilton to conclude that selection favors not only genes that enhance their bearers' ability to reproduce, but also genes that influence their bearers to aid the reproductive efforts of kin.

I can aid the reproductive efforts of my kin by performing any act that provides some fitness benefit to them. This could involve feeding or caring for them as children, feeding or caring for their children, providing them with essential food or resources as adults, or even serving as matchmaker. By performing an act that provides a fitness benefit to a relative, I increase the chances that they will successfully reproduce, and I thereby increase the odds of producing more copies of *my* genes. Thus, I can contribute copies of my genes to future generations *directly*, by producing offspring, or *indirectly*, by helping my relatives reproduce. Accordingly, my fitness— my expected genetic contribution to future generations—has both direct and indirect components. The direct component is a measure of my ability to contribute copies of my genes to future generations by reproducing, whereas the indirect component is a measure of my ability to contribute copies of my genes to future generations by enhancing the reproductive abilities of my kin. Hamilton referred to the sum of the direct and indirect components of fitness as *inclusive fitness*.

Of course, the acts that I perform to enhance the reproductive abilities of my kin exact fitness costs from me, the actor. This involves a rather different kind of fitness cost-benefit analysis than we considered in chapter 1, where the fitness benefit of an act accrues directly to the actor, the same individual who pays the cost of the act. When the actor both pays the cost and accrues the benefit of an act, we can expect the actor to perform an act as long as the cost of the act is less than the benefit of the act (weighted, of course, by the probability that the benefit will ensue). As long as that condition is met, the act, on balance, enhances the fitness of the actor. But under what conditions should we expect individuals to perform acts that are costly to themselves and beneficial to others?

Hamilton argued that we should expect individuals to perform acts that benefit others as long as the cost of the act (to the actor) is less than the benefit of the act (to the recipient of the benefit) weighted by the relatedness of the actor to the recipient of the benefit (since $r$ gives the probability that the benefit to the recipient will in fact redound to the actor's genes). To make this intuitive, let's again employ the technique of representing fitness costs and benefits by whole numbers. Let's suppose that a 1,200-calorie meal provides 12 fitness points to the person who eats it. As long as I don't have to spend more than 11 fitness points obtaining and eating the meal myself, it pays me to obtain the meal and eat it. But under what conditions would it make sense for me to obtain the meal and give it to a sibling to eat? The meal would enhance my sibling's fitness and thereby increase the odds that my sibling's genes will leave copies of themselves. But, of course, for any particular gene I have, there is a probability of 0.5 that my sibling has a copy, hence a probability of 0.5 that my sibling's reproducing will increase the number of copies of any particular gene that *I* possess. Thus, the *inclusive fitness* benefit that accrues to me by feeding my sibling a 12-point meal is 6 points (the 12-point benefit to my sibling weighted by the relatedness of 0.5). Consequently, as long as obtaining the meal for my sibling doesn't cost me more than 5 fitness points, it pays *me*—that is, *my genes*—to give the meal to my sibling. Similarly, as long as it doesn't cost me more than 2 fitness points to obtain the meal, it pays me to give the meal to a niece, since the inclusive fitness benefit to me of feeding my niece a 12-point meal is 3 points (the 12-point benefit to my niece weighted by the relatedness of 0.25).

As the above examples show, if the fitness benefit to the recipients of my acts is assumed to be constant, my willingness to provide that benefit to a relative should vary as a function of my relatedness to that relative. This is because the more distant the relative, the lower the cost it is worthwhile for me to absorb in order to help that relative. Other things being equal, if an act of mine would benefit all my relatives equally, I should be willing to pay twice the cost to provide that benefit to a parent, sibling, or child as I would be to provide it to a niece or nephew, and I should be willing to pay twice the cost to provide that benefit to a niece or nephew as I would be to provide it to a cousin. This reasoning reportedly prompted the English biologist J. B. S. Haldane to quip that he would risk his life to save two siblings or eight cousins.

An interesting implication of Hamilton's theory is that parental care is just an instance of the broader phenomenon of selection for aiding kin. The care that I provide my children increases my inclusive fitness by enhancing the fitness of individuals to whom my relatedness is 0.5. Of course, in the typical case, it pays me more to care for my children than to care for my cousins, since I am more closely related to my children, so I get a higher return on the care that I invest in them. But, it can be just as beneficial to me to feed and care for an infant sibling as to feed and care for my infant child, since my relatedness to both is 0.5.

It is now but a short step to Daly and Wilson's General Formula—namely, that the strength of A's love of B is proportional to the product of B's reproductive value and B's relatedness to A. For, if familial love is the motivational mechanism that causes us to perform acts that benefit kin, and if that motivational mechanism has been designed by selection, then, by Hamilton's theory, strength of familial love should vary (at least partly) as a function of relatedness. Other things being equal, I should love my parents, siblings, and children more than I love my aunts, uncles, nieces, and nephews, and I should love my grandchildren more than I love my cousins. Of course, one thing that isn't always equal is the reproductive value of each of my family members. My children have greater reproductive value than my parents, so although my relatedness to both is the same, by Daly and Wilson's General Formula I should love my children more than my parents. Similarly, since the average reproductive value of children is greater than that of their parents, parents should love their children more than their children love them. But, if reproductive value is equal, I should love members of my immediate family more than I love distant relatives, and I should love equally all family members to whom my relatedness is the same.

With this understanding of Daly and Wilson's General Formula regarding parental love, let's turn to the evidence that Daly and Wilson claim supports their General Formula. Let's first consider the General Formula with respect to the relationship between a parent and its genetic offspring. Since relatedness between parents and their genetic offspring is always 0.5, Daly and Wilson's General Formula entails that parental love of genetic offspring should vary as a function of the offspring's reproductive value. This has a couple of implications. First, since reproductive value increases from infancy to pubescence, parental love of genetic offspring should deepen as offspring mature toward reproductive viability—parents should feel deeper love for their child at age five years than at six months, and that love should deepen further by the time their child is ten. Second, if there are reliable phenotypic cues of reproductive value on the basis of which parents can assess the reproductive value of their offspring, parents should feel deeper love for offspring who exhibit phenotypic cues of high reproductive value than for those who exhibit phenotypic cues of low reproductive value.

Of course, these predictions would be difficult to test directly, since measuring the degree to which a parent feels love for a child, or comparing the degrees to which two different parents feel love for two different children, is well-nigh impossible. But Daly and Wilson argue that parental love serves to *inhibit* a parent's tendencies or impulses to react violently when a child piques the parent's anger. "The child's growing value to the parent may be expected to produce an increasing *parental inhibition against the use of dangerous tactics* in conflict with the child. . . . Putting the point more plainly: Children annoy adults frequently, and the risk that the adult might react so angrily as to damage the child must surely be influenced by the particular adult's degree of concern for the particular child's welfare."[5] If parental love has this inhibitory effect on violent reactions to annoyance and conflict, Daly and Wilson argue, then child maltreatment is a *by-product* of the absence of parental love. As a result, strength of parental love should be negatively correlated with the incidence of child abuse, filicide, and other forms of maltreatment. Thus, it should be possible to test a prediction about strength of parental love using data regarding the incidence of child maltreatment, which are more readily available than data regarding the strength of parental love. In particular, child maltreatment should be rarest in those circumstances in which Daly and Wilson predict parental love and solicitude to be strongest, and it should be most common in those circumstances in which they predict parental love and solicitude to be weakest.

Reformulated with respect to these more easily obtainable data, the two predictions are as follows. First, since reproductive value increases from infancy to pubescence, the incidence of child maltreatment should decline from infancy to pubescence. Second, if there are reliable phenotypic cues of offspring reproductive value, children who exhibit phenotypic cues of low reproductive value should be at greater risk of maltreatment than children who exhibit phenotypic cues of high reproductive value.

Daly and Wilson tested the first of these predictions with data on Canadian child maltreatment fatalities between 1974 and 1983. They found that the filicide rate for children under the age of one year was thirty-four filicides per million children in the population (per year).[6] The rate dropped precipitously to nine filicides per million one-year-old children, and the rate declined steadily from there with increasing age of the child, until the rate was less than one filicide per million pubescent children. This pattern contrasted sharply with the homicide rate for children killed by nonrelatives, which hovered around five homicides per million children from infancy through pubescence. Thus, the declining risk of filicide from infancy to pubescence accords with the first of Daly and Wilson's predictions.

With respect to the second prediction, Daly and Wilson argue that we should expect children "with a variety of imperfections predictive of poor prospects for survival or reproduction" to be at greater risk of maltreatment than children without such "imperfections."[7] These "imperfections" would include "such congenital handicaps as spina bifida, fibrocystic disease, talipes, cleft palate, and Down's syndrome."[8] In a survey of studies of child abuse in Australia, England, and the United States, Daly and Wilson found that "those children who are severely abused include anywhere from two to ten times as many of these congenital problems as one would expect on the basis of their incidence in the population-at-large."[9] In addition, in a study of thirty-five societies represented in the Human Relations Area Files, a large database of ethnographic information on societies around the world, Daly and Wilson found that "deformity" or severe illness was the second most frequently cited reason for infanticide. Thus, children who exhibit phenotypic cues that are potentially predictive of low reproductive value do appear to be at greater risk of maltreatment than children who do not exhibit those phenotypic cues, which accords with the second of Daly and Wilson's predictions. These two findings appear to support the hypothesis that parental solicitude varies partly as a function of the reproductive value of offspring.

In deriving these two specific predictions from Daly and Wilson's General Formula regarding parental love, we held the degree of relatedness between parent and child fixed at 0.5 because that is the relatedness between parents and their genetic children. But many children are cared for by "substitute parents," adults other than genetic parents who are in loco parentis to a child. The most common substitute parents are stepparents, adoptive parents, grandparents, and other relatives (for example, aunts and uncles). If Daly and Wilson's General Formula is correct, the strength of love that substitute parents feel for their children should not be as great as that felt by genetic parents for their children. This leads Daly and Wilson to what they call "*the most obvious prediction* from a Darwinian view of parental motives": "Substitute parents will generally tend to care less profoundly for children than natural parents, with the result that children reared by people other than their natural parents will be more often exploited and otherwise at risk. Parental investment is a precious resource, and selection must favor those parental psyches that do not squander it on nonrelatives."[10] In short, substitute parents should be more likely than genetic parents to maltreat their children.

But not all substitute parents are genetically equal. Grandparents and aunts and uncles have a relatedness of 0.25 to the children for whom they are substitute parents. So, while they should not feel as much love as genetic parents for those children, they are still rather closely related to the children for whom they are substitute parents. Thus, while Daly and Wilson's "most obvious prediction" should lead us to expect grandparents and aunts and uncles to be more likely than genetic parents to maltreat the children for whom they provide care, we should not expect the risk of maltreatment at the hands of these other relatives to be that much greater than the risk at the hands of genetic parents, other things being equal.

Stepparents and unrelated adoptive parents, however, have a relatedness to their stepchildren and adopted children that is effectively zero. As a result, according to Daly and Wilson's General Formula, such parents should feel little to nothing by way of true parental love for their adoptive children or stepchildren (since the reproductive value of the child is, in these cases, multiplied by a relatedness of zero). Nonetheless, stepparents and unrelated adoptive parents are in roles in which they are expected to pay the same fitness costs of parental care that are paid by genetic parents. But, unlike genetic parents, they do not stand to reap any inclusive fitness benefit from the care they provide to their children. This violates the essential logic of inclusive fitness. And Daly and Wilson argue that this should be particularly problematic in the case of stepparenthood. "The stepparent has, after all, usually entered into the relationship out of an attraction to the new mate; the stepchild must frequently enter into the remarriage decision as a cost, not a benefit. Whereas satisfying relationships with nonrelatives ordinarily involve careful reciprocity, parental investment is exceptional: parents tolerate a cumulative imbalance in the flow of resources. With all the good will in the world, stepparents may strive to feel the altruism of a natural parent, but they do not always—

perhaps do not often—succeed."[11] Consequently, if Daly and Wilson's "most obvious prediction" is correct, the children at greatest risk of maltreatment should be those cared for by unrelated substitute parents.

A great deal of Daly and Wilson's research has focused on testing this prediction. And Daly and Wilson have accumulated significant evidence that "stepchildren in Canada, Great Britain, and the United States indeed incur a greatly elevated risk of child maltreatment of various sorts, especially lethal beatings," compared to children who live with both genetic parents.[12] They claim that this evidence provides strong confirmation for their "Darwinian view of parental motives," and their findings regarding stepparental maltreatment have been among the most highly publicized empirical results in Evolutionary Psychology. Because these findings have been so highly publicized, they will be my focus in the remainder of this chapter.

Wilson and Daly began their research to test their "most obvious prediction" in a collaborative study with the psychologist Suzanne Weghorst, analyzing 87,789 cases of child abuse and neglect reported to the American Humane Association in 1976. The case reports included information on the living arrangements of the abuse victims, and Wilson, Daly, and Weghorst classified all cases of abuse and neglect by the following household types: a household in which the adults in loco parentis to the victim were both genetic parents, a household with a genetic parent and a stepparent, a household with a genetic mother only, or a household with a genetic father only. They found the number of child abuse and neglect victims living with both genetic parents to be higher than the number of victims living with a genetic parent and a stepparent. But, the number of children living with both genetic parents is vastly higher than the number of children living in a household with a stepparent. Thus, to test their prediction, it was insufficient to simply obtain numbers of maltreatment victims; they needed to obtain *rates* of maltreatment within each household type (that is, the number of victims per million children living in each household type).

To obtain the rates of maltreatment within each household type, Wilson, Daly, and Weghorst needed data on the numbers of American children living in each household type during 1976. However, since not even the U.S. Census Bureau gathered and maintained such specific data about the living arrangements of children in 1976, they had to estimate how many children lived in each household type. The U.S. Census Bureau had reported that 80 percent of all American children in 1976 lived with "two parents," which included stepparent and adoptive parent households. And

Paul Glick, of the U.S. Census Bureau, had estimated that 10 percent of these children lived with a stepparent. Wilson, Daly, and Weghorst accordingly estimated that 70 percent of American children lived with two genetic parents. They made similar estimates for the percentages of children living with a genetic mother only or a genetic father only. These percentages allowed population estimates of the numbers of children living in each household type, and this made it possible to compute rates of maltreatment for each household type.

Wilson, Daly, and Weghorst then compared these rates with the rate of maltreatment for the population at large (combining all household types). They found that the rate of maltreatment of children in all age groups living with both genetic parents was markedly lower than the rate of maltreatment within the population at large. In contrast, the rate of maltreatment for children under the age of three living with a genetic parent and a stepparent was 4.6 times the rate for children under three within the population at large. The rate of maltreatment for children living with a genetic parent and a stepparent declined with increasing age of the child, but even children aged fourteen to seventeen living with a stepparent were maltreated at a rate 1.6 times that of the population at large. In addition, they found that children under the age of three who lived with a genetic mother only were maltreated at nearly 3 times the rate of maltreatment for that age group within the population at large, and children in the same age group living with a genetic father only were maltreated at a rate more than 7 times that within the population at large.

Daly and Wilson were dissatisfied with these results for a couple of reasons. First, the population estimates of the numbers of children living in various household types, on which the calculation of maltreatment rates was based, were unreliable. In particular, Daly and Wilson found reasons for doubting Glick's estimate that as many as 10 percent of all children lived with a stepparent. And, if that estimate was too high, the calculated rates of maltreatment of children living with a stepparent were too low. Second, the case reports to the American Humane Association came from a number of different states in the U.S., and the criteria for maltreatment varied significantly from one state to the next. Consequently, Daly and Wilson undertook to do a better controlled test of their hypothesis, in which they could eliminate these two problems.

In the study that has become a classic within Evolutionary Psychology, Daly and Wilson analyzed cases of child maltreatment in the municipality of Hamilton-Wentworth in Ontario, Canada, during a one-year period from 1982 to 1983. Their sample consisted of 99 maltreated children under the age of eighteen, who were active cases for the two children's aid societies in Hamilton-Wentworth and who were registered as victims of maltreatment with the Ontario Child Abuse Registry. The children's aid societies were able to provide Daly and Wilson with information about the living arrangements of all 99 children. Grouping abuse victims by age and household type, these 99 cases broke down as shown in table 7.1.[13]

In order to calculate rates of maltreatment for each household type, in 1983 Daly and Wilson conducted their own telephone survey of Hamilton-Wentworth residents, which allowed them to collect very specific and detailed information about 1,286 households in Hamilton-Wentworth. Those 1,286 households included 841 children under the age of eighteen, and each respondent with a child in the household was asked about the relationship of each child in the household to each adult in loco parentis to the child. Daly and Wilson considered any adult who coresided with a child and had responsibilities for caring for that child to be a parent, regardless of the marital status of the adults in the household. If two genetic parents of a child lived with that child, the household was classified as a two-genetic-parent household, regardless of whether the parents were legally married or had a common-law union. Similarly, a male who coresided with a female and one or more of her genetic children, and who shared parental responsibilities for those children, was considered a stepfather of those children regardless of whether he was legally married to

**Table 7.1**
Numbers of Maltreated Children by Household Composition in Hamilton-Wentworth, 1982–1983

|  | Child's age at maltreatment | | |
| --- | --- | --- | --- |
| Parents in household | 0–4 | 5–10 | 11–17 |
| Two genetic parents | 8 | 7 | 13 |
| One genetic parent | 7 | 11 | 16 |
|    Mother only | 7 | 11 | 15 |
|    Father only | 0 | 0 | 1 |
| One genetic parent + one stepparent | 3 | 11 | 14 |
|    Genetic mother + stepfather | 2 | 8 | 11 |
|    Genetic father + stepmother | 1 | 3 | 3 |
| Other substitute parent | 1 | 4 | 4 |
|    Genetic relative | 1 | 1 | 1 |
|    Unrelated adoptive parent | 0 | 1 | 0 |
|    Other nonrelative | 0 | 2 | 3 |

their mother. From their survey data, Daly and Wilson estimated the frequency of different living arrangements of children in the Hamilton-Wentworth area. From these estimates and population estimates derived from the data in table 7.1, Daly and Wilson derived the rates of maltreatment of children in each of the three age groups for each of the different types of living arrangement. They then calculated the *risk* of maltreatment to children in each of the other types of living arrangement *relative to* the risk of maltreatment to a child living with two genetic parents. The results are in table 7.2.[14]

As these results show, children aged from birth to age four living with a single genetic parent were 12.5 times more likely to be victims of maltreatment than similarly aged children living with both genetic parents. Children up to age four living with a genetic parent and a stepparent, in contrast, were 40.1 times more likely to be victims of maltreatment than children living with both genetic parents. From age five to ten, the relative risk to stepchildren dropped sharply, with children living with a genetic parent and a stepparent being 19.4 times more likely to be victims of maltreatment than children living with both genetic parents. And, for children aged eleven to seventeen living with a genetic parent and a stepparent, the relative risk of maltreatment dropped sharply again, reduced effectively by half. In all age groups, however, children living with a genetic parent and a stepparent were at a significantly greater risk of becoming victims of maltreatment than children living with both genetic parents.

Two subsequent studies have corroborated these findings. In one of these studies, Daly and Wilson analyzed a British report on child abuse in England and Wales between 1983 and 1987. They found that children of all ages who lived with a stepparent were approximately 19 times more likely to be registered victims of physical injury than were children who

**Table 7.2**
Relative Risk of Maltreatment by Household Composition in Hamilton-Wentworth, 1982–1983

| Parents in household | Child's age at maltreatment | | |
| --- | --- | --- | --- |
| | 0–4 | 5–10 | 11–17 |
| Two genetic parents | *reference* | *reference* | *reference* |
| One genetic parent | 12.5 | 11.8 | 8.3 |
| One genetic parent + one stepparent | 40.1 | 19.4 | 9.8 |
| Other substitute parent | 3.3 | 13.3 | 11.6 |

lived with both genetic parents.[15] In the other study, the psychiatrists Kwang-iel Kim and Bokja Ko administered a questionnaire to 1,142 third and fourth graders in two elementary schools in Seoul, Korea, that asked about experiences of being battered by family members and about family structure, among other things. Although Kim and Ko did not obtain population data that allowed them to calculate rates of battery for each household type, they nonetheless found the incidence of battery reported in stepfamilies to be higher than should be expected given the presumed frequency of stepfamilies in the population as a whole.

When Daly and Wilson focused on filicide, rather than maltreatment generally, they found the picture to be even more bleak for children living with a substitute parent. In their 1976 U.S. data, they found that a child living with at least one substitute parent was "approximately 100 times as likely to be fatally abused as a child living with natural parents only."[16] In addition, in a study of 147 cases of filicide in Canada between 1974 and 1983 in which the perpetrator had been identified, Daly and Wilson found that children under the age of three were roughly 70 times more likely to be killed by a stepparent than by a genetic parent.[17] As in the Canadian child maltreatment data, the relative risk of filicide decreased with increasing age of the child. But Daly and Wilson found that teenage children were still roughly 15 times more likely to be killed by a stepparent than by a genetic parent.[18] Daly and Wilson take all of these data to provide strong confirmation of their prediction that children who live with substitute parents—in particular, stepparents—are at a greater risk of maltreatment and filicide than children who live with their genetic parents.

Two subsequent studies by other researchers, however, produced results that apparently disconfirm Daly and Wilson's "most obvious prediction." In one study, the psychologists Catherine Malkin and Michael Lamb analyzed cases of physical and fatal abuse reported to the American Humane Association in 1984. Malkin and Lamb compared the frequencies with which genetic parents and stepparents perpetrated minor physical abuse, major physical abuse, and fatal abuse. They found that "the risk of major physical abuse or fatal abuse by biological parents was greater than the risk of major physical abuse or fatal abuse by nonbiological parents. Descriptive data revealed that nonbiological parents were proportionately more likely (93%) to engage in minor physical abuse than were biological parents (87.8%), whereas a greater proportion of biological parents (11%) engaged in major physical abuse than did nonbiological parents (6.5%)."[19] Malkin and Lamb concluded that "biological parents were more rather than less likely than nonbiological parents to abuse severely and to kill rather than cause major physical injuries to their children. These findings thus failed to replicate previous findings about the risks associated with stepparenthood."[20]

But Malkin and Lamb's study merely compared forms of abuse within the population of abused children. They set out to answer the question, *Relative to the population of abused children*, what was the likelihood that a child living with a genetic parent (stepparent) suffered a particular form of abuse? So, what Malkin and Lamb actually found was that, *relative to the populations of children who were abused by stepparents and genetic parents respectively*, stepparents were more likely than genetic parents to perpetrate minor physical abuse whereas stepparents were less likely than genetic parents to perpetrate major physical abuse or fatal abuse. But this tells us nothing about how likely it is for a child living with a stepparent or genetic parents to become a victim of major physical abuse or fatal abuse at all. To obtain this kind of information, we have to ask, *Relative to the population of children living with a genetic parent (stepparent)*, what is the likelihood that a child will be abused? So Malkin and Lamb's results aren't really relevant to Daly and Wilson's prediction. Moreover, in responding to Malkin and Lamb's study, Daly and Wilson point out that "in the data archive that Malkin and Lamb analyzed, 39% of the abuse victims who resided with 'two parents' had a stepparent, compared to an expected value for a same-age sample of US children of less than 5% . . . ; according to the data in this archive, *every* form of abuse was perpetrated at massively higher rates by stepparents than by genetic parents."[21] Thus, Daly and Wilson conclude, Malkin and Lamb's results do not, in fact, disconfirm their "most obvious prediction" after all.

In the other study, the Swedish biologists Hans Temrin, Susanne Buchmayer, and Magnus Enquist analyzed cases of child homicide in Sweden between 1975 and 1995. Of all those child homicides, 139 children under the age of sixteen were killed by an identified adult who was in loco parentis to the victim. Temrin and his colleagues found the homicide rate for children living with both genetic parents to be 3.0 homicides, and the rate for children living with one genetic parent and one stepparent to be 3.4 homicides, per million children (per year). In contrast, they found the rate for children living with only one genetic parent to be 12.6 homicides per million children (per year). Temrin and his colleagues concluded that "our results do not support the conclusion that step-parenthood is the most important risk factor for child homicides in families. Furthermore, the differences in risks between Canada and Sweden suggest that cultural factors influence patterns of child homicide."[22]

Daly and Wilson have responded by pointing out that Temrin and his colleagues calculated homicide rates for *all* children under the age of sixteen, rather than for children of different age groups as Daly and Wilson had done in their studies. Daly and Wilson argue that this method ignores "the fact that the average child in the population at large was substantially older (and therefore more likely to have had time to acquire a stepparent) than the average homicide victim."[23] As a result, they claim, the method used by Temrin and his colleagues artificially reduces the homicide rate for children living in stepfamilies. Daly and Wilson obtained the Swedish data and calculated the homicide rates for children aged one through four only, an age group that accounted for 57 of the 139 homicides. Within that age group Daly and Wilson found the rate for children living with both genetic parents to be 3.8 homicides, and the rate for children living with one genetic parent and one stepparent to be 31.7 homicides, per million children (per year). Thus, Daly and Wilson conclude, when the homicide rates are calculated properly, the Swedish study actually supports their "most obvious prediction."

Daly and Wilson thus argue that neither study undermines their claim that children living with a stepparent are far more likely to be abused than children living with both genetic parents. In their book *The Truth about Cinderella*, Daly and Wilson argue that the reason that children who live with stepparents are at greater risk is that *stepparents are more likely than genetic parents to maltreat or kill their children*. Stepparents, they argue, "don't *want* to do what they feel obliged to do, namely to make a substantial investment of 'parental' effort without receiving the usual emotional rewards."[24] Stepparents suffer a "resentment of pseudo-parental obligation," and this resentment frequently boils over in violent outbursts during conflicts with their stepchildren, whereas the parental love that genetic parents feel for their children typically inhibits violent outbursts when parenting becomes stressful.[25]

To further test the idea that stepparental abuse and filicide is the result of violent outbursts precipitated by resentment, Daly and Wilson did a study of the methods of killing children under the age of five in the Canadian cases of filicide mentioned earlier. Daly and Wilson focused on paternal filicide because, for children under five, "stepparental abuse is overwhelmingly step*paternal* abuse, not necessarily because stepfathers are more dangerous than stepmothers but because small children scarcely ever reside with stepmothers."[26] Daly and Wilson found that stepfathers were much more likely than genetic fathers to kill their children by hitting them, kicking them, or striking them with a blunt object, whereas genetic fathers were more likely to kill their children by shooting them, suffocating them, strangling them, or asphyxiating them with exhaust fumes. In addition, genetic fathers were vastly more likely to commit suicide after killing their children, and significantly more likely to kill their wives in the same violent incident, than were stepfathers. In a study of filicides in England and Wales between 1977 and 1990, Daly and Wilson found the same pattern. Daly and Wilson take these results to indicate that stepfathers typically kill their children in impulsive, violent rages, whereas genetic fathers typically kill their children in premeditated acts of deliberately wider scope than mere filicide. "Thus," they say, "some considerable proportion of men's killings of their genetic offspring appear to have been undertaken as parts of suicidal and/or familicidal projects, in which despondency may be of greater motivational relevance than hostility to the victims. . . . The same cannot be said of cases in which men killed their stepchildren."[27] In other words, stepfathers killed out of unbridled hostility toward their stepchildren.

This study appears to confirm Daly and Wilson's claim that stepparental abuse is the consequence of violent, impulsive outbursts precipitated by simmering resentment over having to fill an unwanted parental role. Since Daly and Wilson argue that parental love serves to inhibit tendencies or impulses to react violently in conflicts with children, their finding that stepparents are more likely than genetic parents to abuse and kill their children out of anger appears to show that stepparents lack the parental love for their stepchildren that genetic parents have for their own children. Daly and Wilson thus conclude that these results support their "most obvious prediction" that substitute parents care less profoundly for their children than do genetic parents. And their results appear to show, more generally, that the strength of parental love varies with the relatedness between parent and child, which supports Daly and Wilson's General Formula that the strength of parental love is proportional to the product of the reproductive value of the child and the child's relatedness to the parent.

The sociologists Jean Giles-Sims and David Finkelhor have been reluctant to blame Daly and Wilson's findings on stepparenthood per se, and they have offered an argument that may have already occurred to readers with a sociological orientation. Giles-Sims and Finkelhor argue that divorce and remarriage rates are higher among lower socioeconomic classes, so that stepfamilies are overrepresented among lower socioeconomic classes. In addition, the rate of violent crime in general is higher among lower socioeconomic classes, and the majority of child maltreatment reports come from lower socioeconomic classes. Thus, they argue, the underlying cause of the elevated risk of child maltreatment could be poverty, and the apparent correlation between stepfamilies and an elevated risk of child maltreatment could simply be a by-product of the overrepresentation of stepfamilies among lower socioeconomic classes.

But Daly and Wilson argue that poverty, or low socioeconomic status, was not a confounding variable in their studies. First, in an analysis of data compiled by the National Center for Health Statistics regarding the living arrangements of children in the United States in 1976, the sociologist Christine Bachrach found no significant socioeconomic differences between households with two genetic parents and those with one genetic parent and a stepparent. Since these data were collected the same year as the American Humane Association's maltreatment data used in Wilson, Daly, and Weghorst's first study, Daly and Wilson argue that the results of that study could not have been confounded by a correlation between poverty and stepparenthood. Second, in their Canadian study, Daly and Wilson found that stepfamilies were not, in fact, overrepresented among lower-income households. Stepfamilies constituted 6.4 percent of the low-income households and 5.3 percent of the high-income households they surveyed. Thus, Daly and Wilson conclude, the correlation between stepparenthood and an elevated risk of maltreatment cannot be explained away as a by-product of a correlation between poverty and stepparenthood.

So far we've considered the evidence that Daly and Wilson offer in support of their claim that patterns of parental love and care accord with predictions derived from general evolutionary considerations. That is, we've considered evidence that parental motivational systems produce *effects* that accord with Daly and Wilson's General Formula. But what kinds of process in those motivational systems *cause* those effects? How, in other words, does the parental *mind* function so as to produce the patterns of behavior that Daly and Wilson claim to have documented? How do parents make "decisions" about parental investment that manage to vary investment according to the reproductive value of a child and the relatedness between parent and child? Do parental psychologies calculate the reproductive value of children and then moderate parental investment accordingly? Do they have mechanisms that process information about relatedness and then calculate the degree to which parental investment will enhance inclusive fitness?

The answer to these last two questions is, of course, no. Daly and Wilson in no way think that parental psychologies have been designed to process information about reproductive value and relatedness. As we saw in our discussion of the evolution of marriage, our motivational systems can be designed to cause us to act in ways that enhance our reproductive success without processing information about reproductive success. Rather, Daly and Wilson argue, the specific process by which parental love becomes established or fails to become established causes parents to treat their children in ways that accord with principles regarding reproductive value and relatedness. Daly and Wilson have offered a theory of *parental attachment*, which is intended to illuminate the workings of the motivational mechanisms underlying parental love and thus explain their findings regarding patterns of child maltreatment. Their theory is designed specifically to account for "maternal bonding," but they make some suggestive remarks about paternal love as well.

According to Wilson and Daly, mothers go through a three-stage process of attachment to their children. The first stage is one of *assessment*, "in the immediate aftermath of the birth, of the child and of how its qualities and present circumstances combine to predict its prospects."[28] During this stage mothers feel relative indifference to their new child, a detachment that allows them to assess the reproductive value of the child and terminate investment if the child's reproductive value appears low. This stage may last for the first few days after birth, but by the end of the first week after birth a mother enters the second stage of bonding, *the establishment of an individualized love* for her child, which is characterized by a feeling that her child is uniquely wonderful and worthy of devotion. The third stage consists of a *gradual deepening of parental love*, which occurs over the course of many years as the child matures into adolescence and young adulthood.

In their description of these three stages, Wilson and Daly mention only maternal love in connection with the first stage, but discuss both maternal and paternal love in connection with the second and third stages. They seem to conceive of paternal attachment as essentially a two-stage process consisting of the establishment of individualized love followed by the gradual deepening of that love. The first stage of paternal attachment, however, is complicated by paternity uncertainty. The very process of childbirth assures a woman of maternity, so the primary task facing a new mother is that of assessing her infant and then, if it is of sufficient quality, developing an attachment to it. Because paternity is uncertain, however, the primary task facing a new father, according to Wilson and Daly, is that of ensuring that he does not invest in another man's offspring. "There are at least two obvious sources of information contributing to a putative father's confidence that he is indeed the sire: his confidence of the mother's sexual fidelity and his assessment of the phenotypic similarity of the child to himself and his blood relatives."[29] Consequently, Wilson and Daly conclude, an "evolutionary psychological view of paternal bonding suggests that perception of paternal resemblance would be correlated with paternal bonding."[30] The process of paternal attachment, then, begins with a postnatal assessment of phenotypic resemblance between father and child (although there may also be an assessment of the child's quality), during which a perceived resemblance presumably triggers the establishment of an individualized love for the child. This stage is then followed by the extended period during which there is a gradual deepening of paternal love.

According to this theory, a positive assessment by a mother or father during a "critical period" in the first several days after birth serves to trigger the establishment of an individualized love for a child. When this love is triggered, it serves as an "inhibition against the use of dangerous tactics in conflict with the child."[31] But a negative assessment by a mother (of a child's quality) or a father (of a child's quality or resemblance to him) may result in a failure to trigger the establishment of an individualized love for a child. According to Daly and Wilson, child maltreatment is a by-product of this failure to "engage the evolved psychology of parental feeling," since that failure involves a failure to engage the inhibition against violent reactions to conflict.[32]

But a negative assessment during the "critical period" for the establishment of individualized parental love isn't the only factor that can result in failure to trigger that love. If parents are not exposed to their child during the "critical period," the mechanisms for the establishment of individualized love can also fail to be engaged. According to Daly and Wilson, the evolved mechanisms of parental attachment are designed for genetic parenthood, where in the normal course of events parents are exposed to, and have contact with, their children immediately after birth. We are designed to develop feelings of deep, individualized love for healthy newborns who are born to us (for women) or resemble us (for men). Since stepchildren are typically older when they are first exposed to their stepparents, the "critical period" for the establishment of individualized love has been missed, and consequently stepchildren don't trigger parental love in their stepparents. As a result, stepparents don't develop the same inhibition against violent reactions to conflict with their stepchildren that parents normally do with respect to their genetic children. And that, according to Daly and Wilson's theory, explains why stepparents are more likely than genetic parents to maltreat their children.

With this understanding of Daly and Wilson's theory in place, let's turn to a critical appraisal of it. In the next section, I'll discuss evidence pertaining to Daly and Wilson's theory, including the evidence they have presented in support of it. In the final section, I'll examine just how much Daly and Wilson's work really tells us about the nature of parental psychology.

## What Is "The Truth about Cinderella"?

The previous section reviewed the evidence Daly and Wilson have offered in support of their General Formula that the strength of a parent's love for a child is proportional to the product of the child's reproductive value and the child's relatedness to the parent. In doing so, it focused primarily on the implication that parental love varies partly as a function of relatedness between parent and child. For this entails Daly and Wilson's "most obvious prediction from a Darwinian view of parental motives"—namely, that "substitute parents will generally tend to care less profoundly for children than natural parents, with the result that children reared by people other than their natural parents will be more often exploited and otherwise at risk."[33] As we saw, Daly and Wilson claim that this prediction is confirmed by their finding that children who live with a stepparent are at far greater risk of maltreatment than children who live with both genetic parents.

In this section, I will analyze the available evidence concerning the "most obvious prediction." The analysis will focus primarily on evidence concerning stepparental maltreatment, since that is the evidence that Daly and Wilson claim confirms their hypothesis. But the "most obvious prediction" claims that children who live with *substitute parents*, not simply those who live with stepparents, will be at greater risk of abuse and neglect than children who live with both genetic parents. If Daly and Wilson's prediction is right, children who live with two genetically unrelated adoptive parents should also be at greater risk of maltreatment than children who live with both genetic parents. So I will also present and discuss some data concerning abuse of adopted children. I will argue that there is no reliable evidence to support the "most obvious prediction."

Before delving into analysis of the evidence, however, I'd like to address a couple of misrepresentations of Daly and Wilson's findings. It's not uncommon for the dissemination of scientific results to resemble the game of telephone, in which an original message is modified radically by the time it reaches the end user. Scientific results published in relatively technical scientific journals often get simplified, distorted, or exaggerated by the time they reach a broader audience. Usually the news media are responsible for such misrepresentations, but popular science writers also sometimes distort the scientific theories and results on which they report. Daly and Wilson's research regarding the risk to stepchildren provides an example of how original results get misrepresented to a broader audience by third-party writings. In this case, however, Evolutionary Psychologists themselves have distorted Daly and Wilson's findings in works intended for broad audiences. Two specific examples are worth pointing out and correcting before we examine the evidence in greater detail.

First, in his undergraduate textbook, *Evolutionary Psychology: The New Science of the Mind*, David Buss presents the data reported here in table 7.2, then says: "These data show that children living with one genetic parent and one stepparent are roughly *40 times* more likely to be physically abused than children living with both genetic parents."[34] In fact, if you check table 7.2 again, you'll see that it is *only children under five*, not children of all age groups, of whom this claim is true. The increased risk to children aged five to ten was less than half, and to children aged eleven to seventeen less than one quarter, of the increased risk to children under five. Of course, even when Buss's exaggeration is corrected, in Daly and Wilson's sample children of all age groups who live with a genetic parent and a stepparent are at greater risk of maltreatment than children who live with both genetic parents, and this does appear to confirm their hypothesis. However, Buss also presents Daly and Wilson's statistics as though they are facts about whole populations, not just facts about their sample. Yet Daly and Wilson's sample was relatively small and perhaps not representative of large populations. So how confident should we be that the rates Daly and Wilson found in their Canadian sample reflect the rates of child maltreatment in large populations? In what follows, I will present results of a study with a far larger and more representative sample than Daly and Wilson's, and it will reveal an increased risk to stepchildren that is of far lesser magnitude than the increased risk claimed by Daly and Wilson, let alone that claimed by Buss's exaggeration. Misrepresentations such as the one in Buss's textbook have great shock value, and they make it appear that Evolutionary Psychology has shown us an *obvious* and deep truth about human psychology. But finding a lower relative risk to stepchildren will open the door to another understanding of the data that show stepchildren to be at greater risk of maltreatment.

The second misrepresentation occurs in Steven Pinker's popular book *The Blank Slate: The Modern Denial of Human Nature*. Pinker says: "The psychologists Martin Daly and Margo Wilson have documented that stepparents are far more likely to abuse a child than are biological parents."[35] In fact, Daly and Wilson have "documented" no such thing. Daly and Wilson found that *children who live with a stepparent and a genetic parent* are more likely to be victims of maltreatment than *children who live with both genetic parents*. Daly and Wilson *inferred* that the elevated risk to stepchildren is due to maltreatment at the hands of stepparents; but they did not *document* that stepparents perpetrated the maltreatment that resulted in this elevated risk. And this is a difference that makes a difference. One of the parents in a stepfamily is a genetic parent. If the elevated risk to children in stepfamilies is due to an elevated risk of maltreatment by a genetic parent, then Daly and Wilson's "most obvious prediction" is not confirmed. That prediction is confirmed only if stepparents (and other substitute parents) are more likely than genetic parents to maltreat a child. Another issue to be examined in this section, then, is the extent to which stepparents, rather than genetic parents, are responsible for the elevated risk to children in stepfamilies.

These issues are intertwined with several others, and the entire thicket of issues will have to be wrestled with in what follows. The best way to begin is by taking a closer look at Daly and Wilson's classic Canadian study.

The first thing to get clear about is precisely what counted as maltreatment in Daly and Wilson's study. Since Daly and Wilson analyzed cases that were active with local children's aid societies, they adopted the definition of maltreatment employed by those societies. Accordingly, they considered behavior toward a child to be maltreatment as long as "the care being provided by those *in loco parentis* is, in the opinion of child welfare professionals, so poor or unreliable as to imperil the child."[36] One notable aspect of this criterion is that it includes not only neglect and physical abuse, but sexual abuse as well. In fact, of the 99 cases of maltreatment that constituted Daly and Wilson's sample, 28 were cases of sexual abuse.[37] The earlier study with American Humane Association data also included cases of sexual abuse, although Daly and Wilson nowhere indicate how many of those cases were sexual abuse.

But sexual abuse and physical abuse appear to be different phenomena with different underlying causes. In a review of available studies of child sexual abuse, the social scientists Hilda and Seymour Parker found that "intrafamilial child sexual abuse is generally not accompanied by physical abuse."[38] Further, nearly all parental sexual abuse is perpetrated by fathers or father substitutes, and the majority of victims of parentally perpetrated sexual abuse are daughters. Parker and Parker also found that stepfathers are overrepresented among child sexual abusers. Indeed, the sociologist

Michael Gordon has reported that stepfathers are perhaps seven times more likely than genetic fathers to sexually abuse one of their children.

Interestingly, however, Parker and Parker found that stepfathers who coresided with their stepdaughters during the first three years of their stepdaughters' lives were no more likely to sexually abuse their daughters than genetic fathers. In addition, they found that fathers who coresided with their daughters during the first three years of their daughters' lives and participated in child care and nurturant tasks were far less likely than other fathers to sexually abuse their daughters. To explain this fact, Parker and Parker hypothesize that caring for a very young child triggers a mechanism that inhibits the subsequent development of sexual desire for that child. This hypothesis is a variant of the Westermarck hypothesis, which has significant empirical support. The Westermarck hypothesis claims that living in close proximity during the first five years of life triggers a mechanism that inhibits the subsequent development of sexual desire between siblings. According to both hypotheses, the postulated inhibitory mechanism has the function of reducing the likelihood of incest, which is important since inbreeding greatly increases the odds that a harmful mutation will be passed on with fatal or debilitating consequences.

As we have seen, Daly and Wilson argue that maltreatment data can test their theory about the nature of the *motivational systems* underlying parental care. In particular, they argue that such data can test their hypothesis about strength of parental love because parental love functions to *inhibit* "the use of dangerous tactics in conflict with the child."[39] Assuming that parental love does have this inhibitory function, the impulses that fail to be inhibited in cases of sexual abuse undoubtedly originate in different motivational systems than the impulses that fail to be inhibited in cases of physical abuse. As a result, the mechanisms of inhibition too are undoubtedly different. A parent who strikes a child in a fit of rage is in a much different psychological state than a stepfather who sexually molests the pubescent stepdaughter who has recently begun sharing his home. Calling these both "lapses of parental love" obscures the fact that cases of sexual abuse are confounded by the troubled sexual motivation of the abuser in a way that cases of physical abuse are not. Humbert Humbert's sexual obsession with Lolita didn't originate in a simple "lack of concern for Lolita's welfare," but in Humbert Humbert's troubled sexuality. It's simply *not* the case that the desires of the sexual abuser are "normal" and widely shared among parents, but inhibited in most parents by a "concern for the particular child's welfare." This is evidenced in Parker and Parker's finding that sexual abuse is typically not accompanied by physical abuse.

For, if "lack of concern for the child's welfare" underlay sexual abuse, that same lack of concern would manifest itself in physical abuse as well. Thus, if the objective is to understand the motivational systems underlying parental care, conflating sexual abuse and physical abuse is problematic. For purposes of understanding parental motivation, as it is manifested in "lapses of parental love" that result in "the use of dangerous tactics in conflict with the child," the focus should be exclusively on nonsexual maltreatment.

If the 28 cases of sexual abuse are removed from Daly and Wilson's Canadian data, however, the sample consists of 71 cases of nonsexual maltreatment. Since stepparents—in particular, stepfathers—probably accounted for a disproportionate share of the 28 cases of sexual abuse, the removal of the sexual abuse cases would probably lower the rate of maltreatment for children living in stepfamilies more than it would lower the rate of maltreatment for children living with both genetic parents. As a result, the relative risks to stepchildren wouldn't be as high as those given in table 7.2.

In addition, the 71 cases of nonsexual maltreatment in Daly and Wilson's sample are cases in which the care was "so poor or unreliable as to imperil the child." Daly and Wilson are explicit that this includes cases of neglect, not simply cases of physical abuse, but they don't report the full range of acts or omissions that were included under this criterion by the children's aid societies that cataloged the cases. This definition, however, is very similar to the standard definition of child maltreatment endorsed by the U.S. National Institute of Child Health and Human Development and employed in most American studies of child maltreatment. According to that standard definition, child maltreatment is any behavior that "(a) is outside the norms of conduct, and (b) entails a substantial risk of causing physical or emotional harm. Behaviors included will consist of actions and omissions, ones that are intentional and ones that are unintentional."[40] As implemented by local agencies reporting maltreatment under this standard, maltreatment includes neglect, and neglect includes such omissions as failure to put a child in a car seat and failure to secure a child with a seat belt while driving.

I am certainly no advocate for the neglectful. But, by any criterion according to which failure to use a car seat or secure a child with a seat belt constitutes maltreatment, every child growing up in America when I did was maltreated. While it is unquestionably desirable to raise consciousness about matters of child safety, and even to penalize those who fail to protect their children to the best of their ability, failure to use a car seat or secure a child with a seat belt should not be conflated with such acts as hitting or kicking a child or stubbing out a cigarette on a child's back. There are, of course, forms of neglect that are effectively abusive and that clearly do betray an utter lack of concern for a child's welfare or life. But the class of unintentional omissions that are considered neglectful changes over time within a society and is different across societies, and it will include unintentional omissions that many reasonable and caring people at some time or in some place do not recognize as endangering their children. The class of *actions* that are designed to *inflict* suffering, however, is an entirely different matter. If we want to understand the "lapses of parental love" that result in "the use of dangerous tactics in conflict with the child," as Daly and Wilson claim, we should use data regarding physical abuse, rather than the amorphous category of maltreatment, to test whether substitute parents are more abusive than genetic parents.

While Daly and Wilson's study employed a criterion of maltreatment that included unintentional omissions considered serious enough to imperil a child, there is no indication of how many of the 71 cases of non-sexual maltreatment in Daly and Wilson's study were cases of unintentional omission. If many were, then the appropriate sample to test their hypothesis would be even smaller than 71 cases. In the absence of definitive information, let's assume that all 71 cases were cases of physical abuse. Although a sample of 71 cases of abuse in Hamilton-Wentworth is large enough to obtain a significant test of whether stepchildren are overrepresented in cases of abuse, it is not large or representative enough to allow confident extrapolation of abuse rates to the population at large (in the manner of the quote from Buss). One question, then, is whether the results that Daly and Wilson obtained in their Canadian sample can be replicated with another, preferably larger and more representative, sample that is composed exclusively of cases of physical abuse, cases of *acts* that *harmed* a child.

Another thing to note about Daly and Wilson's Canadian study is the fact that, of the 99 cases of maltreatment, only one was a case of maltreatment of a child living with unrelated adoptive parents, whereas there were three cases of maltreatment of a child living with a "biological relative" (table 7.1). This, in itself, should raise suspicion about Daly and Wilson's "most obvious prediction," since that prediction claims that children reared by nongenetic parents should be at greater risk than children reared by genetic parents and genetic relatives. Of course, the number of adopted children is vastly smaller than the number of children living with two genetic parents or one genetic parent and a stepparent. So, the fact that Daly and Wilson found only one case of maltreatment of an adopted child could have been due merely to a combination of their relatively small sample size and the relative rarity of adoptive households. A second question, then, is whether abuse in adoptive households would prove equally rare in a study with a larger and more representative sample than Daly and Wilson's. (The rarity of abuse in adoptive households could also be due to adoptive parents' constituting an atypical population, a consideration I will address momentarily.)

In an effort to answer both questions with a study that meets these desiderata, Elliott Smith, the Associate Director of the National Data Archive on Child Abuse and Neglect, and I analyzed child maltreatment data compiled in the Third National Incidence Study of Child Abuse and Neglect (NIS-3), a study contracted by the U.S. Department of Health and Human Services. NIS-3 collected child abuse and neglect data during 1993 from forty-two counties across the United States, which were carefully selected to ensure a nationally representative sample. In each of the counties, data were gathered from two sources. First, child protective service agencies provided information on all cases of child abuse and neglect that were reported to the agencies and accepted by them for investigation. Second, 5,612 professionals who did not work in child protective service agencies reported the cases of abuse and neglect they encountered. These professionals had lines of work in which they were likely to come into contact with maltreated children, and they included social workers, teachers and administrators in public schools, child-care providers in day care centers, hospital workers, and public health officials. All of these professionals were trained by NIS-3 investigators in definitions of abuse and neglect and in methods for detecting and confirming cases of each. Both sources provided detailed reports, on the same standardized form, about the victims, the members of the victims' households, the nature of the abuse or neglect, the severity of the abuse or neglect, and the relationship of the identified perpetrator to the victim, as well as various demographic data regarding the victims and the members of their households.

NIS-3 used two broad standards for classifying maltreatment, the Harm Standard and the Endangerment Standard. The Harm Standard was more restrictive, encompassing acts that met one of the following three degrees of severity:

1. Fatal: maltreatment suspected as a major contributory cause of death,
2. Serious Injury/Condition: professional treatment/remediation needed to alleviate acute present suffering or to prevent significant long-term impairment,
3. Moderate Injury/Condition: behavior problem or physical/mental/emotional condition with observable symptoms lasting at least forty-eight hours.

The Endangerment Standard, in contrast, was more inclusive, including in addition to the above all cases involving acts or unintentional omissions that, in the judgment of the reporting agency or professional, endangered the child's health or safety. These cases were classified under one of the following three degrees of severity:

4. Probable Impairment: no obvious injuries or problems but, in view of the extreme or traumatic nature of the maltreatment, it is probable that the child's mental or emotional health or capabilities have been significantly impaired,
5. Endangered: child's health or safety was or is seriously endangered, but child appears not to have been harmed,
6. Other/Unknown.

As these last three degrees of severity were implemented in the reporting form, they included "knowingly permitted chronic truancy" and "inadequate nurturance/affection."

For the reasons discussed above, Smith and I analyzed only cases that met the Harm Standard. Also for the reasons discussed above, we excluded from our analysis all cases of sexual abuse, and we excluded all cases of physical abuse in which the victim was abused by someone other than a parent in the child's home. Utilizing the information on the living arrangements of each victim, we then followed Daly and Wilson's method of classifying the resulting cases by age of the child and the parental composition of the child's household. Table 7.3 shows the number of cases in each class.

From these data, Elliott Smith was able to derive estimates of the number of abused children in the U.S. population at large for each age group and household type. To calculate rates of abuse for each age group and household type, however, I needed to know how many children of each age group lived in each household type in the United States in 1993. Since the Census Bureau did not collect such data for 1993, I extracted data from the Census Bureau's 1996 Survey of Income and Program Participation (Wave 2, fourth reference month). The 1996 Survey of Income and

**Table 7.3**
Numbers of Physically Abused Children by Household Composition in NIS-3, 1993

| Parents in household | Child's age at maltreatment | | | |
| --- | --- | --- | --- | --- |
| | 0–4 | 5–10 | 11–17 | Total |
| Two genetic parents | 100 | 116 | 115 | 331 |
| One genetic parent | 54 | 89 | 94 | 237 |
| One genetic parent + one stepparent | 21 | 50 | 81 | 152 |
|    Genetic mother + stepfather | 18 | 40 | 64 | 122 |
|    Genetic father + stepmother | 3 | 10 | 17 | 30 |
| Two unrelated adoptive parents | 0 | 1 | 1 | 2 |
| One nongenetic parent | 0 | 1 | 3 | 4 |
| Total | 175 | 257 | 294 | 726 |

Program Participation (SIPP) collected very detailed and comprehensive demographic information about the households within the survey, and unlike earlier Census Bureau surveys it distinguished among genetic, step-, adoptive, and foster relationships within households. (As in Daly and Wilson's survey, two-parent households in both NIS-3 and the 1996 SIPP include both married and unmarried parents.) The SIPP data provided population estimates of the number of children of each age group living in each household type in the United States in 1996. To obtain population estimates of the numbers of children of each age group living in each household type in 1993, I calculated the percentages of all children in the United States in 1996 who were in each age group and living in each household type represented in table 7.3, and I multiplied those percentages by the Census Bureau's figure for the number of children in the United States in 1993. (This method assumes, of course, that the relative proportions of children of each age group living in each household type did not change significantly between 1993 and 1996.) The population estimates for 1993 appear (in thousands) in table 7.4.

These population estimates made it possible to calculate the rates of physical abuse presented in table 7.5.

There are two things to note about the data in table 7.5. First, the risk to children living in a stepfamily relative to the risk of children living with both genetic parents is significantly lower than the relative risk found by Daly and Wilson. Children from birth through age four living in a stepfamily were 8.2 times more likely to be physically abused than children living with both genetic parents, which is drastically lower than the 40-

**Table 7.4**
Estimated Numbers of Children by Age and Household Composition in the United States, 1993 (in thousands)

| Parents in household | Child's age | | | |
| --- | --- | --- | --- | --- |
| | 0–4 | 5–10 | 11–17 | Total |
| Two genetic parents | 13,404 | 14,422 | 14,141 | 41,967 |
| One genetic parent | 4,241 | 5,740 | 6,716 | 16,697 |
| One genetic parent + one stepparent | 378 | 1,582 | 2,961 | 4,921 |
|   Genetic mother + stepfather | 296 | 1,324 | 2,325 | 3,945 |
|   Genetic father + stepmother | 82 | 258 | 636 | 976 |
| Two unrelated adoptive parents | 145 | 250 | 264 | 659 |
| One nongenetic parent | 74 | 118 | 160 | 352 |
| Total | 18,242 | 22,112 | 24,242 | 64,596 |

*Note:* Entries are rounded to the nearest thousand, but nonrounded estimates were used to calculate the abuse rates appearing in subsequent tables.

**Table 7.5**
Estimated Rates of Physical Abuse (per thousand children) by Household Composition in the United States, 1993

| Parents in household | Child's age at maltreatment | | | |
| --- | --- | --- | --- | --- |
| | 0–4 | 5–10 | 11–17 | Overall |
| Two genetic parents | 1.7 | 3.2 | 3.1 | 2.7 |
| One genetic parent | 2.4 | 6.5 | 4.9 | 4.8 |
| One genetic parent + one stepparent | 13.9 | 10.2 | 10.5 | 10.7 |
|   Genetic mother + stepfather | 17.5 | 9.7 | 11.8 | 11.5 |
|   Genetic father + stepmother | 0.9 | 12.8 | 6.0 | 7.4 |
| Two unrelated adoptive parents | n.d.* | 0.2 | 1.7 | 0.8 |
| One nongenetic parent | n.d.* | 0.3 | 8.4 | 3.9 |
| Overall rates | 2.1 | 4.5 | 4.5 | 3.8 |

*The data included no cases of physical abuse in the youngest age group for these household types.

times-greater risk of maltreatment that Daly and Wilson found. Children aged five to ten living in a stepfamily were 3.2 times more likely to be physically abused than children living with both genetic parents (as opposed to Daly and Wilson's 19.4-times-greater risk of maltreatment), and children aged eleven to seventeen living in a stepfamily were 3.4 times more likely to be physically abused than same-aged children living with both genetic parents (compared to Daly and Wilson's 9.8-times-greater risk of maltreatment). Second, the rates of physical abuse of children living with two unrelated adoptive parents were significantly lower than the rates of physical abuse of children living with both genetic parents. I will return to the first of these points later, but for the moment I want to examine the exceptionally low rate of physical abuse of adopted children.

As table 7.5 shows, not only was the risk to adopted children lower than the risk to children living with both genetic parents, but adopted children were at the lowest risk of all children in all age groups. Indeed, despite the fact that an estimated 144,820 children under age five lived with two adoptive parents, NIS-3 did not record a single case of physical abuse of adopted children under five (which is why no rate appears in the corresponding cell of table 7.5). In addition, children aged five to ten living with both genetic parents were 16 times more likely to be physically abused than same-aged children living with two adoptive parents, and children aged eleven to seventeen living with both genetic parents were 1.8 times more likely to be physically abused than same-aged children living with two adoptive parents. The fact that adopted children had the lowest risk of physical abuse of any group appears to provide straightforward falsification of the "most obvious prediction" that children who live with substitute parents should be at greater risk than those living with genetic parents.

There's another angle from which to approach this. Instead of classifying households as Daly and Wilson did, we could aggregate households according to the average relatedness of the parents in the household to the abuse victim. In a two-genetic-parent household, the relatedness of each parent to the abuse victim is 0.5, so the average relatedness between parents and victim in such households is 0.5. The relatedness between parent and victim in a one-genetic-parent household is also 0.5. So the average relatedness between parents and abuse victim is the same in two-genetic-parent and one-genetic-parent households. Consequently, both household types could be treated as households in which the average relatedness between parents and abuse victim is 0.5. Similarly, we could group households containing two nongenetic parents with those containing only one nongenetic parent, since the relatedness of each parent to abuse victim in these households is zero; so the average relatedness between parents and victim in all such households is zero. The third household type would be that in which there is one genetic parent and one stepparent. Since these households consist of a parent whose relatedness to the victim is 0.5 and another whose relatedness is zero, the average relatedness of the parents in these households to the abuse victim is 0.25. With households aggregated in this way, the abuse rates (per thousand children) for each age group within each household type are as shown in table 7.6.

According to the "most obvious prediction," the risk to a child is a function of the relatedness between parents and child. If this is the case, the risk to children should increase with decreasing average relatedness between parents and child. Accordingly, children who live with a genetic parent and a stepparent should be at greater risk than children who live with both genetic parents, as Daly and Wilson argue. But, also, children who live with only nongenetic parents should be at greater risk than those who live in a household with a genetic parent and a stepparent, since the former children should be at greater risk of abuse at the hands of both parents in the household.

As the abuse rates in table 7.6 show, however, this is not the case. In fact, in every age group, households with no genetic parent had a significantly lower rate of abuse than households with a genetic parent and a stepparent. (No rate is reported in the birth-to-four age group for households without a genetic parent because there were no cases of abuse of such children, although an estimated 219,180 children under five lived with only nongenetic parents.) In addition, the rate of abuse for children from birth to age ten who lived with only genetic parents (3.07 per thousand) was more than 20 times greater than the rate of abuse for same-aged

**Table 7.6**
Estimated Rates of Physical Abuse (per thousand children) by Average Relatedness of Parents in Household in the United States, 1993

| Parents in household | Child's age at maltreatment | | | |
| --- | --- | --- | --- | --- |
| | 0–4 | 5–10 | 11–17 | Overall |
| Genetic parent(s) only | 1.9 | 4.1 | 3.6 | 3.3 |
| One genetic parent + one stepparent | 13.9 | 10.2 | 10.5 | 10.7 |
| Nongenetic parent(s) only | n.d.* | 0.2 | 4.2 | 1.9 |

*The data included no cases of physical abuse in the youngest age group for this household type.

children living with only nongenetic parents (0.15), despite the fact that 13.3 percent (or 78,283) of the children living with only nongenetic parents lived with a single stepparent. Thus, contrary to the "most obvious prediction," it appears that only children living with a genetic parent *and* a stepparent, rather than children living with a nongenetic parent, are at greater risk relative to children living with genetic parents. The elevated risk of physical abuse does not appear to be correlated with relatedness per se, but with living in a stepfamily. And this appears to falsify Daly and Wilson's "most obvious prediction."

But perhaps appearances deceive. Daly and Wilson argue that the low rate of abuse in adoptive households should not be taken as a falsification of their "most obvious prediction" because there are mitigating factors that lower the rate of abuse in adoptive households. "Nonrelative adoptions," they say, "are primarily the recourse of childless couples who are strongly motivated to simulate a natural family experience; rather than having their position *in loco parentis* thrust upon them, they have actively sought it. Applicants to adopt are screened by agencies, and many are rejected as unsuitable. . . . Finally, if the adoption (or the marriage) fails, the couple can return the child, which happens more often than is generally realized."[41] The implication is that these factors serve to ensure that adoptive households present a very low risk for child abuse and, consequently, serve to mitigate the natural discrimination against nongenetic children that would otherwise manifest itself in adoptive households. So, Daly and Wilson imply, if just any "unsuitable" couple could adopt, if unwanted children made surprise appearances in the lives of adoptive parents, and if adoptive parents could not simply return unwanted children, the rate of abuse in adoptive households would be far greater than it is and probably greater than the rate in two-genetic-parent homes.

There is no doubt some truth in this argument, and it does appear to explain away the fact that the rate of abuse in adoptive households is much lower than the "most obvious prediction" entails that it should be. But Daly and Wilson's explanation of the low rate of abuse in adoptive households opens a hornet's nest of questions about how we should interpret the available data.

First, Daly and Wilson claim that the rate of abuse in adoptive households is low because adoptive parents "actively sought" parenthood, rather than having it "thrust upon them." In other words, adoptive parents rarely abuse their adopted children because adoptive parents *wanted* their adopted children. In contrast, we have seen Daly and Wilson argue, the relationship between stepparent and stepchild is "thrust upon" the stepparent as an *unwanted* and incidental consequence of the stepparent's sexual relationship with the stepchild's genetic parent. But these arguments raise the possibility that whether a child was *wanted* by its parents is the single most important risk factor in child abuse, regardless of the composition of the household in which the child lives. Indeed, the data showing a higher rate of abuse in stepfamilies than in genetic or adoptive families may not be directly testing whether parental love is conditioned by relatedness at all. For those data may be a by-product of the fact that parental love is conditioned by how much the parents wanted the child and the incidental fact that stepparents are less likely than genetic or adoptive parents to want the parental relationships they have with their children.

Daly and Wilson could respond that, nonetheless, stepparents *are* less likely to want the parental relationships they have with their children and that this is due to an evolved discrimination against investment in unrelated children. But, if this were true, adoptive parents should also be loathe to invest in the unrelated children that they adopt. As we have seen, however, adoptive parents actively want to invest in the unrelated children they adopt. Conversely, as we are about to see, many genetic parents do not want to invest in their (potential) children. So it seems that relatedness per se does not explain whether and to what extent parents want(ed) their children. And, following Daly and Wilson's reasoning, it seems that whether a child was wanted *may* be the most important risk factor for child abuse.

Second, Daly and Wilson maintain that the rate of abuse in adoptive households is low because the process of adoption—which includes the screening of prospective adoptive parents and the ability of adoptive parents to return children—tends to ensure that adoptive parents don't find themselves caring for unwanted children. But there are processes that similarly ensure that genetic parents don't find themselves caring for unwanted children. Genetic mothers and fathers frequently have the prospect of parenthood "thrust upon them" in the form of surprise, unwanted pregnancies. If genetic mothers (or parents) decide that they don't want the children that would issue from these pregnancies, they can either terminate the pregnancy or give up the unwanted child for adoption (and these are family-planning methods that are available only to genetic parents). Whenever genetic parents take one of these actions, an otherwise unwanted child fails to appear in the statistics for genetic-parent households. This means that genetic households, like adoptive households, do not include a significant number of children who would be unwanted were those children actually members of those households. If we reason that the abuse rate in adoptive households *would be higher if* the process of adoption didn't ensure that adoptive parents don't find themselves caring for unwanted children, we should also reason that the abuse rate in genetic-parent households *would be higher if* genetic parents had to care for all the unwanted children that could have been, but in fact were not, members of their households. Thus, the rate of abuse in genetic-parent households would be higher if genetic parents didn't have methods of ensuring that they don't find themselves caring for unwanted children.

To see the potential impact of these family-planning methods on abuse rates, consider the abuse rates obtained from NIS-3. In the United States in 1993, the number of legally terminated pregnancies reported to the Centers for Disease Control and Prevention was 1,330,414.[42] Four states, however, did not report the number of pregnancies that were legally terminated within their borders: Alaska, California, New Hampshire, and Oklahoma. If the number of legally terminated pregnancies per capita was the same in those four states as in the forty-six states that did report, the actual number of legally terminated pregnancies in the United States in 1993 was approximately 1,547,500. In addition, according to estimates by the National Adoption Information Clearinghouse, in the United States in 1993, approximately 120,000 children were adopted.[43] Typically, half of all adoptions are of children younger than age five, and the overwhelming majority of these children have been given up for adoption by their genetic mothers (or parents). Thus, were it not for adoption and pregnancy termination, in 1993 there would have been perhaps 1,600,000 more children under the age of five living with genetic parents than there in fact were. Moreover, these children would have been living with genetic parents who, in fact, decided they did not want to care for those children. If we take Daly and Wilson's argument seriously, these counterfactual, unwanted children would have been at an elevated risk of abuse relative to the actual children who appeared in the 1993 population data. And, if as few as 15 percent of these unwanted children had become victims of abuse, the abuse rate for children under the age of five living in genetic-parent households would have slightly exceeded that for same-aged children living with a genetic parent and a stepparent.

Would as many as 15 percent of these counterfactual, unwanted children have become victims of abuse? That, of course, is an imponderable question. It is similarly imponderable what the rate of abuse in adoptive households would be if the adoption process did not tend to ensure that only suitable adoptive parents end up parenting only wanted children. But these imponderables do present the following dilemma with respect to the interpretation of the available data on abuse rates in different types of household.

On the one hand, we can take the available abuse data at face value. If we do, the fact that the rate of abuse for children from birth to age ten in genetic-parent households was more than 20 times greater than the rate for same-aged children living in non-genetic-parent households proves Daly and Wilson's "most obvious prediction" false. On the other hand, we can accept the argument by which Daly and Wilson explain away the low rate of abuse in adoptive households. If we do, we discount the data from adoptive households on the grounds that it is sufficiently confounded by extraneous factors that it is unusable as evidence against the "most obvious prediction." If we take this option, however, we have to accept that an argument identical to Daly and Wilson's shows that the rates of abuse in genetic-parent households would be much higher than they actually are if genetic parents didn't have methods to exclude unwanted children from the available abuse statistics. In fact, had the counterfactual, unwanted children actually appeared in the data for genetic-parent households, the abuse rates in genetic-parent households could have equaled those for children living in stepfamilies. Consequently, since the ability of genetic parents to exclude unwanted children from their households artificially lowers the abuse rate in genetic households relative to step-households, we can't be confident that the available abuse data provide a true test of Daly and Wilson's "most obvious prediction." Thus, either the data from non-genetic households prove Daly and Wilson's "most obvious prediction" false or the data from genetic households are sufficiently confounded that they can't be compared with stepfamily data in order to confirm their prediction. Either way, Daly and Wilson can't claim that the available data clearly confirm their hypothesis.

This line of argument may strike some readers as too metaphysical. So let's return from a consideration of how counterfactual possibilities affect the interpretation of the data to further consideration of the actual data before us. As we have seen in the NIS-3 data, as well as in Daly and Wilson's original data, there is an elevated risk of child abuse associated with living in a stepfamily (although not with living with a nongenetic parent in general). Daly and Wilson infer that this elevated risk is due to abuse at the hands of stepparents, and this led Pinker to claim that Daly and Wilson "have documented that stepparents are far more likely to abuse a child than are biological parents."[44] But all of the data so far considered have taken *household composition*, rather than *relationship of perpetrator to victim* of child abuse, as the unit of analysis. That is, the data concern the risk of abuse to children *living in households* of varying parental composition, rather than a child's risk of being *abused by* a stepparent or genetic parent. As a result, none of the data directly confirm Daly and Wilson's prediction that stepparents are more likely than genetic parents to abuse their children. Only data concerning the rates of physical abuse for various types of relationship between perpetrator and victim are capable of providing a direct test of the prediction that stepparents are more likely than genetic parents to abuse their children.

One significant study that took as its unit of analysis the relationship of perpetrator to abused child, rather than the composition of the abused child's household, was conducted by the sociologist Richard J. Gelles and the psychiatrist John W. Harrop. Gelles and Harrop analyzed data gathered by the Second National Family Violence Survey, which was an anonymous telephone survey of 6,002 households across the United States in 1985. Households were contacted using random-dialing procedures, and the 6,002 households that made up the survey database were then selected from among those contacted to ensure demographic representativeness. Of the 6,002 households contacted, 3,232 included at least one child under eighteen years of age. Interviewers asked adult respondents about the relationships among members in the household, and they asked how often in the previous year various "conflict tactics" were used by the adult respondent in dealing with a child in the household. The conflict tactics fell under three broad categories: use of rational discussion and agreement, use of verbal and nonverbal expressions of hostility, and use of physical force or violence. The category of "physical force or violence" included a number of items that Gelles and Harrop extracted to form a category of "severe violence." This category of severe violence, on which Gelles and Harrop based their analysis, included "the items that have a high probability of causing an injury—kicked, bit or hit with a fist; hit or tried to hit the child with something; beat up the child; burned or scalded the child; threatened the child with a gun or knife; used a knife or fired a gun."[45]

Gelles and Harrop analyzed the resultant data in order to calculate the rates (per thousand children) at which tactics of severe violence were used on genetic children and stepchildren, and their results appear in table 7.7.[46]

As table 7.7 shows, the rate of abuse by acts of severe violence for stepchildren from infancy to age six is higher than that for genetic children the same age, yet only 1.2 times higher. But the overall rate of severe violence committed by genetic parents is 1.2 times the rate of severe violence committed by stepparents. On the whole, then, there is no substan-

**Table 7.7**
Rates of Severe Violence against Children (per thousand children) in the United States, 1985

| Relationship of victim to perpetrator | Child's age at maltreatment | | | |
| --- | --- | --- | --- | --- |
| | 0–6 | 7–12 | 13–17 | Overall |
| Genetic child | 113 | 124 | 89 | 109 |
| Stepchild | 136 | 53 | 98 | 93 |

tial difference between the rates of severe violence committed by genetic parents and by stepparents. Gelles and Harrop conclude that these "results from the Second National Family Violence Survey did not confirm the hypothesis that non-genetic parents are more violent and abusive towards children than are genetic parents."[47] And they take their results as providing disconfirmation of Daly and Wilson's "biological theory of child maltreatment."

Daly and Wilson have responded to Gelles and Harrop by arguing that self-report data about child abuse are likely to be highly unreliable, since respondents can simply lie about whether and how often they perform abusive acts toward their children. The motivation to lie is perhaps particularly strong when people are asked about behavior as socially unacceptable as child abuse, Daly and Wilson argue, and this calls into question Gelles and Harrop's finding that stepparents are no more likely to abuse their children than genetic parents. "An alternative characterization of this finding," Daly and Wilson quip, "is that when telephoned by a stranger and asked whether they have committed various assaultive acts against their children within the past year, stepparents were no more likely than genetic parents to profess to have done so."[48]

Daly and Wilson are certainly right that we should take self-report data about matters such as child abuse with a large grain of salt. People lie all the time, and we should expect them to lie when asked whether they've hit or kicked their children, even if their responses are protected by anonymity. Indeed, it is well known that people respond to interviews and surveys with answers that they believe will meet with interviewer approval and avoid interviewer disapproval (an effect known as "evaluator apprehension" or "evaluation apprehension"). And there is certainly widespread disapproval of child abuse. But I don't think that this worry justifies Daly and Wilson's wholly dismissive attitude toward Gelles and Harrop's results. For, if Daly and Wilson's interpretation is right, stepparents are far more likely than genetic parents to abuse their children, yet they are no more likely than genetic parents to admit to having abused their children. This conjunction, however, entails that stepparents must be *far* more likely than genetic parents to *lie* about whether they've abused their children. And there is no clear reason why this should be so. Genetic parents should be no less ashamed than stepparents to admit to child abuse, and they should thus be no less motivated to lie about it. Yet genetic parents must be less likely than stepparents to lie about abuse in order for Daly and Wilson to be justified in dismissing Gelles and Harrop's finding.

In addition, the rates of severe violence that Gelles and Harrop found are astonishingly high—indeed, they are vastly higher than the rates of abuse found in NIS-3 (table 7.5). Since the Second National Family Violence Survey simply *asked* people about whether they've abused their children, so that all respondents had the opportunity to lie about it, one would think that a high rate of lying on the part of respondents to the survey would result in rates of severe violence that were not substantially greater than the rates of abuse found in official case reports of physical abuse. Yet the overall rate of severe violence reported by stepparents in Gelles and Harrop's study was 10.6 times greater than the overall rate of physical abuse at the hands of stepparents in NIS-3. If respondents to the Second National Family Violence Survey were lying with the impunity that Daly and Wilson imply, it's inexplicable why they would admit to as much severe violence as they did admit to. So, while the possibility of lying by respondents to the Second National Family Violence Survey means that Gelles and Harrop's results should be met with some skepticism, there is no compelling reason why they should dismissed wholesale. Perhaps Gelles and Harrop's finding that stepparents are no more likely than genetic parents to abuse their children is fairly accurate even if the rates they found are not. And, if their finding is accurate, it falsifies Daly and Wilson's "most obvious prediction."

But Gelles and Harrop's results don't actually contradict Daly and Wilson's finding that there is an elevated risk to children living in stepfamilies. For, if children in stepfamilies are sufficiently more likely to be abused by a genetic parent than are children who live with both genetic parents, it could be the case both that stepparents are no more likely than genetic parents to abuse their children (as per Gelles and Harrop) *and* that children in stepfamilies are more likely to be abused than children living with both genetic parents (as per Daly and Wilson). Gelles and Harrop's results just aren't consistent with Daly and Wilson's *interpretation* of their finding—namely, that stepparental abuse accounts for the elevated risk to children living in stepfamilies. Daly and Wilson require this interpretation of their results for confirmation of their "most obvious prediction," since that prediction is confirmed only if stepparents are more likely than genetic parents to abuse their children. The question, then, is whether the elevated risk to children in stepfamilies is due to stepparental abuse (as Daly and Wilson claim) or is due to at least equal rates of abuse at the hands of genetic parents (which could reconcile Gelles and Harrop's results with those of Daly and Wilson).

As Daly and Wilson point out, the children who are at greatest risk of abuse in stepfamilies are small children, and small children in stepfamilies typically live with a stepfather and a genetic mother. In fact, in the United States in 1993, 80 percent of all children who lived with a genetic parent and a stepparent lived with a genetic mother and a stepfather (table 7.4). Thus, the elevated risk to children who live in stepfamilies derives almost entirely from an elevated risk to children who live with a stepfather. So we can be more specific in the way we formulate the crucial question: Is the elevated risk to children in stepfamilies due to abuse *by stepfathers* (as Daly and Wilson claim) or is it due at least equally to abuse *by genetic mothers* (which would reconcile Gelles and Harrop's findings with those of Daly and Wilson). In other words, are children who live with stepfathers at greater risk than those who live with both genetic parents because stepfathers are more likely to abuse their children than genetic fathers, or are they at greater risk because children are more likely to be abused by their genetic mothers if they live with a genetic mother and a stepfather than if they live with both genetic parents?

To explore this question, I would like first to examine the reasons for thinking that the elevated risk to children living with a stepfather is due to abuse by stepfathers. Then I will examine whether there are reasons for thinking that mothers are more likely to abuse their genetic children if they live with a man who is not the genetic father of those children than if they live with their children's genetic father. The objective of this exploration will be to ascertain whether abuse by genetic mothers might account for enough of the elevated risk to children in stepfamilies that, overall, stepparents are no more likely than genetic parents to abuse their children.

As I have pointed out, Daly and Wilson document an elevated risk to children living with a stepfather, but they do not document that abuse by stepfathers is responsible for the elevated risk. They *infer* that steppaternal abuse accounts for the elevated risk, and their inference is driven by their theoretical commitment to the idea that selection has designed parental psychology to discriminate against investment in unrelated children. Consequently, when they find an elevated risk to children living with a stepfather, they naturally suspect the stepfather, since he is the parent who is unrelated to the victim of abuse. But this presupposes that paternal solicitude is strictly *parenting effort*, whereby males invest in related children, and try to avoid "squandering" parental care on unrelated children, in order to enhance their inclusive fitness. Thus, the idea that stepfathers pose a severe abuse risk to children is part and parcel of the view that paternal solicitude is, and evolved as, parenting effort.

As we saw in chapter 6, however, the evidence favors the hypothesis that male parental care evolved as a form of mating effort, rather than parenting effort. According to the mating effort hypothesis, recall, males evolved to provide parental care because they received in exchange increased paternity opportunities from the mothers of the young to whom they provided care. According to this hypothesis, an inclusive fitness benefit from providing parental care wasn't a precondition for the evolution of male parental care; rather, it was a beneficial by-product of it. The real fitness benefit of paternal care was, instead, an increase in the number of paternity opportunities. For, if a male can secure paternity opportunities from a female by providing care to her children, even if those children are the offspring of another male, the male enhances his chances of having children of his own and thereby transmitting his genes to future generations. So, another male's child can make a contribution to a male's fitness via the opportunities for paternity provided by that child's mother in exchange for parental care provided to the child. The possibility of such fitness payoffs, however, means that we should not expect male psychology to be so unconditionally averse to investing in unrelated children. And this, in turn, means that we should not be so ready to expect that an elevated risk to children in stepfamilies must be due primarily to steppaternal abuse precipitated by an evolved nepotistic psychology that produces sometimes violent resentment in response to substitute parenthood.

There is, in fact, some interesting empirical evidence that stepfathers are less reluctant to invest in stepchildren than Daly and Wilson presuppose and that their investment, and paternal care in general, is a form of mating effort. The anthropologist Kermyt Anderson and his colleagues conducted lengthy interviews of 1,325 randomly selected males over the age of twenty-five in Albuquerque, New Mexico. They interviewed the males about their reproductive and parenting histories, obtaining information about the children the men had sired and the children, both related and unrelated, for whom the men had ever provided parental care. Anderson and his colleagues also gathered information about each of the following categories of investment: the amount of financial support for college provided to the children listed, the amount of other financial expenditures on children aged from birth to twenty-four, and the amount of time spent in activities with children aged five through twelve. Finally, they classified the children of their male subjects according to the relatedness between father and child and the relationship between the father and the child's genetic mother, as shown in table 7.8. Class 1 children were the genetic children of the male and his current mate. Class 2 children were the genetic children of the male and his previous mate. Class 3 children were the male's stepchildren from a current relationship (the genetic children of his current mate). And Class 4 children were the male's stepchildren from a previous relationship (the genetic children of a previous mate).

Each of the four "classes" of children corresponds to a different form of male reproductive effort. Since Class 2 children are genetic children with a former mate, investment in Class 2 children yields no return in the form of paternity opportunities provided by the mothers of those children. Thus, investment in Class 2 children must be strictly a form of parenting effort, whereby a male invests in his genetic child so as to enhance his own fitness by enhancing that of his child. In contrast, investment in Class 3 children must be strictly a form of mating effort, whereby a male invests in his stepchild in order to maximize his paternity opportunities with the child's mother. Investment in Class 1 children, however, can combine both parenting and mating effort, while investment in Class 4 children involves neither parenting nor mating effort.

Anderson and his colleagues found that, in each of the categories of investment, fathers invested the most in Class 1 children (genetic children from current relationships), and they invested the least in Class 4 children (stepchildren from previous relationships). More tellingly, Anderson and his colleagues found that, overall, fathers invested more in Class 3 children (stepchildren from current relationships) than in Class 2 children

**Table 7.8**
Classification of Father-Child Relationships

|  | Child's mother is male's current mate | Child's mother is male's former mate |
|---|---|---|
| Genetic child of male | Class 1 | Class 2 |
| Stepchild of male | Class 3 | Class 4 |

(genetic children from previous relationships). First, fathers spent an average of 16.2 hours per week in activities with Class 3 children, but only 9.5 hours per week in activities with Class 2 children. While this finding could perhaps be explained away as a by-product of the fact that fathers coreside full time with Class 3 children, but probably only see Class 2 children on some weekends, the other findings can't be so easily explained away. For, second, Anderson and his colleagues found that fathers gave 55 percent of Class 2 children money for college, while fathers gave a nearly equal 52 percent of Class 3 children money for college. Third, fathers had spent equal average amounts of money over the course of the previous year on Class 2 and Class 3 children under the age of eighteen. And, fourth, over the course of the previous year, fathers had spent an average (in 1990 dollars) of $1,828 on Class 3 children aged eighteen to twenty-four, whereas they spent an average of $1,535 on same-aged Class 2 children.

The last three of these findings are particularly interesting. If paternal care is strictly parenting effort, we should not expect fathers to spend as much on Class 3 children under the age of eighteen as on same-aged Class 2 children, and we should not expect virtually as many Class 3 children as Class 2 children to receive money for college from their fathers. But these statistics may actually overstate the degree to which fathers are inclined to invest in Class 2 children, since some of the money that fathers invest in non-coresident genetic children under the age of eighteen is typically mandated by divorce settlements, as are some financial contributions to their children's college educations. It's hard to know whether the investments in Class 2 and Class 3 children in these two categories would be equal in the absence of legal compulsion mandating some of the investment in Class 2 children. In contrast, investment in children eighteen and older who are not college students is less likely to be mandated by a divorce settlement. Indeed, for reasons such as these, Anderson and his colleagues contend that the statistics regarding financial expenditures on children aged eighteen to twenty-four are especially revealing of steppaternal psychology. "Because these children are not necessarily dependent on their parents," they argue, "and because they often do not live at home, we expect expenditures on this group of offspring to more closely reflect actual parental preferences."[49] If these expenditures are more revealing of paternal inclinations than expenditures on children under eighteen and financial contributions for college, then the results suggest that males are *more inclined* to invest in stepchildren from current relationships than in genetic children from previous relationships.

Of course, the fact that fathers were found to invest more in genetic children from current relationships than in stepchildren from current relationships does show that paternal care is, in part, parenting effort. But, the fact that fathers were found to invest more in genetic children from current relationships than in genetic children from previous relationships shows that paternal care is also mating effort. And, since fathers were found to invest more in stepchildren from current relationships than in genetic children from previous relationships, paternal care appears to be *primarily* a form of mating effort. If paternal care is primarily mating effort, however, the fitness payoff of paternal care isn't captured by a narrow calculus concerning the relatedness between father and child. Consequently, we should not expect that selection has designed the motivational systems of paternal psychology to allocate paternal solicitude strictly as a function of relatedness between father and child, as Daly and Wilson's view of paternal care as parenting effort would lead us to expect.

If we follow Daly and Wilson in arguing that incidence of abuse is a negative measure of parental solicitude, we can find additional evidence from NIS-3 that paternal solicitude is more closely tied to paternity opportunities with a child's mother than to relatedness between father and child. So far I've presented the data from NIS-3 in terms of the household composition of the abused child in order to facilitate comparison with Daly and Wilson's research. But, in all of the abuse cases in NIS-3, the perpetrators were identified. So the NIS-3 data can also be mined for comparisons of abuse rates between various types of perpetrator-victim relationship. Table 7.9 presents the rates of abuse (per thousand children) at the hands of genetic fathers and stepfathers acting alone within four types of household.

**Table 7.9**
Estimated Rates of Physical Abuse (per thousand children) by a Father Acting Alone in the United States, 1993

| Parents in household | Child's age at maltreatment | | | |
|---|---|---|---|---|
| | 0–4 | 5–10 | 11–17 | Overall |
| Genetic father + genetic mother | 0.7 | 1.3 | 2.2 | 1.4 |
| Genetic father only | 19.8 | 9.8 | 10.1 | 11.4 |
| Genetic father + stepmother | n.d.* | 3.7 | 4.1 | 3.6 |
| Stepfather + genetic mother | 11.1 | 7.1 | 6.1 | 6.8 |

*The data included no cases of physical abuse in the youngest age group for this household type.

Some of the results in table 7.9 conform to Daly and Wilson's "most obvious prediction." For, overall, stepfathers are 4.9 times more likely to abuse their children than genetic fathers in two-genetic-parent homes. But, children younger than five, whom Daly and Wilson believe to be the most likely to be abused by a stepfather, are in fact 1.8 times more likely to be abused by a single genetic father than by a stepfather. In fact, children of all age groups are most likely to suffer paternal abuse at the hands of a single genetic father, and, overall, single genetic fathers are 1.7 times more likely than stepfathers to abuse their children. If child abuse is the flip side of parental solicitude, these results indicate that stepfathers are more solicitous toward their stepchildren than single fathers are toward their genetic children.

These facts don't sit well with the idea that paternal solicitude is parenting effort. For, if it were, stepfathers should exhibit higher rates of abuse than genetic fathers, regardless of whether a genetic father is (still) married to his child's genetic mother, since the relationship with his child's mother doesn't affect relatedness between father and child. The fact that single genetic fathers are more likely than stepfathers to abuse their children, however, does conform to the idea that paternal investment is primarily a form of mating effort. For single genetic fathers are no longer receiving paternity opportunities from the mothers of their children, whereas stepfathers are receiving paternity opportunities in exchange for the parental care they provide to their stepchildren. Thus, paternal abuse is more closely (negatively) correlated with a father's paternity opportunities with a child's mother (hence his potential returns on mating effort) than with relatedness between father and child (hence the father's potential returns on parenting effort).

The *evolutionary reason* that Daly and Wilson have for suspecting that children are at risk from stepfathers is that paternal care is parenting effort and stepfathers are not related to their stepchildren. However, since the evidence favors the mating effort hypothesis regarding the evolution of paternal care, and since patterns of paternal investment and paternal abuse support viewing paternal solicitude as primarily mating effort, we should reject Daly and Wilson's particular evolutionary view of paternal solicitude. As a result, we should not be led to infer, in the absence of concrete evidence, that the elevated risk to children in stepfamilies is due primarily to steppaternal abuse. Of course, as table 7.9 shows, stepfathers are more likely to abuse their children than genetic fathers in two-genetic-parent households. We will return to this datum, but first let's examine whether there are reasons for thinking that some of the elevated risk to children living with a stepfather might be due to abuse by genetic mothers.

The possibility that children living with stepfathers would suffer an elevated risk of abuse at the hands of their genetic mothers is clearly contrary to Daly and Wilson's particular "Darwinian view of parental motives." But it is not without an evolutionary explanation, since women who take their children into a marriage to a man other than the father of those children find themselves facing a *conflict of reproductive interests*. First, the new marriage represents a potential reproductive venture, so mating effort devoted to the new marriage has to detract from the parenting effort devoted to a child from a former marriage. Second, and more important, any children from the new marriage will also demand parenting effort, which will force a mother to make a decision about how to allocate parenting effort among all of her children. From a broadly evolutionary standpoint, we should expect her to allocate parenting effort in a way that will maximize the return on her invested parental care. But what kind of allocation would achieve this?

As Anderson's study and the data about paternal abuse show, a genetic mother can expect a greater investment in her children from a genetic father to whom she is married than from a stepfather. So, if a woman takes her genetic children into a marriage to a man other than their genetic father, she can expect her new husband to invest more in any "new children" they might have together than in any "old children" she brings from her previous relationship. If she invests equally in all her children, her new children will nonetheless flourish more than her old children, since they receive a greater investment from her husband. The return on her investment in her new children will thus be greater than the return on her investment in her old children, despite her equal investment in all. Since this makes her investment in her old children a worse investment than her investment in her new children, equal investment in all her children doesn't appear to be the optimal allocation.

To address this problem, a mother could adjust her allocation in two ways. First, she could invest more in her old children than in her new children, counterbalancing the differential investment by her husband in an effort to make all of her children flourish equally. This tactic, however, would undoubtedly generate conflict with her husband, who is likely to expect at least an equal investment in the children from their marriage, and this could jeopardize the mating effort she is investing in the new marriage. So this option is potentially too costly. Second, she could invest more in her new children than in her old children. This would have the effect of "throwing good money after good," since her new children, who are already flourishing more than her old children because of the higher paternal investment, would flourish even more with the increased investment from her. Of course, her old children would suffer from this allocation. But, depending on the number and "quality" of her children from each marriage, a mother could actually enhance the average fitness of her brood by investing more in her new children at the expense of her old children. Thus, selection could have designed maternal psychology to decrease investment in old children when an increased investment in new children would result in greater average fitness of a woman's brood. And, if an increased risk of abuse is correlated with decreased investment, then, under the conditions in which this allocation of maternal care results, a mother would be more likely to abuse her old children than her new children. Finally, if this were the case, children living with a stepfather would be at an increased risk of abuse at the hands of their genetic mothers relative to children living with both genetic parents.

But, given this reasoning, a mother's remarriage wouldn't be strictly necessary in order for children to suffer an increased risk of abuse at the hands of their genetic mother. As Anderson's study shows, children of single mothers receive lower investments from their genetic fathers than children living with married genetic parents. Consequently, a single mother's investment in her child will not see the returns that it would see if the mother were (still) married to the child's father. Further, if a single mother is seeking a new mate, she is already headed down the path toward the decreased investment in her child that is described above. Of course, a single mother doesn't yet have new children from a new relationship. Thus, while we should expect that a single mother might invest less in her children than a mother who is married to her children's genetic father, she should nonetheless invest more than a remarried mother with new children (since her current children are, to date, her only live prospects for transmitting her genes to the next generation). And, again, if an increased risk of abuse is correlated with decreased investment, a single mother should be more likely to abuse her genetic children than a mother who is married to her children's genetic father, and a remarried mother should be more likely than a single mother to abuse her children from a previous relationship. In short, relative to children living with both genetic parents, a child should be at increased risk of abuse at the hands of a single genetic mother and at even greater risk of abuse at the hands of a remarried genetic mother.

There is significant evidence that the first part of this prediction is true—namely, that genetic children of single mothers are at an elevated risk of maltreatment relative to children living with married genetic parents. Some of the support for this prediction comes from research by the anthropologists Eckart Voland and Peter Stephan, who studied parish records, which spanned the period from 1655 to 1939, in two German communities. First, Voland and Stephan found that "illegitimate" children whose mothers subsequently married men who were not their genetic fathers died in infancy at a rate that was approximately six times greater than that of "illegitimate" children whose mothers subsequently married their acknowledged fathers. Through an examination of the cases, Voland and Stephan were unable to find any explanation other than "maternal manipulation" (infanticide or severe neglect) for this differential incidence of infant mortality. Second, Voland and Stephan found that women who did not go on to marry the fathers of their illegitimate children had a better chance of marrying at all if their illegitimate children died in infancy than if they lived. They further found that women whose illegitimate children lived, and who did not go on to marry at all, had an average of 1.6 children throughout life, whereas women whose illegitimate children died in infancy, and who went on to marry men other than the fathers of those children, had an average of 1.9 children throughout life. These two sets of data suggest that single mothers who do not go on to marry the fathers of their illegitimate children have greater lifetime reproductive success if their illegitimate children die and they marry another man than if their illegitimate children live and they remain unmarried. Since Voland and Stephan found "maternal manipulation" to be the only plausible explanation of the difference in infant mortality, they "interpret the willingness of women to underinvest in their illegitimate children as an adaptive outcome of a sexually selected maternal algorithm that weighs current reproduction against future mating success."[50]

In addition, Daly and Wilson found children of single mothers to suffer an elevated risk of maltreatment. First, Daly and Wilson found that children under the age of five living with a single genetic mother were 12.5 times more likely to be maltreated than same-aged children living with married genetic parents (table 7.2). Similarly, they found that children aged five through ten living with a single genetic mother were 11.8 times more likely to be maltreated, and children aged eleven through seventeen were 8.3 times more likely to be maltreated, than same-aged children living with married genetic parents (table 7.2). Second, in their cross-cultural study of infanticide, Daly and Wilson found that half of all circumstances in which infanticides occurred were tied to the mother's inability to deal with the demands of child rearing and that nearly half of these circumstances concerned a mother's being unmarried or lacking assured paternal support for the child.[51] Third, in their study of infanticide in Canada between 1977 and 1982, Daly and Wilson found that unmarried mothers were between 2.5 and 7 times more likely to kill their infant children than married mothers, depending on maternal age.[52] In fact, they found that, overall, unmarried mothers accounted for 60 percent of all infanticides while accounting for only 12.7 percent of all live births.[53]

Finally, the NIS-3 data show that genetic children of single mothers suffer a greater risk of physical abuse than children living with married genetic parents. Table 7.10 shows the rates of abuse (per thousand children) at the hands of genetic mothers acting alone within three types of household. Overall, children living with a single genetic mother were 5.9 times more likely than children living with both genetic parents to be physically abused by their mothers.

While the results in table 7.10 do support the prediction that children living with single genetic mothers suffer an elevated risk of maltreatment relative to children living with both genetic parents, they do not appear to support the prediction that a child should be at greater risk of maltreatment at the hands of a remarried genetic mother than at the hands of a single genetic mother. Children under the age of five were slightly more likely to be physically abused by a remarried genetic mother than by a single genetic mother, but overall children living with a single genetic mother were 2.7 times more likely than children living with a remarried genetic mother to be abused by a mother acting alone. But, somewhat in keeping with the rationale behind the prediction that children of remarried genetic mothers should be at greatest risk of genetic-maternal abuse, children living with remarried genetic mothers were 2.1 times more likely

**Table 7.10**

Estimated Rates of Physical Abuse (per thousand children) by a Genetic Mother Acting Alone in the United States, 1993

| Parents in household | Child's age at maltreatment | | | |
|---|---|---|---|---|
| | 0–4 | 5–10 | 11–17 | Overall |
| Genetic mother + genetic father | 0.7 | 0.7 | 0.6 | 0.7 |
| Genetic mother only | 1.4 | 6.1 | 4.1 | 4.1 |
| Genetic mother + stepfather | 1.6 | 0.8 | 1.9 | 1.5 |

to be abused by a mother acting alone than were children living with both genetic parents.

Table 7.10, however, doesn't reveal all the facts about genetic-maternal abuse rates. First, children under the age of one year living with a genetic mother and a stepfather were 13.9 times more likely to be abused by a genetic mother acting alone (19.5 children per thousand) than same-aged children living with a single genetic mother (1.4 children per thousand). Second, many victims of abuse were abused by both parents acting in concert. If we turn our attention from cases of abuse at the hands of a genetic mother acting alone to cases of abuse in which a genetic mother was involved, then we do indeed find that children who live with a genetic mother and a stepfather are the most likely to be abused by their genetic mothers. Table 7.11 reports the rates of abuse (per thousand children) within the same three types of household, but here I have divided the under-five age group into three smaller age groups in order to show the very high risk to the youngest children.

As table 7.11 shows, children younger than three suffer a dramatically elevated risk of being abused by a genetic mother if they live with a step-father. And, overall, the results do conform to the prediction that children should be at greater risk of being abused by a genetic mother if they live with a genetic mother and a stepfather than if they live with a single genetic mother. This, in turn, supports the hypothesis, suggested by Voland and Stephan, that mothers exhibit reduced investment in their genetic children when they have married a man who is not the father of those children.

We thus have two conclusions that conspire to suggest that some of the elevated risk to children living with stepfathers is due to abuse by genetic mothers. First, we saw that paternal solicitude is not strongly correlated

**Table 7.11**

Estimated Rates of Physical Abuse (per thousand children) Involving a Genetic Mother in the United States, 1993

| Parents in household | Child's age at maltreatment | | | | | |
|---|---|---|---|---|---|---|
| | <1 | 1–2 | 3–4 | 5–10 | 11–17 | Overall |
| Genetic mother + genetic father | 1.2 | 1.5 | 0.4 | 1.9 | 0.8 | 1.2 |
| Genetic mother only | 1.4 | 2.3 | 0.5 | 6.1 | 4.1 | 4.1 |
| Genetic mother + stepfather | 19.5 | 16.6 | n.d.* | 2.7 | 5.6 | 4.7 |

*The data included no cases of physical abuse in this age group and household type.

with relatedness, but is more closely correlated with the paternity opportunities a male can get in exchange for paternal care. This undermines the
particular evolutionary rationale that leads Daly and Wilson to suspect that
steppaternal abuse is responsible for the elevated risk to children living
with a stepfather. Second, we saw that maternal investment in genetic children decreases with single motherhood and decreases even further with
marriage to a man who is not the father of those children. This suggested
a plausible evolutionary explanation for why children who live with a stepfather might be at greater risk of abuse by a genetic mother than children
who live with both genetic parents. But could abuse by genetic mothers
in stepfamilies account for the elevated risk of abuse suffered by children
living with a genetic mother and a stepfather?

The answer appears to be no. If we look more directly at abuse in stepfamilies, the data do not confirm that genetic mothers are primarily
responsible for the elevated risk to children who live with a genetic mother
and a stepfather. Table 7.12 shows the rates of abuse (per thousand children) according to perpetrator within households comprised of the victim's
genetic mother and stepfather. As these results indicate, children under the
age of one year are slightly more likely to be abused by a genetic mother
than by a stepfather, and children aged one and two are slightly more likely
to be abused by both parents acting in concert than by a stepfather acting
alone. But, children three and older are significantly more likely to be
abused by a stepfather acting alone than by a genetic mother, whether
acting alone or in concert with her husband. Thus, the NIS-3 data do show
that the elevated risk to children living with a stepfather is due primarily
to abuse by the stepfather. Given this result, there appear to be only two
possible conclusions. First, Daly and Wilson could simply be right that

Table 7.12

Estimated Rates of Physical Abuse (per thousand children) in Genetic Mother–
Stepfather Households in the United States, 1993

| Perpetrator | Child's age at maltreatment | | | | | |
| | <1 | 1–2 | 3–4 | 5–10 | 11–17 | Overall |
| --- | --- | --- | --- | --- | --- | --- |
| Genetic mother | 19.5 | 0.4 | n.d.* | 0.8 | 1.9 | 1.5 |
| Stepfather | 19.1 | 15.8 | 7.8 | 7.1 | 6.1 | 6.8 |
| Both parents | n.d.* | 16.2 | n.d.* | 1.9 | 3.8 | 3.2 |

*The data included no cases of physical abuse for these age groups and household
types.

stepparents are more likely than genetic parents to abuse their children. Second, the results from NIS-3, like Daly and Wilson's own results, which appear to support Daly and Wilson's "most obvious prediction," could be unreliable.

As far-fetched as this second option might appear at first glance, there are arguments to be made in its favor. Both Daly and Wilson's sample and the NIS-3 sample consist entirely of officially reported cases of child maltreatment. This means that the samples consist entirely of cases of maltreatment that were brought to the attention of a professional who worked in a capacity concerned with child welfare, were investigated in some way by that professional or others to whom the cases were referred, and were determined to be genuine cases of child maltreatment by those who investigated the cases. Studies that rely on official reports of child maltreatment are thus dependent on the judgments of both those who report the cases to child welfare professionals and the child welfare professionals themselves. Consequently, the factors that go into the judgments about whether apparent harm to a child was genuinely a case of maltreatment can bias the results of the studies that rely on official case reports.

Gelles and Harrop, as well as the sociologist Jean Giles-Sims, point out that child welfare professionals sometimes take the presence of a stepparent in the household into consideration in deciding whether a bruise or broken bone resulted from an accident or from abuse. That is, many child welfare professionals take the presence of a stepparent in a household to be partly *diagnostic* of maltreatment. Accordingly, Gelles and Harrop argue, "injuries to children with non-genetic parents are more likely to be diagnosed and reported as abuse."[54] Thus, the detection and reporting of child maltreatment may be biased in a way that increases the proportional representation of stepfamily cases in the data set of official case reports and decreases the proportional representation of genetic-family cases of maltreatment.

Daly and Wilson are fully aware of the potentially confounding effects of diagnostic bias on their studies. Indeed, they take the issue of diagnostic bias seriously enough to argue repeatedly that it cannot have had a significant effect on their results. They offer the following *single argument* against the confounding effects of diagnostic bias, which they repeat in a number of different publications: "Such biases surely exist, and it is almost impossible to estimate their magnitude, but they cannot begin to account for the facts. The reasoning behind this assertion is as follows. If reporting or detection biases were responsible for the overrepresentation of stepparents among child abusers, then we would expect the bias, and hence the overrepresentation, to diminish as we focused upon increasingly severe and unequivocal maltreatment up to the extreme of fatal batterings. But the actual trend is precisely the opposite."[55] Daly and Wilson then present some of the evidence we have reviewed about comparative rates of homicide and severe abuse in genetic families and stepfamilies.

Of course, the critical question to ask is why Daly and Wilson think that the effects of any diagnostic bias should diminish as the form of abuse becomes increasingly severe. At one point, Daly and Wilson answer this questions as follows: "At the limit, we can be reasonably confident that child murders are usually detected and recorded. Admittedly, some failures to help a newborn live may escape detection and some deliberate smotherings may be successfully disguised as 'sudden infant deaths,' but there is no reason to suppose that these are numerous."[56] If child homicide is "usually detected and recorded," then data regarding child homicide are not confounded by a diagnostic bias, and we can be confident that the comparative rates of genetic-parental and stepparental filicide are accurate. Since Daly and Wilson present evidence that stepparents—in particular, stepfathers—murder their children at far higher rates than do genetic parents, they express confidence that comparable findings with respect to nonfatal abuse must not be confounded by a diagnostic bias on the part of child welfare professionals.

Daly and Wilson base their argument on two sets of homicide statistics. One set consists of the validated cases of child homicide that were reported to the American Humane Association in 1976.[57] The other set consists of child homicides in Canada between 1974 and 1983 that were known to Canadian police departments and cataloged in a governmental homicide archive.[58] There is substantial evidence, however, that "validated" child homicides and those "known to police" are just a proper subset of child maltreatment fatalities in the United States, and there is little reason to doubt that Canada is very similar to the United States in this regard. Indeed, the evidence shows that official case reports of child maltreatment fatalities significantly underreport the number of child fatalities due to abuse and that fatalities at the hands of nongenetic parents are more likely to be reported than those at the hands of genetic parents. So, if Daly and Wilson's argument is the only reason we have for believing that official case reports of child maltreatment are not biased against stepparents, then we truly have no good reason for believing that official case reports are a very reliable source of information about the true comparative rates of child abuse.

One study that demonstrates the extent to which official records can underreport abuse fatalities was conducted by the pediatrician Katherine Christoffel and her colleagues Nora Anzinger and David Merrill. Christoffel and her colleagues examined death certificates and medical examiner's records concerning 437 deaths of children under the age of fifteen in Cook County, Illinois, between 1977 and 1982. In these records, deaths "are assigned one of five 'manners of death': homicide, suicide, accident, natural, or undetermined. Cases that are ruled of an undetermined manner include those in which information is lacking to prove intentional injury or neglect, but in which there is evidence that precludes assigning the death a natural or accidental manner."[59] Of course, deaths for which information was lacking to prove any intentional injury or neglect were typically not prosecuted, for lack of evidence, and were not subsequently recorded as homicides in police records. But they were also cases for which there was physical evidence to preclude attributing the death to sudden infant death syndrome (SIDS), so they were not the purportedly rare cases of disguising a child homicide as SIDS to which Daly and Wilson refer. And there were a not insignificant number of undetermined deaths. Of the 437 deaths that Christoffel and her colleagues examined, 206 (or 47 percent) were coded as having an undetermined manner. Further, Christoffel and her colleagues found that "rates for the undetermined deaths exceeded those for the deaths that were ruled as homicides through age 4 years."[60] Thus, within the class of children whom Daly and Wilson claim to be most at risk, a child's death was more likely to be recorded as undetermined than as a homicide.

A much more thorough investigation of the degree of underreporting of child maltreatment fatalities was conducted by the pediatricians Bernard Ewigman, Coleen Kivlahan, and Garland Land. Ewigman and his colleagues studied all injury fatalities of children under the age of five in Missouri from 1983 to 1986. By classifying a death as an injury fatality if the death certificate listed any external cause as the cause of death, they identified 384 injury fatalities in that age group during the study period. Assuming that official records may underreport the number of child maltreatment fatalities because of insufficient investigation of cases and inadequate communication among law enforcement, departments of family services, and medical professionals, Ewigman and his colleagues gathered information about the 384 decedents from nine different sources of information. "Sources used included birth certificates; law enforcement sources; autopsy reports; fire investigation reports; DFS-substantiated abuse or neglect events that occurred before death; homicide reports to the Federal Bureau of Investigation–Uniform Crime Report (FBI-UCR) system; medical records, including emergency department and inpatient records; and the National Highway Traffic Safety Administration's Fatal Accident Reporting System. The Aid to Families With Dependent Children (AFDC) status of the child was also determined."[61]

By collating all available information from these sources about each injury fatality, Ewigman and his colleagues classified each of the 384 injury fatalities into one of five categories: definite maltreatment, probable maltreatment, possible maltreatment, non-maltreatment, and inadequate information. They classified an injury fatality as being due to "definite maltreatment" if it met any of the following criteria: "Substantiated as child abuse or neglect by the Division of Family Services, perpetrator convicted of homicide, death reported to Federal Bureau of Investigation–Uniform Crime Report, or death coded on death certificate as a maltreatment fatality."[62] And they classified an injury fatality as being due to "probable maltreatment" if there were "findings that strongly suggest maltreatment caused or contributed to the death," where the relevant findings derived from "the clinical history, legal or social services investigations, physical examination, autopsy, radiological examination, toxicology, or death scene investigation."[63]

Of the 384 injury fatalities, Ewigman and his colleagues found that 121 met their definition of "definite maltreatment." Of the 121 definite maltreatment fatalities, only 96 had been substantiated as abuse or neglect fatalities by the Missouri Division of Family Services, and only 47 were recorded as homicides in the Federal Bureau of Investigation–Uniform Crime Report. In addition, only 58 of the 121 definite maltreatment fatalities were coded as homicides on the death certificates, while 27 were coded as accidental deaths, 20 as natural deaths, and 16 as undetermined. Thus, a study of child maltreatment fatalities that relied solely on law enforcement records would have missed a full 60 percent of the definite maltreatment fatalities, and it would have missed more than half of even those cases that were substantiated as abuse or neglect fatalities by the Division of Family Services. Further, a reliance on any single one of these sources of evidence would result in a failure to detect at least 20 percent of the definite maltreatment fatalities.

These disturbing facts clearly belie Daly and Wilson's claim that "we can be reasonably confident that child murders are usually detected and recorded."[64] And the reasons why there are many probable child homicides that are not detected and recorded derive from mundane facts about governmental bureaucracies. As Ewigman and his colleagues explain: "Investigators often lack basic skills, fail to communicate findings with others, and frequently lack access to other professionals' records. . . . Data collection and reporting procedures among health, law enforcement, and social services agencies are not uniform, standardized, or coordinated."[65] That a child fatality is due to abuse is sometimes apparent only to one who takes the time to investigate multiple sources of information about the case, and overworked individuals in underfunded agencies simply don't conduct the sorts of exhaustive investigation required to detect all such abuse fatalities. Overtaxed police forces typically don't undertake homicide investigations unless a medical examiner's autopsy yields a reason to do so, and medical examiners often don't have sufficient grounds for suspecting foul play in the absence of thorough police investigations or case histories from child welfare agencies.

Ewigman and his colleagues also found 25 of the 384 fatalities to meet the definition of probable maltreatment. None of these were coded as homicides on death certificates, while 21 were coded as death by accident and 4 as undetermined. In addition, none of these cases were recorded as maltreatment fatalities in vital statistics or law enforcement records. Given the manners of death coded on the death certificates and the absence of law enforcement records on the cases, presumably none were investigated by law enforcement as possible homicides. But Ewigman and his colleagues found 5 cases of death by unexplained head injury in which the histories given were inconsistent with the physical evidence. The following case exemplifies these 5 cases.

A 4-month-old infant, by the father's history, was discovered dead the morning after the father had placed the infant between two pillows on an adult's bed. The emergency department physician noted facial bruising, which was later confirmed by an autopsy that also revealed a subdural hematoma. The death certificate listed head injury and skull fracture as the cause of death. The medical examiner reported that "death would seem to be related to the head injury, but a precise terminal event is not apparent in the autopsy examination." There were no law enforcement, DFS, or other records. The study forensic pathologist noted that the case raised the suspicion of child abuse or neglect. Manner of death (accident, homicide, or natural) on the death certificate was undetermined.[66]

Another 4 of the 25 probable maltreatment fatalities were cases of death by smoke inhalation in a residential fire of undetermined cause, and the following case exemplifies these.

This 3-year-old died in a residential fire. Accidental manner of death was marked on the death certificate. There were no autopsy, law enforcement, DFS, or medical records. The fire investigation report included photographs documenting that the fire's point of origin was in the child's bedroom, where his charred body was found under a bed with a cigarette lighter nearby. The door to the child's bedroom was locked with a chain. The child's father, who was in charge of the child at the time, escaped without injury. There was no autopsy and no indication in the fire report that DFS or law enforcement had been notified of the case.[67]

Of course, it's far from certain that cases like the above are homicides. But, given the facts of the above case, "probable homicide" is not an unreasonable classification.

Unfortunately, this problem is not confined to Missouri. While Ewigman and his colleagues investigated *all injury fatalities* with an eye to determining which were definitely or probably due to maltreatment, the medical examiner Marcia Herman-Giddens and her colleagues investigated all fatalities of children aged ten and younger that were actually *coded as homicides* in medical examiner records in North Carolina from 1985 to 1994. Herman-Giddens and her colleagues found that, during that period, there were 259 homicides in which the victim was aged ten or younger. Of these, 220 were identified by medical examiners' records as child-abuse homicides, where a homicide was considered to be due to child abuse if a child was killed by an injury purposely inflicted by a person who was responsible for the child's welfare. But, when Herman-Giddens and her colleagues checked these 220 cases against North Carolina's vital records system, maintained by the State Center for Health Statistics, they found that only 68 (or roughly 31 percent) of the cases were coded as child abuse homicides in vital records. To put this fact in another light, 58.7 percent of *all 259 child homicides* in North Carolina during the study period were due to child abuse but not coded as abuse homicides in the vital records system.

Similar results were obtained in a Colorado study by the epidemiologist Tessa Crume and her colleagues. In 1989, Colorado formed a statewide Child Fatality Review Committee (CFRC), which has subsequently reviewed every death of a child under the age of eighteen that occurs in Colorado. The CFRC is a multidisciplinary effort, consisting of professionals from coroner's offices, medicine, social services, law enforcement, criminal justice, mental health, and public health. For every child fatality that an expert physician suspects may not be due entirely to natural causes, the CFRC obtains and reviews any available autopsy report, medical records, law enforcement report, district attorney report, motor vehicle accident report, and social services history. In this respect, the CFRC functions much as Ewigman and his colleagues did in their study, reviewing multiple sources of information about a child fatality in an effort to obtain a complete picture of a child's circumstances so that it can more accurately ascertain whether a fatality was due to maltreatment. Between 1990 and 1998, the CFRC determined that 295 deaths of children aged sixteen and younger were due to maltreatment.

Crume and her colleagues examined the manner of death recorded on the death certificates for these 295 maltreatment fatalities and found that only 147 (or 50 percent) of them were recorded as maltreatment fatalities on death certificates. Of course, this class of maltreatment fatalities includes some fatalities that resulted from unintentional omissions. But, even with respect to causes of death that would include inflicted injury, death certificates failed to code many abuse fatalities as such. The CFRC found 93 cases in which death was caused by bodily force, but 16 (or 17 percent) of those were not coded as maltreatment fatalities on the death certificates. There were 42 fatalities caused by hanging, strangulation, or suffocation, although 27 (or 64 percent) of those cases were not identified as maltreatment on death certificates. And, of 42 deaths caused by drowning or submersion, which the CFRC determined to be maltreatment fatalities, 38 (or 90 percent) were not recorded as maltreatment fatalities on death certificates. "Maltreatment fatality by drowning" is a particularly ambiguous category, of course, since it could include both drownings of children left momentarily unattended and intentional drownings passed off as bathing accidents. So a good many of these may not be homicides. But, when 90 percent of maltreatment fatalities by drowning are not coded as maltreatment fatalities on death certificates, the cases will not receive the investigative scrutiny required to determine which drownings are homicides. On the whole, these statistics show that *we should have no confidence that reliance on law enforcement records or death certificates alone gives anything close to an accurate picture of the number of child maltreatment homicides.* Indeed, Crume and her colleagues summarize their findings rather bluntly: "Estimates that rely on data from vital statistics, child protection services agencies, or law enforcement alone would seriously underestimate the number of child maltreatment fatalities."[68]

Of course, you might be persuaded that official records of child homicides are radically incomplete but still not think that any of this evidence gives reason to believe that the unrecorded homicides differ in any systematic way from the recorded homicides. If that is the case there is still no reason to believe that the homicide records involve a bias against stepparents. But, the fact that possibly half of all child homicides are not recorded as such in precisely the kinds of record on which Daly and Wilson relied does cast serious doubt on any findings based on those records. With as much as 60 percent of child abuse fatalities not recorded as such in official homicide records, there is ample room for diagnostic bias to cloud homicide data. In the absence of clear evidence of abuse, genetic parents will likely not be investigated in cases of child fatality, and the death of the child will be assigned an accidental, natural, or undetermined manner of death, depending on whether the method causing death more closely resembles an accident, death by natural causes, or neither. But, as we have seen, even inflicted injury fatalities may be classified as having an undetermined manner of death if there is insufficient evidence to pursue a charge of homicide against the parents.

More important, Crume and her colleagues actually found direct evidence of a potential diagnostic bias against stepfathers. Crume and her colleagues found that maltreatment fatalities at the hands of "other relatives," which in their analysis included legally married stepfathers, were 1.37 times more likely to be recorded as such on death certificates than maltreatment fatalities at the hands of genetic parents. Moreover, they found that maltreatment fatalities at the hands of "other unrelated" individuals, which in their analysis included "live-in boyfriends" of victims' mothers, were 8.71 times more likely to be recorded as maltreatment fatalities on death certificates than maltreatment fatalities at the hands of genetic parents.[69]

This last fact is particularly important. In both Daly and Wilson's studies and the NIS-3 study, males who lived in a home with a woman and her genetic children were classified as stepfathers, regardless of whether they were legally married to the woman in the household. That is, the category "stepfather" included both legally married stepfathers and common-law stepfathers (which itself included live-in boyfriends). So, many members of the group that accounts for some of the highest child abuse and filicide rates were found by Crume and her colleagues to be far more likely than genetic parents to get caught. Further, when Daly and Wilson examined their Canadian filicide data regarding stepfather-perpetrated filicides, they found that common-law stepfathers accounted for *a full 89 percent* of the filicides that were attributed to stepfathers in police records.[70] In terms of the categories used in Daly and Wilson's studies and the NIS-3 study, then, Crume and her colleagues actually found that common-law stepfathers, who alone almost accounted for the higher rate of filicide among stepfathers, are in a group that is *8.71 times more likely* than genetic parents to have a perpetrated child maltreatment fatality recorded as such. To put this fact in some perspective, we saw in the NIS-3 data that children living with a genetic mother and a stepfather were 4.5 times more likely to be abused by a stepfather than by a genetic mother. Thus, the degree of diagnostic bias exposed by Crume and her colleagues is more than sufficient to account for the greater rate of abuse by stepfathers in official case reports.

This has been a long and wide-ranging section, so let's take stock of where we've arrived. If Daly and Wilson's "most obvious prediction" is correct, then children who live with nongenetic parents should be at greater risk of abuse than children who live with genetic parents. But we have seen several results that don't conform to that prediction. First, we found that children who live with unrelated adoptive parents are even less likely to be abused than children who live with genetic parents. Although Daly and Wilson try to explain away this fact, their very explanation undermines their comparison of rates of abuse in genetic families with those in stepfamilies, which they cite in support of their "most obvious prediction." Second, we saw that children are at far greater risk of being abused by a single genetic father than by a stepfather, a finding that is inconsistent with Daly and Wilson's supposition that paternal solicitude is a function of relatedness. Third, we saw that children who live with stepfathers are more likely to be abused by their genetic mothers than are children who live with both genetic parents, so that some of the elevated risk to children in stepfamilies is due to genetic-maternal abuse. However, fourth, we also saw that, according to official case reports of child abuse, a child living with a stepfather and a genetic mother is 4.5 times more likely to be abused by the stepfather than by the genetic mother (a factor of increased risk that is nowhere near that found by Daly and Wilson in their small sample of maltreatment).

There are, however, reasons to suspect a diagnostic bias against stepparents in official case reports of child abuse, which results in proportionately more cases of abuse by stepparents than by genetic parents being reported and confirmed. Daly and Wilson argue that any effects of such a diagnostic bias must be negligible, since virtually all child homicides should be detected and recorded, and the data on child homicide show that stepparents are far more likely than genetic parents to fatally abuse their children. But several studies have shown that a great many cases of fatal abuse do not appear in official homicide records, so it is far from clear that the comparative rates of homicide at the hands of stepparents and genetic parents are reliable. In addition, one study found that a case of fatal maltreatment is more than eight times more likely to be recorded as such if perpetrated by a (common-law) stepfather than if perpetrated by a genetic parent. Thus, since all of our evidence to date concerning stepparental abuse derives from official case reports, *we simply don't know* whether step-parents are more likely than genetic parents to abuse their children. Like many claims in Evolutionary Psychology, Daly and Wilson's claim that stepparents are more likely than genetic parents to abuse their children goes well beyond the available *reliable* evidence.

## Trying to Understand Parents

Let's stand back now from the foregoing arguments and consider some other issues. Daly and Wilson's stated objective is to provide us with an understanding of the evolved motivational systems that make up the parental mind, not simply to provide us with an evolutionarily based pre-diction about how parents will tend to behave. But suppose, contrary to the arguments of the previous section, that Daly and Wilson actually had convincing evidence that stepparents are more likely than genetic parents to abuse their children. Even that, I will now argue, would not constitute good evidence for their theory about the workings of the evolved motiva-tional systems of the human parent.

It has been extensively and graphically documented (albeit doubted by a few) that male lions who take over a pride typically kill the suckling cubs who were sired by other males. Killing the sucklings brings their mothers into estrus sooner, and this enables the males to sire offspring with those females sooner than they could if they simply waited for the sucklings to be weaned. This behavior among lions is so well documented, and its adap-tive advantages are so apparently clear, that it is widely accepted among those who study animal behavior that male infanticide among lions is an adaptation.

Daly and Wilson recount these facts in chapter 2 of their book *The Truth about Cinderella*, right before launching into chapter 3, "Human Stepfam-ilies," in which they recount the alleged risks of abuse and filicide at the hands of human stepfathers. Alas, the discussion of infanticide-as-adaptation turns out to be nothing but a red herring in the end. For in chapter 5, after they've presented all their evidence of stepparental abuse and homicide, Daly and Wilson set the record straight with the theory I sketched in the first section of this chapter. "Human beings are not like langurs or lions," they inform us. "We know that 'sexually selected infan-ticide' is not a human adaptation because men, unlike male langurs and lions, do not routinely, efficiently dispose of their predecessors' young. . . . Child abuse must therefore be considered a *non-adaptive or maladaptive byproduct* of the evolved psyche's functional organization, rather than an adaptation in its own right. . . . All told, we see little reason to imagine that the average reproductive benefits of killing stepchildren would ever have outweighed the average costs enough to select for specifically infanticidal inclinations."[71]

But, Daly and Wilson argue, "although sexually selected infanticide is clearly not a human adaptation, discriminative parental solicitude just as clearly is."[72] The mechanisms of discriminative parental solicitude, they claim, are designed to cause parents to feel deep love for a child who, first, parents have reason to believe is their genetic offspring and, second, has sufficiently high reproductive value. When these conditions are met, Daly and Wilson argue, parents develop deep parental love for the child, which creates a "parental *inhibition* against the use of dangerous tactics in conflict with the child."[73] Child abuse emerges as a by-product of the adaptation of discriminative parental solicitude when the mechanisms of discriminative parental solicitude are not activated so as to inhibit violent reactions to annoying and conflictual behavior on the part of children. Further, it is the putative fact that child abuse results from a lack of inhibition of violent reactions to conflict with a child that is supposed to justify using evidence about the incidence of child abuse as "reverse assay" evidence about the strength of parental love, which is what Daly and Wilson's General Formula and "most obvious prediction" are actually about. For, if there weren't a connection between parental love and child abuse, via an inhibition of the tendency to abuse, there would be no clear reason why evidence about child abuse could serve to test Daly and Wilson's evolutionary predictions about parental love.

The above account of the psychological mechanisms underlying both parental love and parental child maltreatment presupposes that the *natural, default* psychological state of adults would lead them to react to annoying children with physical violence. Parents only take such good care of their children, when they do, because their deep love for their children *inhibits* this natural tendency. Daly and Wilson confirm that this presupposition underlies their theory of discriminative parental solicitude in a comment on their discovery that the rate of filicide decreases with increasing age of a child. Daly and Wilson say: "When we consider the conspicuous, tempestuous conflicts that occur between teenagers and their parents—conflicts that apparently dwarf those of the preadolescent period—it is all the more remarkable that the risk of parental homicide continues its relentless decline to near zero."[74] In other words, it's remarkable that more parents don't kill their annoying and conflictual teenagers, since the natural impulse is to want to do so. According to this picture of human psychology, we all have the inclination to throttle the screaming infant on the plane, but only its parents are sufficiently besotted by love for the despicable creature "to tenderly alleviate its distress," rather than silence it permanently.[75]

To clarify the presupposition underlying Daly and Wilson's theory of parental psychology, consider an analogy. If you remove the muffler from virtually any car, the car will make a sputtering sound. The muffler serves to inhibit the sound the car would naturally make otherwise. But an older car can sometimes make a sputtering sound when the distributor cap is fouled, or the timing needs to be reset, despite having a muffler in good repair. In such cases, the sputtering sound is caused by an atypical condition in the engine. Daly and Wilson would have us see parental love as a muffler that quiets the natural impulses to respond with physical violence to childish annoyance. In this model, child abuse results when the inhibiting effect of parental love is absent, because people will naturally respond with physical violence to others who are annoying, especially when those others are relatively incapable of fighting back. But there is an alternative model. Physical violence toward children could, instead, be the result of some atypical condition in the engine of the mind, rather than being the mind's default output in the absence of muffling by parental love. In this model, child abuse isn't caused by the *absence* of some psychological factor (inhibition of violent impulses), but is caused by the *presence* of some psychological factors that are not at all widespread in the population of (substitute) parents.

These two models present very different pictures of the etiology of child abuse, and they entail very different procedures with respect to investigating its etiology. According to Daly and Wilson's muffler model, the tendency toward child abuse is typically present in parents, but in some parents the tendency is inhibited by parental love. Given this model, if we are investigating the etiology of child abuse, our investigation would focus on discovering the causal factors responsible for the presence or absence of *the inhibition of the tendency* to abuse. The tendency to abuse itself appears as a background factor, common to both parents who abuse and parents who do not, so the presence of that tendency does not feature in an investigation into what causes one parent to abuse while another does not. The guiding question in this investigation would be, Why is one parent's tendency to abuse inhibited while another parent's tendency is not inhibited? According to the "atypical condition" model, however, the tendency toward child abuse is not typically present in parents, but only makes its appearance in a small percentage of them. Given this model, if we are investigating the etiology of child abuse, our investigation would focus on discovering the causal factors responsible for *the presence of the tendency* to abuse. Rather than appearing as a background condition in our causal investigation into why one parent abuses when another does not, the presence of the tendency to abuse becomes the very thing whose causal origin we seek to understand. The guiding question in this investigation would be, Why does one parent have a tendency to abuse while another parent does not?

Daly and Wilson offer no direct evidence for their muffler model of parental psychology and no evidence against any alternative model (such as the "atypical condition" model). And it's difficult to see how the evidence concerning stepparental abuse that we've considered in this chapter supports their muffler model. For, presumably, the overwhelming majority of stepparents will not have had the early parenting experiences with their stepchildren that Daly and Wilson claim are necessary to activate in them the inhibition of the alleged tendency toward abuse. If child abuse really does result from a failure to establish the individualized love for a child that serves to inhibit physical violence toward it, then child abuse should occur with fairly high frequency among the class of parents that Daly and Wilson claim lack genuine parental love. But, just slightly more than 1 percent of all children who live with a stepparent, and only 1.4 percent of children aged four and younger who live with a stepparent, are reportedly victims of abuse (table 7.5). Further, if we look at perpetrators of abuse in the NIS-3 data, rather than household composition, only 0.6 percent of all children living with a stepparent are abused by the stepparent acting alone, and only 0.3 percent are abused by the stepparent acting in concert with the genetic parent in the home. Even if Daly and Wilson could provide convincing evidence that this rate is substantially higher than the rate of abuse by genetic parents, the low rate of abuse by stepparents, in itself, does not sit well with Daly and Wilson's muffler model of the psychology of child abuse. Thus, there is no reason to accept Daly and Wilson's muffler model. Contrary to their claims, then, their research on stepparental abuse doesn't really illuminate the *psychological mechanisms* of parental care and child maltreatment, evolved or otherwise.

Daly and Wilson's muffler model of the psychology of child maltreatment works together with their theory of parental attachment, as we saw earlier in this chapter. According to their theory of parental attachment, a very brief initial assessment phase is followed by the establishment of an individualized love in infancy, which is then followed by a long-term, gradual deepening of the individualized love. Much child abuse purportedly results from a failure to establish individualized love in infancy, since that love is what subsequently serves to inhibit the use of violence in dealing with a child. Indeed, according to Daly and Wilson's theory, since children under the age of one only rarely acquire stepparents, one of the reasons why children are at higher risk of abuse by stepparents may be the fact that stepparents miss the "critical period" of parenting during which individualized love gets established. And, once that critical period is missed, it is much more difficult to establish individualized love for a child. Since most adoptions, in contrast, occur in infancy, Daly and Wilson have suggested that the adoptive relationship more frequently simulates "a natural family experience," in which individualized love for the child gets established in infancy, with the result that maltreatment rates are comparatively low in adoptive households.[76]

If "a natural family experience" can be simulated between unrelated adoptive parents and adopted child, provided that the adoption occurs early enough to activate the mechanisms that establish individualized love, it should also be possible to simulate it in stepfamilies, provided that the stepfamily is formed early enough in the child's life. As a result, infant stepchildren should be more likely to trigger individualized love in their stepparents than children who are older when the stepfamilies are formed. Thus, given Daly and Wilson's theory of parental attachment, children who begin living with their stepparents as infants should be less likely to be abused by their stepparents than children who don't start living with stepparents until they are past the age at which the parental mind is designed to form an individualized love for a child. In other words, the rates of abuse by stepparents should increase with an increase in the ages at which stepchildren begin to live with their stepparents.

But, if we look at all stepfamilies in the United States in 1993, and we consider only abuse perpetrated by a stepparent in those families, we find that children under the age of one were abused by stepparents at a rate of 16.9 children per thousand, children aged one and two were abused by stepparents at a rate of 11.1 children per thousand, and children aged three and four were abused by stepparents at the rate of 6.5 children per thousand. There is, thus, a steady *decline* in the rate of stepparental abuse of preschoolers as the child's age increases. Children under the age of one were more likely to be abused even than children aged eleven to seventeen. For stepchildren aged five to ten were abused by stepparents at a rate of 7 children per thousand, while stepchildren aged eleven to seventeen were abused by stepparents at a rate of 4.9 children per thousand. Thus, the group of stepchildren who should be most likely to activate the mechanisms of individualized love in their stepparents, and hence should be least likely to be abused if Daly and Wilson's theory of parental attachment is right, are in fact the most likely to be abused at the hands of a stepparent.

Of course, one problem with these data is that they provide only the age of the stepchild *at the time of abuse,* not the age of the stepchild at the time the child began to live with the stepparent. Some of the stepchildren in the one-to-two age group, for example, undoubtedly began living with their stepparents when they were under the age of one. And, according to the prediction we're considering, children who begin living with their stepparents when they are less than a year old will have triggered in their stepparents the establishment of an individualized love for them; this individualized love will have deepened as the children grew older, thereby decreasing the risk that those children would become victims of stepparental abuse at the ages of one or two. So these data don't truly provide an adequate test of the implication of Daly and Wilson's theory that we're examining. And there are, unfortunately, no data that allow us to calculate rates of abuse by stepparents broken down by the ages of stepchildren at the time they began living with their stepparents. But the numbers of children in the older preschooler age groups who began living with their stepparents in infancy can't possibly be large enough to affect the *pattern* in the rates of abuse by stepparents—although those numbers could be large enough to affect the actual rates, if we could distinguish them from the numbers of stepchildren who began living with their stepparents after the age of one.

To see why, consider the fact that in the United States in 1993 there were approximately 26,000 children less than one year old living with a stepparent. Obviously, these children were under the age of one when they began living with a stepparent, so the rate of stepparental abuse of children under the age of one given above is probably fairly accurate for the group of stepchildren who began living with their stepparents when they were under the age of one. In addition, there were approximately 128,000 children aged one or two living with a stepparent. If we assume that the number of infants entering stepfamilies was relatively constant over the couple of years before 1993, approximately 26,000 of these 128,000 children began living in their stepfamilies as infants, so approximately 102,000 children began living with stepparents at the age of one or two. Thus, approximately 80 percent of the stepchildren aged one and two in the above abuse statistics actually began living with their stepparents at the age of one or two. Since this 80 percent will have missed the "critical period" for their stepparents to establish individualized love for them, they should be at greater risk than the 20 percent who began living with their stepparents when they were under the age of one. So, the number of children who began living with their stepparents as infants can't possibly account for the lowered risk to stepchildren aged one and two. Similar reasoning would show that the number of stepchildren aged three and four who began living with their stepparents as infants can't possibly account for the further reduction in risk to stepchildren of that age group.

Of course, the fact that the risk of abuse by a stepparent declines with increasing age of stepchildren does conform to Daly and Wilson's claim that parental love gradually deepens over time. But, parental love is supposed to gradually deepen over time only if it was established in the first place. The problem with stepfamilies, according to Daly and Wilson, is that they typically form when stepchildren are beyond the age at which the parental mind is designed to form an individualized love for a child. Since the vast majority of stepchildren do not begin living with their stepparents in infancy, the purported gradual deepening of parental love over time can't account for the declining risk of stepparental abuse as stepchildren get older. If anything, Daly and Wilson's theory entails that stepchildren who begin living with their stepparents when they are older, but still young enough to be relatively defenseless, should be at greater risk than stepchildren who have the opportunity to trigger the mechanisms of individualized parental love in their stepparents. Yet, as we have just seen, the data show just the opposite pattern.

At this point you might be wondering how my arguments in this section can appeal to precisely the data (drawn from official case reports of child abuse) that I argued in the last section are unreliable. It's true that there is evidence that official case reports of child abuse severely underreport the number of cases of child abuse. But the evidence also showed that abuse by genetic parents is more likely to go unreported than abuse by stepparents. So, of the abuse rates derived from official case reports, the rates of stepparental abuse are the least likely to be affected by any diagnostic bias that results in the underreporting of child abuse. The rates of abuse by genetic parents are the most likely to be affected by underreporting—in a way that underestimates the true rates—and that is what renders suspect a *comparison* of the rates of genetic-parental abuse with the rates of stepparental abuse. Taken in themselves, however, the rates of stepparental abuse derived from NIS-3 are probably the most reliable of all the rates derived from it.

The data regarding patterns of stepparental abuse, then, don't conform to predictions derived from Daly and Wilson's theory of parental attachment. For, if their theory were right, the youngest stepchildren should be the most likely to trigger an attachment in their stepparents (in the way that adopted infants do), and hence they should be the least likely to be victims of stepparental abuse. But the youngest stepchildren are, in fact, the most likely to be abused by stepparents. Not only is there no evidence for their muffler model of child maltreatment, then, but the evidence regarding stepparental abuse is difficult to reconcile with their three-stage theory of parental attachment. Thus, even if there were convincing evidence in support of their "most obvious prediction," Daly and Wilson still would have not succeeded in providing any good evidence for their theory of the psychological mechanisms underlying parental care and child maltreatment. Despite all the fascinating and provocative research, Daly and Wilson have brought us no closer to understanding either the mechanisms underlying the development of parental love for a child or the mechanisms that produce sometimes fatal maltreatment of a child.

The last five chapters critically examined a number of the specific claims Evolutionary Psychologists make about the evolution and nature of human psychology. In this final chapter, I will move away from examination of specific claims about human psychology in order to engage some broader theoretical issues related to Evolutionary Psychology's advertisement that it is "the new science of human nature."

Some of the theoretical issues examined in this chapter are absolutely central to Evolutionary Psychology's claim that there is a universal human nature. That is, the very idea of a universal human nature stands or falls with some of the theoretical arguments considered here. Other theoretical issues engaged in this chapter are more properly "philosophical," since they concern the broader conceptual framework in which the idea of a universal human nature is situated and interpreted. While these issues may be less central to Evolutionary Psychology's narrowly focused *scientific project* of discovering universal psychological adaptations and understanding how they function, they are nonetheless significant. For, in developing and promoting their account of human nature, Evolutionary Psychologists have often endorsed positions on broader philosophical issues, and the positions they've endorsed form part of a widely held, "commonsense" understanding of the idea of human nature. Consequently, it is important to understand both why their philosophical positions are wrong and how those positions help motivate the quest for human nature.

Throughout the discussion of these various theoretical issues, I will be focused on a single theme—that the idea of a universal human nature is deeply antithetical to a truly evolutionary view of our species. Indeed, I will argue, a truly *evolutionary* psychology should abandon the quest for human nature and with it any attempt to discover universal laws of human psychology. As the evolutionary biologist Michael Ghiselin so pithily puts it: "What does evolution teach us about human nature? It tells us that human nature is a superstition."[1] In other words, the idea of human nature is an idea whose time has gone.

## Human Nature: The Very Idea

Let's begin by examining what it *means* to talk of human nature. One possibility is that the concept of human nature could refer to the totality of human behavior and psychology. In this broad sense, human nature would simply be whatever humans happen to do, think, or feel, regardless of whether different humans do, think, or feel differently. If one person is violent, violence is part of human nature, even if another person is not violent. If one person is kind, kindness is part of human nature, despite another person's inveterate unkindness, which is also part of human nature. In this very broad sense, the concept of human nature has no particular *theoretical* meaning; it is merely an abbreviated way of talking about the rich tapestry of human existence. And, if this is what one means by human nature, no one can quibble about the existence of human nature, since the mere existence of humans guarantees the existence of human nature.

But, traditionally, the concept of human nature has never meant simply *whatever* people happen to do, think, or feel. Regardless of the details of the theory of human nature in which it featured, the concept of human nature has traditionally referred to *some* of the things that people do but not to others, to *some* of the things that people think and feel but not to others. Theories of human nature have differed over precisely which aspects of human behavior and psychology constitute human nature, but they have all used the concept of human nature to pick out only a small part of everything about humanity that meets the eye. That is, regardless of the theory of human nature in which it featured, the concept of human nature has traditionally designated only a proper subset of human behavior and mentation, which was claimed to belong to human beings *by their nature* as opposed to behavior and mentation that was claimed not to be owing to or in accordance with that nature. And there are three noteworthy features of this traditional concept of human nature.

First, the concept of human nature has always refered to what is distinctively human about us, to what distinguishes humans from the other animals on the planet. This aspect of its meaning put the *human* in the concept of human nature, and it is what David Buss alludes to when he writes that "humans also have a nature—*qualities that define us as a unique species.*"[2]

Second, the concept of human nature has typically referred only to *biologically based* behavioral or psychological characteristics of human beings. This aspect of its meaning put the *nature* in the concept of human nature, and human *nature* has always been contrasted with human *culture*. As the philosopher Peter Loptson puts it, the characteristics that constitute human nature form a "single unitary nature that humans have, common and generic to all societies they have formed."[3] These characteristics thus form "a fixed unchangeable nature or 'essence' that human beings have," which "is independent of culture."[4] Accordingly, the characteristics that constitute human nature are a consequence solely of our biological properties, whereas characteristics that result from "socialization" in one's culture are not part of human nature. Eating is part of human nature, since it is a biological function, but using a fork to eat is not part of human nature, since fork users are so only by virtue of having been socialized in fork-using cultures. Thus, in accordance with the traditional concept of human nature, culture has been viewed as an "unnatural" imposition that typically transforms, represses, or corrupts what is biologically "natural" for humans.

Third, the biologically grounded characteristics constitutive of human nature have traditionally been assumed to be *universal* among humans. As the philosopher Roger Trigg expresses it: "The concept [of human nature] has implications, particularly that we can assume similarities merely on the basis of membership of one biological species. We will then all have some tendencies, and some likes and dislikes, in common simply because of our common humanity."[5]

In sum, then, regardless of the particular theory of human nature in which it featured, the concept of human nature has traditionally designated biologically based, as opposed to culturally instilled, behavioral and psychological characteristics that are presumed to be universal among, and distinctive to, human beings. Because of this, traditional arguments that there is no human nature have tended to emphasize culture over "nature," to argue that humans are what they are principally because of their cultural socialization and that there is no human "nature" that strongly channels or constrains socialization.

Evolutionary Psychology's conception of human nature is but a minor variation on the traditional concept. Evolutionary Psychologists are clearly committed to the idea that human nature consists of psychological characteristics that are universal among humans. Tooby and Cosmides frequently speak of "the psychological universals that constitute human nature,"[6] and they claim that "theories of human nature make claims about a universal human psychology."[7] Further, Evolutionary Psychologists claim that the psychological universals constitutive of human nature evolved during our lineage's stint as hunter-gatherers, which was well after our lineage diverged from that of our nearest relatives, the chimpanzees. Consequently, our putative psychological universals are supposed to have evolved during hominid history; and, since we are the only surviving hominid species, these putative universals are unique to us and serve to distinguish us from other species. This is why Buss refers to the psychological universals that constitute human nature as the "qualities that define us as a unique species."

However, the contrast between nature and culture that provides the traditional concept of human nature with some of its meaning, and that provides the basis for the traditional arguments that there is no human nature, isn't part of Evolutionary Psychology's conception of human nature. There are two primary reasons for this. First, as we will see in greater detail later in the chapter, Evolutionary Psychologists contend that much of the content in human cultures across the globe is determined by universal psychological characteristics of humans. Evolutionary Psychologists argue that the cultural universality of marriage, for example, is the result of psychological universals that impel people to seek out and remain in long-term reproductive unions. If aspects of culture are determined by universals of human psychology in this way, and if psychological universals constitute human nature, then at least some aspects of culture are manifestations of human nature, rather than "unnatural" external constraints or impositions upon human nature.

Second, from a broad evolutionary standpoint, human culture as a whole is not opposed to human biology, but is part of it. From this standpoint, the practices that constitute human cultures differ only in degree of complexity, not in kind, from the web-spinning habits of spiders. For evolutionary biology is concerned to explain the emergence and characteristics of the various forms of life on our planet, and everything that we humans do we do as the living creatures that evolutionary biology studies. Whatever their potentially detrimental consequences, nuclear power plants differ only in degree of complexity, and degree of manipulation of nature, from beaver dams. And just as beaver dams are unproblematically a consequence of beaver biology, nuclear power plants are a consequence of ours. Within everything that is part of human biology, however, distinctions can be drawn between aspects of human life that are genetically transmitted across generations and aspects of human life that are transmitted in other ways, just as we can draw a *biological distinction* between genotype and phenotype. Accordingly, the biologist John Bonner defines *culture* as "the transfer of information by behavioral means, most particularly the process of teaching and learning," which he distinguishes from "the transmission of genetic information passed by the direct inheritance of genes from one generation to the next."[8] In this sense, culture is present in a vast array of species, and its evolution predated the emergence of modern humans. Thus, *culture is a biological phenomenon*, in the very broadest sense of the word *biology*, despite not being a genetically determined or genetically transmitted phenomenon. Consequently, the traditional arguments that there is no human nature, because humans are what they are due to cultural socialization rather than biology, rest upon a false dichotomy.

Although Evolutionary Psychology's conception of human nature doesn't involve the traditional dichotomy between human biology (nature) and human culture, it is highly dependent on a dichotomy between different biological characteristics of humans. As Tooby and Cosmides say, "the concept of a universal human nature," as employed in Evolutionary Psychology, is "based on a species-typical collection of complex *psychological adaptations*."[9] Evolutionary Psychology's conception of human nature is thus restricted to universal *adaptations*, which constitute only a proper subset of the biological characteristics to which the traditional concept of human nature has applied. If there are universal psychological characteristics that evolved under genetic drift, for example, these would not count as part of human nature for Evolutionary Psychologists, although they would for traditional theories that include in human nature all universal biological traits. Consequently, the contrast between nature and culture that is part of the meaning of the traditional concept of human nature is replaced within Evolutionary Psychology's conception of human nature by the contrast between traits that are universal adaptations and traits that aren't. In sum, then, according to Evolutionary Psychologists, human nature consists of a set of psychological adaptations that are presumed to be universal among, and unique to, human beings.

In the remainder of this chapter, I will argue that Evolutionary Psychology's theory of human nature is multiply problematic. For the most part, these problems are shared by the traditional concept of human nature. So, while my arguments will be directed at Evolutionary Psychology, they will apply in most instances to the traditional concept of human nature as well. For Evolutionary Psychology and the traditional concept of human nature share the idea that human nature consists of universal biological characteristics that "define us as a unique species." *In this sense*, I will argue, there simply is no such thing as human nature. But, since the dichotomy between nature and culture is a false one, I will not be arguing that Evolutionary Psychology's theory of human nature is wrong because it mistakenly emphasizes biology over culture. Rather, I will argue that the idea that there are universal biological characteristics that "define us as a unique species" simply *gets biology wrong* in a number of important ways. To begin exploring these arguments, let's return to Evolutionary Psychology's reasons for claiming that there is a universal human nature.

As we saw in chapter 2, Evolutionary Psychologists offer two arguments for the existence of a universal human nature. One of these I called "the argument from sexual recombination," which contends that the genetics of adaptation necessitates the species universality of all complex adaptations. In chapter 3 I demonstrated a variety of problems with this argument, and I showed how selection can, and frequently does, maintain polymorphisms of complex adaptations within populations. Contrary to the argument from sexual recombination, there is nothing in the nature of adaptation, or of the evolutionary process more generally, that necessitates a universal human nature as Evolutionary Psychologists conceive it. In other words, there are a variety of adaptational and genetic "natures" in human populations. But, while Evolutionary Psychologists typically take the argument from sexual recombination to be a definitive theoretical proof of the existence of a universal human nature, I don't think that that argument accounts for the intuitive pull that the idea of a universal human nature has enjoyed among Evolutionary Psychologists and their followers. That intuitive pull, I believe, is primarily due to another argument that Tooby and Cosmides offer, which I called in chapter 2 "the argument from *Gray's Anatomy*." The argument from *Gray's Anatomy* is largely an appeal to common sense, and it thereby garners tremendous intuitive credibility for Evolutionary Psychology's claim that there is a universal human nature, since it makes the denial of that claim seem quite literally incredible.

The argument from *Gray's Anatomy* is compellingly simple, though not, I will argue, simply compelling. Tooby and Cosmides put it as follows: "the fact that any given page out of *Gray's Anatomy* describes in precise anatomical detail individual humans from around the world demonstrates the pronounced monomorphism present in complex human physiological adaptations. Although we cannot yet directly 'see' psychological adaptations (except as described neuroanatomically), no less could be true of them."[10] Selection, in other words, has designed a universal human anatomy and physiology. As Tooby and Cosmides say, humans have a "universal architecture," in the sense that "everyone has two eyes, two hands, the same set of organs, and so on."[11] Since selection has presumably designed our minds as well as our bodies, the argument goes, we should expect selection to have designed a system of psychological adaptations that is just as universal as the anatomical and physiological adaptations described in *Gray's Anatomy*. Indeed, Tooby and Cosmides boldly claim that, "just as one can now flip open *Gray's Anatomy* to any page and find an intricately detailed depiction of some part of our evolved species-typical morphology, we anticipate that in 50 or 100 years one will be able to pick up an equivalent reference work for psychology and find in it detailed information-processing descriptions of the multitude of evolved species-typical adaptations of the human mind."[12]

Despite its intuitive pull, however, the argument from *Gray's Anatomy* is multiply problematic, and it provides no reason to believe that there will ever be a reference work for psychology containing detailed descriptions of universal and species-typical psychological adaptations. I will discuss just five problems with the argument from *Gray's Anatomy*.

First, the argument relies on a questionable analogy between anatomy and psychology. Even if selection has designed a universal human anatomy, that fact alone doesn't justify the inference that selection has designed a universal human psychology. The features of the environment to which aspects of our anatomy have adapted are, for the most part, relatively stable and relatively simple. For example, the composition of the air, to which our lungs are adapted and whose contents they process, has been relatively stable throughout our evolutionary history. Recent problems with air pollution have precipitated changes in the chemical composition of the air we breathe, but our lungs still process the core chemicals in our air to which they are adapted. In contrast, the human mind has evolved to be responsive to rapidly changing environmental conditions. So the selection pressures that drove psychological evolution differ from those that drove anatomical evolution. Further, as we saw in chapter 3, the selection pressures that drove most of the evolution of human intelligence stemmed primarily from human social life, rather than from the physical environment. But social life doesn't present a uniform condition to which a trait must adapt, in the way that the air presented a relatively uniform condition to which lungs had to adapt. Instead, human social life is characterized by behavioral variation. As a result, the fittest response to the complexities of human social life depends on the behavioral strategies of other humans in the population. This creates frequency-dependent selection, which can result in the evolution of adaptive psychological differences between individuals. Thus, there are reasons why minds could exhibit adaptive differences when and where bodies don't. So, even if there is a universal human anatomy, it doesn't follow that there must be a universal human psychology.

Second, the argument from *Gray's Anatomy* appeals to similarities among people at a relatively coarse scale. But, as the evolutionary biologist David Sloan Wilson points out, "uniformity at the coarsest scale does not imply uniformity at finer scales."[13] Every human may have a brain with two hemispheres, a cortex, an occipital lobe, and so on, just as "everyone has two eyes, two hands, the same set of organs, and so on." But the uniformity at this scale doesn't entail uniformity with respect to psychological mechanisms at a more micro level. Since Evolutionary Psychologists claim that our universal psychological adaptations are modules, which are highly specialized "minicomputers," the universal psychological adaptations they postulate are actually much smaller-scale brain mechanisms than the anatomical structures in the brain that are possessed by most humans. Thus, in order to demonstrate that there are universal psychological adaptations, Evolutionary Psychologists would need to demonstrate psychological uniformity at a much finer scale than that addressed by the argument from *Gray's Anatomy*.

Third, the "coarsest scale" to which the argument from *Gray's Anatomy* appeals is incommensurate with Evolutionary Psychologists' understanding of human nature as constituted by "qualities that define us as a unique species." For the universals appealed to in these arguments typify the whole primate order and sometimes the whole class of mammals and even all vertebrates. For example, all primates have two hands, all mammals have lungs, and all vertebrates have two eyes, a heart, a liver, and a stomach. So the analogical appeal to the coarsest scale of uniformity within our species ("everyone has two eyes, two hands, the same set of organs, and so on") supports no conclusions about universal psychological adaptations that "define us as a unique species," since uniquely human adaptations would have had to evolve during human evolutionary history. Hence, the appeal to very coarse-scale common characteristics supports no conclusion about distinctively *human* universals.

The fourth problem, related to the third, is that the basic structural plan that typifies the "universal architecture" of our species—and that, at ever coarser scales of description, typifies the body plan of our order (primate), class (mammal), and subphylum (vertebrate)—consists primarily of features that have *persisted* down lineages and through speciations for tens to hundreds of millions of years. Although selection probably played a role in designing the basic body plan that now characterizes humans, it did not design that structural plan during human history, but rather during the history of the common ancestor of humans and other primates, mammals, or vertebrates. Consequently, even though all humans may have two eyes, two hands, one nose, and a mouth, it doesn't follow that similarly universal adaptations emerged during comparatively recent human evolutionary history.

Finally, strictly speaking, there is no single human anatomy and physiology possessed by all humans around the world of which *Gray's Anatomy* provides a "detailed" and "precise" description. Approximately 0.25 percent of all humans are born with only one kidney, rather than two, yet nonetheless live reasonably healthy lives. Others are born with three kidneys, yet still live healthy lives (although there are no solid estimates of the incidence of this phenomenon). In addition, somewhere between "one in every 8,000 to 25,000 people is born with a condition known as situs inversus, in which the positions of all the internal organs are reversed relative to the normal situation (situs solitus): the person's heart and stomach lie to the right, their liver to the left, and so on. (The organs are also mirror images of their normal structures.)"[14] There is no more precise estimate of the incidence of situs inversus because it creates no medical complications, so it is typically discovered only incidentally to routine physical examination (if sought) or medical treatment for some other condition. At the physiological level, there are four main blood types in humans (A, B, AB, and O), which are genetically coded for at a single locus. If we move from the four blood types coded for at that one locus to examine broader categories of blood type, there are more than twenty additional blood types in humans. And, moving to the outside of the body, approximately one in every fifteen hundred infants is born with ambiguous genitalia, which do not allow the assignment of a sex. Thus, the idea that *Gray's Anatomy* provides *a single* "detailed" and "precise" picture of the anatomy and physiology of every human on earth is plausible only if one ignores known facts about human anatomical and physiological variation. Although most of us are pretty much the same in a lot of "coarse" details, we are not all cast from the same anatomical and physiological mold, so there is no reason to think that there is a single psychological mold from which we are all cast. Despite its intuitive appeal, the argument from *Gray's Anatomy* provides no good reason to believe in the existence of a universal human nature.

### Essentialism, Part I: "Normal" People

Of course, there is an obvious rejoinder to this last argument. No Evolutionary Psychologist really believes that literally all human beings on earth have precisely the same anatomy or that every single human being on earth possesses all of the characteristics that constitute human nature. Rather, as Cosmides and Tooby say, "a scientific definition of *human nature*" concerns "the uniform architecture of the human mind and brain that reliably develops in *every normal human* just as do eyes, fingers, arms, a heart, and so on."[15] So, *of course* there are some human beings born with only one or with three kidneys, just as some human beings are born without arms. And *of course* there are some human beings born with their organs reversed, just as some human beings are born with three copies of the twenty-first chromosome (which results in Down syndrome). But such individuals are "abnormal," either because of an unusual genetic condition or because of exposure to some "environmental insult" during development. And the concept of an anatomical universal architecture, like the concept of universal human nature, is not intended to apply to cases of developmental "abnormality." Such concepts are intended, rather, to capture only what *all normal human beings* have in common. Thus, the obvious rejoinder goes, pointing out that some human beings depart from the "universal architecture" described in *Gray's Anatomy* doesn't constitute a valid objection to the argument from *Gray's Anatomy*, since that argument presupposes only that *Gray's Anatomy* provides a "precise" and "detailed" description of the anatomy of all *normal* human beings.

It should be clear at this point that any reasonable claim that there exists a universal human nature must be committed to some distinction between normality and abnormality. For, strictly speaking, there are *no* characteristics that are universally distributed among all and only human beings. So any claim about universality must refer only to characteristics that are universally distributed among "normal" humans, rather than characteristics that are distributed among all humans, and the "abnormal" must be conceived as not partaking of human nature. Accordingly, people who don't possess the characteristics definitive of some theory's concept of a universal human nature don't actually constitute counterexamples to the claim that there is a universal human nature, because those who are "abnormal" simply don't count.

This distinction between normality and abnormality, on which all claims regarding a universal human nature must depend, is part and parcel of a doctrine known as *essentialism*. In general, essentialism is a view about what makes *distinct individual entities* of the same kind into distinct individual entities *of the same kind*. Essentialism is the view that there are certain characteristics that *define* a kind, so that two different entities belong to the same kind just in case they both possess the characteristics definitive of that kind. For example, two objects are both samples of the kind *platinum* just in case both of those objects are composed of atoms with atomic number 78. Having atomic number 78 is the characteristic that defines the kind *platinum;* it is the *essence* of platinum. Consequently, any two entities with atomic number 78 are instances of platinum, regardless of whatever other properties (size, shape, or overall weight) they may have. Kinds, such as platinum, that are defined by essential characteristics, which any object must possess to be a member of that kind, are known as *natural kinds*.

While essentialism is comfortably at home in the table of elements, it has also been applied to biological classification at least since the time of Aristotle. Within biological classification, essentialism becomes the view that species are natural kinds. Accordingly, species are defined by characteristics that serve to differentiate them from all other species, and those characteristics are taken to constitute the essence of a species. An organism belongs to a particular species, then, by virtue of possessing the characteristics definitive of that species. But the philosopher of biology Elliott Sober points out that essentialism regarding species typically involves more than the minimal claim that species are defined by sets of unique characteristics. According to Sober, a species' essence does not simply constitute a condition that is necessary and sufficient for membership in that species, but plays an explanatory role as well. As Sober says: "The essentialist hypothesizes that there exists some characteristic unique to and shared by all members of *Homo sapiens* which *explains why they are the way they are.* A species essence will be a causal mechanism that acts on each member of the species, making it the kind of thing that it is."[16]

That Evolutionary Psychology is committed to essentialism regarding species, and that its essentialism underlies its conception of human nature, is often explicit when Evolutionary Psychologists wax theoretical about *Homo sapiens* and human nature. The passage quoted earlier from Buss, in which he speaks of human nature as consisting of "qualities that *define us as a unique species,*" is clearly committed to essentialism regarding species. From the opposite side of the same viewpoint, Cosmides and Tooby write:

"By virtue of being members of the human species, all humans are expected to have the same adaptive mechanisms."[17] In other words, membership in the same species entails the shared possession of the essential characteristics definitive of the species. Elsewhere, in a clear expression of the essentialist view that species are natural kinds, Cosmides and Tooby say, "the species-typical genetic endowments of species, and the common ancestry of larger taxa do cause an indefinitely large set of similarities to be shared among members of a natural kind, as does a common chemical structure for different instances of a substance."[18] Finally, tying essentialism directly to the concept of human nature, the Evolutionary Psychologist Donald Brown writes: "Universals of essence at the level of the individual collectively constitute human nature."[19]

But how can essentialism regarding species be reconciled with the existence of organisms that appear to belong to *Homo sapiens* even though they don't possess all of the "qualities that define us as a unique species"? If species are natural kinds, so that an organism is a member of a species if and only if it possesses the characteristics essential to that species, and if some people don't actually possess all the characteristics that define human nature, which is the essence of *Homo sapiens*, aren't those people not actually human beings? Isn't essentialism committed to claiming that people who lack a characteristic essential to the human species simply aren't human? And, if so, how can essentialism integrally involve a distinction between "normal" and "abnormal" human beings? Aren't "abnormal" humans not actually human, so that, strictly speaking, there is no such thing as an "abnormal" human?

Throughout the history of essentialism there has been a tension between essentialism regarding species and apparent variation within species. The usual way of resolving this tension is to conceive of a species' essence as a *causal mechanism* that produces the phenotypic characteristics considered definitive of membership in that species. This involves what Sober calls the "Natural State Model." According to the Natural State Model, "there is a distinction between the *natural state* of a kind of object and those states which are not natural. These latter are produced by subjecting the object to an *interfering force*. . . . The cause for this divergence from what is natural is that these objects are acted on by interfering forces that prevent them from achieving their natural state by frustrating their natural tendency. Variability within nature is thus to be explained as a deviation from what is natural."[20] When applied within biology, the Natural State Model entails that "there is one path of foetal development which counts as the realization of the organism's natural state, while other developmental results are consequences of unnatural interferences."[21] The Natural State Model consequently explains variation in a species as a result of causal interactions between an essential developmental mechanism and potentially interfering forces.

The distinction between "normal" and "abnormal" characteristics of members of a species derives from the Natural State Model. For, according to the Natural State Model, each member of a species possesses the causal mechanism that produces that species' essential characteristics. When not interfered with, the causal essence of a species thus produces normal members of that species. But various factors can prevent the causal mechanism from producing its normal results, and when it is prevented from doing so it results in species members with abnormal characteristics. Thus, according to this version of essentialism, abnormal humans are still human, since despite their abnormal phenotypes they still possess the developmental mechanism considered essential to humans.

Evolutionary Psychology's essentialism, and hence its conception of human nature, is clearly committed to the Natural State Model. As mentioned in chapter 2, although Evolutionary Psychologists typically identify human nature with a cluster of psychological (phenotypic) adaptations, in a more guarded moment Tooby and Cosmides indicate that their concept of a "universal human nature" is intended to apply primarily at the developmental level and only secondarily at the phenotypic level:

when we use terms such as "evolved design," "evolved architecture," or even "species-typical," "species-standard," "universal," and "panhuman," we are not making claims about every human phenotype all or even some of the time; instead, we are referring to the existence of evolutionarily organized developmental adaptations, whether they are activated or latent. Adaptations are not necessarily expressed in every individual. . . . For this reason, adaptations and adaptive architecture can be discussed and described at (at least) two levels: (1) the level of reliably achieved and expressed organization (as, for example, in the realized structure of the eye), and (2) at the level of the developmental programs that construct such organization.[22]

Thus, universal developmental programs are the causal mechanism that produces "the species-standard physiological and psychological architecture visible in all humans raised in normal environments."[23]

In addition, the more guarded identification of "universal human nature" with "universal developmental programs" underlies Evolutionary Psychologists' commitment to the idea that some aspects of human nature are sexually dimorphic and age differentiated. For, as we saw in chapter 2, Evolutionary Psychologists argue that the sexes have faced different selection pressures, which designed some adaptive morphological and psychological sex differences, and that differences in selection pressures faced across the life cycle created age-differentiated adaptive "coordinated design differences." These adaptive sex and age differences, however, result from universal developmental adaptations, which are programmed to produce sex-specific adaptations in response to the presence or absence of the *SRY* gene and to bring age-specific adaptations "on line" and take them "off line" at appropriate ages.

Despite the existence of adaptive age and sex differences, Evolutionary Psychologists are nonetheless committed to the idea that there are certain things that all humans share. First, all humans share the "universal developmental programs" that produce programmed sex and age differences. And, second, these universal developmental programs produce some morphological and psychological characteristics that are not sex or age differentiated. The latter constitute "the species-standard physiological and psychological architecture visible in all humans raised in normal environments." This "architecture" is "normal," or the "natural state" for humans, and departure from that natural state is presumed to be caused by forces— for example, genetic mutation or "environmental insult"—that interfere with developmental programs and thereby produce "abnormalities." Similarly, there are male and female "architectures" that are "normal," or the "natural state," for human males and human females, and departures from those natural states are caused by interference with universal developmental programs. Consequently, departures from human nature (or male nature or female nature) at the phenotypic level are due to causal interaction between "interfering forces" and a universal human nature at the level of developmental mechanisms.

There are, however, several problems with Evolutionary Psychology's essentialism. There are problems with the Natural State Model, on which the distinction between "normal" and "abnormal" phenotypes depends, and there are problems with essentialism regarding species more generally. These problems don't so much show that the Natural State Model and essentialism can't possibly be right, but they point up that both are inconsistent with contemporary theory and practice within biology. In other words, the Natural State Model and essentialism can't be founded in contemporary evolutionary biology; there is simply nothing evolutionary about them. And any psychological theory that claims to be *evolutionary* must trade in theoretical constructs that can be founded in evolutionary biology. Further, as we will see in the next section, when essentialism regarding species is abandoned, the prospects for the kind of "science of the mind" that Evolutionary Psychology envisions providing disappear with it. In the remainder of this section, let's examine the problems with the Natural State Model.

As we have seen, according to the Natural State Model there is one path of development that results in the "normal" or "natural" state for the organism, and other paths of development are the result of "interfering forces." "Put slightly differently," as Sober says, "for a given genotype, there is a single phenotype which it can have that is the natural one. Or, more modestly, the requirement might be that there is some restricted range of phenotypes which count as natural."[24] The problem with this view is that there is no basis in genetics for the idea that a genotype is associated with a phenotype that is "natural" for it to produce. As Sober says, "when one looks to genetic theory for a conception of the relation between genotype and phenotype, one finds no such distinction between natural state and states which are the results of interference. One finds, instead, the *norm of reaction*, which graphs the different phenotypic results that a genotype can have in different environments."[25] For example, the norm of reaction for a particular genetic strain of corn would be a graph showing the different heights that corn of that genotype would have in each of a range of environments, where the different environments could be characterized by differences in amount of rainfall and sunlight. That is, the norm of reaction would be a graphed function showing that corn with genotype $G_1$ has height phenotype $P_1$ in environment $E_1$, phenotype $P_2$ in environment $E_2$, phenotype $P_3$ in environment $E_3$, and so on. But nothing in the norm of reaction would identify any particular height as "natural" for corn of that genotype. There are simply different heights that corn of that genotype can have under a range of different environmental conditions.

Of course, there may be a phenotype that is the *statistically most frequent* phenotype produced by a particular genotype. And it makes perfect sense to speak of that statistically most frequent phenotype as the "normal" phenotype for that genotype—as long as we bear in mind that by "normal" we mean only what is statistically most frequent. But this sense of "normal" is not at all the sense that has always been intended by proponents of the Natural State Model. For, in this statistical conception of "normal," a diseased phenotype can be normal for a population. If a virus has reached epidemic proportions in a population, for example, it can be statistically normal for members of that population to be diseased. But no proponent of the Natural State Model would consider disease to be the "natural state" for members of that population, despite its frequency in the population. The Natural State Model is after a more robust notion of "normal" phenotype, one that would pick out a phenotype as normal regardless of whether that phenotype is prevalent or even represented at all in a population. But the norm of reaction, which is the geneticist's way of understanding the relation between genotype and phenotype, simply doesn't underwrite such a robust notion of "normal" or "natural" phenotype for a genotype.

Since the norm of reaction doesn't privilege any particular phenotype as "normal" or "natural," but simply identifies which phenotypes result in which environments, one way to save the Natural State Model would be to provide some independent justification for identifying one of the environments specified in the norm of reaction for a genotype as the "natural environment" for that genotype (or identifying a restricted range of environments as being "natural environments"). Derivatively, then, a "natural" phenotype for that genotype would be a phenotype that develops in a "natural environment" for that genotype.

This would be the obvious move for Evolutionary Psychologists to make, since it fits quite naturally with their overall theoretical framework. For, as Tooby and Cosmides say, "the species-standard physiological and psychological architecture" is the architecture that is "visible in all humans *raised in normal environments*."[26] And the "normal environments" are clearly those that closely resemble the environment of evolutionary adaptedness (EEA), the statistical composite of the environments in which our adaptations evolved and to which they are adapted. Indeed, in one of the earliest discussions of the EEA in the Evolutionary Psychology literature, Donald Symons refers to the environments that compose the EEA as the "natural environments" for humans, which he characterizes as "environments to which ancestral populations were exposed for sufficient lengths of time to become adapted to them."[27] Thus, Evolutionary Psychologists could argue, of all the environments specified in the norm of reaction for a genotype, those that closely resemble the EEA are the "natural environments" for that genotype. So, of all the phenotypes specified in a norm of reaction, those that develop in "natural environments" are "normal" phenotypes.

There are, however, two problems with this attempt to specify natural environments for development and, derivatively, to define "normal" phenotypes. First, the EEA is supposed to be a natural environment because that is the environment to which we are adapted, the environment for which we are "designed." But we must bear in mind precisely what talk of being "adapted to" and "designed for" an environment means. These expressions appear to describe some direct relationship between our traits (or genotypes) and the environment; but they in fact do not. For selection never "designs" traits for particular environments in isolation from competing traits. To say that a trait is "adapted to" or "designed for" a particular environment is simply shorthand for saying that the trait was *selected over alternative traits* in that environment. And that, in turn, simply means that individuals with that trait had higher average fitness in that environment than individuals with alternative traits. Thus, to say that a trait is "adapted to" or "designed for" a particular environment emphatically does *not* mean that the trait is a perfect "fit" for that environment, that the trait is the fittest of all possible traits in that environment, or that the trait has higher fitness in that environment than in any other.

If the motivation for identifying a genotype's "natural environment" with its EEA is that the EEA is the environment in which the genotype made the greatest contribution to fitness (by producing a trait that enhanced fitness), then there are undoubtedly other environments that would be better candidates for a genotype's "natural environment." For example, the EEA of a genotype is simply the environment in which that genotype had *higher fitness than available alternative genotypes* in the population. In a different environment, the genotype may have had an even greater fitness advantage over those alternatives. So why not identify the "natural environment" of a genotype with the environment in which the genotype has its highest fitness? Similarly, had a genotype competed in its EEA against a different set of alternative genotypes, one of those alternatives may have had higher fitness than the genotype that was actually selected. Why should a genotype's EEA be the "natural environment" for *that genotype* rather than for some other genotype that would have had higher fitness in that environment? Had a mutation occurred that improved the human eye so that it could see as well at night as during the day, for example, the genotype for that supereye would have been selected over the genotype for the typical human eye in the EEA of the human eye. Why should the EEA of the human eye be the "natural environment" for the human eye rather than for the supereye that would have been selected in that environment had it actually been present in our ancestral population? If a genotype's "natural environment" is defined in terms of a genotype's fitness, there are no principled grounds on which to identify as a genotype's natural environment its EEA rather than an alternative environment in which it would have higher fitness, or to identify a genotype's EEA as *its* natural environment, rather than that of an alternative genotype that would have had higher fitness in that environment. Thus, it is arbitrary to call a genotype's EEA its "natural environment."

Second, calling the EEA the "natural environment" involves defining "natural environment" in terms of *selection*, since the EEA of a trait or genotype is the environment in which it was selected over alternatives. This presumes that what is selected for is somehow more "in accordance with nature" than what is selected against or what is neither selected for nor against. But nothing in evolutionary theory justifies privileging selection in this way. Evolution is change in gene or genotype frequencies across generations in a lineage, and evolutionary theory is concerned to explain *all* such changes. Selection is just *one* of the causes of evolution. Evolution is also caused by mutation, recombination, genetic drift, and migration into and out of populations, and evolutionary theory encompasses these as well. In addition, a trait can increase in frequency because of selection, but it can also increase in frequency because of genetic drift or migration, and evolutionary theory will be there to explain all such changes. Evolutionary theory also explains why traits decrease in frequency and why they sometimes disappear from populations entirely. It also explains why entire species go extinct. All of these processes are natural, each is every bit as real as the others, and evolutionary theory is designed to explain them all, without privileging the process of selection. Thus, an environment in which a trait or genotype is selected for is no more natural than an environment in which it is selected against.

Now, it is true that selection plays a particular explanatory role within evolutionary theory. If we want to explain the process of *adaptation*, selection will be central and indispensable to that explanation. And this fact no doubt underlies Evolutionary Psychology's idea that the EEA is the "natural environment." But, again, adaptation is just one process among many in evolution, and nothing in evolutionary theory privileges the process of adaptation over other processes by considering it more natural than other processes. Similarly, nothing in evolutionary theory privileges traits that are adaptations over traits that are not by considering them a more natural part of an organism's endowment than traits that are not adaptations. We do, of course, appeal to evolutionary theory and the process of selection in order to answer the question, Why is this highly articulated and apparently well designed trait so prevalent in this population? But we also appeal to evolutionary theory to answer the question, Why do humans have an appendix when it serves no apparent function? Which kind of question we ask reflects only *our explanatory interests*. Nothing in evolutionary theory itself justifies the conviction that one question is more important than the other or that one question better reflects what is "natural." Rather, the conviction that one question is more significant than the other is a theoretical vestige of an outdated worldview, as I will argue in greater detail in the final section of this chapter.

Thus, there are no principled reasons deriving from evolutionary theory to designate certain environments in a norm of reaction as "natural environments." And this means that there are no principled reasons deriving from evolutionary theory to designate certain phenotypes in a norm of reaction as "normal" phenotypes. Our best *biological* understanding of the relation between genotype and phenotype is reflected only in the norm of reaction itself, a simple mapping of environments onto phenotypes for any given genotype. The distinction between "normal" and "abnormal" phenotypes, which is central to the Natural State Model, can't be drawn by the norm of reaction. That distinction is imposed on biological theory from a nonbiological worldview.

But the Natural State Model presupposes not only that each genotype is associated with a normal phenotype, which is the organism's natural state, but that for any locus that codes for a trait there is a normal genotype for an organism to have at that locus. That normal genotype is, of course, the genotype that produces the organism's normal phenotype, and alternate genotypes at the same locus are abnormal because they produce abnormal phenotypes. Again, however, there is nothing in genetic theory that allows for a distinction between "normal" and "abnormal" genotypes (unless, again, by "normal" one simply means the genotype that is most common in a population).

The fact is that substantial genetic variation exists in natural populations, human populations included. A genetic analysis of thirty species of mammal found that, on average, those species were genetically polymorphic—that is, more than one genotype occurred—at approximately 20 percent of their loci.[28] While this analysis didn't provide an estimate of the overall genetic polymorphism within humans, a global genetic study of human populations found that the average heterozygosity in human populations ranges from 21 percent to 37 percent.[29] That is, the average percentage of loci at which individuals in a population are heterozygous is anywhere between 21 and 37 percent of loci, depending on the population; the lowest average heterozygosity is found in New Guinea and Australia, and the highest average heterozygosity is found in the populations of the Middle East, western Asia, and southern, central, and eastern Europe. As we saw in chapter 1, heterozygote mating produces genotypic polymorphisms, even when heterozygotes mate with homozygotes. Thus, the high degree of heterozygosity in human populations sustains a prodigious amount of genetic variation in human populations. And genetic theory doesn't label some of the genetic variants "normal" and others "abnormal." From the standpoint of population genetics, there are simply a variety of genotypes that change in frequency across generations. A new mutation, which may or may not increase in frequency under selection, is no more or less normal than a statistically more frequent allele at the same locus. Any distinction between "normal" and "abnormal" genotypes must be imposed on genetic theory from a nonbiological perspective.

Therefore, the Natural State Model, on which any distinction between "normal" and "abnormal" human characteristics must rely, has no basis in biology. Nothing in biology justifies viewing certain phenotypes, but not others, as the "normal" phenotypes for a genotype, and nothing in biology justifies viewing certain genotypes, but not others, as the "normal" genotypes for humans. There is substantial variation in human populations at both the phenotypic and genetic levels, and our best biological theories to date simply do not partition that variation into "normal" and "abnormal" variants. As Sober so nicely puts it: "Our current theories of biological variation provide no more role for the idea of a natural state than our current physical theories do for the notion of absolute simultaneity."[30] To the extent that Evolutionary Psychology's theory of a universal human nature relies on the Natural State Model for a distinction between "normality" (which exemplifies human nature) and "abnormality" (which does not), its theory of human nature has no foundation in biology.

## Essentialism, Part II: Species

The problems with the Natural State Model, however, are merely symptoms of deeper problems with essentialism itself. The distinction between "normal" and "abnormal," which characterizes the Natural State Model, is necessary only if one is antecedently committed to the view that there are certain characteristics that all and only humans share. For, since the claim that there are characteristics that *literally* all and only humans share is an obvious empirical falsehood, it becomes necessary to retreat to the less robust claim that there are characteristics that all and only *normal* humans share. But, if we are not driven to formulate our understanding of species in terms of what *all and only* members of a species have in common, we don't need a category of "abnormal" to which to relegate the individuals in a species that happen to lack one or more of the characteristics we take to be essential to a species, and we then don't need a category of "normal" to contain the individuals that do happen to possess those characteristics.

It is essentialism that forces these categories on us by mandating that our understanding of species in general, and of human beings in particular, be formulated as a claim about what *all and only* certain organisms have in common.

But essentialism about species is absolutely and completely wrong. Essentialism about species takes each species to be a *natural kind*, which is defined by a set of essential properties. This has two significant implications. First, it implies that species are *individuated*—i.e., distinguished from one another—by virtue of their essential properties. If species A and species B are defined by different sets of essential properties, then they are distinct species; if they are defined by the same set of essential properties, then they are, in fact, the same species. Accordingly, every species has its own essence, which is distinct from the essence of any other species, just as every element in the table of elements has its own essential atomic number, which is distinct from the essential atomic numbers of all other elements. Second, it implies that an organism belongs to a species by virtue of possessing the properties essential to that species. If a certain set of characteristics defines a species, then any organism possessing those characteristics belongs to that species, and any organism lacking them doesn't, regardless of what else may be true of those organisms. Thus, the essence of a species constitutes the criterion for belonging to that species, just as atomic number constitutes the criterion for being a particular element.

These implications of the view that species are natural kinds do not accord with the way that biologists individuate species or the way that they assign individual organisms to species. To see why, let's first get a handle on how species are understood according to theory and practice within biology, then let's examine how the view that species are natural kinds conflicts with the biological understanding of species.

When viewed within a relatively brief interval of evolutionary time, a species, in the biological sense, is a group of *interbreeding populations*. When some organisms in one population reproduce with organisms in another population, the genes from the former population are introduced into the latter population, where those genes can then spread as the organisms in the latter population continue to reproduce. When interbreeding occurs between two populations in this way there is *gene flow* between those populations' gene pools. And when there is gene flow between populations, the interbreeding populations constitute a single species.

As we saw in chapter 1, however, each of the interbreeding populations that constitute a species itself belongs to a lineage, a temporally extended sequence of populations, the later of which are descended by reproduction from the earlier. Consider two currently interbreeding populations. Do all the descendant populations in their respective lineages also belong to the same species? That depends. If the populations in those lineages continue to interbreed, then both lineages, not just their earlier populations, belong to the same species. Of course, it needn't be the case that there be continual interbreeding between the populations in two lineages, only that there be at least periodic interbreeding between the populations in those lineages. When there is at least periodic interbreeding between the populations in two or more lineages, those lineages are *reproductively interwoven* (by periodic gene flow) across evolutionary time, and they consequently belong to the same species over a longer stretch of evolutionary time.

However, there may come a time at which populations in two reproductively interwoven lineages become *reproductively isolated* from one another (due, for example, to geographic separation). When populations become reproductively isolated, no further gene flow occurs between them, and those populations then belong to different species. So, lineages can be reproductively interwoven over long stretches of evolutionary time, but then reach a point at which they *branch* because populations in those lineages become reproductively isolated. When this branching occurs, the previously existing species is replaced by two (or more) daughter species. This is much like how the letter *Y* consists of three line segments, where each line segment represents a distinct species. In the species case, of course, the vertical line segment in the *Y* is actually one of the diagonal line segments of another *Y*, so that the representation of how species have diverged over evolutionary time requires an elaborate branching structure. This elaborate branching structure is the "tree of life," which is the goal of biological classification. The tree of life shows how each species is descended from an earlier species, and each node (each point at which a branching occurs) in the tree of life represents a point at which populations became reproductively isolated.

Thus, in the biological sense, a species is a group of reproductively interwoven lineages that lie on a single "line" segment in the tree of life. Each organism in one of these reproductively interwoven lineages is thus descended from earlier organisms in those lineages, and ultimately the genealogy of each organism is traceable to organisms in the ancestral population that started a new branch in the tree of life. When the genealogy of each organism in a group of reproductively interwoven lineages is traced in its entirety, it will crisscross the genealogies of the other organisms in those lineages, and the network of all such genealogies will constitute an elaborate *genealogical nexus* within which each organism is situated. All the organisms in this genealogical nexus will be descended from common ancestors in the population that founded the species, and the genealogical nexus will display the manner in which they are all related. And, according to biological classification, two organisms that are situated within a common genealogical nexus, which lies on a single segment in the tree of life, are classified as belonging to the same species, regardless of the characteristics those organisms happen to possess.

We are now in a position to see how the biological concept of a species conflicts with the view that species are natural kinds. First, what matters for assigning an organism to a species is the *genealogical nexus* in which it is situated (that is, from which organisms it was descended), not the particular traits it happens to possess. This principle of classification differs sharply from that involved in determining the natural kind to which a particular substance happens to belong. If two samples of liquid contain two parts hydrogen and one part oxygen, bonded in the right way, they both belong to the kind *water*, regardless of how those two samples of liquid happened to come about. One sample may have been produced in a lab by a chemist, and the other may have been scooped out of a river. The provenance of the samples is completely inessential to whether they are samples of water. All that matters is whether the samples have the same *intrinsic properties*. This is because water *is* a natural kind. But, when it comes to determining the species to which an organism belongs, provenance trumps intrinsic properties. Thus, species, *as biologists understand them*, do not exhibit the features of natural kinds.

Second, according to the view that species are natural kinds, if species A and species B possess the same essential characteristics, then they are the same species. But this doesn't accord with practices of biological classification. According to biological classification, if all humans ceased to exist today, *Homo sapiens* would be extinct. If, after millions of years, creatures came to roam our planet that were exactly like us, fitting a "precise and detailed description" from *Gray's Anatomy*, and behaved like us in every respect, they would nonetheless not be *Homo sapiens*. Similarly, if we discovered such creatures in another galaxy, they would not be *Homo sapiens* if they had evolved independently of us. For, as biologists see them, terrestrial species are branches in the tree of life that represents the evolution of all living creatures from the first life form on earth. Accordingly, regardless of whether two distinct branches are perfectly identical in all their observable characteristics, they are nonetheless two distinct branches, just as identical twins are two different organisms despite their similarity. So, when one branch on the tree of life terminates, no other branch that may happen to grow further up the tree will be the same branch, regardless of whether it perfectly resembles the lower, terminated branch. This is the significance behind the slogan "extinction is forever." For species are not individuated by their characteristics; they are individuated as segments in the tree of life. If species were individuated by their characteristics, as natural kinds are, then even if a species ceased to exist it could reemerge later, provided that organisms evolved later that possessed the same characteristics as those that had died earlier. Thus, again, *as biologists understand them*, species don't exhibit the features of natural kinds.

Third, species evolve. In fact, one and the same species may evolve so significantly that characteristics that typify a species at one time period cease to typify it at a later time, and another set of characteristics may become typical of that species. If species were natural kinds, however, a species could not undergo such significant change. A lineage undergoing such significant change would have to be classified as one species before the change and another species after it, since the different sets of typical characteristics would constitute the essences of different species. By analogy, given the right chemical intervention, a volume of carbon monoxide could be transformed into carbon dioxide. But it would not be the same *kind* of gas through the change. That is, the kind carbon monoxide *itself* wouldn't become the kind carbon dioxide, but rather a volume of gas would be transformed from an instance of the natural kind *carbon monoxide* into an instance of the natural kind *carbon dioxide*. The natural kinds themselves would remain unchanged. Similarly, if species were natural kinds, a sufficient degree of evolution would simply transform a species into another, distinct natural kind. But, as biologists understand them, species can be radically overhauled by evolution, yet nonetheless remain *one and the same* species. Provided that the evolutionary change occurs *within* a single branch of the tree of life, the lineage is classified as the same species, no matter how radical the evolutionary change. Evolutionary change creates new species only if the change results in the *branching* of a lineage (the reproductive isolation and splitting of two populations). So, again, *as biologists understand them*, species don't exhibit the features of natural kinds.

Indeed, this last point generates something of a dilemma for the essentialist view that species are natural kinds. Consider the dilemma with respect to Evolutionary Psychology's view of *Homo sapiens*. According to Evolutionary Psychologists, there are "qualities that define us as a unique species," but these qualities evolved during our species' history. Indeed, as we saw in chapter 2, Evolutionary Psychologists maintain that our "species-typical architecture" consists of adaptations that evolved to fixation during the Pleistocene and that, by the end of the Pleistocene some 10,000 years ago, those adaptations reflected "completed rather than ongoing selection."[31] But *Homo sapiens* emerged some 150,000 years ago. So, during at least some of our species' evolutionary history, the qualities that purportedly "define us as a unique species" did not typify our species at all, since they had not yet evolved. In order for those qualities to evolve, however, there had to be sufficient *variation* in our species, since evolution can only occur if there is variation. Thus, during a significant stretch of our evolutionary history, *Homo sapiens* had to be characterized by variation rather than by "the qualities that define us as a unique species."

Here, then, is the dilemma. Evolutionary Psychologists must claim either that we are the same species now that we were 150,000 years ago or that we aren't. If Evolutionary Psychologists claim that we are the same species now that we were 150,000 years ago, before the "qualities that define us as a unique species" became "species typical," then those qualities do not, in fact, "define us as a unique species." For, in that case, *Homo sapiens* would have become a unique species before it was characterized by those qualities—indeed, it would have become a unique species despite being characterized by variation. Thus, because *Homo sapiens* remained the same species both before and after the emergence of its alleged "species-typical architecture," no such architecture is essential to the species. On the other hand, if Evolutionary Psychologists claim that we are not the same species now that we were 150,000 years ago, because 150,000 years ago our lineage did not possess the "qualities that define us as a unique species," then Evolutionary Psychology's demarcation of *Homo sapiens* is directly at odds with the standard biological demarcation of our species. In that case, whatever Evolutionary Psychologists are talking about, they can't be talking about human beings *as a biological species*, since *Homo sapiens* is a term of biological art. Clearly this horn of the dilemma is unacceptable, especially for any psychological theory that claims to be evolutionary. So the only viable option is to grasp the first horn of the dilemma. Grasping that horn, however, requires giving up the idea that species are natural kinds.

But, if species aren't natural kinds, if they aren't what they are because of particular essential qualities that define them each as unique species, what are they? The answer to this question comes from the work of the evolutionary biologists Ernst Mayr and Michael Ghiselin and the philosopher of biology David Hull. As they have shown, the only metaphysical category that exhibits the properties biologists ascribe to species is the category of *individual*. The fact that species are individuals, rather than natural kinds, however, remains little known and little appreciated outside of biology proper. Indeed, Mayr has bemoaned the fact that, although taxonomic biologists are effectively unanimous in rejecting the idea that species are natural kinds, accepting that they are individuals instead, cognate areas of inquiry have failed to absorb the idea and its implications. With characteristic spunk, Hull echoes, then responds to, the "considerable consternation" voiced by those who find it difficult to accept that species are individuals rather than natural kinds: *"Biological species cannot possibly have the characteristics that biologists claim they do.* There *must* be characteristics that all and only people exhibit, or at least *potentially* exhibit, or all *normal* people exhibit—at least potentially. I continue to remain dismayed at the vehemence with which these views are expressed in the absence of any explicitly formulated biological foundations for these notions."[32] Hull lampoons these views as exemplary of the attitude, "What do biologists know about biology?"[33] In an attempt to break this impasse, let's examine more closely the idea that species are individuals.

The first task is to get clear about what *individuals* are and how they differ from natural kinds. There are three primary characteristics that define the concept of an individual, three things that make something an individual entity. Individuals are spatiotemporally localized (hence discrete), spatiotemporally continuous, and cohesive. An organism is, by everyone's measure, a paradigm example of an individual, so let's examine these three properties of individuals by seeing how they are exemplified by organisms.

First, each individual is spatiotemporally localized. That is, each individual has a beginning and an end in time, and each individual occupies a specific region of space. For example, an organism's spatial and temporal location constitute the *boundaries* of that organism. No two distinct organisms have precisely the same boundaries, and numerically the same organism cannot have two distinct sets of boundaries (two distinct locations in space and time). Even though a parasite organism may reside within a host organism, it nonetheless occupies a region of space that is properly contained within the region of space occupied by its host. The parasite does not occupy precisely the same region of space as its host. Further, parasite and host virtually never begin and cease to exist at precisely the same moments in time. Thus, organisms are *discrete:* There are points in space and time at which an organism begins and ends, and these points are different from the points at which another organism begins and ends. As Ghiselin says, "an individual occupies a definite position in space and time. It has a beginning and an end. Once it ceases to exist it is gone forever. In a biological context this means that an organism never comes back into existence once it is dead."[34] In this respect, individuals differ from kinds. The individual members of a kind are located at particular regions of space-time, but the kind itself has no particular location in spacetime. Further, since kinds are constituted by their members, kinds are not discrete. The same individuals can belong to more than one kind, in which case the kinds to which they belong overlap rather than having discrete boundaries. Indeed, two different kinds can have precisely the same members, in which case they overlap one another completely.

Second, each individual is spatiotemporally continuous. Each individual exists continuously between its beginning and end in time, and at every moment of its existence it occupies the same or contiguous regions of space. Given its spatiotemporal continuity, an individual's existence can be plotted as a "spacetime worm," a single unbroken line, however squiggly, through the three dimensions of space and the fourth of time. For example, we often identify an organism as the same organism solely because of its spatiotemporal continuity, since in many cases the same individual organism undergoes radical change over time. As Mayr points out, "that caterpillar and butterfly are the same individual is inferred not from any similarity in their appearance but from this continuity."[35] In this respect, also, individuals differ from kinds or classes. A kind is not spatiotemporally continuous, since a kind is constituted by its individual members, and those members are frequently scattered across disparate regions of spacetime. Indeed, kinds are potentially unlimited, in that members of a kind can come into and go out of existence in remote reaches of the universe at any time. Due to some bizarre chemical catastrophe, for example, all water could cease to exist today, but tomorrow we could synthesize more water in a lab. The kind *water* would thus not exhibit temporal continuity. Similarly, even if the only water in existence today were in Brazil, and the only water in existence tomorrow were in Scotland, the Brazilian and Scottish substances would both be water despite the fact that the kind *water* would not exhibit spatial contiguity. This is because all that matters with respect to whether liquids are water is that they possess the right chemical structure, and individual samples of liquid can share that structure without being continuous with one another in time or contiguous with one another in space.

Third, each individual is a cohesive whole. For example, although each individual organism is composed of parts (organs, cells, and so on), and can be broken down into its parts, those parts are not a mere collection, but are *organized* and *functionally integrated*. Indeed, what makes the parts of an organism parts of that organism is the fact that they are functionally integrated with other parts of the organism, the fact that they contribute to the organization that makes up that organism. The functional integration of an organism's parts consists in the fact that those parts causally interact with one another, on a local level, in ways that help to sustain the organism over time and in ways that they do not causally interact with the parts of any other organism. In addition, the parts of an organism need not resemble one another in any respect in order to be parts of the same organism and contribute to its functional organization. Your left lung doesn't resemble your right femur in any interesting respect, and they don't have to share any particular properties in order to be parts of your body. In this respect, again, individuals differ from kinds. The individual members of a kind are not members of that kind because they are functionally integrated or organized in any particular fashion. Rather, individuals are members of the same kind simply by virtue of their similarity to one another.

As Mayr, Ghiselin, and Hull have shown, given the role that the species concept plays in biological theory, species exhibit each of the three characteristics definitive of individuals, just as organisms do. First, each species is spatiotemporally localized, occupying the region of spacetime that is circumscribed by its temporal beginning and end and its spatial borders. More important, each species has a definite location in the tree of life, a definite segment of the tree, with a definite beginning and end. No two species can occupy the same segment of the tree of life, and no one species can occupy two distinct segments. For, as we have seen, when a species goes extinct, numerically the same species cannot come into existence later. Even if other, identical organisms were to come into existence later, they would be classified by biologists as a new species, not as a continuation of the earlier species. Species, then, are spatiotemporally localized and discrete.

Second, each species is spatiotemporally continuous. Each species exists continuously from its temporal beginning to its end, and each species as a whole is spread over the same or contiguous regions of space for every moment of its existence. In this respect, like an organism, a species' existence can be plotted as a "spacetime worm." Further, as Hull points out, the organisms that make up a species are related by descent. "But descent presupposes replication and reproduction, and these processes in turn presuppose spatiotemporal proximity and continuity. When a single gene undergoes replication to produce two new genes, or a single cell undergoes mitotic division to produce two new cells, the end products are spatiotemporally continuous with the parent entity. In sexual reproduction, the propagules, if not the parent organisms themselves, must come into contact. The end result is the successive modification of the same population."[36] Thus, species are spatiotemporally continuous.

Third, species are unified, cohesive wholes, held together by the organizational glue of reproduction. For species consist of interbreeding populations, and both individual populations and groups of interbreeding populations are united by the *reproductive interactions* of organisms. As Mayr points out, this is due to the fact that the organisms that compose a species develop "from the joint gene pool of the species, and that they jointly contribute their genotypes to form the gene pool of the next generation."[37] The contribution of genotypes to the next generation, however, involves a great many causal interactions among organisms. The organisms in a population must structure a great many of their activities around the pursuit of sex with conspecifics, the act of sex with conspecifics, the incubation or gestation of the embryonic products of sex, and the care and protection of live offspring. These causal interactions on a local level between the organisms involved in reproductive activities produce a cohesiveness within populations and species that is much like the functional organization of an organism (which derives from local causal interactions between its parts). Thus, species are unified, cohesive wholes.

Species, then, exhibit all the properties that are definitive of individuals. But, if species are individuals, just like organisms, how are we to understand the relation between organisms and species? According to essentialism, the only individuals are organisms, and species, as natural kinds, are classes of individuals that are united by a shared set of essential properties. Organisms are thus *members* of the classes that are their species. In this respect, essentialists see the relation between organisms and species as just like the relation between organisms and higher taxa such as orders and phyla. In the essentialist's view, higher taxa are also classes of the same individuals that are members of species, but those individuals are united in orders, and so on, by sharing increasingly more inclusive sets of essential properties. In the view that species are individuals, however, organisms are *parts* of species in precisely the way that cells are parts of organisms. In other words, organisms compose a species in precisely the way that cells compose a body.

The parallel between cell/organism and organism/species is worth belaboring for a moment. Cells are clearly individuals: They are spatiotemporally localized (discrete), spatiotemporally continuous, and cohesive. Yet these individuals are unproblematically parts of another, larger individual (an organism). But what makes the cells in an organism all parts of the same, larger individual? It is *not* shared properties that makes cells all parts of the same organism. The cells in your body, for example, aren't cells of *the same body* because they have the same genetic makeup. For, in fact, many of them don't. In the process of mitosis, which created all the cells in your body, mutations occur. As a result, there are genetic differences among many of the cells in your body. They are, nonetheless, all cells *of your body*. Conversely, the cells in the bodies of identical (monozygotic) twins are genetically identical, with the exception of the cells in each twin that contain mutations. But two genetically identical cells from the bodies of two twins are not cells of the same body, despite their genetic identity. So, the genetic makeup of a cell, and its genetic similarity to other cells, is not what determines which body a cell belongs to. Rather, the cells in your body are cells *of your body* because they satisfy two conditions. First, they all descended, via iterated rounds of cell division, from the same zygote. For every cell in your body, there is an unbroken chain of descent via cell division that links it with the same zygote. And, second, those cells that are parts of your body are so because they are causally integrated into the overall organization that makes up your body.

In the same way, organisms that belong to the same species need not share any properties. Sharing properties is not what determines whether two organisms belong to the same species, even if those organisms do share a significant number of properties. In fact, in many cases, organisms that belong to the same species do not resemble one another much at all. In chapter 1, we encountered *Paracerceis sculpta*, a species in which males come in three "morphs" that pursue different mating strategies. Large males are many times the size of small males, and they possess spiked "horns" where small males have only little nubs. Judging by shared properties, the two would be classified as different species, yet they belong to the same species. In addition, in some species in which developmental plasticity is common, individual organisms develop to mimic the appearance of other species. In such cases, different organisms in the species can develop to mimic distinct species, thereby having more observable characteristics in common with those other species than with one another. Thus, similarity is only *incidental* to belonging to the same species; it is not a criterion of it.

Indeed, not only need there be no shared properties among the organisms in a species, but the fact that species are reproductively organized individuals ensures the maintenance of variation among the organisms in a species. For, in meiosis, the early stage of sexual reproduction, gametes are created that contain only half of an organism's genes, and two gametes often contain different halves of an organism's genes. New organisms, or zygotes, are formed by a process that is, in effect, the random sampling of the parental gametes. This ensures that offspring are never genetically identical to either parent, so that every organism in a species (except for monozygotic siblings) is genetically unique. Further, an organism's development is the result of interactions between its genes and its environment, and no two organisms share precisely the same history of interactions with the environment. Consequently, each organism's unique genome encounters a unique environment during development, and the interactions between genome and environment ensure that each organism develops to be phenotypically unique. Of course, the organisms in a species do tend to share a lot of genes, and their developmental environments are often similar in gross outline, so these processes also tend to create some relatively widespread similarities among organisms in the same species *in certain respects*. But, *on the whole*, each organism is phenotypically unique. Thus, the fact that species are reproductively organized individuals actually serves to guarantee and maintain significant genetic and phenotypic variation among the organisms in a species.

One thing that makes this viewpoint difficult to accept is the prevalence of "field guides" of various sorts—for example, Peterson's *Field Guide to Western Birds*. In field guides (or in dictionaries), you find species apparently defined by certain clusters of "field marks." For example, you will find a list of characteristics that identify the rose-breasted grosbeak: Males have a black head and upperparts, white belly, and a bright splash of red on the breast. This gives the impression to the nonspecialist that these characteristics are the qualities that define the rose-breasted grosbeak as a unique species. But this is mistaken. These characteristics are merely *markers*, which aid in identifying the species to which a bird belongs. They do not *define* the species. In the same way, "yellow house on the corner" can be a marker for identifying the house at 17 Primrose Lane, but it is not definitive of that house, since the house could be repainted, or even moved to another location, yet retain its identity as a unique individual house. Indeed, even though reliance on field guides can induce the conviction that species are defined by the characteristics associated with a species' name in a field guide, a little reflection on their use can actually disabuse one of that conviction. The female common redpoll, for example, shares none of the characteristics that "define" the male of the species; instead, it more closely resembles the female pine siskin, which in turn doesn't much resemble the male pine siskin. Nonetheless, field guides are very clear about the species to which the females belong, and they are not classified in those species because of their distinguishing marks. Thus, field marks are rules of thumb for identifying the species of an organism; they should not be conflated with defining characteristics of a species.

Species, then, are larger-scale individuals than organisms, but they are individuals in the same sense that organisms are. And conspecific organisms are *parts* of the same species, in the same sense in which two cells can be parts of the same body. The fact that you and I belong to *Homo sapiens*, then, *does not entail* that "we can assume similarities merely on the basis of membership of one biological species."[38] Similarly, the fact that my heart and my thumbnail both belong to my body does not entail that there are properties they must share. Thus, when Cosmides and Tooby claim that, "*by virtue* of being members of the human species, all humans are expected to have the same adaptive mechanisms," they are simply wrong.[39] They misunderstand the nature of species, they misunderstand what's involved in two organisms' belonging to the same species, and they fail to understand how the reproductive organization of a species/ individual serves to maintain variation among the organism/parts of that species/individual.

But what does the fact that species are individuals and not natural kinds have to do with human nature? What does the fact that organisms are parts of larger individuals, rather than members of a natural kind, have to do with human nature? The implications of these facts for the idea of human nature are surprisingly direct. If species are individuals, and organisms are parts of those individuals, then organisms do not belong to the same species because of shared possession of a set of characteristics that is purportedly the essence of that species. Shared characteristics are not *definitive* of belonging to the same species, they are *incidental* to belonging to the same species. Indeed, since organisms belong to the same species by virtue of being situated within a common genealogical nexus, there need be *no* characteristics that are shared by all the organisms that belong to a species. Thus, if human nature is supposed to be a set of "qualities that define us as a unique species," there is no human nature. As Hull says, if species are individuals, "then particular organisms belong in a particular species because they are part of that genealogical nexus, not because they possess any essential traits. No species has an essence in this sense. Hence there is no such thing as human nature."[40]

But the fact that species are individuals, rather than natural kinds, has additional implications. Evolutionary Psychologists envision that their "new science of the mind" will discover the "Darwinian algorithms" that are processed by universal psychological mechanisms. This discovery would demonstrate to us the universal functioning of the human mind, and the descriptions of that functioning would constitute *laws of thought* or *psychological laws*. The fact that species are individuals, however, entails that there can be no such species-specific psychological laws. To see why, let's begin by examining the nature of laws of nature.

Laws of nature are exceptionless universal generalizations. That is, a law of nature applies to all objects, at any point in space and at any time, that possess the properties mentioned in the law. As such, laws of nature mention no specific individuals. For example, Newton's law of gravitation states that two bodies attract one another with a force that is proportional to the product of their masses divided by the square of the distance between them. Although this law applies to any two bodies in the universe, it makes no mention of any specific individual body. As Ghiselin puts it, "although there are laws about celestial bodies in general, there is no law of nature for Mars or the Milky Way."[41] The reason is that laws of nature are designed to capture *regularities* in nature, and regularities involve the *repetition of nonunique properties* or events. While unique individuals can instantiate a regularity, they do so only insofar as they possess properties that are also possessed by other individuals—in particular, the properties mentioned in the law stating the regularity. In other words, only the *nonunique features* of unique individuals—only those features of an individual that are *or could be* possessed by other individuals—fall under laws of nature. Thus, Ghiselin says, "there are no laws for individuals as such, only for classes of individuals."[42]

However, there aren't laws of nature for just *any* classes of individuals. For example, each individual gold watch is a member of the class of watches and a member of the class of gold things. There are no laws of nature that apply to individual gold watches by virtue of their being *watches*, but there are laws of nature that apply to them by virtue of their being *gold*. This is because, although *watch* is a kind, it is not a *natural* kind; *gold*, on the other hand, is a natural kind. Kinds, in general, are defined by properties, so that an individual is a member of a kind just in case it possesses the property or properties that define the kind. Some properties, however, are such that their different instances don't exhibit precisely the same patterns of causal interaction with other objects. Watches, for example, come in many shapes and sizes, and they are made of many different materials. So the different instances of the property *watch* tend to exhibit different patterns of causal interaction with other objects. Some tarnish or scratch in certain conditions, whereas others don't. Other properties, though, are such that their different instances exhibit the same patterns of causal interaction with certain other properties. Each sample of gold, for example, exhibits a range of causal interactions with certain other properties that is also exhibited by every other sample of gold, since the essence of gold (its atomic number) features in deep and robust regularities in nature. The properties that exhibit uniform patterns of causal interaction with other properties are the ones that define *natural kinds*. Thus, since laws of nature describe exceptionless causal regularities in nature, and since the properties that define natural kinds are properties that interact in regular ways, the classes of individuals to which laws of nature apply are natural kinds. In short, laws of nature serve to capture the regular interactions among the natural kinds that make up our world.

Laws of nature, then, apply to individuals only insofar as those individuals exemplify the natural kinds over which the laws generalize. Given this fact, could there be laws of *specifically human* biology or psychology? That is, could a science that studies properties that are necessarily unique to a single species discover laws of nature that necessarily apply to that species and that species only? There are two ways in which this question can be taken, but the answer in each case is no.

On the one hand, if we are asking whether there could be laws of nature that apply to our species as a whole, and only to our species, the answer is no because *Homo sapiens* is an individual, not a natural kind, and there are no laws of nature that apply exclusively to a single individual. On the other hand, if we are asking whether there could be laws of nature that apply to individual human beings insofar as they possess properties that uniquely *define Homo sapiens*, the answer is still no. For, since *Homo sapiens* is an individual, not a natural kind, individual human beings are not human beings by virtue of instantiating the natural kind *Homo sapiens*. Rather, individual human beings are all human beings by virtue of being *parts* of the same genealogical nexus. And, as we have seen, the individuals that constitute the parts of another, larger individual are not parts of that individual by virtue of being members of the same natural kind.

There are, however, two respects in which this argument must be qualified. First, although there are no laws of nature that apply *exclusively* to human beings, there are laws of nature that apply to *Homo sapiens*. For *Homo sapiens* is a species, and the category of *species* is a natural kind. That is, there are laws of biology, including the laws of evolution, that apply to *all* species. But, the properties that make *Homo sapiens* a *unique* species— the properties that make it a unique segment in the tree of life—will not figure in these laws. Rather, insofar as laws of evolution apply to *Homo sapiens*, they apply to *Homo sapiens* because of properties that it shares with other species—in particular, the properties essential to the natural kind *species.* *

Second, although there are no laws of nature that apply exclusively to *Homo sapiens*, there are many laws of nature that apply to individual human beings. The laws of physics and chemistry apply to individual human beings, and there are laws of biology, including the laws of genetics, that apply to individual human beings. But these laws apply to individual human beings only insofar as humans exemplify properties that are not exclusive to human beings, but that are (or could be) possessed by much larger classes that include human beings. The laws of mechanics, for example, apply to individual human beings, but they apply to us as objects with mass, and mass is not unique to human beings. Similarly, the laws of genetics apply to individual human beings, but they apply to us as developmental systems or as sexually reproducing organisms, and these properties are not unique to humans. Thus, the laws of nature that do apply to individual human beings are not candidates for scientific laws of *human nature*, since they are laws that do not apply exclusively to human beings.

There are, however, more specific reasons why there can be no scientific laws exclusive to *human* psychology. For, if there were psychological laws that applied exclusively to humans, those laws would have to generalize over natural kinds, and those natural kinds would have to be human psychological mechanisms (or aspects of their functioning). In other words, in order for there to be psychological laws, human psychological mechanisms would have to be natural kinds. But, since psychological mechanisms are phenotypic traits, the question of whether psychological mechanisms form natural kinds is really the question of the logic underlying the classification of phenotypic traits. In particular, it is the question of the criteria involved in classifying a trait of two different organisms as "the same" trait (in this case, classifying psychological mechanisms in two individuals as "the same" psychological mechanism). If traits were natural kinds, the criterion involved in classifying a trait of two different organisms as the same trait would simply be whether those two traits shared certain essential properties—namely, the properties definitive of that natural kind of trait. Again, this would be identical to the logic involved in classifying two samples of platinum as the same substance; the two samples are the same substance if they are both composed of atoms with atomic number 78. But this is never the logic involved in the biological classification of a trait in two organisms as instances of the same trait. Indeed, there are two distinct ways of classifying traits as "the same" in biology, and neither of these ways involves identifying shared essential properties, such as could feature in laws of nature.

The traits of two organisms are grouped as "the same" trait by virtue of being either *homologies* or *analogies* (also known as *homoplasies*). Traits of two organisms are *homologous* if those traits derived, possibly with modification, from an equivalent trait in the common ancestor of those organisms.[43] The ancestral trait is determined to be "equivalent" to the derived traits just in case it occupied the same position relative to other parts of the body and had similar connections with those other body parts. For example, the human eye is homologous to the eye of a cat, since the human eye and the cat eye derived from an equivalent eye of an ancestor of both humans and cats, although eyes in both lineages were modified after their divergence. Similarly, human limbs and cat limbs are homologous, since they were both derived from the limbs of a common ancestor. This is the sense in which the human eye and the cat eye are both eyes. As the evolutionary biologist Gunter Wagner puts it: "A large number of characters are certainly derived from the same structure in a common ancestor and are therefore undoubtedly homologous. One simply cannot escape the conclusion that the brain of a rat and a human are actually the 'same' in spite of their obvious differences."[44] In contrast, traits of two organisms are *analogous* if those traits have a similar structure or function, but evolved in those organisms' lineages independently of one another. The human eye and the octopus eye are not derived from the eye of a common ancestor, since the common ancestor to humans and octopuses had no eyes. The human eye and the octopus eye have structural and functional similarities, however, so the human eye is analogous to the octopus eye. Similarly, the wings of the black-capped chickadee are analogous to the wings of the mosquito, since wings evolved separately in birds and insects. They are nonetheless both wings, because of their structural and functional similarities.

Thus, when two organisms are said to have "the same" trait, it means that those organisms possess either homologous traits or analogous traits. There is no other sense, in biology, in which two organisms can be said to have "the same" trait. This is true not only of trait comparisons between species, as in the examples above, but of trait comparisons within a species as well. Your eyes and my eyes are homologous, because they were derived from the eyes of a common ancestor. Of course, the common ancestor from which you and I derived our eyes was far more recent than the common ancestor from which human eyes and cat eyes were derived. Nonetheless, the sense in which your eyes and my eyes are "the same" is that our eyes are homologous. Indeed, all of the traits that you and I share and that are described in "precise anatomical detail" by *Gray's Anatomy* are homologies.

Homologous traits, however, are not classified together by virtue of shared characteristics, let alone by virtue of shared essential characteristics. The human brain and the rat brain are homologous despite many structural differences, and the hind limbs of the crocodile and those of the starling are homologous despite sharing virtually no interesting properties. The same is true of homologous traits *within* species. The eyes of each individual human are not human eyes because they share properties essential to being a human eye, but because they are homologies, traits derived from an equivalent eye in a common ancestor. Indeed, "deformed" eyes, which lack some of the properties of eyes detailed in *Gray's Anatomy*, are nonetheless eyes. And the eyes of the blind are human eyes despite not performing the typical visual function of eyes. Further, male nipples and females nipples are all nipples because they are homologous traits, not because of shared morphological or functional properties (which, in fact, they do not share). This is because, as Wagner says, "homology is assessed regardless of shape or function."[45] In fact, homology is assessed in precisely the way that the species classification of two organisms is assessed—genealogically. Traits of two organisms are homologies if they were derived from an equivalent trait in a common ancestor, regardless of whether they share properties, just as two organisms belong to the same species if they descended from a common ancestor in that species, regardless of whether they share properties. In short, homologies, like the organisms of a species, are unified by descent, not by shared properties.

Two individual instances of a trait (in two distinct organisms), then, are not classed together as homologous by the same logic as two samples of platinum are classed together as the same substance. Instances of natural kinds, like platinum, are classed together because of their intrinsic properties, regardless of their provenance. If we froze the universe at a particular moment of time, for example, we could identify every instance of platinum simply by determining whether objects were composed of atoms with atomic number 78. But, in that frozen instant, we would not be able to identify every instance of a particular homology. For history is everything with respect to determining whether two individual instances of a trait are homologous. Your eyes and my eyes are homologous ("the same") not because of properties they share *at this instant*, but because of chains of descent that reach back from each of us into the past and converge upon a common ancestor. Our eyes are not "the same" because they are connected by common properties at this moment, but because they are connected by that historical *V* of descent, with our common ancestor located at the apex. Thus, the logic by which traits are classified as "the same" (homologous) in biology is very different from the logic by which two entities are classified as instances of the same natural kind. In short, "the same" trait in organisms of the same species are homologies, and homologies are not natural kinds.

If many humans share "the same" psychological mechanism, then what makes their psychological mechanisms the same is their derivation from a common ancestor, not any properties they may happen to share. But no phenotypic traits are inherited directly, by being directly copied as wholes from one generation to another. They are, instead, constructed anew in each generation through the process of development. Indeed, like all phenotypic characteristics of individual human beings, psychological mechanisms develop via the interaction between an individual human's unique genome and the unique sequence of environments to which that individual's genome is exposed. And this process consistently produces variation among the psychological mechanisms possessed by humans, just as it consistently produces variation among all phenotypes. Despite these variations, however, psychological mechanisms in different individual humans remain "the same" mechanism. For what makes them the same is that they are derived from a common ancestor, even if they have been modified in the process. Thus, human psychological mechanisms are not natural kinds, they are homologies, which may exhibit significant variation despite being "the same." Consequently, there can be no *laws* of *human* psychology, since laws of nature apply only to natural kinds.

This doesn't mean, however, that we can't make discoveries regarding human psychology, and it doesn't mean that human minds exhibit no regularities. Even if there are no laws of nature that apply to single individuals as such, individuals can nonetheless be *described*. There are no laws of nature that pertain to you and only you, but those who know you well can give richly detailed descriptions of your physique and personality. And those descriptions can convey to others a great deal of knowledge about you as an individual. Similarly, although there can be no laws of nature that pertain exclusively to human psychology, psychology may one day provide us with richly detailed descriptions of human minds. And some of those descriptions may prove general enough to apply to vast segments of our species *for a particular period of time* (a point on which I will elaborate in the final section of this chapter). In other words, psychology may one day provide us with descriptions of some very widespread regularities among the minds of our conspecifics. But those descriptions will never achieve the status of laws of nature, since laws of nature apply only to instances of natural kinds. Insofar as psychology concerns itself with distinctively *human* cognition and emotion, it must begin to conceive of itself as being in the business of providing *descriptions* of *homologous characteristics*, rather than being in the business of providing laws of thought in the way that physics provides laws of mechanics or chemistry provides laws of chemical bonding.

To conclude, then, since *Homo sapiens* is an individual, not a natural kind, there is no such thing as human nature. And, since human psychological mechanisms are homologies, human psychological mechanisms do not form natural kinds. Consequently, there are no laws of nature that pertain exclusively to human minds, so Evolutionary Psychology can never fulfill its promise to be the "new science of human nature" by discovering the psychological laws that govern the functioning of evolved psychological mechanisms. A truly *evolutionary* science of human psychology will not only abandon the quest for human nature, but, with it, the quest to be a science in the model of physics or chemistry.

### "Human Universals"

But, even if an evolutionary psychology will never discover universal laws of human psychology, isn't it nonetheless possible that there are human universals? And, if there are human universals, wouldn't those universals be excellent candidates for universal human nature, even if there is no human essence?

In fact, Evolutionary Psychologists claim that they already have unearthed a vast number of human universals and that these constitute the core of what they take to be our universal human nature. But there is an ambiguity in the concept of *human universal* that plays a role in many discussions of human nature in the Evolutionary Psychology literature, and that ambiguity infects the concept of *universality* when Evolutionary Psychologists talk of universal human characteristics, such as "universal mate preferences." For example, in his recent book *The Blank Slate: The Modern Denial of Human Nature*, Steven Pinker vigorously defends the idea that there is a universal human nature, by which Pinker means that there are evolved psychological universals. Among the evidence Pinker cites in this defense is a lengthy list of "human universals" compiled by the Evolutionary Psychologist Donald Brown. Brown's list of universals contains such entries as division of labor, food sharing, incest avoidance, marriage, myths, oligarchy, taboos, and trade. But, insofar as these are universals, they are *cultural universals* (that is, phenomena that are present in every culture), not psychological universals. Although every culture may practice incest avoidance, obviously not every individual human is psychologically designed to do so. And things like division of labor and oligarchy are, by their very nature, properties of groups and not of individual humans.

Pinker's appeal to cultural universals to support an argument for psychological universals no doubt stems from Evolutionary Psychology's attempt to synthesize aspects of anthropology, which deals largely with cultures or populations, with aspects of psychology, which deals largely with the properties of individual human minds. Indeed, Brown is an anthropologist, and his intent in compiling his list of universals was to capture what "all societies, all cultures, and all languages have in common."[46] But when anthropological and psychological agendas are in play simultaneously, it becomes easy to shift imperceptibly from talk of cultural universals to talk of psychological universals. And Evolutionary Psychologists' arguments for the existence of a universal human nature often trade on this ambiguity.

The ambiguity is at its most misleading when Evolutionary Psychologists cite cultural universals as *evidence of* psychological universals, as Pinker does in *The Blank Slate*. Sometimes the purported cultural universals cited as evidence of psychological universals are not well documented cultural universals. For example, as we saw in chapter 5, Evolutionary Psychologists were quick to claim, on the basis of a single study in the United States, that a male preference for females with a 0.70 waist-to-hip ratio is culturally universal. But, when the anthropological field work was actually done to find out whether this preference truly is a cultural universal, it was discovered that it isn't. At other times, however, Evolutionary Psychologists cite truly well documented cultural universals as evidence of the existence of psychological universals. But, even if there are many cultural universals, as I believe there are, cultural universals do not actually provide evidence of a universal human nature when that is understood as consisting of psychological universals.

To see why, consider a prominent example of how (putative) cultural universals are interpreted as evidence of psychological universals. As we saw in chapter 5, Buss hypothesizes that selection designed the male mind to prefer nubility in a mate and the female mind to prefer status, and he argues that these preferences should consequently be universal among individual men and women. To test these hypotheses, Buss conducted mate-preference surveys in thirty-three countries. But, in these surveys,

Buss did *not* find that *every individual* man and woman in every culture around the world possessed the hypothesized mate preferences. In fact, Buss's surveys revealed significant numbers of individual men and women whose mate preferences did not conform to his hypotheses. What Buss actually found was that the *averages* of individual survey responses *in (almost) every culture* conformed reasonably closely to the hypothesized responses. That is, Buss found that *the average male* in (almost) every culture expressed a preference for a younger mate and that *the average female* in (almost) every culture expressed a preference for a mate with a higher socioeconomic status. Although Buss interpreted these results as providing confirmation for his hypotheses, averages are actually properties of populations, not properties of individual humans. In other words, even if they are taken at face value, what Buss's survey results show is not that particular preferences are psychological universals, but that particular *average preferences* are *cultural universals*. Taking those survey results as evidence of a universal human nature involves inferring psychological universals from cultural universals, which is a fallacy analogous to that of inferring that every human is five feet, eight inches tall on the basis of discovering that the average height in every culture is five feet, eight inches.

While the inference from cultural universals to psychological universals (hence human nature) is indeed fallacious, in the hands of Evolutionary Psychologists the inference isn't quite the bald confusion that my height analogy makes it out to be. For, in the hands of Evolutionary Psychologists, the inference from cultural universals to psychological universals is aided and abetted by Tooby and Cosmides' theory of culture and the origins of cultural universals. To properly appraise the role of cultural universals in Evolutionary Psychologists' discussions of human nature, then, we should examine this theory of culture.

According to Tooby and Cosmides, *culture* consists of "any mental, behavioral, or material commonalities shared across individuals, from those that are shared across the entire species down to the limiting case of those shared only by a dyad."[47] Tooby and Cosmides claim that cultural contents—specific mental, behavioral, or material commonalities—can be generated by one of three causal mechanisms.

First, Tooby and Cosmides argue that our (allegedly) universal psychological adaptations "not only constitute regularities in themselves but they impose within and across cultures all kinds of regularities on human life, as do the common features of the environments we inhabit."[48] For example, since every ("normal") human's mind is "preequipped" with the same presuppositions and expectations about the mental functioning and behavioral propensities of other humans, when humans interact their shared "knowledge" of one another generates some highly patterned forms of interaction. And, since the psychological adaptations that generate these behavioral patterns are universal, the patterns of behavioral interaction that they generate emerge everywhere that people interact. Further, since our universal psychological adaptations are also "preequipped" with a great deal of "knowledge" of the nonsocial world, when those adaptations encounter universal and evolutionarily recurrent features of the nonsocial environment they generate universal patterns of behavioral interaction with, and material utilization of, the nonsocial environment. Thus, Tooby and Cosmides claim, our universal psychological adaptations generate universal cultural contents, which Tooby and Cosmides call *metaculture*.

Second, as we saw in chapter 2, universal psychological adaptations can generate differences among individuals when individuals encounter different environments or developmental conditions. And the local conditions encountered by different human populations around the world obviously differ in a number of ways. "As a result," Tooby and Cosmides argue, "humans in groups can be expected to express, in response to local conditions, a variety of organized within-group similarities that are not caused by social learning or transmission. Of course, these generated within-group similarities will simultaneously lead to systematic differences between groups facing different conditions."[49] For example, food sharing within a culture varies as a function of the degree to which luck is a factor in successful foraging, which in turn varies as a function of the types of food available in the local conditions encountered by a population. So differences between populations in food resources can generate differences in cultural practices of food sharing. Similarly, styles of clothing vary as a function of the local climatological conditions to which a population is exposed. The fact that southern Italians wear linen in March while the Inuit wear fur is a function of a common human nature responding differentially to differences in local climate. Were those populations to swap conditions, after some time they would presumably adopt different cultural practices of dress. Thus, Tooby and Cosmides claim, the interactions between our universal psychological adaptations and the local conditions encountered by populations generate within-group similarities and between-group differences in some cultural contents. Tooby and Cosmides call the cultural contents generated in this way *evoked culture*, to designate cultural contents that are "evoked" from a universal human nature by differences in local conditions.

Third, Tooby and Cosmides argue, some cultural contents have their origins within the mind of a single individual, who then transmits to others a novel idea or behavior. Since these cultural contents originate by spreading from one individual to others, like a contagion, Tooby and Cosmides call such cultural contents *epidemiological culture*. As Tooby and Cosmides put it: "This subset of cultural phenomena is restricted to (1) those representations or regulatory elements that exist originally in at least one mind that (2) come to exist in other minds because (3) observation and interaction between the source and the observer cause inferential mechanisms in the observer to recreate the representations or regulatory elements in his or her own psychological architecture."[50] For example, if someone comes up with a new idea for how to catch fish, and that novel idea proves an effective method for catching fish, that individual's interaction with others can result in their adopting the same method of catching fish, and this new idea can begin to spread in the individual's population. Epidemiological culture thus encompasses such phenomena as baseball, bell-bottoms, the hokey-pokey, and television.

Interestingly, once an aspect of epidemiological culture becomes widespread in a population, it becomes an aspect of the local conditions to which that population responds. This change in local conditions, in turn, precipitates a change in the mental and behavioral responses that are "evoked" from the psychological mechanisms in the members of that population. Thus, epidemiological culture can feed into, and precipitate changes in, evoked culture. For example, once radio or television becomes a stable aspect of the cultural landscape, it further transforms culture by evoking novel reactions from evolved psychological mechanisms. Similarly, Evolutionary Psychologists would argue, although pornographic magazines and videos originated through epidemiological culture, once they became a fixture of the cultural landscape they became an aspect of the local conditions to which new generations responded. The patterns of consumption and use of pornographic materials by new generations thus became aspects of evoked culture, as evolved sexual responses encountered a sexual environment populated not only by fellow humans, but by a wealth of pornographic representations of fellow humans as well.

The above theory of culture underwrites the frequent inference by Evolutionary Psychologists from cultural universals to psychological universals. For, according to this theory of culture, cultural universals are aspects of metaculture, which is generated by interactions among psychological universals and interactions between psychological universals and universal features of the nonsocial environment. In short, cultural universals are directly *generated by* psychological universals. As Tooby and Cosmides say, "the way in which such a universal psychology would lead to cultural universals is straightforward."[51] In fact, given this theory of culture, the causal mechanisms that generate evoked culture and epidemiological culture are, by their very nature, mechanisms that act within populations and thereby produce cultural differences between populations (although some epidemiological culture may spread between populations). The only causal mechanism that is capable of generating true cultural universals, according to the theory, is the activity of psychological universals. Thus, Evolutionary Psychologists tend to see cultural universals as evidence of underlying psychological universals because they see psychological universals as the only plausible mechanism for producing cultural universals. In this way, Evolutionary Psychologists tend to see the inference from cultural universals to psychological universals as an instance of a standard pattern of inferring causes from their effects, where Tooby and Cosmides' theory of culture provides the account of how psychological universals cause cultural universals.

But cultural universals may have emerged without having been generated by psychological universals. Indeed, there are at least two other causal mechanisms that could have produced some cultural universals, and each of these could have operated in the absence of psychological universals. So, psychological universals can't be inferred from cultural universals in the way that a cause is inferred from its effect, because cultural universals may have had causes other than psychological universals. Precisely how a cultural universal emerged cannot be determined just with a bit of armchair theorizing about the nature of culture, but must be determined through extensive empirical investigation into the etiology of each cultural universal on a case-by-case basis. Thus, cultural universals *in themselves* cannot provide evidence of psychological universals. There must always be independent evidence of the existence of psychological universals. To see why, let's examine two other causal mechanisms by which cultural universals could have emerged.

One causal mechanism by which cultural universals could emerge in the absence of psychological universals is frequency-dependent selection. To see how, let's return to the simple model of frequency-dependent selection that we discussed in chapter 1, the Hawk-Dove game, which is a contest between two individuals for some resource (for example, food, a mate, or territory). Hawks engage in these contests by attacking and escalating until they either win or get seriously injured, while Doves engage with threatening displays, but never attack, and withdraw when attacked. Given the fitness payoffs in the game we examined, a stable polymorphism consisting of 75 percent Hawks and 25 percent Doves would evolve in a population.

Now, suppose that we took a simple statistical survey of a population consisting of 75 percent Hawks and 25 percent Doves. Suppose, in particular, that we asked the individuals in the population which tactic they employed in contests over resources, and respondents were to answer with a 2 if they played Hawk and a 1 if they played Dove. We would find the *average response* to be 1.75, an average that is very much toward the Hawkish end of the scale. There are two points to consider regarding this example.

First, suppose that prior to our survey we had reasoned that, given the fitness payoff of winning a resource, selection should have favored aggressive pursuit of resources. After all, we could have reasoned, there are only individuals who win resources and those who don't. Those who win resources enjoy enhanced fitness, while those who don't win resources have nothing. So, we could have argued, selection should have favored those who aggressively pursued resources, since they would have had higher average fitness than those who didn't. Thus, we would have predicted, individuals should have evolved to pursue the Hawk strategy. When we then looked at the statistical results of our survey, and found the average response to be far closer to Hawk than Dove, we could have convinced ourselves that our hypotheses about the past action of selection and the present natures of the individuals in the population were confirmed. In fact, however, our hypothesis about the past action of selection would be mistaken, since there had actually been frequency-dependent selection for a stable polymorphism of Hawks and Doves, rather than selection for Hawks. Our hypothesis about the present natures of the individuals in the population would also be mistaken, since 25 percent of the individuals in the population are Doves "by nature." In other words, the Doves aren't simply "abnormal" Hawks, but were actually selected to be Doves. The fact that the results of our survey appeared to confirm our hypotheses was a spurious consequence of our taking the statistical properties of the population as evidence for the phenotypic properties of the individuals in the population.

Second, suppose that Hawk and Dove are the only available strategies to pursue in competitions for a resource. Suppose further that the resource for which individuals compete is the same in every population, as is the fitness payoff of acquiring that resource. Given these suppositions, the same stable polymorphism of Hawks and Doves would evolve in each population. As a result, there would be uniformity at the population level despite diversity among the individuals in each population. To put this point another way, under the fitness payoffs assumed in the above example, every population would be Hawkish *on average*, so that Hawkishness would be a *cultural universal* (that is, each population's culture would be predominantly characterized by aggressiveness). Despite the cultural universality of Hawkishness, however, the phenotypes of individuals would be polymorphic. Indeed, frequency-dependent selection would act within each population to maintain a balanced polymorphism of Hawks and Doves *within* populations, which would nonetheless produce a Hawkish regularity *across* populations because the various populations all face the same cost-benefit structure in competing for the same essential resource.

To ascend from this concrete example to the more abstract theoretical point that it illustrates, frequency-dependent selection within a population can produce and maintain the same balanced polymorphism of psychological phenotypes in every culture. When the psychological morphs within a polymorphism interact with one another within each culture, their interactions will produce a patterned regularity that will be a fixture of the cultural landscape. Since the same morphs will be interacting in the same ways in every culture, there will consequently be a patterned regularity of interactions *across* cultures, and this patterned regularity will thereby be a cultural universal. Further, this cultural universal will actually be causally *generated* by the interactions among diverse psychological morphs within each culture. Whereas Tooby and Cosmides argue that cultural universals must be generated by psychological universals, this argument presents an alternative. For, even if we assume that cultural universals are generated by the psychological mechanisms of the individuals within each culture, frequency-dependent selection could generate cultural universals out of a balanced polymorphism of psychological phenotypes within each culture. Thus, even if cultural universals are generated by psychological mechanisms, systematic psychological *differences* among individuals within populations could generate cultural universals as easily as psychological universals could.

Of course, in order for frequency-dependent selection to produce and maintain precisely the same balanced polymorphism in different populations, several conditions would have to be met. First, the resource for which individuals compete would have to provide the same fitness benefit in every population. For example, in the Hawk-Dove game we've considered, if the fitness payoff of winning the resource were higher or lower, selection would produce and maintain a different ratio of Hawks to Doves. This doesn't mean that the resource for which there is competition must be the same in every population, but only that the fitness benefit of winning a resource must be the same. Second, in every population, individuals would have to compete for a resource by "choosing" a competitive strategy from the same set of alternative strategies. For example, frequency-dependent selection could produce the same stable polymorphism of Hawks and Doves in every population only if Hawk and Dove were among the competitive strategies from which the individuals in every population had to "choose." Third, the fitness costs associated with each of the available strategies would have to be the same in every population. For example, if Hawk were a costlier strategy in one population than in another, the payoff for playing Hawk would be different in those two populations, and the evolutionarily stable ratio of Hawks to Doves would differ accordingly.

These conditions would have to be met in order for precisely *the same ratio* of alternative strategies to be evolutionarily stable in different populations. But, as long as individuals in different populations "choose" from among the same set of alternative strategies in competing for resources, different populations could have *similar* stable ratios even if the fitness costs and benefits of the resources and the competing strategies differed somewhat. To illustrate, consider again the Hawk-Dove game. If the fitness value of the resource for which Hawks and Doves compete varied from population to population, the stable ratio of Hawks to Doves would vary from population to population as well. If we conducted surveys of the competitive strategies in each population, where Hawk is *2* and Dove is *1* as described above, we might find that population averages ranged from, say, 1.62 to 1.84. Each of these populations would still be predominantly Hawkish, so that Hawkishness would still be a cultural universal (that is, in every culture aggressiveness would dominate competitive interpersonal interactions). Indeed, we might find that the population averages all clustered around a central tendency, so that despite some variation in stable ratios across populations there would be a discernible overall tendency of all populations toward a specific degree of Hawkishness. In such a case, we would detect some degree of cultural variation in competitive interpersonal interactions, but Hawkishness would still be a fairly robust cultural universal.

The real question, of course, is whether the mechanism I have just described underlies any human cultural universals. To that question, I think, the answer is a resounding "maybe." For example, individuals in every culture compete to mate with members of the opposite sex, and the fitness-benefit structure of matings with members of the opposite sex is likely very similar across cultures. In addition, the set of behavioral strategies that individuals can employ to attract and retain mates is probably pretty much the same for everyone; in every culture, individuals probably have the same small set of tactics available to them to woo and keep members of the opposite sex. Thus, mating behavior, which includes mate preferences, is an aspect of human life with respect to which it is quite possible that selection would produce and maintain similar stable polymorphisms across cultures. Indeed, as I argued in chapter 5, mate preferences probably are polymorphic. But, polymorphic male and female mate preferences are nonetheless compatible with average population preferences that cluster around a central mate-preference tendency (which is actually what Buss claims to have found).

Bear in mind that it need not be the case that the resources for which individuals compete in every culture be precisely the same; it need only be the case that individuals "choose" from the same set of strategies to compete for resources of equal fitness value. In addition, the fitness costs of the strategies from which individuals "choose" need not be identical across cultures in order for the population averages from all cultures to cluster closely around a central tendency. Thus, cultural universals could be generated by psychological polymorphisms, provided that individuals across cultures competed for any resources of roughly equal fitness value by "choosing" from the same set of strategies, which could vary somewhat in their fitness costs across cultures. Given the centrality of resource acquisition to survival and reproduction, and given that all humans require some of the same resources in order to survive and reproduce (where members of the opposite sex are reproductive resources), it is a distinct possibility that frequency-dependent selection has produced or maintained some similar stable polymorphisms across cultures. Such polymorphisms would entail psychological variation within cultures, but they would nonetheless generate cross-cultural universals. Consequently, cultural universals are not actually evidence of psychological universals. For each cultural universal discovered, only additional empirical investigation can reveal whether that universal is generated by psychological universals or by a stable polymorphism of psychological variation. Whenever Evolutionary Psychologists infer the existence of psychological universals from the discovery of a cultural universal, they are substituting armchair reasoning for the necessary empirical investigation.

Whereas Evolutionary Psychologists assume that cultural universals would have to be generated by evolved psychological universals, we've just seen how evolved psychological polymorphisms could also generate cultural universals. Both of these alternatives, however, are predicated on the assumption that cultural universals are directly caused by evolved psychological mechanisms without the necessary contribution of any other causal factors. According to Evolutionary Psychology, a culturally universal phenomenon is causally generated in each culture by the psychological adaptations of the inhabitants of that culture. Since the psychological adaptations that generate a given cultural phenomenon are present in all humans, the same cultural phenomenon just happens to be generated in every culture. But its causal generation in each culture is independent of its generation in other cultures. Similarly, according to the alternative I've sketched, the same cultural phenomenon is generated in every culture by the presence of a psychological polymorphism in every culture, so that the presence of that phenomenon in each culture is *causally independent* of its presence in other cultures. In both cases, the presence of a cultural phenomenon causally depends only on the psychologies of the individuals in that culture; it does not causally depend on anything that is happening, or has happened, in any other culture.

But some cultural universals may have emerged without having been generated directly by evolved psychological mechanisms, let alone by universal psychological mechanisms. Some cultural phenomena may be present in all cultures because those phenomena were present in the culture of the ancestral human population from which all extant cultures have descended. For example, suppose that there is a certain ritual that is performed in every culture. Suppose that the precise details and structure of the ritual vary from culture to culture, but that the ritual is recognizably the same in every culture. This ritual could have originated *epidemiologically* in the ancestral human population from which all living humans are descended. That is, the performance of, or idea for, the ritual could have originated with one or a few humans in the ancestral population and then spread through the population via observation and interaction between the source individual(s) and others in the population. The performance of the ritual could have then been continually repeated and taught to subsequent generations, and it could have thereby become a cultural fixture of the ancestral population. As that population expanded, and groups split off and began to disperse across the globe (into Europe, Asia, and Australia) to form new and relatively independent populations, the ritual would have been transmitted to new populations. As those populations then evolved relatively independently of one another, the ritual could have undergone modification over time in each of the splinter populations. As a result, the performance of the ritual would begin to take different forms in different populations. If we did a cross-cultural study in the present day, we would thus find that some variant of the ritual is performed in every culture. In short, we would find that the ritual is a cultural universal.

Thus, the existence of a cultural universal may signal only a common origin of all the world's cultures, rather than common psychological adaptations among all the world's peoples. For, rather than being independently generated within every culture by human psychologies, some cultural universals may have been produced epidemiologically within the ancestral human culture, and they may have then merely persisted in human cultures throughout the process of population expansion and divergence. In this way, some current cultural universals may have a common *cultural* origin, rather than common *psychological* origins. To put it yet another way, some cultural universals may be *cultural homologies*—cultural traits that derived, possibly with modification, from a cultural trait of the ancestral human population from which we all evolved.

There is, in fact, some intriguing evidence of cultural homology, although the phenomenon of cultural homology has been little studied. Consider the universality of the incest taboo. Evolutionary Psychologists argue that the incest taboo is universal among all cultures because it reflects a universal psychological aversion to incest. As we saw in chapter 7, there is good evidence that sexual desire is inhibited between individuals who experience prolonged and intimate exposure to one another during early childhood and that sexual desire is also inhibited in father-daughter pairs in which the father is actively involved in providing care for the daughter in early childhood. Given the well-known deleterious effects of inbreeding, it is difficult not to interpret these facts as the product of an adaptive psychological mechanism, which is designed to inhibit sexual desire for family members. And Evolutionary Psychologists argue that this adaptive psychological mechanism is given expression in disapprovals of incest throughout human cultures. The incest taboo is thus taken to be a clear example of how a purportedly universal psychological adaptation can causally generate a cultural universal.

But Evolutionary Psychology's account of the incest taboo is problematic, for the psychological aversion to sex with childhood associates can't begin to explain the facts about the incest taboo in all the world's cultures.

As the anthropologist William Durham points out, the incest taboo varies widely from culture to culture with respect to the degree of relatedness of the individuals between whom sex is taboo. In some cultures, only sex between siblings is taboo, whereas in other cultures the taboo extends to sex between fifth cousins. Moreover, Durham has shown that this variation is not explained by variation in the likelihood of intimate childhood association of relatives between whom sex is taboo. For example, first cousins are no more likely to be reared together in cultures where sex between first cousins is taboo than in cultures where sex between first cousins is not taboo. Since an inhibition of sexual desire for those with whom one was reared can only work to avert sex with those with whom one was reared, even the universality of such a mechanism can't explain why there would be taboos against sex with relatives with whom children are consistently *not* reared. Thus, the incest taboo *as a cultural phenomenon* can't simply be generated by an evolved aversion to sex with intimate childhood associates. While that psychological mechanism may be perfectly real, and while it may also be an adaptation, it is simply insufficient to account for the extent and complexities of the incest taboo as a cultural phenomenon.

Durham argues, instead, that in all cultures the incest taboo is based on minimizing the sum of the costs of inbreeding and the costs of outbreeding. Durham argues that in each culture there is a recognition of the deleterious effects of inbreeding, so that every culture recognizes certain reproductive costs associated with inbreeding. In each culture, however, there are also social and reproductive costs involved in outbreeding. These costs vary from culture to culture as a function of such things as degree of access to unrelated mates. As a result, the sum of the costs of inbreeding and the costs of outbreeding varies from culture to culture. Where the costs of outbreeding are low, the sum will be low, and the incest taboo will extend to include a wider range of relatives, such as third and fourth cousins. Where the costs of outbreeding are high, the sum will also be high, and the incest taboo will be restricted to siblings or first cousins. Not only did Durham find that this pattern held in a study of sixty cultures in the Human Relations Area Files, but he found that all sixty of these cultures were related by descent. Thus, Durham concludes, the evidence suggests "that all existing incest taboos are related by descent to one, or a few, ancestral prohibitions," so that existing incest taboos "may all be cultural homologs—locally refined variations on the same ancestral theme."[52]

Evolutionary Psychologists also point out that myths are culturally universal, and they argue that myth is an expression of the functioning of universal psychological adaptations. Among the culturally universal myths are creation myths—myths about the creation of the universe, in general, and of humans, in particular. But creation myths appear to be cultural homologies. For, in a study of all Indo-European creation myths, the anthropologist Bruce Lincoln found systematic structural similarities among the historical creation myths from Europe, the Middle East, and Asia (including the Judeo-Christian creation myth). These similarities, Lincoln argues, indicate descent with modification from a common "proto-Indo-European" creation myth, which Lincoln argues was the myth of the population from which all Indo-European populations descended. And that myth arguably took hold in the ancestral population through epidemiological culture. Thus, extant creation myths appear to be cultural homologies, rather than direct expressions of universal innate psychological adaptations.

Similarly, in chapter 6 we saw Evolutionary Psychologists argue that marriage is a cultural universal, where marriage is defined as an implicit reproductive contract. We saw how marriage, in this sense, could have evolved, and we saw how certain needs and desires could have evolved along with it. We also saw that, although it is not an essential feature of marriage, in the vast majority of the world's cultures marriage typically involves some sort of ritual solemnization of a mateship before the community. In fact, communal solemnization rituals, or "marriage ceremonies," are such a ubiquitous accompaniment of marriage that some anthropologists have taken them to be the defining feature of marriage. While the formation of long-term mateships is explicable as the causal product of evolved psychological needs and desires, the cultural phenomenon of the marriage ceremony is not as easily explicable in the same way. Rather, it is possible that the cultural variants of the marriage ceremony are cultural homologies, cultural ceremonies that are all descended from an ancestral marriage ceremony, which was elaborated and modified in a variety of ways in different populations and which disappeared entirely in a few populations.

Thus, cultural universals are not necessarily the causal product of psychological universals, as Evolutionary Psychologists suppose. In fact, there are (at least) two other mechanisms that would generate cultural universals in the absence of psychological universals. First, universal psychological polymorphisms could generate cultural universals despite systematic psychological variation within each culture. Second, some cultural universals may be cultural homologies, cultural traits that originated epidemiologically in an ancestral human population and were then transmitted, possibly with modification, down different lineages as human populations diverged and spread across the globe. As a result, cultural universals do not provide evidence of a universal human nature, if human nature is understood to consist of universal psychological adaptations, which is how Evolutionary Psychologists understand it. There are several processes that could have produced any given cultural universal, and only extensive, and often very difficult, empirical investigation can reveal how a cultural universal was produced and whether it has any connection to evolved psychological mechanisms, let alone universal psychological adaptations. In the absence of such empirical investigation, the existence of cultural universals provides no evidence for Evolutionary Psychology's claims about the existence of psychological universals.

**Please Be Patient; Evolution Isn't Finished with Us Yet**

But suppose that Evolutionary Psychologists were able to provide the necessary independent evidence of some psychological universals. Indeed, suppose they were able to provide independent evidence that at least some of these psychological universals are adaptations. Would those discoveries vindicate Evolutionary Psychology's theory of a universal human nature? In the remainder of this chapter, I will argue that it would not. Even if there were some psychological universals, Evolutionary Psychology's theory of human nature would not represent a truly *evolutionary* interpretation of the significance of those universals. In fact, there are two respects in which Evolutionary Psychology would distort a truly evolutionary understanding of any discovered psychological universals.

First, even if there are psychological universals, at least some of them are likely the result of genetic drift, rather than selection, since some portion of all fixated traits in a population are typically due to drift. This is not to say that a psychological universal due to drift must have evolved independently by drift *in each of the world's populations*. Rather, it is possible that a psychological trait evolved to fixation under genetic drift in our species' ancestral (founder) population. The best available evidence indicates that our species evolved from a single, relatively small population, and it is very easy for traits to drift to fixation in small populations. Once fixated, the trait could have simply persisted, without being significantly modified, as human populations expanded and diverged. In this way, a psychological trait that we discovered to be universal could have emerged under drift very early in our species' history.

Now, I do not cite this possibility in order to argue that some psychological universals evolved by drift or to debate the likelihood that any given proportion of whatever psychological universals there may be evolved by drift rather than selection. Rather, I cite this possibility to draw attention to how a drift-fixated psychological trait would figure in Evolutionary Psychology's theory of a universal human nature. For Evolutionary Psychologists argue that drift-fixated traits are not typically incorporated into the "functional design" of an organism, and Evolutionary Psychology's theory of human nature is focused on the "functional design" of the human mind. For this reason, Evolutionary Psychologists would not take a drift-fixated psychological trait to be part of human nature, despite its universality. Indeed, Evolutionary Psychology's conception of human nature is expressly restricted to universal psychological *adaptations*. But, a drift-fixated psychological trait would be every bit as efficacious in causing behavior as a selection-fixated psychological trait would be. Indeed, whereas universal adaptations would explain some aspects of behavior, a drift-fixated psychological trait would undoubtedly figure indispensably in the explanation of other aspects of behavior. Nonetheless, Evolutionary Psychologists would not count that trait as part of human nature. But why should the concept of human nature be restricted to adaptations, rather than applied to the totality of psychological traits that have evolved by any evolutionary process?

This question returns us to the issue of adaptationism, although not adaptationism in the way that Stephen Jay Gould understood it. As we saw in chapter 3, and contrary to Gould, Evolutionary Psychology does not suppose that all evolved aspects of the human mind are adaptations. In that sense, it is not adaptationist. But Evolutionary Psychology *is* adaptationist in the sense that it conceives of adaptations as occupying a more central place in our psychologies than any other psychological traits— indeed, so central a place that *only* psychological adaptations constitute our *nature*.

Privileging adaptations in this way, however, and viewing them as "natural" in a way that other traits are not, has no foundation in evolutionary theory proper. In fact, to view adaptations as "central" to an organism's "nature," in a way that nonadaptations are not, is to adopt what the philosopher of biology Peter Godfrey-Smith calls a form of *natural theology*. It is a form of natural theology because a central focus on adaptations is a theoretical vestige of the theological worldview that held sway prior to the development of evolutionary theory. To see why, let's take a brief excursus into intellectual history.

In *Natural Theology*, first published in 1802, the Reverend William Paley asks us to imagine finding a watch on the ground. Upon examining the watch, we would find it to be composed of a number of intricate parts that are complexly interconnected in ways necessary to produce the observable motions of the hands, which successfully tell the time. The inescapable conclusion, Paley argues, would be that the watch is *designed*, "that its several parts are framed and put together for a purpose."[53] The existence of such complex design requires explanation, Paley argues, and he claims that there is only one plausible explanation: "the inference, we think, is inevitable, that the watch must have had a maker."[54] For, as Paley says: "There cannot be design without a designer; contrivance, without a contriver; order, without choice; arrangement, without any thing capable of arranging; subserviency and relation to a purpose, without that which could intend a purpose; means suitable to an end, and executing their office in accomplishing that end, without the end ever having been contemplated, or the means accommodated to it. Arrangement, disposition of parts, subserviency of means to an end, relation of instruments to a use, imply the presence of intelligence and mind."[55]

Further, Paley argues, when we turn our attention to "the works of nature," we find "contrivances" that exhibit an even greater degree of complex design than is exhibited by watches: "I mean that the contrivances of nature surpass the contrivances of art, in the complexity, subtilty, and curiosity of the mechanism: and still more, if possible, do they go beyond them in number and variety: yet, in a multitude of cases, are not less evidently mechanical, not less evidently contrivances, not less evidently accommodated to their end, or suited to their office, than are the most perfect productions of human ingenuity."[56] The eye, Paley argues, is an instrument that exhibits remarkably complex design for the purpose of vision. In fact, the design of the eye varies with the needs of its function. For the lens of the eye of a fish is rounder than that of terrestrial animals, which adapts the fish eye to the refractory properties of water. Since the complex design of the watch leads to the conclusion that it was created by an intelligent watchmaker, Paley contends, the complex design of organs such as the eye, and of the organisms that possess numerous complexly interconnected organs, must similarly lead to the conclusion that they were created by an intelligent being—namely, God.

This and similar arguments became known as the *argument from design*, since the basic idea is that the existence of complex design in nature presupposes the existence of an intelligent designer. Subscribers to the argument from design also maintain that the complex, purposeful design within organic form reveals the Creator's "works." Complex design within nature, they claim, reveals the natural order that conforms to God's intentions in creating the universe and the life forms within it. In short, complex design *is* what God created.

For the majority of educated Westerners, the argument from design, in one form or another, provided the intellectual framework for understanding nature throughout the better part of the nineteenth century. More important, the argument from design set the terms of the debate between creationists and *naturalists*, those who believed that all of nature came to be through the operation of laws of nature, without any intervention by an intelligent being. For the argument from design posed the challenge that any naturalistic theory had to overcome: Provide a convincing explanation of how complex design could have emerged without the intervention of an intelligent being. Thus, throughout the nineteenth century, *the* problem that naturalistic theories had to solve was the problem of complex design.

This was the intellectual context within which Darwin developed his theory of evolution. Indeed, Darwin had read Paley and had been impressed by Paley's argument from design. As a result, the problem of complex design—the problem of what Darwin called "organs of extreme perfection and complication"—became Darwin's own litmus test for his theory of evolution. In an extended argument, Darwin took on Paley's own example of the eye in order to demonstrate that the process of natural selection was capable of creating "organs of extreme perfection and complication." The process by which it does so, as we saw in chapter 1, consists of iterated rounds of modification to a preexisting trait followed by retention of modifications that prove beneficial and elimination of those that prove detrimental. Darwin thereby provided a naturalistic solution to the problem of complex design, meeting Paley's challenge, and his theory of evolution accordingly became a viable explanation of the origins of life. In fact, a forceful demonstration of how decisively Darwin's theory of natural selection answered Paley's challenge is provided by the evolutionary biologist Richard Dawkins in his book *The Blind Watchmaker*, the title of which is an allusion to Paley's argument.

But, while natural selection was the mechanism that met Paley's challenge, there has always been much more to evolutionary theory than explaining how "organs of extreme perfection and complication" arose by natural selection. For one thing, the process of selection itself doesn't result only in complex adaptations. Selection also eliminates traits from populations and, arguably, eliminates entire groups or populations. Since Darwin's time, it has also become clear that selection can sometimes prevent a population from becoming optimally adapted to its environment. For another thing, there is much more to evolution than natural selection. Selection is just one force among many that drive the process of evolution, and these forces are all implicated in having generated the diversity of life forms on earth. Further, all of these evolutionary forces can affect the form and characteristics of organisms as well as the diversity of life. Explaining the diversity of life, past extinctions, and both adaptive and nonadaptive evolution within populations are all among the problems with which evolutionary theory deals. Thus, there are actually numerous problems concerning organic form and the diversity of life to which evolutionary theory provides, and aspires to provide, solutions.

Given that the problem of complex design is but one among many problems in evolutionary theory, why should it be accorded a central status? The answer, of course, is that it shouldn't be accorded a central status, because it doesn't occupy a central place within the array of problems that evolutionary theory addresses. This can be seen by examining any introductory textbook in evolutionary biology. The problem of complex design was actually *Paley's problem*. It was the problem that nineteenth-century theologians used to challenge naturalistic accounts of the origins and complexity of life, and they chose that problem because they thought it to be unsolvable by naturalistic theories. There is nothing *in the nature of things* that dictates that the problem of complex design is central to understanding life on earth. There is nothing *in the nature of things* that mandates that we should consider explaining complex design to be more important than explaining, say, the Cambrian explosion, the unprecedented and since unequaled proliferation of species between 535 and 525 million years ago. Rather, a focus on the problem of complex design reflects the *explanatory interests* of Paley and the nineteenth-century natural theologians. Thus, to see natural selection, and the creation of complex design, as the centerpiece of evolutionary theory is to retain the problem that was created by Paley and the theologians and merely to replace their solution to the problem with a naturalistic solution. That is, to retain a focus on the problem of complex design is to adopt naturalism, but only within the framework of natural theology. It is to view the significance of evolutionary theory through a lens that was ground by natural theologians.

But evolutionary theory has triumphed over Paley and the natural theologians. No one committed to allowing the evidence to decide between evolutionary theory and natural theology can see creationism as a viable alternative to evolutionary theory. And once evolutionary theory is accepted as an account of the origins and diversity of life, there is no longer any reason to draw our problems from the framework of natural theology to which Darwin responded in the middle of the nineteenth century. There is no longer any reason to view evolutionary theory through the lens of a preevolutionary, theological worldview. Indeed, to truly accept evolutionary theory as an account of the diversity of life is to allow evolutionary theory itself to determine which are the interesting and important problems about organic form and the diversity of life. However, when evolutionary theory itself is taken as the *source of problems* about the nature of life, rather than as simply the source of solutions to preevolutionary problems, the problem of adaptation becomes merely one among, and on a par with, many problems with which evolutionary theory deals. Once we take evolutionary theory on its own terms, rather than on Paley's terms, we can see that there is no sense in which evolution is *all about* adaptation in the way that God's creation *was* all about complex design.

Thus, to see adaptations as central to human "nature" in a way that nonadaptations are not—to see human "nature" as consisting exclusively of adaptations—is to view the human organism through the theoretical prism of natural theology. It is to replace God with Natural Selection as the Creator, but to still maintain that the Creator's "intention," as manifested in what was selected for, represents the "nature" of our species, departure from which is "abnormal." But this exclusive focus on adaptations in Evolutionary Psychology's theory of human nature does not derive from evolutionary theory itself, and it receives no justification from evolutionary theory. Rather, this focus is a preevolutionary interpretation of the human organism; it is a theoretical vestige of natural theology. Consequently, Evolutionary Psychology's adaptation-centered theory of human nature is in no true sense *evolutionary*.

In order to forestall any potential misunderstanding, let me be very clear about what I am claiming. I am *not* claiming that humans possess no psychological adaptations, and I am *not* claiming (as we saw Gould claim) that human psychological adaptations constitute a small and insignificant part of human psychology. Rather, I am claiming only that *there is no basis in evolutionary theory* for maintaining that psychological adaptations are constitutive of human "nature" in a way that psychological traits that aren't adaptations are not. There undoubtedly are adaptations in every species, but adaptations do not represent the "order of nature" or the raison d'être of evolution. The belief that they do is an imposition upon evolutionary theory that derives from a preevolutionary worldview.

Let's turn now to the second respect in which Evolutionary Psychology's theory of human nature represents a distortion of a truly evolutionary view of life. As we saw in chapter 2, Evolutionary Psychologists believe that the totality of human psychological universals "reflects completed rather than ongoing selection."[57] We saw in chapter 3, however, that selection is continuing to modify traits and trait frequencies in human populations. There has been significant adaptive evolution in human physiological and morphological traits in the past few thousand years, and there is clear evidence that ongoing environmental changes continue to drive adaptive evolution in those traits. Since human psychological evolution is driven largely by human social life, the profound changes in human social life over the past several thousand years, which I detailed in chapter 3, are assuredly driving ongoing evolution in human psychological traits as well. In short, human populations have been evolving since the Pleistocene and they continue to evolve.

This means that any psychological universals we might happen to discover—*if* we were to discover any at all—are temporally contingent. For any psychological universals we might happen to discover in the present did not characterize our species in the past and are subject to change as our species continues to evolve. Today's universals were not yesterday's universals, and today's universals may be possessed by only a fraction of our species, or even extinguished altogether, tomorrow. Thus, any psychological universals we might happen to discover in the present would not characterize *Homo sapiens* per se, but would only characterize our species at this particular moment in evolutionary time.

When the world is viewed under the aspect of evolutionary time, however, the present doesn't occupy a privileged position. *Even if* our species hasn't undergone any significant evolution in the past 10,000 years, which is assuredly contrary to fact, those 10,000 years are just a blip in evolutionary time. Indeed, 10,000 years represents a mere 7 percent, at most, of our own species' evolutionary history to date. When we view our species under the aspect of evolutionary time, the present is just one of many vantage points from which we could take a snapshot of the traits, psychological or otherwise, that characterize our species. And any psychological universals that may happen to characterize our species in the present—or even over the past 10,000 years—are no more "central" to our species, no more a part of our species' "nature," than psychological traits that may have characterized our species 100,000 years ago or that may characterize our species 100,000 years from now. Any focus on present psychological universals, then, is merely an artifact of our occupying the present while we study ourselves. But, while we must always, of necessity, study ourselves from the vantage point of the present, it is *temporal provincialism* to interpret present facts about us as more significant than past or (necessarily unknowable) future facts about us. Thus, even if there are psychological universals that now characterize our species, and even if those universals have characterized our species for 10,000 years, it is a mistake to think, as Evolutionary Psychologists do, that these universals reveal to us the "nature" of our species, in any interesting sense of the word *nature*.

Evolutionary Psychology's temporal provincialism, however, is but a symptom of its vestigial natural theology. For natural theology is a *product theory*, a theory designed to explain how certain products came into existence. Paley and his fellow natural theologians viewed the organic world as consisting of life forms that were *finished products*, with fixed, unchanging natures. In this respect, they viewed species as similar to watches. A watch has a fixed, unchanging design, which is embodied by a finished watch that keeps time. If we want to explain how something as complex as a watch has come to be, we attempt to discover a process that could have resulted in that finished product (the watch). Our understanding of the process, and the explanatory function that appeal to the process serves, is conditioned entirely by the finished product. For the finished product, the outcome of the process, represents the *end point* of the process we are trying to understand. The process itself then gets conceptualized as nothing more than a series of events that lead up to the production of the finished product and that *terminates* with its appearance. This, in fact, was the conceptual framework within which Paley and the natural theologians understood creation by God. Species were conceived as finished products, and creation was conceived as the process by which God produced those finished products. Once those products were created, the process of creation terminated, and God rested.

In viewing the psychological adaptations that constitute human nature as the result of "completed rather than ongoing selection," Evolutionary Psychology perpetuates this aspect of natural theology. For it thereby views psychological adaptations as finished products, which must be explained by appeal to a process that terminated with those products. It differs from natural theology only with respect to the process to which it appeals in order to explain the finished products. Whereas natural theology appeals to creation by God, Evolutionary Psychology appeals to evolution by natural and sexual selection. In this way, however, Evolutionary Psychology retains the structure of the theoretical framework of natural theology. And, within that structure, Evolutionary Psychology simply views evolutionary theory as an alternative to creation by God as an explanation of the *production* of complex psychological design. Evolutionary Psychology thereby treats evolutionary theory as a *product theory*, a theory designed to explain how particular products (for example, adaptations) came to be.

But evolutionary theory is not a product theory, and evolution is not a watchmaker, blind or otherwise. Evolutionary theory is purely a *process theory*. Evolution, as we saw in chapter 1, is *change across generations* within lineages. Some of these changes occur across generations within a single species, and such changes are known collectively as *microevolution*, which is what we've been discussing throughout this book. More technically, as we have seen, microevolution is change in gene or genotype frequencies across generations within a population. But other transgenerational changes involve the branching of lineages, which occurs when populations become reproductively isolated. Those changes result in the creation of new species, many of which eventually go extinct. So, other transgenerational changes in lineages result in the creation and extinction of species, and such changes are known collectively as *macroevolution*. Whether we're dealing with microevolution or macroevolution, however, we're dealing with *change across generations*. And evolutionary theory is designed to explain these changes. That is, the objective of evolutionary theory is to discover all the principles that govern transgenerational change and to thereby explain the origins of species and the changes that occur within them. In short, evolution is a *process*, and evolutionary theory is designed to explain the dynamics of that process. Evolutionary theory is designed to explain *change*.

Thus, evolutionary theory is designed to serve a much different function than the function served by the creationism of the natural theologians. For evolutionary theory is not designed to explain the creation of some pretheoretically specified products. Indeed, in evolution there are no *products* in any robust sense of the term. We can, of course, now look at nature and see a variety of organisms with particular constellations of genetic and phenotypic properties. But the organisms we now see do not represent the final products of evolution. Rather, they represent *the current stage of the process* of evolution. Evolutionary theory explains the origins and characteristics of the organisms we now see only insofar as they are embedded within the process of change that evolutionary theory explains. It does not explain the origins and characteristics of the organisms we now see in the same way that creationism explains them but by appealing to different kinds of creation event. For evolutionary theory and creationism are actually designed to explain different phenomena. Evolutionary theory explains a process, whereas creationism explains products.

When we view ourselves through the theoretical prism of evolutionary theory, then, we don't simply get a new explanation of how we came to be the way that we are, as Evolutionary Psychology supposes. Rather, we get a new understanding of *what* we are. We are not a species with a fixed "nature" that was created by "millions of years of selection." We are not a product. We are a work in progress, which can only be considered "completed," in the most tenuous sense of the term, upon extinction. And whatever properties we may now possess—psychological or otherwise, universal or otherwise—are but radically contingent and momentary stages of that work in progress. Even if our species has been characterized by the same properties for longer than recorded history, which is assuredly contrary to fact, those properties would be no less contingent and momentary and no more a part of our "nature" than any other properties. Indeed, if we could view the world under the aspect of evolutionary time, we would be able to *see* the momentary character of such properties, and they would appear as no more central to our species' identity than teenage pimples are to a person's total identity from the womb to the tomb. While a teenager may feel that their entire existence is wrapped up in a pimple at the moment they've got it, if we are to take a truly evolutionary view of our species we need to recognize the insignificance of the present: Our species was not always as it is now, and it will not remain as it is now. Taking a truly evolutionary view of ourselves will involve relinquishing the temporal provincialism that Evolutionary Psychology's theory of human nature offers us.

Thus, if we learn to see ourselves as evolutionary theory teaches us to see ourselves, we will not be tempted by Evolutionary Psychology's theory of human nature. For we will learn to see our current adaptations—even if some of those *are* universal psychological adaptations—under the aspect of evolutionary time. When we do, we will recognize that evolution isn't finished with us yet, and our current adaptations will appear no more definitive of our "nature" than past or future adaptations. We will also recognize that there is no evolutionary justification for conceiving of our adaptations as the properties that we have "by nature." When we do, universal adaptations will appear no more definitive of our "nature" than nonuniversal adaptations or nonadaptations. We will then see why Michael Ghiselin says that evolution teaches us that human nature is a superstition. Indeed, if we learn to see ourselves as *evolutionary theory* teaches us to see ourselves, rather than as Evolutionary Psychology urges us to see ourselves, we will see that human nature is just as great a superstition as the creation myth of natural theologians.

# Epilogue

Evolutionary Psychology is a deeply ambitious enterprise. It presents us with a Grand Unified Theory of the structure and evolution of the human mind, and its proponents have busily gathered some provocative evidence for a number of intriguing hypotheses derived from that Grand Unified Theory—hypotheses about many of the most intimate aspects of our lives. As I have argued throughout this book, however, Evolutionary Psychology is wrong in almost every detail. The problem isn't that it rests on "one big mistake," but that it makes little mistakes at nearly every theoretical and empirical turn. In short, the picture of ourselves that Evolutionary Psychology offers fails to provide us with an accurate evolutionary understanding of human psychology.

This is not to say, however, that there has been no progress whatsoever in understanding human behavior and mentality from an evolutionary perspective. Indeed, I believe that there has been. For example, the work of Kristen Hawkes on the "grandmother hypothesis," briefly discussed in chapter 5, and the work of both Hawkes and her colleagues and Barbara Smuts and David Gubernick on the evolution of male parental care, discussed in chapter 6, represent the sort of progress that I believe has been made in applying evolutionary theory to human behavior. But such progress has been piecemeal; the understanding thus gained is not (yet) unified within a single theoretical framework.

In short, even though Evolutionary Psychology fails to provide us with an accurate Grand Unified Theory of the evolution of human psychology, there is no alternative Grand Unified Theory yet available. We really don't yet know how to understand the rich panoply of human psychology from an evolutionary perspective. Perhaps someday we will achieve that understanding. But that day is not at hand, and it is certainly not at hand in the form of Evolutionary Psychology. Coming to terms with the mistakes of Evolutionary Psychology, however, may help us eventually to achieve a new and improved evolutionary psychology.

# Notes

## Introduction

1. Beynon 1994.
2. Dawkins 1989, p. 20.
3. Rose and Rose 2000, p. 3.
4. Gould 1997.
5. Daly and Wilson 1999, p. 48.
6. Thornhill and Palmer 2000, p. 115.
7. Maynard Smith 1995, p. 46.
8. Caporael 2001, p. 608; Barrett, Dunbar and Lycett 2002, p. 1.
9. Buss 1999, p. xix.
10. Kennair 2003, p. 30.

## Chapter 1

1. Darwin 1859/1964, p. 186.
2. Sober 1984, p. 211.

## Chapter 2

1. Futuyma 1998, p. 579; whole phrase italicized in original.
2. Cosmides and Tooby 1987, p. 281.
3. Cosmides and Tooby 1987, p. 282; whole sentence italicized in original.
4. Crook and Crook 1988, p. 98.
5. Symons 1990, p. 435.
6. Tooby and Cosmides 1990b, p. 386.

7. Tooby and Cosmides 1990b, p. 388.

8. Cosmides and Tooby 1997, p. 85.

9. Pinker 1997, p. 386.

10. Cosmides, Tooby, and Barkow 1992, p. 5.

11. Cosmides, Tooby, and Barkow 1992, p. 5.

12. Tooby and Cosmides 1992, p. 110.

13. Pinker 1997, p. 21; emphasis added.

14. Tooby and Cosmides 1995, p. xiv.

15. Symons 1992, p. 142.

16. Symons 1992, p. 142.

17. Cosmides and Tooby 1994, p. 93.

18. Tooby and Cosmides 1992, p. 113.

19. Tooby and Cosmides 1995, p. xiii; emphasis added.

20. Buss 1995, p. 6.

21. Buss 1995, p. 6.

22. Tooby and Cosmides 1992, p. 68.

23. Buss 1995, p. 6.

24. Symons 1992, p. 139.

25. Tooby and Cosmides 1990b, pp. 380–381.

26. Cosmides, Tooby, and Barkow 1992, p. 5.

27. Tooby and Cosmides 1990a, p. 19.

28. Tooby and Cosmides 1992, p. 38.

29. Tooby and Cosmides 1992, p. 45.

30. Tooby and Cosmides 1992, p. 45.

31. Tooby and Cosmides 1992, p. 38.

32. Tooby and Cosmides 1992, p. 78.

33. Tooby and Cosmides 1992, pp. 78–79.

34. Symons 1995, p. 84.

35. Tooby and Cosmides 1992, p. 79.

36. Tooby and Cosmides 1990a, p. 24.

37. Buss 1995, p. 11.

38. Tooby and Cosmides 1990a, p. 55.

39. Cosmides, Tooby, and Barkow 1992, p. 5; emphasis added.

40. Tooby and Cosmides 1992, p. 82.

41. Crawford 1998, p. 280.

42. Crawford 1998, p. 280.

43. Tooby and Cosmides 1992, p. 45.

44. Tooby and Cosmides 1992, p. 84.

45. Tooby and Cosmides 1992, p. 45.

46. Tooby and Cosmides 1990a, p. 46.

47. Tooby and Cosmides 1990a, p. 46.

48. Tooby and Cosmides 1992, p. 81.

49. Tooby and Cosmides 1992, p. 82.

## Chapter 3

1. Gould 1997, p. 51.

2. Gould and Lewontin 1979, pp. 584–585.

3. Gould 1997, p. 50.

4. Gould and Vrba 1982, p. 6.

5. Gould and Vrba 1982, p. 6.

6. Gould 1997, p. 52; emphasis added.

7. Gould 1991, p. 57; emphasis added.

8. Gould 1991, p. 57.

9. Pinker 1997a, p. 174; emphasis added.

10. Pinker 1997b, pp. 55–56.

11. Gould and Lewontin 1979, p. 588.

12. Gould and Lewontin 1979, p. 587.

13. Gould 1997, pp. 50–51.

14. Gould 1997, p. 51.

15. Gould 1997, p. 51.

16. Gould 1997, p. 51.

17. Gould 1997, p. 51.

18. Gould 1997, p. 51.

19. Gould 1997, p. 51.

20. Buss 1992, p. 249.

21. Tooby and Cosmides 1992, pp. 68–69.

22. Tooby and Cosmides 1992, p. 67.

23. Cosmides and Tooby 1994, p. 96; emphasis added.

24. Tooby and Cosmides 1992, p. 76.

25. Thornhill 1997, p. 11.

26. Buss 1998, p. 29.

27. Kelly 1995, pp. 25–26.

28. Gittleman et al. 1996; Böhning-Gaese and Oberrath 1999.

29. Pinker 1997b, p. 56.

30. Lewontin 1983b, p. 76.

31. Sterelny and Griffiths 1999, p. 331.

32. Laland, Odling-Smee, and Feldman 2000, p. 137.

33. Cosmides and Tooby 1994, p. 96.

34. Tooby and Cosmides 1990b, pp. 380–381.

35. Cosmides, Tooby, and Barkow 1992, p. 5.

36. Wilson 1994, p. 226.

37. Laland, Odling-Smee, and Feldman 2000, p. 132.

38. Tooby and Cosmides 1992, p. 79; emphasis added.

39. Wilson 1994, p. 232.

40. Tooby and Cosmides 1992, p. 45.

41. Tooby and Cosmides 1992, p. 45.

42. Tooby and Cosmides 1992, p. 78.

43. Symons 1995, p. 84.

44. Wilson 1994, pp. 227–228.

45. Tooby and Cosmides 1990a, p. 48.

46. Tooby and Cosmides 1990a, p. 46.

47. Tooby and Cosmides 1990a, p. 24.

48. Tooby and Cosmides 1990a, pp. 38–39.

49. Tooby and Cosmides 1992, p. 45.

50. Crawford 1998, p. 280.

51. Crawford 1998, p. 280.

52. Tooby and Cosmides 1992, p. 82; emphasis added.

53. Tooby and Cosmides 1992, p. 45.

54. Symons 1992, p. 139.

55. Tooby and Cosmides 1992, p. 84.

56. Tooby and Cosmides 1990a, p. 47; emphasis added.

57. Tooby and Cosmides 1992, p. 84.

58. Tooby and Cosmides 1992, p. 84.

59. Quoted in Lewin 1984, p. 1328.

## Chapter 4

1. Pinker 1997, p. 21.

2. Tooby and Cosmides 1995, p. xiii; emphasis added.

3. Cosmides and Tooby 1997, p. 81.

4. Cosmides and Tooby 1997, p. 78.

5. Tooby and Cosmides 1992, p. 59.

6. Cosmides and Tooby 1997, p. 82.

7. Tooby and Cosmides 1995, p. xiv.

8. Cosmides and Tooby 1997, p. 84.

9. Tooby and Cosmides 1992, p. 113.

10. Pinker 1997, pp. 21 and 32.

11. Tooby and Cosmides 1992, pp. 81–82; emphasis added.

12. Deacon 1997, p. 194.

13. Pinker 1997, p. 32.

14. Futuyma 1998, p. 227.

15. Symons 1992, p. 142.

16. Cosmides and Tooby 1994, p. 92.

17. Cosmides and Tooby 1994, p. 90.

18. Cosmides and Tooby 1994, pp. 91–92.

19. Tooby and Cosmides 1992, p. 39.

20. Symons 1992, p. 142.

21. Cosmides and Tooby 1994, p. 92.

22. Cosmides and Tooby 1994, p. 93.

23. Tooby and Cosmides 1992, p. 34.

24. Ellis 1992, p. 268.

25. Wright 1994, pp. 259–261; emphasis added.

26. Symons 1992, p. 143.

27. Trivers 1971, p. 48.

28. Cosmides 1989, p. 196.

29. Cosmides 1989, p. 197.

30. Cosmides and Tooby 1992, p. 180.

31. Cosmides 1989, p. 264.

32. Gigerenzer and Hug 1992, p. 154.

33. Fiddick, Cosmides, and Tooby 2000, p. 28.

34. Cosmides and Tooby 1992, p. 180; emphasis added.

35. Fiddick, Cosmides, and Tooby 2000, p. 70.

36. Fiddick, Cosmides, and Tooby 2000, p. 57.

37. Sperber, Cara, and Girotto 1995, p. 83.

38. Cosmides 1989, p. 217.

39. Fiddick, Cosmides, and Tooby 2000, p. 57.

40. Gerrans 2002, p. 316.

41. Tooby and Cosmides 1992, p. 29; emphasis added.

42. Tooby and Cosmides 1992, p. 66.

## Chapter 5

1. Kenrick and Keefe 1992, p. 78.

2. Buss 1999, p. 134.

3. Ellis 1992, p. 268.

4. Buss 1992, p. 250.

5. Buss 1999, p. 136.

6. Buss 1999, p. 139.

7. Buss 1992, p. 250.

8. Buss 1994, pp. 51 and 25.

9. Buss 1994, p. 25.

10. Buss 1989, p. 9.

11. Buss 1989, p. 9.

12. Kenrick and Keefe 1992, p. 85.

13. Kenrick and Keefe 1992, p. 79.

14. Kenrick and Keefe 1992, p. 88.

15. Kenrick, Keefe, Gabrielidis, and Cornelius 1996, p. 1505.

16. Kenrick, Keefe, Gabrielidis, and Cornelius 1996, p. 1506; emphasis added.

17. Kenrick, Keefe, Gabrielidis, and Cornelius 1996, p. 1505; emphasis added.

18. Buss 1999, p. 136; emphasis added.

19. Buss 1999, p. 104.

20. Ellis 1992, p. 268.

21. Ellis 1992, p. 268.

22. Ellis 1992, p. 274.

23. Sadalla, Kenrick, and Vershure 1987, p. 733.

24. Sadalla, Kenrick, and Vershure 1987, p. 733.

25. Townsend and Levy 1990a, p. 376.

26. Ellis 1992, p. 270.

27. Kenrick and Keefe 1992, p. 85.

28. Ellis 1992, p. 268; emphasis added.

29. Kenrick, Sadalla, Groth, and Trost 1990, p. 103.

30. Buss 1989, p. 41.

31. Wiederman and Allgeier 1992, p. 122.

32. Buss 1989, p. 3.

33. Pérusse 1993, p. 275.

34. Buss 1994, p. 63.

35. Stevens, Owens, and Schaefer 1990, p. 69.

36. Umberson and Hughes 1987; Hamermesh and Biddle 1994; Mulford, Orbell, Shatto, and Stockard 1998.

37. De Waal 2000, p. 24.

38. Gagneux, Boesch, and Woodruff 1999, p. 20.

39. Buss 1999, p. 352.

40. Buss 1999, p. 184.

41. Ellis 1992, p. 269.

## Chapter 6

1. Buckle, Gallup, and Rodd 1996, p. 364.
2. Wilson and Daly 1992, p. 309; emphasis added.
3. Daly and Wilson 1988, p. 187.
4. Daly and Wilson 1996, p. 15.
5. Symons 1985, p. 142.
6. Symons 1985, p. 141.
7. Fisher 1992, p. 73.
8. Fisher 1992, p. 74.
9. Buss 2000, p. 223.
10. Buss 1994, p. 126.
11. Buss 1999, p. 162.
12. Twain 1991, p. 38.
13. Smith 1984, p. 602.
14. Fisher 1992, p. 90.
15. Kinsey, Pomeroy, and Martin 1948, p. 585.
16. Buss 2000, p. 16.
17. Buss 2000, p. 160.
18. Buss 2000, p. 162.
19. Buss 2000, p. 159.
20. Buss 2000, p. 159; emphasis added.
21. Gangestad, Thornhill, and Garver 2002, p. 975.
22. Buss 2000, p. 162.
23. Buss 2000, p. 173.
24. Greiling and Buss 2000, p. 935.
25. Greiling and Buss 2000, p. 960.
26. Adams, Gold, and Burt 1978; Hill 1988; Stanislaw and Rice 1988; Regan 1996.
27. Gangestad 2001, p. 67.
28. Greiling and Buss 2000, p. 935; emphasis added.
29. Daly, Wilson, and Weghorst 1982, p. 12.
30. Buss et al. 1999, p. 126; emphasis added.
31. Buss 2000, p. 4.

32. Buss et al. 1999, p. 125.

33. Buss 2000, p. 4.

34. Buss 1999, p. 325.

35. Buss 1999, p. 326.

36. Buss 1994, p. 129.

37. Buss 2000, p. 61.

38. Buss 2000, p. 30.

39. Buss, Larsen, Westen, and Semmelroth 1992, p. 252.

40. Data from Buss, Larsen, Westen, and Semmelroth 1992; Geary, Rumsey, Bow-Thomas, and Hoard 1995; Buunk, Angleitner, Oubaid, and Buss 1996; DeSteno and Salovey 1996a; Buss et al. 1999; Pietrzak, Laird, Stevens, and Thompson 2002.

41. Buss, Larsen, Westen, and Semmelroth 1992, p. 252.

42. Data from Buss, Larsen, Westen, and Semmelroth 1992; Buunk, Angleitner, Oubaid, and Buss 1996; Harris and Christenfeld 1996a; Buss et al. 1999.

43. Buss 1999, p. 326.

44. Symons 1979, p. 292.

45. Buss et al. 1999, p. 130.

46. Data from Buss et al. 1999; Wiederman and Kendall 1999.

47. Buss et al. 1999, p. 132.

48. Data from Buss et al. 1999.

49. Buss et al. 1999, p. 132.

50. Data from Buss et al. 1999.

51. Buss, Larsen, and Westen 1996, p. 374.

52. Clark 1989, p. 64.

53. Harris 2000, pp. 1089–1090.

54. Symons 1979, p. 246.

55. Buunk, Angleitner, Oubaid, and Buss 1996, p. 362.

56. Buss, Larsen, Westen, and Semmelroth 1992, pp. 254–255.

57. Harris 2000, p. 1086.

58. Daly, Wilson, and Weghorst 1982, p. 12.

59. Wilson and Daly 1992, pp. 310–311; emphasis added.

60. Buss 2000, p. 125; emphasis added.

61. Buss 2000, p. 122.

## Chapter 7

1. Daly and Wilson 1988b, p. 83.

2. Daly and Wilson 1995, p. 1274.

3. Daly and Wilson 1988b, p. 73.

4. Daly and Wilson 1995, p. 1274.

5. Daly and Wilson 1988b, p. 75; emphasis added.

6. Daly and Wilson 1988b, p. 76.

7. Daly and Wilson 1981, p. 410.

8. Daly and Wilson 1981, p. 411.

9. Daly and Wilson 1988b, p. 72.

10. Daly and Wilson 1988b, p. 83; emphasis added.

11. Daly and Wilson 1985, p. 209.

12. Daly and Wilson 2001, p. 288.

13. Daly and Wilson 1985, p. 201.

14. Daly and Wilson 1985, p. 202.

15. Daly and Wilson 1999, pp. 32–33.

16. Daly and Wilson 1988b, p. 89.

17. Daly and Wilson 1988b, p. 89; 1988a, p. 520.

18. Daly and Wilson 1999, p. 32.

19. Malkin and Lamb 1994, p. 125.

20. Malkin and Lamb 1994, p. 129.

21. Daly and Wilson 2001, p. 289.

22. Temrin, Buchmayer, and Enquist 2000, p. 945.

23. Daly and Wilson 2001, p. 290.

24. Daly and Wilson 1988b, p. 93.

25. Daly and Wilson 1999, p. 30.

26. Daly and Wilson 1994a, p. 208.

27. Daly and Wilson 1994a, p. 212.

28. Wilson and Daly 1994, pp. 90–91.

29. Wilson and Daly 1994, p. 93.

30. Wilson and Daly 1994, p. 93.

31. Daly and Wilson 1988b, p. 75.

32. Daly and Wilson 1999, p. 38.

33. Daly and Wilson 1988b, p. 83.

34. Buss 1999, pp. 202–203; emphasis in original.

35. Pinker 2002, p. 164.

36. Daly and Wilson 1985, p. 207.

37. Daly and Wilson 1985, pp. 206–207.

38. Parker and Parker 1986, p. 533.

39. Daly and Wilson 1988b, p. 75.

40. Christoffel et al. 1992, p. 1033.

41. Daly and Wilson 1985, p. 206.

42. Herndon et al. 2002.

43. National Adoption Information Clearinghouse 2002.

44. Pinker 2002, p. 164.

45. Gelles and Harrop 1991, p. 80.

46. Gelles and Harrop 1991, p. 81.

47. Gelles and Harrop 1991, p. 80.

48. Daly and Wilson 1991, p. 423.

49. Anderson, Kaplan, and Lancaster 1999, p. 421.

50. Voland and Stephan 2000, p. 465.

51. Daly and Wilson 1988b, p. 48.

52. Daly and Wilson 1988b, p. 65.

53. Daly and Wilson 1987, p. 208.

54. Gelles and Harrop 1991, p. 79.

55. Daly and Wilson 1988b, p. 88.

56. Daly and Wilson 1999, p. 31.

57. Daly and Wilson 1988b, pp. 88–89.

58. Daly and Wilson 1988b, p. 89; 1999, p. 32.

59. Christoffel, Anzinger, and Merrill 1989, p. 1403.

60. Christoffel, Anzinger, and Merrill 1989, p. 1405.

61. Ewigman, Kivlahan, and Land 1993, p. 330.

62. Ewigman, Kivlahan, and Land 1993, p. 331.

63. Ewigman, Kivlahan, and Land 1993, p. 331.

64. Daly and Wilson 1999, p. 31.

65. Ewigman, Kivlahan, and Land 1993, p. 335.

66. Ewigman, Kivlahan, and Land 1993, p. 333.

67. Ewigman, Kivlahan, and Land 1993, p. 334.

68. Crume et al. 2002, p. 5.

69. Crume et al. 2002, p. 4, and Crume, personal communication.

70. Daly and Wilson 2001, p. 291.

71. Daly and Wilson 1999, pp. 37–38; emphasis added.

72. Daly and Wilson 1999, p. 38.

73. Daly and Wilson 1988b, p. 75.

74. Daly and Wilson 1988b, pp. 76–77.

75. Daly and Wilson 1999, p. 34.

76. Daly and Wilson 1985, p. 206.

## Chapter 8

1. Ghiselin 1997, p. 1.

2. Buss 1999, p. 47; emphasis added.

3. Loptson 1995, p. 1.

4. Loptson 1995, p. 19.

5. Trigg 1988, p. 4.

6. Tooby and Cosmides 1990a, p. 19.

7. Tooby and Cosmides 1990a, p. 18.

8. Bonner 1980, p. 9.

9. Tooby and Cosmides 1990a, p. 17; emphasis added.

10. Tooby and Cosmides 1992, p. 38.

11. Tooby and Cosmides 1992, p. 78.

12. Tooby and Cosmides 1992, pp. 68–69.

13. Wilson 1994, p. 224.

14. Izpisúa Belmonte 1999, p. 47.

15. Cosmides and Tooby 1997, p. 72; emphasis added.

16. Sober 1994, p. 205; emphasis added.

17. Cosmides and Tooby 1992, p. 211.

18. Cosmides and Tooby 1994, p. 101.

19. Brown 1991, p. 50.

20. Sober 1994, p. 210.

21. Sober 1994, p. 222.

22. Tooby and Cosmides 1992, p. 82.

23. Tooby and Cosmides 1992, p. 78.

24. Sober 1994, p. 222.

25. Sober 1994, p. 222.

26. Tooby and Cosmides 1992, p. 78; emphasis added.

27. Symons 1979, p. 32.

28. Lewontin 1995, p. 41.

29. Cavalli-Sforza, Menozzi, and Piazza 1994, p. 141.

30. Sober 1994, p. 214.

31. Tooby and Cosmides 1990b, pp. 380–381.

32. Hull 1989a, p. 12; emphasis added.

33. Hull 1989a, p. 17.

34. Ghiselin 1997, p. 41.

35. Mayr 1988, p. 343.

36. Hull 1989b, p. 85.

37. Mayr 1988, p. 344.

38. Trigg 1988, p. 4.

39. Cosmides and Tooby 1992, p. 211; emphasis added.

40. Hull 1978, p. 358.

41. Ghiselin 1997, p. 45.

42. Ghiselin 1997, p. 45.

43. See Futuyma 1998, p. 109.

44. Wagner 1989, p. 51.

45. Wagner 1989, p. 51.

46. Brown 1991, p. 130.

47. Tooby and Cosmides 1992, p. 117.

48. Tooby and Cosmides 1992, p. 89.

49. Tooby and Cosmides 1992, p. 116.

50. Tooby and Cosmides 1992, p. 118.

51. Tooby and Cosmides 1992, p. 209.

52. Durham 1991, p. 357.

53. Paley 1805, p. 2.

54. Paley 1805, p. 3.

55. Paley 1805, pp. 12–13.

56. Paley 1805, pp. 19–20.

57. Tooby and Cosmides 1990b, pp. 380–381.

# Bibliography

## Introduction

Barrett, Louise, Robin Dunbar, and John Lycett (2002). *Human Evolutionary Psychology*. Princeton: Princeton University Press.

Beynon, Mike, producer (1994). *Desmond Morris' The Human Animal: The Biology of Love* (television program). London: BBC.

Buller, David J. (2000). Evolutionary Psychology. In M. Nani and M. Marraffa (eds.), *A Field Guide to the Philosophy of Mind*. An official electronic publication of the Department of Philosophy of University of Rome 3 (http://host.uniroma3.it/progetti/kant/field/ep.htm).

Buss, David M. (1994). *The Evolution of Desire: Strategies of Human Mating*. New York: Basic Books.

Buss, David M. (1999). *Evolutionary Psychology: The New Science of the Mind*. Boston: Allyn and Bacon.

Buss, David M. (2000). *The Dangerous Passion: Why Jealousy Is as Necessary as Love and Sex*. New York: Free Press.

Caporael, Linnda R. (2001). Evolutionary Psychology: Toward a Unifying Theory and a Hybrid Science. *Annual Review of Psychology* 52: 607–628.

Daly, Martin, and Margo Wilson (1999). *The Truth about Cinderella: A Darwinian View of Parental Love*. New Haven, CT: Yale University Press.

Dawkins, Richard (1989). *The Selfish Gene* (2nd ed.). Oxford: Oxford University Press.

Downes, Stephen M. (2001). Some Recent Developments in Evolutionary Approaches to the Study of Human Cognition and Behavior. *Biology and Philosophy* 16: 575–595.

Gould, Stephen Jay (1997). Evolution: The Pleasures of Pluralism. *New York Review of Books* 44(11): 47–52.

Kennair, Leif Edward Ottesen (2003). Essay Review: An Alternative Paradigm After All? *Human Nature Review* 3: 24–35.

Kuhn, Thomas S. (1996). *The Structure of Scientific Revolutions* (3rd ed.). Chicago: University of Chicago Press.

Maynard Smith, John (1995). Genes, Memes, and Minds. *New York Review of Books* 42(19): 46.

Pinker, Steven (1997). *How the Mind Works*. New York: Norton.

Pinker, Steven (2002). *The Blank Slate: The Modern Denial of Human Nature*. New York: Viking.

Rose, Hilary, and Steven Rose (2000). Introduction. In H. Rose and S. Rose (eds.), *Alas, Poor Darwin: Arguments against Evolutionary Psychology* (pp. 1–13). London: Jonathan Cape.

Thornhill, Randy, and Craig T. Palmer (2000). *A Natural History of Rape: Biological Bases of Sexual Coercion*. Cambridge, MA: MIT Press.

Wright, Robert (1994). *The Moral Animal: Evolutionary Psychology and Everyday Life*. New York: Vintage.

## Chapter 1

Alcock, John (1993). *Animal Behavior: An Evolutionary Approach* (5th ed.). Sunderland, MA: Sinauer Associates.

Bergstrom, Carl T., and Peter Godfrey-Smith (1998). On the Evolution of Behavioral Heterogeneity in Individuals and Populations. *Biology and Philosophy* 13: 205–231.

Brandon, Robert N. (1990). *Adaptation and Environment*. Princeton: Princeton University Press.

Cade, William H. (1981). Alternative Male Strategies: Genetic Differences in Crickets. *Science* 212: 563–564.

Darwin, Charles (1859/1964). *On the Origin of Species*. Cambridge, MA: Harvard University Press.

Dawkins, Richard (1980). Good Strategy or Evolutionarily Stable Strategy? In G. W. Barlow and J. Silverberg (eds.), *Sociobiology: Beyond Nature/Nurture?* (pp. 331–367). Boulder, CO: Westview Press.

Dawkins, Richard (1986). *The Blind Watchmaker*. London: Penguin Books.

Dawkins, Richard (1989). *The Selfish Gene* (2nd ed.). Oxford: Oxford University Press.

Endler, John A. (1986). *Natural Selection in the Wild*. Princeton: Princeton University Press.

Futuyma, Douglas J. (1998). *Evolutionary Biology* (3rd ed.). Sunderland, MA: Sinauer Associates.

Godfrey-Smith, Peter (1998). *Complexity and the Function of Mind in Nature*. New York: Cambridge University Press.

Greene, Erick (1989). A Diet-Induced Developmental Polymorphism in a Caterpillar. *Science* 243: 643–646.

Gross, Mart R. (1996). Alternative Reproductive Strategies and Tactics: Diversity within Sexes. *Trends in Ecology and Evolution* 11: 92–98.

Gross, Mart R., and Joe Repka (1998). Stability with Inheritance in the Conditional Strategy. *Journal of Theoretical Biology* 192: 445–453.

Harvey, I. F. (1994). Strategies of Behaviour. In P. J. B. Slater and T. R. Halliday (eds.), *Behaviour and Evolution* (pp. 106–149). Cambridge, UK: Cambridge University Press.

Hofmann, Hans A., Mark E. Benson, and Russell D. Fernald (1999). Social Status Regulates Growth Rate: Consequences for Life-History Strategies. *Proceedings of the National Academy of Sciences* 96: 14171–14176.

Kaplan, Jonathan, and Massimo Pigliucci (2001). Genes "for" Phenotypes: A Modern History View. *Biology and Philosophy* 16: 189–213.

Lewontin, Richard (1978). Adaptation. *Scientific American* 239(3): 212–230.

Lewontin, Richard (1995). *Human Diversity*. New York: Scientific American Library.

Maynard Smith, John (1976). Evolution and the Theory of Games. *American Scientist* 64: 41–45.

Maynard Smith, John (1981). Evolutionary Games. In G. G. E. Scudder and J. L. Reveal (eds.), *Evolution Today* (pp. 1–6). Pittsburgh, PA: Hunt Institute.

Maynard Smith, John (1982). *Evolution and the Theory of Games*. New York: Cambridge University Press.

Maynard Smith, John, and G. A. Parker (1976). The Logic of Asymmetric Contests. *Animal Behaviour* 24: 159–175.

Mayr, Ernst (1988). Cause and Effect in Biology. In *Toward a New Philosophy of Biology: Observations of an Evolutionist* (pp. 24–37). Cambridge, MA: Harvard University Press.

Moran, Nancy A. (1992). The Evolutionary Maintenance of Alternative Phenotypes. *American Naturalist* 139: 971–989.

Pigliucci, Massimo (1996). How Organisms Respond to Environmental Changes: From Phenotypes to Molecules (and Vice Versa). *Trends in Ecology and Evolution* 11: 168–173.

Ridley, Mark (1996). *Evolution* (2nd ed.). Cambridge, MA: Blackwell Science.

Shuster, Stephen M. (1989). Male Alternative Reproductive Strategies in a Marine Isopod Crustacean (*Paracerceis sculpta*): The Use of Genetic Markers to Measure Differences in the Fertilization Successes among α-, β- and γ-males. *Evolution* 43: 1683–1698.

Shuster, Stephen M. (1992). The Reproductive Behavior of α-, β-, and γ-male Morphs in *Paracerceis sculpta*, a Marine Isopod Crustacean. *Behaviour* 121(3–4): 231–258.

Shuster, Stephen M., and M. J. Wade (1991). Equal Mating Success among Male Reproductive Strategies in a Marine Isopod. *Nature* 350: 608–610.

Sober, Elliott (1984). *The Nature of Selection*. Cambridge, MA: MIT Press.

Sober, Elliott (1993). *Philosophy of Biology*. Boulder, CO: Westview Press.

Stearns, Stephen C. (1989). The Evolutionary Significance of Phenotypic Plasticity. *BioScience* 39: 436–445.

Sterelny, Kim, and Philip Kitcher (1988). The Return of the Gene. *Journal of Philosophy* 85: 339–361.

Travis, Joseph (1994). Evaluating the Adaptive Role of Morphological Plasticity. In P. C. Wainwright and S. M. Reilly (eds.), *Ecological Morphology: Integrative Organismal Biology* (pp. 99–122). Chicago: University of Chicago Press.

Via, Sara, Richard Gomulkiewicz, Gerdien de Jong, Samuel M. Scheiner, Carl D. Schlichting, and Peter H. Van Tienderen (1995). Adaptive Phenotypic Plasticity: Consensus and Controversy. *Trends in Ecology and Evolution* 10: 212–217.

West-Eberhard, Mary Jane (1989). Phenotypic Plasticity and the Origins of Diversity. *Annual Review of Ecology and Systematics* 20: 249–278.

## Chapter 2

Brown, Donald E. (1991). *Human Universals*. New York: McGraw-Hill.

Buss, David M. (1995). Evolutionary Psychology: A New Paradigm for Psychological Science. *Psychological Inquiry* 6: 1–30.

Cosmides, Leda, and John Tooby (1987). From Evolution to Behavior: Evolutionary Psychology as the Missing Link. In J. Dupré (ed.), *The Latest on the Best: Essays on Evolution and Optimality* (pp. 277–306). Cambridge, MA: MIT Press.

Cosmides, Leda, and John Tooby (1994). Origins of Domain Specificity: The Evolution of Functional Organization. In L. A. Hirschfeld and S. A. Gelman (eds.), *Mapping the Mind: Domain Specificity in Cognition and Culture* (pp. 85–116). New York: Cambridge University Press.

Cosmides, Leda, and John Tooby (1997). The Modular Nature of Human Intelligence. In A. B. Scheibel and J. W. Schopf (eds.), *The Origin and Evolution of Intelligence* (pp. 71–101). Sudbury, MA: Jones and Bartlett.

Cosmides, Leda, John Tooby, and Jerome H. Barkow (1992). Introduction: Evolutionary Psychology and Conceptual Integration. In J. H. Barkow, L. Cosmides, and J. Tooby (eds.), *The Adapted Mind: Evolutionary Psychology and the Generation of Culture* (pp. 3–15). New York: Oxford University Press.

Crawford, Charles (1998). Environments and Adaptations: Then and Now. In C. Crawford and D. L. Krebs (eds.), *Handbook of Evolutionary Psychology* (pp. 275–302). Mahwah, NJ: Lawrence Erlbaum.

Crook, John H., and Stamati J. Crook (1988). Tibetan Polyandry: Problems of Adaptation and Fitness. In L. Betzig, M. Borgerhoff Mulder, and P. Turke (eds.), *Human Reproductive Behaviour: A Darwinian Perspective* (pp. 97–114). Cambridge, UK: Cambridge University Press.

Dawkins, Richard (1989). *The Selfish Gene* (2nd ed.). Oxford: Oxford University Press.

Draper, Patricia, and Henry Harpending (1982). Father Absence and Reproductive Strategy: An Evolutionary Perspective. *Journal of Anthropological Research* 38: 255–273.

Draper, Patricia, and Henry Harpending (1987). Parent Investment and the Child's Environment. In Jane B. Lancaster et al. (eds.), *Parenting across the Life Span: Biosocial Dimensions* (pp. 207–235). New York: Aldine de Gruyter.

Fodor, Jerry A. (1983). *The Modularity of Mind.* Cambridge, MA: MIT Press.

Futuyma, Douglas J. (1998). *Evolutionary Biology* (3rd ed.). Sunderland, MA: Sinauer Associates.

Jones, Steve, Robert Martin, and David Pilbeam (eds.) (1992). *The Cambridge Encyclopedia of Human Evolution.* Cambridge, UK: Cambridge University Press.

Lewin, Roger (1998). *Principles of Human Evolution.* Malden, MA: Blackwell Science.

Pinker, Steven (1994). *The Language Instinct.* New York: HarperPerennial.

Pinker, Steven (1997). *How the Mind Works.* New York: Norton.

Raff, Rudolf A. (1996). *The Shape of Life: Genes, Development, and the Evolution of Animal Form.* Chicago: University of Chicago Press.

Symons, Donald (1987). If We're All Darwinians, What's the Fuss About? In C. Crawford, M. Smith, and D. Krebs (eds.), *Sociobiology and Psychology: Ideas, Issues, and Applications* (pp. 121–146). Hillsdale, NJ: Lawrence Erlbaum.

Symons, Donald (1990). Adaptiveness and Adaptation. *Ethology and Sociobiology* 11: 427–444.

Symons, Donald (1992). On the Use and Misuse of Darwinism in the Study of Human Behavior. In J. H. Barkow, L. Cosmides, and J. Tooby (eds.), *The Adapted Mind: Evolutionary Psychology and the Generation of Culture* (pp. 137–159). New York: Oxford University Press.

Symons, Donald (1995). Beauty Is in the Adaptations of the Beholder: The Evolutionary Psychology of Human Female Sexual Attractiveness. In P. R. Abramson and S. D. Pinkerton (eds.), *Sexual Nature, Sexual Culture* (pp. 80–118). Chicago: University of Chicago Press.

Tooby, John, and Leda Cosmides (1990a). On the Universality of Human Nature and the Uniqueness of the Individual: The Role of Genetics and Adaptation. *Journal of Personality* 58: 17–67.

Tooby, John, and Leda Cosmides (1990b). The Past Explains the Present: Emotional Adaptations and the Structure of Ancestral Environments. *Ethology and Sociobiology* 11: 375–424.

Tooby, John, and Leda Cosmides (1992). The Psychological Foundations of Culture. In J. H. Barkow, L. Cosmides, and J. Tooby (eds.), *The Adapted Mind: Evolutionary Psychology and the Generation of Culture* (pp. 19–136). New York: Oxford University Press.

Tooby, John, and Leda Cosmides (1995). Foreword. In Simon Baron-Cohen, *Mindblindness: An Essay on Autism and Theory of Mind* (pp. xi–xviii). Cambridge, MA: MIT Press.

## Chapter 3

Betzig, Laura (1998). Not Whether to Count Babies, but Which. In C. Crawford and D. L. Krebs (eds.), *Handbook of Evolutionary Psychology: Ideas, Issues, and Applications* (pp. 265–273). Mahwah, NJ: Lawrence Erlbaum.

Böhning-Gaese, Katrin, and Reik Oberrath (1999). Phylogenetic Effects on Morphological, Life-History, Behavioural and Ecological Traits of Birds. *Evolutionary Ecology Research* 1: 347–364.

Buss, David M. (1992). Mate Preference Mechanisms: Consequences for Partner Choice and Intrasexual Competition. In J. H. Barkow, L. Cosmides, and J. Tooby (eds.), *The Adapted Mind: Evolutionary Psychology and the Generation of Culture* (pp. 249–266). New York: Oxford University Press.

Buss, David M. (1998). Sexual Strategies Theory: Historical Origins and Current Status. *Journal of Sex Research* 35: 19–31.

Buss, David M., Martie G. Haselton, Todd K. Shackelford, April L. Bleske, and Jerome C. Wakefield (1998). Adaptations, Exaptations, and Spandrels. *American Psychologist* 53: 533–548.

Cavalli-Sforza, Luigi Luca (2000). *Genes, Peoples, and Languages* (Mark Seielstad, trans.). New York: North Point Press.

Cosmides, Leda, and John Tooby (1994). Origins of Domain Specificity: The Evolution of Functional Organization. In L. A. Hirschfeld and S. A. Gelman (eds.), *Mapping the Mind: Domain Specificity in Cognition and Culture* (pp. 85–116). New York: Cambridge University Press.

Cosmides, Leda, John Tooby, and Jerome H. Barkow (1992). Introduction: Evolutionary Psychology and Conceptual Integration. In J. H. Barkow, L. Cosmides, and J. Tooby (eds.), *The Adapted Mind: Evolutionary Psychology and the Generation of Culture* (pp. 3–15). New York: Oxford University Press.

Crawford, Charles (1998). Environments and Adaptations: Then and Now. In C. Crawford and D. L. Krebs (eds.), *Handbook of Evolutionary Psychology* (pp. 275–302). Mahwah, NJ: Lawrence Erlbaum.

Davies, Paul Sheldon (1996). Discovering the Functional Mesh: On the Methods of Evolutionary Psychology. *Minds and Machines* 6: 559–585.

De Chadarevian, Soraya (1998). Of Worms and Programmes: *Caenorhabditis elegans* and the Study of Development. *Studies in History and Philosophy of Biological and Biomedical Sciences* 29(1): 81–105.

Diamond, Jared (1991). *The Rise and Fall of the Third Chimpanzee*. London: Vintage.

Foley, Robert (1996). The Adaptive Legacy of Human Evolution: A Search for the Environment of Evolutionary Adaptedness. *Evolutionary Anthropology* 4(6): 194–203.

Francis, Richard C., and George W. Barlow (1993). Social Control of Primary Sex Differentiation in the Midas Cichlid. *Proceedings of the National Academy of Sciences* 90: 10673–10675.

Gangestad, Steven W. (1997). Evolutionary Psychology and Genetic Variation: Non-Adaptive, Fitness-Related and Adaptive. In G. R. Bock and G. Cardew (eds.), *Characterizing Human Psychological Adaptations* (pp. 212–223). Chichester, UK: Wiley.

Gangestad, Steven W., and Jeffrey A. Simpson (1990). Toward an Evolutionary History of Female Sociosexual Variation. *Journal of Personality* 58: 69–96.

Gangestad, Steven W., and Jeffrey A. Simpson (1993). Development of a Scale Measuring Genetic Variation Related to Expressive Control. *Journal of Personality* 61: 133–158.

Gittleman, John L., C. Gregory Anderson, Mark Kot, and Hang-Kwang Luh (1996). Comparative Tests of Evolutionary Lability and Rates Using Molecular Phylogenies. In P. H. Harvey, A. J. Leigh Brown, J. Maynard Smith, and S. Nee (eds.), *New Uses for New Phylogenies* (pp. 289–307). New York: Oxford University Press.

Gould, Stephen Jay (1991). Exaptation: A Crucial Tool for an Evolutionary Psychology. *Journal of Social Issues* 47: 43–65.

Gould, Stephen Jay (1997). Evolution: The Pleasures of Pluralism. *New York Review of Books* 44(11): 47–52.

Gould, Stephen Jay, and Richard C. Lewontin (1979). The Spandrels of San Marco and the Panglossian Paradigm: A Critique of the Adaptationist Programme. *Proceedings of the Royal Society of London B* 205: 581–598.

Gould, Stephen Jay, and Elisabeth S. Vrba (1982). Exaptation: A Missing Term in the Science of Form. *Paleobiology* 8: 4–15.

Grantham, Todd, and Shaun Nichols (1999). Evolutionary Psychology: Ultimate Explanations and Panglossian Predictions. In V. G. Hardcastle (ed.), *Where Biology Meets Psychology: Philosophical Essays* (pp. 47–66). Cambridge, MA: MIT Press.

Griffiths, Paul E. (1997). *What Emotions Really Are: The Problem of Psychological Categories*. Chicago: University of Chicago Press.

Humphrey, Nicholas K. (1976). The Social Function of Intellect. In P. P. G. Bateson and R. A. Hinde (eds.), *Growing Points in Ethology* (pp. 303–318). Cambridge, UK: Cambridge University Press.

Irons, William (1998). Adaptively Relevant Environments versus the Environment of Evolutionary Adaptedness. *Evolutionary Anthropology* 6: 194–204.

Jacob, François (1982). *The Possible and the Actual*. Seattle: University of Washington Press.

Kaplan, Jonathan M. (2002). Historical Evidence and Human Adaptations. *Philosophy of Science* 69: S294–S304.

Kelly, Robert L. (1995). *The Foraging Spectrum: Diversity in Hunter-Gatherer Lifeways*. Washington, D.C.: Smithsonian Institution Press.

Laland, Kevin N., John Odling-Smee, and Marcus W. Feldman (2000). Niche Construction, Biological Evolution and Cultural Change. *Behavioral and Brain Sciences* 23: 131–175.

Lewin, Roger (1984). Why Is Development So Illogical? *Science* 224: 1327–1329.

Lewontin, Richard C. (1983a). Gene, Organism and Environment. In D. S. Bendall (ed.), *Evolution from Molecules to Men* (pp. 273–285). Cambridge, UK: Cambridge University Press.

Lewontin, Richard C. (1983b). The Organism as the Subject and Object of Evolution. *Scientia* 118: 65–82.

Lloyd, Elisabeth A., and Marcus W. Feldman (2002). Evolutionary Psychology: A View from Evolutionary Biology. *Psychological Inquiry* 13: 150–156.

Odling-Smee, F. John, Kevin N. Laland, and Marcus W. Feldman (1996). Niche Construction. *American Naturalist* 147: 641–648.

Oyama, Susan (2000). *The Ontogeny of Information: Developmental Systems and Evolution* (2nd ed.). Durham, NC: Duke University Press.

Pinker, Steven (1997a). *How the Mind Works*. New York: Norton.

Pinker, Steven (1997b). Letter to the Editors. *New York Review of Books* 44(15): 55–56.

Pinker, Steven, and Paul Bloom (1992). Natural Language and Natural Selection. In J. H. Barkow, L. Cosmides, and J. Tooby (eds.), *The Adapted Mind: Evolutionary Psychology and the Generation of Culture* (pp. 451–493). New York: Oxford University Press.

Plotkin, Henry (1998). *Evolution in Mind: An Introduction to Evolutionary Psychology*. Cambridge, MA: Harvard University Press.

Raff, Rudolf A. (1996). *The Shape of Life: Genes, Development, and the Evolution of Animal Form*. Chicago: University of Chicago Press.

Reznick, David N., Mark J. Butler, F. Helen Rodd, and Patrick Ross (1996). Life-History Evolution in Guppies (*Poecilia reticulata*) 6. Differential Mortality as a Mechanism for Natural Selection. *Evolution* 50: 1651–1660.

Reznick, David N., Frank H. Shaw, F. Helen Rodd, and Ruth G. Shaw (1997). Evaluation of the Rate of Evolution in Natural Populations of Guppies (*Poecilia reticulata*). *Science* 275: 1934–1937.

Rose, Michael R., and George V. Lauder (1996). Post-Spandrel Adaptationism. In M. R. Rose and G. V. Lauder (eds.), *Adaptation* (pp. 1–8). New York: Academic Press.

Ross, Robert M., George S. Losey, and Milton Diamond (1983). Sex Change in a Coral-Reef Fish: Dependence of Stimulation and Inhibition on Relative Size. *Science* 221: 574–575.

Sterelny, Kim (1995). The Adapted Mind. *Biology and Philosophy* 10: 365–380.

Sterelny, Kim (2003). *Thought in a Hostile World: The Evolution of Human Cognition.* Malden, MA: Blackwell.

Sterelny, Kim, and Paul E. Griffiths (1999). *Sex and Death: An Introduction to Philosophy of Biology.* Chicago: University of Chicago Press.

Symons, Donald (1992). On the Use and Misuse of Darwinism in the Study of Human Behavior. In J. H. Barkow, L. Cosmides, and J. Tooby (eds.), *The Adapted Mind: Evolutionary Psychology and the Generation of Culture* (pp. 137–159). New York: Oxford University Press.

Symons, Donald (1995). Beauty Is in the Adaptations of the Beholder: The Evolutionary Psychology of Human Female Sexual Attractiveness. In P. R. Abramson and S. D. Pinkerton (eds.), *Sexual Nature, Sexual Culture* (pp. 80–118). Chicago: University of Chicago Press.

Thornhill, Randy (1997). The Concept of an Evolved Adaptation. In G. R. Bock and G. Cardew (eds.), *Characterizing Human Psychological Adaptations* (pp. 4–13). Chichester, UK: Wiley.

Tooby, John, and Leda Cosmides (1990a). On the Universality of Human Nature and the Uniqueness of the Individual: The Role of Genetics and Adaptation. *Journal of Personality* 58: 17–67.

Tooby, John, and Leda Cosmides (1990b). The Past Explains the Present: Emotional Adaptations and the Structure of Ancestral Environments. *Ethology and Sociobiology* 11: 375–424.

Tooby, John, and Leda Cosmides (1992). The Psychological Foundations of Culture. In J. H. Barkow, L. Cosmides, and J. Tooby (eds.), *The Adapted Mind: Evolutionary Psychology and the Generation of Culture* (pp. 19–136). New York: Oxford University Press.

Tooby, John, and Leda Cosmides (2000). Toward Mapping the Evolved Functional Organization of the Mind and Brain. In M. S. Gazzaniga (ed.), *The New Cognitive Neurosciences* (pp. 1167–1178). Cambridge, MA: MIT Press.

Wilson, David Sloan (1994). Adaptive Genetic Variation and Human Evolutionary Psychology. *Ethology and Sociobiology* 15: 219–235.

Wilson, David Sloan (1998). Game Theory and Human Behavior. In L. A. Dugatkin and H. K. Reeve (eds.), *Game Theory and Animal Behavior* (pp. 261–282). New York: Oxford University Press.

## Chapter 4

Adams, David B., Alice Ross Gold, and Anne D. Burt (1978). Rise in Female-Initiated Sexual Activity at Ovulation and Its Suppression by Oral Contraceptives. *New England Journal of Medicine* 299: 1145–1150.

Allman, John (1999). *Evolving Brains*. New York: Scientific American Library.

Baron-Cohen, Simon (1995). *Mindblindness: An Essay on Autism and Theory of Mind*. Cambridge, MA: MIT Press.

Beaman, C. Philip (2002). Why Are We Good at Detecting Cheaters? A Reply to Fodor. *Cognition* 83: 215–220.

Bechtel, William (2003). Modules, Brain Parts, and Evolutionary Psychology. In S. J. Scher and F. Rauscher (eds.), *Evolutionary Psychology: Alternative Approaches* (pp. 211–227). Boston: Kluwer.

Bloom, Paul, and Tim P. German (2000). Two Reasons to Abandon the False Belief Task as a Test of Theory of Mind. *Cognition* 77: B25–B31.

Buller, David J., and Valerie Gray Hardcastle (2000). Evolutionary Psychology, Meet Developmental Neurobiology: Against Promiscuous Modularity. *Brain and Mind* 1: 307–325.

Changeux, Jean-Pierre (1985). *Neuronal Man: The Biology of Mind* (Laurence Garey, trans.). New York: Oxford University Press.

Changeux, Jean-Pierre, and A. Danchin (1976). Selective Stabilization of Developing Synapses as a Mechanism for the Specification of Neural Networks. *Nature* 264: 705–712.

Cheng, Patricia W., and Keith J. Holyoak (1985). Pragmatic Reasoning Schemas. *Cognitive Psychology* 17: 391–416.

Cheng, Patricia W., and Keith J. Holyoak (1989). On the Natural Selection of Reasoning Theories. *Cognition* 33: 285–313.

Cosmides, Leda (1989). The Logic of Social Exchange: Has Natural Selection Shaped How Humans Reason? Studies with the Wason Selection Task. *Cognition* 31: 187–276.

Cosmides, Leda, and John Tooby (1987). From Evolution to Behavior: Evolutionary Psychology as the Missing Link. In J. Dupré (ed.), *The Latest on the Best: Essays on Evolution and Optimality* (pp. 277–306). Cambridge, MA: MIT Press.

Cosmides, Leda, and John Tooby (1992). Cognitive Adaptations for Social Exchange. In J. H. Barkow, L. Cosmides, and J. Tooby (eds.), *The Adapted Mind: Evolutionary Psychology and the Generation of Culture* (pp. 163–228). New York: Oxford University Press.

Cosmides, Leda, and John Tooby (1994). Origins of Domain Specificity: The Evolution of Functional Organization. In L. A. Hirschfeld and S. A. Gelman (eds.), *Mapping the Mind: Domain Specificity in Cognition and Culture* (pp. 85–116). New York: Cambridge University Press.

Cosmides, Leda, and John Tooby (1997). The Modular Nature of Human Intelligence. In A. B. Scheibel and J. W. Schopf (eds.), *The Origin and Evolution of Intelligence* (pp. 71–101). Sudbury, MA: Jones and Bartlett.

Cowie, Fiona (1999). *What's Within? Nativism Reconsidered*. New York: Oxford University Press.

Cummins, Denise Dellarosa, and Robert Cummins (1999). Biological Preparedness and Evolutionary Explanation. *Cognition* 73: B37–B53.

Cummins, Denise, Robert Cummins, and Pierre Poirier (2003). Cognitive Evolutionary Psychology without Representational Nativism. *Journal of Experimental and Theoretical Artificial Intelligence* 15: 143–159.

Davies, Paul Sheldon, James H. Fetzer, and Thomas R. Foster (1995). Logical Reasoning and Domain Specificity: A Critique of the Social Exchange Theory of Reasoning. *Biology and Philosophy* 10: 1–37.

Deacon, Terrence W. (1997). *The Symbolic Species: The Co-evolution of Language and the Brain*. New York: Norton.

Duchaine, Bradley, Leda Cosmides, and John Tooby (2001). Evolutionary Psychology and the Brain. *Current Opinion in Neurobiology* 11: 225–230.

Edelman, Gerald M. (1992). *Bright Air, Brilliant Fire: On the Matter of the Mind*. New York: Basic Books.

Edgington, Dorothy (1995). On Conditionals. *Mind* 104: 235–329.

Ellis, Bruce J. (1992). The Evolution of Sexual Attraction: Evaluative Mechanisms in Women. In J. H. Barkow, L. Cosmides, and J. Tooby (eds.), *The Adapted Mind: Evolutionary Psychology and the Generation of Culture* (pp. 267–288). New York: Oxford University Press.

Elman, Jeffrey L., Elizabeth A. Bates, Mark H. Johnson, Annette Karmiloff-Smith, Domenico Parisi, and Kim Plunkett (1996). *Rethinking Innateness: A Connectionist Perspective on Development*. Cambridge, MA: MIT Press.

Fiddick, Laurence, Leda Cosmides, and John Tooby (2000). No Interpretation without Representation: The Role of Domain-Specific Representations and Inferences in the Wason Selection Task. *Cognition* 77: 1–79.

Fodor, Jerry (2000). *The Mind Doesn't Work That Way: The Scope and Limits of Computational Psychology*. Cambridge, MA: MIT Press.

Fodor, Jerry (2002). Reply to Beaman. *Cognition* 83: 221.

Futuyma, Douglas J. (1998). *Evolutionary Biology* (3rd ed.). Sunderland, MA: Sinauer Associates.

Gerrans, Philip (2002). The Theory of Mind Module in Evolutionary Psychology. *Biology and Philosophy* 17: 305–321.

Gierer, Alfred, and Christian M. Muller (1995). Development of Layers, Maps, and Modules. *Current Opinion in Neurobiology* 5: 91–97.

Gigerenzer, Gerd, and Klaus Hug (1992). Domain-Specific Reasoning: Social Contracts, Cheating, and Perspective Change. *Cognition* 43: 127–171.

Goldman-Rakic, Patricia S., M. Isseroff, M. Schwartz, and N. Bugbee (1983). The Neurobiology of Child Development. In F. Plum and V. Mountcastle (eds.), *The Handbook of Child Development* (pp. 282–331). Bethesda, MD: American Physiological Society.

Gould, Elizabeth, Alison J. Reeves, Michael S. A. Graziano, and Charles G. Gross (1999). Neurogenesis in the Neocortex of Adult Primates. *Science* 286: 548–552.

Innocenti, Giorgio M. (1995). Exuberant Development of Connections, and Its Possible Permissive Role in Cortical Evolution. *Trends in Neurosciences* 18: 397–402.

Johnson, Mark H. (1993). Constraints on Cortical Plasticity. In M. H. Johnson (ed.), *Brain Development and Cognition* (pp. 703–721). Cambridge, MA: Blackwell.

Karmiloff-Smith, Annette (1992). *Beyond Modularity: A Developmental Perspective on Cognitive Science*. Cambridge, MA: MIT Press.

La Cerra, Peggy, and Roger Bingham (1998). The Adaptive Nature of the Human Neurocognitive Architecture: An Alternative Model. *Proceedings of the National Academy of Sciences* 95: 11290–11294.

Leslie, Alan M. (2000). "Theory of Mind" as a Mechanism of Selective Attention. In M. S. Gazzaniga (ed.), *The New Cognitive Neurosciences* (pp. 1235–1247). Cambridge, MA: MIT Press.

Lloyd, Elisabeth A. (1999). Evolutionary Psychology: The Burdens of Proof. *Biology and Philosophy* 14: 211–234.

Manktelow, K. I., and D. E. Over (1990). Deontic Thought and the Selection Task. In K. J. Gilhooly, M. T. G. Keane, R. H. Logie, and G. Erdos (eds.), *Lines of Thinking: Reflections on the Psychology of Thought: Representation, Reasoning, Analogy and Decision Making* (pp. 153–164). New York: Wiley.

Murray, John B. (1996). Psychophysiological Aspects of Autistic Disorders: Overview. *Journal of Psychology* 130: 145–158.

Nowakowski, R. S. (1993). Basic Concepts of CNS Development. In M. H. Johnson (ed.), *Brain Development and Cognition* (pp. 54–92). Cambridge, MA: Blackwell.

Over, David E. (2003). From Massive Modularity to Metarepresentation: The Evolution of Higher Cognition. In D. E. Over (ed.), *Evolution and the Psychology of Thinking: The Debate* (pp. 121–144). Hove, UK: Taylor and Francis.

Pascalis, Olivier, Michelle de Haan, and Charles A. Nelson (2002). Is Face Processing Species-Specific during the First Year of Life? *Science* 296: 1321–1323.

Peterson, Candida C., and Michael Siegal (2000). Insights into Theory of Mind from Deafness and Autism. *Mind and Language* 15: 123–145.

Pinker, Steven (1994). *The Language Instinct*. New York: HarperPerennial.

Pinker, Steven (1997). *How the Mind Works*. New York: Norton.

Pinker, Steven (2002). *The Blank Slate: The Modern Denial of Human Nature*. New York: Viking.

Popper, Karl (1992). Science: Conjectures and Refutations. In *Conjectures and Refutations: The Growth of Scientific Knowledge* (pp. 33–55). New York: Routledge.

Quartz, Steven R. (2003). Innateness and the Brain. *Biology and Philosophy* 18: 13–40.

Samuels, Richard (1998). Evolutionary Psychology and the Massive Modularity Hypothesis. *British Journal for the Philosophy of Science* 49: 575–602.

Shapiro, Lawrence, and William Epstein (1998). Evolutionary Theory Meets Cognitive Psychology: A More Selective Perspective. *Mind and Language* 13: 171–194.

Sperber, Dan, Francesco Cara, and Vittorio Girotto (1995). Relevance Theory Explains the Selection Task. *Cognition* 57: 31–95.

Sperber, Dan, and Vittorio Girotto (2002). Use or Misuse of the Selection Task? Rejoinder to Fiddick, Cosmides, and Tooby. *Cognition* 85: 277–290.

Stanislaw, Harold, and Frank J. Rice (1988). Correlation between Sexual Desire and Menstrual Cycle Characteristics. *Archives of Sexual Behavior* 17: 499–508.

Sterelny, Kim (2003). *Thought in a Hostile World: The Evolution of Human Cognition*. Malden, MA: Blackwell.

Stone, Valerie E., Leda Cosmides, John Tooby, Neal Kroll, and Robert T. Knight (2002). Selective Impairment of Reasoning about Social Exchange in a Patient with Bilateral Limbic System Damage. *Proceedings of the National Academy of Sciences* 99: 11531–11536.

Sugiyama, Lawrence S., John Tooby, and Leda Cosmides (2002). Cross-cultural Evidence of Cognitive Adaptations for Social Exchange among the Shiwiar of Ecuadorian Amazonia. *Proceedings of the National Academy of Sciences* 99: 11537–11542.

Symons, Donald (1992). On the Use and Misuse of Darwinism in the Study of Human Behavior. In J. H. Barkow, L. Cosmides, and J. Tooby (eds.), *The Adapted*

*Mind: Evolutionary Psychology and the Generation of Culture* (pp. 137–159). New York: Oxford University Press.

Thompson, Richard F. (1993). *The Brain: A Neuroscience Primer*. New York: W. H. Freeman.

Tooby, John, and Leda Cosmides (1992). The Psychological Foundations of Culture. In J. H. Barkow, L. Cosmides, and J. Tooby (eds.), *The Adapted Mind: Evolutionary Psychology and the Generation of Culture* (pp. 19–136). New York: Oxford University Press.

Tooby, John, and Leda Cosmides (1995). Foreword. In S. Baron-Cohen, *Mindblindness: An Essay on Autism and Theory of Mind* (pp. xi–xviii). Cambridge, MA: MIT Press.

Trivers, Robert L. (1971). The Evolution of Reciprocal Altruism. *Quarterly Review of Biology* 46: 35–57.

Wong, Rachel O. L. (1999). Retinal Waves and Visual System Development. *Annual Review of Neuroscience* 22: 29–47.

Wright, Robert (1994). *The Moral Animal: Evolutionary Psychology and Everyday Life*. New York: Vintage.

## Chapter 5

Boyd, Robert, and Joan B. Silk (2000). *How Humans Evolved* (2nd ed.). New York: Norton.

Burger, Jerry M., and Mica Cosby (1999). Do Women Prefer Dominant Men? The Case of the Missing Control Condition. *Journal of Research in Personality* 33: 358–368.

Buss, David M. (1989). Sex Differences in Human Mate Preferences: Evolutionary Hypotheses Tested in 37 Cultures. *Behavioral and Brain Sciences* 12: 1–49.

Buss, David M. (1992). Mate Preference Mechanisms: Consequences for Partner Choice and Intrasexual Competition. In J. H. Barkow, L. Cosmides, and J. Tooby (eds.), *The Adapted Mind: Evolutionary Psychology and the Generation of Culture* (pp. 249–266). New York: Oxford University Press.

Buss, David M. (1994). *The Evolution of Desire: Strategies of Human Mating*. New York: Basic Books.

Buss, David M. (1999). *Evolutionary Psychology: The New Science of the Mind*. Boston: Allyn and Bacon.

Buss, David M., Max Abbott, Alois Angleitner, Armen Asherian, Angela Biaggio, Angel Blanco-Villasenor, M. Bruchon-Schweitzer, et al. (1990). International Preferences in Selecting Mates: A Study of 37 Cultures. *Journal of Cross-Cultural Psychology* 21: 5–47.

Buston, Peter M., and Stephen T. Emlen (2003). Cognitive Processes Underlying Human Mate Choice: The Relationship between Self-Perception and Mate Preference in Western Society. *Proceedings of the National Academy of Sciences* 100: 8805–8810.

Buunk, Bram P., Pieternel Dijkstra, Douglas T. Kenrick, and Astrid Warntjes (2001). Age Preferences for Mates as Related to Gender, Own Age, and Involvement Level. *Evolution and Human Behavior* 22: 241–250.

Caporael, Linnda R. (1989). Mechanisms Matter: The Difference between Sociobiology and Evolutionary Psychology. *Behavioral and Brain Sciences* 12: 17–18.

Clutton-Brock, T. H. (1991). *The Evolution of Parental Care*. Princeton: Princeton University Press.

Daly, Martin, and Margo Wilson (1983). *Sex, Evolution, and Behavior* (2nd ed.). Belmont, CA: Wadsworth.

De Waal, Frans (1998). *Chimpanzee Politics: Power and Sex among Apes* (rev. ed.). Baltimore: Johns Hopkins University Press.

De Waal, Frans (2000). Survival of the Rapist: Review of *A Natural History of Rape*, by Randy Thornhill and Craig T. Palmer. *New York Times Book Review* (April 2), pp. 24–25.

Doyle, Rodger (2000). By the Numbers: Women and the Professions. *Scientific American* 282(4): 30.

Dupré, John (1993). Scientism, Sexism and Sociobiology: One More Link in the Chain. *Behavioral and Brain Sciences* 16: 292.

Eagly, Alice H., and Wendy Wood (1999). The Origins of Sex Differences in Human Behavior: Evolved Dispositions versus Social Roles. *American Psychologist* 54: 408–423.

Elder, Glen H. (1969). Appearance and Education in Marriage Mobility. *American Sociological Review* 34: 519–533.

Ellis, Bruce J. (1992). The Evolution of Sexual Attraction: Evaluative Mechanisms in Women. In J. H. Barkow, L. Cosmides, and J. Tooby (eds.), *The Adapted Mind: Evolutionary Psychology and the Generation of Culture* (pp. 267–288). New York: Oxford University Press.

Ellis, Lee (1995). Dominance and Reproductive Success among Nonhuman Animals: A Cross-Species Comparison. *Ethology and Sociobiology* 16: 257–333.

Eskenazi, B., A. J. Wyrobek, E. Sloter, S. A. Kidd, L. Moore, S. Young, and D. Moore (2003). The Association of Age and Semen Quality in Healthy Men. *Human Reproduction* 18: 447–454.

Euler, Harald A., and Barbara Weitzel (1996). Discriminative Grandparental Solicitude as Reproductive Strategy. *Human Nature* 7: 39–59.

Ford, W. C. L., Kate North, Hazel Taylor, Alexandra Farrow, M. G. R. Hull, Jean Golding, and ALSPAC Study Team (2000). Increasing Paternal Age Is Associated with Delayed Conception in a Large Population of Fertile Couples: Evidence for Declining Fecundity in Older Men. *Human Reproduction* 15: 1703–1708.

Gagneux, Pascal, Christophe Boesch, and David S. Woodruff (1999). Female Reproductive Strategies, Paternity and Community Structure in Wild West African Chimpanzees. *Animal Behaviour* 57: 19–32.

Gangestad, Steven W., and Randy Thornhill (1997). The Evolutionary Psychology of Extrapair Sex: The Role of Fluctuating Asymmetry. *Evolution and Human Behavior* 18: 69–88.

Grammer, Karl (1992). Variations on a Theme: Age Dependent Mate Selection in Humans. *Behavioral and Brain Sciences* 15: 100–102.

Hamermesh, Daniel S., and Jeff E. Biddle (1994). Beauty and the Labor Market. *American Economic Review* 84: 1174–1194.

Hawkes, Kristen (2003). Grandmothers and the Evolution of Human Longevity. *American Journal of Human Biology* 15: 380–400.

Hawkes, Kristen, James F. O'Connell, and Nicholas G. Blurton Jones (1997). Hadza Women's Time Allocation, Offspring Provisioning, and the Evolution of Long Postmenopausal Life Spans. *Current Anthropology* 38: 551–577.

Hawkes, Kristen, James F. O'Connell, Nicholas G. Blurton Jones, Helen Alvarez, and Eric L. Charnov (1998). Grandmothering, Menopause, and the Evolution of Human Life Histories. *Proceedings of the National Academy of Sciences USA* 95: 1336–1339.

Hrdy, Sarah Blaffer (1997). Raising Darwin's Consciousness: Female Sexuality and the Prehominid Origins of Patriarchy. *Human Nature* 8: 1–49.

Hyde, Janet Shibley, and John D. DeLamater (2000). *Understanding Human Sexuality* (7th ed.). Boston: McGraw-Hill.

Irons, William (1979). Cultural and Biological Success. In N. A. Chagnon and W. Irons (eds.), *Evolutionary Biology and Human Social Behavior: An Anthropological Perspective* (pp. 257–272). North Scituate, MA: Duxbury Press.

Jankowiak, William R., Elizabeth M. Hill, and James M. Donovan (1992). The Effects of Gender and Sexual Orientation on Attractiveness Judgments: An Evolutionary Interpretation. *Ethology and Sociobiology* 13: 73–85.

Kalmijn, Matthijs (1991). Status Homogamy in the United States. *American Journal of Sociology* 97: 496–523.

Kalmijn, Matthijs (1994). Assortative Mating by Cultural and Economic Occupational Status. *American Journal of Sociology* 100: 422–452.

Kalmijn, Matthijs (1998). Intermarriage and Homogamy: Causes, Patterns, Trends. *Annual Review of Sociology* 24: 395–421.

Kenrick, Douglas T., and Richard C. Keefe (1992). Age Preferences in Mates Reflect Sex Differences in Reproductive Strategies. *Behavioral and Brain Sciences* 15: 75–133.

Kenrick, Douglas T., Richard C. Keefe, Cristina Gabrielidis, and Jeffrey S. Cornelius (1996). Adolescents' Age Preferences for Dating Partners: Support for an Evolutionary Model of Life-History Strategies. *Child Development* 67: 1499–1511.

Kenrick, Douglas T., Edward K. Sadalla, Gary Groth, and Melanie R. Trost (1990). Evolution, Traits, and the Stages of Human Courtship: Qualifying the Parental Investment Model. *Journal of Personality* 58: 97–116.

Laumann, Edward O., John H. Gagnon, Robert T. Michael, and Stuart Michaels (1994). *The Social Organization of Sexuality: Sexual Practices in the United States.* Chicago: University of Chicago Press.

Leonard, Janet L. (1989). *Homo sapiens*: A Good Fit to Theory, but Posing Some Enigmas. *Behavioral and Brain Sciences* 12: 26–27.

Lloyd, Elisabeth (forthcoming). *Something about Eve: Bias in Evolutionary Explanations of Female Sexuality.* Cambridge, MA: Harvard University Press.

Mare, Robert D. (1991). Five Decades of Educational Assortative Mating. *American Sociological Review* 56: 15–32.

Marlowe, Frank, and Adam Wetsman (2001). Preferred Waist-to-Hip Ratio and Ecology. *Personality and Individual Differences* 30: 481–489.

Mulford, Matthew, John Orbell, Catherine Shatto, and Jean Stockard (1998). Physical Attractiveness, Opportunity, and Success in Everyday Exchange. *American Journal of Sociology* 103: 1565–1592.

Pérusse, Daniel (1993). Cultural and Reproductive Success in Industrial Societies: Testing the Relationship at the Proximate and Ultimate Levels. *Behavioral and Brain Sciences* 16: 267–322.

Pérusse, Daniel (1994). Mate Choice in Modern Societies: Testing Evolutionary Hypotheses with Behavioral Data. *Human Nature* 5: 255–278.

Popenoe, David, and Barbara Dafoe Whitehead (2000). The State of Our Unions: The Social Health of Marriage in America, 2000. A Report of The National Marriage Project (http://marriage.rutgers.edu/SOOU/NMPAR2000.pdf).

Rasmussen, Jeffrey Lee, D. W. Rajecki, Anita A. Ebert, Kathy Lagler, Candice Brewer, and Elizabeth Cochran (1998). Age Preferences in Personal Advertisements: Two Life History Strategies or One Matching Tactic? *Journal of Social and Personal Relationships* 15: 77–89.

Sadalla, Edward K., Douglas T. Kenrick, and Beth Vershure (1987). Dominance and Heterosexual Attraction. *Journal of Personality and Social Psychology* 52: 730–738.

Simpson, Jeffrey A., and Steven W. Gangestad (1992). Sociosexuality and Romantic Partner Choice. *Journal of Personality* 60: 31–51.

Singh, Devendra (1993). Body Shape and Women's Attractiveness: The Critical Role of Waist-to-Hip Ratio. *Human Nature* 4: 297–321.

Singh, Devendra, and Suwardi Luis (1995). Ethnic and Gender Consensus for the Effect of Waist-to-Hip Ratio on Judgment of Women's Attractiveness. *Human Nature* 6: 51–65.

Stevens, Gillian, Dawn Owens, and Eric C. Schaefer (1990). Education and Attractiveness in Marriage Choices. *Social Psychology Quarterly* 53: 62–70.

Symons, Donald (1979). *The Evolution of Human Sexuality*. New York: Oxford University Press.

Symons, Donald (1995). Beauty Is in the Adaptations of the Beholder: The Evolutionary Psychology of Human Female Sexual Attractiveness. In P. R. Abramson and S. D. Pinkerton (eds.), *Sexual Nature, Sexual Culture* (pp. 80–118). Chicago: University of Chicago Press.

Tassinary, Louis G., and Kristi A. Hansen (1998). A Critical Test of the Waist-to-Hip-Ratio Hypothesis of Female Physical Attractiveness. *Psychological Science* 9: 150–155.

Taylor, Patricia Ann, and Norval D. Glenn (1976). The Utility of Education and Attractiveness for Females' Status Attainment through Marriage. *American Sociological Review* 41: 484–498.

Townsend, John Marshall (1998). *What Women Want—What Men Want: Why the Sexes Still See Love and Commitment So Differently*. New York: Oxford University Press.

Townsend, John Marshall, and Gary D. Levy (1990a). Effects of Potential Partners' Costume and Physical Attractiveness on Sexuality and Partner Selection. *Journal of Psychology* 124: 371–389.

Townsend, John Marshall, and Gary D. Levy (1990b). Effects of Potential Partners' Physical Attractiveness and Socioeconomic Status on Sexuality and Partner Selection. *Archives of Sexual Behavior* 19: 149–164.

Townsend, John Marshall, and Laurence W. Roberts (1993). Gender Differences in Mate Preference among Law Students: Divergence and Convergence of Criteria. *Journal of Psychology* 127: 507–528.

Trivers, Robert L. (1972). Parental Investment and Sexual Selection. In B. Campbell (ed.), *Sexual Selection and the Descent of Man* (pp. 136–179). Chicago: Aldine de Gruyter.

Umberson, Debra, and Michael Hughes (1987). The Impact of Physical Attractiveness on Achievement and Psychological Well Being. *Social Psychology Quarterly* 50: 227–236.

Van den Berghe, Pierre L. (1992). Wanting and Getting Ain't the Same. *Behavioral and Brain Sciences* 15: 116–117.

Voracek, Martin, and Maryanne L. Fisher (2002). Shapely Centrefolds? Temporal Change in Body Measures: Trend Analysis. *British Medical Journal* 325: 1447–1448.

Wallen, Kim (1992). Evolutionary Hypothesis Testing: Consistency Is Not Enough. *Behavioral and Brain Sciences* 15: 118–119.

Weinberg, Martin S., and Colin J. Williams (1980). Sexual Embourgeoisment? Social Class and Sexual Activity: 1938–1970. *American Sociological Review* 45(1): 33–48.

Wetsman, Adam, and Frank Marlowe (1999). How Universal Are Preferences for Female Waist-to-Hip Ratios? Evidence from the Hadza of Tanzania. *Evolution and Human Behavior* 20: 219–228.

Wiederman, Michael W., and Elizabeth Rice Allgeier (1992). Gender Differences in Mate Selection Criteria: Sociobiological or Socioeconomic Explanation? *Ethology and Sociobiology* 13: 115–124.

Yu, Douglas W., and Glenn H. Shepard (1998). Is Beauty in the Eye of the Beholder? *Nature* 396: 321–322.

## Chapter 6

Adams, David B., Alice Ross Gold, and Anne D. Burt (1978). Rise in Female-Initiated Sexual Activity at Ovulation and Its Suppression by Oral Contraceptives. *New England Journal of Medicine* 299: 1145–1150.

Bailey, J. Michael, Steven Gaulin, Yvonne Agyei, and Brian A. Gladue (1994). Effects of Gender and Sexual Orientation on Evolutionarily Relevant Aspects of Human Mating Psychology. *Journal of Personality and Social Psychology* 66: 1081–1093.

Baker, R. Robin, and Mark A. Bellis (1993). Human Sperm Competition: Ejaculate Manipulation by Females and a Function for the Female Orgasm. *Animal Behaviour* 46: 887–909.

Baker, R. Robin, and Mark A. Bellis (1995). *Human Sperm Competition: Copulation, Masturbation, and Infidelity.* New York: Chapman and Hall.

Bell, Robert R., and Dorthyann Peltz (1974). Extramarital Sex among Women. *Medical Aspects of Human Sexuality* 8: 10–31.

Bell, Robert R., Stanley Turner, and Lawrence Rosen (1975). A Multivariate Analysis of Female Extramarital Coitus. *Journal of Marriage and the Family* 37: 375–384.

Bellis, Mark A., and R. Robin Baker (1990). Do Females Promote Sperm Competition? Data for Humans. *Animal Behaviour* 40: 997–999.

Betzig, Laura L. (1989). Causes of Conjugal Dissolution: A Cross-Cultural Study. *Current Anthropology* 30: 654–676.

Birkhead, Tim (2000). *Promiscuity: An Evolutionary History of Sperm Competition.* Cambridge, MA: Harvard University Press.

Brewer, Devon D., John J. Potterat, Sharon B. Garrett, Stephen Q. Muth, Jr., John M. Roberts, Danuta Kasprzyk, Daniel E. Montano, and William W. Darrow (2000).

Prostitution and the Sex Discrepancy in Reported Number of Sexual Partners. *Proceedings of the National Academy of Sciences* 97: 12385–12388.

Brown, Norman R., and Robert C. Sinclair (1999). Estimating Number of Lifetime Sexual Partners: Men and Women Do It Differently. *Journal of Sex Research* 36: 292–297.

Buckle, Leslie, Gordon G. Gallup, and Zachary A. Rodd (1996). Marriage as a Reproductive Contract: Patterns of Marriage, Divorce, and Remarriage. *Evolution and Human Behavior* 17: 363–377.

Buss, David M. (1988). From Vigilance to Violence: Tactics of Mate Retention in American Undergraduates. *Ethology and Sociobiology* 9: 291–317.

Buss, David M. (1994). *The Evolution of Desire: Strategies of Human Mating.* New York: Basic Books.

Buss, David M. (1999). *Evolutionary Psychology: The New Science of the Mind.* Boston: Allyn and Bacon.

Buss, David M. (2000). *The Dangerous Passion: Why Jealousy Is as Necessary as Love and Sex.* New York: Free Press.

Buss, David M., Randy J. Larsen, and Drew Westen (1996). Sex Differences in Jealousy: Not Gone, Not Forgotten, and Not Explained by Alternative Hypotheses. *Psychological Science* 7: 373–375.

Buss, David M., Randy J. Larsen, Drew Westen, and Jennifer Semmelroth (1992). Sex Differences in Jealousy: Evolution, Physiology, and Psychology. *Psychological Science* 3: 251–255.

Buss, David M., Todd K. Shackelford, Lee A. Kirkpatrick, Jae C. Choe, Hang K. Lim, Mariko Hasegawa, Toshikazu Hasegawa, and Kevin Bennett (1999). Jealousy and the Nature of Beliefs about Infidelity: Tests of Competing Hypotheses about Sex Differences in the United States, Korea, and Japan. *Personal Relationships* 6: 125–150.

Buunk, Bram P., Alois Angleitner, Viktor Oubaid, and David M. Buss (1996). Sex Differences in Jealousy in Evolutionary and Cultural Perspective: Tests from the Netherlands, Germany, and the United States. *Psychological Science* 7: 359–363.

Chesser, Eustace (1956). *The Sexual, Marital and Family Relationships of the English Woman.* London: Hutchinson's Medical Publications.

Clark, Andy (1989). *Microcognition: Philosophy, Cognitive Science, and Parallel Distributed Processing.* Cambridge, MA: MIT Press.

Daly, Martin, and Margo Wilson (1983). *Sex, Evolution, and Behavior* (2nd ed.). Belmont, CA: Wadsworth.

Daly, Martin, and Margo Wilson (1988). *Homicide.* New York: Aldine de Gruyter.

Daly, Martin, and Margo Wilson (1996). Evolutionary Psychology and Marital Conflict. In D. M. Buss, and N. M. Malamuth (eds.), *Sex, Power, Conflict: Evolutionary and Feminist Perspectives* (pp. 9–28). New York: Oxford University Press.

Daly, Martin, Margo Wilson, and Suzanne J. Weghorst (1982). Male Sexual Jealousy. *Ethology and Sociobiology* 3: 11–27.

DeSteno, David A., and Peter Salovey (1996a). Evolutionary Origins of Sex Differences in Jealousy? *Psychological Science* 7: 367–372.

DeSteno, David A., and Peter Salovey (1996b). Genes, Jealousy, and the Replication of Misspecified Models. *Psychological Science* 7: 376–377.

Einon, Dorothy (1994). Are Men More Promiscuous than Women? *Ethology and Sociobiology* 15: 131–143.

Ellis, Bruce J., and Donald Symons (1990). Sex Differences in Sexual Fantasy: An Evolutionary Psychological Approach. *Journal of Sex Research* 27: 527–555.

Fisher, H. E. (1992). *Anatomy of Love: The Natural History of Monogamy, Adultery and Divorce*. New York: Norton.

Gangestad, Steven W. (2001). Adaptive Design, Selective History, and Women's Sexual Motivations. In J. A. French, A. C. Kamil, and D. W. Leger (eds.), *Evolutionary Psychology and Motivation* (pp. 37–74). Lincoln: University of Nebraska Press.

Gangestad, Steven W., and Randy Thornhill (1997). The Evolutionary Psychology of Extrapair Sex: The Role of Fluctuating Asymmetry. *Evolution and Human Behavior* 18: 69–88.

Gangestad, Steven W., Randy Thornhill, and Christine E. Garver (2002). Changes in Women's Sexual Interests and Their Partners' Mate-Retention Tactics across the Menstrual Cycle: Evidence for Shifting Conflicts of Interest. *Proceedings of the Royal Society of London B* 269: 975–982.

Geary, David C., Michael Rumsey, C. Christine Bow-Thomas, and Mary K. Hoard (1995). Sexual Jealousy as a Facultative Trait: Evidence from the Pattern of Sex Differences in Adults from China and the United States. *Ethology and Sociobiology* 16: 355–383.

Glass, Shirley P., and Thomas L. Wright (1985). Sex Differences in Type of Extramarital Involvement and Marital Dissatisfaction. *Sex Roles* 12: 1101–1120.

Glass, Shirley P., and Thomas L. Wright (1992). Justifications for Extramarital Relationships: The Association between Attitudes, Behaviors, and Gender. *Journal of Sex Research* 29: 361–387.

Gough, E. K. (1959). The Nayars and the Definition of Marriage. *Journal of the Royal Anthropological Institute of Great Britain and Ireland* 89: 23–34.

Greiling, Heidi, and David M. Buss (2000). Women's Sexual Strategies: The Hidden Dimension of Extra-Pair Mating. *Personality and Individual Differences* 28: 929–963.

Harris, Christine R. (2000). Psychophysiological Responses to Imagined Infidelity: The Specific Innate Modular View of Jealousy Reconsidered. *Journal of Personality and Social Psychology* 78: 1082–1091.

Harris, Christine R. (2002). Sexual and Romantic Jealousy in Heterosexual and Homosexual Adults. *Psychological Science* 13: 7–12.

Harris, Christine R. (2003). A Review of Sex Differences in Sexual Jealousy, Including Self-Report Data, Psychophysiological Responses, Interpersonal Violence, and Morbid Jealousy. *Personality and Social Psychology Review* 7: 102–128.

Harris, Christine R., and Nicholas Christenfeld (1996a). Gender, Jealousy, and Reason. *Psychological Science* 7: 364–366.

Harris, Christine R., and Nicholas Christenfeld (1996b). Jealousy and Rational Responses to Infidelity across Gender and Culture. *Psychological Science* 7: 378–379.

Hawkes, Kristen, Alan R. Rogers, and Eric L. Charnov (1995). The Male's Dilemma: Increased Offspring Production Is More Paternity to Steal. *Evolutionary Ecology* 9: 662–677.

Hill, Elizabeth M. (1988). The Menstrual Cycle and Components of Human Female Sexual Behaviour. *Journal of Social and Biological Structures* 11: 443–455.

Hoogland, John L. (1998). Why Do Female Gunnison's Prairie Dogs Copulate with More than One Male? *Animal Behaviour* 55: 351–359.

Kinsey, Alfred C., Wardell B. Pomeroy, and Clyde E. Martin (1948). *Sexual Behavior in the Human Male*. Philadelphia: W. B. Saunders.

Kinsey, Alfred C., Wardell B. Pomeroy, Clyde E. Martin, and Paul H. Gebhard (1953). *Sexual Behavior in the Human Female*. Philadelphia: W. B. Saunders.

Laumann, Edward O., John H. Gagnon, Robert T. Michael, and Stuart Michaels (1994). *The Social Organization of Sexuality: Sexual Practices in the United States*. Chicago: University of Chicago Press.

Lovejoy, C. Owen (1981). The Origin of Man. *Science* 211: 341–350.

Macintyre, Sally, and Anne Sooman (1991). Non-Paternity and Prenatal Genetic Screening. *Lancet* 338: 869–871.

Marlowe, Frank (2000). Paternal Investment and the Human Mating System. *Behavioural Processes* 51: 45–61.

Marlowe, Frank (2001). Male Contribution to Diet and Female Reproductive Success among Foragers. *Current Anthropology* 42: 755–760.

Paul, Luci, Mark A. Foss, and MaryAnn Baenninger (1996). Double Standards for Sexual Jealousy: Manipulative Morality or a Reflection of Evolved Sex Differences? *Human Nature* 7: 291–324.

Pietrzak, Robert H., James D. Laird, David A. Stevens, and Nicholas S. Thompson (2002). Sex Differences in Human Jealousy: A Coordinated Study of Forced-Choice,

Continuous Rating-Scale, and Physiological Responses on the Same Subjects. *Evolution and Human Behavior* 23: 83–94.

Pound, Nicholas, and Martin Daly (2000). Functional Significance of Human Female Orgasm Still Hypothetical. *Behavioral and Brain Sciences* 23: 620–621.

Regan, Pamela C. (1996). Rhythms of Desire: The Association between Menstrual Cycle Phases and Female Sexual Desire. *Canadian Journal of Human Sexuality* 5: 145–156.

Sagarin, Brad J., D. Vaughn Becker, Rosanna E. Guadagno, Lionel D. Nicastle, and Allison Millevoi (2003). Sex Differences (and Similarities) in Jealousy: The Moderating Influence of Infidelity Experience and Sexual Orientation of the Infidelity. *Evolution and Human Behavior* 24: 17–23.

Sheets, Virgil L., and Marlow D. Wolfe (2001). Sexual Jealousy in Heterosexuals, Lesbians, and Gays. *Sex Roles* 44: 255–276.

Smith, Robert L. (1984). Human Sperm Competition. In R. L. Smith (ed.), *Sperm Competition and the Evolution of Animal Mating Systems* (pp. 601–659). New York: Academic Press.

Smuts, Barbara B., and David J. Gubernick (1992). Male-Infant Relationships in Nonhuman Primates: Paternal Investment or Mating Effort? In B. S. Hewlett (ed.), *Father-Child Relations: Cultural and Bio-Social Contexts* (pp. 1–30). Hawthorne, NY: Aldine de Gruyter.

Sperber, Dan (1996). *Explaining Culture: A Naturalistic Approach.* Oxford, UK: Blackwell.

Stanislaw, Harold, and Frank J. Rice (1988). Correlation between Sexual Desire and Menstrual Cycle Characteristics. *Archives of Sexual Behavior* 17: 499–508.

Symons, Donald (1979). *The Evolution of Human Sexuality.* New York: Oxford University Press.

Symons, Donald (1985). Darwinism and Contemporary Marriage. In K. David (ed.), *Contemporary Marriage: Comparative Perspectives on a Changing Institution* (pp. 99–125). New York: Russell Sage Foundation.

Tavris, Carol, and Susan Sadd (1975). *The Redbook Report on Female Sexuality.* New York: Delacorte Press.

Terman, Lewis M. (1938). *Psychological Factors in Marital Happiness.* New York: McGraw-Hill.

Thompson, Anthony P. (1983). Extramarital Sex: A Review of the Research Literature. *Journal of Sex Research* 19: 1–22.

Thornhill, Randy, and Steven W. Gangestad (1999). Facial Attractiveness. *Trends in Cognitive Sciences* 3: 452–460.

Thornhill, Randy, and Steven W. Gangestad (1999). The Scent of Symmetry: A Human Sex Pheromone That Signals Fitness? *Evolution and Human Behavior* 20: 175–201.

Thornhill, Randy, Steven W. Gangestad, and Randall Comer (1995). Human Female Orgasm and Mate Fluctuating Asymmetry. *Animal Behaviour* 50: 1601–1615.

Twain, Mark (1991). *Letters from the Earth*. New York: HarperPerennial.

Van Schaik, Carel P., and Andreas Paul (1996). Male Care in Primates: Does It Ever Reflect Paternity? *Evolutionary Anthropology* 5: 152–156.

Wiederman, Michael W. (1997). Extramarital Sex: Prevalence and Correlates in a National Survey. *Journal of Sex Research* 34: 167–174.

Wiederman, Michael W., and Elizabeth Rice Allgeier (1993). Gender Differences in Sexual Jealousy: Adaptionist or Social Learning Explanation? *Ethology and Sociobiology* 14: 115–140.

Wiederman, Michael W., and Erica Kendall (1999). Evolution, Sex, and Jealousy: Investigation with a Sample from Sweden. *Evolution and Human Behavior* 20: 121–128.

Wiederman, Michael W., and Lisa LaMar (1998). "Not with Him You Don't!": Gender and Emotional Reactions to Sexual Infidelity during Courtship. *Journal of Sex Research* 35: 288–297.

Wilson, Margo, and Martin Daly (1992). The Man Who Mistook His Wife for a Chattel. In J. H. Barkow, L. Cosmides, and J. Tooby (eds.), *The Adapted Mind: Evolutionary Psychology and the Generation of Culture* (pp. 289–322). New York: Oxford University Press.

Wilson, Margo, and Martin Daly (1996). Male Sexual Proprietariness and Violence against Wives. *Current Directions in Psychological Science* 5: 2–7.

Wolf, Arthur P. (1966). Childhood Association, Sexual Attraction, and the Incest Taboo: A Chinese Case. *American Anthropologist* 68: 883–898.

Wolf, Arthur P. (1970). Childhood Association and Sexual Attraction: A Further Test of the Westermarck Hypothesis. *American Anthropologist* 72: 503–515.

## Chapter 7

Anderson, Kermyt G., Hillard Kaplan, David Lam, and Jane Lancaster (1999). Paternal Care by Genetic Fathers and Stepfathers II: Reports by Xhosa High School Students. *Evolution and Human Behavior* 20: 433–451.

Anderson, Kermyt G., Hillard Kaplan, and Jane Lancaster (1999). Paternal Care by Genetic Fathers and Stepfathers I: Reports from Albuquerque Men. *Evolution and Human Behavior* 20: 405–431.

Bachrach, Christine A. (1983). Children in Families: Characteristics of Biological, Step-, and Adopted Children. *Journal of Marriage and the Family* 45: 171–179.

Buss, David M. (1999). *Evolutionary Psychology: The New Science of the Mind*. Boston: Allyn and Bacon.

Cashell, Alan W. (1987). Homicide as a Cause of the Sudden Infant Death Syndrome. *American Journal of Forensic Medicine and Pathology* 8: 256–258.

Christoffel, Katherine K., Nora K. Anzinger, and David A. Merrill (1989). Age-Related Patterns of Violent Death, Cook County, Illinois, 1977 through 1982. *American Journal of Diseases of Children* 143: 1403–1409.

Christoffel, Katherine K., Peter C. Scheidt, Phyllis F. Agran, Jess F. Kraus, Elizabeth McLoughlin, and Jerome A. Paulson (1992). Standard Definitions for Childhood Injury Research: Excerpts of a Conference Report. *Pediatrics* 89: 1027–1034.

Crume, Tessa L., Carolyn DiGuiseppi, Tim Byers, Andrew P. Sirotnak, and Carol J. Garrett (2002). Underascertainment of Child Maltreatment Fatalities by Death Certificates, 1990–1998. *Pediatrics* 110(2): e18.

Daly, Martin, and Margo Wilson (1981). Abuse and Neglect of Children in Evolutionary Perspective. In R. D. Alexander, and D. W. Tinkle (eds.), *Natural Selection and Social Behavior: Recent Research and New Theory* (pp. 405–416). New York: Chiron Press.

Daly, Martin, and Margo Wilson (1985). Child Abuse and Other Risks of Not Living with Both Parents. *Ethology and Sociobiology* 6: 197–210.

Daly, Martin, and Margo Wilson (1987). Children as Homicide Victims. In R. J. Gelles and J. B. Lancaster (eds.), *Child Abuse and Neglect: Biosocial Dimensions* (pp. 201–214). New York: Aldine de Gruyter.

Daly, Martin, and Margo Wilson (1988a). Evolutionary Social Psychology and Family Homicide. *Science* 242: 519–524.

Daly, Martin, and Margo Wilson (1988b). *Homicide*. New York: Aldine de Gruyter.

Daly, Martin, and Margo Wilson (1991). A Reply to Gelles: Stepchildren *Are* Disproportionately Abused, and Diverse Forms of Violence *Can* Share Causal Factors. *Human Nature* 2: 419–426.

Daly, Martin, and Margo Wilson (1994a). Some Differential Attributes of Lethal Assaults on Small Children by Stepfathers versus Genetic Fathers. *Ethology and Sociobiology* 15: 207–217.

Daly, Martin, and Margo Wilson (1994b). Stepparenthood and the Evolved Psychology of Discriminative Parental Solicitude. In S. Parmigiani and F. S. v. Saal (eds.), *Infanticide and Parental Care* (pp. 121–134). Chur, Switzerland: Harwood.

Daly, Martin, and Margo Wilson (1995). Discriminative Parental Solicitude and the Relevance of Evolutionary Models to the Analysis of Motivational Systems. In M. S. Gazzaniga (ed.), *The Cognitive Neurosciences* (pp. 1269–1286). Cambridge, MA: MIT Press.

Daly, Martin, and Margo Wilson (1996). Violence against Stepchildren. *Current Directions in Psychological Science* 5: 77–81.

Daly, Martin, and Margo Wilson (1999). *The Truth about Cinderella: A Darwinian View of Parental Love*. New Haven, CT: Yale University Press.

Daly, Martin, and Margo Wilson (2001). An Assessment of Some Proposed Exceptions to the Phenomenon of Nepotistic Discrimination against Stepchildren. *Annales Zoologici Fennici* 38: 287–296.

Ewigman, Bernard, Coleen Kivlahan, and Garland Land (1993). The Missouri Child Fatality Study: Underreporting of Maltreatment Fatalities among Children Younger than Five Years of Age, 1983 through 1986. *Pediatrics* 91: 330–337.

Geary, David C. (2000). Evolution and Proximate Expression of Human Paternal Investment. *Psychological Bulletin* 126: 55–77.

Gelles, Richard J. (1991). Physical Violence, Child Abuse, and Child Homicide: A Continuum of Violence, or Distinct Behaviors? *Human Nature* 2: 59–72.

Gelles, Richard J., and John W. Harrop (1991). The Risk of Abusive Violence among Children with Non-genetic Caretakers. *Family Relations* 40: 78–83.

Giles-Sims, Jean (1997). Current Knowledge about Child Abuse in Stepfamilies. *Marriage and Family Review* 26: 215–230.

Giles-Sims, Jean, and David Finkelhor (1984). Child Abuse in Stepfamilies. *Family Relations* 33: 407–413.

Glick, Paul C. (1989). Remarried Families, Stepfamilies, and Stepchildren: A Brief Demographic Profile. *Family Relations* 38: 24–27.

Gordon, Michael (1989). The Family Environment of Sexual Abuse: A Comparison of Natal and Stepfather Abuse. *Child Abuse and Neglect* 13: 121–130.

Hamilton, W. D. (1964). The Genetical Evolution of Social Behaviour (I and II). *Journal of Theoretical Biology* 7: 1–16, 17–52.

Herman-Giddens, Marcia E., Gail Brown, Sarah Verbiest, Pamela J. Carlson, Elizabeth G. Hooten, Eleanor Howell, and John D. Butts (1999). Underascertainment of Child Abuse Mortality in the United States. *Journal of the American Medical Association* 282(5): 463–467.

Herndon, Joy, Lilo T. Strauss, Sara Whitehead, Wilda Y. Parker, Linda Bartlett, and Suzanne Zane (2002). Abortion Surveillance—United States, 1998. In *Surveillance Summaries*, April 13, 2002. *Morbidity and Mortality Weekly Report* 51 (no. SS-3), pp. 1–32.

Kim, Kwang-Iel, and Bokja Ko (1990). An Incidence Survey of Battered Children in Two Elementary Schools of Seoul. *Child Abuse and Neglect* 14: 273–276.

Malkin, Catherine M., and Michael E. Lamb (1994). Child Maltreatment: A Test of Sociobiological Theory. *Journal of Comparative Family Studies* 25: 121–133.

Marlowe, Frank (1999). Showoffs or Providers? The Parenting Effort of Hadza Men. *Evolution and Human Behavior* 20: 391–404.

National Adoption Information Clearinghouse (2002). Adoption: Numbers and Trends. Retrieved 2003 from the U. S. Department of Health and Human Services, Administration for Children and Families, National Adoption Information Clearinghouse (http://www.calib.com/naic/pubs/s_number.doc).

Parker, Hilda, and Seymour Parker (1986). Father-Daughter Sexual Abuse: An Emerging Perspective. *American Journal of Orthopsychiatry* 56: 531–549.

Perrot, L. J., and S. Nawojczyk (1988). Nonnatural Death Masquerading as SIDS (Sudden Infant Death Syndrome). *American Journal of Forensic Medicine and Pathology* 9: 105–111.

Pinker, Steven (2002). *The Blank Slate: The Modern Denial of Human Nature.* New York: Viking.

Schaik, Carel P. van (2000). Infanticide by Male Primates: The Sexual Selection Hypothesis Revisited. In C. P. van Schaik and C. H. Janson (eds.), *Infanticide by Males and Its Implications* (pp. 27–60). New York: Cambridge University Press.

Sedlak, Andrea J., and Diane D. Broadhurst (1996). Executive Summary of the Third National Incidence Study of Child Abuse and Neglect. Retrieved 2003 from the U. S. Department of Health and Human Services, Administration for Children and Families, National Clearinghouse on Child Abuse and Neglect Information (http://nccanch.acf.hhs.gov/pubs/statsinfo/nis3.cfm).

Stiffman, Michael N., Patricia G. Schnitzer, Patricia Adam, Robin L. Kruse, and Bernard G. Ewigman (2002). Household Composition and Risk of Fatal Child Maltreatment. *Pediatrics* 109: 615–621.

Temrin, Hans, Susanne Buchmayer, and Magnus Enquist (2000). Step-parents and Infanticide: New Data Contradict Evolutionary Predictions. *Proceedings of the Royal Society of London B* 267: 943–945.

Temrin, Hans, Johanna Nordlund, and Helena Sterner (2004). Are Stepchildren Overrepresented as Victims of Lethal Parental Violence in Sweden? *Proceedings of the Royal Society of London B* 271: S124–S126.

Voland, Eckart, and Peter Stephan (2000). "The Hate That Love Generated": Sexually Selected Neglect of One's Own Offspring in Humans. In C. P. van Schaik and C. H. Janson (eds.), *Infanticide by Males and Its Implications* (pp. 447–465). New York: Cambridge University Press.

Wilson, Margo, and Martin Daly (1987). Risk of Maltreatment of Children Living with Stepparents. In R. J. Gelles and J. B. Lancaster (eds.), *Child Abuse and Neglect: Biosocial Dimensions* (pp. 215–232). New York: Aldine de Gruyter.

Wilson, Margo, and Martin Daly (1994). The Psychology of Parenting in Evolutionary Perspective and the Case of Human Filicide. In S. Parmigiani and F. S. vom Saal (eds.), *Infanticide and Parental Care* (pp. 73–104). Chur, Switzerland: Harwood.

Wilson, Margo, Martin Daly, and Suzanne J. Weghorst (1980). Household Composition and the Risk of Child Abuse and Neglect. *Journal of Biosocial Science* 12: 333–340.

Wolfner, Glenn D., and Richard J. Gelles (1993). A Profile of Violence toward Children: A National Study. *Child Abuse and Neglect* 17: 197–212.

## Chapter 8

Amundson, Ron (1994). Two Concepts of Constraint: Adaptationism and the Challenge from Developmental Biology. *Philosophy of Science* 61: 556–578.

Bonner, John T. (1980). *The Evolution of Culture in Animals*. Princeton, NJ: Princeton University Press.

Brown, Donald E. (1991). *Human Universals*. New York: McGraw-Hill.

Buller, David J. (2000). Evolutionary Psychology. In M. Nani and M. Marraffa (eds.), *A Field Guide to the Philosophy of Mind*. An official electronic publication of the Department of Philosophy of University of Rome 3 (http://host.uniroma3.it/progetti/kant/field/ep.htm).

Buss, David M. (1999). *Evolutionary Psychology: The New Science of the Mind*. Boston: Allyn and Bacon.

Cavalli-Sforza, L. Luca, Paolo Menozzi, and Alberto Piazza (1994). *The History and Geography of Human Genes*. Princeton: Princeton University Press.

Cosmides, Leda, and John Tooby (1987). From Evolution to Behavior: Evolutionary Psychology as the Missing Link. In J. Dupré (ed.), *The Latest on the Best: Essays on Evolution and Optimality* (pp. 277–306). Cambridge, MA: MIT Press.

Cosmides, Leda, and John Tooby (1992). Cognitive Adaptations for Social Exchange. In J. H. Barkow, L. Cosmides, and J. Tooby (eds.), *The Adapted Mind: Evolutionary Psychology and the Generation of Culture* (pp. 163–228). New York: Oxford University Press.

Cosmides, Leda, and John Tooby (1994). Origins of Domain Specificity: The Evolution of Functional Organization. In L. A. Hirschfeld, and S. A. Gelman (eds.), *Mapping the Mind: Domain Specificity in Cognition and Culture* (pp. 85–116). New York: Cambridge University Press.

Cosmides, Leda, and John Tooby (1997). The Modular Nature of Human Intelligence. In A. B. Scheibel and J. W. Schopf (eds.), *The Origin and Evolution of Intelligence* (pp. 71–101). Sudbury, MA: Jones and Bartlett.

Dawkins, Richard (1986). *The Blind Watchmaker*. London: Penguin Books.

Deacon, Terrence W. (1997). *The Symbolic Species: The Co-evolution of Language and the Brain*. New York: Norton.

Durham, William H. (1991). *Coevolution: Genes, Culture, and Human Diversity.* Stanford: Stanford University Press.

Futuyma, Douglas J. (1998). *Evolutionary Biology* (3rd ed.). Sunderland, MA: Sinauer Associates.

Ghiselin, Michael T. (1997). *Metaphysics and the Origin of Species.* Albany: State University of New York Press.

Godfrey-Smith, Peter (1999). Adaptationism and the Power of Selection. *Biology and Philosophy* 14: 181–194.

Hull, David L. (1978). A Matter of Individuality. *Philosophy of Science* 45: 335–360.

Hull, David L. (1980). Individuality and Selection. *Annual Review of Ecology and Systematics* 11: 311–332.

Hull, David L. (1989a). On Human Nature. In *The Metaphysics of Evolution* (pp. 11–24). Albany: State University of New York Press.

Hull, David L. (1989b). The Ontological Status of Species as Evolutionary Units. In *The Metaphysics of Evolution* (pp. 79–88). Albany: State University of New York Press.

Izpisúa Belmonte, Juan Carlos (1999). How the Body Tells Left from Right. *Scientific American* 280(6): 46–51.

Lewontin, Richard (1995). *Human Diversity.* New York: Scientific American Library.

Lincoln, Bruce (1975). The Indo-European Myth of Creation. *History of Religions* 15: 121–145.

Loptson, Peter (1995). *Theories of Human Nature.* Peterborough, Canada: Broadview Press.

Mayr, Ernst (1976). *Evolution and the Diversity of Life.* Cambridge, MA: Harvard University Press.

Mayr, Ernst (1982). *The Growth of Biological Thought: Diversity, Evolution, and Inheritance.* Cambridge, MA: Harvard University Press.

Mayr, Ernst (1988). The Ontology of the Species Taxon. In *Toward a New Philosophy of Biology: Observations of an Evolutionist* (pp. 335–358). Cambridge, MA: Harvard University Press.

Paley, William (1805). *Natural Theology* (9th ed.). London: R. Faulder.

Sober, Elliott (1993). *Philosophy of Biology.* Boulder, CO: Westview Press.

Sober, Elliott (1994). Evolution, Population Thinking, and Essentialism. In *From a Biological Point of View: Essays in Evolutionary Philosophy* (pp. 201–232). New York: Cambridge University Press.

Sterelny, Kim, and Paul E. Griffiths (1999). *Sex and Death: An Introduction to Philosophy of Biology.* Chicago: University of Chicago Press.

Stevenson, Leslie, and David L. Haberman (1998). *Ten Theories of Human Nature* (2nd ed.). New York: Oxford University Press.

Symons, Donald (1979). *The Evolution of Human Sexuality*. New York: Oxford University Press.

Tooby, John, and Leda Cosmides (1989). Evolutionary Psychology and the Generation of Culture, Part I: Theoretical Considerations. *Ethology and Sociobiology* 10: 29–49.

Tooby, John, and Leda Cosmides (1990a). On the Universality of Human Nature and the Uniqueness of the Individual: The Role of Genetics and Adaptation. *Journal of Personality* 58: 17–67.

Tooby, John, and Leda Cosmides (1990b). The Past Explains the Present: Emotional Adaptations and the Structure of Ancestral Environments. *Ethology and Sociobiology* 11: 375–424.

Tooby, John, and Leda Cosmides (1992). The Psychological Foundations of Culture. In J. H. Barkow, L. Cosmides, and J. Tooby (eds.), *The Adapted Mind: Evolutionary Psychology and the Generation of Culture* (pp. 19–136). New York: Oxford University Press.

Trigg, Roger (1988). *Ideas of Human Nature: An Historical Introduction*. Oxford, UK: Blackwell.

Wagner, Gunter P. (1989). The Biological Homology Concept. *Annual Review of Ecology and Systematics* 20: 51–69.

Wilson, David Sloan (1994). Adaptive Genetic Variation and Human Evolutionary Psychology. *Ethology and Sociobiology* 15: 219–235.

# Index